T0376785

*THE PICKERING MASTERS*

THE SELECTED WORKS OF
MARGARET OLIPHANT

# CONTENTS OF THE EDITION

## Part I: Literary Criticism and Literary History

Volume 1
Literary Criticism, 1854–69

Volume 2
Literary Criticism, 1870–6

Volume 3
Literary Criticism, 1877–86

Volume 4
*The Victorian Age of English Literature* (1892)

## Part II: Literary Criticism, Autobiography, Biography and Historical Writing

Volume 5
Literary Criticism, 1887–97

Volume 6
*The Autobiography and Letters of Mrs M. O. W. Oliphant* (1899)

Volume 7
Writings on Biography I

Volume 8
Writings on Biography II

Volume 9
Historical Writing

## Part III: Novellas and Shorter Fiction, Essays on Life-Writing and History, Essays on European Literature and Culture

Volume 10
Novellas

Volume 11
Short (Domestic) Fiction

Volume 12
Supernatural Tales

Volume 13
Essays on Life-Writing and History

Volume 14
Essays on European Literature and Culture

## Part IV: *The Chronicles of Carlingford*

Volume 15
Preliminary Tales: 'The Executor', 'The Rector' and 'The Doctor's Family'

Volume 16
*Salem Chapel*

Volume 17
*The Perpetual Curate*

Volume 18
*Miss Marjoribanks*

Volume 19
*Pheobe, Junior*

## Part V: Major Novels

Volume 20
*Hester*

Volume 21
*The Wizard's Son*

Volume 22
*Kirsteen*

## Part VI: Major Novels

# THE SELECTED WORKS OF MARGARET OLIPHANT

Part V: Major Novels

### General Editors

Joanne Shattock and Elisabeth Jay

Volume 21

*The Wizard's Son*

### Edited by

Elisabeth Jay

LONDON AND NEW YORK

First published 2015 by Pickering & Chatto (Publishers) Limited

Published 2016 by Routledge
2 Park Square, Milton Park, Abingdon, Oxon OX14 4RN
711 Third Avenue, New York, NY 10017, USA

*Routledge is an imprint of the Taylor & Francis Group, an informa business*

© Taylor & Francis 2015
© Editorial material Elisabeth Jay 2015

To the best of the Publisher's knowledge every effort has been made to contact
relevant copyright holders and to clear any relevant copyright issues.
Any omissions that come to their attention will be remedied in future editions.

All rights reserved, including those of translation into foreign languages.
No part of this book may be reprinted or reproduced or utilised in any form or
by any electronic, mechanical, or other means, now known or hereafter
invented, including photocopying and recording, or in any information storage
or retrieval system, without permission in writing from the publishers.

Notice:
Product or corporate names may be trademarks or registered trademarks, and
are used only for identification and explanation without intent to infringe.

BRITISH LIBRARY CATALOGUING IN PUBLICATION DATA

Oliphant, Mrs. (Margaret), 1828–1897.
The selected works of Margaret Oliphant.
Part 5, Major novels. – (The Pickering masters)
I. Title II. Series III. Shattock, Joanne. IV. Jay, Elisabeth.
823.8-dc23

ISBN-13: 978-1-85196-600-4 (set)

Typeset by Pickering & Chatto (Publishers) Limited

# CONTENTS

| | |
|---|---|
| Acknowledgements | ix |
| Abbreviations | xi |
| Introduction | xiii |
| Select Bibliography | xxvii |
| *The Wizard's Son* | 1 |
| Editorial Notes | 409 |
| Textual Variants | 433 |
| Silent Corrections | 457 |

# ACKNOWLEDGEMENTS

I am grateful as always for the genial collaborative discussions with my co-general editor, Joanne Shattock, which have characterized the enterprise of *The Selected Works of Margaret Oliphant,* as also for her eagle-eye in reading through the editorial material for this volume. Once again the ability to pursue allusions to Margaret Oliphant's other work has been greatly aided by the extensive bibliographical work of John Stock Clarke.

# ABBREVIATIONS

| | |
|---|---|
| *BM* | *Blackwood's Edinburgh Magazine.* |
| *Clarke (1986)* | *Margaret Oliphant: A Bibliography*, compiled by J. S. Clarke, Victorian Fiction Research Guides 11 (St Lucia, Queensland: Department of English, University of Queensland, 1986). |
| *Clarke (1997)* | *Margaret Oliphant (1828–1897): Non-Fictional Writings. A Bibliography*, compiled by J. S. Clarke, Victorian Fiction Research Guides 26 (St Lucia, Queensland: Department of English, University of Queensland, 1997). |
| *Coghill* | *The Autobiography and Letters of Mrs. M. O. W. Oliphant*, ed. Mrs Harry [Annie] Coghill (Edinburgh and London: Blackwood, 1899). |
| *CM* | *Cornhill Magazine.* |
| *Jay (1990)* | *The Autobiography of Margaret Oliphant. The Complete Text*, ed. and intro. E. Jay (Oxford: Oxford University Press, 1990). |
| *Jay (1995)* | E. Jay, *Mrs Oliphant: 'A Fiction to Herself': A Literary Life* (Oxford: Clarendon Press, 1995). |
| *MacM* | *Macmillan's Magazine.* |
| *MOWO* | Margaret Oliphant Wilson Oliphant (1828–97). |
| *Selected Works* | *The Selected Works of Margaret Oliphant*, gen. ed. by J. Shattock and E. Jay, The Pickering Masters, 25 vols (London: Pickering & Chatto, 2011–16). |

# INTRODUCTION

In *The Wizard's Son* MOWO sought to marry her recent interest in the supernatural with her long-acknowledged mastery of the fiction of domestic realism. Indeed, the germ of this novel's plot had been contained in 'The Secret Chamber' (1876), one of her earliest 'Stories of the Seen and the Unseen', in which a young aristocrat faces a hereditary rite of passage.[1] Based on a popular legend surrounding the Earls of Strathmore and their family seat, Glamis Castle, the short story begins in the strain of a tourist pamphlet for visitors to a Scottish pile, and concludes with a guided tour of the castle by the young man whose twenty-first birthday has been the occasion for summoning the guests who accompany him. The heart of the tale focuses more narrowly on the tension experienced in such families between safeguarding long-term material interests, and prioritizing individual moral judgement: this struggle is incarnated in a trio composed of the current head of the family, his son and a ghostly ancestor, 'dressed in a long robe of dark colour, embroidered with strange lines and angles'.[2]

Many of these elements reappear in *The Wizard's Son*. The landscape of the west coast of Argyll, and the economic challenges faced by its landlords and crofters, are fleshed out in greater detail, thanks to a holiday MOWO took with her twenty-four year old son, Cyril, in the late summer of 1881.[3] The choric role of the visitors to this remote region is parcelled out between a wealthy Glasgow magnate and the various house-guests he invites to his loch-side holiday home, and acquaintances from the hero's upbringing in the English Home Counties. Since the moral dilemma at the heart of the tale remained the same, it is pertinent to ask what changes MOWO wrought to justify publishing this novel so very few years after its associated short story.

The most obvious change is that to the milieu of the protagonist's upbringing. The novel's central character, Walter Methven, has been brought up in the south of England in 'limited' (p. 7) but comfortable middle-class circumstances by his mother, the widow of a long-dead captain. Unlike his fictional progenitor, 'John Randolph, Lord Lindores', scion of the noble Gowrie family, and 'a young man of great character and energy', who by age twenty-one has already made his public mark at school and university, besides having 'made more than one great

– xiii –

speech' at the Oxford Union,[4] Walter, who has enjoyed the same educational opportunities, is, at twenty-four, an idle, sulky hedonist, already felt to be past his prime. The local community 'had ceased now to speak of the great things that Walter would do. They asked, "*What* was he going to do?" in an entirely altered tone' (p. 9). The nickname 'July' (Julia) of his childhood playmate, the penniless niece of the local clergyman, with whom he continues to conduct a flirtatious dalliance, confirms that neither is in the first, optimistic flush of youth. In 'The Secret Chamber', Lindores, who enjoys good relations with his proud father, has been raised in the knowledge that his coming-of-age ceremony will involve a mysterious 'trial' reserved for each successive heir apparent. The fatherless Walter's unanticipated elevation to the peerage, and the strange condition on which his patrilineal inheritance is to be held, come out of the blue to disrupt the claustrophobic tension of the Methven household in aptly-named 'Sloebury'.

MOWO had rarely written anything better than the opening serial episodes analysing the unhappy Methven household, comprising the mother, embittered by her powerlessness to motivate the recalcitrant son, and both unsentimentally observed by Cousin Sophia, a self-centred spinster. Despite MOWO's oft-declared disapproval of basing characters on living 'originals',[5] it is hard to avoid the conclusion that in this case she had the materials close to hand. Cousin Annie Walker, who having attached herself to the Oliphant household in 1866, would contract a surprising late marriage just as MOWO was putting the finishing touches to *The Wizard's Son* was one possible candidate. The other spinster who frequently occupied the uncomfortable position of the fictional Cousin Sophie was Fanny Tulloch, daughter of MOWO's old friend Principal Tulloch of St Andrews, who would descend for lengthy visits to the Oliphant household. Dependent upon MOWO's goodwill as their hostess, they witnessed the worsening relationship between her and her oldest son, Cyril, at close quarters, without necessarily fully sympathizing with the maternal emotional investment which made his indolence so distressing.

By 1882, when MOWO embarked on this novel, Cyril had failed to fulfil the early academic promise he had shown at Eton. Instead, having run up considerable bills on entertaining himself at Oxford, he had finally only taken a second-class degree. This had been 'a great disappointment' to his mother, causing her 'a keen moment of pain', although characteristically she subsequently admitted to herself that the result was 'not disgraceful after all'.[6] Despite her attempts to persuade him to take the next career step favoured by many of his contemporaries and proceed to the bar,[7] Cyril remained at home, where he showed little enthusiasm for anything beyond a social life which included tennis, cricket, a worrying propensity to the alcoholism which had afflicted MOWO's older brother, Willie, and the cultivation of acquaintances, both male and female, whom his mother deplored.

*Introduction* xv

In the late summer of 1882 Cyril accompanied his mother on the tour of the western coast of Scotland, which would prove so important for the setting of *The Wizard's Son*. A letter written to her younger son, recounting an exasperating misadventure which had left her on board a ferry which took her beyond her initial disembarkation point and left her soaking wet, penniless and 'very cross', at a port further along the shores of the Isle of Arran, suggests that Cyril could not even be trusted to keep an eye on her 'special boxes' containing the materials necessary for the work which underwrote the expenses of this holiday.[8] The fact that by October 1883, when she was still writing the later serial parts of this novel, she had been forced to rent out her beloved Windsor home and move to rented accommodation in Ealing in order to finance Cyril's short-lived venture of becoming private secretary to the Governor of Ceylon, is likely to have made her hopeful and apprehensive in equal parts.[9]

Looking back after Cyril had died in his early thirties, 'leaving a love-song or two behind him and the little volume of 'De Musset', of which much was so well done, and yet some so badly done, and nothing more to show for his life', MOWO recalled how, despite feeling herself condemned 'to watch it all going on day by day and year by year', they had both clung to the belief that '*Tout peut se reparer*', and that 'when the moment came' he would 'right himself and recover lost way'. Only, 'the moment, God bless him! did not come till God took it in His own hands'.[10]

In *The Wizard's Son* MOWO assumed the providential role of the writer to imagine 'that moment' of spiritual crisis. Just as some twentieth-century feminist novels sometimes felt it necessary to resort to magic realism to bring about the longed-for utopia which would put an end to the oppression their fictions had so acutely diagnosed, so MOWO uses the supernatural in this novel to suggest the apocalyptic dimensions of the shock it will take to shatter and remake the easy habits into which a young man like Walter Methven has fallen. This is not the same as saying that the novel can simply be dismissed as a maternal wish-fulfilment fantasy, for en route to Walter's salvation, the novel exacts a full look at the worst.

Mrs. Methven's mixture of humiliation, self-blame and angry frustration at her inability to motivate or shame her adult son into taking responsibility for his own life, and the consequent wedge she drives between them against her own deepest wishes, are represented with a degree of self-awareness on MOWO's part that make disturbingly poignant reading. However, a portrait that could so easily have settled into a piece of prolonged self-exculpation, is prevented from doing so by MOWO's ability to skewer her creation with the remorseless objectivity of a butterfly collector adding yet another trophy to the collection. Her ability to redirect her reader's sympathies with little more than one well-placed word is shown to perfection in a passage from the first chapter which threatens to make George Eliot's well-known prompt to her readers, 'Dorothea, but why always Dorothea? Was her point of view the only possible one with regard to this marriage?' appear crude by comparison.[11] Having spent a paragraph summarizing and to an extent castigating the Sloebury community's unsympathetic judgement of Mrs. Methven, the narrator suggests that the mother's consciousness of such gossip,

> added to the impatience and indignation and pain with which she contemplated the course of affairs, which she was without strength to combat, yet could not let alone. Now and then, indeed, she did control herself so far as to let them alone, and then there was nothing but tranquillity and peace in the house. But she was a conscientious woman, and, poor soul! she had a temper – the complacency and calm with which her son went upon his way, the approval he showed of her better conduct when she left him to his own devices, struck in some moments with such sudden indignation and pain, that she could no longer control herself (pp. 10–11).

'Conscientious' is the pivotal word on which this passage turns. Just as it seems that we are being urged to endorse the self-restraint that brings about the cessation of domestic warfare, there is a sudden reversal reminding us of the painstaking judgmentalism of her son's behavior that prompts Mrs. Methven's 'conscience' to dictate that the fight is maintained. Scarcely have we had time to absorb this moral recalibration, before the part played by Mrs. Methven's 'temper' is introduced. However, even then we are not allowed to settle easily into pitying contempt for her lack of self-control: the sheer audacity of Walter's casually adopting an attitude of moral approval for a course of behavior which permits him to continue his selfish hedonism uninterrupted leaves the reader, like the mother, almost breathless. Mrs. Methven, of course, is not endowed with the need for unremitting hard work that can make MOWO's role seem heroic in the face of her sons' indolence, and so she has to be granted her apotheosis in the contrast between the stoic self-restraint she shows in the novel's dénouement, and the emotional collapse of her companion, a mother endowed with many dutiful sons and a much-loved daughter.

The novel neither spares nor glamourizes Mrs Methven's only son, Walter. He is no mere idler, requiring only the opportunity provided by his sudden good fortune to galvanize him into a purposeful life. Always keeping just within the bounds of the sayable, in a novel designed with an eye to the suitability for family reading, MOWO nevertheless lets us know that this 'sad bad boy' has 'gone further...than the ordinary'; further that is than such misdemeanours as being 'nasty to his mother', or gambling (p. 338). These accusations are tempered by being spoken by July to a rival at a stage when the former is still anxious to keep open the option of becoming Lady Erradean. Nevertheless, even the practical, fair-minded Katie Williamson, mulling over her rejection of Walter's proposal, reflects upon his 'Gambling, wine, even the spells of such women as Katie blushed to think of' (p. 325).

MOWO therefore faced two problems with Walter as the novel's protagonist. First, how was she to create interest in a young man notable at the start of the novel for little beyond obstinacy and a certain prickly vanity? – a question partly answered by propelling him swiftly, in adventure-story mode, through Edin-

*Introduction* xvii

burgh, Argyll and London. The Scottish part of the novel with its Edinburgh lawyers and antiquaries; Glasgow magnate; bailiffs and crofters also suggested how much she had learnt from her hero, Sir Walter Scott, whom she had recently praised for the way he had revealed the multifariousness of Scottish life.[12]

The second problem was how to transform the easily-led ne'er-do-well portrayed in the bulk of the novel into, if not a heroic figure, at least a man capable of facing up to his adult responsibilities. In a Christmas ghost story such as 'The Secret Chamber' it had been relatively easy to resort to the efficacy of a prop such as 'an old sword with cross handle' which could be viewed either 'as a weapon', or 'as a religious symbol' as the instrument with which to rout a diabolic ancestor,[13] but from a novel which in its accounts of Sloebury, and of the various London milieux open to a newly-enriched and ennobled young man, made full use of MOWO's long-established skills as a master of realist fiction, more was demanded.

Attempting to give social and psychological reality to the mundane temptations Walter faces in Sloebury, MOWO created the character of a newcomer to the country town, a Captain Underwood who acts as something of a Pied Piper for the town's idle youth, encouraging them in their drinking, smoking and cardplaying. Every so often MOWO throws out a hint that this worldly bachelor is of the devil's party. Introduced as something of a man of mystery, he possesses 'burning hazel eyes' (p. 17) and confesses to having 'knocked about the world a great deal', (p. 27) yet finally he turns out to be little more than a long-time 'hanger-on' in the house of Erradean. As the embodiment of the louche way of life to which Walter may eventually succumb, Captain Underwood works well as a comparator by which we are led to feel that Walter still retains gentlemanly instincts, but those occasional intimations of Underwood's demonic nature indicate something of the problem MOWO was facing in blending psychological character-study with a long-established literature of spiritual crisis. Underwood's dual nature is indicative of the problem she would face in portraying the Wizard, or Warlock Lord.

Put at its simplest, are we to understand the Warlock Lord as an inner voice of spiritual temptation, or to see him as a spectral presence? Does his room in a ruined tower, swathed in rich materials, furnished with astronomical models, and equipped with a lamp apparently carrying magical powers, and where the heir is summoned once a year to his ritual trial, place him firmly within the world of romance and fairy-tale? If so why does he also appear from time to time in the guise of a modern nineteenth-century gentleman, and more puzzling still, why does he make himself visible to a Glasgow magnate and his companions, while veiling his presence from the Erradean servants? Walter, it is suggested, is wrong to assume that he will simply find himself in a version of a Gothic tale such as *The Mysteries of Udolpho*, where 'all the mysteries ... turned out, he remembered, quite explainable' (pp. 88–9). If, however, we are to interpret the Wizard Lord as the voice of Walter's inner demons, how personal a confrontation can this be when he appears to each successive Lord Erradean in turn, and also confronts the novel's heroine, Oona, with her own inner doubts? Such questions may seem perversely logical in the face of a tale whose title advertises its praeternatural concerns, but also suggest the range of literary genres MOWO was tapping into within this novel as she sought to examine a number of personal spiritual preoccupations.

From the time of wrestling Jacob at Penuel,[14] the literature of spiritual crisis has often been expressed in the language of somatic encounter. John Bunyan's spiritual autobiography, *Grace Abounding to the Chief of Sinners* (1666) endows 'The Tempter', both with dialogue and the power to affect the sinner physically. James Hogg's *The Private Memoirs and Confessions of a Justified Sinner* (1824), which mingled physical assault, with the Gothic, psychological exploration, and a world populated by angels and demons, was less popular than 'the Ettrick Shepherd's' more conventional works in the Victorian period, but given its Scottish setting and the author's connection with *Blackwood's Magazine* it would be surprising if MOWO had not heard of it. However, the literature of spiritual conflict referenced within this tale is more often the allegorical worlds of Dante, on whose life and work she had published a volume in *Blackwood's Foreign Classics for English Readers* (1877), Spenser's *Faerie Queene* (1590–6), or Bunyan's *The Pilgrim's Progress* (1678). The to-ing and fro-ing between conceiving of the Wizard Lord as a metaphysical presence, a psychological phenomenon, and an allegorical concept is central to the dynamic of the novel and also indicative of the dilemmas MOWO, as an intelligent and devout Victorian Christian, wanted to explore within the novel. It was her determination to address these theological issues that in a sense bedevilled a simpler story-line devoted to addressing Walter's personal problems

Convinced that materialism, in its various guises, was the major challenge facing nineteenth-century Christianity, MOWO raised the question of scientific materialism in the encounters between Walter and Katie, the kindly, commonsensical daughter of the Glaswegian magnate. Katie is the fictional descendant of previous MOWO female protagonists such as the heroines of *Miss Marjoribanks* (1866), or *Phoebe, Junior* (1876). Shrewd, capable and wealthy, she admits to herself, after she has turned Walter down, that she could have 'pull[ed] him through ... She would have fought the very devils for him and brought him off' (p. 325). Given that the reader is inclined to agree with Katie that she has been poorly treated by Walter, the narrator's concluding remarks on this episode, seem at first sight to be curiously critical of her: 'Katie thought of Dante's nameless sinner who made "the great refusal". She had lost perhaps the one great opportunity of her life' (p. 325). Dante's 'nameless sinner' is briefly singled out in limbo amongst the hordes who have failed to take an unequivocal stand: these include the angels who failed to engage on either God's or Satan's side in the great fight in heaven, remaining true only to themselves. So, the narrator implies, if Katie, after repeatedly asserting that praeternatural manifestations always have a physical explanation, has been permit-

*Introduction*                                                                                   xix

ted to recognize the reality of Walter's fight with 'devils', her failure to live up to this moment of spiritual vision will haunt her for the rest of her life.

Katie, as the heiress of the cheerily hospitable Glaswegian magnate, who puts such faith in his steam-powered yacht and the other modern comforts with which he surrounds himself, also serves as an embodiment of the material interests the Wizard Lord wishes the heads of the Erradean family to prioritize in their dealings with others. 'It is all for materialism, for profit, for personal advantage – the most self-interested, the least ideal of ages' MOWO wrote of the nineteenth-century,[15] and the suddenness of Walter's inheritance exposes him and the reader to the path which leads from a reasonable desire to safeguard the lot of one's family, to a hard-nosed economic materialism that ends by imprisoning even the most privileged in a world of compromised ideals. Since Walter had never, prior to his inheritance, shown any signs of selfless idealism, to represent its sacrifice as his greatest challenge may seem a little surprising. MOWO was, however, very aware of having been faced with similar challenges herself. Raised by her mother to take considerable pride in her Oliphant heritage,[16] as her boys grew to maturity she became increasingly conscious of the financial worth now attached to her name, and of the hope that they would play their part in cementing this achievement. However, family-related events were to confront her with a sharp contrast between aspiring to achieve her highest personal goals, and the need to accept second best for the good of 'the race' (p. 329). When her destitute oldest brother arrived on her doorstep with three of his children in 1870, she 'remembered making a kind of pretence to myself that I had to think it over, to make a great decision, to give up what hopes I might have had of doing now my very best'. In later years she taught herself to see her sacrifice of the highest artistic aspirations as a matter of necessity:

> Which was God and which was mammon in that individual case it would be hard to say, perhaps; for once in a way mammon, meaning the money which fed my flock, was in a kind of a poor way God, so far as the necessities of that crisis went.[17]

To demonstrate how insidious such temptations can be, MOWO subjects even the heroine of the novel, Oona Forrester, to a moment of doubt as to her own motives.

Raised in virginal purity on a remote Scottish island, and with a name designed to invoke the associations of Una, symbol of true religion in Spenser's *Faerie Queene*, Oona, has seen marriage to Walter as a matter of selflessly responding to his needs, until the Wizard Lord suggests to her that it will be very much for her worldly advantage: 'the blow fell upon her with crushing effect. Every word had truth in it; her mother would be satisfied; the family would profit by it wherever they were scattered; and she would be the first to reap the advantage' (p. 378).

Although contemporary reviews on the whole praised the character of Oona, for modern tastes she is too saintly and self-sacrificial a figure, despite her occasional moments of pique or hauteur with her rivals. Rather than being the heroine of a domestic romance, she belongs more properly to another genre on which MOWO had very recently been working: her 'Little Pilgrim' series.[18] These tales which she admitted became so 'personal' to her that it hurt to publish them,[19] celebrated women's altruism as salvific work, and so pulled against the conviction that had long permeated her literary reviewing and fiction: namely, that however wise or virtuous, women simply did not possess the domestic power to deter their menfolk from immoral or self-destructive behavior.[20] Only when their sons were children could women impose their will, or bring their moral influence to bear, and so the Little Pilgrim stories were particularly inclined to image female salvific work through the mother–child bond. When Oona, acting as an emissary of Christ, accepts Walter, in one of the strangest proposal scenes ever penned, the subsequent narrative commentary makes Oona's quasi-maternal, spiritualized role only too clear.

> To Oona it seemed that life itself became glorious in this service. It raised her above all earthly things. She looked at him with the pity of an angel, with something of the tenderness of a mother, with an identification and willingness to submit which was pure woman (p. 346).

MOWO's substantial revisions, between the serialized version and the first edition, to the scenes in which the Warlock Lord is finally vanquished are therefore significant.[21] Whatever MOWO's first inclinations to make Oona into a transfigured version of Walter's mother ('like his mother' only 'brilliant with celestial certainty' (p. 344)), she recognized that Oona could not take on a Christ-like role of sacrificial substitute for Walter. The initial version in which Oona, almost possessed herself, routs the wizard alone, does not fulfil the terms of the prophecy of Walter's fairy godmother-cum-spiritual counsellor, Miss Milnathort, that it will take 'two souls that are one ... two of one mind – and that one mind set intent upon good, not evil' (p. 240), to withstand the Wizard Lord. Nor could such mediation do the work of individual decision-making and commitment required of Walter, either in theological or aesthetic terms. Both versions, however, concur in allowing the Wizard to depart from his stronghold in the ruins for an unspecified time, but with the tones of Oona's plea that God pardon him ringing in his ears. MOWO had always inclined to the liberal side in the contested matter of the infinity of eternal punishment, and her first Little Pilgrim story had suggested that redemption might be extended to Satan himself. As one of her later tales of the afterlife, expressed it: 'there is that which is beyond hope yet not beyond love'.[22]

If Oona is somewhat hamstrung by the allegorical role she is required to play, the novel makes up for this with the two other female characters to whom Walter at various times seems attracted, Katie Williamson and Julia ('July') Herbert. Their contrasting circumstances are designed to offer food for thought about women's position. All three have only one parent still living, but while Katie's motherless state allows her to reign supreme in her doting father's household,

*Introduction* xxi

Oona and Julia are ultimately bound by their mother's whims and limited means in all practical matters. Nevertheless, for all the wealth and enviable freedoms she enjoys, Katie remarks to Oona that in the matter of marriage, a decision which determines so much in a woman's life, she is as helpless as Oona or Julia:

> We have a great deal to put up with, being women, but we can't help ourselves. Of course the process will go on in his own mind. He will not be so brutal as to let us see that he is weighing and considering (p. 233).

The women's self-respect must therefore lie in the repudiation of the rivalry into which 'the marriage competition' is commonly presumed to throw them. Katie at least commands the financial means to preserve her own dignity, by being able to arrange an instant retreat to Scotland when Walter disappoints the general expectation that he will propose during the London season, whereas Julia Herbert is forced into a series of increasingly flagrant stratagems in pursuit of Walter, and these, moreover, involve her in having to be grateful for the minor favours handed out to her as a poor relation. Despite the contempt from Katie and Oona that her provocatively forward behavior and arch remarks win, the narrator urges the reader to comprehend the last 'desperate struggle' of 'the husband-hunting girl' whose only alternative is to sink into the role of 'governess, or even a seamstress' (p. 288), and for whom flirtation provides the thrill of the chase, and 'all those developments of pleasure, so-called, which are impossible to a woman'. As MOWO reminds the reader, ' She cannot dabble a little in vice as a man can do, and yet return again, and be no worse thought of than before'. It is a mark of the generous compass of MOWO's imagination that she can both make us squirm at Julia's over-vivacious, insinuating manner and lead us to sympathize with her predicament. Her masterly stroke in having Julia wish, out of womanly compassion, to go to comfort her old enemy, Mrs. Methven, because she recognizes that as a mother Mrs. Methven 'has only him in all the world', but also to revert to type in the admission that she can afford this generosity 'now I have got one who is going to stand by me' (p. 418), is as fine a piece of psychology as George Eliot's allowing Rosamond Lydgate to admit her own culpability to her rival, only to retreat to her habitual sense of self-righteousness: 'But now I have told you, and he cannot reproach me any more'.[23]

In order to sustain these comparisons between the three girls, or indeed the two mothers, over the course of a novel which initially ran for seventeen months, MOWO faced the technical challenge of moving the characters among places as disparate as small town Sloebury, the plays, exhibitions and parties of the London season, and the remoter reaches of rural Scotland selected as a suitably wild setting for the preternatural episodes. This is largely achieved by making restlessness, punctuated by periods of aimless sociability, part of the character of a protagonist who is driven to confess that he has been 'wandering about the face of the earth, seeking I don't know what' (p. 236), a sentence which neatly incorporates a satanic echo[24] with a note of existential desperation. Rather than merely leaving this as a device for moving the story along, MOWO uses the journeys back and forth to his ancestral inheritance as a barometer of Walter's mental state. Since she came from a generation still able to recall the earlier north-south travel by paddle-steamer, for MOWO the railways still characterized the scientific and technological advances of 'the age of progress'.[25] In Walter's sudden flight from Kinloch Houran, after his first encounter with the Wizard Lord, the conflict between the metaphysical nature of his recent experience and his desire to find logical, materialist explanations for the phenomena he has witnessed, comes to a head in a railway carriage hurtling him south. The modern lights along the river and the great bridge at Newcastle are a reassuring antithesis to 'the old, ruinous house in which he had been compelled to shut himself up, the wonderful solitude, full of superstitious suggestions, into which he had been plunged' (p. 169). Yet the change in pace from the tranquil boat and waggonette travel along the loch shores, and the 'leisurely friendly trains on the Highland railway, with their broad large windows for the sake of the views' to the 'ploughing and plunging' (p. 169) of the express train, tell a counter-tale of 'excited nerves, shaken health' and uneasy slumbers.

The range of places visited in the course of this novel also called upon MOWO's talent for differing styles of dialogue. *The Wizard's Son* shows her equally at home managing the dialect of the western coast of Scotland, without causing readers undue puzzlement or irritation, as in reproducing the male clubland slang indulged in by Walter and his Sloebury intimates. By now MOWO was capable of slipping dexterously within a single sentence between different registers, as in the following passage:

> The maids who were going to bed, and who heard all this, thought it was beautiful to hear his lordship speaking like that, quite natural to his mother; but that missus was that hard it was no wonder if they didn't get on; and Cousin Sophia from her virgin retirement, where she sat in her dressing-gown reading a French novel, and very much alive to every sound, commented in her own mind, closing her book, in the same sense. "Now she will just go and hold him at arm's length while the boy's heart is melting, and then break her own," Miss Merivale said to herself (p. 51).

The adjective 'virgin', working in combination with the relaxed attire, and private indulgence in the much-bruited hard-boiled cynicism of French novels, also economically conveys Cousin Sophie's self-protective detachment from the passions stirring between mother and son.

A capacity worthy of Henry James, for exploiting the interplay between the rhythms and imagery of narrative comment and crisply managed dialogue, is evident in the close of this early chapter:

*Introduction*                                                                    xxiii

He [Walter] paused a moment, as if doubtful what to do; there was something in
her hasty withdrawal which for an instant disposed him to follow, and she paused
breathless, with a kind of hope, in the half-light of the little hall; but the next moment
his footsteps sounded clear and quick on the pavement, going away. Mrs. Methven
waited until they were almost out of hearing before she closed the door. Angry, baffled, helpless, what could she do? She wiped a hot tear from the corner of her eye
before she went into the drawing-room, where her companion, always on the alert,
had already turned up the light of the lamp, throwing an undesired illumination upon
her face, flushed and troubled from this brief controversy.

"I thought you were never coming in," said Miss Merivale, "and that open door
sends a draught all through the house."

"Walter detained me for a moment to explain some arrangements he has to make
for to-morrow," Mrs. Methven said with dignity. "He likes to keep me au courant of
his proceedings."

Miss Merivale was absolutely silenced by this sublime assumption, notwithstanding the flush of resentment, the glimmer of moisture in the mother's eye (p. 14).

The half-light of the hall echoes the caesuras in the prose rhythms to emphasize the
indeterminacy of the outcome of this encounter and serves as the back-drop to the
bright light Cousin Sophia is anxious to cast upon the proceedings. The 'sublim-
ity' before which Cousin Sophia temporarily quails lies as much in Mrs. Methven's
ability to outdo her with a French phrase as in the boldness of the lie she tells.

The points in this novel which were always going to be the hardest for MOWO
to negotiate are the transitions between social realism and the moments of spiritual crisis, often in Walter's case delivered in a dialogue which seems strangely
remote from his clubland persona. This undoubtedly grates on today's reader.
However, there are also wonderful moments when MOWO undercuts the overwrought rhetoric she has used to convey the intensity of the psychodrama, by
juxtaposing it with the comic or with more mundane concerns. Walter's extraordinary proposal to Oona, for instance, takes place in a boat accompanied by the
*sotto voce* commentary of its steersman, a loyal retainer of Oona's family who
intermittently attempts to warn his young mistress of Walter's supposed insanity by a series of grimaces and mute entreaties. An even more clearly contrived
release of tension occurs between two chapters in the January 1884 portion of
the serialized novel (III, XI and XII).[26] One chapter ends with Walter:

down, down on his knees – down to the dust, hiding his face in gratitude unutterable. He ceased to think of what it was he had been struggling and contending for;
he forgot his enemy, his danger, himself altogether, and, overawed, sank at the feet of
love, which alone can save (p. 360).

When the next chapter begins Walter has been repositioned so as to allow the
narrator to view him from a greater distance and offer a worldly *bon mot* before
returning him to the compassionate attentions of his elderly valet.

> LORD ERRADEEN was found next morning lying on his bed full dressed sleeping like a child. A man in his evening dress in the clear air of morning is at all times a curious spectacle, and suggestive of many uncomfortable thoughts...(p. 360)

Such disjunctures, even when highlighted by the author, do mean that the novel also has a tendency to fracture into its component parts. The chapters dealing with the London season, which *en passant* include a comic account of the performance of Tennyson's play, *The Falcon* (pp. 201–4), are a world away from the scenes detailing the plight of Scottish crofters, and such socio-economic concerns though carefully-wrought and illustrative of the moral decisions Walter must make, are very different in tone from the episodes where Walter wrestles with his inner demons. *The Wizard's Son*, then, is by no means MOWO's most perfectly-crafted novel, but to omit it from the fiction profiled in this edition of her *Selected Works*, would be to diminish the sense of MOWO's range and ambition.

This novel is a clear marker of her increasing interest in the metaphysical both as a subject for her short stories, and in her personal life. Only a few months after the serialization of *The Wizard's Son* had finished, MOWO was once again in Scotland with both her sons. The summer of 1884 was 'a very black moment': Cyril had been sent back from Ceylon after a very short trial in his post there, and his younger brother seemed bent on joining his brother in disporting themselves in the evenings at the Golf Club in St Andrews. Feeling herself as powerless to intervene, as Mrs. Methven had with Walter, MOWO 'went up round the Club to see if I could get a glimpse of them through the lighted windows, but could not'.

> I was very miserable, crying to God for them, both, feeling more miserable almost than I had ever done before – when suddenly there came upon me a great quiet and calm, and I seemed stilled and a heavenly peace came over me – I thought after it must have been the peace that passeth all understanding'.[27]

Perhaps working through her problems in the denouement of *The Wizard's Son* had enabled MOWO to see, like Miss Milnathort, long crippled by a loved-one's shortcomings, 'That is what all our troubles will be when the end comes: just a dream! and good brought out of evil and pardon given to many, many a one that men are just willing to give over and curse instead of blessing' (p. 425).

Notes

1.  See *Selected Works*, vol. 12, pp. 3–25. I have written elsewhere about this story in Jay (1995), pp. 159–61.
2.  *Selected Works*, vol. 12, p. 13.
3.  See Coghill, p. 305; *Selected Works*, vol. 6, p. 208; and Correspondence of Margaret Oliphant with Alexander Macmillan and other members of the publishing house 1858–95, 5 September 1881, Macmillan Archive, British Library [hereafter BL], Add.MS54919 f. 129, vol. 134.
4.  *Selected Works*, vol. 12, p. 6.
5.  MOWO's periodic discussion of the use of 'originals', and the critical problems raised by

*Introduction*                                                         xxv

such attributions, are more fully discussed in Jay (1995), pp. 2, 259.

6.  Jay (1990), p.152; and *Selected Works*, vol. 6, p. 106.

7.  Macmillan Archive, BL, Add.MS54919 f. 77, vol. 134, contains a letter asking Mr Macmillan to stand surety for Cyril's application to the Inner Temple.

8.  Coghill, p. 305; and *Selected Works*, vol. 6, p. 208.

9.  3 October 1883, Macmillan Archive, BL, Add.MS54919 f. 152, vol. 134.

10. Jay (1990), pp. 152–3; and *Selected Works*, vol. 6, pp. 106–7.

11. G. Eliot, *Middlemarch,* ed. D. Carroll (1874; Oxford: Clarendon Press, 1992), pp. 271–2.

12. M. O. W. Oliphant, *The Literary History of England in the End of the Eighteenth and Beginning of the Nineteenth Century*, 3 vols (London Macmillan & Co., 1882), vol. 2, pp. 94–180.

13. *Selected Works*, vol. 12, p. 11.

14. Genesis 32:22–32.

15. M. O. W. Oliphant, 'Laurence Oliphant', *BM*, 145 (February 1889), pp. 280–96, on p. 296.

16. Jay (1990), p. 21; and *Selected Works*, vol. 6, p. 21.

17. Jay (1990), p. 132; and *Selected Works*, vol. 6, p. 92

18. M. O. W. Oliphant, 'A Little Pilgrim in the Unseen', *MacM* (May 1882), pp. 1–19; and M. O. W. Oliphant, 'The Little Pilgrim Goes Up Higher', *MacM* (September 1882), pp. 337–55. The theological implications of these tales are discussed at greater length in Jay (1995), pp. 170–80.

19. Coghill, p. 430; and *Selected Works*, vol. 6, p. 289.

20. Jay (1995), pp. 81–3.

21. See the Textual Variants for *Selected Works*, vol. 13, ch. 13.

22. M. O. W. Oliphant, 'On the Dark Mountains', *BM*, 144 (November 1888), pp. 646–63, on p. 663.

23. Eliot, *Middlemarch*, p. 787.

24. Job 1:7: 'And the LORD said unto Satan, Whence comest thou? Then Satan answered the LORD, and said, From going to and fro in the earth, and from walking up and down in it'.

25. M. O. W. Oliphant, ''Tis Sixty Years Since', *BM*, 161 (May 1897), pp. 599–64, on pp. 601–2; and *Selected Works*, vol. 13, pp. 445–74.

26. Writing to the publisher from Heidelberg in December 1883, MOWO hoped that the last numbers of *The Wizard's Son* 'will tell' because they had 'cost her more work than a whole volume', 4 December 1883, Macmillan Archive, BL, Add.MS54919 f. 153, vol. 134.

27. Jay (1990), pp. 52–3; and *Selected Works*, vol. 6, pp. 394–5.

# SELECT BIBLIOGRAPHY

## Manuscript

Correspondence of Margaret Oliphant with Alexander Macmillan and other members of the publishing house 1858–95, Macmillan Archive, British Library, Add.MS54919.

## Online Publications

*Dictionary of the Scots Language*, at http://www.dsl.ac.uk/.

## Printed

Arnold, M., *The Complete Prose Works of Matthew Arnold*, ed. R. H.Super, 10 vols (Ann Arbor, MI: University of Michigan Press, 1960–74).

Austen, J., *Persuasion*, ed. J. Todd and A. Blank (1817; Cambridge: Cambridge University Press, 2006).

Brown, S. J., 'Scotland and the Oxford Movement', *The Oxford Movement: Europe and the Wider World 1830–1930* (Cambridge: Cambridge University Press, 2012).

Bunyan, J., *Pilgrim's Progress from This World to That Which Is to Come; Delivered Under the Similitude of a Dream,* ed. J. B.Wharey, 2nd edn, revsd. R. Sharrock (1678; Oxford:

Clarendon Press, 1960).

—, *Grace Abounding to the Chief of Sinners,* ed. R. Sharrock (1666; Oxford, Clarendon Press, 1962).

Byron, G. G., *Byron's Letters and Journals*, ed. L. A. Marchand, 12 vols (London: John Murray, 1973–82), vol. 2.

—, *The Poetical Works of Lord Byron* (London: Oxford University Press, 1935).

Clarke, J. S., *Margaret Oliphant: A Bibliography* (St Lucia, Queensland: University of Queensland, 1986).

—, *Margaret Oliphant (1828–1897): Non-Fictional Writings. A Bibliography*, compiled by J. S. Clarke, Victorian Fiction Research Guide 26 (St Lucia, Queensland: Department of English, University of Queensland, 1997).

Eliot, G., *Middlemarch,* ed. D. Carroll (1874; Oxford: Clarendon Press, 1992).

– xxvii –

Graham, R., *John Knox: Democrat* (London: Robert Hale, 2001).

Henderson, D. M., *Highland Soldier: A Social Study of the Highland Regiments 1820–1920* (Edinburgh: John Donaldson, 1989).

Hogg, J., *The Private Memoirs and Confessions of a Justified Sinner*, ed. J. Carey (1824; London: Oxford University Press, 1969).

Hunt, L., *The Poetical Works of Leigh Hunt*, ed. H. S. Milford (London: Oxford University Press, 1923).

Huxley, T., 'On the Hypothesis that Animals are Automata, and Its History' (1874), *Collected Essays*, 8 vols (London: Macmillan, 1893).

Jay, E. (ed.), *The Autobiography of Margaret Oliphant: The Complete Text* (Oxford: Oxford University Press, 1990).

—, 'Margaret Oliphant', in J. John (ed.), *Oxford Bibliographies in Victorian Literature* (New York: Oxford University Press, 2011), at http://www.oxfordbibliographies.com/view/document/obo-9780199799558/obo-9780199799558–0048.xml [accessed 27 October 2014].

—, *Mrs Oliphant: 'A Fiction to Herself': A Literary Life* (Oxford: Clarendon Press, 1995).

Magnus, P., *Gladstone: A Biography* (1963; London: Penguin, 2001).

Mitchell, S., *Daily Life in Victorian England* (Westport, CT: Greenwood Press, 1996).

Oliphant, M.O.W.O., 'Giacomo Leopardi', *BM*, 98 (October 1865), pp. 459–80.

—, *Miss Marjoribanks,* 3 vols (Edinburgh and London: William Blackwood & Sons, 1866), in *Selected Works*, vol. 18.

—, 'Novels', *BM*, 102 (September 1867), pp. 257–80, in *Selected Works*, vol. 1, pp. 367–96.

—, 'Alexandre Dumas', *BM*, 114 (July 1873), pp. 111–30, in *Selected Works*, vol. 14, pp. 165–84.

—, 'The Early Years of Dante', *CM*, 32 (October 1875), pp. 471–89.

—, 'Giacomo Leopardi', *CM* (September 1876), pp. 341–57, in *Selected Works*, vol. 14, pp. 287–302.

—, 'The Secret Chamber', *BM*, 120 (December 1876), pp. 709–29, in *Selected Works*, vol. 12, pp. 3–25.

—, *Phoebe, Junior,* 3 vols (London: Hurst and Blackett, 1876), in *Selected Works*, vol. 19.

—, *The Makers of Florence* (London: Macmillan & Co.,1876).

—, *Dante* (Edinburgh and London: William Blackwood & Sons, 1877).

—, *He That Will Not When He May*, 3 vols (London: Macmillan & Co., 1880).

—, 'A Little Pilgrim in the Unseen', *MacM* (May 1882), pp. 1–19.

—, 'The Little Pilgrim Goes Up Higher', *MacM* (September 1882), pp. 337–55.

—, *The Literary History of England in the End of the Eighteenth and Beginning of the Nineteenth Century*, 3 vols (London: Macmillan & Co., 1882).

—, *Hester: A Story of Contemporary Life,* 3 vols (London: Macmillan & Co.,1883), in *Selected Works*, vol. 20.

—, *Sir Tom*, 3 vols (London: Macmillan & Co., 1884).

—, 'On the Dark Mountains', *BM*, 144 (November 1888), pp. 646–63.

*Select Bibliography*      xxix

—, Laurence Oliphant', *BM*, 145 (February 1889), pp. 280–96.

—, *Kirsteen: The Story of a Scotch Family Seventy Years Ago* (London: Macmillan & Co., 1890), in *Selected Works*, vol. 22.

—, ''Tis Sixty Years Since', *BM*, 161 (May 1897) pp. 599–64, in *Selected Works*, vol. 13, pp. 445–74.

—, *The Autobiography and Letters of Mrs. M. O. W. Oliphant*, ed. Mrs H. Coghill (Edinburgh and London: Blackwood, 1899), in *Selected Works*, vol. 6.

Prochaska, F. K., *Women and Philanthropy in Nineteenth-century England* (Oxford: Oxford University Press, 1980).

Radcliffe, A., *The Mysteries of Udolpho: A Romance*, ed. B. Dobrée (London: Oxford University Press, 1966).

Scott, W., *The Lives of the Novelists* (1825; London: Henry Frowde, Oxford University Press, 1906).

—, *The Poetical Works of Sir Walter Scott*, ed. J. L. Robertson (London: Oxford University Press, 1964).

—, *The Edinburgh Edition of the Waverley Novels*, ed. J. H. Alexander et al., 30 vols (Edinburgh: Edinburgh University Press, 2007–12).

Spenser, E., *The Poetical Works of Edmund Spenser*, ed. J. C. Smith and E. de Selincourt (London: Oxford University Press, 1965).

Tennyson, A., *The Poems of Tennyson*, ed. C. Ricks, 3 vols (Harlow: Longman, 1987).

Trollope, A., *An Autobiography*, intro. M. Sadleir (1883; London, Oxford University Press, 1968).

Winter, A., *Mesmerized: Powers of Mind in Victorian Britain* (Chicago and London: University of Chicago Press, 1998).

# THE WIZARD'S SON

This text is based upon the first three-volume edition published by Macmillan and Co., in May 1884, rather than upon the novel's first appearance in serial form in *MacM* (November 1882–March 1884). There is firm evidence for preferring the first edition. Writing in October 1883 to protest against the decision by John Morley, *MacM*'s editor, to reduce the length of each number as the novel approached its conclusion, MOWO vowed, 'I will revise it carefully for republication instead'.[1] Accordingly, the major alterations reflect definite artistic decisions, rather than minor pieces of stylistic tidying, although these too feature, together with the normal small typographical changes.

In effect Morley's decision resulted in extending the novel across seventeen months in the magazine. When this idea had been first mooted back in May 1883, the date when Morley took over the editorship of *MacM* after six episodes of *The Wizard's Son* had already appeared, MOWO declared it be a matter of indifference as long as she enjoyed the same 'room'.[2] However, as the pages per issue began to diminish (May 1883's generous allowance of twenty-five pages had been cut to thirteen by February 1884) this told against her normally expansive style. The need to continue producing three chapters per issue, despite making them shorter than usual, exerted pressure on the pace of the concluding chapters, and also explains the rather unusual unevenness of chapter distribution between the three volumes: while the first volume contains a conventional fifteen chapters, the second contains seventeen, and the third, nineteen. Part of MOWO's strategy in making her revisions appears to have been the decision to make quite extensive cuts between the serial and the first edition in volumes II and III. Since Morley's cuts to the page length of each episode had not taken effect until chapter 10 of the second volume, possibly the imbalance between the more expansive middle volume and the shorter chapters of the third volume struck MOWO as she re-read. There were also alterations, discussed in the Introduction, she wished to make in the interests of the thematic coherence of the novel. In making these more substantial revisions, she is unlikely to have been influenced by the novel's critical reception in the press, since, apart from a couple of admiring references to the initial episodes of November and December 1882,[3]

– 1 –

there were no major reviews until the novel's first edition appeared in May 1884. Mixed though these were, there was a degree of unanimity in both the praise for the way in which the novel's women figures were drawn, and the criticism directed at the creation of the warlock-lord.

Contracts drawn up prior to publication will have led to the novel's simultaneous publication in one-volume form by Macmillan's New York branch. Two other one-volume American editions appeared that year, published respectively by J. W. Lovell (Lovell's Library, vol. 6, no. 326) and by Harper (Franklin Square Library). Such American editions are usually assumed to be piracies, printed without the permission of either the author or the legitimate publisher. However, an 1883 letter to Macmillan, expressing her surprise that she had received a cheque from Harper which she had assumed would in this instance be paid direct to Macmillan, suggests that Macmillan had reached an accommodation with their American competitor, and possibly also indicates that MOWO, like George Eliot and other authors popular with a transatlantic readership, may have arrived at some settlement with them for each republication of her work not already under her publisher's copyright.[4] However, in the case of *Littell's Living Age* of Boston, their practice of serializing the novel towards the end of each month, between 21 April and 29 March 1884, suggests that this was to allow time for copies of each month's number to reach America before being swiftly pirated.

*The Wizard's Son* had formed part of a three-novel deal proposed to Macmillan by MOWO. She had raised the matter with George Lillie Craik, the partner who handled the publisher's financial arrangements, as early as November 1881, suggesting the firm pay her £1700 for three novels (*The Wizard's Son, Hester,* and *Sir Tom*), though she would reserve the rights to the Tauchnitz editions, destined for the European market. The Tauchnitz edition of *The Wizard's Son* duly appeared in three volumes, rather than their usual two-volume format, in 1884. Perhaps feeling that negotiations about European copyright agreements were at a tricky stage, MOWO also suggested the insertion of a clause covering her rights in event of change. In addition she had received confirmation from the Tillotson agency that she would receive £300 for the prior publication of *Sir Tom* as a newspaper serial.[5] By the following summer, in principle still anxious to proceed with this package, MOWO had changed her mind about the terms, now asking for a two-year agreed income of £1,000 per annum, paid quarterly.[6] She claimed that the negotiations over separate novels only delayed her work and annoyed her, but assuming that she could have commanded £750 per novel – the price the publishing house of Macmillan had paid in 1878 for *He That Will Not When He May* – in effect she was sacrificing £250, and potentially submitting greater control of her on-going writing to the publisher than would have been involved in an outright fee.

Macmillan's was very prompt in following up the 1884 three-volume edition with a one-volume English edition, which appeared in the same year. Given the novel's ghostly theme, it may have been considered especially suitable for the Christmas market. The 1884 one-volume edition is hard to come by these days, and it may have been the realization that this had been too short a run that led Macmillan to reprint it in their Globe series in 1888, and then again in their 'three-and-sixpenny series' in 1894: this last was to prove the final issue of the novel until the current volume. The 1894 one-volume edition, clearly states on the verso of the flyleaf that it is a reprint of the 1884 one-volume edition, rather than a new edition, and since it is the last printing of the novel MOWO could have seen, I have used this for a final comparison in the Textual Variants listed at the end of the volume.

The relation between the copy text, (the first, three-volume edition of 1884), the serialization, and the one-volume reprint is inconsistent. The first volume of text as it appears in the one-volume edition appears to have been based upon the serial version rather than upon the three-volume first edition, an unusual procedure possibly predicated upon the frequency with which new errors had been introduced between the serial and the first edition. A further piece of evidence for claiming that the printers initially followed the serial edition is provided by the word 'clanjamfry' (p. 431, n. 76) which would have been unfamiliar to them: it appears correctly in unhyphenated form in the first three-volume edition, but in the subsequent one-volume edition as 'clan-jamfry', presumably because of a failure to recognize that the hyphen was a product of the word being split over two lines in the magazine's narrow columns. By volumes two and three, however, there was little choice but to use the first edition as the source text, since these volumes contained chapters in which MOWO had, as promised, significantly revised the plot.

Where variations in punctuation occur in each of the editions consulted, this may well have been the result of decisions made by the different type-setters involved, since in her handwritten manuscripts MOWO was notoriously fond of using the em dash in lieu of more formal punctuation. Moreover, successive printers' preferences seem to have operated in matters such as the hyphenation of such words and phrases as 'down-stairs', or 'by-the-by'.

Please note that there can be significant variances not only between different editions of texts but also differences between individual extant copies. Any variances between our printed text and other original texts have to be considered in this light.

Every effort has been made to reproduce this text as closely to the original as possible without actually replicating the original typography. Original capitalization and punctuation has been retained and only the most significant typographical errors have been amended where they undermine the understanding of the text. All silent corrections to obvious mistakes in the copy text are listed in the Silent Corrections. In addition, the title pages for volumes two and three, which replicate the information on the initial title page have been omitted, and the volume number inserted before the opening chapters of volumes II and III.

4 *The Selected Works of Margaret Oliphant, Volume 21*

The serialization of *The Wizard's Son* corresponds as follows with the two book formats:

| MacM volume number and date | MacM page numbers | Chapters in three-volume edition | Chapters in one-volume edition |
|---|---|---|---|
| 47 (November 1882) | 1–20 | i, 1–3 | 1–3 |
| 47 (December 1882) | 86–107 | i, 4–6 | 4–6 |
| 47 (January 1883) | 161–83 | i, 7–9 | 7–9 |
| 47 (February 1883) | 241–63 | i, 10–12 | 10–12 |
| 47 (March 1883) | 321–45 | i, 13–15 | 13–15 |
| 47 (April 1883) | 417–36 | ii, 1–3 | 16–18 |
| 48 (May 1883) | 1–25 | ii, 4–6 | 19–21 |
| 48 (June 1883) | 85–108 | ii, 7–9 | 22–4 |
| 48 (July 1883) | 165–81 | ii, 10–12 | 25–7 |
| 48 (August 1883) | 261–76 | ii, 13–15 | 28–30 |
| 48 (September 1883) | 378–93 | ii, 16–17, iii, i | 31–3 |
| 48 (October 1883) | 504–22 | iii, 2–4 | 34–6 |
| 49 (November 1883) | 56–73 | iii, 5–7 | 37–9 |
| 49 (December 1883) | 132–48 | iii, 8–10 | 40–2 |
| 49 (January 1884) | 202–20 | iii, 11–13 | 43–5 |
| 49 (February 1884) | 279–92 | iii, 14–16 | 46–8 |
| 49 (March 1884) | 368–83 | iii, 17–19 | 49–51 |

The serial instalments are indicated in this edition by \*\*\*.

## Notes

1. Correspondence of Margaret Oliphant with Alexander Macmillan and other members of the publishing house 1858–95, 3 October 1883, Macmillan Archive, British Library [hereafter BL], Add.MS54919. f.152, vol. 134.
2. 23 May 1883, Macmillan Archive, BL, Add.MS54919. f.142, vol. 134.
3. *Illustrated London News* (11 November 1882), p. 495; and *Illustrated London News* (9 December 1882), p. 611.
4. 1 March, 1883, Macmillan Archive, BL, Add.MS54919. f.136, vol. 134.
5. 25 November 1881, Macmillan Archive, BL, Add.MS54919. f.33, vol. 134.
6. 28 July 1882, Macmillan Archive, BL, Add.MS54919. f.125, vol. 134.

# THE WIZARD'S SON

A Novel

BY

MRS. OLIPHANT

AUTHOR OF 'THE CURATE IN CHARGE,' 'YOUNG MUSGRAVE,' ETC.

IN THREE VOLUMES
VOL. I.

London
MACMILLAN AND CO.
1884

*[The Right of Translation and Reproduction is Reserved]*

LONDON:
R. CLAY, SONS AND TAYLOR, PRINTERS,
BREAD STREET HILL

# THE WIZARD'S SON, VOLUME I

## CHAPTER I.

THE Methvens[1] occupied a little house in the outskirts of a little town where there was not very much going on of any description, and still less which they could take any share in, being, as they were, poor and unable to make any effective response to the civilities shown to them. The family consisted of three persons – the mother, who was a widow with one son; the son himself, who was a young man of three or four and twenty; and a distant cousin of Mrs. Methven's, who lived with her, having no other home. It was not a very happy household. The mother had a limited income and an anxious temper; the son a somewhat volatile and indolent disposition, and no ambition at all as to his future, nor anxiety as to what was going to happen to him in life. This, as may be supposed, was enough to introduce many uneasy elements into their joint existence; and the third of the party, Miss Merivale, was not of the class of the peacemakers to whom Scripture allots a special blessing.[2] She had no amiable glamour in her eyes, but saw her friends' imperfections with a clearness of sight which is little conducive to that happy progress of affairs which is called 'getting on.' The Methvens were sufficiently proud to keep their difficulties out of the public eye, but on very many occasions, unfortunately, it had become very plain to themselves that they did not 'get on.' It was not any want of love. Mrs. Methven was herself aware, and her friends were in the constant habit of saying, that she had sacrificed everything for Walter. Injudicious friends are fond of making such statements, by way, it is to be supposed, of increasing the devotion and gratitude of the child to the parent:[a] but the result is, unfortunately, very often the exact contrary of what is desired – for no one likes to have his duty in this respect pointed out to him, and whatever good people may think, it is not in itself an agreeable thought that 'sacrifices' have been made for one, and an obligation placed upon one's shoulders from the beginning of time, independent of any wish or claim upon the part of the person served. The makers of sacrifices have seldom the reward which surrounding spectators, and in many cases themselves, think their due. Mrs. Methven herself would probably have been at a loss to name what were the special sacrifices she had made for Walter. She had remained a widow, but that she would have been eager to add was no sacrifice. She had pinched herself more or less to find the means for his education, which had been of what is supposed in England to be the best kind:[a] and she had, while he was a boy, subordinated her own tastes and pleasures to his, and eagerly sought out everything that was likely to be agreeable to him. When they took their yearly money[b] – as it is considered necessary for him[c] – places that Walter liked, or where he could find amusement, or had friends, were eagerly sought for. 'Women,' Mrs. Methven said, 'can make themselves comfortable anywhere; but a boy, you know, is quite different.' 'Quite,' Miss Merivale would say: 'Oh, if you only knew them as well as we do; they are creatures entirely without resources. You must put their toys into their very hands.' 'There is no question of toys with Walter – he has plenty of resources. It is not that,' Mrs. Methven would explain, growing red. 'I hope I am not one of the silly mothers that thrust their children upon everybody:[d] but, of course, a boy must be considered. Everybody who has had to do with men – or boys – knows that they must be considered.' A woman whose life has been mixed up with these troublesome beings feels the superiority of her experience to those who know nothing about them. And in this way, without spoiling him or treating him with ridiculous devotion, as the king of her fate, Walter had been 'considered' all his life.

For the rest, Mrs. Methven had, it must be allowed, lived a much more agreeable life in the little society of Sloebury when her son was young than she did now that he had come to years, mis-named, of discretion.[4] Then she had given her little tea-parties, or even a small occasional dinner, at which her handsome boy would make his appearance when it was holiday time, interesting everybody; or, when absent, would still furnish a very pleasant subject of talk to the neighbours, who thought his mother did a great deal too much for him, but still were pleased to discuss a boy who was having the best of educations, and at a public school. In those days she felt herself very comfortable in Sloebury, and was asked to all the best houses, and felt a modest pride in the certainty that she was able to offer something in return. But matters were very different when Walter was four-and-twenty instead of fourteen. By that time it was apparent that he was not going to take the world by storm, or set the Thames on fire;[5] and, though she had been too sensible to brag, Mrs. Methven had thought both these things possible, and perhaps had allowed it to be perceived that she considered something great, something out of the way, to be Walter's certain career. But twenty-four is, as she said herself, so different! He had been unsuccessful in some of his examinations, and for others he had not been 'properly prepared.' His mother did not take refuge in the thought that the examiners were partial or the trials unfair; but there was naturally always a word as to the reason why he did not succeed – he had not been 'properly pre-

The Wizard's Son, Volume I                                    9

pared.' He knew of one only a few days before the eventful moment, and at this time of day, she asked indignantly, when everything is got by competition, how is a young man who has not 'crammed' to get the better of one who has? The fact remained that at twenty-four, Walter, evidently a clever fellow, with a great many endowments, had got nothing to do; and, what was worse – a thing which his mother, indeed, pretended to be unconscious of, but which everybody else in the town remarked upon – he was not in the least concerned about this fact, but took his doing nothing quite calmly as the course of nature, and neither suffered from it, nor made any effort to place himself in a different position. He 'went in for' an examination when it was put before him as a thing to do, and took his failure more than philosophically when he failed, as, as yet, he had always done: and, in the mean time, contentedly lived on, without disturbing himself, and tranquilly let the time go by – the golden time which should have shaped his life.

This is not a state of affairs which can bring happiness to any household. There is a kind of parent – or rather it should be said of a mother, for no parent of the other sex is supposed capable of so much folly – to whom everything is good that her child, the cherished object of her affections, does; and this is a most happy regulation of nature, and smoothes[a] away the greatest difficulties of life for many simple-hearted folk, without doing half so much harm as is attributed to it; for disapproval has little moral effect, and lessens the happiness of all par-ties, without materially lessening the sins of the erring. But, unfortunately, Mrs. Methven was not of this happy kind. She saw her son's faults almost too clearly, and they gave her the most poignant pain. She was a proud woman, and that he should suffer in the opinion of the world was misery and grief to her. She was stung to the heart by disappointment in the failure of her many hopes and pro-jects for him. She was stricken with shame to think of all the fine things that had been predicted of Walter in his boyish days, and that not one of them had come true. People had ceased now to speak of the great things that Walter would do. They asked '*What* was he going to do?' in an entirely altered tone, and this went to her heart. Her pride suffered the most terrible blow. She could not bear the thought; and though she maintained a calm face to the world, and represented herself as entirely satisfied, Walter knew otherwise, and had gradually replaced his old careless affection for his mother by an embittered opposition and resist-ance to her, which made both their lives wretched enough. How it was that he did not make an effort to escape from her continual remonstrances, her appeals and entreaties, her censure and criticism, it is very difficult to tell. To have gone away, and torn her heart with anxiety, but emancipated himself from a yoke which it was against the dignity of his manhood to bear, would have been much more natural. But he had no money, and he had not the energy to seize upon any way of providing for himself. Had such an opportunity fallen at his feet he would probably have accepted it with fervour; but Fortune did not put herself out of the way to provide for him, nor he to be provided for. Notwithstanding the many scenes which took place in the seclusion of that poor little house, when the mother, what with love, shame, mortification, and impatience, would all but rave in impotent passion, appealing to him, to the pride, the ambition, the principle which so far as could be seen the young man did not possess, Walter held upon his way with an obstinate pertinacity, and did nothing. How he managed to do this without losing all self-respect and every better feeling it is impossible to say; but he did so somehow, and was still 'a nice enough fellow,' notwithstanding that everybody condemned him; and had not even lost the good opinion of the little society, though it was unanimous in blame. The only way in which he responded to his mother's remonstrances and complaints was by seeking his pleasure and such occupation as contented him – which was a little cricket now and then, a little lawn-tennis, a little flirtation – as far away from her as possible; and by being as little at home as possible. His temper was a little spoilt by the scenes which awaited him when he went home; and these seemed to justify to himself his gradual separation from his mother's house; but never induced him to sacrifice, or even modify, his own course. He appeared to think that he had a justification for his conduct in the opposition it met with; and that his pride was involved in the necessity for never giving in. If he had been let alone, he represented to himself, everything would have been different; but to yield to this perpetual bullying was against every instinct. And even the society which disapproved so much gave a certain encouragement to Walter in this point of view: for it was Mrs. Methven whom everybody blamed.[6] It was her ridiculous pride, or her foolish indulgence, or her sinful backing-up of his natural indolence; even some people thought it was her want of comprehension of her son which had done it, and that Walter would have been entirely a different person in different hands. If she had not thought it a fine thing to have him appear as a useless fine gentleman above all necessity of working for his living, it was incredible that he could have allowed the years to steal by without making any exertion. This was what the town decided, not without a good deal of sympathy for Walter. What could be expected? Under the guidance of a foolish mother, a young man always went wrong; and in this case he did not go wrong, poor fellow! he only wasted his existence, nothing worse. Sloebury had much consideration for the young man.

Perhaps it added something to the exasperation with which Mrs. Methven saw all her efforts fail that she had some perception of this, and knew that it was supposed to be her fault. No doubt in her soul it added to the impatience and indignation and pain with which she contemplated the course of affairs, which she was without strength to combat, yet could not let alone. Now and then, indeed, she did control herself so far as to let them alone, and then there was nothing but tranquillity and peace in the house. But she was a conscientious woman, and, poor soul! she had a temper – the very complacency and calm with which her son went upon his way, the approval he showed of her better conduct when she left him to his own devices, struck her in some moments with such sudden indignation and pain, that she could no longer contain herself. He, who might have been anything he pleased, to be nothing! He, of whom everybody had predicted such great things! At such moments the sight of Walter smiling, strolling along with his hands in his pockets, excited her almost to frenzy. Poor lady! So many women would have been proud of him – a handsome young fellow in flannels, with his cricket bat or his racquet when occasion served. But love and injured pride were bitter in her heart, and she could not bear the sight. All this while, however, nobody knew anything about the scenes that arose in the little house, which preserved a show of happiness and tender union long after the reality was gone. Indeed, even Miss Merivale, who had unbounded opportunities of knowing, took a long time to make up her mind that Walter and his mother did not 'get on.'

Such was the unfortunate state of affairs at the time when this history begins. The Methvens were distantly connected, it was known, with a great family in Scotland, which took no notice whatever of them, and, indeed, had very little reason so to do, Captain Methven being long since dead, and his widow and child entirely unknown to the noble house, from which it was so great an honour to derive a little, much-diluted, far-off drop of blood, more blue and more rich than the common. It is possible that had the connection been by Mrs. Methven's side she would have known more about it, and taken more trouble to keep up her knowledge of the family. But it was not so, and she had even in her younger days been conscious of little slights and neglects which had made her rather hostile than otherwise to the great people from whom her husband came. 'I know nothing about the Erradeens,' she would say; 'they are much too grand to take any notice of us: and I am too proud to seek any notice from them.'

'I am afraid, my dear, there is a good deal in that,' said old Mrs. Wynn, the wife of the old rector, shaking her white head. This lady was a sort of benign embodiment of justice in Sloebury. She punished nobody, but she saw the right and wrong with a glance that was almost infallible, and shook her head though she never exacted any penalty.

Here Miss Merivale would seize the occasion to strike in –

'Prejudice is prejudice,' she said, 'whatever form it takes. A lord has just as much chance of being nice as an – apothecary.' This was said because the young doctor,[7] newly admitted into his father's business, who thought no little of himself, was within reach, and just then caught Miss Merivale's eye.

'That is a very safe speech, seeing there are neither lords nor apothecaries here,' he said with the blandest smile. He was not a man to be beaten at such a game.

'But a lord may have influence, you know. For Walter's sake I would not lose sight of him,' said Mrs. Wynn.

'You cannot lose sight of what you have never seen: besides, influence is of no consequence nowadays. Nobody can do anything for you – save yourself,' said Mrs. Methven with a little sigh. Her eyes turned involuntarily to where Walter was. He was always in the middle of everything that was going on. Among the Sloebury young people he had a little air of distinction, or so at least his mother thought. She was painfully impartial, and generally, in her anxiety, perceived his bad points rather than his good ones; but as she glanced at the group, love for once allowed itself to speak, though always with an accent peculiar to the character of the thinker. She allowed to herself that he had an air of distinction, a something more than the others – alas, that nothing ever came of it! The others[a] all, or almost all, were already launched in the world. They were doing or trying to do something – whereas Walter! But she took care that nobody should hear that irrepressible sigh.

'I am very sorry for it,' said Mrs. Wynn, 'for there are many people who would never push for themselves, and yet do very well indeed when they are put in the way.'

'I am all for the pushing people,' said Miss Merivale. 'I like the new state of affairs. When every one stands for himself, and you get just as much as you work for, there will be no grudges and sulkings with society. Though I'm a Tory, I like every man to make his own way.'[8]

'A lady's politics are never to be calculated upon,' said the Rector,[b] who was standing up against the fire on his own hearth, rubbing his old white hands. 'It is altogether against the principles of Toryism, my dear lady, that a man should make his own way. It is sheer democracy.[9] As for that method of examinations,[10] it is one of the most levelling principles of the time – it is one of Mr. Gladstone's instruments for the destruction of society. When the son of a cobbler is just as likely to come to high command as your son or mine, what is to become of the country?' the old clergyman said, lifting those thin white hands.

Mr. Gladstone's name was as a firebrand[11] thrown into the midst of this peaceable little country community. The speakers all took fire. They thought that there was no doubt about what was going to come of the country. It was going to destruction as fast as fate could carry it. When society had dropped to pieces, and the rabble had come uppermost, and England had become a mere name, upon which all foreign nations should trample,[12] and wild Irishmen[13] dance war dances, and Americans expectorate,[14] then Mr. Gladstone would be seen in his true colours. While this was going on, old Mrs. Wynn sat in her easy-chair and shook her head. She declared always that she was no politician. And young Walter Methven, attracted by the sudden quickening of the conversation which naturally attended the introduction of this subject, came forward, ready in the vein of opposition which was always his favourite attitude.

'Mr. Gladstone must be a very great man,' he said. 'I hear it is a sign of being in society when you foam at the mouth at the sound of his name.'

'You young fellows think it fine to be on the popular side; but wait till you are my age,' cried one of the eager speakers. 'It will not matter much to me. There will

*The Wizard's Son, Volume I* 13

be peace in my days.'[15] 'But wait,' cried another, 'and see how you will like it when everything topples down together, the crown and the state, and the aristocracy, and public credit,[16] and national honour, and property, and the constitution, and –'

So many anxious and alarmed politicians here spoke together that the general voice became inarticulate, and Walter Methven, representing the opposition, was at liberty to laugh.

'Come one, come all!' he cried, backed up by the arm of the sofa, upon which Mrs. Wynn sat shaking her head. 'It would be a fine thing for me and all the other proletarians. Something would surely fall our way.'

His mother watched him, standing up against the sofa, confronting them all, with her usual exasperated and angry affection. She thought, as she looked at him, that there was nothing he was not fit for. He was clever enough for Parliament;[17] he might have been prime minister – but he was nothing! nothing, and likely to be nothing, doing nothing, desiring nothing. Her eye fell on young Wynn, the rector's nephew, who had just got a fellowship at his college,[18] and on the doctor's son, who was just entering into a share of his father's practice, and on Mr. Jeremy the young banker, whose attentions fluttered any maiden to whom he might address them. They were Walter's contemporaries, and not one of them was worthy, she thought, to be seen by the side of her boy; but they had all got before him in the race of life. They were something and he was nothing. It was not much wonder if her heart was sore and angry. When she turned round to listen civilly to something that was said to her, her face was contracted and pale. It was more than she could bear. She made a move to go away before any of the party was ready, and disturbed Miss Merivale in the midst of a *tête-à-tête,* which was a thing not easily forgiven.

Walter walked home with them in great good humour, but his mother knew very well that he was not coming in. He was going to finish the evening elsewhere. If he had come in would she have been able to restrain herself? Would she not have fallen upon him, either in anger or in grief, holding up to him the examples of young Wynn and young Jeremy and the little doctor? She knew she would not have been able to refrain, and it was almost a relief to her, though it was another pang, when he turned away at the door.

'I want to speak to Underwood about to-morrow?'[a] he said.

'What is there about to-morrow? Of all the people in Sloebury Captain Underwood is the one I like least,' she said. 'Why must you always have something to say to him when every one else is going to bed?'

'I am not going to bed, nor is he,' said Walter lightly.

Mrs. Methven's nerves were highly strung. Miss Merivale had passed in before them, and there was nobody to witness this little struggle, which she knew would end in nothing, but which was inevitable. She grasped him by the arm in her eagerness and pain.

'Oh, my boy!' she said, 'come in, come in, and think of something more than the amusement of tomorrow. Life is not all play, though you seem to think so.

For once listen to me, Walter – oh, listen to me! You cannot go on like this. Think of all the others; all at work, every one of them, and you doing nothing.'

'Do you want me to begin to do something now,' said Walter, 'when you have just told me everybody was going to bed?'

'Oh! if I were you,' she cried in her excitement, 'I would rest neither night nor day. I would not let it be said that I was the last, and every one of them before me.'

Walter shook himself free of her detaining hold. 'Am I to be a dustman, or a scavenger, or – what?' he said,[a] contemptuously. 'I know no other trades that are followed at this hour.'

Mrs. Methven had reached the point at which a woman has much ado not to cry in the sense of impotence and exasperation which such an argument brings. 'It is better to do anything than to do nothing,' she cried, turning away from him and hastening in at the open door.

He paused a moment, as if doubtful what to do; there was something in her hasty withdrawal which for an instant disposed him to follow, and she paused breathless, with a kind of hope, in the half-light of the little hall; but the next moment his footsteps sounded clear and quick on the pavement, going away. Mrs. Methven waited until they were almost out of hearing before she closed the door. Angry, baffled, helpless, what could she do? She wiped a hot tear from the corner of her eye before she went into the drawing-room, where her companion, always on the alert, had already turned up the light of the lamp, throwing an undesired illumination upon her face, flushed and troubled from this brief controversy.

'I thought you were never coming in,' said Miss Merivale, 'and that open door sends a draught all through the house.'

'Walter detained me for a moment to explain some arrangements he has to make for to-morrow,' Mrs. Methven said with dignity. 'He likes to keep me *au courant*[19] of his proceedings.'

Miss Merivale was absolutely silenced by this sublime assumption, notwithstanding the flush of resentment, the glimmer of moisture in the mother's eye.

# CHAPTER II.

WALTER walked along the quiet, almost deserted street with a hasty step and a still hastier rush of disagreeable thoughts. There was, he felt, an advantage in being angry, in the sensation of indignant resistance to a petty tyranny. For a long time past he had taken refuge in this from every touch of conscience and sense of time lost and opportunities neglected. He was no genius, but he was not so dull as not to know that his life was an entirely unsatisfactory one, and himself in the wrong altogether; everything rotten in the state of his existence, and a great deal that must be set right one time or another in all his habits and ways. The misfortune was that it was so much easier to put off this process till to-morrow than to begin it to-day. He had never been roused out of the boyish condition of mind in which a certain resistance to authority was natural, and opposition to maternal rule and law a sort of proof of superiority and independence. Had this been put into words, and placed before him as the motive of much that he did, no one would have coloured more angrily or resented more hotly the suggestion; and yet in the bottom of his heart he would have known it to be true. All through his unoccupied days he carried with him the sense of folly, the consciousness that he could not justify to himself the course he was pursuing. The daily necessity of justifying it to another was almost the sole thing that silenced his conscience. His mother, who kept 'nagging' day after day, who was never satisfied, whose appeals he sometimes thought theatrical, and her passion got up, was his sole defence against that self-dissatisfaction which is the severest of all criticisms. If she would but let him alone, leave him to his own initiative, and not perpetually endeavour to force a change which to be effectual, as all authorities agreed, must come of itself! He was quite conscious of the inadequacy of this argument, and in his heart felt that it was a poor thing to take advantage of it; but yet, on the surface of his mind, put it forward and made a bulwark of it against his own conscience. He did so now as he hurried along, in all the heat that follows a personal encounter. If she would but let him alone! But he could not move a step anywhere, could not make an engagement, could not step into a friend's rooms, as he was going to do now, without her interference. The relations of a parent to an only child are not the same as those that exist between a father and mother and the different members of a large family. It has been usual to consider them in one particular light as implying the closest union and mutual devotion. But there is another point of view in which to consider the question. They are so near to each other, and the relationship so close, that there is a possibility of opposition and contrariety more trying, more absorbing, than any other except that between husband and wife. A young son does not always see the necessity of devotion to a mother who is not very old, who has still many sources of pleasure apart from himself, and who is not capable, perhaps, on her side, of the undiscriminating worship which is grandmotherly, and implies a certain weakness and dimness of perception in the fond eyes that see everything in a rosy, ideal light. This fond delusion is often in its way a moral agent, obliging the object of it to fulfil what is expected of him, and reward the full and perfect trust which is given so unhesitatingly. But in this case it was not possible. The young man thought, or persuaded himself, that his mother's vexatious watch over him, and what he called her constant suspicion and doubt of him, had given him a reason for the disgust and impatience with which he turned from her control. He pictured to himself the difference which a father's larger, more generous sway would have made in him;[20] to that he would have answered, he thought, like a ship to its helm, like an army to its general. But this petty rule, this perpetual fault-finding, raised up every faculty in opposition. Even when he meant the best, her words of warning, her reminders of duty, were enough to set him all wrong again. He thought, as a bad husband often thinks when he is conscious of the world's disapproval, that it was her complaints that were the cause. And when he was reminded by others, well-meaning but injudicious, of all he owed to his mother, his mind rose yet more strongly in opposition, his spirit refused the claim. This is a very different picture from that of the widow's son whose earliest inspiration is his sense of duty to his mother, and adoring gratitude for her care and love – but it is perhaps as true a one. A young man may be placed in an unfair position by the excessive claim made upon his heart and conscience in this way, and so Walter felt it. He might have given all that, and more, if nothing had been asked of him; but when he was expected to feel so much, he felt himself half justified in feeling nothing. Thus the situation had become one of strained and continual opposition. It was a kind of duel, in which the younger combatant at least – the assailed person, whose free-will and independence were hampered by such perpetual requirements – never yielded a step. The other might do so, by turns throwing up her arms altogether, but not he.

It was with this feeling strong in his mind, and affecting his temper as nothing else does to such a degree, that he hastened along the street towards the rooms occupied by Captain Underwood, a personage whom the ladies of Sloebury were unanimous in disliking. Nobody knew exactly where it was that he got his military title. He did not belong to any regiment in her Majesty's service. He had not even the humble claim of a militia[21] officer; yet nobody dared say that there was anything fictitious about him, or stigmatise the captain as an impostor. Other captains and colonels and men-at-arms of undoubted character supported his claims; he belonged to one or two well-known clubs. An angry woman would sometimes fling an insult at him when her husband or son came home penniless after an evening in his company, wondering what they could see in an underbred fellow who was no more a captain (she would say in her wrath) than she was; but of these assertions there was no proof, and the vehemence of them naturally made the captain's[a] partisans more and more eager in his favour. He had not been above six months in Sloebury, but everybody knew him. There was scarcely an evening in which half-a-dozen men did not congregate in his rooms, drawn together by that strange attraction which makes people meet who do not care in the least for each other's company, nor have anything to say to each other, yet are possibly less vacant in society than when alone, or find the murmur of many voices, the smoke of many cigars, exhilarating and agreeable. It was not every evening that the cards were produced. The captain[b] was wary; he frightened nobody; he did not wish to give occasion to the tremors of the ladies, whom he would have conciliated even, if he had been able; but there are men against whom the instinct of all women rises, as there are women from whom all men turn. It was only now and then that he permitted play. He spoke indeed strongly against it on many occasions. 'What do you want with cards?' he would say. 'A good cigar and a friend to talk to ought to be enough for any man.' But twice or thrice in a week his scruples would give way. He was a tall, well-formed man, of an uncertain age, with burning hazel eyes, and a scar on his forehead got in that mysterious service to which now and then he made allusion, and which his friends concluded must have been in some foreign legion, or with Garibaldi,[22] or some other irregular warfare. There were some who thought him a man, old for his age, of thirty-five, and some who, concluding him young for his age, and well preserved, credited him with twenty years more; but thirty-five or fifty-five, whichever it was, he was erect and strong, and well set up, and possessed an amount of experience and apparent knowledge of the world, at which the striplings of Sloebury admired and wondered, and which even the older men respected, as men in the country respect the mention of great names and incidents that have become historical. He had a way of recommending himself even to the serious, and would now and then break forth, as if reluctantly, into an account of some instance of faith or patience on the battlefield or the hospital which made even the rector declare that to consider Underwood as an irreligious man was both unjust and unkind. So strong was the prejudice of the women, however, that Mrs. Wynn, always charitable, and whose silent protest was generally only made when the absent were blamed, shook her head at this testimony borne in favour of the Captain. She had no son to be led away, and her husband it need not be said, considering his position, was invulnerable; but with all her charity she could not believe in the religion of Captain Underwood. His rooms were very nice rooms in the best street in Sloebury, and if his society was what is called 'mixed,' yet the best people were occasionally to be met there, as well as those who were not the best.

There was a little stir in the company when Walter entered. To tell the truth, notwithstanding the wild mirth and dissipation which the ladies believed to go on in Captain Underwood's rooms, the society assembled there was at the moment dull and in want of a sensation. There had not been anything said for the course of two minutes at least. There was no play going on, and the solemn puff of smoke from one pair of lips after another would have been the height of monotony had it not been the wildest fun and gratification. The men in the room took pipes and cigars out of their mouths to welcome the new-comer. 'Hallo, Walter!' they all said in different tones; for in Sloebury the use of Christian names was universal, everybody having known everybody else since the moment of their birth.

'Here comes Methven,' said the owner of the rooms (it was one of his charms, in the eyes of the younger men, that he was not addicted to this familiarity), 'in the odour of sanctity. It will do us all good to have an account of the rector's party. How did you leave the old ladies, my excellent boy?'

'Stole away like the fox, by Jove,' said the hunting man, who was the pride of Sloebury.

'More like the mouse with the old cats after it,' said another wit.

Now Walter had come in among them strong in his sense of right and in his sense of wrong, feeling himself at the same moment a sorry fool and an injured hero, a sufferer for the rights of man; and it would have been of great use to him in both these respects to have felt himself step into a superior atmosphere, into the heat of a political discussion, or even into noisy amusement, or the passion of play – anything which would rouse the spirits and energies, and show the action of a larger life. But to feel his own arrival a sort of godsend in the dulness, and to hear nothing but the heavy puff of all the smoke, and the very poor wit with which he was received, was sadly disconcerting, and made him more and more angry with himself and the circumstances which would give him no sort of support or comfort.

'The old ladies,' he said, 'were rather more lively than you fellows. You look as if you had all been poisoned in your wine, like the men in the opera, and expected the wall to open and the monks and the coffins to come in.'[23]

'I knew that Methven would bring us some excellent lesson,' said Captain Underwood. 'Remember that we have all to die. Think, my friends, upon your latter end.'

'Jump up here and give us a sermon, Wat.'

'Don't tease him, he's dangerous.'

'The old ladies have been too much for him.'

This went on till Walter had settled down into his place, and lighted his pipe like the rest. He looked upon them with disenchanted eyes; not that he had ever entertained any very exalted opinion of his company; but to-night he was out of sympathy with all his surroundings, and he felt it almost a personal offence that there should be so little to attract and excite in this manly circle which thought so much more of itself than of any other, and was so scornful of the old ladies who after all were not old ladies: but the graver members of the community in general, with an ornamental adjunct of young womankind. On ordinary occasions no doubt Walter would have chimed in with the rest, but to-night he was dissatisfied and miserable, not sure of any sensation in particular, but one of scorn and distaste for his surroundings. He would have felt this in almost any conceivable case, but in the midst of this poor jesting and would-be wit, the effect was doubled. Was it worth while for this to waste his time, to offend the opinion of all his friends? Such thoughts must always come in similar circumstances. Even in the most brilliant revelry there will be a pause, a survey of the position, a sense, however unwilling, that the game is not worth the candle. But here! They were all as dull as ditch water, he said to himself. Separately there was scarcely one whom he would have selected as an agreeable companion, and was it possible by joining many dulnesses together to produce a brilliant result? There was no doubt that Walter's judgment was jaundiced that evening; for he was not by any means so contemptuous of his friends on ordinary occasions; but he had been eager to find an excuse for himself, to be able to say that here was real life and genial society in place of the affected solemnity of the proper people. When he found himself unable to do this, he was struck as by a personal grievance, and sat moody and abstracted, bringing a chill upon everybody, till one by one the boon companions strolled away.

'A pretty set of fellows to talk of dulness,' he cried, with a little burst, 'as if they were not dull beyond all description themselves.'

'Come, Methven, you are out of temper,' said Captain Underwood. 'They are good fellows enough when you are in the vein for them. Something has put you out of joint.'

'Nothing at all,' cried Walter, 'except the sight of you all sitting as solemn as owls pretending to enjoy yourselves. At the rectory one yawned indeed, it was the genius of the place[24] – but to hear all those dull dogs laughing at that, as if they were not a few degrees worse! Is there nothing but dulness in life? Is everything the same – one way or another – and nothing to show for it all, when it is over, but tediousness and discontent?'

Underwood looked at him keenly with his fiery eyes.

'So you've come to that already, have you?' he said. 'I thought you were too young and foolish.'

'I am not so young as not to know that I am behaving like an idiot,' Walter said. Perhaps he had a little hope of being contradicted and brought back to his own esteem.

But instead of this, Captain Underwood only looked at him again and laughed.

'I know,' he said: 'the conscience has its tremors, especially after an evening at the rectory. You see how well respectability looks, how comfortable it is.'

'I do nothing of the sort,' Walter cried indignantly. 'I see how dull you are, you people who scoff at respectability, and I begin to wonder whether it is not better to be dull and thrive than to be dull and perish. They seem much the same thing so far as enjoyment goes.'

'You want excitement,' said the other carelessly. 'I allow there is not much of that here.'

'I want something,' cried Walter. 'Cards even are better than nothing. I want to feel that I have blood in my veins.'

'My dear boy, all that is easily explained. You want money. Money is the thing that mounts the blood in the veins. With money you can have as much excitement, as much movement as you like. Let people say what they please, there is nothing else that does it,' said the man of experience. He took a choice cigar leisurely from his case as he spoke. 'A bit of a country town like this, what can you expect from it? There is no go in them. They risk a shilling, and go away frightened if they lose. If they don't go to church on Sunday they feel all the remorse of a villain in a play. It's all petty here – everything's petty, both the vices and the virtues. I don't wonder you find it slow. What I find it, I needn't say.'

'Why do you stop here, then?' said Walter, not unnaturally, with a momentary stare of surprise. Then he resumed, being full of his own subject. 'I know I'm an ass,' he said. 'I loaf about here doing nothing when I ought to be at work. I don't know why I do it; but neither do I know how to get out of it. You, that's quite another thing. You have no call to stay. I wonder you do: why do you? If I were as free as you, I should be off – before another day.'

'Come along then,' said Underwood, good-humouredly. 'I'll go if you'll go.'

At this Walter shook his head.

'I have no money you know. I ought to be in an office or doing something. I can't go off to shoot here or fish there, like you.'

'By and by – by and by. You have time enough to wait.'

Walter gave him a look of surprise.

'There is nothing to wait for,' he said. 'Is that why you have said so many things to me about seeing life? I have nothing. We've got no money in the family. I may wait till doomsday, but it will do nothing for me.'

'Don't be too sure of that,' said Underwood. 'Oh, you needn't devour me with your eyes. I know nothing of your family affairs. I suppose of course that by and by,[a] in the course of nature –'

'You mean,' said Walter, turning pale, 'when my mother dies. No, I'm not such a wretched cad as that: if I didn't know I should get next to nothing then, I –' (His conscience nearly tripped this young man up, running into his way so hurriedly that he caught his foot unawares.) Then he stopped and grew red, staring at his companion. 'Most of what she has dies with her, if that's what you're thinking of. There is nothing in that to build upon. And I'm glad of it,' the young man cried.

'I beg your pardon, Methven,' said the other. 'But it needn't be that; there are other ways of getting rich.'

'I don't know any of them, unless by work: and how am I to work? It is so easy to speak. What can I work at? and where am I to get it? – there is the question. I hear enough on that subject – as if I were a tailor or a shoemaker that could find something to do at any corner. There is no reason in it,' the young man said, so hotly, and with such a flush of resentful obstinacy, that the fervour of his speech betrayed him. He was like a man who had outrun himself, and paused, out of breath.

'You'll see; something will turn up,' said Underwood, with a laugh.

'What can turn up? – nothing. Suppose I go to New Zealand and come back at fifty with my fortune made – Fifty's just the age, isn't it, to begin to enjoy yourself,' cried Walter, scornfully; 'when you have not a tooth left, nor a faculty perfect?' He was so young that the half-century appeared to him like the age of Methusaleh,[25] and men who lived to that period as having outlived all that is worth living for. His mentor laughed a little uneasily, as if he had been touched by this chance shot.

'It is not such a terrible age after all,' he said. 'A man can still enjoy himself when he is fifty; but I grant you that at twenty-four it's a long time to wait for your pleasure.

However, let us hope something will turn up before then. Supposing, for the sake of argument, you were to come in to your fortune more speedily, I wonder what you would do with it – eh? you are such a terrible fellow for excitement. The turf?'

'All that is folly,' said Walter, getting up abruptly. 'Nothing more, thanks. I am coming in to no fortune. And you don't understand me a bit,' he said, turning at the door of the room, to look back upon the scene where he had himself spent so many hours, made piquant by a sense of that wrongdoing which supplies excitement when other motives fail. The chairs standing about as their occupants had thrust them away from the table, the empty glasses upon it, the disorder of the room, struck him with a certain sense of disgust. It was a room intended by nature to be orderly and sober, with heavy country-town furniture, and nothing about it that could throw any grace on disarray. The master of the place stood against the table swaying a somewhat heavy figure over it, and gazing at the young man with his fiery eyes. Walter's rudeness did not please him, any more than his abrupt withdrawal.

'Don't be too sure of that,' he said, with an effort to retain his good-humoured aspect. 'If I don't understand you, I should like to know who does? and when that fortune comes, you will remember what I say.'

'Pshaw!' Walter cried, impatiently turning away. A nod of his head was all the good-night he gave. He hurried down as he had hurried up, still as little contented, as full of dissatisfaction as when he came. This man who thought he understood him, who intended to influence him, revolted the young man's uneasy sense of independence, as much as did the bond of more lawful authority. Did Underwood, *too*, think him a child not able to guide himself? It was very late by this time, and the streets very silent. He walked quickly home through the wintry darkness of November, with a mind as thoroughly out of tune as it is possible to imagine. He had gone to Underwood's in the hot impulse of opposition, with the hope of getting rid temporarily, at least, of the struggle within him; but he had not got rid of it. The dull jokes of the assembled company had only made the raging of the inward storm more sensible,[26] and the jaunty and presumptuous misconception with which his host received his involuntary confidences afterwards, had aggravated instead of soothing his mind. Indeed, Underwood's pretence at knowing all about it, his guesses and attempts to sound his companion's mind, and the blundering interpretation of it into which he stumbled, filled Walter with double indignation and disgust. This man too he had thought much of, and expected superior intelligence from – and all that he had to say was an idiotic anticipation of some miraculous coming into a fortune which Walter was aware was as likely to happen to the beggar on the streets as to himself. He had been angry with nature and his mother when he left her door; he was angry with everybody when he returned to it, though his chief anger of all, and the root of all the others, was that anger with himself, which burnt within his veins, and which is the hardest of all others to quench out.

## CHAPTER III.

WALTER was very late next morning as he had been very late at night. The ladies had breakfasted long before, and there was a look of reproach in the very table-cloth left there so much after the usual time, and scrupulously cleared of everything that the others had used, and arranged at one end, with the dish kept hot for him, and the small teapot just big enough for one, which was a sermon in itself. His mother was seated by the fire with her weekly books, which she was adding up. She said scarcely anything to him, except the morning greeting, filling out his tea with a gravity which was all the more crushing that there was nothing in it to object to, nothing to resent. Adding up accounts of itself is not cheerful work; but naturally the young man resented this seriousness all the more because he had no right to do so. It was intolerable, he felt, to sit and eat in presence of that silent figure partly turned away from him, jotting down the different amounts on a bit of paper, and absorbed in that occupation as if unconscious of his presence. Even scolding was better than this; Walter was perfectly conscious of all it was in her power to say. He knew by heart her remonstrances and appeals. But he disliked the silence more than all. He longed to take her by the shoulders, and cry, 'What is it? What have you got to say to me? What do you mean by sitting there like a stone figure, and *meaning* it all the same!' He did not do this, knowing it would be foolish, and gave[a] his constant antagonist a certain advantage; but he longed to get rid of some of his own exasperation by such an act. It was with a kind of force over himself that he ate his breakfast, going through all the forms, prolonging it to the utmost of his power, helping himself with deliberate solemnity in defiance of the spectator, who seemed so absorbed in her own occupation, but was, he felt sure, watching his every movement. It was not, however, until he had come to an end of his prolonged meal and of his newspaper, that his mother spoke.

'Do you think,' she said, 'that it would be possible for you to write that letter to Mr. Milnathort of which I have spoken so often, to-day?'

'Oh, quite possible,' said Walter, carelessly.

'Will you do it, then? It seems to me very important to your interests. Will you really do it, and do it to-day?'

'I'll see about it,' Walter said.

'I don't ask you to see about it. It is nothing very difficult. I ask you to do it at once – to-day.'

He gazed at her for a moment with an angry obstinacy.

'I see no particular occasion for all this haste. It has stood over a good many days. Why should you insist so upon it now?'

'Every day that it has been put off has been a mistake. It should have been done at once,' Mrs. Methven said.

The Wizard's Son, Volume I    23

'I'll see about it,' he said carelessly; and he went out of the room with a sense of having exasperated her as usual, which was almost pleasant.

At the bottom of his heart he meant to do what his mother had asked of him: but he would not betray his good intentions. He preferred to look hostile even when he was in the mind to be obedient. He went away to the little sitting-room which was appropriated to him, where his pipes adorned the mantelpiece, and sat down to consider the situation. To write a letter was not a great thing to do, and he fully meant to do it; but after he had mused a little angrily upon the want of perception which made his mother adopt that cold and hectoring tone, when if she had asked him gently he would have done it in a minute, he put forth his hand and drew a book towards him. It was not either a new or an entertaining book, but it secured his idle attention until he suddenly remembered that it was time to go out. The letter was not written, but what did that matter? The post did not go out till the afternoon, and there was plenty of time between that time and this to write half-a-dozen letters. It would do very well, he thought, when he came in for lunch. So he threw down the book and got his hat and went out.

Mrs. Methven, who was on the watch, hearing his every movement, came into his room after he was gone, and looked round with eager eyes to see if the letter was written, if there was any trace of it. Perhaps he had taken it out with him to post it, she thought: and though it was injurious to her that she should not know something more about a piece of business in which he was not the sole person concerned, yet it gave her a sort of relief to think that so much at least he had done. She went back to her books with an easier mind. She was far from being a rich woman, but her son had known none of her little difficulties, her efforts to make ends meet. She had thought it wrong to trouble his childhood with such confidences, and he had grown up thinking nothing on the subject, without any particular knowledge of, or interest in, her affairs, taking everything for granted. It was her own fault, she said to herself, and so it was to some extent. She would sometimes think that if she had it to do over again she would change all that. How often do we think this, and with what bitter regret, in respect to the children whom people speak of as wax in our hands, till we suddenly wake up and find them iron! She had kept her difficulties out of Walter's way, and instead of being grateful to her for so doing, he was simply indifferent, neither inquiring nor caring to know. Her own doing! It was easier to herself, yet bitter beyond telling, to acknowledge it to be so. Just at this time, when Christmas was approaching, the ends took a great deal of tugging and coaxing to bring them together. A few of Walter's bills had come in unexpectedly, putting her poor balance altogether wrong. Miss Merivale contributed a little, but only a little, to the housekeeping; for Mrs. Methven was both proud and liberal, and understood giving better than receiving. She went back to the dining-room, where all her books lay upon the table, near the fire. Her reckoning had advanced[a] much since she had begun it, with Walter sitting at breakfast. Her faculties had been all absorbed in him and what he was doing. Now she addressed herself to her accounts with a strenuous effort. It is hard work to balance a small sum of money against a large number of bills, to settle how to divide it so as that everybody shall have something, and the mouths of hungry creditors be stopped. Perhaps we might say that this was one of the fine arts – so many pounds here, so many there, keeping credit afloat, and the wolf of debt from the door. Mrs. Methven was skilled in it. She went to this work, feeling all its difficulty and burden: yet, with a little relief, not because she saw any way out of her difficulties, but because Walter had written that letter. It was always something done, she thought, in her simplicity, and something might come of it, some way in which he could get the means of exercising his faculties, perhaps of distinguishing himself even yet.

Walter for his part strolled away through the little town in his usual easy way. It was a fine, bright, winterly morning, not cold, yet cold enough to make brisk walking pleasant, and stir the blood in young veins. There was no football going on, nor any special amusement. He could not afford to hunt, and the only active winter exercise which he could attain was limited to this game – of which there was a good deal at Sloebury – and skating, when it pleased Providence to send ice, which was too seldom. He looked in upon one or two of his cronies, and played a game of billiards, and hung about the High Street to see what was going on. There was nothing particular going on, but the air was fresh, and the sun shining, and a little pleasant movement about, much more agreeable at least than sitting in a stuffy little room writing a troublesome letter which he felt sure would not do the least good. Finally, he met Captain Underwood, who regarded him with a look which Walter would have called anxious had he been able to imagine any possible reason why Underwood should entertain any anxiety on his account.

'Well! any news?' the captain cried.

'News! What news should there be in this dead-alive place?' Walter said.

The other looked at him keenly as if to see whether he was quite sincere, and then said, 'Come and have some lunch.'

He was free of all the best resorts in Sloebury, this mysterious man. He belonged to the club, he was greatly at his ease in the hotel – everything was open to him. Walter, who had but little money of his own, and could not quite cut the figure he wished, was not displeased to be thus exhibited as the captain's foremost ally.

'I thought you might have come into that fortune, you are looking so spruce,' the captain said, and laughed. But though he laughed he kept an eye on the young man as if the pleasantry meant more than appeared. Walter felt a momentary irritation with this, which seemed to him a very bad joke; but he went with the captain all the same, not without a recollection of the table at home, at which, after waiting three quarters of an hour or so, and watching at the window for his coming, the ladies would at last sit down. But he was not a child to be forced to

*The Wizard's Son, Volume I*     25

attendance at every meal, he said to himself. The captain's attentions to him were great, and it was a very nice little meal that they had together.

'I expect you to do great things for me when you come into your fortune. You had better engage me at once as your guide, philosopher, and friend,' he said, with a laugh. 'Of course you will quit Sloebury, and make yourself free of all this bondage.'

'Oh, of course,' said Walter, humouring the joke, though it was so bad a one in every way.

He could not quarrel with his host at his own table, and perhaps after all it was more dignified to take it with good humour.

'You must not go in for mere expense,' the captain said; 'you must make it pay. I can put you up to a thing or two. You must not go into the world like a pigeon to be plucked. It would effect my personal honour if a pupil of mine – for I consider you as a pupil of mine, Methven, I think I have imparted to you a thing or two. You are not quite the simpleton you used to be, do you think you are?'

Walter received this with great gravity, though he tried to look as if he were not offended.

'Was I a simpleton?' he said. 'I suppose in one's own case one never sees.'

'Were you a simpleton!' said the other, with a laugh, and then he stopped himself, always keenly watching the young man's face, and perceiving that he was going too far. 'But I flatter myself you could hold your own at whist with any man now,' the captain said.

This pleased the young man; his gravity unbended a little; there was a visible relaxation of the corners of his mouth. To be praised is always agreeable. Moral applause, indeed, may be taken with composure, but who could hear himself applauded for his whist-playing without an exhilaration of the heart? He said, with satisfaction, 'I always was pretty good at games,' at which his instructor laughed again, almost too much for perfect good breeding.

'I like to have young fellows like you to deal with,' he said, 'fellows with a little spirit, that are born for better things. Your country-town young man is as fretful and frightened when he loses a few shillings as if it were thousands. But that's one of the reasons why I feel you're born to luck, my boy. I know a man of liberal breeding whenever I see him, he is not frightened about a nothing. That's one of the things I like in you, Methven. You deserve a fortune, and you deserve to have me for your guide, philosopher, and friend.'

All this was said by way of joke; but it was strange to see the steady watch which he kept on the young man's face. One would have said a person of importance whom Underwood meant to try his strength with, but guardedly, without going too far, and even on whom he was somehow dependent, anxious to make a good impression. Walter, who knew his own favour to be absolutely without importance, and that Underwood above all, his host and frequent entertainer, could be under no possible delusion on the subject, was puzzled, yet flattered, feeling that only some excellence on his part, undiscovered by any of his other acquaintances, could account for this. So experienced a person could have 'no motive' in thus paying court to a penniless and prospectless youth. Walter was perplexed, but he was gratified too. He had not seen many of the captain's kind; nobody who knew so many people or who was so much at his ease with the world. Admiration of this vast acquaintance, and of the familiarity with which the captain treated things and people of which others spoke with bated breath, had varied in his mind with a fluctuating sense that Underwood was not exactly so elevated a person as he professed to be, and even that there were occasional vulgarities in this man of the world. Walter felt these, but in his ignorance represented to himself that perhaps they were right enough, and only seemed vulgar to him who knew no better. And to-day there is no doubt he was somewhat intoxicated by this flattery. It must be disinterested, for what could he do for anybody? He confided to the captain more than he had ever done before of his own position. He described how he was being urged to write to old Milnathort. 'He is an old lawyer in Scotland – what they call a writer[27] – and it is supposed he might be induced to take me into his office, for the sake of old associations. I don't know what the associations are, but the position does not smile upon me,' Walter said.

'Your family then is a Scotch family?' said the captain with a nod of approval. 'I thought as much.'

'I don't know that I've got a family,' said Walter.

'On the contrary, Methven is a very good name. There are half-a-dozen[a] baronets at least, and a peer – you must have heard of him, Lord Erradeen.'

'Oh yes, I've heard of him,' Walter said with a conscious look.

If he had been more in the world he would have said 'he is a cousin of mine,' but he was aware that the strain of kindred was very far off, and he was at once too shy and too proud to claim it. His companion waited apparently for the disclosure, then finding it did not come opened the way.

'If he's a relation of yours, it's to him you ought to write; very likely he would do something for you. They are a curious family. I've had occasion to know something about them.'

'I think you know everybody, Underwood.'

'Well, I have knocked about the world a great deal; in that way one comes across a great many people. I saw a good deal of the present lord at one time. He was a very queer man – they are all queer. If you are one of them you'll have to bear your share in it. There is a mysterious house they have – You would think I was an idiot if I told you half the stories I have heard –'

'About the Erradeens?'

'About everybody,' said the captain evasively. 'There is scarcely a family, that, if you go right into it, has not something curious about them. We all have; but those that last and continue keep it on record. I could tell you the wildest tales about So-and-so and So-and-so, very ordinary people to look at, but with stories that would make your hair stand on end.'

'We have nothing to do with things of that sort. My people have always been straightforward and above-board.'[a]

'For as much as you know, perhaps; but go back three or four generations and how can you tell? We have all of us ancestors that perhaps were not much to brag of.'

Walter caught Underwood's eye as he said this, and perhaps there was a twinkle in it, for he laughed.

'It is something,' he said, 'to have ancestors at all.'

'If they were the greatest blackguards in the world,' the captain said with a responsive laugh, 'that's what I think. You don't want any more of my revelations? Well, never mind, probably I shall have you coming to me some of these days quite humbly to beg for more information. You are not cut out for an attorney's office. It is very virtuous, of course, to give yourself up to work and turn your back upon life.'

'Virtue be hanged,' said Walter, with some excitement, 'it is not virtue, but necessity, which I take to be the very opposite. I know I'm wasting my time, but I mean to turn over a new leaf. And as the first evidence of that, as soon as I go home I shall write to old Milnathort.'

'Not to-day,' said Underwood, looking at his watch; 'the post has gone; twenty-four hours more to think about it will do you no harm.'

Walter started to his feet, and it was with a real pang that he saw how the opportunity had escaped him, and his intention in spite of himself been balked; a flush of shame came over his face. He felt that, if never before, here was a genuine occasion for blame. To be sure, the same thing had happened often enough before, but he had never perhaps so fully intended to do what was required of him. He sat down again with a muttered curse at himself and his own folly. There was nothing to be said for him. He had meant to turn over a new leaf, and yet this day was just like the last. The thought made his heart sick for the moment. But what was the use of making a fuss and betraying himself to a stranger? He sat down again, with a self-disgust which made him glad to escape from his own company. Underwood's talk might be shallow enough, perhaps his pretence at knowledge was not very well founded, but he was safer company than conscience, and that burning and miserable sense of moral impotence which is almost worse than the more tragic stings of conscience. To find out that your resolution is worth nothing, after you have put yourself to the trouble of making it, and that habit is more strong than any motive, is not a pleasant thing to think of. Better let the captain talk about Lord Erradeen, or any other lord in the peerage. Underwood, being encouraged with a few questions, talked very largely on this subject. He gave the young man many pieces of information, which indeed he could have got in Debrett[28] if he had been anxious on the subject; and as the afternoon wore on they strolled out again for another promenade up and down the more populous parts of Sloebury, and there fell in with other idlers like themselves; and when the twilight yielded to the more cheerful light of the lamps, betook themselves to whist, which was sometimes played in the captain's rooms at that immoral hour. Sloebury, even the most advanced portion of it, had been horrified at the thought of whist before dinner[29] when the captain first suggested it, but that innocent alarm had long since melted away. There was nothing dangerous about it, no stakes which any one could be hurt by losing. When Walter, warned by the breaking up of the party that it was the hour for dinner, took his way home also, he was the winner of a sixpence or two, and no more;[a] there had been nothing wrong in the play. But when he turned the corner of Underwood's street and found himself with the wind in his face on his way home, the revulsion of feeling from something like gaiety to a rush of disagreeable anticipations, a crowd of uncomfortable thoughts, was pitiful. In spite of all our boastings of home and home influence, how many experience this change the moment they turn their face in the direction of that centre where it is conventional to suppose all comfort and shelter is! There is a chill, an abandonment of pleasant sensations, a preparation for those that are not pleasant. Walter foresaw what he would find there with an impatience and resentment which were almost intolerable. Behind the curtain, between the laths of the Venetian blind, his mother would be secretly on the outlook watching for his return; perhaps even she had stolen quietly to the door, and, sheltered in the darkness of the porch, was looking out; or, if not that, the maid who opened the door would look reproachfully at him, and ask if he was going to dress, or if she might serve the dinner at once: it must have been waiting already nearly half an hour. He went on very quickly, but his thoughts lingered and struggled with the strong disinclination that possessed him. How much he would have given not to go home at all! how little pleasure he expected when he got there! His mother most likely would be silent, pale with anger, saying little, while Cousin Sophia would get up a little conversation. She would talk lightly about anything that might have been happening, and Walter would perhaps exert himself to give Sophia back her own, and show his mother that he cared nothing about her displeasure. And then when dinner was over, he would hurry out again, glad to be released. Home: this was what it had come to be: and nothing could mend it so far as either mother or son could see. Oh, terrible incompatibility, unapproachableness of one soul to another! To think that they should be so near, yet so far away. Even in the case of husband and wife the severance is scarcely so terrible; for they have come towards each other out of different spheres, and if they do not amalgamate, there are many secondary causes that may be blamed, differences of nature and training and thought. But a mother with her child, whom she has brought up, whose first opinions she has implanted, who ought naturally to be influenced by her ways of thinking, and even by prejudices and superstitions in favour of her way! It was not, however, this view of the question which moved the young man. It was the fact of his own bondage, the compulsion he was under

The Wizard's Son, Volume I                    29

to return to dinner, to give some partial obedience to the rules of the house, and to confess that he had not written that letter to Mr. Milnathort.

When he came in sight of the house, however, he became aware insensibly, he could scarcely tell how, of some change in its aspect: what was it? It was lighted up in the most unusual way. The window of the spare room was shining not only with candlelight, but with firelight, his own room was lighted up; the door was standing open, throwing out a warm flood of light into the street, and in the centre of this light stood Mrs. Methven with her white shawl over her head, not at all concealing herself, gazing anxiously in the direction from which he was coming.

'I think I will send for him,' he heard her say; 'he has, very likely, stepped into Captain Underwood's, and he is apt to meet friends there who will not let him go.'

Her voice was soft – there was no blame in it, though she was anxious. She was speaking to some one behind her, a figure in a great coat.[a] Walter was in the shadow and invisible. He paused in his surprise to listen.

'I must get away by the last train,' he heard the voice of the muffled figure say somewhat pettishly.

'Oh, there is plenty of time for that,' cried his mother; and then she gave a little cry of pleasure, and said, 'And, at a good moment, here he is!'

He came in somewhat dazzled, and much astonished, into the strong light in the open doorway. Mrs. Methven's countenance was all radiant and glowing with pleasure. She held out her hand to him eagerly.

'We have been looking for you,' she cried; 'I have had a great surprise. Walter, this is Mr. Milnathort.'

Puzzled, startled, and yet somewhat disappointed, Walter paused in the hall, and looked at a tall old man with a face full of crotchets[30] and intelligence, who stood with two great coats[b] unbuttoned, and a comforter[31] half unwound from his throat, under the lamp. His features were high and thin, his eyes invisible under their deep sockets.

'Now, you will surely take off your coat, and consent to go up-stairs, and make yourself comfortable,' said Mrs. Methven, with a thrill of excitement in her voice. 'This is Walter. He has heard of you all his life. Without any reference to the nature of your communication, he must be glad, indeed, to make your acquaintance –'

She gave Walter a look of appeal as she spoke. He was so much surprised that it was with difficulty he found self-possession to murmur a few words of civility. A feeling that Mr. Milnathort must have come to look after that letter which had never been written came in with the most wonderfully confusing, half ludicrous effect into his mind, like one of the inadequate motives and ineffable conclusions of a dream. Mr. Milnathort made a stiff little bow in reply.

'I will remain till the last train. In the mean time the young gentleman had better be informed, Mrs. Methven.'

She put out her hands again. 'A moment – give us a moment first.'

The old lawyer stood still and looked from the mother to the son. Perhaps to his keen eyes it was revealed that it would be well she should have the advantage of any pleasant revelation.

'I will,' he said, 'madam, avail myself of your kind offer to go up-stairs and unroll myself out of these trappings of a long journey; and in the mean time you will, perhaps, like to tell him the news yourself: he will like it all the better if he hears it from his mother.'

Mrs. Methven bowed her head, having, apparently, no words at her command: and stood looking after him till he disappeared on the stairs, following the maid, who had been waiting with a candle lighted in her hand. When he was gone, she seized Walter hurriedly by the arm, and drew him towards the little room, the nearest, which was his ordinary sitting-room. Her hand grasped him with unnecessary force in her excitement. The room was dark – he could not see her face, the only light in it being the reflection of the lamp outside.

'Oh, Walter!' she cried; oh, my boy! I don't know how to tell you the news. This useless life is all over for you, and another – oh, how different – another – God grant it happy and great, oh, God grant it! blessed and noble! –'

Her voice choked with excitement and fast-coming tears. She drew him towards her into her arms.

'It will take you from me – but what of that, if it makes you happy and good? I have been no guide to you, but God will be your guide: His leadings were all dark to me, but now I see –'

'Mother,' he cried, with a strange impulse he could not understand, putting his arm round her, 'I did not write that letter: I have done nothing I promised or meant to do. I am sick to the heart to think what a fool and a cad I am – for the love of God tell me what it is!'

\*\*\*

# CHAPTER IV.

ALL Sloebury was aware next morning that something of the most extraordinary character had happened to young Walter Methven. The rumour even reached the club on the same evening. First the report was that he had got a valuable appointment, at which the gentlemen shook their heads; next that he had come into a fortune: they laughed with one accord at this. Then, as upon a sudden gale of wind, there blew into the smoking-room, then full of tobacco, newspapers, and men, a whisper which made everybody turn pale. This was one reason, if not the chief, why that evening was one of the shortest ever known at the club, which did not indeed generally keep very late hours, but still was occupied by its *habitués*[32] till ten or eleven o'clock, when the serious members would go away, leaving only the boys, who never could have enough of it. But on that evening even the young men cleared off about ten or so. They wanted to know what it meant. Some of them went round to Captain Underwood's where Walter was so often to be found, with a confidence that at least Underwood would know; the more respectable members of society went home to their families to spread the news, and half-a-dozen mothers at least went to bed that night with a disagreeable recollection that they had individually and deliberately 'broken off' an incipient flirtation or more, in which Walter had been one of the parties concerned. But the hopeful ones said to themselves, 'Lizzie has but to hold up her little finger to bring him back.' This was before the whole was known. The young men who had hurried to Captain Underwood's were received by that gentleman with an air of importance and of knowing more than he would tell, which impressed their imaginations deeply. He allowed that he had always known that there was a great deal of property, and perhaps a title concerned, but declared that he was not at liberty to say any more. Thus the minds of all were prepared for a great revelation; and it is safe to say that from one end of Sloebury to the other Walter's name was in everybody's mouth. It had been always believed that the Methvens were people of good connections, and of later years it had been whispered by the benevolent as a reason for Walter's inaction that he had grand relations, who at the proper moment would certainly interfere and set everything right for him. Others, however, were strenuous in their denial and ridicule of this, asking, was his mother a woman to conceal any advantages she had? – for they did not understand the kind of pride in which Mrs. Methven was so strong. And then it was clear that not only did the grand relations do nothing for Walter, but he did not even have an invitation from them, and went from home only when his mother went to the sea-side. Thus there was great doubt and wonder, and in some quarters an inclination to treat the rumour as a canard,[33] and to postpone belief. At the same time everybody believed it, more or less, at the bottom of their hearts, feeling that a thing so impossible must be true.

But when it burst fully upon the world next morning along with the pale November daylight, but much more startling, that Walter Methven had succeeded as the next heir to his distant cousin, who was the head of the family, and was now Lord Erradeen, a great potentate, with castles in the Highlands and fat lands further south, and moors and deer forests and everything that the heart of man could think of, the town was swept not only by a thrill of wonder, but of emotion. Nobody was indifferent to this extraordinary romance. Some, when they had got over the first bewilderment, received it with delightful anticipations, as if the good fortune which had befallen Walter was in some respects good fortune also for themselves; whereas many others were almost angry at this sudden elevation over their heads of one who certainly did not deserve any better, if indeed half so well as they did. But nobody was indifferent. It was the greatest excitement that had visited Sloebury for years – even it might be said for generations. Lord Erradeen! it took away everybody's breath.

32        *The Selected Works of Margaret Oliphant, Volume 21*

Among the circle of Walter's more intimate acquaintance, the impression made was still deeper, as may be supposed. The commotion in the mind of the rector, who indeed was old enough to have taken it with more placidity, was such that he hurried in from morning service without taking off his cassock. He was a good Churchman, but[34] not so far gone as to walk about the world in that ecclesiastical garment.

'Can you imagine what has happened?' he said, bursting in upon Mrs. Wynn, who was delicate and did not go to church in the winter mornings. 'Young Walter Methven, that you all made such a talk about – '

This was unfair, because she had never made any talk – being a woman who did not talk save most sparingly. She was tempted for a moment to forestall him by telling him she already knew, but her heart failed her, and she only shook her head a little in protest against this calumny, and waited smilingly for what he had to say. She could not take away from him the pleasure of telling this wonderful piece of news.

'Why it was only the night before last he was here – most of us rather disapproving of him, poor boy,' said the rector. 'Well, Lydia, that young fellow that was a good-for-nothing, you know – doing nothing, never exerting himself: well, my dear! the most extraordinary thing has happened – the most wonderful piece of good fortune –'

'Don't keep me on tenterhooks, Julius; I have heard some buzzing of talk already.'

'I should think you had! the town is full of it; they tell me that everybody you meet on the streets – Lydia!' said the rector with solemnity, drawing close to her to make his announcement more imposing, 'that boy is no longer simple Mr. Walter Methven. He is Lord Erradeen –'

'Lord what?' cried the old lady. It was part of her character to be a little deaf, or rather hard of hearing, which is the prettier way of stating the fact. It was supposed by some that this was one of the reasons why, when any one was blamed, she always shook her head.

'Lord Er-ra-deen; but bless me, it is not the name that is so wonderful, it is the fact. Lord Erradeen – a great personage – a man of importance. You don't show any surprise, Lydia! and yet it is the most astonishing incident without comparison that has happened in the parish these hundred years.'

'I wonder what his mother is thinking,' Mrs. Wynn said.

'If her head is turned nobody could be surprised. Of course, like every other mother, she thinks her son worthy of every exaltation.'

'I wish she was of that sort,' the old lady said.

'Every woman is of that sort,' said the rector with hasty dogmatism; 'and, in one way, I am rather sorry, for it will make her feel she was perfectly right in encouraging him, and that would be such a terrible example for others. The young men will all take to idling –'

'But it is not the idling, but the fact that there is a peerage in the family –'

'You can't expect,' cried the rector, who was not lucid, 'that boys or women either will reason back so far as that. It will be a bad example: and, in the mean time, it is a most astonishing fact. But you don't seem in the least excited. I thought you would have jumped out of your chair – out of the body almost.'

'I am too rheumatic for that,' said Mrs. Wynn with a smile: then, 'I wonder if she will come and tell me,' the old lady said.

'I should think she does not know whether she is on her head or her heels,' cried the rector; 'I don't feel very sure myself. And Walter! What a change, to be sure, for that boy! I hope he will make a good use of it. I hope he will not dart off with Underwood and such fellows and make a fool of himself. Mind, I don't mean that I think so badly of Underwood,' he added after a moment, for this was a subject on which, being mollified as previously mentioned, the rector took the male side of the question. Mrs. Wynn received the protest in perfect silence, not even shaking her head.

'But if he took a fancy for horses or that sort of thing,' Mr. Wynn added with a moment's hesitation; then he brightened up again – 'of course it is better that he should know somebody who has a little experience in any case; and you will perceive, my dear, there is a great difference between a penniless youth like Walter Methven getting such notions in his head which lead only to ruin, and young Lord Erradeen dabbling a little in amusements which, after all, have no harm in them if not carried too far, and are natural in his rank – but you women are always prejudiced on such a point.'

'I did not say anything, my dear,' the old lady said.

'Oh, no, you don't say anything,' cried the rector fretfully, 'but I see it in every line of your shawl and every frill of your cap. You are just stiff with prejudice so far as Underwood is concerned, who really is not at all a bad fellow when you come to know him, and is always respectful to religion, and shows a right feeling – but one might as well try to fly as to convince you when you have taken a prejudice.'

'Mrs. Wynn made no protest against this. She said only, 'It is a great ordeal for a boy to pass through. I wonder if his mother –' And here she paused, not having yet, perhaps, formulated into words the thoughts that arose in her heart.

'It is to be hoped that she will let him alone,' the rector said; 'she has indulged him in everything hitherto; but just now, when he is far better left to himself, no doubt she will be wanting to interfere.'

'Do you think she has indulged him in everything?' said the old lady; but she did not think it necessary to accuse her husband of prejudice. Perhaps he understood Captain Underwood as much better as she understood Mrs. Methven; so she said nothing more. She was the only individual in Sloebury who had any notion of the struggle in which Walter's mother had wrecked so much of her own peace.

'There cannot be any two opinions on that subject,' said the rector. 'Poor lad! You will excuse me, my dear, but I am always sorry for a boy left to a woman's training. He is either a mere milksop[35] or a ne'er-do-well. Walter is not a milksop, and here has Providence stepped in, in the most wonderful way, to save him from being the other: but that is no virtue of hers. You will stand up, of course, for your own side.'

The old lady smiled and shook her head. 'I think every child is the better for having both its parents, Julius, if that is what you mean.'

This was not exactly what he meant, but it took the wind out of the rector's sails. 'Yes, it is an ordeal for him,' he said, 'but, I am sure, if my advice can do him any good, it is at his service; and, though I have been out of the way of many things for some time, yet I dare say the world is very much what it was, and I used to know it well enough.'

'He will ask for nobody's advice,' said Mrs. Wynn.

'Which makes it all the more desirable he should have it,' cried the rector; and then he said, 'Bless me! I have got my cassock on still. Tell John to take it down to the vestry – though, by the way, there is a button off, and you might as well have it put on for me, as it is here.'

Mrs. Wynn executed the necessary repair of the cassock with her own hands. Though she was rheumatic, and did not care to leave her chair oftener than was necessary, she had still the use of her hands, and she had a respect for all the accessories of the clerical profession. She was sitting examining the garment to see if any other feeblenesses were apparent, in which a stitch in time might save after labours, when, with a little eager tap at the door, another visitor came in. This was a young lady of three or four and twenty, with a good deal of the beauty which consists in fresh complexion and pleasant colour. Her hair was light brown, warm in tone; her eyes were brown and sparkling; her cheeks and lips bloomed with health. She had a pretty figure, full of life and energy – everything, in short, that is necessary to make up a pretty girl, without any real loveliness or deeper grace. She came in quickly, brimming over, as was evident, with something which burst forth as soon as she had given the old lady the hasty conventional kiss of greeting, and which, as a matter of course, turned out to be the news of which Sloebury was full.

'Did you ever hear anything so wonderful?' she said. 'Walter Methven, that nobody thought anything of – and now he is turned into a live lord! a real peer of parliament! they say. I thought mamma would have fainted when she heard it.'

'Why should your mamma faint when she heard of it, July? It is very pleasant news.'

'Oh, Aunt Lydia! don't you know why? I am so angry: I feel as if I should never speak to her again. Don't you remember? And I always thought you had some hand in it. Oh, you sit there and look so innocent, but that is because you are so deep.'

'Am I deep?' the old lady asked with a smile.

'You are the deepest person I ever knew: you see through us all, and you just throw in a word; and then, when people act upon it, you look so surprised. I heard you myself remark to mamma how often Walter Methven was at our house.'

'Yes, I think I did remark it,' Mrs. Wynn said.

'And what was the harm? He liked to come, and he liked me; and I hope you don't think I am the sort of person to forget myself and think too much about a man.'

'I thought you were letting him be seen with you too often, July, that is true.'

'You thought it might keep others off that were more eligible? Well, that is what I supposed you meant, for I never like to take a bad view. But, you see, there was somebody that was eligible; and here has he turned, all at once, into the very best match within a hundred miles. If mamma had only let things alone, what prospects might be opening upon me now!'

'Half-a-dozen[a] girls, I am afraid, may say just the same,' said Mrs. Wynn.

'Well, what does that matter? He had nothing else to do. When a young man has nothing to do he must be making up to somebody. I don't blame him a bit; that is what makes us girls always ready for a flirtation. Time hangs so heavy on our hands. And only think, Aunt Lydia, if things had been allowed to go on (and I could always have thrown him off if anything better turned up), only think what might have happened to me now. I might be working a coronet in all my new handkerchiefs,'[36] cried the girl: 'only imagine! oh, oh, oh!'

And she pretended to cry; but there was a sparkle of nervous energy all the same in her eyes, as if she were eager for the chase, and scarcely able to restrain her impatience. Mrs. Wynn shook her head at her visitor with a smile.

'You are not so worldly as you give yourself out to be,' she said.

'Oh, that just shows how little you know. I am as worldly as ever woman was. I think of nothing but how to establish myself, and have plenty of money. We want it so! Oh, I know you are very good to us – both my uncle and you; but mamma is extravagant, and I am extravagant, and naturally all that anybody thinks of is to have what is necessary and decent for us. We have to put up with it, but I hate what is necessary and decent. I should like to go in satin and lace to-day even if I knew I should be in rags tomorrow; and to think if you had not interfered that I might have blazed in diamonds, and gone to court, and done everything I want to do! I could strangle you, Aunt Lydia, and mamma too!' Upon which Miss July (or Julée, which was how her name was pronounced) gave Mrs. Wynn a sudden kiss and took the cassock out of her hands. 'If it wants any mending I will do it,' she said; 'it will just give me a little consolation for the moment. And you will have time to think and answer this question: Is it too late now?'

'July, dear, it hurts me to hear you talk so – you are not so wild as you take credit for being.'

'I am not wild at all, Aunt Lydia,' said the girl, appropriating Mrs. Wynn's implements, putting on her thimble, threading her needle, and discovering at one glance the little rent in the cassock which the old lady had been searching for in vain, 'except with indignation to think what I have lost – if I have lost it. It is all very well to speak, but what is a poor girl to do? Yes, I know, to make just enough to live on by teaching, or something of that sort; but that is not what I want. I want to be well off. I am so extravagant, and so is mamma. We keep ourselves down, we don't spend money; but we hate it so! I would go through a great many disagreeables if I could only have enough to spend.'

'And is Walter one of the disagreeables you would go through?'

'Well, no; I could put up with him very well. He is not at all unpleasant. I don't want him, but I could do with him. Do you really think it is too late? Don't you think mamma might call upon Mrs. Methven and say how delighted we are; and just say to him, you know, in a playful way (mamma could manage that very well), 'We cannot hope to see you now in our little house, Lord Erradeen!' and then of course he would be piqued (for he's very generous), and say, 'Why?' And mamma would say, 'Oh, we are such poor little people, and you are now a great man.' Upon which, as sure as fate, he would be at the Cottage the same evening. And then!' July threw back her head, and expanded her brown eyes with a conscious power and sense of capability, as who should say – Then it would be in my own hands. – 'Don't you think that's very good for a plan?' she added, subsiding quickly to the work, which she executed as one to the manner born.

'I don't think anything of it as a plan – and neither do you; and your mother would not do it, July,' the old lady said.

'Ah,' said July, throwing back her head, 'there you have hit the blot,[37] Aunt Lydia. Mamma wouldn't do it! She could, you know. When she likes she is the completest humbug![38] – but not always. And she has so many notions about propriety, and what is womanly, and so forth – just like you. Poor women have no business with such luxuries. I tell her we must be of our time, and all that sort of thing; but she won't see it. No, I am afraid that is just the difficulty. It all depends on mamma – and mamma won't. Well, it is a little satisfaction to have had it all out with you. If you had not interfered, you two, and stopped the poor boy coming – '

At this juncture John threw open the door, and with a voice which he reserved for the great county ladies, announced 'Mrs. Methven.' John had heard the great news too.

'— Stopped the poor boy coming,' July said. The words were but half out of her mouth when John opened the door, and it was next to impossible that the new visitor had not heard them. A burning blush covered the girl's face. She sprang to her feet with the cassock in her arms, and gazed at the new comer. Mrs. Methven for the first moment did not notice this third person. She came in with the content and self-absorption of one who has a great wonder to tell. The little world of Sloebury and all its incidents were as nothing to her. She went up to old Mrs. Wynn with a noiseless swiftness.

'I have come to tell you great news,' she said.

'Let me look at you,' said the old lady. 'I have heard, and I scarcely could believe it. Then it is all true?'

'I am sorry I was not the first to tell you. I think such a thing must get into the air. Nobody went out from my house last night, and yet everybody knows. I saw even the people in the street looking at me as I came along. Mrs. Wynn, you always stood up for him; I never said anything, but I know you did. I came first to you. Yes, it is all true.'

The old lady had known it now for several hours, and had been gently excited, no more. Now her eyes filled with tears, she could not have told why.

'Dear boy! I hope God will bless him, and make him worthy and great,' she said, clasping her old hands together. 'He has always been a favourite with me.'

'He is a favourite with everybody,' said July. No one had noticed her presence, and she was not one that could remain unseen. 'Everybody is glad; there is not one that doesn't wish him well.'

Did she intend to strike that *coup*[39] for herself which her mother was not to be trusted to make? Mrs. Wynn thought so with a great tremor, and interrupted her in a tone that for her was hurried and anxious.

'July speaks nothing but the truth, Mrs. Methven; there is nobody that does not like Walter; but I suppose I ought now to drop these familiarities and call him Lord Erradeen?'

'He will never wish his old friends to do that,' said Mrs. Methven. She already smiled with a gracious glance and gesture: and the feeling that these old friends were almost too much privileged in being so near to him, and admitted to such signs of friendship, came into her mind; but she did not care to have July share her expansion. 'Miss Herbert,' she said, with a little bow, 'is very good to speak so kindly. But everybody is kind. I did not know my boy was so popular. Sunshine,' she added, with a smile, 'brings out all the flowers.'

She had not sat down, and she evidently did not mean to do so while July remained. There was something grand in her upright carriage, in her air of superiority, which had never been apparent before. She had always been a woman, as Sloebury people said, who thought a great deal of herself; but no one had ever acknowledged her right to do so till now. On the other hand, July Herbert was well used to the cold shade. Her mother was Mrs. Wynn's niece, but she was none the less poor for that, and as July was not a girl to be easily put down, she was acquainted with every manner of polite snubbing known in the society of the place. This of standing till she should go was one with which she was perfectly familiar, and in many cases it afforded her pleasure to subject the operator to great personal inconvenience; but on the present occasion she was not disposed to exercise this power. She would have conciliated Walter's mother if she could have done so, and on a rapid survey of the situation she decided that the best plan was to yield.

'I must go and tell mamma the great news,' she said. 'I am sure she will never rest till she rushes to you with her congratulations; but I will tell her you are tired of congratulations already – for of course it is not a thing upon which there can be two opinions' July laid down the cassock as she spoke. 'I have mended all there is to mend, Aunt Lydia; you need not take any more trouble about it. Good-bye for the moment. You may be sure you will see one or other of us before night.'

They watched her silently as she went out of the room. Mrs. Methven saying nothing till the door had closed, Mrs. Wynn with a deprecatory smile upon her face. She did not altogether approve of her grandniece. But neither was she willing to hand her over to blame. The old lady felt the snub July had received more than the girl herself did. She looked a little wistfully after her. She was half angry when as soon as July disappeared Mrs. Methven sank down upon a chair near her, huge billows of black silk rising about her, for she had put on her best gown. Mrs. Wynn thought that the mother, whose child, disapproved by the world, had been thus miraculously lifted above its censures, should have been all the more tolerant of the other who had met no such glorious fate. But she reflected that *they never see it,* which was her favourite expression of wonderment, yet explanation of everything. There were so many things that *they* ought to learn by; but they never saw it. It was thus she accounted with that shake of her head for all the errors of mankind.

Mrs. Methven for her part waited till even the very step of that objectionable Julia Herbert had died away. She had known by instinct that if *that* girl should appear she would be on the watch to make herself agreeable to Walter's mother. 'As if he could ever have thought of her,' she said to herself. Twenty-four hours before Mrs. Methven would have been glad to think that Walter 'thought of' any girl who was at all in his own position. She would have hailed it as a means of steadying him, and making him turn seriously to his life. But everything was now changed, and this interruption had been very disagreeable. She could scarcely turn to her old friend now with the effusion and emotion which had filled her when she came in. She held out her hand and grasped that of the old lady.

'I don't need to tell you what I am feeling,' she said. 'It is all like a tumultuous sea of wonder and thankfulness. I wanted it, for I was at my wits' end.'

Mrs. Wynn was a little chilled too, but she took the younger woman's hand.

'You did not know what was coming,' she said. 'You wanted one thing, and Providence was preparing another.'

'I don't know if that is how to state it; but at all events I was getting to feel that I could not bear it any longer, and trying for any way of setting things right: when the good came in this superlative way. I feel frightened when I think of it. After we knew last night I could do nothing but cry. It took all the strength from me. You would have thought it was bad news.'

'I can understand that.' The old lady relinquished the hand which she had been holding. 'To be delivered from any anxieties you may have had in such a superlative way, as you say, is not the common lot – most of us have just to fight them out.'

Mrs. Methven already felt herself far floated away from those that had to fight it out. The very words filled her heart with an elation beyond speech.

'And this morning,' she said, 'to wake and to feel it must be folly, and then to realise that it was true! One knows so well the other sort of waking when the shock and the pang come all over again. But to wake up to this extraordinary, incredible well-being – one might say happiness!'

The tears of joy were in her eyes, and in those tears there is something so strange, so rare, that the soul experienced in life looks upon them almost with more awe than upon the familiar ones of grief which we see every day. The old lady melted, and her chill of feeling yielded to a tender warmth. Yet what a pity that They never see it! How much more perfect it would have been if the woman in her happiness had been softened and kind to all those whom nothing had happened to! Imperceptibly the old lady in her tolerant experience shook her gentle old head. Then she gave herself in full sympathy to hear all the wonderful details.

# CHAPTER V.

THE sentiments of the spectators in such a grand alteration of fortune may be interesting enough, and it is in general more easy to get at them than at those which fill the mind of the principal actor. In the present case it is better to say of the principal subject of the change, for Walter could not be said to be an actor at all. The emotions of the first evening it would indeed be impossible to describe. To come in from his small country-town society, to whom even he was so far inferior that every one of them had facilities of getting and spending money which he did not possess, and to sit down, all tremulous and guilty, feeling himself the poorest creature, opposite to the serious and important personage who came to tell him, with documents as solemn as himself, that this silly youth who had been throwing away his life for nothing, without even the swell of excitement to carry him on, had suddenly become, without deserving it, without doing anything to bring it about, an individual of the first importance – a peer, a proprietor, a great man. Walter could have sobbed as his mother did, had not pride kept him back. When they sat down at table in the little dining-room there were two at least of the party who ate nothing, who sat and gazed at each other across the others with white faces and blazing eyes. Mr. Milnathort made a good dinner, and sat very watchful, making also his observations, full of curiosity and a certain half-professional interest. But Cousin Sophy was the only one who really got the good of this prodigious event. She asked if they might not have some champagne to celebrate the day. She was in high excitement but quite self-controlled, and enjoyed it thoroughly. She immediately began in her thoughts to talk of my young cousin Lord Erradeen. It was a delightful advancement which would bring her no advantage, and yet almost pleased her more than so much added on to her income; for Miss Merivale was not of any distinction in her parentage, and suddenly to find herself cousin to a lord went to her heart: it was a great benefit to the solitary lady fond of society, and very eager for a helping hand to aid her up the ascent. And it was she who kept the conversation going. She even flirted a little, quite becomingly, with the old lawyer, who felt her, it was evident, a relief from the high tension of the others, and was amused by the vivacious middle-aged lady, who for the moment had everything her own way. After dinner there was a great deal of explanation given, and a great many facts made clear, but it is to be doubted whether Walter knew very well what was being said. He listened with an air of attention, but it was as if he were listening to some fairy tale. Something out of the *Arabian Nights*[40] was being repeated before him. He was informed how the different branches of his family had died out one after another. 'Captain Methven was aware that he was in the succession,' the lawyer said; and Mrs. Methven cast a thought back, half-reproachful, half-approving upon her husband, who had been dead so long that his words and ways were like shadows to her, which she could but faintly recall. Would it have been better if he had told her? After pursuing this thought a long time she decided that it would not, that he had done wisely – yet felt a little visionary grudge and disappointment to think that he had been able to keep such a secret from her. No doubt it was all for the best. She might have distracted herself with hopes, and worn out her mind with waiting. It was doubtful if the support of knowing what was going to happen would really have done her any good; but yet it seemed a want of trust in her, it seemed even to put her in a partially ridiculous position now, as knowing nothing, not having even an idea of what was coming. But Walter did not share any of these goings back upon the past. He had scarcely known his father, nor was he old enough to have had such a secret confided to him for long after Captain Methven died. He thought nothing of that. He sat with an appearance of the deepest attention, but unaware of what was being said, with a vague elation in his mind, something that seemed to buoy him up above the material earth. He could not bring himself down again. It was what he remembered to have felt when he was a child when some long-promised pleasure was coming – to-morrow. Even in that case hindrances might come in. It might rain to-morrow, or some similar calamity might occur. But rain could not affect this. He sat and listened and did not hear a word.

Next morning Walter awoke very early, before the wintry day had fully dawned. He opened his eyes upon a sort of paling and whitening of everything – a grey perception of the walls about him, and the lines of the window marked upon the paleness outside. What was it that made even these depressing facts exhilarate him and rouse an incipient delight in his mind, which for the moment he did not understand? Then he sat up suddenly in his bed. It was cold, it was dark. There was no assiduous servant to bring hot water or light his fire – everything was chilling and wretched; and he was not given to early rising. Ordinarily it was an affair of some trouble to get him roused, to see that he was in time for a train or for any early occupation. But this morning he found it impossible to lie still; an elasticity in him, an elation and buoyancy, which he almost felt, with a laugh, might float him up to the ceiling, like the mediums,[41] made him jump up, as it were in self-defence. It buoyed him, it carried him as on floating pinions into a limitless heaven. What was it? Who was he? The chill of the morning brought him a little to himself, and then he sat down in his shirt-sleeves and delivered himself up to the incredible, and laughed low and long, with a sense of the impossibility of it that brought tears to his eyes. He Lord Erradeen, Lord Anything! He a peer, a great man! he with lands and money and wealth of every sort, who last night had been pleased to win two sixpences! After the buoyancy and sensation of rising beyond the world altogether, which was a kind of physical consciousness of something great that had happened before he was awake, came this sense of the ludicrous, this incredulity and confused amusement. He dressed himself in this mood, laughing low from time to time, to himself, as if it were some game which was being played upon him, but of which he was in the secret, and not to be deceived, however artfully it might be managed. But when he was dressed and ready to go down-stairs[a] – by which time daylight had fully struggled forth upon a wet and clammy world – he stopped himself short with a sudden reminder that to-day this curious practical joke was to extend its career and become known to the world. He laughed again, but then he grew grave, standing staring at the closed door of his bedroom, out of which he was about to issue – no longer a nobody – in a new character, to meet the remarks, the congratulations of his friends. He knew that the news would fly through the little town like lightning; that people would stop each other in the streets and ask, 'Have you heard it? – is it true?' and that throughout the whole place there would be a sort of revolution, a general change of positions, which would confuse the very world. He knew vaguely that whatever else might happen he would be uppermost. The people who had disapproved of him, and treated him *de haut en bas*,[42] would find this to be impossible any longer. He would be in a position which is to be seen on the stage and in books more frequently than in common life – possessed of the power of making retribution, of punishing the wicked, and distributing to the good tokens of his favour. It is a thing we would all like to do, to avenge ourselves (within due Christian and social limits) on the persons who have despised us, and to reward those who have believed in us, showing the one how right they were, and the other how wrong they were, with a logic that should be undeniable. There is nobody who has ever endured a snub – and who has not? – who would not delight in doing this; but the most of us never get such a supreme gratification, and Walter was to have it. He was going to see everybody abashed and confounded who had ever treated him with contumely. Once more he felt that sensation of buoyancy and elation as if he were spurning earth with his foot and ready to soar into some sort of celestial sphere. And then once more he laughed to himself. Was it possible?

could it be? would anybody believe it? He thought there would be an explosion of incredulous laughter through all the streets; but then, when that was over, both friends and foes would be forced to believe it – as he himself was forced to believe.

With that he opened his door, and went down-stairs[a] into the new world. He stumbled over the housemaid's pail, of course, but did not call forth any frown upon that functionary's freckled forehead[43] as he would have done yesterday. On the contrary, she took away the pail, and begged his pardon with awe – being of course entirely blameless. He paused for a moment on the steps as he faced the raw morning air going out, and lo! the early baker, who was having a word with cook at the area[44] over the rolls, turned towards him with a reverential look, and pulled off his cap. These were the first visible signs of Walter's greatness; they gave him a curious sort of conviction that after all the thing was true.

There was scarcely anybody about the Sloebury streets except bakers and milkmen at this hour. It was a leisurely little town, in which nothing particular was doing, no manufactures or business to demand early hours; and the good people did not get up early. Why should they? the day was long enough without that: so that Walter met no one in his early promenade. But before he got back there were symptoms that the particular baker who had taken off his cap had whispered the news to others of his fraternity, who, having no tie of human connection, such as supplying the family with rolls, to justify a salutation, only stared at him with awe-stricken looks as he went past. He felt he was an object of interest even to the policeman going off duty, who being an old soldier, saluted with a certain grandeur as he tramped by. The young man took an aimless stroll through the half-awakened district. The roads were wet, the air raw: it was not a cheerful morning; damp and discouragement breathed in the air; the little streets looked squalid and featureless in shabby British poverty; lines of low, two-storied brick, all commonplace and monotonous. It was the sort of morning to make you think of the tediousness to which most people get up every day, supposing it to be life, and accepting it as such with the dull content which knows no better; a life made up of scrubbing out of kitchens and sweeping out of parlours, of taking down shutters and putting them up again; all sordid, petty, unbroken by an exhilarating event. But this was not what struck Walter as he floated along in his own wonderful atmosphere, seeing nothing, noting everything with the strange vision of excitement. Afterwards he recollected with extraordinary vividness a man who stood stretching his arms in shirt sleeves[b] above his head for a long, soul-satisfying yawn, and remembered to have looked up at the shop-window within which he was standing, and read the name of ROBINSON in gilt letters. Robinson, yawning in his shirt-sleeves, against a background of groceries, pallid in the early light, remained with him like a picture for many a day.

When he got back the breakfast table was spread, and his mother taking her place at it. Mr. Milnathort had not gone away as he intended by the night train.

*The Wizard's Son, Volume I*          43

He had remained in Mrs. Methven's spare room, surrounded by all the attentions and civilities that a household of women, regarding him with a sort of awe as a miraculous messenger or even creator of good fortune, could show to a bachelor gentleman, somewhat prim and old-fashioned in his habits and ways. It was his intention to leave Sloebury by the eleven o'clock train, and he had arranged that Walter should meet him in Edinburgh within a week, to be made acquainted with several family matters, in which, as the head of the house, it was necessary that he should be fully instructed. Neither Walter nor his mother paid very much attention to these arrangements, nor even remarked that the old lawyer spoke of them with great gravity. Mrs. Methven was busy making tea, and full of anxiety that Mr. Milnathort should breakfast well and largely, after what she had always understood to be the fashion of his country; and as for Walter, he was not in a state of mind to observe particularly any such indications of manner. Cousin Sophia was the only one who remarked the solemnity of his tone and aspect.

'One would suppose there was some ordeal to go through,' she said in her vivacious way.

'A young gentleman who is taking up a large fortune and a great responsibility will have many ordeals to go through, madam,' Mr. Milnathort said in his deliberate tones: but he did not smile or take any other notice of her archness. It was settled accordingly, that after a few days for preparation and leave-taking, young Lord Erradeen should leave Sloebury. 'And if I might advise, alone,' Mr. Milnathort said, 'the place is perhaps not just in a condition to receive ladies. I would think it wiser on the whole, madam, if you deferred your coming till his lordship there has settled everything for your reception.'

'*My* coming?' said Mrs. Methven. The last twelve hours had made an extraordinary difference in her feelings and faith; but still she had not forgotten what had gone before, nor the controversies and struggles of the past. 'We must leave all that for after consideration,' she said.

Walter was about to speak impulsively, but old Milnathort stopped him with a skilful interruption –

'It will perhaps be the wisest way,' he said; 'there will be many things to arrange. When Lord Erradeen has visited the property, and understands everything about it, then he will be able to –'

Walter heard the name at first with easy unconsciousness: then it suddenly blazed forth upon him as his own name. His mother at the other end of the table felt the thrill of the same sensation. Their eyes met; and all the wonder of this strange new life suddenly gleamed upon them with double force. It is true that the whole condition of their minds was affected by this revelation, that there was nothing about them that was not full of it, and that they were actually at this moment discussing the business connected with it. Still it all came to life now as at the first moment at the sound of this name, Lord Erradeen! Walter could not help laughing to himself over his coffee.

'I can't tell who you mean,' he said. 'You must wait a little until I realise what Walter Methven has got to do with it.'

Mrs. Methven thought that this was making too much of the change. She already wished to believe, or at least to persuade Mr. Milnathort to believe, that she was not so very much surprised after all.

'Lord Erradeen,' she said, 'is too much amused at present with having got a new name to take the change very seriously.'

'He will soon learn the difference, madam,' said Mr. Milnathort. 'Property is a thing that has always to be taken seriously: and of all property the Erradeen lands. There are many things connected with them that he will have to set his face to in a way that will be far from amusing.'

The old lawyer had a very grave countenance – perhaps it was because he was a Scotchman. He worked through his breakfast with a steady routine that filled the ladies with respect. First fish, then kidneys, then a leg of the partridge that had been left from dinner last night; finally he looked about the table with an evident sense of something wanting, and though he declared that it was of no consequence, avowed at last, with some shyness, that it was the marmalade for which he was looking: and there was none in the house! Mr. Milnathort was full of excuses for having made such a suggestion. It was just a Scotch fashion he declared; it was of no consequence. Mrs. Methven, who held an unconscious conviction that it was somehow owing to him that Walter had become Lord Erradeen, was made quite unhappy by the omission.

'I shall know better another time,' she said regretfully. They were all still under the impression more or less that it was his doing. He was not a mere agent to them, but the god, out of the machinery,[45] who had turned darkness into light. He justified this opinion still more fully before he went away, putting into Walter's hand a cheque-book from a London bank, into which a sum of money which seemed to the inexperienced young man inexhaustible, had been paid to his credit. The old gentleman on his side seemed half-embarrassed, half-impatient after a while by the attention shown him. He resisted when Walter declared his intention of going to the railway to see him off.

'That is just a reversal of our positions,' he said.

At this Mrs. Methven became a little anxious, fearing that perhaps Walter's simplicity might be going too far. She gave him a word of warning when the cab drove up for Mr. Milnathort's bag. It was not a very large one, and Walter was quite equal to the condescension of carrying it to the station if his mother had not taken that precaution. She could not make up her mind that he was able to manage for himself.

'You must remember that after all he is only your man of business,' she said, notwithstanding all the worship she had herself been paying to this emissary of fortune. It was a relief to shake hands with him, to see him drive away from the door, leaving behind him such an amazing, such an incalculable change. Some-

The Wizard's Son, Volume I                                    45

how it was more easy to realise it when he was no longer there. And this was what Walter felt when he walked away from the railway, having seen with great satisfaction the grizzled head of the old Scotsman nod at him from a window of the departing train. The messenger was gone; the thing which he had brought with him, did that remain? Was it conceivable that it was now fixed and certain not to be affected by anything that could be done or said? Walter walked steadily enough along the pavement, but he did not think he was doing so. The world around him swam in his eyes once more. He could not make sure that he was walking on solid ground, or mounting up into the air. How different it was from the way in which he had come forth yesterday, idle, half-guilty, angry with himself and everybody, yet knowing very well what to do, turning with habitual feet into the way where all the other idlers congregated, knowing who he should meet and what would happen. He was separated from all that as if by an ocean. He had no longer anything to do with these foolish loungers. His mother had told him a thousand times in often varied tones that they were not companions for him; to-day he recognised the fact with a certain disgust. He felt it more strongly still when he suddenly came across Captain Underwood coming up eagerly with outstretched hands.

'I hope I am the first to congratulate you, Lord Erradeen,' he said. 'Now you will know why I asked you yesterday, Was there any news –'

'Now I shall know? I don't a bit; what do you mean? Do you mean me to believe that *you* had any hand in it?' Walter cried, with a tone of mingled incredulity and disdain.

'No hand in it, unless I had helped to put the last poor dear lord out of the way. I could scarcely have had that; but if you mean did I know about it, I certainly did, as you must if you had been a little more in the world.'

'Why didn't you tell me then?' said Walter. He added somewhat hotly, with something of the sublime assumption of youth: 'Waiting for a man to die would never have suited me. I much prefer to have been, as you say, out of the world –'

'Oh, Lord! I didn't mean to offend you,' said the captain. 'Don't get on a high horse. Of course, if you'd known your Debrett[46] as I do, you would have seen the thing plain enough. However, we needn't quarrel about it. I have always said you were my pupil, and I hope I have put you up to a few things that will be of use on your entry into society.'

'Have you?' said Walter. He could not think how he had ever for a moment put up with this underbred person. Underwood stood before him with a sort of jaunty rendering of the appeal with which grooms and people about the stable remind a young man of what in his boyish days they have done for him – an appeal which has its natural issue in a sovereign. But he could not give Underwood a sovereign,[47] and it was perhaps just a little ungenerous to turn in the first moment of his prosperity from a man who, from whatever purpose, had been serviceable to him in his poverty. He said, with an attempt to be more friendly: 'I know, Underwood, you have been very kind.'

'Oh, by Jove! kind isn't the word. I knew you'd want a bit of training; the best thoroughbred that ever stepped wants that; and if I can be of any use to you in the future, I will. I knew old Erradeen; I've known all about the family for generations. There are a great many curious things about it, but I think I can help you through them,' said the captain with a mixture of anxiety and swagger. There had always been something of this same mixture about him, but Walter had never been fully conscious what it was till now.

'Thank you,' he said; 'perhaps it will be better to let that develop itself in a natural way. I am going to Scotland in a week, and then I shall have it at first hand.'

'Then I can tell you beforehand you will find a great many things you won't like,' said Underwood, abruptly. 'It is not for nothing that a family gets up such a reputation. I know two or three of your places. Mulmorrel, and the shooting-box on Loch Etive, and that mysterious old place at Kinloch-houran. I have been at every one of them. It was not everybody, I can tell you, that old Erradeen would have taken to that place. Why, there is a mystery at every corner. There is –'

Walter held up his hand to stay this torrent. He coloured high with a curious sentiment of proprietorship and the shrinking of pride from hearing that which was his discussed by strangers. He scarcely knew the names of them, and their histories not at all. He put up his hand: 'I would rather find out the mysteries for myself,' he said.

'Oh,' cried Underwood, 'if you are standing on your dignity, my lord, as you like, for that matter. I am not one to thrust my company upon any man if he doesn't like it. I have stood your friend, and I would again; but as for forcing myself upon you now that you've come to your kingdom –'

'Underwood,' cried the other, touched in the tenderest point, 'if you dare to insinuate that this has changed me, I desire never to speak to you again. But it is only, I suppose, one of the figures of speech that people use when they are angry. I am not such a cad as you make me out. Whether my name is Methven or Erradeen – I don't seem to know very well which it is –'

'It is both,' the other cried with a great laugh, and they shook hands, engaging to dine together at the hotel that evening. Underwood, who was knowing in such matters, was to order the dinner, and two or three of 'the old set,' were to be invited. It would be a farewell to his former comrades, as Walter intended; and with a curious recurrence of his first elation he charged his representative to spare no expense. There was something intoxicating and strange in the very phrase.

As he left Underwood and proceeded along the High Street, where, if he had not waved his hand to them in passing with an air of haste and pre-occupation, at least every second person he met would have stopped him to wish him joy, he suddenly encountered July Herbert. She was going home from the vicarage, out of which his mother had politely driven her; and it seemed the most wonderful luck to July to get him to herself, thus wholly unprotected, and with nobody even to see what she was after. She went up to him, not with Underwood's eagerness, but with a pretty frank pleasure in her face.

'I have heard a fairy tale,' she said, 'and it is true –'[a]

'I suppose you mean about me,' said Walter. 'Yes, I am afraid it is true. I don't exactly know who I am at present.'

'Afraid!' cried July. 'Ah, you know you don't mean that. At all events, you are no longer just the old Walter whom we have known all our lives.'

There was another girl with her whom Walter knew but slightly, but who justified the plural pronoun.

'On the contrary, I was going to say, when you interrupted me –'

'I am so sorry I interrupted you.'

'That though I did not know who I was in the face of the world, I was always the old Walter, &c. A man, I believe, can never lose his Christian name.'

'Nor a woman either,' said July. 'That is the only thing that cannot be taken from us. We are supposed, you know, rather to like the loss of the other one.'

'I have heard so,' said Walter, who was not unaccustomed to this sort of fencing. 'But I suppose it is not true.'

'Oh,' said July, 'if it were for the same reason that makes you change your name, I should not mind. But there is no peerage in our family that I know of, and I should not have any chance if there were, alas! Good-bye, Lord Erradeen. It is a lovely name! And may I always speak to you when I meet you, though you are such a grand personage? We do not hope to see you at the Cottage now, but mamma will like to know that you still recognise an old friend.'

'I shall come and ask Mrs. Herbert what she thinks of it all,' Walter said.

July's brown eyes flashed out with triumph as she laughed and waved her hand to him. She said –

'It will be too great an honour,' and curtseyed; then laughed again as she went on, casting a glance at him over her shoulder.

He laughed too; he was young, and he was gratified even by this undisguised provocation, though he could not help saying to himself, with a slight beat of his heart, how near he was to falling in love with that girl! What a good thing it was that he did not – *now!*

As for July, she looked at him with a certain ferocity, as if she would have devoured him. To think of all that boy had it in his power to give if he pleased, and to think how little a poor girl could do!

# CHAPTER VI.

MRS. METHVEN was conscious of a new revival of the old displeasure when Walter informed her of the engagement he had formed for the evening. She was utterly disappointed. She had thought that the great and beneficial shock of this new life would turn his character altogether, and convert him into that domestic sovereign, that object of constant reference, criticism, and devotion which every woman would have every man be. It was a wonderful mortification and enlightenment to find that without even the interval of a single evening devoted to the consideration of his new and marvellous prospects, and that talking over which is one of the sweetest parts of a great and happy event, he should return – to what? – to wallowing in the mire, as the Scripture says,[48] to his old billiard-room acquaintances, the idlers and undesirable persons with whom he had formed associations. Could there be anything more unsuitable than Lord Erradeen in the midst of such a party, with Underwood, and perhaps worse than Underwood. It wounded her pride and roused her temper, and, in spite of all her efforts, it was with a lowering brow that she saw him go away. Afterwards, indeed, when she thought of it, as she did for hours together, while cousin Sophia talked, and she languidly replied, maintaining a conversation from the lips outward, so poor a substitute for the evening's talking over and happy consultation she had dreamed of – Mrs. Methven was more just to her son. She tried always to be just, poor lady. She placed before herself all the reasons for his conduct. That he should entertain the men who, much against her wish and his own good, yet in their way had been kind to and entertained him, was natural. But to do it this first evening was hard, and she could not easily accept her disappointment. Afterwards she reminded herself with a certain stern philosophy that because Walter had owned a touch of natural emotion, and had drawn near to her and confessed himself in the wrong, that was no reason why his character should be changed in a moment. There were numbers of men who on occasion felt and lamented their misdoing, yet went on again in the same way. He had been no doubt startled, as some are by calamity, by the more extraordinary shock of this good fortune; but why should he for that abandon all the tastes and occupations of his former life? It was she, she said to herself, with some bitterness, who was a fool. The fact was that Walter meant no harm at all, and that it was merely the first impulse of a half-scornful liberality, impatience of the old associations, which he had tacitly acknowledged were not fit for him, that led him back to his former companions. He felt afterwards that it would have been in better taste had he postponed this for a night. But he was very impatient and eager to shake himself free of them, and enter upon his new career.

Something of the same disappointed and disapproving sentiment filled Mrs. Methven's mind when she heard of his visit to the Cottage. She knew no reason why he should take a special leave of July Herbert; if he knew himself a reason, which he did not disclose, that was another matter. Thoughts like this embittered the preparations for his departure, which otherwise would have been so agreeable. She had to see after many things which a young man of more wealth, or more independent habits, would have done for himself – his linen, his portmanteau,[49] most of the things he wanted, except the tailor part of the business; but it was not until the last evening that there was any of the confidential consultation, for which her heart had longed. Even on that last day Walter had been very little indoors. He had been busy with a hundred trifles, and she had begun to make up her mind to his going away without a word said as to their future relations, as to whether he meant his mother to share any of the advantages of his new position, or to drop her at Sloebury as something done with, which he did not care to burden himself with, any more than the other circumstances of his past career. She did so little justice to the real generosity of her son's temper in the closeness of her contest with him, and the heat of personal feeling, that she had begun to make up her mind to this, with what pain and bitterness it is unnecessary to say.

She had even begun to make excuses for her own desertion in the tumult of endless thought upon this one subject which possessed her. She would be just; after all, was it not better perhaps that she should be left in the little house which was her independent home, for which she owed nothing to any one? If any unnecessary sense of gratitude made him offer her reluctantly a share in his new life, that would be humiliation indeed. If, as was apparent, her society, her advice, her love were nothing to him, was it not far better that both should recognise the situation, and view things in their true light? This the proud woman had made up her mind to, with what depth of wounded tenderness and embittered affection who could say? She had packed for him with her own hands, for all his permanent arrangements were to be made after he had left Sloebury, and to change her household in consequence of an alteration of fortune which, according to all appearances, would not concern her, was, she had proudly decided, quite out of the question. She packed for him as in the days when he was going to school, when he was a boy, and liked everything better that had been done by his mother. A woman may be pardoned for feeling such a difference with a passionate soreness and sense of downfall. In those days how she had thought of the time when he would be grown up, when he would understand all her difficulties and share all her cares, and in his own advancement make her triumphant and happy! God forgive me, she said to herself, now he has got advancement far above my hopes, and I am making myself wretched thinking of myself. She stopped and cried a little over his new linen. No, he was right; if it must be allowed that they did not 'get on,' it was indeed far better in the long run that there should be no false sentiment, no keeping up of an untenable position. Thank God she required nothing; she had enough; she wanted neither luxury nor grandeur, and her home, her natural place was here, where she had lived so many years, where she could disarm all comment upon Walter's neglect of her, by saying that she preferred the place where she had lived so long, and where she had so many friends. Why, indeed, should she change her home at her time of life? No doubt he would come back some time and see her; but after all why should her life be unsettled because his was changed? It was he who showed true sense in his way of judging the matter, she said to herself with a smile, through the hastily dried and momentary tears.

50 *The Selected Works of Margaret Oliphant, Volume 21*

Walter came in when the packing was just about concluded. He came half way up the stairs and called 'Mother, where are you?' as he had often done when he was a boy and wanted her at every turn, but as he never did now. This touched and weakened her again in her steady resolution to let him see no repining in her. 'Are you packing for me?' he called out again; 'what a shame while I have been idling! But come down, mother, please, and leave that. You forget we have everything to settle yet.'

'What is there to settle?' she said, with a certain sharpness of tone which she could not quite suppress, coming out upon the landing. The maids who were going to bed, and who heard all this, thought it was beautiful to hear his lordship speaking like that, quite natural to his mother; but that missus was that hard it was no wonder if they didn't get on; and Cousin Sophia from her virgin retirement, where she sat in her dressing-gown reading a French novel,[50] and very much alive to every sound, commented in her own mind, closing her book, in the same sense. 'Now she will just go and hold him at arm's length while the boy's heart is melting, and then break her own,' Miss Merivale said to herself. Thus everybody was against her and in favour of the fortunate young fellow who had been supping on homage and flattery, and now came in easy and careless to make everything straight at the last moment. Mrs. Methven on her side was very tired, and tremulous with the exertion of packing. It would have been impossible for her to banish that tone out of her voice. She stood in the subdued light upon the stairs looking down upon him, leaning on the banister to support herself; while he, with all the light from below upon his face, ruddy with the night air, and the applauses, and his own high well-being, looked up gaily at her. He had shaken off all his old irritability in the confidence of happiness and good fortune that had taken possession of him. After a moment he came springing up the stairs three at a time.

'You look tired, mother, while I have been wasting my time. Come down, and let us have our talk. I'll do all the rest to-morrow,' he said, throwing his arm round her and leading her down-stairs. He brought her some wine first of all and a footstool, and threw himself into the easy task of making her comfortable. 'Now,' he said, 'let's talk it all over,' drawing a chair to her side.

All this was quite new upon Walter's part – or rather quite old, belonging to an age which had long ago gone.

'Isn't it rather late for that?' she said, with a faint smile.

'Yes, and I am ashamed of myself; but, unfortunately, you are so used to that. We must settle, however, mother. I am to go first of all to Kinloch-houran, which Milnathort says is not a place for you. Indeed, I hear – ' here he paused a little as if he would have named his authority, and continued, 'that it is a ruinous sort of place; and why I should go there, I don't know.'

'Where did you hear?' she said, with quick suspicion.

'Well, mother, I would rather not have mentioned his name; but if you wish to know, from Underwood. I know you are prejudiced against him. Yes, it is prejudice, though I don't wonder at it. I care nothing for the fellow; but still it comes out, which is rather strange, that he knows these places, and a good deal about the Erradeens.'

'Is that, then,' cried the mother quickly, 'the reason of his being here?'

'He never said so, nor have I asked him,' answered Walter, with something of his old sullenness; but then he added –'The same thought has crossed my own mind, mother, and I shouldn't wonder if it were so.'

'Walter,' she said, 'a man like that can have but one motive – the desire to aggrandise himself. For heaven's sake, don't have anything to do with him; don't let him get an influence over you.'

'You must have a very poor opinion of me, mother,' he said, in an aggrieved tone.

She looked at him with a curious gaze, silenced, as it seemed. She loved him more than anything in the world, and thought of him above everything; and yet perhaps in that wrath with those we love which works like madness in the brain, it was true what he said – that she had a poor opinion of him. Extremes meet, as the proverb says.[51] However, this was a mystery too deep for Walter to enter into.

'Don't let us waste words about Underwood,' he said. 'I care nothing for the fellow; he is vulgar and presuming – as you always said.'

Partly, no doubt, this avowal was made with the intention of pleasing his mother; at the same time it proved the great moral effect of promotion in rank. Lord Erradeen saw with the utmost distinctness what Walter Methven had only glimpsed by intervals. And it is impossible to describe how this speech pleased Mrs. Methven. Her tired eyes began to shine, her heart to return to its brighter hopes.

'The thing is, what arrangements you wish me to make,' said Walter. 'What are you going to do? I hear Mulmorrel is a handsome house, but it's November, and naturally it is colder in the north. Do you think you would care to go there now, or wait till the weather is better? It may want furnishing, for any-thing I know; and it appears we've got a little house in town.'

'Walter,' she said, in a voice which was husky and tremulous, 'before you enter upon all this – you must first think, my dear. Are you sure it will be for your comfort to have me with you at all? Wouldn't you rather be free, and make your own arrangements, and leave me – as I am?'

'MOTHER?' the young man cried. He got up suddenly from where he was sitting beside her, and pushed away his chair, and stood facing her, with a sudden paleness and fiery eyes that seemed to dazzle her. He had almost kicked her footstool out of his way in his excitement and wounded feeling. 'Do you mean to say you want to have nothing to do with me?' he said.

'Oh! my boy, you could not think so. I thought that was what – you meant. I wish only what is for your good.'

'Would it be for my good to be an unnatural cad?' said the young man, with rising indignation –' a heart-less, ill-conditioned whelp, with no sense and no feeling? Oh, mother! mother! what a poor opinion you must have of me!' he cried; and so stung was he with this blow that sudden tears sprang to his eyes. 'All because I'm a fool and put everything off to the last moment,' he added, in a sort of undertone, as if explaining it to himself. 'But I'm not a beast for all that,' he said, fiercely.

She made him no reply, but sat and gazed at him with a remorse and compunction, which, painful sentiments as they are, were to her sweet as the dews from heaven. Yes, it appeared that through all her passionate and absorbing tenderness she had had a poor opinion of him. She had done him injustice. The conviction was like a new birth. That he should be Lord Erradeen was nothing in comparison of being,[a] as he thus proved himself, good and true, open to the influences of affection and nature. She could not speak, but her eyes were full of a thousand things; they asked him mutely to forgive her. They repented, and were abashed and rejoiced all in one glance. The young man who had not been nearly so heartless as she feared, was now not nearly so noble as she thought: but he was greatly touched by the crisis, and by the suggestion of many a miserable hour which was in her involuntary sin against him and in her penitence. He came back again and sat close by her, and kissed her tremulously.

'I have been a cad,' he said. 'I don't wonder you lost all faith in me, mother.'

'Not that, not that,' she said faintly; and then there was a moment of exquisite silence, in which, without a word, everything was atoned for, and pardon asked and given.

And then began perhaps the happiest hour of Mrs. Methven's life, in which they talked over everything and decided what was to be done. Not to give up the house in Sloebury at present, nor indeed to do anything at present, save wait till he had made his expedition into Scotland and seen his new property, and brought her full particulars. After he had investigated everything and knew exactly the capabilities of the house, and the condition in which it was, and all the necessities and expediencies, they would then decide as to the best thing to be done; whether to go there, though at the worst time of the year, or to go to London, which was an idea that pleased Walter but alarmed his mother. Mrs. Methven did her best to remember what were the duties of a great landed proprietor and to bring them home to her son.

'You ought to spend Christmas at your own place,' she said. 'There will be charities and hospitalities and the poor people to look after.'

She did not know Scotland, nor did she know very well what it was to be a great country magnate. She had been but a poor officer's daughter herself, and had married another officer, and been beaten about from place to place before she settled down on her small income at Sloebury. She had not much more experience than Walter himself had in this respect; indeed, if the truth must be told, both of them drew their chief information from novels, those much-abused sources of information, in which the life of rural potentates is a favourite subject, and not always described with much knowledge. Walter gravely consented to all this, with a conscientious desire to do what was right: but he thought the place would most likely be gloomy for his mother in winter, and that hospitalities would naturally be uncalled for so soon after the death of the old lord.

'What I would advise would be Park Lane,' he said, with a judicial tone. 'Milnathort said that it was quite a small house.'

'What is a small house in Park Lane would look a palace at Sloebury,' Mrs. Methven said: 'and you must not begin on an extravagant footing, my dear.'

'You will let us begin comfortably, I hope,' he said; 'and I must look for a nice carriage for you, mother.'

Walter felt disposed to laugh as he said the words, but carried them off with an air of easy indifference as if it were the most natural thing in the world: while his mother on her side could have cried for pleasure and tenderness.

'You must not mind me, Walter; we must think what is best for yourself,' she said, as proud and pleased as if she had twenty carriages.

'Nothing of the sort,' he said. 'We are going to be comfortable, and you must have everything that is right first of all.'

What an hour it was! now and then there will be given to one individual out of a class a full measure of recompense heaped and overflowing, out of which the rest may get a sympathetic pleasure though they do not enjoy it in their own persons. Mrs. Methven had never imagined that this would come to her, but lo! in a moment it was pouring upon her in floods of consolation. So absorbing was this happy consultation that it was only when her eyes suddenly caught the clock on the mantelpiece, and saw that the hands were marking a quarter to two! that Mrs. Methven startled awoke out of her bliss.

'My poor boy! that I should keep you up to this hour talking, and a long journey before you to-morrow!' she cried.

She hustled him up to his room after this, talking and resisting gaily to the very door. He was happy too with that sense of happiness conferred, which is always sweet, and especially to youth in the delightful, easy sense of power and beneficence. When he thought of it he was a little remorseful, to think that he had possessed the power so long and never exercised it, for Walter was generous enough to be aware that the house in Park Lane and the carriage were not the occasions of his mother's blessedness. 'Poor mother,' he said to himself softly. He might have made her a great deal more happy if he had chosen before these fine things were dreamt of. But Mrs. Methven remembered that no more. She begged pardon of God on her knees for misjudging her boy, and for once in her life was profoundly, undoubtingly happy, with a perfection and fulness of content which perhaps could only come after long experience of the reverse. After such a moment a human creature, if possible, should die, so as to taste nothing less sweet: for the less sweet, to be sure, must come back if life goes on, and at that moment there was not a cloud or a suggestion of darkness upon the firmament. She grudged falling asleep, though she was very tired, and so losing this beautiful hour; but nature[a] is wilful and will seldom abdicate the night for joy, whatever she may do for grief.

Next morning she went to the station with him to see him away. Impossible to describe the devotion of all the officials to Lord Erradeen's comfort on his journey. The station-master kindly came to superintend this august departure, and the porters ran about contending for his luggage with an excitement which made, at least, one old gentleman threaten to write to the *Times*. There was nothing but 'my lord' and 'his lordship' to be heard all over the station; and so many persons came to bid him good-bye and see the last of him, as they said, that the platform was quite inconveniently crowded. Among these, of course, was Captain Underwood, whose fervent – 'God bless you, my boy' – drowned all other greetings. He had, however, a disappointed look – as if he had failed in some object. Mrs. Methven, whose faculties were all sharpened by her position, and who felt herself able to exercise a toleration which, in former circumstances, would have been impossible to her, permitted him to overtake her as she left the place, and acknowledged his greeting with more cordiality, or, at least, with a less forbidding civility than usual. And then a wonderful sight was seen in Sloebury. This *bête noir*[52] of the feminine world, this man[b] whom every lady frowned upon, was seen walking along the High Street, side by side, in earnest conversation with one of the women who had been most unfavourable to him. Was she listening to an explanation, a justification, an account of himself, such as he had not yet given, to satisfy the requirements of the respectability of Sloebury? To tell the truth, Mrs. Methven now cared very little for any such explanation. She did not remember, as she ought to have done, that other women's sons might be in danger from this suspicious person, though her own was now delivered out of his power. But she was very curious to know what anybody could tell her of Walter's new possessions, and of the family which it was rather humiliating to know so little about. It was she, indeed, who had begun the conversation after his first remark upon Walter's departure and the loss which would result to Sloebury.

'You know something about the Erradeens, my son tells me,' she said almost graciously.

'Something! I know about as much as most people. I knew he was the heir, which few, except yourselves, did,' the captain said. He cast a keen glance at her when he said, 'except yourselves.'

'Indeed,' said Mrs. Methven, 'that is scarcely correct, for Walter did not know, and I had forgotten. I had, indeed, lost sight of my husband's family and the succession seemed so far off.'

It was thus that she veiled her ignorance and endeavoured to make it appear that indifference on her part, and a wise desire to keep Walter's mind unaffected by such a dazzling possibility, had been her guiding influence. She spoke with such modest gravity that Captain Underwood, not used to delusion under that form, was tempted into a sort of belief. He looked at her curiously, but her veil was down, and her artifice, if it was an artifice, was of a kind more delicate than any to which he was accustomed.

'Well!' he said, 'then it was not such a surprise to you as people thought? Sloebury has talked of nothing else, I need not tell you, for several days; and everybody was of opinion that it burst upon you like a thunderbolt.'

'Upon my son, yes,' Mrs. Methven said with a smile. He looked at her again, and she had the satisfaction of perceiving that this experienced man of the world was taken in.

'Well, then,' he said, 'you will join with me in wishing him well out of it: you know all the stories that are about.'

'I have never been at Mulmorrel – my husband's chances in his own lifetime were very small, you know.'

'It isn't Mulmorrel, it is that little ruined place where something uncanny is always said to go on – oh, *I* don't know what it is; nobody does but the reigning sovereign himself, and some hangers-on, I suppose. I have been there. I've seen the mysterious light, you know. Nobody can ever tell what window it shows at, or if it is any window at all. I was once with the late man – the late lord, he who died the other day – when it came out suddenly. We were shooting wildfowl, and his gun fell out of his hands. I never saw a man in such a funk. We were a bit late, and twilight had come on before we knew.'

'So then you actually saw something of it yourself?' Mrs. Methven said. She had not the remotest idea what this was, but if she could find out something by any means she was eager enough to take advantage of it.

'No more than that; but I can tell you this: Erradeen was not seen again for twenty-four hours. Whether it was a call to him or what it was I can't undertake to say. He never would stand any questioning about it. He was a good fellow enough, but he never would put up with anything on that point. So I can only wish Walter well through it, Mrs. Methven. In my opinion he should have had some one with him; for he is young, and, I dare say, he is fanciful.'

'My son, Lord Errradeen,' said Mrs. Methven with dignity, 'is man enough, I hope, to meet an emergency. Perhaps you think him younger than he is.' She propounded this delicately as, perhaps, a sort of excuse for the presumption of the Christian name.

Underwood grew very red: he was disappointed and irritable. 'Oh, of course you know best,' he said. 'As for my Lord Erradeen (I am sure I beg your pardon for forgetting his dignity), I dare say he is quite old enough to take care of himself – at least, we'll hope so; but a business of that kind will upset the steadiest brain, you know. Old Erradeen had not a bad spirit of his own, and *he* funked it. I confess I feel a little anxious for your boy; he's a nice fellow, but he's nervous. I was in a dozen minds to go up with him to stand by him; but, perhaps, it is better not, for the best motives get misconstrued in this world. I can only wish him well out of it,' Captain Underwood said, taking off his hat, and making her a fine bow as he stalked away.

It is needless to say that this mysterious intimation of danger planted daggers in Mrs. Methven's heart. She stopped aghast: and for the moment the idea of running back to the station, and signalling that the train was to be stopped came into her mind. Ridiculous folly! Wish him well out of it? What, out of his great fortune, his peerage, his elevation in the world? Mrs. Methven smiled indignantly, and thought of the strange manifestations under which envy shows itself. But she went home somewhat pale, and could not dismiss it from her mind as she wished to do. Well out of it! And there were moments when, she remembered, she had surprised a very serious look on the countenance of Mr. Milnathort. Was Walter going unwarned, in the elation and happy confidence of his heart, into some danger unknown and unforeseen? This took her confidence away from her, and made her nervous and anxious. But after all, what folly it must be: something uncanny and a mysterious light! These were stories for Christmas, to bring a laugh or a shiver from idle circles round the fire. To imagine that they could effect anything in real life was a kind of madness; an old-fashioned, exploded superstition. It was too ridiculous to be worthy a thought.

\*\*\*

# CHAPTER VII.

Walter arrived in Edinburgh on a wintry morning white and chill. A sort of woolly shroud wrapped all the fine features of the landscape. He thought the dingy turrets of the Calton Jail[53] were the Castle, and was much disappointed, as was natural. Arthur's Seat[54] and the Crags were as entirely invisible as if they had been a hundred miles away, and the cold crept into his very bones after his night's journey, although it had been made luxuriously, in a way very different from his former journeyings. Also it struck him as strange and uncomfortable that nobody was aware of the change in his position, and that even the railway porter, to whom he gave a shilling (as a commoner he would have been contented with sixpence), only called him 'Sir,' and could not perceive that it would have been appropriate to say my lord. He went to an hotel, as it was so early, and found only a dingy little room to repose himself in, the more important part of the house being still in the hands of the housemaids. And when he gave his name as Lord Erradeen, the attendants stared at him with a sort of suspicion. They looked at his baggage curiously, and evidently asked each other if it was possible he could

*The Wizard's Son, Volume I* 57

be what he claimed to be. Walter had a half-consciousness[a] of being an impostor, and trying to take these surprised people in. He thawed, however, as he eat his breakfast, and the mist began to rise, revealing the outline of the Old Town.[55] He had never been in Edinburgh before; he had rarely been anywhere before. It was all new to him, even the sense of living in an inn. There was a curious freedom about it, and independence of all restraint, which pleased him. But it was very strange to be absolutely unknown, to meet the gaze of faces he had never seen before, and to be obliged always to explain who he was. It was clear that a servant was a thing quite necessary to a man who called himself by a title, a servant not so much to attend upon him as to answer for him, and be a sort of guarantee to the world. Now that he was here in Edinburgh, he was not quite sure what to do with himself. It was too early to do anything. He could not disturb old Milnathort at such an hour. He must let the old man get to his office and read his letters before he could descend upon him. So that on the whole Walter, though sustained by the excitement of his new position, was altogether chilled and not at all comfortable, feeling those early hours of grim daylight hang very heavily on his hands. He went out after he had refreshed and dressed – and strolled about the fine but foreign street. It looked quite foreign to his inexperienced eyes. The Castle[56] soared vaguely through the grey mist; the irregular line of roofs and spires crowning the ridge threw itself up vaguely against a darker grey behind. There was a river of mist between him and that ridge, running deep in the hollow, underneath the nearer bank, which was tufted with spectral bushes and trees, and with still more spectral white statues glimmering through. On the other side of the street, more cheerful and apparent, were the jewellers' shops full of glistening pebbles and national ornaments. Everybody knows that it is not these shops alone, but others of every luxurious kind, that form the glory of Prince's Street.[57] But Walter was a stranger and foreigner; and in the morning mists the shining store of cairngorms[58] was the most cheerful sight that met his eye.

Mr. Milnathort's office was in a handsome square, with a garden in the centre of it, and another statue holding possession of the garden. For the first time since he left home, Walter felt a little thrill of his new importance when he beheld the respectful curiosity produced among the clerks by the statement of his name. They asked his lordship to step in with an evident sensation. And for Walter himself to look into that office where his mother had so strongly desired that he should find a place, had the most curious effect. He felt for the moment as if he were one of the serious young men peeping from beyond the wooden railing that inclosed the office, at the fortunate youth whose circumstances were no different from their own. He did not realise at that moment the unfailing human complacency which would have come to his aid in such circumstances, and persuaded him that the gifts of fortune had nothing to do with real superiority. He thought of the possible reflections upon himself of the other young fellows in their lowly estate as if he had himself been making them. He was sorry for them all, for the contrast they must draw, and the strange sense of human inequality that they must feel. He was no better than they were – who could tell? perhaps not half as good. He felt that to feel this was a due tribute from Lord Erradeen in his good fortune to those who might have been Walter Methven's fellow-clerks, but who had never had any chance of being Lord Erradeen. And then he thought what a good thing it was that he had never written that letter to Mr. Milnathort, offering himself for a desk in the office. He had felt really guilty on the subject at the time. He had felt that it was miserable of him to neglect the occasion thus put before him of gaining a livelihood. Self-reproach, real and unmistakable, had been in his mind; and yet what a good thing he had not done it: and how little one knows what is going to happen! These were very ordinary reflections, not showing much depth; but it must be recollected that Walter was still in a sort of primary state of feeling, and had not had time to reach a profounder level.

Mr. Milnathort made haste to receive him, coming out of his own room on purpose, and giving him the warmest welcome.

'I might have thought you would come by the night train.[59] You are not old enough to dislike night travelling as I do; but I will take it ill, and so will my sister, if you stay in an hotel, and your room ready for you in our little place. I think you will be more comfortable with us, though we have no grandeur to surround you with. My sister has a great wish to make your acquaintance, my Lord Erradeen. She has just a wonderful acquaintance with the family, and it was more through her than any one that I knew just where to put my hand upon you, when the time came.'

'I did not like to disturb you so early,' Walter said.

'Well, perhaps there is something in that. We are not very early birds: and as a matter of fact, Alison did not expect you till about seven o'clock at night. And here am I in the midst of my day's work. But I'll tell you what I'll do for you. We'll go round to the club, and there your young lordship will make acquaintance with somebody that can show you something of Edinburgh. You have never been here before? It is a great pity that there is an easterly haar,[60] which is bad both for you and the objects you are wanting to see. However, it is lifting, and we'll get some luncheon, and then I will put you in the way. That is the best thing I can do for you. Malcolm, you will send down all the documents relative to his lordship's affairs to Moray Place,[61] this afternoon; and you can tell old Symington to be in attendance in case Lord Erradeen should wish to see him. That is your cousin the late lord's body servant. He is a man of great experience, and you might wish –; but all that can be settled later on. If Drysdales should send over about that case of theirs, ye will say, Malcolm, that I shall be here not later than three in the afternoon; and if old Blairallan comes fyking,[62] ye can say I am giving the case my best attention; and if it's that big north-country fellow about his manse and his augmentation –'[63]

'I fear that I am unpardonable,' said Walter, 'in interfering with your valuable time.'

'Nothing of the sort. It is not every day that a Lord Erradeen comes into his inheritance; and as there are, may be, things not over-cheerful to tell you at night, we may as well make the best of it in the morning,' said the old lawyer. He got himself into his coat as he spoke, slowly, not without an effort. The sun was struggling through the mist as they went out again into the streets, and the mid-day gun from the Castle[64] helped for a moment to disperse the haar, and show the noble cliff on which it rears its head aloft. Mr. Milnathort paused to look with tender pride along the line – the houses and spires lifting out of the clouds, the sunshine breaking through, the crown of St. Giles's[65] hovering like a visible sign of rank over the head of the throned city, awakened in him that keen pleasure and elation in the beauty of his native place which is nowhere more warmly felt than in Edinburgh. He waved his hand towards the Old Town in triumph. 'You may have seen a great deal, but ye will never have seen anything finer than that,' he said.

'I have seen very little,' said Walter; 'but everybody has heard of Edinburgh, so that it does not take one by surprise.'

'Ay, that is very wisely said. If it took you by surprise, and you had never heard of it before, the world would just go daft over it. However, it is a drawback of a great reputation that ye never come near it with your mind clear.' Having said this the old gentleman dismissed the subject with a wave of his hand, and said, in a different tone, 'You will be very curious about the family secrets you are coming into, Lord Erradeen.'

Walter laughed.

'I am coming to them with my mind clear,' he said. 'I know nothing about them. But I don't believe much in family secrets. They belong to the middle ages. Nowadays we have nothing to conceal.'

Mr. Milnathort listened to this blasphemy with a countenance in which displeasure struggled with that supreme sense that the rash young man would soon know better, which disarms reproof. He shook his head.

'You may say we can conceal but little,' he said, 'which is true enough, but not altogether true either. Courage is a fine thing, Lord Erradeen, and I am always glad to see it; and if you have your imagination under control, that will do ye still better service. In most cases it is not only what we see, but what we think we are going to see, that daunts us. Keep you your head cool, that is your best defence in all emergencies. It is better to be too bold than not to be bold enough, notwithstanding the poet's warning to yon warrior-maid of his.'[66].

These last words made Walter stare, for he was not very learned in poetry at the best, and was totally unprepared to hear Spenser from the lips of the old Scottish lawyer. He was silent for a little in mere perplexity, and then he said, with a laugh –

60    *The Selected Works of Margaret Oliphant, Volume 21*

'You speak of danger as if we were on the eve of a battle. Are there giants to encounter or magicians? One would think we were living in the dark ages,' Walter cried with a little impatience.

Mr. Milnathort said nothing more. He led the young man into one of the great stone palaces which form the line of Prince's Street, and which was then the seat of the old original club of Edinburgh society.[67] Here Walter found himself in the midst of a collection of men with marked and individual faces, each one of whom ought to be somebody, he thought. Many of them were bound about the throat with white ties, like clergymen,[68] but they did not belong to that profession. It gave the young man a sense of his own importance, which generally deserted him in Mr. Milnathort's presence, and of which he felt himself to stand in need, to perceive that he excited a great deal of interest among these grave and potent signors. There was a certain desire visible to make his acquaintance and to ascertain his political opinions, of which Walter was scarcely aware as yet whether he had any. It was suggested at once that he should be put up for the club, and invitations to dinner began to be showered upon him. He was stopped short in his replies to those cordial beginnings of acquaintance by Mr. Milnathort, who calmly assumed the guidance of his movements. 'Lord Erradeen,' he said, 'is on his way West. Business will not permit him to tarry at this moment. We hope he will be back ere long, and perhaps stay a while in Edinburgh, and see what is to be seen in the way of society.' This summary way of taking all control of his own movements from him astounded Walter so much that he merely stared at his old tyrant or vizier, and in his confusion of surprise and anger did not feel capable of saying anything, which, after all, was the most dignified way; for, he said to himself, it was not necessary to yield implicit obedience even if he refrained from open protest upon these encroachments on his liberty. In the mean time it was evident that the old lawyer did not intend him to have any liberty at all. He produced out of the recesses of the club library a beaming little man in spectacles, to whom he committed the charge of the young stranger.

'Mr. Bannatyne,' he said, 'knows Edinburgh as well as I know my chambers, and he will just take you round what is most worth seeing.'

When Walter attempted to escape with a civil regret to give his new acquaintance trouble he was put down by both with eagerness.

'The Old Town is just the breath of my nostrils,' said the little antiquary.

'It cannot be said that it's a fragrant breath,' said old Milnathort; 'but since that is so, Lord Erradeen, you would not deprive our friend of such a pleasure: and we'll look for you by five or six at Moray Place, or earlier if you weary, for it's soon dark at this time of the year.'

To find himself thus arrested in the first day of his emancipation and put into the hands of a conductor was so annoying yet so comic that Walter's resentment evaporated in the ludicrous nature of the situation and his consciousness that otherwise he would not know what to do with himself. But sight-seeing requires a warmer inspiration than this, and even the amusement of beholding his companion's enthusiasm over all the dark entries and worn-out inscriptions was not enough to keep Walter's interest alive. His own life at this moment was so much more interesting than anything else, so much more important than those relics of a past which had gone away altogether out of mortal ken. When the blood is at high pressure in our veins, and the future lying all before us, it is very difficult to turn back, and force our eager eyes into contemplation of scenes with which we ourselves have little or no connection. The antiquary, however, was not to be baulked. He looked at his young companion with his head on one side like a critical bird. 'You are paying no attention to me,' he said half pathetically; 'but 'cod,[69] man (I beg your pardon, my lord!), ye *shall* be interested before I'm done.' With this threat he hurried Walter along to the noisiest and most squalid part of that noble but miserable street which is the pride of Edinburgh, and stopped short before a small but deep doorway, entering from a short flight of outside stairs. The door was black with age and neglect, and showed a sort of black cave within, out of which all kind of dingy figures were fluttering. The aspect of the muddy stairs and ragged wayfarers was miserable enough, but the mouldings of the lintel, and the spiral staircase half visible at one side, were of a grim antiquity, and so was the lofty tenement above, with its many rows of windows and high-stepped gable.

'Now just look here,' said Mr. Bannatyne, 'these arms[70] will tell their own story.'

There was a projecting boss of rude, half-obliterated carving on the door.

'I cannot make head nor tail of it,' said the young man; his patience was beginning to give way.

'Lord Erradeen,' cried the other with enthusiasm, 'this is worth your fattest farm; it is of more interest than half your inheritance; it is as historical as Holyrood.[71] You are just awfully insensible, you young men, and think as little of the relics that gave you your consequences in the world –!' He paused a little in the fervour of his indignation, then added – 'But there are allowances to be made for you as you were bred in England, and perhaps are little acquainted – My lord, this is Me'even's Close, bearing the name even now in its decay. It was my Lord Methven's lodging in the old time. Bless me! can your young eyes not read the motto that many people have found so significant? Look here,' cried Walter's cicerone,[72] tracing with his stick the half-effaced letters, 'Baithe Sune and Syne.'[73]

Young Lord Erradeen began, as was natural, to feel ashamed of himself. He felt a pang of discomfort too, for this certainly bore no resemblance to the trim piece of modern Latin about the conquering power of virtue which was on his father's seal. The old possibility that he might turn out an impostor after all gleamed across his mind. 'Does this belong to me?' he added with some eagerness, to veil these other and less easy sentiments.

'I know nothing about that,' said Mr. Bannatyne with a slight tone of contempt. 'But it was the Lord of Methven's lodging in the days when Scots lords lived in the Canongate[74] of Edinburgh.' Then he added, 'There is a fine mantelpiece up-stairs which you had better see. Oh nobody will have any objection, a silver key[75] opens every door hereabout. If it should happen to be yours, my lord, and I were you,' said the eager little man, 'I would clear out the whole clan-jamfry[76a] and have it thoroughly cleaned, and make a museum of the place. You would pick up many a curious bit as the auld houses go down. This way, to the right, and mind the hole in the wall. The doors are all carved, if you can see them for the dirt, and you'll not often see a handsomer room.'

It was confusing at first to emerge out of the gloom of the stairs into the light of the great room, with its row of windows guiltless of either blind or curtain, which was in possession of a group of ragged children, squatting about in front of the deep, old-fashioned chimney, over which a series of elaborate carvings rose to the roof. The room had once been panelled, but half of the woodwork had been dragged down, and the rest was in a deplorable state. The contrast of the squalor and wretchedness about him, with the framework of the ancient, half-ruined grandeur, at once excited and distressed Walter. There was a bed, or rather a heap of something covered with the bright patches of an old quilt, in one corner, in another an old corner cupboard fixed into the wall, a rickety table and two chairs in the middle of the room. The solemn, unsheltered windows, like so many hollow, staring eyes, gazed out through the cold veil of the mist upon the many windows of an equally tall house on the other side of the street, the view being broken by a projecting pole thrust forth from the middle one, upon which some dingy clothes were hanging to dry. The children hung together, getting behind the biggest of them, a ragged, handsome girl, with wild, elf locks, who confronted the visitors with an air of defiance. The flooring was broken in many places, and dirty beyond description. Walter felt it intolerable to be here, to breathe the stifling atmosphere, to contemplate this hideous form of decay. He thought some one was looking at him from behind the torn panels. 'This is horrible,' he said. 'I hope I have nothing to do with it.' Disgust and a shivering, visionary dread was in his voice.

'Your race has had plenty to do with it,' said the antiquary. 'It was here, they say, that the warlock-lord[77] played most of his pliskies.[78] It was his 'warm study of deals' like that they made for John Knox[79] on the other side of the street. These walls have seen strange sights: and if you believe in witchcraft, as one of your name ought –'

'Why should one of my name believe in witchcraft? It appears,' he said, with petulance, 'that I know very little about my name.'

'So I should have said,' said the antiquary, dryly. 'But no doubt you have heard of your great ancestor, the warlock-lord? I am not saying that I admire the character in the abstract; but an ancestor like that is fine for a family. He was mixed up in all the doings of the time, and he made his own out of every one of them. And then he's a grand historical problem to the present day, which is no small distinction. You never heard of that? Oh, my lord, that's just not possible! He was the one whose death was never proved nor nothing about him, where he was buried, or the nature of his end, or if he ever came to an end at all; his son would never take the title, and forbade *his* son to do it: but by the time you have got to the second generation you are not minding so much. I noticed that the late lord would never enter into conversation on the subject. The family has always been touchy about it. It was the most complete disappearance I can recollect hearing of. Most historical puzzles clear themselves up in time: but this never was cleared up. Of course it has given rise to legends. You will perhaps be more interested in the family legends, Lord Erradeen?'

'Not at all,' said Walter, abruptly. 'I have told you I know very little about the family. What is it we came to see? – not this wretched place which makes me sick. The past should carry off its shell with it, and not leave these old clothes to rot here.'

'Oh!' cried little Mr. Bannatyne, with a shudder. 'I never suspected I was bringing in an iconoclast. That mantelpiece is a grand work of art, Lord Erradeen. Look at that serpent twisted about among the drapery – you'll not see such work now; and the ermine on that mantle just stands out in every hair, for all the grime and the smoke. It is the legend beneath the shield that is most interesting in the point of view of the family. It's a sort of rhyming slogan, or rather it's an addition to the old slogan, 'Live, Me'even,' which everybody knows.'

Walter felt a mingled attraction and repulsion which held him there unde-cided in front of the great old fireplace, like Hercules[80] or any other hero between the symbolical good and evil. He had a great curiosity to know what all this meant mingled with an angry disinclination impossible to put into words. Mr. Bannatyne, who of course knew nothing of what was going on in his mind, took upon himself the congenial task of tracing the inscription out. It was doggerel, bad enough to satisfy every aspiration of an antiquary. It was as follows: –

'Né fleyt atte Helle, né fond for Heeven,
Live, Me'even.'

'You will see how it fits in with the other motto,' cried the enthusiast. ''Baithe Sune and Syne,' which has a grand kind of indifference to time and all its changes that just delights me. And the other has the same sentiment, 'Neither frightened for hell nor keen about heaven. It is the height of impiety,' he said, with a sub-dued chuckle; 'but that's not inappropriate – it's far from inappropriate; it is just, in fact, what might have been expected. The warlock lord –'

'I hope you won't think me ungrateful,' cried Walter, 'but I don't think I want to know any more about that old ruffian. There is something in the place that oppresses me.' He took out from his pocket a handful of coins. (It was with the pleasure of novelty that he shook them together, gold and silver in one shin-ing heap, and threw half a dozen of them to the little group before the fire.) 'For heaven's sake let us get out of this!' he said, nervously. He could not have explained the sentiment of horror, almost of fear, that was in his mind. 'If it is mine,' he said, as they went down the spiral stair, groping against the black humid wall, 'I shall pull it down and let in some air and clear the filth away.'

'God bless me!' cried the antiquary in horror and distress, 'you will never do that. The finest street in Christendom, and one of the best houses! No, no, Lord Erradeen, you will never do that!'

When Mr. Bannatyne got back to the club, he expressed an opinion of Lord Erradeen, which we are glad to believe further experience induced him to modify. He declared that old Bob Milnathort had given him such a handful as he had not undertaken for years. 'Just a young Cockney!'[81] he said, 'a stupid Englishman! with no more understanding of history, or even of the share his own race has had in it, than that collie dog – indeed, Yarrow is far more intelligent, and a brute that is conscious of a fine descent. I am not saying that there are not fine lads among some of those English-bred young men, and some that have the sense to like old-fashioned things. But this young fellow is just a Cockney, he is just a young cynic. Pull down the house, said he? Spoil the first street in Europe! We'll see what the Town Council – not to say the Woods and Forests – will say to that, my young man! And I hope I have Bailie[82] Brown under my thumb!' the enraged antiquary cried.

Meantime Walter made his way through the dark streets in a tremor of excitement and dislike of which he could give no explanation to himself. Why should the old house have affected him so strongly![a] There was no reason for it that he knew. Perhaps there was something in the suddenness of the transition from the comfortable English prose of Sloebury to all these old world scenes and suggestions which had a disenchanting effect upon him. He had not been aware that he was more matter of fact than another, less likely to be affected by romance and historical associations. But so it had turned out. The grimy squalor of the place, the bad atmosphere, the odious associations, had either destroyed for him all the more attractive prejudices of long family descent, and a name which had descended through many generations – or else, something more subtle still, some internal influence, had communicated that loathing and sickness of the heart. Which was it? He could not tell. He said to himself, with a sort of scorn at himself, that probably the bourgeois atmosphere of Sloebury had made him incapable of those imaginative flights for which the highest and the lowest classes have a mutual aptitude. The atmosphere of comfort and respectability was against it. This idea rather exasperated him, and he dwelt upon it with a natural perversity because he hated to identify himself as one of that stolid middle class which is above or beneath fanciful impulses. Then he began to wonder whether all this might not be part of a deep-laid scheme on the part of old Milnathort to get him, Walter, under his power. No doubt it was arranged that he should be brought to that intolerable place, and all the spells of the past called forth to subdue him by his imagination if never through his intellect. What did they take him for? He was no credulous Celt, but a sober-minded Englishman,[83] not likely to let his imagination run away with him, or to be led by the nose by any *diablerie,*[84] however skilful. They might make up their minds to it, that their wiles of this kind would meet with no success. Walter was by no means sure who he meant by *they,* or why they should endeavour to get him into their power; but he wanted something to find fault with – some way of shaking off the burden of a mental weight which he did not understand, which filled him with discomfort and new sensations which he could not explain. He could almost have supposed (had he believed in mesmerism,[85] according to the description given of it in fiction –) that he was under some mesmeric influence, and that some expert, some adept, was trying to decoy him within some fatal circle of impression. But he set his teeth and all his power of resistance against it. They should not find him an easy prey.

# CHAPTER VIII.

THE drawing-room in Moray Place[86] seemed in the partial gloom very large and lofty. It must be remembered that Walter was accustomed only to the comparatively small rooms of an English country town where there was nobody who was very rich – and the solid, tall Edinburgh houses were imposing to him. There was no light but that which came from a blazing fire, and which threw an irregular ruddy illumination upon everything, but no distinct vision. He saw the tall windows indefinitely draped, and looking not unlike three colossal women in abundant vague robes standing against the wall. In a smaller room behind, which opened from this, the firelight was still brighter, but still only partially lit up the darkness. It showed, however, a table placed near the fire, and glowing with bright reflections from its silver and china; and just beyond that, out of the depths of what looked like an elongated easy-chair, a piece of whiteness, which was a female countenance. Walter, confused at his entrance, made out after a moment that it was a lady, half reclining on a sort of invalid *chaise longue,*[87] who raised herself slightly to receive him, with a flicker of a pair of white, attenuated hands. 'You are very welcome, Lord Erradeen,' she said, in a sweet, feeble voice. 'Will you excuse my rising – for I'm a great invalid – and come and sit down here beside me? I have been looking for you this half-hour past.' The hand which she held out to him was so thin that he scarcely felt its light pressure. 'If you have no objection,' said Miss Milnathort, 'we will do with the firelight for a little longer. It is my favourite light. My brother sent me word I was to expect you, and after your cold walk you will be glad of a cup of tea.' She did not pause for any reply, but went on, drawing the table towards her, and arranging everything with the skill of an accustomed hand. 'I am just a cripple creature,' she said. 'I have had to learn to serve myself in this way, and Robert is extraordinarily thoughtful. There is not a mechanical convenience invented but I have it before it is well out of the brain that devised it; and that is how I get on so well with no backbone to speak of. All this is quite new to you,' she said, quickly shaking off one subject and taking up another, with a little swift movement of her head.

'Do you mean – Edinburgh, or –'

'I mean everything,' said the lady. 'Edinburgh will be just a bit of scenery in the drama that is opening upon you, and here am I just another tableau. I can see it all myself with your young eyes. You can scarcely tell if it is real.'

'That is true enough,' said Walter, 'and the scenery all turns upon the plot so far: which is what it does not always do upon the stage.'

'Ay!' said Miss Milnathort, with a tone of surprise, 'and how may that be? I don't see any particular significance in Holyrood. It is where all you English strangers go, as if Edinburgh had no meaning but Queen Mary.'

'We did not go to Holyrood. We went to Lord Methven's Lodging, as I hear it is called: which was highly appropriate.'

'Dear me,' said the lady, 'do you mean to tell me that John Bannatyne had that sense in him? I will remember that the next time Robert calls him an auld foozle.[88] And so you saw the lodging of Methven? I have never seen it myself. Did it not make your heart sick to see all the poverty and misery in that awful street? Oh yes, I'm told it's a grand street: but I never have the heart to go into it. I think the place should die with the age that gave it birth.'

This was a sentiment so entirely unlike what Walter had expected to hear, that for the moment it took from him all power of reply. 'That would be hard upon antiquity,' he said at length, 'and I don't know what the artists would say, or our friend Mr. Bannatyne.'

'He would have me burnt for a witch,' the invalid said with a sweet little laugh; and then she added, 'Ah, it is very well to talk about art; but there was great sense in that saying of the old Reformers, 'Ding down the nest, and the crows will flee away.'[89]

'I expected,' said Walter, 'to find you full of reverence for the past, and faith in mysteries and family secrets, and – how can I tell? – ghosts perhaps.' He laughed, but the invalid did not echo his laugh. And this brought a little chill and check to his satisfaction. The sense that one has suddenly struck a jarring note is highly uncomfortable when one is young. Walter put back his chair a little, not reflecting that the firelight revealed very little of his sudden blush.

'I have had no experience in what you call ghosts,' she said, gravely. 'I cannot, to tell the truth, see any argument against them, except just that we don't see them; and I think that's a pity, for my part.'

To this, as it was a view of the subject equally new to him, Walter made no reply.

'Take you care, Lord Erradeen,' she resumed hastily, 'not to let yourself be persuaded to adopt that sort of nomenclature.' There was a touch of Scotch in her accent that naturalised the long word, and made it quite in keeping. 'Conclude nothing to be a ghost till you cannot account for it in any other way. There are many things that are far more surprising,' she said; then, shaking off the subject once more with that little movement of her head, 'You are not taking your tea. You must have had a tiring day after travelling all night. That is one of the modern fashions I cannot make up my mind to. They tell me the railway is not so wearying as the long coach journeys we used to make in the old time.'

'But you – can scarcely remember the old coach journeys? Why, my mother –'

'Very likely I am older than your mother; and I rarely budge out of this corner. I have never seen your mother, but I remember Captain Methven long long ago, who was not unlike the general outline of you, so far as I can make out. When the light comes you will see I am an old woman. It is just possible that this is why I am so fond of the firelight,' she said with a laugh; 'for I'm really very young though I was born long ago. Robert and me, we remember all our games and plays in a way that people that have had children of their own never do. We are just boy and girl still, and I've known us, after a long talk, forget ourselves altogether, and talk of papa and mamma!' She clapped her hands together at this, and went into a peal of genuine laughter, such as is always infectious. Walter laughed too, but in a half-embarrassed, half-unreal way. All was so strange to him, and this curious introduction into a half-seen, uncomprehended world the most curious of all.

'I would like to know a little about yourself,' she resumed after a moment. 'You were not in the secret that it was you who were the kin? It was strange your father should have left you in the dark.'

'I can't remember my father,' said Walter, hastily.

'That makes little difference; but you were always a strange family. Now you, Robert tells me, you're not so very much of an Erradeen – you take after your mother's side. And I'm very very glad to hear it. It will perhaps be you, if you have the courage, that will put a stop to – many things. There are old rhymes upon that subject, but you will put little faith in old rhymes; I none at all. I believe they are just made up long after the occasion, just for the sake of the fun, or perhaps because some one is pleased with himself to have found a rhyme. Now that one that they tell me is in the Canongate – that about 'Live, Me'even –"

'I thought you said you didn't know it?'

'I have never seen it; but you don't suppose I am ignorant of the subject, Lord Erradeen? Do you know I have been here stretched out in my chair these thirty years? and what else could I give my attention to, considering all things? Well, I do not believe in that. Oh, it's far too pat! When a thing is true it is not just so terribly in keeping. I believe it was made up by somebody that knew the story just as we do; probably a hundred years or more after the event.'

Walter did not say that he was quite unacquainted with the event. His interest perhaps, though he was not aware of it, was a little less warm since he knew that Miss Milnathort was his mother's contemporary rather than his own; but he had come to the conclusion that it was better not to ask any direct questions. The light had faded much, and was now nothing more than a steady red glow in place of the leaping and blazing of the flames. He scarcely saw his entertainer at all. There were two spots of brightness which moved occasionally, and which represented her face and the hands which she had clasped together (when they were not flickering about in incessant gesture) in her lap. But there was something altogether quaint and strange in the situation. It did not irritate him as the men had done. And then she had the good sense to agree with him in some respects, though the *mélange*[90] of opinions in her was remarkable, and he did not understand what she would be at. There was an interval of quiet in which neither of them said anything, and then a large step was audible coming slowly up-stairs,[a] and through the other drawing room.[b]

'Here is Robert,' the invalid said with a smile in her voice. It was nothing but a tall shadow that appeared, looming huge in the ruddy light.

'Have you got Lord Erradeen with you, Alison? and how are you and he getting on together?' said old Milnathort's voice.

Walter rose hastily to his feet with a feeling that other elements less agreeable were at once introduced, and that his pride was affronted by being discussed in this easy manner over his head.

'We are getting on fine, Robert. He is just as agreeable as you say, and I have great hopes will be the man. But you are late, and it will soon be time for dinner. I would advise you to show our young gentleman to his room, and see that he's comfortable. And after dinner, when you have had your good meal, we'll have it all out with him.'

'I am thinking, Alison, that there is a good deal we must go over that will be best between him and me.'

'That must be as you please, Robert, my man,' said the lady, and Walter felt like a small child who is being discussed over his head by grown-up persons, whom he feels to be his natural enemies. He rose willingly, yet with unconscious offence, and followed his host to his room, inwardly indignant with himself for having thus impaired his own liberty by forsaking his inn. The room however was luxuriously comfortable, shining with firelight, and a grave and respectable servant in mourning, was arranging his evening clothes upon the bed.

'This is Symington,' said Mr. Milnathort, 'he was your late cousin's body-servant. The late Lord Erradeen gave him a very warm recommendation. There might be things perhaps in which he would be of use.'

'Thanks,' said Walter, impulsively. 'I have a man coming. I am afraid the recommendation is a little too late.'

This unfortunately was not true; but the young man felt that to allow himself to be saddled with a sort of governor in the shape of the late lord's servant was more than could be required of him; and that he must assert himself before it was too late.

'You will settle that at your pleasure, my lord,' said old Milnathort, and he went away shutting the door carefully, his steady, slow step echoing along the passage. The man was not apparently in the least daunted by Walter's irritation. He went on mechanically, lightly brushing out a crease, and unfolding the coat

*The Wizard's Son, Volume I*  69

with that affectionate care which a good servant bestows upon good clothes. Walter longed to have brought his old coat with him that everything should not have been so distressingly new.

'That will do,' he said, 'that will do. It is a pity to give you so much trouble when, as I tell you, I have another man engaged.'

'It is no trouble, my lord; it is a pleasure. I came out of attachment to the family. I've been many years about my late lord. And however ye may remind yourself that you are but a servant, and service is no heritage, yet it's not easy to keep yourself from becoming attached.'

'My good man,' said Walter, half impatient, half touched,[a] 'you never saw me in your life before. I can't see how you can have any attachment to me.'

Symington had a long face, with a somewhat lugubrious expression, contradicted by the twinkle of a pair of humorous, deep-set eyes. He gave a glance up at Walter from where he stood fondling the lappels of the new coat.

'There are many kinds of attachments, my lord,' he said oracularly; 'some to the person and some to the race. For a number of years past I have, so to speak, just identified myself with the Erradeens. It's not common in England, so far as I can hear, but it's just our old Scots way. I will take no other service. So, being free, if your lordship pleases, I will just look after your lordship's things till the other man comes.'

Walter perceived in a moment by the way Symington said these words that he had no faith whatever in the other man. He submitted accordingly to the ministrations of the family retainer, with a great deal of his old impatience, tempered by a sense of the humour of the situation. It seemed that he was never to have any control over himself. He had barely escaped from the tutelage of home when he fell into this other which was much more rigid. 'Poor mother!' he said to himself, with an affectionate recollection of her many cares, her anxious watchfulness; and laughed to himself at the thought that she was being avenged.

Mr. Milnathort's table was handsome and liberal; the meal even too abundant for the solitary pair who sat alone at a corner of the large table, amid a blaze of light. Miss Milnathort did not appear.

'She never comes down. She has never sat down at table since she had her accident, and that is thirty years since.'

There was something in Mr. Milnathort's tone as he said this that made Walter believe that her accident too had something to do with the family. Everything tended towards that, or sprang from it. Had he been to the manner born, this would no doubt have seemed to him natural enough; but as it was he could not keep himself from the idea either that he was being laughed at, or that some design was hidden beneath this constant reference. The dinner, however, went off quietly. It was impossible to discuss anything of a private character in the presence of Milnathort's serious butler, and of the doubly grave apparition of Symington, who helped the other to wait.

Walter had never dined so solemnly before. It must be added, however, that he had seldom dined so well. It was a pity that he was so little knowing in this particular. Mr. Milnathort encouraged him through the repast by judicious words of advice and recommendation. He was very genial and expansive at this most generous moment of the day. Fond of good fare himself he liked to communicate and recommend it, and Walter's appetite was excellent, if perhaps his taste was uncultivated. The two noiseless attendants circulating about the table served them with a gravity in perfect keeping with the importance of the event, which was to the old lawyer the most interesting of the day.

When they were left alone finally, the aspect of affairs changed a little. Mr. Milnathort cleared his throat, and laid aside his napkin. He said –

'We must not forget, Lord Erradeen, that we have a great deal of business to get through. But you have had a fatiguing day, and probably very little sleep last night' –

'I slept very well, I assure you,' Walter replied cheerfully.

'Ay, ay, you are young,' said Mr. Milnathort, with a half-sigh.[a] 'Still all the financial statements, and to give you a just view of all that's coming to you, will take time. With your permission we'll keep that till to-morrow. But there's just a thing or two –. Lord save us!' he cried suddenly, 'you're not the kind of person for this. There is many a one I know that would have liked it all the better – till they knew – for what's attached to it. I thought as much when I first set eyes upon you. This will be one that will not take it all for gospel, I said to myself – one that will set up his own judgment, and demand the reason why.'

Walter, a little uncertain at first how to take this, ended by being gratified with such an estimate of himself. It showed, he felt, more perception than he had looked for, and he answered, with a little complacency, 'I hope you think that is the right way of approaching a new subject.'

'I am not unbiased myself,' said the lawyer, 'and I have had to do with it all my life. There are conditions connected with your inheritance, Lord Erradeen, that may seem out of the way to a stranger. If you had succeeded in the way of nature, as your father's son, they would not have been new to you, and you would have been prepared. In that way it is hard upon you. There was one of your ancestors that laid certain conditions, as I was saying, upon every heir. He was one that had, as you may say, a good right to do that, or whatever else he pleased, seeing he was the making of the family. In old days it was no more than a bit small highland lairdship. It was he that gave it consequence; but he has held a heavy hand upon his successors ever since.'

'Would it be he by any chance of whom Mr. Bannatyne was discoursing to me,' said Walter, 'under the title of the warlock-lord?'

'Ah! John Bannatyne took that upon him?' cried Mr. Milnathort with vivacity. His eyes gleamed from under his deep-set brows. 'The less a man knows the more ready he is to instruct the world: but I never thought he would take that upon him. So you see, as I was saying, there are certain formalities to go through. It is understood that once a year, wherever he may be, Lord Erradeen should pass, say a week, say two or three days, in the old castle of Kinloch Houran,[91] which is the old seat of the family, the original of the Methven race.'

Walter had been listening with some anxiety. He drew a long breath as Mr. Milnathort came to a pause. 'Is that all?' he cried, with a voice of relief. Then he laughed. 'I was winding myself up to something heroic, but if it is only a periodical retirement to an old castle – to think, I suppose, upon one's sins and examine one's conscience –'

'Something very like that,' said the old man, somewhat grimly.

'Well! It might be a great inconvenience; but there is nothing very appalling in the prospect, if that is all.'

'It is all, Lord Erradeen – if ye except what passes there, a thing that is your own concern, and that I have never pried into for my part. And just this beside, that you are expected there at once and without delay.'

'Expected – at once and without delay.' Walter grew red with anger at these peremptory words. 'This sounds a little arbitrary,' he said. 'Expected? by whom? and to what purpose? I don't understand –'

'Nor do I, my young lord. But it's so in the documents, and so has it been with every Lord of Erradeen up to this period. It is the first thing to be done. Before you come into enjoyment of anything, or take your place in the country, there is this visit – if you like to call it a visit: this – sojourn: not a long one, at least, you may be thankful – to be made –'

'To what purpose?' Walter repeated, almost mechanically. He could not, himself, understand the sudden tempest of resistance, of anger, of alarm that got up within him. 'There is reason in everything,' he said, growing pale. 'What is it for? What am I to do?'

'Lord Erradeen, a minute since you said, was that all? And now you change colour: you ask why, and wherefore –'

Walter made a great effort to regain command of himself. 'It is inconsistent, I allow,' he said. 'Somehow, the order to go now is irritating and unpleasant. I suppose it's simple enough, a piece of tyranny such as people seem to think they may indulge in after they're dead. But it is abominably arbitrary and tyrannical. What good does the old beggar think –'

'Hold your peace,' cried Mr. Milnathort, with a little trepidation. 'We have no right to call names, and I would not like it to be thought –' Here he paused with a sort of uneasy smile, and added, 'I am speaking nonsense,' with a vague glance about him. 'I think we might join my sister up-stairs;[a] and, as she knows just as much as I do, or, maybe, more, you can speak as freely as you please before her – oh, quite freely. But, my dear young lord, call no names!' cried Mr. Milnathort. He got up hurriedly, leaving his wine which he had just filled out,[92] a demonstration of sincerity which made a great impression upon Walter: and threw open the door. 'Putting off the business details till tomorrow, I know nothing else that we cannot discuss before Alison,' he said.

Walter was much startled when he went back to the inner drawing-room and found it lighted. Miss Milnathort did not employ any of those devices by which light is softened to suit the exigencies of beauty which has passed its prime. The light (alas for the prejudices of the æsthetic reader) was gas;[93] and, though it was slightly disguised by means of opal glass, it still poured down in a brilliant flood, and the little room was almost as light as day. She lay in her *chaise longue* placed under this illumination. Her face was preternaturally young, almost childish, small, and full of colour, her hair snow-white. She seemed to have been exempted from the weight of years, in compensation, perhaps, for other sufferings; her skin was smooth and unwrinkled, her eyes full of dewy brightness like those of a girl. Her dress, so far as it was visible, was white, made of cashmere or some other woollen material, solid and warm, but with lace at the neck, and pretty ribbons breaking the monotony of the tint. She looked like a girl dressed for some simple party, who had lain there waiting for the little festivity to begin, for no one could imagine how many years. Her hands were soft and round and young like her face. The wind had not been allowed to visit her cheek too roughly for a lifetime. What had happened before the event which she and her brother had both referred to as her 'accident' belonged to a period which had evidently nothing to do with the present. Walter saw at a glance that every possible convenience which could be invented for an invalid surrounded her. She had a set of book-shelves at one side with vacant spaces where she could place the book she was reading. Tables that wheeled towards her at a touch, with needlework, with knitting, with drawing materials, were arranged within reach. One of these made into a desk and put itself across her couch by another adaptation. It was evident that the tenderest affection and care had made this prison of hers into a sort of museum of every ingenuity that had ever been called to the help of the suffering. She lay, or rather sat, for that was her general position, with an air of pleasant expectation on her face, and received them with smiles and hands held out. 'Come away, come away,' she said in her soft Scotch. 'I have been wearying for you.' Walter thought there was something of age in her voice, but that might have been only the Scotch, and the unusual form of her salutation. She pointed out a chair to him carefully placed for her convenience in seeing and hearing. 'Come and tell me what you think about it all,' she said.

'I have not heard much,' said Walter, 'to think about: except that I am to go away directly, which does not please me at all, Miss Milnathort.'

'Oh, you will come back, you will come back,' she said.

'I hope so: but the reason why I should go doesn't seem very plain. What would happen, I wonder, if I didn't?' Walter said, lightly. He was surprised to see how much effect was produced upon his companions by this very simple utterance. Miss Milnathort put her hands together, as if to clasp them in triumph.

Her brother stood looking down upon the others, with his back to the light, and an air of alarmed displeasure.

'One result would be that certain of the lands would pass to the next heir,' he said; 'besides, perhaps – other penalties: that I would not incur, Lord Erradeen, if I were you.'

'What penalties? But do you think at this time of day,' said Walter, 'that ridiculous conditions of this kind that can mean nothing could really be upheld by the law – now that bequests of all kinds are being interfered with, and even charities?'[94]

'Robert, that is true. There was the Melville mortification[95] that you had so much trouble about, and that was a charity. How much more, as young Lord Erradeen is saying, when it is just entirely out of reason.'

'You should hold your peace on legal subjects, Alison. What can you know about them? I disapprove of all interference with the will of a testator, Lord Erradeen. I hold it to be against the law, and against that honour and honesty that we owe to the dead as well as the living. But there has always been a license allowed in respect to charities. So far as they are intended to be for the good of the poor, we have a right to see that the testator's meaning is carried out, even if it be contrary to his stipulations. But in a private case there is no such latitude. And you must always respect the testator's meaning, which is very clear in this case, as even you will allow, Alison.'

'Ay, clear enough,' cried the young-old lady, shaking her white head. 'But I'm on your side, Lord Erradeen. I would just let them try their worst, and see what would come of it, if, instead of a lame woman, I was a young man, lively and strong like you.'

'The question is,' said Walter, 'for I have become prudent since I have had property – whether for such an insignificant affair it is worth while losing a substantial advantage, as Mr. Milnathort says? And then, perhaps, a new man like myself, coming into an antiquated routine, there would be a sort of discourtesy, a want of politeness –' He laughed. 'One ought, I suppose, to be on one's best behaviour in such circumstances,' he said.

Miss Milnathort's countenance fell a little. She did not make any reply; but she had been listening with an air so eager and full of vivacity, anxious to speak, that the young man at once perceived the disappointment in her expressive little face. He said quickly –

'That does not please you? What would you have me to do?' with an involuntary sense that she had a right to an opinion.

Mr. Milnathort at this moment sat heavily down on the other side, giving great emphasis to his interruption by the sound of his chair drawn forward, a sound which she protested against with a sudden contraction of her forehead, putting up a delicate hand.

'I beg your pardon, my dear, for making a noise. You must not consult Alison, Lord Erradeen; she is prejudiced on one side – and I – perhaps I am, if not prejudiced, yet biased, on the other. You must act on your own instinct, which, as far as I can judge, is a just one. It would be a great incivility, as you say, for a

74 *The Selected Works of Margaret Oliphant, Volume 21*

far-away collateral,[96] that is really no more than a stranger, to set himself against the traditions of a house.'

Walter did not much like to hear himself described as a far-away collateral. It sounded like a term of reproach, and as he did not choose to say anything more on this matter, he made the best change of subject he could.

'I wonder,' he said, 'what would happen with any of the fantastic old feudal tenures if a new heir, a new man like myself, should simply refuse to fulfil them.'

'Mostly they take a pride and a pleasure in fulfilling them,' said the old lawyer.

'But suppose,' cried Walter, 'for the sake of argument, that a new Duke of Marlborough should say, 'What rubbish! Why should I send that obsolete old flag to Windsor?'[97] That is a modern instance; or suppose – '

'Just that,' cried Miss Milnathort, striking in with a flicker of her pretty hands. 'Suppose young Glenearn should refuse when he comes of age to hear a word about that secret cha'mer —'[98]

'What would happen?' said Walter, with a laugh of profane and irreverent youth.

Mr. Milnathort rose to his full height; he pushed back his chair with an indignant movement.

'You may as well ask me,' he said, 'what would happen if the pillars of the earth should give way. It is a thing that cannot be, at least till the end of all things is at hand. I will ring for prayers, Alison. My Lord Erradeen is young; he knows little; but this kind of profane talk is not to be justified from you and me.'

Then the bell was rung; the servants came trooping up-stairs,[a] and Symington gave Walter a sidelong look as he took his seat behind their backs. It seemed to assert a demure claim of proprietorship, along with a total want of faith in the 'other man.' Young Lord Erradeen found that it was all he could do to restrain an irreverent laugh. The position was so comic, that his original sense of angry resistance disappeared before it. He was going off against his will to pass through a mysterious ordeal in an old ruined house, under charge of a servant whom he did not want, and in obedience to a stipulation which he disowned. He was not half so free an agent as he had been when he was poor Walter Methven, knocking about the streets of Sloebury and doing much what he liked, though he thought himself in bondage. Bondage! he did not know in the old days what the word would mean.

# CHAPTER IX.

THE day on which Walter set out for Kinloch Houran was fine and bright, the sky very clear, the sun shining, the hills standing out against the blue, and every line of the tall trees clearly marked upon the transparent atmosphere. It was not till two days after the conversation above recorded – for there had been much to explain, and Walter was so little acquainted with business that instructions of various kinds were necessary. Miss Milnathort was visible much earlier

*The Wizard's Son, Volume I*  75

than usual on the morning of his departure, and he was admitted to see her. She was paler than before, and her little soft face was full of agitation; the corners of her mouth turned down, and her upper lip, which was a trifle too long, quivering. This added rather than took away from her appearance of youth. She was like a child who had exhausted itself with crying, and still trembled with an occasional sob. She stretched up her arms to him as if she would have put them round his neck, and bade God bless him with a tremulous voice.

'You must have plenty of courage,' she said; 'and you must never, never give up your own way.'

Walter was touched to the heart by this look of trouble on the innocent, young-old face.

'I thought it was always right to give up one's own way,' he said, in the light tone which he had come to employ with her.

She made an effort to smile in response.

'Oh yes, oh yes, it's the fashion to say so. You are a self-denying race, to believe yourselves; but this time you must not yield.'

'To whom am I supposed to be about to yield?' he asked. 'You may be sure I sha'n't unless I can't help myself.'

The tears overflowed her bright[a] old eyes; her hands shook as they held his.

'God bless you! God bless you!' she said. 'I will do nothing but pray for you, and you will tell me when you come back.'

He left her lying back upon her cushions sobbing under her breath. All this half-perplexed, half-amused the young man. She was a very strange little creature, he felt, neither old nor young; there was no telling the reason of her emotion. She was so much indulged in all her whims, like a spoiled child, that perhaps these tears were only her regrets for a lost playmate. At the same time Walter knew that this was not so, and was angry with himself for the thought. But how find his way out of the perplexity? He shook it off, which is always the easiest way; and soon the landscape began to attract his attention, and he forgot by degrees that there was anything very unusual in the circumstances of his journey. It was not till the first long stage of this journey was over that he was suddenly roused to a recollection of everything involved, by the appearance of Symington at the carriage window, respectfully requesting to know whether he had wanted anything. Walter had not remembered, or if he had remembered had thought no more of it, that this quietly officious retainer had taken all trouble from him at the beginning of his journey, as he had done during his stay in Mr. Milnathort's house.

'What! are you here?' he said, with surprise, and a mixture of amusement and offence.

'I beg your pardon, my lord,' said Symington, with profound and serious respect, yet always a twinkle in his eye, 'but as the other man did not turn up – and your lordship could scarcely travel without some attendance –'

76          *The Selected Works of Margaret Oliphant, Volume 21*

He had to rush behind to get his place in the train in the midst of his sentence, and Walter was left to think it over alone. In the balance between anger and amusement the latter fortunately won the day. The comic side of the matter came uppermost. It seemed to him very droll that he should be taken possession of, against his will, by the valet who professed an attachment to the race, not to the individual members of it, whose head was garlanded with crape[99] in the quaint Scotch way for Walter's predecessor, and who had 'identified himself with the Erradeens.' He reminded himself that he was in the country of Caleb Balderstone and Ritchie Moniplies,[100] and he resigned himself to necessity. Symington's comic yet so respectful consciousness that 'the other man' was a mere imagination, was joke enough to secure his pardon, and Walter felt that though the need of attendance was quite new in his life, that it might be well on his arrival in a strange country and a lonely ruined house, to have some one with him who was not ignorant either of the locality or the household.

The country increased in interest as he went on, and by and by he forgot himself in gazing at the mountains which appeared in glimpses upon the horizon, then seemed to draw nearer, closing in upon the road, which led along by the head of one loch after another, each encompassed by its circle of hills. Walter knew very little about Scotland. He thought it a barren and wild country, all bleak and gloomy, and the lavish vegetation of the west filled him with surprise and admiration. The sun was near its setting when the railway journey came to an end, and he found himself at a village station, from which a coach ran to Kinloch Houran. It appeared that there was no other vehicle to be had, and though it was cold there was nothing else for it but to clamber up on the top of the rude coach, which was a sort of *char-à-banc*[101] without any interior. Walter felt that it would become him ill, notwithstanding his new rank, to grumble at the conveyance, upon which there mounted nimbly a girl whom he had remarked when leaving Edinburgh, and whom he had watched for at all the pauses of the journey. He thought her the very impersonation of all he had ever heard of Scotch beauty, and so would most observers to whom Scotland is a new country. The native Scot is aware that there are as many brown locks as golden, and as many dark maidens as fair ones in his own country; but notwithstanding, to the stranger it is the fair who is the type. This young lady was warmly clothed in dark tweed, of the ruddy heathery hue which is now so general,[102] not long enough to conceal her well-shod feet, closely fitting, and adapted for constant walking and movement. She seemed to be met by friends all along the route. From the carriage window Walter saw her look out with little cries of pleasure. 'Oh, is that you, Jack?' 'Oh, Nelly, where are you going?' 'Oh, come in here, there is room in this carriage,' and such like. She was always leaning out to say a word to somebody, either of farewell or welcome. 'You will remember me to your mother,' old gentlemen would call to her, as the train went on. Walter was greatly in want of amusement, and he was at the age when a girl is always interesting. She became to him the heroine of the journey. He felt that he was collecting a great deal of information about her as they travelled on, and had begun to wonder whether he should ever find out who she was, or see any more of her, when he perceived her, to his delight, getting out, as he himself did, at Baldally. She was met by a respectable woman servant, who took possession of her baggage, while the young lady herself ran across the road to the coach, and with a hearty greeting to John the coachman darted up to the seat immediately behind him, where her maid presently joined her. Walter, and a personage of the commercial traveller class, shared the coachman's seat in front, and Symington and some other humbler passengers sat behind. The coach was adapted for summer traffic, so that there were several lines of empty seats between the two sets of travellers. It gave Walter a great deal of pleasure to hear the soft voice of his fellow-traveller pouring forth, low yet quite audible, an account of her journey to her maid, who was evidently on the most confidential terms with her young mistress.

'Has mamma missed me – much?' she asked after the little Odyssey was over.

'Oh, Miss Oona, to ask that,' cried the woman; 'how should we no miss you?' and then there ensued a number of details on the home side. The girl had been on a visit in Edinburgh, and had gone to balls, and 'seen everything.' On the other hand many small matters, faithfully reported, had filled up the time of separation. Walter listened to all this innocent interchange with great amusement and interest as the coach made its way slowly up the ascents of the hilly road. It was not in itself an agreeable mode of progression: the wind was icy cold, and swept through and through the unfortunates who faced it in front, sharpening into almost absolute needle points of ice when the pace quickened, and the noisy, jolting vehicle lumbered down the further side of a hill, threatening every moment to pitch the passengers into the heathery bog on one side or the other. He tried to diminish his own discomfort by the thought that he took off the icy edge of the gale and sheltered the little slim creature in her close ulster[103] behind, about whose shoulders the maid had wound the snowy mass of a great white knitted shawl. The low sun was in their faces as they toiled and rattled along, and the clear wintry blue of the sky was already strewn with radiant rosy masses of cloud. When they reached the highest point of the road the dazzling gleam of the great loch lying at their feet and made into a mirror of steel by the last blaze of the sun before it disappeared, dazzled the young man, who could see nothing except the cold intolerable brightness; but in a moment more the scene disclosed itself. Hills all purple in the sunset, clothed with that ineffable velvet down which softens every outline, opened out on either side, showing long lines of indistinct green valleys and narrower ravines that ran between, all converging towards the broad and noble inland sea fringed with dark woods and broken with feathery islands, which was the centre of the landscape. The wonderful colour of the sky reflected in the loch, where everything found a reflection, and every knoll and island floated double, changed the character of the scene and neutralised the dazzling coldness of the great water-mirror. Walter's involuntary exclamation at this sight stopped for a moment all the conversation going on. 'By Jove,' he said, 'how glorious!' They all stopped talking, the coachman, the traveller, the woman behind, and looked at him. Big John the driver, who knew everybody, eyed him with a slightly supercilious air, as one who felt that the new-comer could not be otherwise than contemptible, more or less, even though his sentiments were irreproachable. 'Ay, sir – so that's your opinion? most folk have been beforehand with ye,' said John.

The commercial traveller added, condescendingly, 'It is cold weather for touring, sir; but it's a grand country, as ye say.' And then they resumed their conversation.

The young lady behind was far more sympathetic. She made a distinct pause, and when she spoke again it was with a flattering adoption of Walter's tone to point out to her companion how beautiful the scene was.

'The isle is floating too, Mysie – look! If we could get there soon enough we might land upon one of those rosy clouds.'

Walter gave a grateful glance behind him, and felt that he was understood.

'That is just your poetry, Miss Oona,' said the maid; 'but, bless me, I have never told ye: there has been the light lighted in the castle these two nights past. We have just thought upon you all the time, and how much taken up you would be about it, your mamma and me.'

'The light on the castle!' cried the young lady; and at this the coachman, turning slightly round, entered into the conversation.

'That has it,' he said; 'I can back her up in that; just as clear and as steady as a star. There are many that say they never can see it; but they would be clever that had not seen it these two past nights.'

'Who says they cannot see it?' said the girl, indignantly.

John gave a little flick to his leader, which made the whole machine vibrate and roll.

'Persons of the newfangled kind that believe in nothing,' he said. 'They will tell ye it cannot be – so how can you see it? though it is glinting in their faces all the time.'

'You are meaning me, John,' said the traveller on the box-seat; 'and there's truth in what you say. I've seen what you call the light, and no doubt it has the appearance of a light; but if ye tell me it's something supernatural, there can be no doubt I will answer ye that there's nothing supernatural. If you were to tell me ye had seen a ghost, I would just reply in the same way. No, my man, I'm not impeachin' your veracity. You saw something, I'll allow; but no' a ghost, for there are no ghosts to see.'

'That's just an awfu' easy way of settlin' the question,' said the maid from behind – and then she went on in a lower tone: 'This will be the third night since it began, and we've a' seen it on the Isle. Hamish, he says the new lord maun be of a dour kind to need so many warnings. And he's feared ill will come of it; but I say the new lord, no' bein' here away nor of this country at all, how is he to ken?'

The girl's voice was now quite low, almost a whisper: but Walter being immediately in front of her could still hear. 'Has anything been heard,' she said, 'of the new lord?'

'Very little, Miss Oona, only that he's a young lad from the south with no experience, and didna even know that he was the heir; so how could he ken? as I say to Hamish. But Hamish he insists that it's in the blood, and that he would ken by instinck; and that it shows an ill-will,ᵃ and ill will come of it.'

'If I were he,' cried the girl, 'I would do the same. I would not be called like that from the end of the world wherever I was.'

'Oh, whisht, Miss Oona. It is such an auld, auld story; how can the like of you say what should be done?'

'I would like myself,' said the traveller, 'to come to the bottom of this business. What is it for, and who has the doing of it? The moment you speak of a light ye pre-suppose a person that lights it and mainy adjuncks and accessories. Now there's nobody, or next to nobody, living in that auld ruin. It's some rendeyvouss, I can easily understand that. The days of conspiracies are gone by, or I would say it was something against the state; but whatever it is, it must have a purpose, and mortal hands must do it, seeing there are no other. I have heard since ever I began to travel this country of the Kinloch Houran light, but I never heard a reason assigned.'

'It's the living lord,' cried the maid, 'as everybody knows! that is called to meet with –'

Here the young lady interfered audibly –

'Mysie, not a word!' The woman's voice continued, stifled as if a hand had been laid on her mouth.

'With them that are – with ane that is – I'm saying nothing, Miss Oona, but what all the loch is well aware –'

'It's just a ferlie¹⁰⁴ of this part of the world,' said John the driver; 'nae need of entering into it with them that believe naething. I'm no what ye call credulous mysel'; but when it comes to the evidence of a man's ain senses –'

'And what have your senses said to ye, my fine fellow? that there's a queer kind of a glimmer up upon the auld tower? So are there corpse-candles,¹⁰⁵ if I'm not mistaken, seen by the initiated upon your burial isle – what do you call it?'

'And wha has a word to say gainst that?' cried the driver angrily; whilst Mysie behind murmured – 'It's well seen ye have naething to do with any grave there.'

Now Walter was as entirely free from superstition as any young man need be; but when he heard the laugh with which the sceptic greeted these protests, he had the greatest mind in the world to seize him by the collar and pitch him into the bog below. Why? but the impulse was quite unreasonable and defied explanation. He had as little faith in corpse-candles as any bagman¹⁰⁶ever had, and the embarrassed and uneasy consciousness he had that the end of his journey was inexplicable, and its purpose ridiculous, led him much more to the conclusion that he was being placed in a ludicrous position, than that there was anything solemnly or awfully mysterious in it. Nevertheless, so far from ranging himself upon the side of the enlightened modern who took the common-sense view of these Highland traditions, his scorn and impatience of him was beyond words. For his own part he had not been sufficiently self-possessed to join in the discussion; but at this moment he ventured a question –

'Is this old castle you speak of – ' here he paused not knowing how to shape his inquiry; then added 'uninhabited?' for want of anything better to say.

'Not altogether,' said John; 'there is auld Macalister and his wife that live half in the water, half out of the water. And it's the story in the parish that there are good rooms; aye ready for my lord. But I can tell ye naething about that, for I'm always on the road, and I see nothing but a wheen[107] tourists in the summer, that are seeking information, and have none to give, puir creatures. There's a new lord just come to the title; ye will maybe have met with him if ye're from the south, for he's just an English lad.'

'England, my man John, is a wide road,' said the traveller; 'there are too many for us all to know each other as ye do in a parish; this gentleman will tell ye that.'

John's satirical explanation that he had not suspected Mr. Smith, whose northern accent was undoubted, of being an Englishman, saved Walter from any necessity of making a reply; and by this time the coach was rattling down upon a little homely inn, red-roofed and white-walled, which stood upon a knoll, overlooking the loch, and was reflected in all its brightness of colour in that mirror. The ground shelved rapidly down to the water-side, and there were several boats lying ready to put out into the loch – one a ponderous ferry boat, another a smaller, but still substantial and heavy, cobble,[108] in which a man with a red shirt and shaggy locks was standing up relieved against the light. Walter jumped down hurriedly with the hope of being in time to give his hand to the young lady, who perhaps had divined his purpose, for she managed to alight on the other side and so balk him. The landlady of the little inn had come out to the door, and there was a great sound of salutations and exclamations of welcome. 'But I mustna keep you, Miss Oona, and your mamma countin' the moments; and there's two or three parcels,' the woman said. The air had begun to grow a little brown, as the Italians say, that faint veil of gathering shade which is still not darkness, was putting out by degrees the radiance of the sky, and as Walter stood listening all the mingled sounds of the arrival rose together in a similar mist of sound, through which he sought for the soft little accents of the young lady's voice amid the noises of the unharnessing, the horses' hoofs and ostler's pails, and louder tones. Presently he saw her emerge from the group with her maid, laden with baskets and small parcels, and embarking under the conduct of the man in the red shirt,

*The Wizard's Son, Volume I* 81

whom she greeted affectionately as Hamish, assume her place in the stern, and the ropes of the rudder, with evident use and wont. To watch her steer out into the darkening loch, into the dimness and cold, gave the young man a vague sensation of pain. It seemed to him as if the last possible link with the human and sympathetic was detaching itself from him. He did not know her indeed, but it does not take a long time or much personal knowledge to weave this mystic thread between one young creature and another. Most likely, he thought, she had not so much as noticed him: but she had come into the half-real dream of his existence, and touched his hand, as it were, in the vague atmosphere which separates one being from another. Now he was left with nothing around him but the darkening landscape and the noisy little crowd about the coach; no one who could give him any fellowship or encouragement in the further contact which lay before him with the mysterious and unknown.

After a few moments the landlady came towards him, smoothing down her white apron, which made a great point in the landscape, so broad was it and so white. She smiled upon him with ingratiating looks.

'Will you be going north, sir?' she said; 'or will you be biding for the night? Before we dish up the dinner and put the sheets on the bed we like to know.'

'Who is that young lady that has just gone away?' said Walter, not paying much attention; 'and where is she going? It is late and cold for the water. Do you ever get frozen here?'

'That is Miss Oona of the Isle,' said the landlady; 'but as I was saying, sir, about the beds –'

'Are the islands inhabited then?' said Walter; 'and where is Kinloch Houran? Does one go there by water too?'

'No, Mistress Macgregor,' said Symington's voice on the other side; 'my lord will not bide here to-night I've been down to the beach, and there is a boat there, but not your lordship's own, any more than there was a carriage waiting at Baldally. We must just put our pride in our pockets, my lord, and put up with what we can get. When your lordship's ready we're all ready.'

By this time Big John and all the others were standing in a group staring at Lord Erradeen with all their eyes. John explained himself in a loud voice, but with an evident secret sense of shame.

'Hoo was I to ken?[109] A lord has name[110] business to scour the country like that, like ony gangrel[111] body – sitting on the seat just like the rest of us – Mr. Smith and him and me. Lord! hoo was I to ken? If you hear nae good of yourself, it is just your ain[112] blame. I was thinking of no lord or any such cattle.[113] I was just thinking upon my beasts. As for a lord that gangs about like you, deceiving honest folk, I wouldna give that for him,' John said, snapping his finger and thumb. His voice sank at the end, and the conclusion of the speech was but half audible. Mrs. Macgregor interposing her round, soft intonation between the speaker and the stranger.

'Eh, my lord, I just beg your pardon! I had no notion – and I hope your lordship found them a' civil. Big John is certainly a little quick with his tongue – 'I hope you're not supposing, Mistress Macgregor, that his lordship would fash himself about Big John,' said Symington, who had now taken the direction of affairs. Walter, to tell the truth, did not feel much inclination to enter into the discussion. The gathering chill of the night had got into his inner man. He went down towards the beach slowly pondering, taking every step with a certain hesitation It seemed to him that he stood on the boundary between the even ground of reality and some wild world of fiction which he did not comprehend, but had a mingled terror and hatred of. Behind him everything was homely and poor enough; the light streamed out of the open doors and uncovered windows, the red roof had a subdued glow of cheerfulness in the brown air, the sounds about were cheerful, full of human bustle and movement, and mutual good offices. The men led the horses away with a certain kindness; the landlady, with her white apron, stopped to say a friendly word to Big John, and interchanged civilities with the other humble passengers who were bringing her no custom, but merely passing her door to the ferry-boat that waited to take them across the loch. Everywhere there was a friendly interchange, a gleam of human warmth and mutual consolation. But before him lay the dark water, with a dark shadow of mingled towers and trees lying upon it at some distance. He understood vaguely that this was Kinloch Houran, and the sight of it was not inviting. He did not know what it might be that should meet him there, but whatever it was it repelled and revolted him. He seemed to be about to overpass some invisible boundary of truth and to venture into the false, into regions in which folly and trickery reigned. There was in Walter's mind all the sentiment of his century towards the supernatural. He had an angry disbelief in his mind, not the tranquil contempt of the indifferent. His annoyed and irritated scorn perhaps was nearer faith than he supposed; but he was impatient of being called upon to give any of his attention to those fables of the past which imposture only could keep up in the present. He felt that he was going to be made the victim of some trick or other. The country people evidently believed, indeed, as was natural enough to their simplicity; but Walter felt too certain that he would see the mechanism behind the most artful veil to believe it possible that he himself could be taken in, even for a moment. And he had no desire to find out the contemptible imposture. He felt the whole business contemptible; the secluded spot, the falling night, the uninhabited place, were all part of the jugglery. Should he voluntarily make himself a party to it, and walk into the snare with his eyes open? He felt sure, indeed, that he would remain with his eyes open all the time, and was not in the least likely to submit to any black art that might be exercised upon him. But he paused, and asked himself was it consistent with the dignity of a reasonable creature, a full-grown man, to allow himself to be drawn into any degrading contact with this jugglery at all?

The boat lay on the beach with his baggage already in it, and Symington standing respectful awaiting his master's pleasure. Symington, no doubt, was the god out of the machinery who had the *fin mot*[114] of everything and all the strings in his hand. What if he broke the spell peremptorily and retired to the ruddy fireside of the inn and defied family tradition? He asked himself again what would come of it? and replied to himself scornfully that nothing could come of it. What law could force him to observe an antiquated superstition? It was folly to threaten him with impossible penalties. And even if a thing so absurd could happen as that he should be punished in purse or property for acting like a man of sense instead of a fool, what then? The mere possibility of the risk made Walter more disposed to incur it. It was monstrous and insufferable that he should be made to carry out a tyrannical, antiquated stipulation by any penalty of the law. It would be better to fight it out once for all. All the sense of the kingdom would be with him, and he did not believe that any judge could pronounce against him. Here Symington called, with a slight tone of anxiety, 'We are all ready, my lord, and waiting.' This almost decided Walter. He turned from the beach, and made a few hasty steps up the slope.

But then he paused again, and turning round faced once more the darkening water, the boat lying like a shadow upon the beach, the vague figures of the men about it. The ferry-boat had pushed off and was lumbering over the water with great oars going like bats' wings, and a noisy human load. The other little vessel with that girl had almost disappeared. He thought he could see in the darkness a white speck like a bird, which was the white shawl that wrapped her throat and shoulders. Her home lay somewhere in the centre of these dark waters, a curious nest for such a creature. And his? He turned again towards the dark, half-seen towers and gables. Some of them were so irregular in outline that they could be nothing but ruins. He began to think of the past, mute, out of date, harmless to affect the life that had replaced it, which had taken refuge there. And he remembered his own argument about the courtesy that the living owed to the dead. Well! if it was so, if it was as a politeness, a courtesy to the past, it might be unworthy a gentleman to refuse it. And perhaps when all was said it was just a little cowardly to turn one's back upon a possible danger, upon what at least the vulgar thought a danger. This decided him. He turned once more, and with a few rapid steps reached the boat. Next moment they were afloat upon the dark loch. There had been no wind to speak of on shore, but the boat was soon struggling against a strong running current, and a breeze which was like ice. The boatmen showed dark against the gleaming loch, the rude little vessel rolled, the wind blew. In front of them rose the dark towers and woods all black without a sign of human habitation. Walter felt his heart rise at last with the sense of adventure. It was the strangest way of entering upon a fine inheritance.

\*\*\*

# CHAPTER X.

KINLOCH HOURAN CASTLE stands out of the very waters of Loch Houran, with its ruined gables and towers clothed with ivy. From the water it looked like nothing but a roofless and deserted ruin. One tower in the centre stood up above the jagged lines of the walls, with something that looked like a ruined balcony or terrace commanding the landscape. The outline was indistinct, for the trees that had got footing in the ruined chambers below grew high and wild, veiling the means by which it was sustained at that altitude: but the little platform itself was very visible, surrounding the solid block of the tower, which showed no window or opening, but looked as if it might yet outlive centuries. As the boat approached, Walter saw the rowers whisper, and give significant looks at Symington, who sat respectfully on one of the cross seats, not to put himself in the way of his master, who occupied the other alone. Hoarse whispers breathed about the other end of the boat, and Symington was progged[115] in the shoulders with an occasional oar. 'Will ye no' be letting him see't?' the rowers said. Walter's faculties were eagerly acute in the strangeness of everything around him; the sense that he was going to an impossible house – to a ruin – on an impossible errand, seemed to keep him on the alert in every particular of his being. He could see through the dusk, he could hear through the whistle of the wind and the lashing of the water upon the boat's side, which was like the roar of a mimic storm; and he was not even insensible to the comic element in Symington's face, who waved away the oar with which he was poked, and replied with words and frowns and looks full of such superiority of information, that a burst of sudden nervous laughter at the sight relieved Walter's excitement. He felt that a thrill of disapproval at this went through the boat, and the men in the bow shook their bonnets as they rowed.

'It's nothing to laugh at, my lord,' said old Symington, 'though I'm not one – and I make no question but your lordship is not one – to lose my presence o' mind. Yon's the phenomenon that they wanted me to call your lordship's attention to,' he added, jerking his arm, but without turning his head, in the direction of the tower.

'The light?' Walter said. He had been about to ask what the meaning of it might be. It had not been visible at all when they started, but for the last moment or two had been growing steadily. The daylight was waning every minute, and no doubt (he thought) it was this that made the light more evident. It shone from the balcony or high roof-terrace which surrounded the old tower. It was difficult to distinguish what it was, or identify any lamp or beacon as the origin of it. It seemed to come from the terrace generally, a soft, extended light, with nothing fiery in it, no appearance of any blaze or burning, but a motionless, clear shining, which threw a strange glimmer upwards upon the solid mass of the tower, and downwards upon the foliage, which was black and glistening, and upon the surface of the water. 'Yon's the phenomenon,' said Symington, pointing with a jerk of his elbow. The light brought out the whole mass of rugged masonry and trees from the rest of the landscape, and softly defined it against the darker background.

'How is it done?' said the young man, simply. He perceived the moment after that his tone was like that of the bagman on the coach, and shivered at the thought. So soft and steady was the light that it had not seemed to him extraordinary at all.

'What do you mean by a phenomenon?' he asked, hastily. He remembered suddenly that the young lady on the coach had spoken of this light, and taken it, so to speak, under her protection.

'If your lordship has ainy desire to inquire into my opinion,' said old Symington, 'though I doubt that's little likely, I would say it was just intended to work on the imagination. Now and then, indeed, it's useful in the way of a sign – like a person waving to you to come and speak; but to work on the imagination, that's what I would say.'

Walter looked up at the light which threw a faint glimmer across the dark water, showing the blackness of the roughened ripple, over which they were making their way, and bringing into curious prominence the dark mass of the building rising out of it. It was not like the moon, it was more distinct than starlight, it was paler than a torch: nor was there any apparent central point from which it came. There was no electric light in those days,[116] nor was Loch Houran a probable spot for its introduction: but the clear colourless light was of that description. It filled the visitor with a vague curiosity, but nothing more.

'To work on – whose imagination? and with what object?' he said.

But as he asked the question the boat shot forward into the narrow part of the loch, and rounded the corner of the ruin. Anything more hopeless as a place to which living passengers, with the usual encumbrances of luggage, were going, could not well be conceived; but after a few minutes' rowing, the boat ran in to some rude steps on the other side of the castle, where there were traces of a path leading up across the rough grass to a partially visible door. All was so dark by this time that it was with difficulty that Walter found the landing; when he had got ashore, and his portmanteau had been put out on the bank, the men in the boat pushed off with an energy and readiness which proved their satisfaction in getting clear of the castle and its traditions. To find himself left there, with an apparently ruined house behind him, his property at his feet, his old servant by his side, night closing in around, and the dark glistening water lapping up on the stones at his feet, was about as forlorn a situation as could be imagined.

'Are we to pass the night here?' he said, in a voice which could not help being somewhat querulous.

The sound of a door opening behind interrupted his words, and turning round he saw an old man standing in the doorway, with a small lamp in his hand. He held it up high over his head to see who the new-comers were; and Walter, looking round, saw a bowed and aged figure – a pale old face, which might have been made out of ivory, so bloodless was it, the forehead polished and shining, some grey locks escaping at the side of a black skull-cap, and eyes looking out keenly into the darkness.

'It is just his lordship, Macalister,' said old Symington.

The young man, who was so strange to it all, stood with a sort of helplessness between the two old men who were familiar with each other and the place and all its customs.

'Come away, then, come away,' cried the guardian of the house, with a shrill voice that penetrated the stillness sharply. 'What are ye biding there for in the dark?'

'And who's to carry up my lord's portmanteau?'[117] said Symington.

'His portmanteau!' cried the other, with a sort of eldritch[118] laugh. 'Has he come to bide?'

This colloquy held over him exasperated Walter, and he seized the portmanteau hastily, forgetting his dignity.

'Lend a hand, Symington, and let us have no more talk,' he said.

There is a moment when the most forlorn sensations and the most dismal circumstances become either ludicrous or irritating. The young man shook off his sense of oppression and repugnance as be hastened up the slope to the door, while the lantern, flashing fitfully about, showed now the broken path, now the rough red masonry of the ruin, which was scarcely less unlike a ruin on this side than on the other. The door gave admittance into a narrow passage only, out of which a spiral staircase ascended close to the entrance, the passage itself apparently leading away into the darkness to a considerable distance. At the end of it stood a woman with a lighted candle peering out at the stranger as the man had done. He seemed to realise the stories which every one has read of a belated traveller unwillingly received into some desolate inn, which turns out to be the headquarters of a robber-band, and where the intruder must be murdered ere the morning.

'This is your way, my lord,' said the shrill old man, leading the way up the spiral stair. The whole scene was like a picture. The woman holding up her light at the end of the long passage, the old man with his lamp, the dark corners full of silence and mystery, the cold wind blowing as through an icy ravine. And the sensations of the young man, who had not even had those experiences of adventure which most young men have in these travelling days, whom poverty and idleness had kept at home in tame domestic comfort, were very strange and novel. He seemed to himself to be walking into a romance, not into any real place, but into some old storybook, a mystery of Udolpho,[119] an antiquated and conventional region of gloom and artificial alarms.

'Come this way, my lord; come this way,' said the old man; 'the steps are a bit worn, for they're auld, auld – as auld as the house. But we hope you'll find everything as comfortable as the circumstances will permit. We have had just twa three days to prepare, my mistress and me; but we've done our best, as far,' he added, 'as the circumstances will permit. This way, this way, my lord.'

*The Wizard's Son, Volume I*                     87

At the head of the stair everything was black as night. The old man's lamp threw his own somewhat fantastic shadow upon the wall of a narrow corridor as he held it up to guide the new-comer. Close to the top of the staircase, however, there opened a door, through which a warm light was showing, and Walter, to his surprise, found himself in a comfortably-furnished room with a cheerful fire, and a table covered for dinner, a welcome end to the discomfort and gloom of the arrival. The room was low, but large, and there were candles on the mantelpiece and table which made a sort of twinkling illumination in the midst of the dark panelled walls and dark furniture. The room was lined with books at one end. It was furnished with comfortable sofas and chairs of modern manufacture. There was a curious dim mirror over the mantelshelf in a heavy gilt frame of old carving, one or two dim old portraits hung opposite, the curtains were drawn, the fire was bright, the white tablecloth with an old-fashioned silver vase in the middle, and the candles burning, made a cheerful centre of light. At the further end was another door, open, which admitted to a bed-room, dim, but comfortable in the firelight. All this was encouraging. Walter threw himself into a chair with a sense that the situation altogether was improving. Things cannot be so very bad when there is a fire and lights, and a prospect of dinner. He began to laugh at himself, when he had taken off his coat, and felt the warmth of the glowing fire. Everything around him was adapted for comfort. There was a little want of light which left all the corners mysterious, and showed the portraits dimly, like half-seen spectators, looking down from the wall; but the comfortable was much more present than the weird and uncanny which had so much predominated on his arrival. And when a dinner, which was very good and carefully cooked, and a bottle of wine, which, though he had not very much skill in that subject, Walter knew to be costly and fine, had been served with noiseless care by Symington, the young man began to recover his spirits, and to think of the tradition which required his presence here, as silly indeed, but without harm. After dinner he seated himself by the fire to think over the whole matter. It was not yet a fortnight since this momentous change had happened in his life. Before that he had been without importance, without use in the world, with little hope, with nothing he cared for sufficiently to induce him to exert himself one way or another. Now after he had passed this curious probation, whatever it was, what a life opened before him! He did not even know how important it was, how much worth living. It shone before him indistinctly as a sort of vague, general realisation of all dreams. Wealth – that was the least of it; power to do whatever he pleased; to affect other people's lives, to choose for himself almost whatever pleased him. He thought of Parliament, even of government, in his ignorance: he thought of travel, he thought of great houses full of gaiety and life. It was not as yet sufficiently realised to make him decide on one thing or another. He preferred it as it was, vague – an indefinite mass of good things and glories to come. Only this ordeal, or whatever it was – those few days more or less that he was bound to remain at Kinloch Houran, stood between him and his magnificent career. And after all, Kinloch Houran was nothing very terrible. It might be like the mysteries of Udolpho outside; but all the mysteries of Udolpho turned out, he remembered, quite explainable,[120] and not so very alarming after all; and these rooms, which bore the traces of having been lived in very lately, and which were quite adapted to be lived in, did not seem to afford much scope for the mysterious. There were certain points, indeed, in which they were defective, a want of air, something which occasionally caught at his respiration, and gave him a sort of choked and stifled sensation; but that was natural enough, so carefully closed as everything was, curtains drawn, every draught warded off. Sometimes he had an uneasy feeling as if somebody had come in behind him and was hanging about the back of his chair. On one occasion he even went so far as to ask sharply, 'Is it you, Symington?' but, looking back, was ashamed of himself, for of course there was nobody there. He changed his seat, however, so as to face the door, and even went the length of opening it, and looking out to see if there was any one about. The little corridor seemed to ramble away into a darkness so great that the light of his candle did no more than touch its surface – the spiral staircase looked like a well of gloom. This made him shiver slightly, and a half-wish[a] to lock his door came over him, of which he felt ashamed as he turned back into the cheerful light.

After all, it was nothing but the sensation of loneliness which made this impression. He went back to his chair and once more resumed his thoughts – or rather was it not his thoughts – nay, his fancies – that resumed him, and fluttered about and around, presenting to him a hundred swiftly changing scenes? He saw visions of his old life, detached scenes which came suddenly up through the darkness and presented themselves before him – a bit of Sloebury High Street, with a group of his former acquaintances now so entirely separated from him; the little drawing-room at the cottage, with Julia Herbert singing him a song; Underwood's rooms on that particular night when he had gone in, in search of something like excitement, and had found everything so dull and flat. None of these scenes had any connection with his new beginning in life. They all belonged to the past, which was so entirely past and over. But these were the scenes which came with a sort of perversity, all broken, changing like badly managed views in a magic lantern,[121] produced before him without any will of his. There was a sort of bewildering effect in the way in which they swept along, one effacing another, all of them so alien to the scene in which he found himself. He had to get up at last, shaking himself as free of the curious whirl of unwonted imagination as he could. No doubt his imagination was excited; but happily not, he said to himself, by anything connected with the present scene in which he found himself. Had it been roused by these strange surroundings, by the darkness and silence that were about him, by the loneliness to which he was so unused, he felt that there was no telling what he might see or think he saw; but fortunately it was not in this way that his imagination worked. His pulse was quick, however, his heart beating, a quite involuntary excitement in all his bodily faculties. He got up hastily and went to the bookshelves, where he found, to his surprise, a large collection of novels and light literature. It seemed to Walter that his predecessor, whom he had never seen – the former Lord Erradeen, who inhabited these rooms not very long ago – had been probably, like himself, anxious to quench the rising of his fancy in the less exciting course of a fictitious drama, the conventional excitements of a story. He looked over the shelves with a curious sympathy for this unknown person, whom indeed be had never thought much upon before. Did that unknown know who was to succeed him? Did he ever speculate upon Walter as Walter was now doing upon him? He turned over the books with a strange sense of examining the secrets of his predecessor's mind. They were almost all books of adventure and excitement. He took down, after a moment, a volume of Dumas,[122] and returned to his easy-chair by the fire, to lose himself in the breathless ride of d'Artagnan[123] and the luckless fortunes of the three companions. It answered the purpose admirably. A sudden lull came over his restless fancy. He was in great comfort externally, warmed and fed and reposing after a somewhat weary day, and the spell of the great story-teller got hold of him. He was startled out of this equable calm when Symington came in to light the candles in his bedroom and bring hot water, and offer his services generally. Symington regarded him with an approval which he did not think it worth his while to dissemble.

'That's right, my lord, that's right,' he said. 'Reading's a very fine thing when you have too much to occupy your thoughts.'

Walter was amused by this deliverance, and happily not impatient of it. 'That is a new reason for reading,' he said.

'But it is a real just one, if your lordship will permit me to say so. Keep you to your book, my lord; it's just fine for putting other things out of your head. It's Dumas's you're reading? I've tried that French fellow myself, but I cannot say that I made head or tail of him. He would have it that all that has happened in history was just at the mercy of a wheen[124] adventurers, two or three vagrants of Frenchmen. No, no. I may believe a great deal, but I'm not likely to believe that.'

'I see you are a critic, Symington; and do you read for the same reason that you have been suggesting to me? – because you have too much to occupy your thoughts?'

'Well, pairtly, my lord, and pairtly just in my idle hours to pass the time. I have made up your fire and lighted the candles, and everything is in order. Will I wait upon your lordship till you're inclined for your bed? or will I – ' Symington made a significant pause, which it was not very difficult to interpret.

'You need not wait,' Walter said; and then, with an instinct which he was half ashamed of, he asked hurriedly, 'Whereabouts do you sleep?'

'That is just about the difficulty,' said old Symington. 'I'm rather out of call if your lordship should want anything. The only way will just be to come down the stairs, if your lordship will take the trouble, and ring the big bell. It would waken a' the seven sleepers if it was rung at their lug:[125] and I'm not so ill to waken when there is noise enough. But ye have everything to your hand, my lord. If you'll just give a glance into the other room, I can let you see where everything is. There is the spirit-lamp, not to say a small kettle by the fire, and there's –'

'That will do,' said Walter. 'I shall not want anything more to-night.'

The old servant went away with a glance round the room, in which Walter thought there was some anxiety, and stopped again at the door to say 'Good night, my lord. It's not that I am keen for my bed – if your lordship would like me to bide, or even to take a doze upon a chair –'

'Go to bed, old Sym.,' said the young man with a laugh. The idea of finding a protector in Symington was somewhat ludicrous. But these interruptions disturbed him once more, and brought back his excitement: he felt a sort of pang as he heard the old servant's heavy step going down the winding stair, and echoing far away, as it seemed, into the bowels of the earth. Then that extreme and blighting silence which is like a sort of conscious death came upon the place. The thick curtains shut out every sound of wind and water outside as they shut out every glimpse of light. Walter heard his pulse in his ears, his heart thumping like the hammer of a machine. The whole universe seemed concentrated in that only living breathing thing, which was himself. He tried to resume his book, but the spell of the story was broken. He could no longer follow the fortunes of Athos, Porthos, and Aramis.[126] Walter Methven thrust himself in front of these personages, and, though he was not half so amusing, claimed a superior importance by right of those pulses that clanged in his head like drums beating. He said to himself that he was very comfortable, that he had never expected to be so well off. But he could not regain his composure or sense of well-being. It was a little better when he went into his bed-room, the mere movement and passage from one room to another being of use to him. The sense of oppression and stagnation, however, soon became almost greater here than in the sitting-room. One side of the room was entirely draped in close-drawn curtains, so that it was impossible to make out even where the windows were. He drew them aside with some trouble, for the draperies were very heavy, but not to much advantage. At first it seemed to him that there were no windows at all; then he caught sight of something like a recess high in the wall; and climbing up, found the hasp of a rough shutter, which covered a small square window built into a cave of the deep masonry. That this should be the only means of lighting an almost luxurious sleeping chamber, bewildered him more and more; but it would not open, and let in no air, and the atmosphere felt more stifling than ever in this revelation of the impossibility of renewing it. Finally, he went to bed with a sort of rueful sense that there was the last citadel and refuge of a stranger beset by imaginations in so weird and mysterious a place. He did not expect to sleep, but he determined that he would not, at least, be the sport of his own fancies.

It astonished Walter beyond measure to find himself waking in broad daylight, with Symington moving softly about the room, and a long window, the existence of which he had never suspected, facing him as he looked up from his pillows, after a comfortable night's sleep. Mingled shame and amusement made him burst into an uneasy laugh, as he realised this exceedingly easy end of his tribulations.

'Mrs. Macalister,' said Symington, 'would like well to know when your lordship is likely to be ready, to put down the trout at the right moment: for it's an awful pity to spoil a Loch Houran trout.'

# CHAPTER XI.

To insist upon the difference between an impression made when we arrive, tired and excited at night, in a strange place, and that which the same scene produces in the early freshness and new life of the morning, would be to deliver ourselves over to the reign of the truism. It would, however, have been impossible to feel this with more force than Walter felt it. His sensations of alarm and excitement struck him not only as unjustifiable but ludicrous. He laughed once more when he came out of his chamber into the warm and genial room, which had seemed to him so mysterious and dark on the previous night. There were windows upon either side of the fire-place,[a] each in a deep recess like a small room, so great was the thickness of the wall. They looked out upon the mountains, upon the narrow end of the loch, all bubbling and sparkling in the sunshine, and down upon the little grassy slope rough and uncared for, yet green, which was the only practicable entrance to the castle. The windows were not large, and the room still not very light, though the sunshine which poured in at one side made a most picturesque effect of light and shade. The portraits on the wall were better than they had seemed, and had lost the inquisitive air of dissatisfied inspection which Walter's imagination had given them. The book-shelves[b] at the end gave relief to the room, with their cheerful gilding and the subdued tone of their bindings. Walter thought of the chamber in the *Pilgrim's Progress* turned towards the sunrising, the name of which was Peace.[127] But peace was not the thing most suggested at Kinloch Houran by any of the accessories about, and a vision of the chilliness of the gray light in the afternoon, and the force of the east wind when it came, crossed his mind in true nineteenth century[c] criticism of the more poetical view. But in the mean time, the policy of enjoying the present was undeniable, especially when that present took the form of a Loch Houran trout, fresh from the water, and cooked as fish only are under such conditions. He looked back upon the agitations of the evening, and the reluctant angry sentiment with which he had come to this old house of his family, with amused incredulity and shame. To think that he could be such an impressionable fool! He dismissed it all lightly from his mind as he hurried over his breakfast, with the intention of getting out at once and exploring everything about. He had even newspapers upon his table along with the fresh scones, the new-made butter, all the fresh provisions of the meal. To be sure, it was Glasgow and not London from which they came – but the world's history was no less instant in them, flashing from all parts of the world into this home of the ancient ages.

His first inspection was of the castle itself, which he undertook under the auspices of old Symington and old Macalister, both eager to explain and describe what it had been, as well as what it was. What it was did not consist of very much. 'My lord's rooms,' those in which he had spent the night, were the only habitable portion of the great pile. He was led through the roofless hall, with its musicians' gallery still perched high up and overshadowed with canopies of ashen boughs, vigorous though leafless; the guard-room, the supposed kitchen with its large chimney, the oblong space from east to west which was supposed to have been the chapel. All was a little incoherent in the completeness of ruin. There was little of the stimulation of family pride to be got out of those desolate places. The destruction was too complete to leave room even for the facile web of imagination. The Crusader,[128] about whom there was a legend a little too picturesque and romantic to be true, or the lady who was only saved by his sudden appearance from unfaithfulness, were not more easy to conjure up within the inclosure of those shapeless walls than on any unremarkable spot where the story might have been told. Walter grew a little weary as Symington and the old guardian of the house argued as to which was this division of the castle, and which that. He left them discussing the question, and climbed up by a rude stair which had been half improvised from the ruined projections of the masonry, to the crumbling battlements above. From thence he looked down upon a scene which was older than the oldest ruin, yet ever fresh in perennial youth: the loch stretched out like a great mirror under the wintry blue of the sky and the dazzling blaze of the sunshine, reflecting everything, every speck of cloud above and every feathery twig and minute island below. There was no need to make believe, to simulate unfelt enthusiasm, or endeavour to connect with unreal associations this wonderful and glorious scene. Perhaps there was in his mind something more in harmony with the radiance of nature than with the broken fragments of a history which he had no skill to piece up into life again. He stood gazing upon the scene in a rapture of silent delight. The hills in their robes of velvet softness, ethereal air-garments more lovely than any tissue ever woven in mortal loom, drew aside on either hand in the blue space and dazzling atmosphere to open out this liquid vale of light, with its dark specks of islets, its feathery banks, all rustling with leafless trees. Every outline and detail within its reach was turned into a line, a touch, more sweet by the flattering glory of the still water in which everything was double. The morning freshness and sheen were still unbroken.

*The Wizard's Son, Volume I*          93

It was like a new creation lying contemplating itself in the first ecstasy of consciousness. Walter was gazing upon this wonderful scene when the sharp voice of old Macalister made him start, and take a step aside which almost had serious consequences: for he stepped back unwarily upon the crumbling wall, and might have fallen but for the violent grip of the old man, who clutched him like a shaky, with a grasp which was vigorous yet trembling.

'Lord's sake take care,' he cried. His face flushed, then paled again with genuine emotion. 'Do you think we have a store of young lads like you, that you will risk your life like yon? and just in the place where the lady fell. You have given me such a start I canna breathe,' he cried.

To tell the truth, looking back upon it, Walter himself did not like the look of the precipice which he had escaped.

'Where the lady fell?' he asked with a little eagerness, as he came to the battlement.

'Oh ay. I seldom bother my head about what's happened, so to speak, two or three days since. It was just there she fell. She has been bedridden ever since, from a' I hear, which just shows the folly of venturing about an auld place without somebody that knows how to take care of ye. What would have come of you yoursel', that is the maister of a', if auld Sandy Macalister had not been there?'

'Thank you, Macalister, you shall find me grateful,' said Walter; 'but who was this lady? two or three days ago, did you say?'

'Years – years; did I no say years? Oh ay, it may be longer, twenty or thirty. I'm meaning just naething in a life like mine. She had some silly story of being frightened with a gentleman that she thought she saw. They are keen about making up a story – women folk. She was just the sister to the man of business, ye'll have heard of her –[a] a pretty bit thing, if that was of any consequence; but, Lord's sake, what's that atween you and me, and you ignorant of everything?' the old man said. 'Do you see the chimneys yonder, and the gable end with the crow steps, as they call it, just pushing out among the trees? That's just your ain shooting-box – they call it Auchnasheen. I'll tell you the meanings of the names another time. Out beyond yonder, the big house away at the point, it's a new place built for his diversion by one of your new men. Yon island far away that's bare and green is the island of Rest, where all the loch was once buried: and atween us and that there's another isle with a gable end among the trees which is just the last place that's left to an auld race to plant their feet upon. It's a bonnie piece of water; you that's come from the south you'll never have seen the like. I'll tell you all the stories of the divers places, and how they're connected with the Me'vens that are chiefs of Loch Houran; for I wouldna give a button for that new-fangled title of the Lords Erradeen.'

'It has lasted however for some centuries,' said Walter, with a sudden sense of displeasure which he felt to be absurd enough.

'And what is that in a family?' said old Macalister, 'I think nothing of it. A hundred years or two that never counts one way nor another; it's nae antiquity. If that nonsense were true about the Warlock lord, he would be but twa hundred and fifty at the present speaking, or thereabouts, and a' that have ever thought they saw him represent him as a fine personable man. I have never had that pleasure myself,' the old man said with his shrill laugh. 'Where are you going, my young gentleman? Ye'll just go down like a stane and end in a rattle of dust and mortar, if you'll no be guided by me.'

'Let you his lordship alone, Sandy,' cried the voice of Symington, intermingled with pants and sobs as he climbed up to the parapet. 'Ye must not occupy my lord's time with your old craiks.[129] You would perhaps like, my lord, to visit Auchnasheen, where the keeper will be on the outlook: or may be it would be better to organise your day's shooting for to-morrow, when you have lookit a little about you: or ye would perhaps like to take a look at the environs, or see the factor,[130] who is very anxious as soon as your lordship has a moment –'

'Oh! and there is the minister that can tell ye a' about the antiquities, my lord: and traces out the auld outline of the castle grandly, till ye seem to see it in all its glory –'

'Or –' Symington had begun, when Walter turned at bay. He faced the old men with a half-laughing[a] defiance. 'I see plenty of boats about,' he said. 'I am going out to explore the loch. I want no attendance, or any help, but that you will be good enough to leave me to myself.'

'We'll do that, my lord. I will just run and cry upon Duncan that is waiting about –'

The end of all this zeal and activity was that when Walter found himself at last free and on the shining bosom of the loch, he was in a boat too heavy for his own sole management, sharing the care of it with Duncan, who was of a taciturn disposition and answered only when spoken to. This made the arrangement almost as satisfactory as if he had been alone, for Duncan was quite willing to obey and yield a hearty service without disturbing his young master with either questions or remarks. He was a large young man, strong and well knit though somewhat heavy, with a broad smiling face, red and freckled, with honest blue eyes under sandy eyelashes, and a profusion of strong and curly reddish hair. He beamed upon Lord Erradeen with a sort of friendly admiration and awe, answering, 'Ay, my lord,' and 'No, my lord,' always with the same smile of general benevolence and readiness to comply with every desire. When they had got beyond hail of the castle, from which Symington and Macalister watched them anxiously, Duncan mutely suggested the elevation of a mast and setting of the sail which the vessel was furnished with, to which Walter assented with eagerness: and soon they were skimming along before a light wind as if they had wings. And now began perhaps the most pleasurable expedition that Walter had ever made in his life. Escaped

*The Wizard's Son, Volume I*    95

from the ruinous old pile, within which he had feared he knew not what, escaped too from the observation and inspection of the two old men so much better acquainted with the history of his family than himself, whom he felt to be something between keepers and schoolmasters – fairly launched forth upon the world, with nothing to consult but his own pleasure, Walter felt his spirits rise to any height of adventure. There was not indeed any very wild adventure probable, but he was not much used to anything of the kind, and the sense of freedom and freshness in everything was intoxicating to the young man. The small boat, the rag of a sail, the lively wind that drove them along, the rushing ripple under their keel, all delighted him. He held the helm with a sense of pleasure almost beyond anything he had ever known, feeling all the exhilaration of a discoverer in a new country, and for the first time the master of himself and his fate. Duncan said nothing, but grinned from ear to ear, when the young master in his inattention to, or to tell the truth ignorance of, the capabilities of the boat, turned the helm sharply, bringing her up to the wind in such a way as to threaten the most summary end for the voyage. He kept his eye upon the rash steersman, and Walter was not aware of the risks he ran. He directed his little vessel now here, now there, with absolute enjoyment, running in close ashore to examine the village, turning about again in a wild elation to visit an island, running the very nose of the boat into the rocky banks or feathery bushwood. How it was that no harm came as they thus darted from point to point Duncan never knew. He stood up roused to watchfulness, with his eyes intent on the movements of his master ready to remedy any indiscretion. It was in the nature of such undeserved vigilance that the object of it was never aware of it, but to be sure Duncan had his own life to think of too.

They had thus swept triumphantly down the loch, the wind favouring, and apparently watching over the rash voyager as carefully, as and still more disinterestedly than Duncan. The motion, the air, the restless career, the novelty, and the freedom enchanted Walter. He felt like a boy in his first escapade, with an intoxicating sense of independence and scorn of danger which gave zest to the independence. At every new zigzag he made, Duncan but grinned the more. He uttered the Gaelic name of every point and isle, briefly, with guttural depth, out of his chest, as they went careering along before the wind. The boat was like an inquisitive visitor, too open for a spy, poking in to every corner. At length they came to an island standing high out of the water, with a rocky beach, upon which a boat lay carefully hauled up, and a feathery crest of trees, fine clumps of fir, fringed and surrounded by a luxuriant growth of lighter wood. In the midst of this fine network of branches, such as we call bare, being leafless, but which in reality are all astir with life restrained, brown purple buddings eager to start and held in like hounds in a leash – rose the solid outline of a house, built upon the ridge of rock, and appearing like a shadow in the midst of all the anatomy of the trees.

'That will be joost the leddy's,'[131] cried Duncan; at which Walter's heart, so light in his bosom, gave an additional leap of pleasure. He steered it so close that Duncan's vigilance was doubly taxed, for the least neglect would have sent the little vessel ashore. Walter examined the little landing, the rocky path that led up the bank, winding among the trees, and as much as could be made out of the house, with keen interest. The man with the red shirt, who had been the young lady's boatman on the previous day, appeared at the further point as they went on. He was fishing from a rock that projected into the water, and turning to gaze upon the unwary boat, with astonished eyes, shouted something in Gaelic to Duncan, who nodded good-humouredly a great many times, and replied with a laugh in the same tongue –

'Yon will joost be Hamish,' said Duncan.

'What is he saying?' cried Walter.

'He will just be telling us to mind where we are going,' said Duncan, imperturbable.

'Tell him to mind his own business,' cried Walter, with a laugh. 'And who is Hamish, and who is the leddy? Come, tell me all about it.' His interest in the voyage flagged a little at this point.

Duncan thus interrogated was more put to it than by the dangerous course they had hitherto been running.

'It will joost be the leddy,' he said; 'and Hamish that's her man: and they will joost be living up there like ither persons, and fearing God: fery decent folk – oh, joost fery decent folk.'

'I never doubted that. But who are they, and what are they? And do you mean to say they *live* there, on that rock, in winter, so far north?'

Walter looked up at the dazzling sky, and repented his insinuation: but he was, alas, no better than an Englishman, when all was said, and he could not help a slight shiver as he looked back. Hamish, who had made a fine point of colour on his projecting rock, had gone from that point, and was visible in his red shirt mounting the high crest of the island with hurried appearances and disappearances as the broken nature of the ground made necessary. He had gone, there seemed little doubt, to intimate to the inhabitants the appearance of the stranger. This gave Walter a new thrill of pleasure, but it took away his eagerness about the scenery. He lay back languidly, neglecting the helm, and as he distracted Duncan's attention too, they had nearly run aground on the low beach of the next island. When this difficulty was got over, Walter suddenly discovered that they had gone far enough, and might as well be making their way homeward, which was more easily said than done; for the wind, which had hitherto served their purpose nobly, was no longer their friend. They made a tack[a] or two, and crept along a little, but afterwards resigned themselves to ship the sail and take to the oars, which was not so exhilarating nor so well adapted to show the beauty of the landscape. It took them some time to make their way once more past the rocky point, and along the edge of the island which attracted Walter's deepest interest, but to which he could not persuade Duncan to give any name.

'It will joost be the leddy's,' the boatman insisted on saying, with a beaming face; but either his English or his knowledge was at fault, and he went no further.

Walter's heart beat with a kind of happy anxiety, a keen but pleasant suspense, as he swept his oar out of the water, and glanced behind him to measure how near they were to the landing, at which he had a presentiment something more interesting than Hamish might be seen. And as it turned out, he had not deceived himself. But what he saw was not what he expected to see.

The lady on the bank was not his fellow-traveller of yesterday. She was what Walter to himself, with much disappointment, called an old lady, wrapped in a large furred mantle and white fleecy wrap about her head and shoulders. She stood and waved her hand as Walter's boat came slowly within range.

'You will be joost the leddy,' said Duncan of the few words; and with one great sweep of his oar he turned the boat towards the landing. It was the man's doing, not the master's; but the master was not sorry to take advantage of this sudden guidance. It was all done in a moment, without intention. Hamish stood ready to secure the boat, and before he had time to think, Walter found himself on the little clearing above the stony bit of beach, hat in hand, glowing with surprise and pleasure, and receiving the warmest of welcomes.

'You will forgive me for just stopping you on your way,' the lady said; 'but I was fain to see you, Lord Erradeen, for your father and I were children together. I was Violet Montrose. You must have heard him speak of me.'

'I hope,' said Walter, with his best bow, and most ingratiating tone, 'that you will not consider it any fault of mine; but I don't remember my father; he died when I was a child.'

'Dear me,' cried the lady; 'how could I be so foolish! Looking at you again; I see you would not be old enough for that: and, now I remember, he married late, and died soon after. Well, there is no harm done. We are just country neighbours, and as I was great friends with Walter Methven some five-and-forty years ago –'

'I hope,' said the young man with a bow and smile, 'that you will be so good as to be friends with Walter Methven now: for that is the name under which I know myself.'

'Oh, Lord Erradeen,' the lady said with a little flutter of pleasure. Such a speech would be pretty from any young man; but made by a young lord, in all the flush of his novel honours, and by far the greatest potentate of the district, there was no one up the loch or down the loch who would not have been gratified. 'It is just possible,' she said, after a momentary pause, 'that having been brought up in England, and deprived of your father so early, you may not know much about your neighbours, nor even who we are, in this bit island of ours. We are the Forresters of Eaglescairn, whom no doubt ye have heard of; and I am one of the last of the

Montroses – alas! that I should say so. I have but one of a large family left with me; and Oona and me, we have just taken advantage of an old family relic that came from my side of the house, and have taken up our habitation here. I hear she must have travelled with you yesterday on the coach, not thinking who it was. Oh, yes; news travels fast at this distance from the world. I think the wind blows it, or the water carries it. All the loch by this time is aware of Lord Erradeen's arrival. Indeed,' she added, with a little laugh, 'you know, my lord, we all saw the light.'

She was a woman over fifty, but fair and slight, with a willowy figure, and a complexion of which many a younger woman might have been proud; and there was a little airiness of gesture and tread about her, which probably thirty years before had been the pretty affectations, half-natural, half-artificial, of a beauty, and which still kept up the tradition of fascinating powers. The little toss of her head, the gesture of her hands, as she said the last words, the half-apologetic laugh as if excusing herself for a semi-absurdity, were all characteristic and amusing.

'You know,' she added, 'in the Highlands we are allowed to be superstitious,' and repeated the little laugh at herself with which she deprecated offence.

'What is it supposed to mean?' Walter asked somewhat eagerly. 'Of course there is some natural explanation which will be simple enough. But I prefer to take the old explanation, if I knew what it was.'

'And so do we,' she said quickly. 'We are just ready to swear to it, man and woman of us on the loch. Some say it is a sign the head of the house is coming – some that it is a call to him to come and meet – Dear me, there is Oona calling. And where is Hamish? I will not have the child kept waiting,' said the lady, looking round her with a little nervous impatience.

She had begun to lead the way upward by a winding path among the rocks and trees, and now paused, a little breathless, to look down towards the landing-place, and clap her hands impatiently.

'Hamish is away, mem,' said the woman whom Walter had seen on the coach, and who now met them coming down the winding path. She looked at him with a cordial smile, and air of kindly welcome. It was evident that it did not occur to Mysie that her salutations might be inappropriate. 'You're very welcome, sir, to your ain country,' she said with a courtesy, which was polite rather than humble. Walter felt that she would have offered him her hand, on the smallest encouragement, with a kindly familiarity which conveyed no disrespect.

'You should say my lord, Mysie,' her mistress remarked.

'Deed, mem, and so I should; but when you're no much in the way o't, ye get confused. I said, as soon as I heard the news, that it would be the young gentleman on the coach, and I had just a feeling a' the time that it was nae tourist, but a kent[132] face. Hamish is away, mem. I tell him he hears Miss Oona's foot on the bank, before ever she cries upon him; and yonder he is just touching the shore, and her ready to jump in.'

*The Wizard's Son, Volume I*    99

The party had reached a little platform on the slope. The path was skilfully engineered between two banks, clothed with ferns and grasses, and still luxuriant with a vivid green, though the overhanging trees were all bare. Here and there a little opening gave a point of repose and extended view. Mrs. Forrester paused and turned round to point out to her visitor the prospect that now lay before them. She was a little breathless and glad of the pause, but it did not suit her character to say so. She pointed round her with a little triumph. They were high enough to see the loch on either side, looking down upon it through the fringe of branches. Opposite to this was the mainland which at that spot formed a little bay, thickly wooded with the dark green of the fir woods, amid which appeared the gables of a sort of ornamental cottage. Nearer the eye was the road, and underneath the road on the beach stood a little slight figure in the closely-fitting garb which Walter recognised. She had evidently been set down from a waggonette full of a lively party which waited on the high road to see her embark. It was impossible to hear what they were saying, but the air was full of a pleasant murmur of voices.

'It is the young Campbells of Ellermore,' said Mrs. Forrester, waving her handkerchief towards the group. 'Oona has been spending last night with them, and they have brought her back. They will all be astonished, Mysie, to see me standing here with a gentleman. Dear me, they will all be saying who has Mrs. Forrester got with her?'

'They will think,' said Mysie, 'just that it's Mr. James or Mr. Ronald come home.'

'Ah, Mysie, if that could be!' said the lady of the isle: and she put her hands together, which were thin and white, and ornamented by a number of rings, with a pretty conventional gesture of maternal regret. Walter stood looking on with mingled amazement and pleasure: pleased as if he were at a play with all the new indications of domestic history which were opening to him, and with a sense of enjoyment through all his being. When the girl sprang into the boat, and Hamish, conspicuous in his red shirt, pushed off into the loch, the tumult of good-byes became almost articulate. He laughed to himself under his breath, remembering all the greetings he had heard along the line of railway, the recognitions at every station.

'Your daughter seems to know everybody,' he said.

'And how could she help knowing every person,' cried Mysie, taking the words, as it were, out of her mistress's mouth, 'when she was born and brought up on the loch, and never one to turn her back upon a neebor, gentle or simple, but just adored wherever she goes?'

'Oh, whisht, Mysie, whisht! we are partial,' said Mrs. Forrester with her little antiquated graces; and then she invited Lord Erradeen to continue his walk.

It was the full blaze of day, and the view extended as they went higher up to the crest of rock upon which the house was set. It was built of irregular reddish stone, all cropped with lichens where it was visible, but so covered with clinging plants that very little of the walls could be seen. The rustic porch was built something like a bee-hive, with young, slim-growing saplings for its pillars, and chairs placed within its shelter. There were some flower-beds laid out around, in which a few autumn crocuses had struggled into pale bloom – and a number of china roses hung half opened against the sides of the house. The roofs were partly blue slates, that most prosaic of comfortable coverings, and partly the rough red tiles of the country, which shone warm through the naked boughs.

'Every hardy plant could bear

Loch Katrine's keen and searching air,'[133]

was garlanded about the house, the little lawn was as green as velvet, the china roses were pale but sweet. Behind the house were the mossed apple-trees of a primitive orchard among the rocky shelves. It lay smiling in the sun, with the silver mirror of the lake all round, and every tint and outline doubled in the water. From the door the dark old castle of Kinloch Houran stood out against the silent darkness of the hill. Little rocky islets, like a sport of nature, too small to be inhabited by anything bigger than rabbits, lay all reflected in broken lines of rock and brushwood, between Walter's old castle and this romantic house. They were so visible, one to the other, that the mere position seemed to form a link of connection between the inhabitants.

'We cannot but take an interest in you, you see, Lord Erradeen, for we can never get out of sight of you,' said Mrs. Forrester.

'And I think the old place looks better from here than any other view I have seen,' Walter added almost in the same breath.

They laughed as they spoke together. It was not possible to be more entirely 'country neighbours.' The young man had a fantastic feeling that it was a sort of flattery to himself that his house should be so entirely the centre of the land-scape. He followed the lady into the house with a little reluctance, the scene was so enchanting. Inside, the roofs were low, but the rooms well-sized and comfort-able. They were full of curiosities of every kind: weapons from distant countries, trophies of what is called 'the chase,'[134] hung upon the wall of the outer hall. The drawing-room was full of articles from India and China, carved ivories, mon-sters in porcelain, all the wonders that people used to send home before we got Japanese shops at every corner.[135] An air of gentle refinement was everywhere, with something, too, in the many ornaments, little luxuries, and daintinesses which suggested the little *minauderies*[136] of the old beauty, the old-fashioned airs and graces that had been irresistible to a previous generation.

'You will just stay and eat your luncheon with us, Lord Erradeen. I might have been but poor company, an old woman as I'm getting; but, now that Oona is coming, I need not be too modest; for, though there will not be a grand lunch-eon, there will be company, which is always something. And sit down and tell me something about your father and the lady he married, and where you have been living all this time.'

*The Wizard's Son, Volume I* 101

Walter laughed. 'Is it all my humble history you want me to tell you?' he said. 'It is not very much. I don't remember my father, and the lady he married is – my mother, you know. The best mother – But I have not been the best of sons. I was an idle fellow, good-for-nothing a little while ago. Nobody knew what was going to come of me. I did nothing but loaf, if you know what that means.'

'Ah, that I do,' said Mrs. Forrester; 'that was just like my Jamie. But now they tell me he is the finest officer –'

Walter paused, but the lady was once more entirely attention, listening with her hands clasped, and her head raised to his with an ingratiating sidelong look. He laughed. 'They all made up their minds I was to be good-for-nothing –'

'Yes,' murmured Mrs. Forrester, softly, half closing her eyes and shaking her head, 'that was just like my Bob – till he took a thought: and now he is planting coffee in Ceylon and doing well. Yes? and then?'

'An old man arrived one evening,' said Walter, half laughing,[a] 'and told me – that I was Lord Erradeen. And do you know, from that moment nobody, not even I myself, would believe that I had ever loafed or idled or been good for nothing.'

There was a pause, in which Walter thought he heard some one move behind him. But no sound reached Mrs. Forrester, who responded eagerly –

'My son, the present Eaglescairn, was just of the same kind,' she said, reflectively. She had a comparison ready for every case that could be suggested – 'till he came of age. It was in the will that they were to come of age only at twenty five,[b] and till then I had a sore time. Oh, Oona, my dear, is that you? And had you a pleasant evening.[c] Here is young Lord Erradeen that has come in, most kindly, I'm sure, to tell me about his father, that I knew so well. And it appears you met upon the coach yesterday. Come away, my dear, come away! And that was just most curious that, knowing nothing of one another, you should meet upon the coach.'

Oona came in lightly, in her out-door[d] dress. She gave Walter a look which was very friendly. She had paused for a moment at the door, and she had heard his confession. It seemed to Oona that what he said was generous and manly. She was used to forming quick impressions. She had been annoyed when she had heard from Hamish of the visitor, but her mind changed when she heard what he said. She came up to him and held out her hand. The fresh air was in her face, which Walter thought was like the morning, all bright and fresh and full of life. She made him a little curtsey with much gravity, and said in the pretty voice which was so fresh and sweet, and with that novelty of accent which had amused and delighted the young man, 'You are welcome to your own country[e] Lord Erradeen.'

'Now that is very pretty of you, Oona,' cried her mother. 'I never thought you would remember to pay your little compliment, as a well-bred person should; for, to tell the truth, she is just too brusque – it is her fault.'

'Hamish told me what to say,' said Oona, with a glance of provocation. 'He is a very well-bred person. He told me I was to bid my lord welcome to his own.'

'Oh, my dear, you need not take away the merit of it, as if you had not thought of it yourself,' said the mother, aggrieved; 'but run away and take off your hat, and let us have our lunch, for Lord Erradeen has been all the morning on the water and he will be hungry, and you are all blown about with the wind.'

The young people exchanged looks, while Mrs. Forrester made her little protest. There was a sort of laughing interchange between them, in which she was mocking and he apologetic. Why, neither could have said. They understood each other, though they by no means clearly understood each what he and she meant. There was to be a little war between them, all in good-humour and good-fellowship, not insipid agreement and politeness. The next hour was, Walter thought, the most pleasant he had ever spent in his life. He had not been ignorant of such enjoyments before. When we said that various mothers in Sloebury had with the first news of his elevation suffered a sudden pang of self-reproach, to think how they had put a stop to certain passages, the end of which might now have been to raise a daughter to the peerage, it must have been understood that Walter was not altogether a novice in the society of women; but this had a new flavour which was delightful to him. It had been pleasant enough in the cottage, when Julia Herbert sang, and on other occasions not necessary to enter into. But on this romantic isle, where the sound of the loch upon the rocks made a soft accompaniment to everything, in a retirement which no vulgar interruption could reach, with the faded beauty on one side, scarcely able to forget the old pretty mannerisms of conquest even in her real maternal kindness and frank Highland hospitality, and the girl, with her laughing defiance on the other, he felt himself to have entered a new chapter of history. The whole new world into which he had come became visible to him in their conversation. He heard how he himself had been looked for, and how 'the whole loch' had known something about him for years before he had ever heard of Loch Houran. 'We used to know you as the 'English lad,'' Oona said, with her glance of mischief. All this amused Walter more than words can say. The sun was dropping towards the west before – escorted to the landing-place by both the ladies, and taken leave of as an old friend – he joined the slow-spoken Duncan and addressed himself to the homeward voyage. Duncan had not been slow of speech in the congenial company of Hamish. They had discussed the new-comer at length, with many a shaft of humour and criticism, during the visit which Duncan had paid to the kitchen. He blushed not now, secure in the stronghold of his unknown tongue, to break off in a witty remark at Walter's expense as he turned to his master his beaming smile of devotion. They set off together, master and man, happy yet regretful, upon their homeward way. And it was a tough row back to Kinloch Houran against the fresh and not too quiet Highland wind.

## CHAPTER XII.

THE castle looked more grim and ruined than ever as Walter set foot once more upon the rough grass of the mound behind. He dismissed the smiling Duncan with regret. As he went up to the door, which now stood open, he thought to himself with relief that another day would finish his probation here, and that already it was more than half over; but next moment remembered that the end of his stay at Kinloch Houran would mean also an end of intercourse with his new friends, which gave a different aspect to the matter altogether. At the door of the castle old Macalister was waiting with a look of anxiety.

'Ye'll have had no luncheon,' he said, 'and here's Mr. Shaw the factor waiting to see ye.'

Macalister had not the manners of Symington, and Walter already felt that it was a curious eccentricity on the part of the old man to leave out his title. The factor was seated waiting in the room up-stairs; he was a middle-aged man, with grizzled, reddish locks, the prototype in a higher class of Duncan in the boat. He got up with a cordial friendliness which Walter began to feel characteristic, but which was also perhaps less respectful than might have been supposed appropriate, to meet him. He had a great deal to say of business which to Walter was still scarcely intelligible. There were leases to renew, and there was some question about a number of crofter families, which seemed to have been debated with the former lord, and to have formed the subject of much discussion.

'There is that question about the crofters[137] at the Truach-Glas,' Mr. Shaw said.

'What crofters? or rather what are crofters? and what is the question and where is the Truach-Glas?' Lord Erradeen said.

He pronounced it, alas! Truack,[138] as he still called loch, lock – which made the sensitive natives shudder. Mr. Shaw looked at him with a little disapproval. He felt that the English lad should have been more impressed by his new inheritance, and more anxious to acquire a mastery of all the facts connected with it. If, instead of wandering about the loch all the morning, he had been looking up the details of the business and the boundaries of the estate, and studying the map! But that not being the case, of course there was nothing to be done but to explain.

'I had thought that Mr. Milnathort would have put the needs of the estate more clearly before you. There are several questions to be settled. I don't know what may be your views as to a landlord's duties, Lord Erradeen –'

'I have no views,' said Walter; 'I am quite impartial. You must recollect that I have only been a landlord for a fortnight.'

'But I suppose,' said the factor somewhat severely, 'that the heir to such a fine property has had some kind of a little training?'

'I have had no training – not the slightest. I had no information even that I was the heir to any property. You must consider me as entirely ignorant, but ready to learn.'

Shaw looked at him with some surprise, but severely still. 'It is very curious,' he said, as if that too had been Walter's fault, 'that you did not know you were the heir. We knew very well here; but the late lord was like most people, not very keen about his successor; and then he was a comparatively young man when he died.'

'I know nothing of my predecessor,' said Walter. 'What was the cause of his death? I should like to hear something about him. Several of them must have died young, I suppose, or I, so far off, could never have become the heir.'

The factor looked at him keenly, but with doubtful eyes. 'There are secrets in all families, my Lord Erradeen,' he said.

'Are there? I thought that was rather an old-fashioned sentiment. I don't think, except that I was not always virtuously occupied, that there was any secret in mine.'

'And I am sure there is no secret in mine,' said Mr. Shaw, energetically; 'but then you see I am not, and you were not till a very recent date, Lord Erradeen. There is a kind of something in the race that I will not characterise. It is a kind of a melancholy turn; the vulgar rumours ye will have heard, to which I attach no credence. It is little worth while living in the nineteenth century,' the factor said with emphasis, 'if ye are to be subject to delusions like that.'

'I tell you I am quite ignorant; and, except by hints which I could not understand, Mr. Milnathort did not give me any information. Speak plainly, I want to know what the mystery is; why am I here in this tumble-down old place?' Walter cried with an accent of impatience.

Shaw kept a watchful eye upon him, with the air of a man whom another is trying to deceive.

'It is something in the blood, I'm thinking,' the factor said. 'They all seem to find out there's a kind of contrariety in life, which is a thing we all must do to be sure, but generally without any fatal effects. After a certain age they all seem to give way to it. I hope that *you*, my lord, being out of the direct line, will escape: the populace – if ye can accept their nonsense – say it's a – well, something supernatural – a kind of an influence from him they call the Warlock Lord.' Shaw laughed, but somewhat uneasily, apologetically. 'I think shame to dwell upon such absurdity,' he said.

'It does sound very absurd.'

'That is just it – nonsense! not worth the consideration of sensible men. And I may say to you, that are, I hope, of a more wholesome mind, that they are terribly given up to caprice in this family. The Truach-Glas crofters have been up and down twenty times. The late lord made up his mind he would let them stay, and then that they must go, and again that he would just leave them their bits of places, and then that he would help them to emigrate; and after all, I had the order that they were to be turned out, bag and baggage. I could not find it in my heart to do it. I just put off, and put off, and here he is dead; and another,' said Shaw, with a suppressed tone of satisfaction, 'come to the throne. And you're a new man and a young man, and belong to your own century, not to the middle ages,' the factor cried with a little vehemence. Then he stopped himself, with a 'I beg your pardon, my lord; I am perhaps saying more than I ought to say.'

Walter made no reply. He was not sure that he did not think the factor was going too far, for though he knew so little of his family, he already felt that it was something not to be subjected to discussion by common men. These animadversions touched his pride a little; but he was silent, too proud to make any remark. He said, after a pause-

'I don't know that I can give my opinion without a further acquaintance with the facts. If I were to do so on so slight a knowledge, I fear you might think that a caprice too.'

The factor looked at him with a still closer scrutiny, and took the hint. There is nothing upon which it is so necessary to understand the permitted limit of observation as in the discussion of family peculiarities. Though he was so little responsible for this, and even so little acquainted with them, it was impossible that Lord Erradeen should not associate himself with his race. Mr. Shaw got out his papers, and entered upon the questions in which the opinion of the new proprietor was important, without a word further about the late lord and the family characteristics. He explained to Walter at length the position of the crofters, with their small holdings, who in bad seasons got into arrears with their rents, and sometimes became a burden upon the landlord, in whom, so far north, there was some admixture of a Highland chief. The scheme of the estate altogether was of a mixed kind. There were some large sheep farms and extensive moors still intermingled with glens more populated than is usual in these regions. Some of them were on lands but recently acquired, and the crofters in particular were a burden transmitted by purchase, which the father of the last lord had made. It was believed that there had been some covenant in the sale by which the rights of the poor people were secured, but this had fallen into forgetfulness, and there was no reason in law why Lord Erradeen should not exercise all the rights of a proprietor and clear the glen, as so many glens had been cleared. This was the first question that the new lord would have to decide. The humble tenants were all under notice to leave, and indeed were subject to eviction as soon as their landlord pleased. It was with a kind of horror that Walter listened to this account of his new possibilities.

'Eviction!' he said; 'do you mean the sort of thing that happens in Ireland?'[139] He held his breath in unfeigned dismay and repugnance. 'I thought there was nothing of the sort here.'

'Ireland is one thing, and Scotland another,'[140] said the factor. 'We are a law-abiding people. No man will ever be shot down behind a hedge by a Highlander:

so if you should resolve to turn them out to-morrow, my lord, ye need stand in no personal fear.'

Walter put aside this somewhat contemptuous assurance with a wave of his hand.

'I have been told of a great many things I could do,' he said, 'in this last fort-night; but I never knew before that I could turn out a whole village full of people if I chose, and make their houses desolate.'

It was a new view altogether of his new powers. He could not help returning in thought to all the prepossessions of his former middle-class existence, where arbitrary power was unknown, and where a mild, general beneficence towards 'the poor' was the rule. He said, half to himself, 'What would my mother say?' and in the novelty of the idea, half laughed. What a thrill it would send through the district visitors,[141] the managers of the soup kitchen, all the charitable peo-ple! There suddenly came up before him a recollection of many a conversation he had heard, and taken no note of – of consultations how to pay the rent of a poor family here and there, how to stop a cruel landlord's mouth. And that he should appear in the character of a cruel landlord! No doubt it would have been easy to show that the circumstances were quite different. But in the mean time the son of Mrs. Methven could not throw off the traditions in which he had been brought up. He contemplated the whole matter from a point of view altogether different even from that of Mr. Shaw, the factor. Shaw was prepared to prove that on the whole the poor crofters were not such bad tenants, and that sheep farms and deer forests, though more easily dealt with, had some disadvantages too; for there was Paterson of Inverchory that had been nearly ruined by a bad lambing season, and had lost the half of his flock; and as for the shootings, was there not the dreadful example before them of the moors at Finlarig, where everything had been shot down, and the game fairly exterminated by a set of fellows that either did not know what they were doing, or else were making money of it, and not pleasure. The very veins in Shaw's forehead swelled when he spoke of this.

'I would like to have had the ducking of him,' he cried; 'a man with a grand name and the soul of a henwife, that swept out the place as if he had done it with a broom, and all for the London market; grant me patience! You will say,' added Shaw, 'that the thing to do at Inverchory is to get a man with more capital now that John Paterson's tack is done; and that there's few sportsmen like Sir John. That's all very true; but it just shows there are risks to be run in all ways, and the poor folk at Truach-Glas would never lead you into losses like that.'

Walter, however, did not pay much attention even to this view. His mind had not room at the moment for Paterson of Inverchory, who was behind with the rent, or Sir John, who had devastated the moors. He did not get beyond the primitive natural horror of what seemed to him an outrage of all natural laws and kindness. He had not been a landowner long enough to feel the sacred right of property. He turn the cottagers out of their poor little homes for the sake of a few pounds more or less of which he stood in no need? The very arguments against taking this step made him angry. Could anybody suppose he could do it? he, Walter Methven! As for the Erradeen business, and all this new affair altogether – good heavens, if anybody thought he would purchase it by that! In short, the young man, who was not born a grand seigneur,[142] boiled up in right-eous wrath, and felt it high scorn and shame that it could be supposed of him that he was capable, being rich, of oppressing the poor – which was the way in which he put it, in his limited middle-class conditions of thought.

Mr. Shaw was half-gratified, half-annoyed by the interview. He said to the minister with whom he stopped to dine, and who was naturally much interested about the new young man, that assuredly the young fellow had a great deal of good in him, but he was a trifle narrow in his way of looking at a question, 'which is probably just his English breeding,' the factor said. 'I would have put the Crofter question before him in all its bearings; but he was just out of himself at the idea of eviction – like what happened in Ireland, he said. I could not get him to go into the philosophy of it. He just would not hear a word. Nothing of the kind had ever come his way before, one could see, and he was just horrified at the thought.'

'I don't call that leemited, I call it Christian,' the minister said, 'and I am not surprised he should have a horror of it. I will go and see him in the morning, if you think it will be well taken, for I'm with him in that, heart and soul.'

'Yes, yes, that's all in your way,' said Mr. Shaw; 'but I am surprised at it in a young man. There is a kind of innocence about it. But I would not wonder after a little if he should change his mind, as others have done.'

'Do you form any theory in your own thoughts, Shaw,' said the minister, 'as to what it is that makes them so apt to change?'

'Not I,' cried the factor, with a shrug of his shoulders; and then he added hurriedly, 'you've given me a capital dinner, and that whisky is just excellent: but I think I must be going my ways, for already it's later than I thought.'

Mr. Cameron, who was minister of the parish, was, like Walter, a stranger to the district and its ways. He was a great antiquary and full of curiosity about all the relics of the past, and he had an enlightened interest in its superstitions too. But Shaw was a Loch Houran man. He had a reverence for the traditions which of course he vowed he did not believe, and though he was very ready to make this statement in his own person he did not like to hear outsiders, as he called the rest of the world, discussing them disrespectfully? So he desired his dog-cart[143] to be 'brought round,' and drove home in the clear, cold night, warm at his heart, good man, because of the good news for the Crofters, but a little dissatisfied in his mind that the new lord should be doing this simply as a matter of sentiment, and not from a reasonable view of the situation. 'Provided even that he keeps of that mind,' the factor said to himself.

Walter subsided out of his just indignation when the business part of the interview ended, and he came out to the open air to see Mr. Shaw away.

'This must all be put in order,' he said, as he accompanied his visitor to the boat.

Shaw looked at him with a little curiosity mingled with a slight air of alarm.

'Auchnasheen being so near,' he said, 'which is a very comfortable place, there has never been much notice taken of the old castle.'

'But I mean to take a great deal of notice of it,' the young man said with a laugh. 'I shall have some of the antiquaries down and clear out all the old places.'

His laugh seemed to himself to rouse the echoes, but it called forth no responsive sound from his companion, and he caught a glimpse of old Macalister in the distance shaking his old head. This amused yet slightly irritated Walter, in the sense of power which alternated with a sense of novelty and unreality in his mind.

'So you object to that?' he said to the old man. 'You don't like your privileges invaded?'

'It's no that,' said Macalister; 'but ye'll never do it. I've a lang, lang acquaintance with the place, and I've witnessed many a revolution, if I may say sae. One was to pull down the auld wa's altogether; another was to clean it a' out like you. But it's never been done. And it'll never be done. I'm just as sure o' that as your young lordship is that you have a' the power in your hands.'

Walter turned away with a little disdain in his laugh. It was not worth while arguing out the matter with Macalister. Who should prevent him from doing what he liked with his old house? He could not but reflect upon the curious contradictions with which he was beset. He was supposed to be quite capable of turning out a whole village out of their homes, and making them homeless and destitute; but he was not supposed capable of clearing out the blocked-up passage and rooms of an old ruin! He smiled with a kind of scornful indignation as he went up to his sitting-room. By this time the afternoon had lost all light and colour. It was not dark, but neither was it day. A greyness had come into the atmosphere; the shadows were black, and had lost all transparency. The two windows made two bars of a more distinct greyness in the room, with a deep line of shade in the centre between, which was coloured, but scarcely lighted up, by the fire. He could not but think with a sense of relief that the three days which were all he believed that were necessary for his stay at Kinloch Houran were half over at least. Another night and then he would be free to go. He did not mean to go any further than to Auchnasheen, which was exactly opposite to the island; and then, with a smile creeping about the corners of his mouth, he said to himself, that he could very well amuse himself for a few days, what with the shooting and what with –

And it would be comfortable to get out of this place, where the air, he could not tell why, seemed always insufficient. The wainscot, the dark hangings, the heavy old walls, seemed to absorb the atmosphere. He threw up the window to get a little air, but somehow the projecting masonry of the old walls outside seemed to intercept it. He felt an oppression in his breast, a desire to draw long breaths, to get more air into his lungs. It was the same sensation which he had felt last night, and he did not contemplate with any pleasure the idea of another long evening alone in so strange an atmosphere. However, he must make the best of it. He went to the bookshelf and got down again his *Trois Mousquetaires*.[144] When the candles were lighted, he would write a dutiful long letter to his mother, and tell her all that had been going on about him, especially that barbarous suggestion about the cottagers.

'Fancy me in the character of a rapacious landlord, turning a whole community out of doors!' he said to himself, concocting the imaginary letter, and laughed aloud with a thrill of indignation.

Next moment he started violently, and turned round with a wild rush of blood to his head, and that sort of rallying and huddling together of all the forces of his mind which one feels in a sudden catastrophe. It was, however, no loud alarm that had sounded. It was the clear and distinct vibration of a voice close to him, replying calmly to his thought.

'Is there anything special in you to disqualify you for doing a disagreeable duty?' some one said.

Walter had started back at the first sound, his heart giving a bound in him of surprise – perhaps of terror. He had meant to take that great chair by the fire as soon as he had taken his book from the shelf, so that it must (he said to himself in instantaneous self-argument) have been vacant then. It was not vacant now. A gentleman sat there, with his face half turned towards the light looking towards the young man; his attitude was perfectly easy, his voice a well-bred and cultivated voice. There seemed neither hurry nor excitement about him. He had not the air of a person newly entered, but rather of one who had been seated there for some time at his leisure, observing what was going on. He lifted his hand with a sort of deprecating yet commanding gesture.

'There is no occasion,' he said, in his measured voice, 'for alarm. I have no intention of harming you, or any one. Indeed I am not aware that I have any power of harm.'

Never in his life before had Walter's soul been swept by such violent sensations. He had an impulse of flight and of deadly overwhelming terror, and then of sickening shame at his own panic. Why should he be afraid? He felt dimly that this moment was the crisis of his life, and that if he fled or retreated he was lost. He stood his ground, grasping the back of a chair to support himself.

'Who are you?' he said.

'That is a searching question,' said the stranger, with a smile. 'We will come to it by and by. I should like to know in the first place what there is in you which makes it impossible to act with justice in certain circumstances?'

The air of absolute and calm superiority with which he put this question was beyond description.

Walter felt like a criminal at the bar.

'Who are you?' he repeated hoarsely. He stood with a curious sense of being supported only by the grasp which he had taken of the back of the chair, feeling himself a mere bundle of impulses and sensations, hardly able to keep himself from flight, hardly able to keep from falling down at the feet of this intruder, but holding to a sort of self-restraint by his grasp upon the chair. Naturally, however, his nerves steadied as the moments passed. The first extreme shock of surprise wore away. There was nothing to alarm the most timid in the countenance upon which he gazed. It was that of a handsome man who had scarcely turned middle age, with grey but not white hair very thin on the forehead and temples, a high delicate aquiline nose, and colourless complexion. His mouth closed somewhat sternly, but had a faint melting of a smile about it, by movements which were ingratiating and almost sweet. The chief thing remarkable about the stranger, however, besides the extraordinary suddenness of his appearance, was the perfect composure with which he sat, like a man who not only was the most important person wherever he went, but also complete master of the present scene. It was the young man who was the intruder, not he.

'I will tell you presently who I am,' he said. 'In the mean time explain to me why you should be horrified at a step which better men than yourself take every day. Sit down.' The stranger allowed himself to smile with distinct intention, and then said in a tone of which it is impossible to describe the refined mockery, 'You are afraid?'

Walter came to himself with another sensible shock: his pride, his natural spirit, a certain impulse of self-defence which never forsakes a man, came to his aid. He was inclined to say 'No,' with natural denial of a contemptuous accusation; but rallying more and more every moment, answered with something like defiance,

'Yes – or rather I am not afraid. I am startled. I want to know how you come here, and who you are who question me – in my own house.'

'You are very sure that it is your own house? You mean to have it restored and made into a piece of sham antiquity – if nothing prevents?'

'What can prevent? if I say it is to be done,' cried the young man. His blood seemed to curdle in his veins when he heard the low laugh with which alone the stranger replied. 'May I ask you – to withdraw or to tell me who you are?' he said. His voice trembled in spite of himself. The words left his lips quite sturdily, but quivered when they got into the air, or so in the fantastic hurry of his mind he thought.

'If I refuse, what then?' the stranger said.

These two individuals confronted each other, defying each other, one angry and nervous, the other perfectly calm. In such circumstances only one result is sure: that he who retains his self-possession will have the mastery. Walter felt himself completely baffled. He could not turn out with violence a dignified and serious visitor, who assumed indeed an intolerable superiority, and had come in without asking leave, but yet was evidently a person of importance – if nothing more. He stared at him for a moment, gradually becoming familiarized with the circumstances. 'You are master of the situation,' he said, with a hard-drawn breath.

'I suppose I can do nothing but submit. But if politeness on my part requires this of me, it requires on yours some information. Your name, your object?'

They looked at each other once more for a moment.

'When you put it in that way, I have nothing to say,' said the stranger, with great courtesy; 'but to acknowledge your right to require –'

At that moment the door opened hurriedly, and Symington came in.

'Your lordship will be wanting something?' he said. 'I heard your voice. Was it to light the lights? or would it be for tea, or –'

He gave a sort of scared glance round the room, and clung to the handle of the door, but his eyes did not seem to distinguish the new-comer in the failing twilight.

'I did not call; but you may light the candles,' Walter said, feeling his own excitement, which had been subsiding, spring up again, in his curiosity to see what Symington's sensations would be.

The old man came in reluctantly. He muttered something uneasily in his throat. 'I would have brought a light if I had known. You might have cried down the stairs. It's just out of all order to light the lights this gate,'[145] he muttered. But he did not disobey. He went round the room lighting one after another of the twinkling candles in the sconces. Now and then he gave a scared and tremulous look about him; but he took no further notice. The stranger sat quite composedly, looking on with a smile while this process was gone through. Then Symington came up to the table in front of which Walter still stood.

'Take a seat, my lord, take a seat,' he said. 'It's no canny to see you standing just glowering frae ye,[146] as we say in the country. You look just as if you were seeing something. And take you your French fallow that you were reading last night. It's better when you're by yourself in an auld house like this, that has an ill-name, always to do something to occupy your thoughts.'

Walter looked at the stranger, who made a little gesture of intelligence with a nod and smile; and old Symington followed the look, still with that scared expression on his face.

'Your lordship looks for all the world as if you were staring at something in that big chair; you must be careful to take no fancies in your head,' the old servant said. He gave a little nervous laugh, and retreated somewhat quickly towards the door. 'And talk no more to yourself; it's an ill habit,' he added, with one more troubled glance round him as he closed the door.

***

# CHAPTER XIII.

'AND so you have made acquaintance with the young lord – tell us what kind of person he is, Mrs. Forrester – tell us what you think of him, Oona.'

This was the unanimous voice which rose from the party assembled on the second day after Walter's visit in the drawing-room in the Isle.

It was by no means out of the world, though to all appearances so far removed from its commotions. A low cottage-mansion on the crest of a rock, in the middle of Loch Houran, six miles from the railway at the nearest spot on which you could land, and with a mile or so of water, often rough, between you and the post-office, is it possible to imagine a more complete seclusion? and yet it was not a seclusion at all. Oona cared very little for the roughness of the water between the Isle and the post-office, and Hamish nothing at all, and news came as constantly and as regularly to the two ladies on their island as to any newspaper – news from all quarters of the world. The mail days were almost as important to them – in one way far more important than to any merchant in his office. Budgets came and went every week, and both Oona and her mother would be busy till late at night, the little gleam of their lighted windows shining over the dark loch, that no one might miss his or her weekly letter. These letters went up into the hill countries in India, far away to the borders of Cashmere, round the world to Australia, dropt midway into the coffee groves of Ceylon.[147] When one of the boys was quartered in Canada, to which there is a mail three times a week, *that* looked like next parish, and they thought nothing of it.[148] Neither need it be supposed that this was the only enlivenment of their lives. The loch, though to the tourist it looks silent enough, was in fact fringed by a number of houses in which the liveliest existence was going on. The big new house at the point, which had been built by a wealthy man of Glasgow, with every possible splendour, threw the homelier houses of the native gentry a little into the shade; but nobody bore him any malice, his neighbours being all so well aware that their own 'position' was known and unassailable, that his finery and his costliness gave them no pang. They were all a little particular about their 'position:' but then nobody on the loch could make any mistake about that, or for a moment imagine that Mr. Williamson from Glasgow could rival the Scotts of Inverhouran, the Campbells of Ellermore, of Glentruan, and half a dozen names beside, or the Forresters of Eaglescairn, or the old Montroses, who, in fact, were a branch of the Macnabs, and held their house on the Isle from that important but extinct clan. This was so clearly understood that there was not an exception made to the Williamsons, who knew their place, and were very nice, and made a joke of their money, which was their social standing ground. They had called their house, which was as big as a castle, in the most unobtrusive manner, Birkenbraes, thus proving at once that they were new people and Lowlanders: so much better taste, everybody said, than any pretence at Highland importance or name. And this being once acknowledged, the gentry of the loch adopted the Williamsons cordially, and there was not a word to be said. But all the Campbells about, and those excellent Williamsons, and a few families who were not Campbells, yet belonged to Loch Houran, kept a good deal of life 'on the loch,' which was a phrase that meant in the district generally. And the Isle was not a dull habitation, whatever a stranger might think. There was seldom a day when a boat or two was not to be seen, sometimes for hours together, drawn up upon the rocky beach. And the number of persons entertained by Mrs. Forrester at the early dinner which was politely called luncheon[149] would have appeared quite out of proportion with her means by any one unacquainted with Highland ways. There was trout from the loch, which cost nothing except Hamish's time, a commodity not too valuable, and there was grouse during the season, which cost still less, seeing it came from all the sportsmen about. And the scones, of every variety known in Scotland, which is a wide word, were home-made. So that hospitality reigned, and yet Mrs. Forrester, who was a skilled housekeeper and Mysie, to whom the family resources were as her own, and its credit still more precious than her own, managed somehow to make ends meet.

On this particular afternoon the drawing-room with all its slim sofas and old-fashioned curiosities was full of Campbells, for young Colin of Ellermore was at home for his holiday, and it was a matter of course that his sisters and Tom, the youngest, who was at home reading (very little) for his coming examination, should bring him to the Isle. Colin was rather a finer gentleman than flourished by nature upon the loch. He had little company ways which made his people laugh; but when he had been long enough at home to forget these he was very nice they all said. He was in London, and though in trade, in 'tea,' which is rather aristocratic, he was in society too.

'What kind of person is he, Mrs. Forrester? Tell us what you think of him, Oona,' was what this youthful band said.

'Well, my dears,' said Mrs. Forrester, 'he is just a very nice young man. I don't know how I can describe him better, for young men now-a-days are very like one another. They all wear the same clothes – not but what,' she added graciously, 'I would know Colin anywhere for a London gentleman with his things all so well made: but Lord Erradeen was just in a kind of tweed suit, and nothing remarkable. And his hands in his pockets, like all of ye. But he answered very nicely when I spoke to him, and said he was more used to Walter Methven than to any other name, and that to be neighbourlike would just be his pleasure. It is not possible to be more pleasant and well-spoken than the young man was.'

'Oh, but I want a little more,' cried Marjorie Campbell; 'that tells nothing; is he fair, or is he dark? is he tall or is he little – is he –'

'He couldn't be little,' cried Janet, indignantly, 'or he would not be a hero: and I've made up my mind he's to be a hero. He'll have to do something grand, but I don't know what: and to spoil it all with making him small –'

'Heroes are all short,' said Tom, 'and all the great generals. You don't want weedy, long-legged fellows like Colin and the rest of them. But you know they all run to legs in our family, all but me.'

'All this is irrelevant,' said Colin with a smile which was somewhat superior, 'and you prevent Mrs. Forrester from giving us the masterly characterisation which I know is on her lips.'

'You are just a flatterer,' said that simple lady, shaking her finger at him; 'there was no character coming from my lips. He is just a fine simple-hearted young man. It appears he never knew what he was heir to, and has no understanding even now, so far as I could learn, about the Erradeens. He told me he had been a thoughtless lad, and, as well as I could judge just a handful to his poor mother; but that all that was over and gone.'

'You are going too far, mamma,' said Oona. 'He said he had 'loafed.' Loafing means no harm, does it, Colin? It means mere idleness, and no more.'

'Why should you think I am an authority on the subject?' said Colin. 'I never loaf: I go to the City every day. When I come back I have to keep up society, so far as I can, and hunt about for invitations, otherwise I should never be asked out. That is not loafing, it is hard work.'

'Ask me, Oona,' said young Tom; 'I can tell you. It is the nicest thing in the world. It means just doing nothing you are wanted to do, taking your own way, watching nature, don't you know, and studying men, and that sort of thing, which all the literary people say is better than cramming. But only it does not pay in an exam.'

'Oh, hold your tongue, Tommy,' cried his sister. 'You will fail again, you know you will, and papa will be in despair. For you are not like Colin, who is clever; you are good for nothing but soldiering, and next year you will be too old.'

'It's a shame,' cried Tom hotly, 'to make a fellow's commission depend upon his spelling.[150] What has spelling to do with it? But I'm going into the militia,[151] and then I shall be all right.'

'And did Erradeen,' said Colin to Mrs. Forrester, 'let out any of the secrets of his prison-house?'[a]

'Bless me, he looked just as cheerful as yourself or even as Tom. There was nothing miserable about him,' Mrs. Forrester replied. 'He had been all the morning enjoying himself on the loch, and he came up and ate his lunch just very hearty, and as happy as possible, with Oona and me. He was just very like my own Ronald or Rob: indeed I think there's something in his complexion and his way of holding himself that is very like Rob; and took my opinion about the old castle, and what was the meaning of the light on the tower. Indeed,' added Mrs. Forrester with a laugh, 'I don't know if it is anything in me that draws people to tell me their stories, but it is a very general thing, especially for young persons, to ask for my advice.'

'Because you're so kind,' said Janet Campbell, who was romantic and admired the old beauty.

'Because you're so clever,' said Marjorie, who had a turn for satire.

*The Wizard's Son, Volume I*     115

Oona, whose ear was very quick for any supposed or possible ridicule, such as her mother's little foibles occasionally laid her open to, turned quickly round from Tom, leaving him speaking, and with a little heightened colour interposed.

'We are opposite to the castle night and day,' she said. 'We cannot go out to the door or gather a flower without seeing it; and at night there it is in the moonlight. So naturally we are better acquainted with what happens than anybody else can be.'

'And do you really, really believe in the light?' said Marjorie.

Ellermore lay quite at the other end of the great loch, among another range of hills, and was shut out from personal acquaintance with the phenomena of Kinloch Houran. Colin gave a slight laugh, the faintest possible indication of incredulity, to repeat with an increase of force the doubt in his sister's tone. Oona was not without a healthful little temper, which showed in the flash of her eye and the reddening of her cheek. But she answered very steadily, with much suppressed feeling in her tone –

'What do you call believing?' she said. 'You believe in things you cannot see? then I don't believe in the Kinloch Houran light. Because I see it, and have seen it a hundred times as clear as day.'

At this there was a little pause among the party of visitors, that pause of half-amused superiority and scepticism, with which all believers in the mysterious are acquainted. And then Marjorie, who was the boldest, replied –

'Papa says it is a sort of phosphorescence, which is quite explainable: and that where there is so much decaying matter, and so much damp, and so much –'

'Faith, perhaps,' said Colin, with that slight laugh; 'but we are outsiders, and we have no right to interfere with the doctrines of the loch. Oona, give us that credit that we are outside the circle, and you must not send us to the stake.'

'Oh, my dears,' said Mrs. Forrester, 'and that is quite true. I have heard very clever men say that there was nothing made so much difference in what you believed as just the place you were born in, and that people would go the stake, as you say, on one side of the border for a thing they just laughed at on the other.'

This, which was a very profound deliverance for Mrs. Forrester, she carried off at the end with a pretty profession of her own disabilities.

'I never trust to my own judgment,' she said. 'But Oona is just very decided on the subject, and so are all our people on the isle, and I never put myself forward one way or another. Are you sure you will not take a cup of tea before you go? a cup of tea is never out of place. It is true that the day is very short, and Colin, after his town life, will be out of the way of rowing. You are just going across by the ferry, and then driving? Well, that is perhaps the best way. And in that case there is plenty of time for a cup of tea. Just ring the bell, or perhaps it will be safer, Oona, if you will cry upon Mysie and tell her to lose no time. Just the tea, and a few of the cream scones, and a little cake. She need not spread the table as there is so little time.'

116 *The Selected Works of Margaret Oliphant, Volume 21*

The interlude of the tea and the cream scones made it late before the visitors got away. Their waggonette was visible waiting for them on the road below Auchnasheen, and five minutes were enough to get them across, so that they dallied over this refreshment with little thought of the waning afternoon. Then there was a little bustle to escort them down to the beach, to see them carefully wrapped up, to persuade Marjorie that another 'hap'[152] would be desirable, and Janet that her 'cloud'[153] should be twisted once more about her throat. The sunset was waning when at last they were fairly off, and the loch lay in a still, yellow radiance, against which every tree and twig, every rock and stone, stood out dark in full significance of outline. It was cold, and Mrs. Forrester shivered in her furred cloak.

'The shore looks so near that you could touch it,' she said; 'there will be rain to-morrow, Oona.'

'What does it matter about to-morrow?' cried the girl; 'it's beautiful to-night. Go in, mamma, to the fireside; but I will stay here and see them drive away.'

The mother consented to this arrangement, which was so natural; but a moment afterwards came back and called from the porch, where she stood sheltered from the keen and eager air,

'Oona! Come in, my dear. That Colin one, with his London ways, will think you are watching him.'

There was something sublime in the fling of Oona's head, and the erection of her slim figure, as she rejected the possibility.

'Watching *him!*' She was too proud even to permit herself to resent it.

'Ah! but you never can tell what a silly lad may take into his head,' said Mrs. Forrester; and, having thus cleared her conscience, she went in and took off her cloak, and shut the drawing-room door, and made herself very comfortable in her own cosy chair in the ruddy firelight. She laid her head back upon the soft cushions and looked round her with a quiet sense of content. Everything was so comfortable, so pretty and homelike; and by-and-by[a] she permitted herself, for ten minutes or so, to fall into a soft oblivion. 'I just closed my eyes,' was Mrs. Forrester's little euphuism to herself.

Meanwhile Oona stood and looked at sky and sea and shore. The soft plash of the oars came through the great stillness, and, by-and-by,[b] there was the sound of the boat run up upon the shingle, and the noise of the disembarkation, the voices swelling out in louder tones and laughter. As they waved their hands in a final good-night to the watcher on the isle before they drove away, the young people, as Mrs. Forrester had said, laughed and assured Colin that it was not for them Oona stood out in the evening chill. But, as a matter of fact, there was nothing so little in Oona's mind. She was looking round her with that sort of exaltation which great loneliness and stillness and natural beauty so naturally give: the water gleaming all round, the sky losing its orange glow and melting into soft primrose tints the colour of the daffodil.

*The Wizard's Son, Volume I*          117

'The holy time is quiet as a nun
Breathless with adoration.' [154]

All the sensations that belong to such a moment are exquisite; a visionary elevation above the earth and all things earthly, a soft pensiveness, an elation, yet wistful
longing* of the soul. Before her the old castle of Kinloch Houran lay gloomy and
dark on the edge of the water. If she thought of anything it was of the young neighbour, to whom she felt so strangely near in wonder and sympathy. Who might be
with him at that moment in the ghostly quiet? What thoughts, what suggestions,
were being placed before him? Oona put her hands together, and breathed into the
still air a wish of wondering and wistful pity which was almost a prayer. And then,
rousing herself with a slight shiver and shake, she turned and went in, shutting out
behind her the lingering glory of the water and sky.

Mysie was lighting the candles when she went in, and Mrs. Forrester had
opened her eyes. Two candles on the mantelpiece and two on the table were
all the ladies allowed themselves, except on great occasions, when the argand
lamp,[155] which was the pride of the household, was lighted in honour of a visitor. The warmth of this genial interior was very welcome after the cold of the
twilight, and Oona brought her work to the table, and the book from which her
mother was in the habit of reading aloud. Mrs. Forrester thought she improved
her daughter's mind by these readings; but, to tell the truth, Oona's young soul,
with all the world and life yet before it, often fled far enough away while her
mother's soft voice, with the pretty tricks of elocution, which were part of her
old-fashioned training, went on. Never was there a prettier indoor scene. In
the midst of that great solitude of woods and water, the genial comfort of this
feminine room, so warm, so softly lighted, so peaceful and serene, struck the
imagination like a miracle. Such a tranquil retirement would have been natural
enough safely planted amid the safeguards and peaceful surroundings of a village: but in being here there was a touching incongruity. The little play of the
mother's voice as she read with innocent artifice and the simple vanity which
belonged to her, the pretty work, of no great use, with which the girl was busy,
both heightened the sense of absolute trust with which they lived in the bosom
of nature. A sudden storm, one could not but think, might have swept them
away into the dark gleaming water that hemmed them round. They were not
afraid: they were as safe as in a citadel. They were like the birds in their nests;
warm and soft, though in the heart of Loch Houran. Mrs. Forrester was reading a historical novel, one of the kind which she thought so good for improving
Oona's mind; amusing, yet instructing her. But Oona's mind, refusing to be
improved, was giving only a mechanical attention. It was away making a little
pilgrimage of wonder about the mystic house which was so near them, longing
to know, and trying to divine, what was going on there.

But when the afternoon closes in at four o'clock, and the candles are lighted shortly after, the night is long. It seemed endless on this occasion, because of the too early tea, which Mrs. Forrester had thought it would be 'just a farce' to produce again at six o'clock, their usual hour; and from half-past four till nine, when the small and light repast known in the house under the pleasantly indefinite name of 'the tray' made its appearance, is a long time. There had been two or three interruptions of a little talk, and the book had been laid down and resumed again, and Oona's work had dropped two or three times upon her knee, when Mysie, coming in, announced that it was just an uncommon fine night, though all the signs (including the glass, which, however, does not always count in the west of Scotland) pointed to rain, and that Hamish was going to take advantage of the moonlight to do an errand at the village above Auchnasheen. Would Miss Oona like to go? It was just awfu' bonny, and with plenty of haps she could take no harm, Mysie said. To see how the girl sprang from her seat was a proof of the gentle tedium that had stolen upon her soul.

'But, my dear, it will be cold, cold. I am afraid of you catching cold, Oona,' Mrs. Forrester cried.

'Oh, mother, no. I never catch cold; and besides, if I did, what would it matter? Tell him I'm coming, Mysie; tell him to wait for me. I'll put on my thick ulster,[156] or the fur cloak, if you like.'

'Certainly, the fur cloak, Oona. I will not hear of it without that. But, my dear, just think, Hamish will have to leave you in the boat while he goes to the village; and what would you do, Oona, if there is any one on the road?'

'Do, mamma? Look at them, to see if I knew them. And, if it was a stranger, just sit still and say nothing.'

'But, my dear! It might be somebody that would speak to you, and – annoy you, Oona.'

'There is no person up the loch or down the loch that would dare to do that, mem,' said Mysie, composedly.

'How can we tell? It might be some tourist or gangrel[157] body.'

'Annoy *me!*' said Oona, as if indeed this suggestion was too far-fetched for possibility. 'If anything so ridiculous happened I would just push out into the loch. Don't you trouble, mother, about me.'

Mrs. Forrester got up to envelop her child's throat in fold after fold of the fleecy white 'cloud.' She shook her head a little, but she was resigned, for such little controversies occurred almost daily. The evening had changed when Oona ran lightly down the bank to the boat in which Hamish was waiting. Everything about was flooded with the keen, clear white moonlight, which in its penetrating chilly fashion was almost more light than day. The loch was shining like silver, but with a blackness behind the shining, and all the shadows were like midnight profound in inky gloom. The boat seemed to hang suspended in the keen atmosphere rather than to float, and the silence was shrill, and seemed to cut into the soul. It was but a few minutes across the cold white glittering strait that lay between the isle and the mainland. Hamish jumped out with an exaggerated noise upon the slippery shingle, and fastened the boat with a rattle of the ring to which it was attached, which woke echoes all around both from land and water, everything under the mingled influence of winter and night being so still. A chance spectator would have thought that the mother had very good cause for her alarm, and that to sit there in the rough boat absolutely alone, like the one living atom in a world all voiceless and asleep, was not a cheerful amusement for a girl. But Oona had neither fear nor sense of strangeness in an experience which she had gone through so often. She called out lightly to Hamish to make haste, and looked after him as he set out on the white road, the peculiarities of his thick-set figure coming out drolly in the curious dab of foreshortened shadow flung upon the road by his side. She laughed at this to herself, and the laugh ran all about with a wonderful cheerful thrill of the silence. How still it was! When her laugh ceased, there was nothing but the steps of Hamish in all the world – and by and by even the steps ceased, and that stillness which could be felt settled down. There was not a breath astir, not enough to cause the faintest ripple on the beach. Now and then a pebble which had been pushed out of its place by the man's foot toppled over, and made a sound as if something great had fallen. Otherwise not a breath was stirring; the shadows of the fir-trees looked as if they were gummed upon the road. And Oona held her breath; it seemed almost profane to disturb the intense and perfect quiet. She knew every hue of every rock, and the profile of every tree. And presently, which no doubt was partly because of this perfect acquaintance, and partly because of some mesmeric consciousness in the air, such as almost invariably betrays the presence of a human being, her eyes fixed upon one spot where the rock seemed higher than she had been used to. Was it possible that somebody was there? She changed her place to look more closely; and so fearless was the girl that she had nearly jumped out of the boat to satisfy herself whether it was a man or a rock. But just when she was about making up her mind to do so, the figure moved, and came down towards the beach. Oona's heart gave a jump; several well-authenticated stories which she had heard from her childhood came into her mind with a rush. She took the end of the rope softly in her hand so as to be able to detach it in a moment. To row back to the isle was easy enough.

'Is it you, Miss Forrester?' a voice said.

Oona let go the rope, and her heart beat more calmly. 'I might with more reason cry out, Is it you, Lord Erradeen? for if you are at the old castle you are a long way from home, and I am quite near.'

'I am at Auchnasheen,' he said. A great change had come over his tone; it was very grave; no longer the airy voice of youth which had jested and laughed on the Isle. He came down and stood with his hand on the bow of the boat. He looked very pale, very serious, but that might be only the blackness of the shadows and the whiteness of the light.

'Did you ever see so spiritual a night?' said Oona. 'There might be anything abroad; not fairies, who belong to summer, but serious things.'

'Do you believe then in – ghosts?' he said.

'Ghosts is an injurious phrase. Why should we call the poor people so who are only – dead?' said Oona. 'But that is a false way of speaking too, isn't it? for it is not because they are dead, but living, that they come back.'

'I am no judge,' he said, with a little shiver. 'I never have thought on the subject. I suppose superstition lingers longer up among the mountains.'

'Superstition!' said Oona, with a laugh. 'What ugly words you use!'

Once more the laugh seemed to ripple about, and break the solemnity of the night. But young Lord Erradeen was as solemn as the night, and his countenance was not touched even by a responsive smile. His gravity produced upon the girl's mind that feeling of visionary panic and distrust which had not been roused by the external circumstances. She felt herself grow solemn too, but struggled against it.

'Hamish has gone up with some mysterious communication to the game-keeper,' she said; 'and in these long nights one is glad of a little change. I came out with him to keep myself from going to sleep.'

Which was not perhaps exactly true: but there had arisen a little embarrassment in her mind, and she wanted something to say.

'And I came out – ' he said; then paused. 'The night is not so ghostly as the day,' he added, hurriedly; 'nor dead people so alarming as the living.'

'You mean that you disapprove of our superstitions, as you call them,' said Oona. 'Most people laugh and believe a little; but I know some are angry and think it wrong.'

'I — angry! That was not what I meant. I meant — It is a strange question which is living and which is — To be sure, you are right, Miss Forrester. What is dead cannot come in contact with us, only what is living. It is a mystery altogether.'

'You are not a sceptic then?' said Oona. 'I am glad of that.'

'I am not — anything. I don't know how to form an opinion. How lovely it is, to be sure,' he burst out all at once; 'especially to have some one to talk to. That is the great charm.'

'If that is all,' said Oona, trying to speak cheerfully, 'you will soon have dozens of people to talk to, for everybody in the county – and that is a wide word – is coming to call. They will arrive in shoals as soon as they know.'

'I think I shall go – in a day or two,' he said.

At this moment the step of Hamish, heard far off through the great stillness, interrupted the conversation. It had been as if they two were alone in this silent world; and the far-off step brought in a third and disturbed them. They were silent, listening as it came nearer and nearer, the sound growing with every repetition. When Hamish appeared in the broad white band of road coming from between the shadows of the trees the young man dropped his hand from the bow of the boat. He had not spoken again, nor did Oona feel herself disposed to speak. Hamish quickened his pace when he saw another figure on the beach.

'Ye'll no' have been crying upon me, Miss Oona,' he said, with a suspicious look at the stranger.

'Oh no, Hamish!' cried Oona, cheerfully. 'I have not been wearying at all, for this is Lord Erradeen that has been so kind as to come and keep me company.'

'Oh, it'll be my Lord Erradeen?' said Hamish, with a curious look into Walter's face.

Then there was a repetition of the noises with which the still loch rang, the rattle of the iron ring, the grating of the bow on the shingle as she was pushed off. Hamish left no time for leave-taking. There were a few yards of clear water between the boat and the beach when Oona waved her hand to the still figure left behind. 'My mother will like to see you to-morrow,' she cried, with an impulse of sympathy. 'Good night.'

He took his hat off, and waved his hand in reply, but said nothing, and stood motionless till they lost sight of him round the corner of the isle. Then Hamish, who had been exerting himself more than usual, paused a little.

'Miss Oona,' he said, 'yon will maybe be the young lord, but maybe no. I would not be speaking to the first that comes upon the loch side —'

'Oh, if you are beginning to preach propriety —' the girl cried.

'It'll not be propriety, it will just be that they're a family that is not canny. Who will tell you if it's one or if it's the other? Did ye never hear the tale of the leddy that fell off the castle wall?'

'But this is not the castle,' cried Oona, 'and I know him very well – and I'm sorry for him, Hamish. He looks so changed.'

'Oh, what would you do being sorry for him? He has nothing ado with us – nothing ado with us,' Hamish said.

And how strange it was to come in again from that brilliant whiteness and silence – the ghostly loch, the visionary night – into the ruddy room full of fire-light and warmth, all shut in, sheltered, full of companionship.

'Come away, come away to the fire; you must be nearly frozen, Oona, and I fear ye have caught your death of cold,' her mother said.

Oona remembered with a pang the solitary figure on the water's edge, and wondered if he were still standing there forlorn. A whole chapter of life seemed to have interposed between her going and coming, though she had been but half an hour away.

# CHAPTER XIV.

Two days after this night scene there was a gathering such as was of weekly occurrence in the Manse of Loch Houran parish. The houses were far apart, and those of the gentry who were old-fashioned enough to remain for the second service, were in the habit of spending the short interval between in the minister's house, where an abundant meal, called by his housekeeper a cold collation, was spread in the dining-room for whosoever chose to partake. As it was the fashion in the country to dine early on Sunday, this repast was but sparingly partaken of, and most of the company, after the glass of wine or milk, the sandwich or biscuit, which was all they cared to take, would sit round the fire in the minister's library, or examine his books, or, what was still more prized, talk to him of their own or their neighbours' affairs. The minister of Loch Houran was one of those celibates who are always powerful ecclesiastically, though the modern mind is so strongly opposed to any artificial manufacture of them such as that which the Church of Rome in her wisdom has thought expedient. We all know the arguments in favour of a married clergy,[158] but those on the other side of the question it is the fashion to ignore. He who has kept this natural distinction by fair means, and without compulsion, has however an unforced advantage of his own which the most Protestant and the most matrimonial of polemics will scarcely deny. He is more safe to confide in, being one, not two. He is more detached and individual; it is more natural that all the world about him should have a closer claim upon the man who has no nearer claims to rival those of his spiritual children. Mr. Cameron was one of this natural priesthood. If he had come to his present calm by reason of passion and disappointment in his past, such as we obstinately and romantically hope to have founded the tranquillity of subdued, sunny, and sober age, nobody could tell. An old minister may perhaps be let off more easily in this respect than an old monk; but he was the friend and consoler of everybody; the depositary of all the secrets of the parish; the one adviser of whose disinterestedness and secrecy every perplexed individual was sure. He did all that man could do to be absolutely impartial and divide himself, as he divided his provisions, among his guests as their needs required. But flesh is weak, and Mr. Cameron could not disown one soft place in his heart for Oona Forrester, of which that young person was quite aware. Oona was his pupil and his favourite, and he was, if not her spiritual director, which is a position officially unknown to his Church, at least her confidant in all her little difficulties, which comes to much the same thing: and this notwithstanding the fact that Mrs. Forrester attended the parish church under protest, and prided herself on belonging to the Scottish Episcopal community, the Church of the gentry,[159] though debarred by providence from her privileges. Mrs. Forrester at this moment, with her feet on the fender, was employed in bewailing this sad circumstance with another

*The Wizard's Son, Volume I*                                    123

landed lady in the same position; but Oona was standing by the old minister's side, with her hand laid lightly within his arm, which was a pretty way she had when she was with her oldest friend. It did not interfere with this attitude, that he was exchanging various remarks with other people, and scarcely talking to Oona at all. He looked down upon her from time to time with a sort of proud tenderness, as her grandfather might have done. It pleased the old man to feel the girl's slim small fingers upon his arm. And as there were no secrets discussed in this weekly assembly her presence interrupted nothing. She added her word from time to time, or the still readier comment of smiles and varying looks that changed like the Highland sky outside, and were never for two minutes the same. It was not, however, till Mr. Shaw, the factor, came in, that the easy superficial interest of all the parish talk quickened into something more eager and warm in her sympathetic countenance. Shaw's ruddy face was full of care; this was indeed its usual expression, an expression all the more marked from the blunt and open simplicity of its natural mood to which care seemed alien. The puckers about his hazel grey eyes, the lines on his forehead which exposure to the air had reddened rather than browned, were more than usually evident. Those honest eyes seemed to be remonstrating with the world and fate. They had an appearance half-comic to the spectator, but by no means comic to their own consciousness of grieved interrogation as if asking every one on whom they turned, 'Why did you do it?' 'Why did you let it be done?' It was this look which he fixed upon the minister, who indeed was most innocent of all share in the cause of his trouble.

'I told you,' he said, 'the other day, about the good intentions of our young lord. I left various things with him to be settled that would bide no delay – things that had been waiting for the late Lord Erradeen from day to day. And all this putting off has been bad, bad. There's those poor crofters that will have to be put out of their bits of places to-morrow. I can hold off no longer without his lordship's warrant. And not a word from him – not a word!' cried the good man, with that appealing look, to which the natural reply was, It is not my fault. But the minister knew better, and returned a look of sympathy, shaking his white head.

'What has become of the young man? they tell me he has left the castle.'

'He is not far off – he is at Auchnasheen; but he is just like all the rest, full of goodwill one day, and just inaccessible the next – just inaccessible!' repeated the factor. And what am I to do? I am just wild to have advice from somebody. What am I to do?'

'Can you not get at him to speak to him?' the minister asked.

'I have written to know if he will see me. I have said I was waiting an answer, but there's no answer comes. They say he's on the hill all day, though the keepers know nothing about his movements, and he does not even carry a gun. What am I to do? He sees nobody; two or three have called, but cannot get at him. He's always out – he's never there. That old Symington goes about wringing his hands. What says he? he says, 'This is the worst of a'; this is the worst of a'. He's just got it on him –"

'What does that mean?'

'Can I tell what that means? According to the old wives it is the weird[160] of the Methvens; but you don't believe such rubbish, nor do I. It has, maybe, something to do with the drainage, or the water, or the sanitary arrangements, one way or the other!' cried the factor with a harsh and angry laugh.

Then there was a momentary pause, and the hum of the other people's talk came in, filling up with easier tones of conversation the somewhat strained feeling of this: 'He's a good shot and a fine oar, and just a deevil for spunk and courage: and yet because he's a little vague in his speaking!' 'But, I say, we must put up with what we can get, and though it's a trial the surplice is not just salvation.' 'And it turned out to be measles, and not fever at all, and nothing to speak of; so we just cheated the doctors.' These were the broken scraps that came in to fill up the pause.

'I saw Lord Erradeen the other night,' said Oona, whose light grasp on the old minister's arm had been tightening and slackening all through this dialogue, in the interest she felt. Both of the gentlemen turned to look at her inquiringly, and the girl blushed – not for any reason, as she explained to herself indignantly afterwards, but because it was a foolish way she had; but somehow the idea suggested to all their minds was not without an effect upon the events of her after-life.[a]

'And what did he say to you? and what is he intending? and why does he shut himself up and let all the business hang suspended like yon fellow Machomet's coffin?'[161] cried the factor, with a guttural in the prophet's name which was due to the energy of his feelings. He turned upon Oona those remonstrating eyes of his, as if he had at last come to the final cause of all the confusion, and meant to demand of her, without any quibbling, an answer to the question, Why did you do it? on the spot.

'Indeed, he said very little to me, Mr. Shaw. He looked like a ghost, and he said – he was going away in a day or two.'

Sudden reflection in the midst of what she was saying made it apparent to Oona that it was unnecessary to give all the details of the interview. Mr. Cameron, for his part, laid his large, soft old hand tenderly upon hers which was on his arm, and said, in the voice which always softened when he addressed her –

'And where would that be, my bonnie Oona, that you met with Lord Erradeen?'

'It was on the beach below Auchnasheen,' said Oona, with an almost indignant frankness, holding her head high, but feeling, to her anger and distress, the blush burn upon her cheek. 'Hamish had some errand on shore, and I went with him in the boat. I was waiting for him, when some one came down from the road and spoke to me. I was half-frightened, for I did not know any one was there. It was Lord Erradeen.'

'And what? – and why? – and –'

The factor was too much disturbed to form his questions reasonably, even putting aside the evident fact that Oona had no answer to give him. But at this moment the little cracked bell began to sound, which was the warning that the hour of afternoon service approached. The ladies rose from their seats round the fire, the little knots of men broke up. 'Oona, my dear, will ye come and tie my bonnet? I never was clever at making a bow,' said Mrs. Forrester; and the minister left his guests to make his preparations for church. Mr. Shaw felt himself left in the lurch. He kept hovering about Oona with a quick decision in his own mind, which was totally unjustified by any foundation; he went summarily through a whole romance, and came to its conclusion in the most matter-of-fact and expeditious way. 'If that comes to pass now!' he said to himself. '*She's* no Me'ven; there's no weird on her; he can give her the management of the estates, and all will go well. She has a head upon her shoulders, though she is nothing but a bit girlie – and there will be me to make everything plain!' Such was the brief epitome of the situation that passed in the factor's mind. He was very anxious to get speech of Oona on the way to church, and it is to be feared that Mr. Cameron's excellent afternoon discourse (which many people said was always his best, though as it was listened to but drowsily the fact may be doubted) made little impression upon Shaw, though he was a serious man, who could say his say upon religious subjects, and was an elder, and had sat in the Assembly in his day. He had his opportunity when the service was over, when the boats were being pushed off from the beach, and the carriages got under way, for those who had far to go. Mrs. Forrester had a great many last words to say before she put on her furred mantle and her white cloud, and took her place in the boat; and Mysie, who stood ready with the mantle to place it on her mistress's shoulders, had also her own little talks to carry on at that genial moment when all the parish – or all the loch, if you like the expression better – stood about exchanging friendly greetings and news from outlying places. While all the world was thus engaged, Oona fell at last into the hands of the factor, and became his prey.

'Miss Oona,' he said, 'if ye will accord me a moment, I would like well, well, to know what's your opinion about Lord Erradeen.'

'But I have no opinion!' cried Oona, who had been prepared for the attack. She could not keep herself from blushing (so ridiculous! but I will do it, she said to herself, as if that 'I' was an independent person over whom she had no control), but otherwise she was on her guard. 'How could I have any opinion when I have only seen Lord Erradeen twice – thrice?' she added, with a heightening of the blush, as she remembered the adventure of the coach.

'Twice – thrice; but that gives you facilities – and ladies are so quick-witted. I've seen him but once,' said the factor. 'I was much taken with him, that is the truth, and was so rash as to think our troubles were over; but here has everything fallen to confusion in the old way. Miss Oona, do you use your influence if you should see his lordship again.'

'But, Mr. Shaw, there is no likelihood that I shall see him again – and I have no influence.'

'Oh no, you'll not tell me that,' said the factor, shaking his head, with a troubled smile. 'Them that are like you, young and bonnie, have always influence, if they like to use it. And as for seeing him again, he will never leave the place, Miss Oona, without going at least to bid you good-bye.'

'Lord Erradeen may come to take leave of my mother,' said Oona, with dignity. 'It is possible, though he did not say so; but even if he does, what can I do? I know nothing about his affairs, and I have no right to say anything to him – no right, more than any one else who has met him three times.'

'Which is just no person – except yourself, so far as I can learn,' the factor said.

'After all, when you come to think of it, it is only once I have seen him,' said Oona, 'for the night on the loch was by chance, and the day on the coach I did not know him; so that after all I have only, so to speak, seen him once, and how could I venture to speak to him about business? Oh no, that is out of the question. Yes, mamma, I am quite ready. Mr. Shaw wishes, if Lord Erradeen comes to bid us goodbye that we should tell him –'

'Yes?' said Mrs. Forrester, briskly, coming forward, while Mysie arranged around her her heavy cloak. 'I am sure I shall be very glad to give Lord Erradeen any message. He is a very nice young man, so far as I can judge; people think him very like my Ronald, Mr. Shaw. Perhaps it has not struck you? for likenesses are just one of the things that no two people see. But we are very good friends, him and me: he is just a nice simple gentlemanly young man – oh, very gentlemanly. He would never go away without saying good-bye. And I am sure I shall be delighted to give him any message. That will do, Mysie, that will do; do not suffocate me with that cloak. Dear me, you have scarcely left me a corner to breathe out of. But, Mr. Shaw, certainly – any message –'

'I am much obliged to you; but I will no doubt see Lord Erradeen myself, and I'll not trouble a lady about business,' said the factor. He cast a look at Oona, in which with more reason than usual his eyes said, How could you do it? And the girl was a little compunctious. She laughed, but she felt guilty, as she took her mother's arm to lead her to the boat. Mrs. Forrester had still a dozen things to say, and waved her hands to the departing groups on every side, while Shaw, half-angry, stood grimly watching the embarkation.

'There are the Kilhouran Campbells driving away, and I have not had a word with them: and there is old Jess, who always expects to be taken notice of: and the Ellermore folk, that I had no time to ask about Tom's examination: and Mr. Cameron himself, that I never got a chance of telling how well I liked the sermon. Dear me, Oona, you are always in such a hurry! And take care now, take care; one would think you took me for your own age. But I am not wanting to be hoisted up either,

as if I were too old to know how to step into a boat. Good-bye, Mr. Shaw, good-bye,'
Mrs. Forroster added cheerfully, waving her hand as she got herself safely established
in the bow, and Hamish, not half so picturesque as usual in his Sunday clothes,
pushed off the boat. 'Good-bye, and I'll not forget your message.' She even kissed her
hand, if not to him, to the parish in general, in the friendliness of her heart.

Mr. Shaw had very nearly shaken his clenched fist in reply. Old fool he called
her in his heart, and even launched an expletive (silently) at Oona, 'the heartless
monkey,' who had betrayed him to her mother. He went back to the manse with
Mr. Cameron, when all the little talks and consultations were over and everybody gone, and once more poured out the story of his perplexities.

'If I do not hear from him, I'll have to proceed to extremities to-morrow, and it
is like to break my heart,' he said. 'For the poor folk have got into their heads that I
will stand their friend whatever happens, and they are just keeping their minds easy.'

'But, man, they should pay their rents,' said Mr. Cameron, who, when all was
said that could be said in his favour, was not a Loch Houran man.

'Rents! where would you have them get the siller? Their bit harvest has failed,
and the cows are dry for want of fodder. If they have a penny laid by they must
take it to live upon. They have enough ado to live, without thinking of rents.'

'But in that case, Shaw,' said the minister, gravely – 'you must not blame me
for saying so, it's what all the wise men say – would they not do better to emigrate, and make a new start in a new country, where there's plenty of room?'

'Oh, I know that argument very well,' said Shaw, with a snort of indignation. 'I
have it all at my fingers' ends. I've preached it many a day. But what does it mean,
when all's done? It means just sheep or it means deer, and a pickle[162] roofless houses
standing here and there, and not a soul in the glen. There was a time even when I
had just an enthusiasm for it – and I've sent away as many as most. But after all,
they're harmless, God-fearing folk; the land is the better of them, and none the
worse. There's John Paterson has had great losses with his sheep, and there's yon
English loon that had the shooting, and shot every feather on the place; both the
one and the other will be far more out of his lordship's pocket than my poor bit
crofters. I laid all that before him; and he showed a manful spirit, that I will always
say. No, minister, it was not to argue the case from its foundations that I came to
you. I know very well what the economists say. I think they're not more than half
right, though they're so cocksure. But if you'll tell me what I should do –'

This, however, was what Mr. Cameron was not capable of. He said, after an
interval, 'I will go to-morrow and try if I can see him, if you think it would not
be ill taken.'

'To-morrow is the last day,' said the factor gloomily: and after a little while
he followed the example of all the others, and sent for his dog-cart and drove
himself away. But a more anxious man did not traverse any road in Great Britain

on that wintry afternoon: and bitter thoughts were in his heart of the capricious family, whose interests were in his hands, and to whom he was almost too faithful a servant. 'Oh, the weird of the Me'vens!' said Mr. Shaw to himself, 'if they were not so taken up with themselves and took more thought for other folk we would hear little of any weirds. I have no time for weirds. I have just my work to do and I do it. The Lord preserve us from idleness, and luxury, and occupation with ourselves!' Here the good man in his righteous wrath and trouble and disappointment was unjust, as many a good man has been before.

When Hamish had pushed off from the beach, and the little party were afloat, Oona repented her of that movement of mingled offence and *espièglerie*[163] which had made her transfer the factor's appeal from herself to her mother: and it was only then that Mrs. Forrester recollected how imperfect the communication was. 'Bless me,' Mrs. Forrester said, 'I forgot to ask after all what it was he wanted me to say. That was a daft like[a] thing, to charge me with a message and never to tell me what it was. And how can I tell my Lord Erradeen! I suppose you could not put back, Hamish, to inquire? – but there's nobody left yonder at the landing that I can see, so it would be little use. How could you let me do such a silly thing, Oona, my dear?'

'Most likely, mamma, we shall not see Lord Erradeen and so no harm will be done.'

'Not see Lord Erradeen! Do ye think then, Oona, that he has no manners, or that he's ignorant how to behave? I wonder what has made ye take an ill-will at such a nice young man. There was nothing in him to justify it, that I could see. And to think I should have a message for him and not know what it is! How am I to give him the message when it was never given to me? I just never heard of such a dilemma. Something perhaps of importance, and me charged to give it, and not to know what it was!'

'Maybe, mem,' said Mysie from the other end of the boat, with that serene certainty that her mistress's affairs were her own, which distinguishes an old Scotch family retainer, 'maybe Miss Oona will ken.'

'Oh, yes, I suppose I know,' said Oona, reluctantly. 'It is something about the cotters[164] at the Truach-Glas, who will be turned out to-morrow unless Lord Erradeen interferes; but why should we be charged with that? We are very unlikely to see Lord Erradeen, and to-morrow is the day.'

This piece of information caused a great excitement in the little party. The cotters to be turned out!

'But no, no, that was just to frighten you. He will never do it,' said Mrs. Forrester, putting on a smile to reassure herself after a great flutter and outcry. 'No, no; it must just have been to give us all a fright. John Shaw is a very decent man. I knew his father perfectly well, who was the minister at Rannoch, and a very good preacher. No, no, Oona, my dear – he could never do it; and yon fine lad

*The Wizard's Son, Volume I*     129

that is so like my Ronald (though you will not see it) would never do it. You need not look so pale. It is just his way of joking with you. Many a man thinks it pleasant to tell a story like that to a lady just to hear what she says.'

'Eh, but it's ill joking with poor folks' lives,' cried Mysie, craning over Hamish's shoulder to hear every word.

'It's none joking,' said Hamish, gruffly, between the sweep of his oars.

'It's none joking, say ye? Na, it's grim earnest, or I'm sair mistaken,' said the woman. 'Eh, Miss Oona, but I would gang round the loch on my bare feet, Sabbath though it be, rather than no give a message like yon.'

'How can we do it?' cried Oona; 'how are we to see Lord Erradeen? I am sure he will not come to call; and even if he did come to-morrow in the afternoon it would be too late.'

'My dear,' said Mrs. Forrester, 'we will keep a look out in the morning. Hamish will just be fishing at the point, and hail him as soon as he sees him. For it was in the morning he came before.'

'Oh, mem!' cried Mysie, 'but would you wait for that? It's ill to lippen to a young man's fancy. He might be late of getting up (they're mostly lazy in the morning), or he might be writing his letters, or he might be seeing to his guns, or there's just a hundred things he might be doing. What would ye say if, maybe, Miss Oona was to write one of her bonnie little notties on that awfu' bonnie paper, with her name upon't, and tell him ye wanted to see him at ten o'clock or eleven o'clock, or whatever time you please?'

'Or we might go over to-night in the boat,' said Hamish, laconically.

Mrs. Forrester was used to take much counsel. She turned from one to the other with uncertain looks. 'But, Oona,' she said, 'you are saying nothing! and you are generally the foremost. If it is not just nonsense and a joke of John Shaw's –'

'I think,' said Oona, 'that Mr. Shaw will surely find some other way; but it was no joke, mother. Who would joke on such a subject? He said if Lord Erradeen called we were to use our influence.'

'That would I,' said Mrs. Forrester, use my influence. I would just tell him, You must not do it. Bless me, a young man new in the country to take a step like that and put every person against him! No, no, it is not possible: but a lady,' she added, bridling a little with her smile of innocent vanity, 'a lady may say anything – she may say things that another person cannot. I would just tell him, You must not do it! and that would be all that would be needed. But bless me, Oona, how are we to use our influence unless we can see him? – and I cannot see how we are to get at him.'

'Oh, mem!' cried Mysie, impeding Hamish's oars as she stretched over his shoulder, 'just one of Miss Oona's little notties!'

130     *The Selected Works of Margaret Oliphant, Volume 21*

But this was a step that required much reflection, and at which the anxious mother shook her head.

# CHAPTER XV.

It had rained all night, and the morning was wet and cold; the water dull like lead, the sky a mass of clouds; all the bare branches of the trees dropping limp in the humid air. Mrs. Forrester, on further thought, had not permitted Oona to write even the smallest of her 'bit notties' to Lord Erradeen; for, though she lived on an isle in Loch Houran, this lady flattered herself that she knew the world. She indited a little epistle of her own, in which she begged him to come and see her upon what she might call a matter of business – a thing that concerned his own affairs. This was carried by Hamish, but it received no reply. Lord Erradeen was out. Where could he be out on a Sabbath day at night, in a place where there were no dinner parties, nor any club, nor the temptations of a town, but just a lonely country place? Nor was there any answer in the morning, which was more wonderful still. It was ill-bred, Mrs. Forrester thought, and she was more than ever glad that her daughter had not been involved in the matter. But Hamish had information which was not communicated to the drawing-room, and over which Mysie and he laid their heads together in the kitchen. The poor young gentleman was off his head altogether, the servants said. The door was just left open, and he came in, nobody knew when. He could not bear that anybody should say a word to him. There had been thoughts among them of sending for his mother, and old Symington showed to Hamish a telegram prepared for Mr. Milnathort, acquainting him with the state of affairs, which he had not yet ventured to send – 'For he will come to himself soon or syne,'[165] the old man said; 'it's just the weird of the Me'vens that is upon him.' Symington was indifferent to the fate of the poor crofters. He said 'the factor will ken what to do.' He was not a Loch Houran man.

On the Monday, however, the feeling of all the little population on the isle ran very high. The wet morning, the leaden loch, the low-lying clouds oppressed the mental atmosphere, and the thought of the poor people turned out of their houses in the rain, increased the misery of the situation in a way scarcely to be expected in the west, where it is supposed to rain for ever. At eleven o'clock Oona appeared in her thickest ulster and her strongest boots.

'I am going up to see old Jenny,' she said, with a little air of determination.

'My dear, you will be just wet through; and are you sure your boots are thick enough? You will come back to me with a heavy cold, and then what shall we all do? But take some tea and sugar in your basket, Oona,' said her mother. She went with the girl to the door in spite of these half-objections,ᵃ which did not mean anything. 'And a bottle of my ginger cordial might not be amiss – they all like it, poor bodies! And, Oona, see, my dear, here are two pound notes. It's all I have of change, and it's more than I can afford; but if it comes to the worst – But surely, surely John Shaw, that is a very decent man, and comes of a good family, will have found the means to do something!'

The kind lady stood at the door indifferent to the wet which every breath of air shook from the glistening branches. It had ceased to rain, and in the west there was a pale clearness, which made the leaden loch more chilly still, yet was a sign of amelioration. Mrs. Forrester wrung her hands, and cast one look at the glistening woods of Auchnasheen, and another at the dark mass, on the edge of the water, of Kinloch Houran. She did not know whether to be angry with Lord Erradeen for being so ill-bred, or to compassionate him for the eclipse which he had sustained. But, after all, he was a very secondary object in her mind in comparison with Oona, whose course she watched in the boat, drawing a long line across the leaden surface of the water. She was just like the dove out of the ark,[166] Mrs. Forrester thought.

The little hamlet of Truach-Glas was at some distance from the loch. Oona walked briskly along the coach road for two miles or thereabouts, then turned up to the left on a road which narrowed as it ascended till it became little more than a cart track, with a footway at the side. In the broader valley below a substantial farmhouse, with a few outlying cottages, was the only point of habitation, and on either side of the road a few cultivated fields, chiefly of turnips and potatoes, were all that broke the stretches of pasture, extending to the left as high as grass would grow, up the dark slopes of the hills. But the smaller glen on the right had a more varied and lively appearance, and was broken into small fields bearing signs of cultivation tolerably high up, some of them still yellow with the stubble of the late harvest, the poor little crop of oats or barley which never hoped to ripen before October, if then. A mountain stream, which was scarcely a thread of water in the summer, now leaped fiercely enough, turbid and swollen, from rock to rock in its rapid descent. The houses clustered on a little tableland at some height above the road, where a few gnarled hawthorns, rowans, and birches were growing. They were poor enough to have disgusted any social reformer, or political economist;[167] grey growths of rough stones, which might have come together by chance, so little shape was there in the bulging walls. Only a few of them had even the rough chimney at one end wattled with ropes of straw, which showed an advanced civilisation. The others had nothing but the hole in the roof, which is the first and homeliest expedient of primitive ventilation. It might have been reasonably asked what charm these hovels could have to any one to make them worth struggling for. But reason is not lord of all.[a]

There was no appearance of excitement about the place when Oona, walking quickly, and a little out of breath, reached the foremost houses. The men and boys were out about their work, up the hill, or down the water, in the occupations of the day; and indeed there were but few men, at any time, about the place. Three out of the half-dozen houses were tenanted by 'widow women,' one with boys who cultivated her little holding, one who kept going with the assistance of a hired lad, while the third lived upon her cow, which the neighbours helped her to take care of. The chief house of the community, and the only one which bore something of a comfortable aspect, was that of Duncan Fraser, who had the largest allotment of land, and who, though he had fallen back so far with his rent as to put himself in the power of the law, was one of the class which as peasant proprietors are thought to be the strength of France.[168] If the land had been his own he would have found existence very possible under the hard and stern conditions which were natural to him, and probably would have brought up for the Church, Robbie his eldest boy, who had got all the parish school could give him, and was still dreaming, as he cut the peats or hoed the potatoes, of Glasgow College[169] and the world. Of the other two houses, one was occupied by an old pair whose children were out in the world, and who managed, by the contributions of distant sons and daughters, to pay their rent. The last was in the possession of a 'weird-less'[170] wight, who loved whisky better than home or holding, and whose wife and children toiled through as best they could the labour of their few fields.[b]

There were about twenty children in the six houses, all ruddy, weatherbeaten, flaxen-haired, the girls tied up about their shoulders in little tartan shawls, and very bare about their legs; the boys in every kind of quaint garments, little bags of trousers, cobbled out of bigger garments by workwomen more frugal than artistic. The rent had failed, for how was money to be had on these levels? but the porridge had never altogether failed. A few little ones were playing 'about the doors' in a happy superiority to all prejudices on the subject of mud and puddles. One woman was washing her clothes at her open door. Old Jenny, whom Oona had come to see, was out upon her doorstep, gazing down the glen to watch the footsteps of her precious 'coo,' which a lass of ten with streaming hair was leading out to get a mouthful of wet grass. Jenny's mind was always in a flutter lest something should happen to the cow.

'Ye would pass her by upon the road, Miss Oona,' the old woman said, 'and how would ye think she was looking? To get meat to her, it's just a' my thought; but I canna think she will be none the worse for a bit mouthfu' on the hill.'

'But, Jenny, have you nothing to think of but the cow? It will not be true then, that the time of grace is over, and that the sheriff's officers are coming to turn you all out?'

'The sheriff's officers!' cried Jenny. She took the edge of her apron in her hand and drew the hem slowly through her fingers, which was a sign of perplex-

*The Wizard's Son, Volume I* 133

ity: but yet she was quite composed. 'Na, na, Miss Oona, they'll never turn us out. What wad I be thinking about but the coo? She's my breadwinner and a' my family. Hoots no, they'll never turn us out.'

'But Mr. Shaw was in great trouble yesterday. He said this was the last day –'

'I never fash'd my thoom about it,'[171] said Jenny. 'The last day! It's maybe the last, or the first, I would never be taking no notice. For the factor, he's our great friend, and he would not be letting them do it. No, no; it would but be his jokes,' the old woman said.

Was it his jokes? This was the second time the idea had been presented to her; but Oona remembered the factor's serious face.

'You all seem very quiet here,' she said; 'not as if any trouble was coming. But has there not been trouble, Jenny, about your rent or something?'

'Muckle trouble,' said Jenny; 'they were to have taken the coo. What would have become of me if they had ta'en the coo? Duncan, they have ta'en his, puir lad. To see it go down the brae was enough to break your heart. But John Shaw he's a kind man; he would not be letting them meddle with us. He just said 'It's a lone woman; my lord can do without it better than the old wife can do without it,' he said. He's a kind man, and so my bonnie beast was saved. I was wae for Duncan; but still, Miss Oona, things is no desperate so lang as you keep safe your ain coo.'

'That is true,' said Oona with a little laugh. There must, she thought, be some mistake, or else Mr. Shaw had found Lord Erradeen, and without the help of any influence had moved him to pity the cotters. Under this consolation she got out her tea and sugar, and other trifles which had been put into the basket. It was a basket that was well known in the neighbourhood, and had conveyed many a little dainty in time of need. Jenny was grateful for the little packets of tea and sugar which she took more or less as a right, but looked with a curious eye at the 'ginger cordial' for which Mrs. Forrester was famous. It was not a wicked thing like whisky, no, no: but it warmed ye on a cold day. Jenny would not have objected to a drop. While she eyed it there became audible far off voices down the glen, and sounds as of several people approaching, sounds very unusual in this remote corner of the world. Jenny forgot the ginger cordial and Oona ran to the door to see what it was, and the woman who had been washing paused in her work, and old Nancy Robertson, she whose rent was paid, and who had no need to fear any sheriff's officers, came out to her door. Even the children stopped in their game.[a]

The voices were still far off, down upon the road, upon which there was a group of men, scarcely distinguishable at this distance. Simon Fraser's wife, she who had been washing, called out that it was Duncan talking to the factor; but who were those other men? A sense of approaching trouble came upon the women. Nelly Fraser wiped the soapsuds[b] from her arms, and wrung her hands still fresh from her tub. She was always prepared for evil, as is natural to a woman with a 'weirdless"[a] husband. Old Jenny, for her part, thought at once of the coo. She flew, as well as her old legs would carry her, to the nearest knoll, and shrieked to the fair-haired little lass who was slowly following that cherished animal to bring Brockie back. 'Bring her back, ye silly thing. Will ye no be seeing – but I mauna say that,' she added in an undertone. 'Bring back the coo! Bring her back! Jessie, my lamb, bring back the coo.' What with old Jenny shrieking, and the voices in the distance, and something magnetic and charged with disorder in the air, people began to appear from all the houses. One of the widow's sons, a red and hairy lad, came running in, in his heavy boots, from the field where he was working. Duncan Fraser's daughter set down a basket of peat which she was carrying in, and called her mother to the door.[b]

'There's my father with the factor and twa-three strange men,' said the girl, 'and oh, what will they be wanting here?' Thus the women and children looked on with growing terror, helpless before the approach of fate, as they might have done two centuries before, when the invaders were rapine and murder, instead of calm authority and law.

When Oona made her appearance half an hour before everything had been unquestioning tranquillity and peace. Now, without a word said, all was alarm. The poor people did not know what was going to happen, but they felt that something was going to happen. They had been living on a volcano, easily, quietly, without thinking much of it. But now the fire was about to blaze forth. Through the minds of those that were mothers there ran a calculation as swift as light. 'What will we do with the bairns? what will we do with Granny? and the bits of plenishing?'[172] they said to each other. The younger ones were half pleased[c] with the excitement, not knowing what it was. Meantime Duncan and Mr. Shaw came together up the road, the poor man arguing with great animation and earnestness, the factor listening with a troubled countenance and sometimes shaking his head. Behind them followed the servants of the law, those uncomfortable officials to whom the odium of their occupation clings, though it is no fault of theirs.

'No, Mr. Shaw, we canna pay. You know that as well as I do; but oh, sir, give us a little time. Would you turn the weans[173] out on the hill and the auld folk? What would I care if it was just to me? But think upon the wake[174] creatures – my auld mother that is eighty, and the bairns. If my lord will not let us off there's some of the other gentry that are kind and will lend us a helping hand. Oh, give us time! My lord that is young and so well off, he canna surely understand. What is it to him? and to us it's life and death.'

'Duncan, my man,' said the factor, 'you are just breaking my heart. I know all that as well as you; but what can I do? It is the last day, and we have to act or we just make fools of ourselves. My lord might have stopped it, but he has not seen fit. For God's sake say no more for I cannot do it. Ye just break my heart!'

*The Wizard's Son, Volume I*  135

By this time the women were within hearing, and stood listening with wistful faces, turning from one to another. When he paused they struck in together, moving towards him eagerly.

'Oh, Mr. Shaw, you've always been our friend,' cried Duncan's wife; 'you canna mean that you've come to turn us out to the hill, with all the little ones and granny?'

'Oh, sir!' cried the other, 'have pity upon me that has nae prop nor help but just a weirdless man.'

'Me, I have nae man ava,[175] but just thae hands to travail for my bairns,' said a third.

And then there came a shriller tone of indignation.

'The young lord, he'll just get a curse – he'll get no blessing.'

The factor made a deprecating gesture with his hands 'I can do nothing, I can do nothing,' he said. 'Take your bairns down the glen to my housekeeper Marg'ret; take them down to the town, the rest of ye – they shall not want. Whatever I can do, I'll do. But for God's sake do not stop us with your wailin', for it has to be done; it is no fault of mine.'

This appeal touched one of the sufferers at least with a movement of fierce irony. Duncan uttered a short, sharp laugh, which rung strangely into the air, so full of passion. 'Haud your tongues, women,' he cried, 'and no vex Mr. Shaw; you're hurting his feelings,' with a tone impossible to describe, in which wrath and misery and keen indignation and ridicule contended for the mastery. He was the only man in the desolate group. He drew a few steps apart and folded his arms upon his breast, retiring in that pride of despair which a cotter ruined may experience no less than a king vanquished, from further struggle or complaint. The women neither understood nor noted the finer meaning in his words. They had but one thought, the misery before them. They crowded round the factor, all speaking in one breath, grasping his arm to call his attention – almost mobbing him with distracted appeals, with the wild natural eloquence of their waving hands and straining eyes.

Meanwhile there were other elements, some comic enough, in the curious circle round. Old Nancy Robertson had not left the doorstep where she stood keenly watching in the composure and superiority of one whom nobody could touch, who had paid her rent, and was above the world. It was scarcely possible not to be a little complacent in the superiority of her circumstances, or to refrain from criticising the unseemly excitement of the others. She had her spectacles on her nose, and her head projected, and she thought they were all like play-actors with their gesticulations and cries. 'I wouldna be skreighin'[176] like that – no me,' she said. Round about the fringe of children gaped and gazed, some stolid with amaze, some pale in a vague sympathetic misery, none of them quite without a certain enjoyment of this extraordinary episode and stimulation of excitement. And old Jenny, awakened to no alarm about her cottage, still stood upon her knoll, with her whole soul intent upon the fortunes of Brockie, who had met the sheriff's officers in full career. The attempts of her little guardian to turn the cow back from her whiff of pasture had only succeeded in calling the special attention of these invaders. They stopped short, and one of them taking a piece of rope from his pocket secured it round the neck of the frightened animal, who stood something like a woman in a similar case, looking to left and to right, not knowing in her confusion which way to bolt, though the intention was evident in her terrified eyes. At this Jenny gave a shriek of mingled rage and terror, which in its superior force and concentrated passion rang through all the other sounds, silencing for the moment even the wailing of the women – and flung herself into the midst of the struggle. She was a dry, little, withered old woman, nimble and light, and ran like a hare or rabbit down the rough road without a pause or stumble.

'My coo!' cried Jenny, 'ye sallna tak' her; ye sall tak' my heart's blood first. My coo! Miss Oona, Miss Oona, will you just be standing by, like nothing at all, and letting them tak' my coo? G'way, ye robbers,' Jenny shrieked, flinging one arm about the neck of the alarmed brute, while she pushed away its captor with the other. Her arm was still vigorous, though she was old. The man stumbled and lost his hold of the rope; the cow, liberated, tossed head and tail into the air and flung off to the hill-side like a deer. The shock threw Jenny down and stunned her. This made a little diversion in the dismal scene above.

And now it became evident that whatever was to be done must be done, expression being exhausted on the part of the victims, who stood about in a blank of overwrought feeling awaiting the next move. The factor made a sign with his hand, and sat down upon a ledge of rock opposite the cottages, his shaggy eyebrows curved over his eyes, his hat drawn down upon his brows. A sort of silent shock ran through the beholders when the men entered the first cottage: and when they came out again carrying a piece of furniture, there was a cry, half savage in its wild impotence. Unfortunately the first thing that came to their hands was a large wooden cradle, in which lay a baby tucked up under the big patchwork quilt, which bulged out on every side. As it was set down upon its large rockers on the uneven ground the little sleeper gave a startled wail; and then it was that that cry, sharp and keen, dividing the silence like a knife, burst from the breasts of the watching people. It was Nelly Fraser's baby, who had the 'weirdless' man. She stood with her bare arms wrapped in her apron beside her abandoned washing-tub, and gazed as if incapable of movement, with a face like ashes, at the destruction of her home. But while the mother stood stupefied, a little thing of three or four, which had been clinging to her skirts in keen baby wonder and attention, when she saw the cradle carried forth into the open air immediately took the place of guardian. Such an incident had never happened in all little Jeanie's experience before. She trotted forth, abandoning all alarm, to the road in which it was set down, and, turning a little smiling face of perfect content to the world, began to rock it softly with little coos of soothing and rills of infant laughter. The sombre background round, with all its human misery, made a dismal foil to this image of innocent satisfaction. The factor jumped up and turned his back upon the scene altogether, biting his nails and lowering his brows in a fury of wretchedness. And at last the poor women began to stir and take whispered counsel with each other. There was no longer room for either hope or entreaty; the only thing to be thought of now was what to do.

The next cottage was that of Nancy Robertson, who still held her position on her doorstep, watching the proceedings with a keen but somewhat complacent curiosity. They gave her an intense sense of self-importance and superiority, though she was not without feeling. When, however, the men, who had warmed to their work, and knew no distinction between one and another, approached her, a sudden panic and fury seized the old woman. She defied them shrilly, flying at the throat of the foremost with her old hands. The wretchedness of the poor women whose children were being thrust out shelterless did not reach the wild height of passion of her whose lawful property was threatened.

'Villains!' she shrieked, 'will ye break into my hoose? What right have ye in my hoose? I'll brack your banes afore you put a fit into my hoose.'

'Whist, whist, wife,' said one of the men; 'let go now, or I'll have to hurt ye. You canna stop us. You'll just do harm to yourself.'

'John Shaw, John Shaw,' shrieked Nancy, 'do ye see what they're doing? and me that has paid my rent, no like those weirdless fuils. Do ye hear me speak? I've paid my rent to the last farden. I've discharged a' my debts, as I wuss ithers would discharge their debts to me.' Her voice calmed down as the factor turned and made an impatient sign to the men. 'Ye see,' said Nancy, making a little address to her community, 'what it is to have right on your side. They canna meddle with me. My man's auld, and I have everything to do for mysel,' but they canna lay a hand on me.

'Oh, hold your tongue, woman,' cried Duncan Fraser. 'If ye canna help us, ye can let us be.'

'And wha says that I canna help ye? I am just saying – I pay my debts as I wuss that ithers should pay their debts to me: and that's Scripter,'[177] said Nancy; but she added, 'I never said I would shut my door to a neebor: ye can bring in Granny here; I'm no just a heart of stane like that young lord.'

The women had not waited to witness Nancy's difficulties. Most of them had gone into their houses, to take a shawl from a cupboard, a book from the 'drawers-head.'[178] One or two appeared with the family Bible under their arm. 'The Lord kens where we are to go, but we must go somewhere,' they said. There was a little group about Oona and her two pound notes. The moment of excitement was over, and they had now nothing to do but to meet their fate. The factor paced back and forward on the path, going out of his way to avoid here and there a pile of poor furniture. And the work of devastation went on rapidly: it is so easy, alas, to dismantle a cottage with its but and ben. Duncan Fraser did not move till two or three had been emptied. When he went in to bring out his mother, there was a renewed sensation among the worn-out people who were scarcely capable of any further excitement. Granny was Granny to all the glen. She was the only survivor of her generation. They had all known her from their earliest days. They stood worn and sorrow-stricken, huddled together in a little crowd, waiting before they took any further steps, till Granny should come.

But it was not Granny who came first. Some one, a stranger even to the children, whose attention was so easily attracted by any novelty, appeared suddenly round a corner of the hill. He paused at the unexpected sight of the little cluster of habitations; for the country was unknown to him; and for a moment appeared as if he would have turned back. But the human excitement about this scene caught him in spite of himself. He gazed at it for a moment trying to divine what was happening, then came on slowly with hesitating steps. He had been out all the morning, as he had been for some days before. His being had sustained a great moral shock, and for the moment all his holds on life seemed gone. This was the first thing that had moved him even to the faintest curiosity. He came forward slowly, observed by no one. The factor was still standing with his back to the woeful scene, gloomily contemplating the distant country, while Oona moved about in the midst of the women, joining in their consultations, and doing her best to rouse poor Nelly, who sat by her baby's cradle like a creature dazed and capable of no further thought. There was, therefore, no one to recognise Lord Erradeen as he came slowly into the midst of this tragedy, not knowing what it was. The officials had recovered their spirits as they got on with their work. Natural pity and sympathetic feeling had yielded to the carelessness of habit and common occupation. They had begun to make rough jokes with each other, to fling the cotters' possessions carelessly out of the windows, to give each other catches with a 'Hi! tak' this,' flinging the things about. Lord Erradeen had crossed the little bridge, and was in the midst of the action of the painful drama, when they brought out from Duncan's house his old mother's chair. It was cushioned with pillows, one of which tumbled out into the mud and was roughly caught up by the rough fellow who carried it; and flung at his companion's head, with a laugh and jest. It was he who first caught sight of the stranger, a new figure among the disconsolate crowd. He gave a whistle to his comrade to announce a novelty, and rattled down hastily out of his hands the heavy chair. Walter was wholly roused by the strangeness of this pantomime. It brought back something to his mind, though he could scarcely tell what. He stepped in front of the man and asked, 'What does this mean?' in a hasty and somewhat imperious tone; but his eyes answered his question almost before he had asked it. Nelly Fraser with her pile of furniture, her helpless group of children, her stupefied air of misery, was full in the foreground, and the ground was strewed with other piles. Half of the houses in the hamlet were already gutted. One poor woman was lifting her

*The Wizard's Son, Volume I*     139

bedding out of the wet, putting it up upon chairs; another stood regarding hers helplessly, as if without energy to attempt even so small a salvage.

'What is the meaning of all this?' the young man cried imperiously again.

His voice woke something in the deep air of despondency and misery which had not been there before. It caught the ear of Oona, who pushed the women aside in sudden excitement. It roused – was it a faint thrill of hope in the general despair? Last of all it reached the factor, who, standing gloomily apart, had closed himself up in angry wretchedness against any appeal. He did not hear this, but somehow felt it in the air, and turned round, not knowing what the new thing was. When he saw Lord Erradeen, Shaw was seized as with a sudden frenzy. He turned round upon him sharply, with an air which was almost threatening.

'What does it mean?' he said. 'It means your will and pleasure, Lord Erradeen, not mine. God is my witness, no will of mine. You brute!' cried the factor, suddenly, 'what are you doing? Stand out of the way, and let the honest woman pass. Get out of her way, I tell you, or I'll send ye head foremost down the glen!'

This sudden outcry, which was a relief to the factor's feelings, was addressed not to Walter, but to the man who, coming out again with a new armful, came rudely in the way of the old Granny, to whom all the glen looked up, and who was coming out with a look of bewilderment on her aged face, holding by her son's arm. Granny comprehended vaguely, if at all, what was going on. She gave a momentary glance of suspicion at the fellow who pushed against her, then looked out with a faint smile at the two gentlemen standing in front of the door. Her startled mind recurred to its old instincts with but a faint perception of anything new.

'Sirs,' she said, in her feeble old voice, 'I am distressed I canna ask ye in; but I'm feckless[179] mysel, being a great age, and there's some flitting[180] going on, and my good-daughter she is out of the way.'

'Do you hear that, my lord?' cried Shaw; 'the old wife is making her excuses for not asking you into a house you are turning her out of at the age of eighty-three. Oh, I am not minding if I give ye offence! I have had enough of it. Find another factor, Lord Erradeen. I would rather gather stones upon the fields than do again what I have done this day.'

Walter looked about like a man awakened from a dream. He said, almost with awe –

'Is this supposed to be done by me? I know nothing of it, nor the reason. What is the reason? I disown it altogether as any act of mine.'

'Oh, my lord,' cried Shaw, who was in a state of wild excitement, 'there is the best of reasons. Rent – your lordship understands that – a little more money lest your coffers should not be full enough. And as for these poor bodies, they have so much to put up with, a little more does not matter. They have not a roof to their heads, but that's nothing to your lordship. You can cover the hills with sheep, and they can – die – if they like,' cried the factor, avenging himself for all he had suffered. He turned away with a gesture of despair and fury. 'I have done enough; I wash my hands of it,' he cried.

Walter cast around him a bewildered look. To his own consciousness he was a miserable and helpless man; but all the poor people about gazed at him, wistful, deprecating, as at a sort of unknown, unfriendly god, who had their lives in his hands. The officers perhaps thought it a good moment to show their zeal in the eyes of the young lord. They made a plunge into the house once more, and appeared again, one carrying Duncan's bed, a great, slippery, unwieldy sack of chaff, another charged with the old, tall, eight-day clock, which he jerked along as if it had been a man hopping from one foot to another.

'We'll soon be done, my lord,' the first said in an encouraging tone, 'and then a' the commotion will just die away.'

Lord Erradeen had been lost in a miserable dream. He woke up now at this keen touch of reality, and found himself in a position so abhorrent and antagonistic to all his former instincts and traditions, that his very being seemed to stand still in the horror of the moment. Then a sudden passionate energy filled all his veins. The voice in which he ordered the men back rang through the glen. He had flung himself upon one of them in half-frantic rage, before he was aware what he was doing, knocking down the astounded official, who got up rubbing his elbow, and declaring it was no fault of his; while Walter glared at him, not knowing what he did. But after this encounter with flesh and blood Lord Erradeen recovered his reason. He turned round quickly, and with his own hands carried back Granny's chair. The very weight of it, the touch of something to do, brought life into his veins. He took the old woman from her son's arm, and led her in reverently, supporting her upon his own: then going out again without a word, addressed himself to the manual work of restoration. From the moment of his first movement, the whole scene changed in the twinkling of an eye. The despairing apathy of the people gave way to a tumult of haste and activity. Duncan Fraser was the first to move.

'My lord!' he cried; 'if you are my lord,' his stern composure yielding to tremulous excitement, 'if it's your good will and pleasure to let us bide, that's all we want. Take no trouble for us; take no thought for that.' Walter gave him a look, almost without intelligence. He had not a word to say. He was not sufficiently master of himself to express the sorrow and anger and humiliation in his awakened soul; but he could carry back the poor people's things, which was a language of nature not to be misunderstood. He went on taking no heed of the eager assistance offered on all sides. 'I'll do it, my lord. Oh, dinna you trouble. It's ower much kindness. Ye'll fyle your fingers;[181] ye'll wear out your strength. We'll do it; we'll do it,' the people cried.

The cottagers' doors flew open as by magic; they worked all together, the women, the children, and Duncan Fraser, and Lord Erradeen. Even Oona joined, carrying the little children back to their homes, picking up here a bird in a cage, there a little stunted geranium or musk in a pot. In half an hour it seemed, or less,

The Wizard's Son, Volume I          141

the whole was done, and when the clouds that had been lowering on the hills and darkening the atmosphere broke and began to pour down torrents of rain upon the glen, the little community was housed and comfortable once more.

While this excitement lasted Walter was once more the healthful and vigorous young man who had travelled with Oona on the coach, and laughed with her on the Isle. But when the storm was over, and they walked together towards the loch, she became aware of the difference in him. He was very serious, pale, almost haggard now that the excitement was over. His smiling lips smiled no longer, there was in his eyes, once so light-hearted and careless, a sort of hunted, anxious look.

'No,' he said, in answer to her questions, 'I have not been ill; I have had – family matters to occupy me: and of this I knew nothing. Letters? I had none, I received nothing. I have been occupied, too much perhaps, with – family affairs.'

Upon this no comment could be made, but his changed looks made so great a claim upon her sympathy that Oona looked at him with eyes that were almost tender in their pity. He turned round suddenly and met her glance.

'You know,' he said, with a slight tremble in his voice, 'that there are some things – they say in every family – a little hard to bear. But I have been too much absorbed – I was taken by surprise. It shall happen no more.' He held his head high, and looked round him as if to let some one else see the assurance he was giving her. 'I promise you,' he added, in a tone that rang like a defiance, 'it shall happen no more!' Then he added hurriedly with a slight swerve aside, and trembling in his voice, 'Do you think I might come with you? Would Mrs. Forrester have me at the Isle?'

\*\*\*

END OF VOL. I.

# THE WIZARD'S SON, VOLUME II

## CHAPTER I.[a]

WHEN Walter seated himself beside Oona in the boat, and Hamish pushed off from the beach, there fell upon both these young people a sensation of quiet and relief for which one of them at least found it very difficult to account. It had turned out a very still afternoon. The heavy rains were over, the clouds broken up and dispersing, with a sort of sullen stillness, like a defeated army making off in dull haste, yet not without a stand here and there, behind the mountains. The loch was dark and still, all hushed after the sweeping blasts of rain, but black with the reflections of gloom from the sky. There was a sense of safety, of sudden quiet, of escape, in that sensation of pushing off, away from all passion and agitation upon this still sea of calm. Why Oona, who feared no one, who had no painful thoughts or associations to flee from, should have felt this she could not tell. The sense of interest in, and anxiety for, the young man by her side was altogether different. That was sympathetic and definable; but the sensation of relief was something more. She looked at him with a smile and sigh of ease as she gathered the strings of the rudder into her hands.

'I feel,' she said, 'as if I were running away, and had got safe out of reach; though there is nobody pursuing me that I know of,' she added, with a faint laugh of satisfaction.

The wind blew the end of the white wrapper round her throat towards her companion, and he caught it as she had caught the rudder ropes.

'It is I that am pursued,' he said, 'and have escaped. I have a feeling that I am safe here. The kind water, and the daylight, and you – but how should *you* feel it? It must have gone from my mind to yours.'

'The water does not look so very kind,' said Oona, 'except that it separates us from the annoyances that are on land – when there are annoyances.'

She had never known any that were more than the troubles of a child before.

'There is this that makes it kind. If you were driven beyond bearing, a plunge down there and all would be over –'

– 143 –

144          *The Selected Works of Margaret Oliphant, Volume 21*

'Lord Erradeen!'

'Oh, I don't mean to try. I have no thought of trying; but look how peaceful, how deep, all liquid blackness! It might go down to the mystic centre of the earth for anything one knows.'

He leant over a little, looking down into those depths profound which were so still that the boat seemed to cut through a surface which had solidity; and in doing this put the boat out of trim, and elicited a growl from Hamish.

It seemed to Oona, too, as if there was something seductive in that profound liquid depth, concealing all that sought refuge there. She put out her hand and grasped his arm in the thrill of this thought.

'Oh, don't look down,' she said. 'I have heard of people being caught, in spite of themselves, by some charm in it.' The movement was quite involuntary and simple; but, on second thoughts, Oona drew away her hand, and blushed a little. 'Besides, you put the boat out of trim,' she said.

'If I should ever be in deadly danger,' said Walter, with the seriousness which had been in his face all along, 'will you put out your hand like that, without reflection, and save me?'

Oona tried to laugh again; but it was not easy; his seriousness gained upon her, in spite of herself.

'I think we are talking nonsense, and feeling nonsense; for it seems to me as if we had escaped from something. Now Hamish is pleased; the boat is trimmed.[1] Don't you think,' she said, with an effort to turn off graver subjects, 'that it is a pity those scientific people who can do everything should not tunnel down through that centre of the earth you were speaking of, straight through to the other side of the world? Then we might be dropped through to Australia without any trouble. I have a brother there; indeed I have a brother in most places. Mamma and I might go and see Rob now and then, or he might come home for a dance, poor fellow; he was always very fond of dancing.'

Thus she managed to fill up the time till they reached the isle. It lay upon the surface of that great mirror, all fringed and feathered with its bare trees; the occasional colour in the roofs gleaming back again out of the water; a little natural fastness, safe and sure. As Oona was later in returning than had been expected, the little garrison of women in the isle was all astir and watching for her coming. Out of one of the upper windows there was the head of a young maid visible, gazing down the loch; and Mrs. Forrester, in her furred cloak, was standing in the porch, and Mysie half way down to the beach, moving from point to point of vision.

'They are all about but old Cookie,' said Oona. 'It is a terrible business when I am late. They think everything that is dreadful must have happened, and that makes a delightful sensation when I get home safe and well. I am every day rescued from a watery grave, or saved from some dreadful accident on shore, in my

*The Wizard's Son, Volume II*     145

mother's imagination. She gives herself the misery of it, and then she has the pleasure of it,' cried the girl, with the amused cynicism of youth.

'But to-day you bring a real fugitive with you – an escaped – what shall I call myself? – escaped not from harm, but from doing harm – which is the most dangerous of the two.'

'You will never do harm to the poor folk,' said Oona, looking at him with kind eyes.

'Never, while I am in my senses, and know. I want you to promise me something before we land.'

'You must make haste, then, and ask; for there is Mysie ready with the boat-hook,' said Oona, a little alarmed.

'Promise me – if it ever occurs that harm is being done in my name, to make me know it. Oh, not a mere note sent to my house; I might never receive it like the last; but to make me know. See me, speak to me, think even: – and you will save me.'

'Oh, Lord Erradeen, you must not put such a responsibility on me. How can I, a girl that is only a country neighbour –'

'Promise me!' he said.

'Oh, Lord Erradeen, this is almost tyrannical. Yes, if I can – if I think anything is concealed from you. Here I am, Mysie, quite safe; and of course mamma has been making herself miserable. I have brought Lord Erradeen to luncheon,' Oona said.

'Eh, my lord, but we're glad to see you,' said Mysie, with the gracious ease of hospitality. 'They said you were going without saying good-bye, but I would never believe it. It is just his lordship, mem, as I said it was,' she called to Mrs. Forrester, who was hastening down the slope.

The mistress of the island came down tripping, with her elderly graces, waving her white delicate hands.

'Oh, Oona, my dear, but I'm thankful to see you, and nothing happened,' she cried; 'and ye are very welcome, Lord Erradeen. I thought you would never go away without saying good-bye. Come away up to the house. It is late, late, for luncheon; but there will be some reason; and I never have any heart to take a meal by myself. Everything is ready: if it's not all spoiled?' Mrs. Forrester added, turning round to Mysie, as she shook hands with the unexpected guest.

'Oh, no fear of that, mem,' said the factotum,[2] 'we're well enough used to waiting in this house: an hour, half an hour, is just nothing. The trout is never put down to the fire till we see the boat; but I maun away[3] and tell cook.'

'And you will get out some of the good claret,' Mrs. Forrester cried. 'Come away – come away, Lord Erradeen. We have just been wondering what had become of you. It is quite unfriendly to be at Auchnasheen and not come over to see us. Oona, run, my dear, and take off your things. Lord Erradeen will take charge of me. I am fain of an arm when I can get one, up the brae. When the boys were at home I always got a good pull up. And where did you foregather, you two? I am glad Oona had the sense to bring you with her. And I hope the trout will not be spoiled,' she said with some anxiety. 'Mysie is just too confident – far too confident. She is one that thinks nothing can go wrong on the isle.'

'That is my creed too,' said Walter with an awakening of his natural inclination to make himself agreeable, and yet a more serious meaning in the words.

'Oh fie!' said Mrs. Forrester, shaking her head, 'to flatter a simple person like me! We have but little, very little to offer; the only thing in our favour is that it's offered with real goodwill. And how do you like Auchnasheen? and are you just keeping it up as it was in the old lord's time? and how is Mary Fleming, the housekeeper, that was always an ailing body?' These questions, with others of the same kind, answered the purpose of conversation as they ascended to the house – with little intervals between, for Mrs. Forrester was a little breathless though she did not care to say so, and preferred to make pauses now and then to point out the variations of the landscape. 'Though I know it so well, I never find it two days the same,' she said. None of these transparent little fictions, so innocent, so natural, were unknown to her friends, and the sight of them had a curiously strengthening and soothing effect upon Walter, to whom the gentle perseverance of those amiable foibles, so simple and evident, gave a sense of reality and nature which had begun to be wanting in his world. His heart grew lighter as he watched the 'ways' of this simple woman, about whose guiles and pretences even there was no mystery at all, and whose little affectations somehow seemed to make her only more real. It gave him a momentary shock, however, when she turned round at her own door, and directed his attention to his old castle lying in lines of black and grey upon the glistening water. He drew her hastily within the porch.

'It gets colder and colder,' he said; 'the wind goes through and through one. Don't let me keep you out in the[a] chilly air.'

'I think you must have caught a little cold,' said Mrs. Forrester, concerned, 'for I do not find it so chilly for my part. To be sure, Loch Houran is never like your quiet landward places in England: we are used up here to all the changes. Oona will be waiting for us by this time; and I hope you are ready for your dinner, Lord Erradeen, for I am sure I am. I should say for your lunch: but when it comes to be so far on in the day as this, these short winter days, Oona and me, we just make it our dinner.[4] Oh, there you are, my dear! Lord Erradeen will like to step into Ronald's room and wash his hands, and then there will be nothing to wait for but the trout.'

When they were seated at the table, with the trout cooked to perfection as fish only is where it is caught, Mrs. Forrester pressing him to eat with old-fashioned anxiety, and even Mysie, who waited at table, adding affectionate importunities, Walter's heart was touched with a sense of the innocence, the kindness, the gentle nature about him. He felt himself cared for like a child, regarded indeed as a sort of larger child to be indulged with every dainty they could think of, and yet in some ineffable way protected and guided too by the simple creatures round him. The mistress and the maid had little friendly controversies as to what was best for him.

*The Wizard's Son, Volume II*                                               147

'I thought some good sherry wine, mem, and him coming off the water, would be better than yon cauld clairet.'

'Well, perhaps you are right, Mysie; but the young men nowadays are all for claret,' Mrs. Forrester said.

'Just a wee bittie more of the fish, my lord,' said Mysie, in his ear.

'No, no, Mysie,' cried her mistress. 'You know there are birds coming. Just take away the trout, it is a little cold, and there's far more nourishment in the grouse.'

'To my mind, mem,' said Mysie, 'there is nothing better than a Loch Houran trout.'

All this had the strangest effect upon Walter. To come into this simple house was like coming back to nature, and that life of childhood in which there are no skeletons or shadows. Even his mother had never been so sheltering, so safe, so real. Mrs. Methven had far more intellect and passion than Mrs. Forrester. It had been impossible to her to bear the failure of her ideal in her boy. Her very love had been full of pain and trouble to both. But this other mother was of a different fashion. Whatever her children did was good in her eyes; but she protected, fed, took care of, extended her soft wings over them as if they still were in the maternal nest. The innocence of it all moved Walter out of himself.

'Do you know,' he said at last, 'what I have come from to your kind, sheltering house, Mrs. Forrester? Do you know what everybody, even your daughter, thought of me two hours ago?'

'I never thought any harm of you, Lord Erradeen,' said Oona, looking up hastily.

'Harm of him! Dear me, Oona, you are far, very far, from polite. And what was it they thought of you?' asked Mrs. Forrester. 'Oona is so brusque, she just says what she thinks; but sure am I it was nothing but good.'

'They thought,' said Walter, with an excitement which grew upon him as he went on, 'that I, who have been poor myself all my life, that never had any money or lands till a few weeks ago, that I was going to turn poor women and children out of their houses, out upon the world, out to the wet, cold mountain-side,[a] without a shelter in sight. They thought I was capable of that. An old woman more than eighty, and a lot of little children! They thought I would turn them out! Oh, not the poor creatures themselves, but others; even Miss Oona. Is thy servant a dog –' cried the young man in a blaze of fiery agitation, the hot light of pain shining through the involuntary moisture in his eyes. 'Somebody says that in the Bible, I know. Is thy servant a dog that he should do this thing?'[5]

'Oh, my dear!' cried Mrs. Forrester, in her sympathy, forgetting all distinctions, and only remembering that he was very like her Ronald, and was in trouble, 'nobody, nobody thought you would do that. Oh no, no, fie no! nobody had such a thought. If I could believe it of Oona I would not speak to her – I would – no,[b] no, it was never believed. I, for one, I knew you would never do it. I saw it,' cried the kind lady, 'in your eyes!'

148      *The Selected Works of Margaret Oliphant, Volume 21*

Though Walter had no real confidence in the independent judgment which she asserted so unhesitatingly, yet he was consoled by the softness of the words, the assurance of the tone.

'I did not think such things ever happened in Scotland,' he said. 'It is Ireland one thinks of:[6] and[a] that it should be supposed I would do it, has hurt me more than I can say–a stranger who had no one to stand up for me.'

'That was just the way of it,' said Mrs. Forrester, soothingly. 'We think here that there is something strange in English ways. We never know how a thing will appear to them – that is how it was. But I said all through that it was impossible, and I just wrote to you last night (you would get my letter?) that you must not do it – for fear you might not have understood how it was.'

'But there is another side to it,' said Oona, 'we must not forget, mother. Sometimes it is said, you know, that the poor folk can do no good where they are. We can all understand the shock of seeing them turned out of their houses: but then people say they cannot live there – that it would be better for themselves to be forced to go away.'

'That is true, Oona,' said her mother, facing round: 'it is just a kind of starvation. When old Jenny went there first (she was in my nursery when I had one) there was just a perpetual craik about her rent. Her man was one of the Frasers, and a well-doing, decent man, till he died, poor fellow, as we must all do: and since that I have heard little about it, for I think it was just out of her power to pay anything. Duncan Fraser, he is a very decent man, but I remember the minister was saying if he was in Glasgow or Paisley, or some of those places, it would be better for his family. I recollect that the minister did say that.'

'So, Lord Erradeen,' said Oona, 'without being cruel you might:[b] but I – we all like you ten times better that you couldn't,' said the girl impulsively.

'Ay, that we do,'[c] said her mother, ready to back up every side, 'that we do.[d] But I am not surprised. I knew that there was nothing unkind either in your heart or your face.'

'There was no time,' said Walter, 'to think what was wise, or take into consideration, like a benevolent tyrant, what could be done for their good, without consulting their inclinations: which is what you mean, Miss Forrester –'

Oona smiled, with a little heightened colour. It was the commencement of one of those pretty duels which mean mutual attraction rather than opposition. She said, with a little nod of her head, 'Go on.'

'But one thing is certain,' he said, with the almost solemn air which returned to his face at intervals, 'that I will rather want shelter myself than turn another man out of his house, on any argument – far less helpless women and children. Did you laugh? I see no laughing in it,' the young man cried.

'Me – laugh!' cried Mrs. Forrester, though it was at Oona he had looked. 'If I laughed it was for pleasure. Between ourselves, Lord Erradeen (though they might perhaps be better away), turning out a poor family out of their house is a thing I could never away with. Oona may say what she likes – but it* is not Christian. Oh, it's not Christian! I would have taken them in, as many as Mysie could have made room for: but I never could say that it was according to Christianity. Oh no, Lord Erradeen! I would have to be poor indeed – poor, poor indeed – before I would turn these poor folk away.'

'There would be no blessing upon the rest,' said Mysie, behind her mistress's chair.

'That is settled then,' said Walter, whose heart grew lighter and lighter. 'But that is not all. Tell me, if I were a benevolent despot, Miss Forrester – you who know everything – what should I do now? – for it cannot stop there.'

'We'll go into the drawing-room before you settle that,' said Mrs. Forrester. 'Dear me, it is quite dark; we will want the candles, Mysie. There is so little light in the afternoon at this time of the year. I am sorry there is no gentleman to keep you in countenance with your glass of wine, Lord Erradeen. If you had been here when my Ronald or Jamie, or even Rob, was at home! But they are all away, one to every airt,[7] and the house is very lonely without any boys in it. Are you coming with us? Well, perhaps it will be more cheerful. Dear me, Mysie, you have left that door open, and we will just be perished with the cold.'

'Let me shut it,' Walter said.

He turned to the open door with a pleasant sense of taking the place of one of those absent boys whom the mother regretted so cheerfully, and with a lighter heart than he could have thought possible a few hours ago. But at the first glance he stood arrested with a sudden chill that seemed to paralyse him. It was almost dark upon the loch; the water gleamed with that polished blackness through which the boat had cut as through something solid; but blacker now, shining like jet against the less responsive gloom of the land and hills. The framework of the doorway made a picture of this night scene, with the more definite darkness of the old castle in the centre, rising opaque against the softer distance. Seeing that Lord Erradeen made a sudden pause, Oona went towards him, and looked out too at the familiar scene. She had seen it often before, but it had never made the same impression upon her. 'Oh, the light – the light again!' she said, with a cry of surprise. It came up in a pale glow as she was looking, faint, but throwing up in distinct revelation the mass of the old tower against the background. Walter, who seemed to have forgotten what he had come to do, was roused by her voice, and with nervous haste and almost violence shut the door. There was not much light in the little hall, and they could see each other's faces but imperfectly, but his had already lost the soothed and relieved expression which had replaced its agitated aspect. He scarcely seemed to see her as he turned round, took up his hat from the table, and went on confusedly before her, forgetting ordinary decorums, to the drawing-room, where Mrs. Forrester had already made herself comfortable in her usual chair, with the intention of for a few moments 'just closing her eyes.' Mysie had not brought the lights, and he stood before the surprised lady like a dark shadow, with his hat in his hand.

'I have come to take my leave,' he said; 'to thank you, and say good-bye.'

'Dear me,' said Mrs. Forrester, rousing herself, 'you are in a great hurry, Lord Erradeen. Why should you be so anxious to go? You have nobody at Auchnasheen to be kept waiting. Toots! you must just wait now you are here for a cup of tea at least, and it will take Hamish a certain time to get out the boat.'

'I must go,' he said, with a voice that trembled: then suddenly threw down his hat on the floor and himself upon a low chair close to her, 'unless,' he said, 'unless – you will complete your charity by taking me in for the night. Will you keep me for the night? Put me in any corner. I don't mind – only let me stay.'

'Let you stay!' cried the lady of the isle. She sprang up as lightly as a girl at this appeal, with no further idea of 'closing her eyes.' 'Will I keep you for the night? But that I will, and with all my heart! There is Ronald's room, where you washed your hands, just all ready, nothing to do but put on the sheets, and plenty of his things in it in case you should want anything. Let you stay!' she cried, with delighted excitement, 'it is what I would have asked and pressed you to do. And then we can do something for your cold, for I am sure you have a cold; and Oona and you can settle all that business about the benevolent tyrant, which is more than my poor head is equal to. Oona, my dear, will you tell Mysie? – where is Mysie? I will just speak to her myself. We must get him better of his cold, or what will his mother think? He must have some more blankets, or an eider-down, which will be lighter, and a good fire.'

If her worst enemy had asked hospitality from Mrs. Forrester, she would have forgotten all her wrongs and opened her doors wide; how much more when it was a friend and neighbour![a] The demand itself was a kindness. She tripped away without a thought of her disturbed nap, and was soon heard in colloquy with Mysie, who shared all her sentiments in this respect. Oona, who stood silent by the fire, with a sense that she was somehow in the secret, though she did not know what it was, had a less easy part. The pang of sympathy she felt was almost intolerable, but she did not know how to express it. The quiet room seemed all at once to have become the scene of a struggle, violent though invisible, which she followed dumbly with an instinct beyond her power to understand. After an interval of silence which seemed endless, he spoke.

'It must be intended that we should have something to do with each other,' he said, suddenly. 'When you are there I feel stronger. If your mother had refused me, I should have been lost.'

'It was impossible that she should have refused you, Lord Erradeen.'

'I wish you would not call me by that ill-omened name. It is a horror to me; and then if all that is true – How is it possible that one man should lord it over

*The Wizard's Son, Volume II* 151

an entire race for so long? Did you ever hear of a similar case? Oh! don't go away. If you knew what an ease it is to speak to you! No one else understands. It makes one feel as if one were restored to natural life to be able to speak of it, to ask advice. Nothing,' he cried suddenly, getting up, picking up his hat as if about to leave the house, 'nothing – shall induce me to go –'

'Oh, no, no!' she cried, 'you must not go;' though she could not have told why.

He put down the hat again on the table with a strange laugh. 'I was going then,' he said, 'but I will not. I will do exactly as you say.' He came up to her where she stood full of trouble watching him. 'I dare say you think I am going wrong in my head, but it is not that. I am being dragged – with ropes. Give me your hand to hold by. There! that is safety, that is peace. You hand is as soft – as snow,' cried the young man. His own were burning, and the cool fresh touch of the girl's hand seemed to diffuse itself through all his being. Oona was as brave in her purity as the other Una, the spotless lady of romance,[8] and would have shrunk from no act of succour. But it agitated her to have this strange appeal for help made to her. She did not withdraw her hand, but yet drew away a little, alarmed, not knowing what to do.

'You must not think,' she said, faltering, 'that any one – has more power over another than – he permits them to have.'

She spoke like one of the oracles, not knowing what she said; and he listened with a slight shake of his head, not making any reply. After a moment he yielded to the reluctance which made itself felt in her, and let her hand go.

'Will you come with me outside?' he said; 'not there, where that place is. I think the cold and the night do one good. Can we go out the other way?'

Oona accepted this alternative gladly. 'We can go to the walk, where it is always dry,' she said, with an assumption of cheerfulness. 'It looks to the south, and that is where the flowers grow best.' As she led the way through the hall, Walter took up Mrs. Forrester's furred cloak which hung there, and put it round her with a great deal of tenderness and care. The girl's heart beat as he took this office upon him, as one of her brothers might have done. It was the strangest conjunction. He was not thinking of her at all, she felt, save as affording some mysterious help in those mysterious miseries: and yet there was a sweetness in the thought he took, even at this extraordinary moment, for her comfort. There could have been no such dangerous combination of circumstances for Oona, whose heart was full of the early thrill of romance, and that inextinguishable pity and attraction towards the suffering which tells for so much in the life of women. A softness and melting of the heart indescribable came over her as she felt his light touch on her shoulders, and found herself enveloped as it were, in his shadow and the sentiment of his presence. He was not thinking of her, but only of his need of her, fantastic though that might be. But her heart went out towards him with that wonderful feminine impulse which is at once inferior and superior, full of dependence, yet full of help. To follow all his movements and thoughts as well as she could with wistful secondariness; yet to be ready to guide, to save, when need was – to dare anything for that office. There had never been aught[a] in Oona's life to make her aware of this strange, sweet, agitating position– the one unchangeable form of conjunction for the two mortal companions[b] who have to walk the ways of earth together. But his mind was pre-occupied with other thoughts than her, while hers were wholly bent upon him and his succour. It was dangerous for her, stealing her heart out of her breast in the interest, the sympathy, the close contact involved; but of none of these things was he aware in the pre-occupation of his thoughts.

They walked up and down for a time together, behind the house, along the broad walk, almost a terrace, of the kitchen garden, where there was a deep bor-der filled in summer with every kind of old-fashioned flowers. It was bare now, with naked fruit-trees against the wall, but the moon was hid in clouds, and it was impossible to see anything, except from the end of the terrace the little landing-place below, and the first curves of the walk leading up to the house, and all round the glimmer of the loch. The stillness had been broken by the sound of a boat, but it was on the Auchnasheen side, and though Oona strained her eyes she had not been able to see it, and concluded that, if coming to the isle at all, it must have touched the opposite point, where there was a less easy, but possible, landing-place. As they reached the end of the terrace, however, she was startled to see a figure detach itself from the gloom and walk slowly towards the house.

'The boat must have run in under the bushes, though I cannot see it,' she said; 'there is some one coming up the walk.'

Walter turned to look with momentary alarm, but presently calmed down. 'It is most likely old Symington, who takes a paternal charge of me,' he said.

Soon after they heard the steps, not heavy, but distinctly audible, crushing the gravel, and to Oona's great surprise, though Walter, a stranger to the place, took no notice of the fact, these footsteps, instead of going to the door, as would have been natural, came round the side of the house and approached the young pair in their walk. The person of the new-comer was quite unknown to Oona. He took off his hat with an air of well-bred courtesy – like a gentleman, not like a servant – and said –

'I am reluctant to interrupt such a meeting, but there is a boat below for Lord Erradeen.'

Walter started violently at the sound of the voice, which was, notwithstand-ing, agreeable and soft, though with a tone of command in it. He came to a sudden stop, and turned round quickly as if he could not believe his ears.

'There is a boat below,' the stranger repeated, 'and it is extremely cold; the men are freezing at their oars. They have not the same delightful inspiration as their master[c] – who forgets that he has business to settle this final night –'

*The Wizard's Son, Volume II*          153

Walter gave a strange cry, like the cry of a hunted creature. 'In God's name,' he exclaimed, 'what have you to do here?'

'My good fellow,' said the other, 'you need not try your hand at exorcising; others have made that attempt before you. Is Circe's island[9] shut to all footsteps save yours? But, even then, you could not shut out me. I must not say Armida's garden[10] in this state of the temperature –' he said.

'Who is it?' asked Oona in great alarm under her breath.

'Let me answer you,' the intruder said. 'It is a sort of a guardian who has the first right to Lord Erradeen's consideration. Love, as even the copybooks will tell, ought to be subordinate to duty.'

'Love!' cried Oona, starting from the young man's side. The indignant blood rushed to her face. She turned towards the house in sudden anger and shame and excitement. Circe! Armida! Was it she to whom he dared to apply these insulting names.

Walter caught her cloak with both hands.

'Do you not see,' he said, 'that he wants to take you from me, to drive you away, to have me at his mercy? Oona! you would not see a man drown and refuse to hold out your hand?'

'This is chivalrous,' said the stranger, 'to put a woman between you and that – which you are afraid to meet.'

To describe the state of excited feeling and emotion in which Oona listened to this dialogue, would be impossible. She was surprised beyond measure, yet, in the strange excitement of the encounter, could not take time to wonder or seek an explanation. She had to act in the mean time, whatever the explanation might be. Her heart clanged in her ears. Tenderness, pity, indignation, shame, thrilled through her. She had been insulted, she had been appealed to by the most sacred voice on earth–the voice of suffering. She stood for a moment looking at the two shadows before her, for they were little more.

'And if he is afraid why should not he turn to a woman?' she said with an impulse she could scarcely understand. 'If he is afraid, I am not afraid. This isle belongs to a woman. Come and tell her, if you will, what you want. Let my mother judge, who is the mistress of this place. Lord Erradeen has no right to break his word to her for any man: but if my mother decides that you have a better claim, he will go.'

'I will abide by every word she says,' Walter cried.

The stranger burst into a laugh.

'I am likely to put forth my claim before such a tribunal!' he said. 'Come, you have fought stoutly for your lover. Make a virtue of necessity now, and let him go.'

'He is not my lover,' cried Oona; 'but I will not let him go.' She added after a moment, with a sudden change of tone, coming to herself, and feeling the extraordinary character of the discussion. 'This is a very strange conversation to occur here. I think we are all out of our senses. It is like the theatre. I don't know your name, sir, but if you are Lord Erradeen's guardian, or a friend of his, I invite you to come and see my mother. Most likely,' she added, with a slight faltering, 'she will know you as she knows all the family.' Then, with an attempt at playfulness, 'If it is to be a struggle between this gentleman and the ladies of the isle, Lord Erradeen, tell him he must give way.'

The stranger took off his hat and made her a profound bow.

'I do so on the instant,' he said.

The two young people stood close together, their shadows confounded in one, and there did not seem time to draw a breath before they were alone, with no sound or trace remaining to prove that the discussion in which a moment before their hearts had been beating so loudly had ever existed at all. Oona looked after the stranger with a gasp. She clung to Walter, holding his arm tight.

'Where has he gone?' she cried in a piercing whisper. She trembled so after her boldness that she would have fallen but for his sustaining arm. 'Who is he? Where has he gone? That is not the way to the beach. Call after him, call after him, and tell him the way.'

Walter did not make any reply. He drew her arm closer threw[a] his, and turned with her towards the house. As for Oona, she seemed incapable of any thought but that this strange intruder might be left on the isle.

'He will get into the orchard and then among the rocks. He will lose himself,' she cried; 'he may fall[b] into the water. Call to him, Lord Erradeen – or stop, we will send Hamish. Here is Hamish. Oh, Hamish! the gentleman has taken the wrong way –'

'It will just be a boat that has come for my lord,' said Hamish. 'I tellt them my lord was biding all night, but nothing would satisfee them, but I had to come up and get his lordship's last word.'

'Oh, he is not going, Hamish! but there is a gentleman –'

Walter interrupted her with an abruptness that startled Oona.

'Let them see that every one is on board – and return at once,' he said.

'Oh there will just be everybody on board that ever was, for none has come ashore,' said Hamish. 'What was you saying about a gentleman, Miss Oona? There will be no gentleman. It is joost Duncan and another man with him, and they cried upon me, Hamish! and I answered them. But there will be no gentleman at all,' Hamish said.

# CHAPTER II.[c]

It was very dark upon Loch Houran that night. Whether nature was aware of a dark spirit, more subtle and more powerful than common man, roaming about in the darkness, temporarily baffled by agencies so simple that their potency almost amused while it confounded him – and shrank from the sight of him, who could tell? but it was dark, as a night in which there was a moon somewhere ought never to have been. The moon was on the wane, it was true, which is never like her earlier career, but all trace and influence of her were lost in the low-lying cloud, which descended from the sky like a hood, and wrapped everything in gloom. The water only seemed to throw a black glimmer into the invisible world where all things brooded in silence and cold, unseen, unmoving. The only thing that lived and shone in all this mysterious still universe was one warm window,[a] full of light, that shone from the isle. It was a superstition of the simple mistress of the house that there should be no shutter or curtain there, so that any late 'traveller by land or water' might be cheered by this token of life and possible help. Had that traveller, needing human succour, been led to claim shelter there, it would have been accorded fearlessly. 'Exceeding peace had made Ben Adhem bold.'[11] The little innocent household of defenceless women had not a fear. Hamish only, who perhaps felt a responsibility as their sole possible defender, might have received with suspicion such an unexpected guest.

The mysterious person already referred to – whose comings and goings were not as those of other men, and whose momentary discomfiture by such simple means perplexed yet partially amused him, as has been said, passed by that window at a later hour and stood for a moment outside. The thoughts with which, out of the external cold and darkness, which affected him not at all, he regarded the warm interior where simple human souls, sheltering themselves against the elements, gathered about their fire, were strange enough. The cold, which did not touch him, would have made them shiver; the dark, which to his eyes was as the day, would have confused their imaginations and discouraged their minds; and yet together by their fire they were beyond his power. He looked in upon their simplicity and calm and safety with that sense of the superiority of the innocent which at the most supreme moment will come in to dash all the triumphs of guile, and all the arts of the schemer. What he saw was the simplest cheerful scene, the fire blazing, the lamp burning steadily, a young man and a girl seated together, not in any tender or impassioned conjunction, but soberly discussing, calculating, arguing, thought to thought and face to face; the mother, on the other side, somewhat faded, smiling, not over wise, with her book, to which she paid little attention, looking up from time to time, and saying something far from clever. He might have gone in among them, and she would have received him with that same smile and offered him her best, thinking no evil. He had a thousand experiences of mankind, and knew how their minds could be worked upon and their imaginations inflamed, and their ambitions roused. Was he altogether baffled by this simplicity, or was there some lingering of human ruth in him, which kept him from carrying disturbance into so harmless a scene? or was it only to estimate those forces that he stood and watched them, with something to learn, even in his vast knowledge, from this unexpected escape of

156 *The Selected Works of Margaret Oliphant, Volume 21*

the fugitive, and the simple means by which he had been baffled for the moment, and his prey taken from him? For the moment! – that was all.

'Come, come now,' Mrs. Forrester said. 'You cannot argue away like that, and fight all night. You must make up your bits of differences, and settle what is to be done; for it is time we had the Books,[12] and let the women and Hamish get to their beds. They are about all day, and up early in the morning, not like us that sit with our hands before us. Oona, you must just cry upon Mysie, and let them all come ben. And if you will hand me the big Bible that is upon you table – since you are so kind, Lord Erradeen.'

At this simple ceremonial – the kindly servant-people streaming in, the hush upon their little concerns, the unison of voices, from Oona's, soft with youth and gentle breeding, to the rough bass of Hamish, in words that spectator knew as well as any – the same eyes looked on, with feelings we cannot attempt to fathom. Contempt, envy, the wonder of the wise over the everlasting, inexplicable superiority of the innocent, were these the sentiments with which he gazed? But in the night and silence there was no interpreter of these thoughts. How he came or went was his own secret. The window was closed soon after, the lights extinguished, and the darkness received this little community of the living and breathing, to keep them warm and unseen and unconscious till they should be claimed again by the cheerful day.

The household, however, though it presented an aspect of such gentle calm, was not in reality so undisturbed as it appeared. In Oona's chamber, for one, there was a tumult of new emotions which to the girl were incomprehensible, strange, and terrible, and sweet. Lord Erradeen was but a new acquaintance, she said to herself, as she sat over her fire, with everything hushed and silent about her; nevertheless the tumult of feeling in her heart was all connected with him. Curiously enough, the strange encounter in the garden–of which she had received no explanation–had disappeared from her thoughts altogether. The rise and sudden dawn of a new life in her own being was more near and momentous than any mysterious circumstances, however unlike the common. By-and-by[a] she might come to that–in the mean time a sentiment '*nova, sola, infinita*,'[13] occupied all her consciousness. She had known him during the last week only: three times in all, on three several days, had they met; but what a change these three days had made in the life that had been so free and so sweet, full of a hundred interests, without any that was exclusive and absorbing. In a moment, without knowing what was coming, she had been launched into this new world of existence. She was humbled to think of it, yet proud. She felt herself to have become a sort of shadow of him, watching his movements with an anxiety which was without any parallel in her experience, yet at the same time able to interpose for him, when he could not act for himself, to save him. It seemed to Oona suddenly, that everything else had slipped away from her, receding into the distance. The things that had occupied her before were now in the background. All the stage of life was filled with him, and the events of their brief intercourse had become the only occupation of her thoughts. She wondered and blushed as she wandered in that maze of recollections, at her own boldness in assuming the guidance of him; yet felt it to be inevitable – the only thing to be done. And the strange new thrill which ran through her veins when he had appealed to her, when he had implored her to stand by him, came back with an acute sweet mixture of pleasure and pain. She declared to herself, Yes! – with a swelling of her heart – she would stand by him, let it cost her what it might. There had been no love spoken or thought of between them. It was not love: what was it? Friendship, fraternity, the instinctive discovery of one by another, that divination which brings those together who can help each other. It was he, not she, who wanted help–what did it matter which it was? in giving or in receiving it was a new world. But whether it was a demon or an angel that had thus got entrance into that little home of peace and security – who could tell? Whatever it was, it was an inmate hitherto unknown, one that must work changes both in earth and Heaven.

Everything that could trouble or disturb had vanished from the dark world outside before Oona abandoned her musings – or rather before she felt the chill of the deep night round her, and twisted up her long hair, and drew aside the curtains from her window as was her custom that she might see the sky from her bed. There had been a change in the midnight hours. The clouds at last had opened, and in the chasm made by their withdrawal was the lamp of the waning moon 'lying on her back' with a sort of mystic disturbance and ominous clearness, as if she were lighting the steps of some evil enterprise, guiding a traitor or a murderer to the refuge of some one betrayed. Oona shivered as she took refuge in the snow-white nest which had never hitherto brought her anything but profound youthful repose, and the airy flitting dreams of a soul at rest. But though this momentary chill was impressed upon her senses, neither fear nor discouragement were in her soul. She closed her eyes only to see more clearly the face of this new influence in her life, to feel her pulses tingle as she remembered all the events of the three days' Odyssey,[14] the strange magical history that had sprung into being in a moment, yet was alive with such endless interest, and full of such a chain of incidents. What was to be the next chapter in it? Or was it to have another chapter? She felt already with a deep drawing of her breath, and warned herself that all would probably end here, and everything relapse into vacancy – a conclusion inconceivable, yet almost certain, she said to herself. But this consciousness only excited her the more. There was something in it of that whirl of desperation which gives a wild quickening to enjoyment in the sensation of momentariness and possible ending – the snatching of a fearful joy.

This sudden end came, however, sooner than she thought; they had scarcely met at the breakfast table when Lord Erradeen begged Mrs. Forrester to allow him to send for his servant, and make his arrangements for his departure from the isle, instead of returning to Auchnasheen. 'I have not felt safe or at ease, save here, since I came to the loch,' he said, looking round him with a grateful sense of the cheerful quiet and security. His eyes met those of Oona, who was somewhat pale after her long vigil and broken rest. She had recognised at once with a pang the conclusion she had foreseen, the interruption of her new history which was implied in the remorseless unintentional abruptness of this announcement. He was going away; and neither felt any inducement to stay, nor any hesitation in announcing his resolution. She had known it would be so, and yet there was a curious pang of surprise in it which seemed to arrest her heart. Notwithstanding, as in duty bound, she met his look with a smile in her eyes.[a]

'Hoots,' said Mrs. Forrester, 'you flatter the isle, Lord Erradeen. We know that is just nonsense; but for all that, we take it kind that you should like our little house. It will always be found here, just faithful and friendly, whenever you come back. And certainly ye shall send for your man or make what arrangements suits you. There's the library quite free and at your service for any writing you may have to do, and Hamish will take any message to Auchnasheen, or wherever you please. The only thing that grieves me is that you should be so set on going to-day.'

'That must be – that must be!' cried Walter: and then he began to make excuses and apologies. There were circumstances which made it indispensable – there were many things that made him anxious to leave Auchnasheen. No, it was not damp – which was the instant suggestion of Mrs. Forrester. There were other things. He was going back to Sloebury to his mother (Mrs. Forrester said to England), and it was so recently that he had entered upon his property, that there was still a great deal to do. After he had made this uncompromising statement of the necessities that he had to be guided by, he looked across the table at Oona once more.

'And Miss Forrester is so kind as to take in hand for me the settlement of the cotters.[b] It will be her doing. I hope they will not blame me for that alarm yesterday, which was no fault of mine; but the new arrangement will be your doing altogether.'

'I shall not take the credit,' said Oona. 'I had not even the boldness to suggest it. It was your own thought, and they will bless you so, that wherever you are, at Sloebury or the end of the world, you must feel your heart warm –'

She said this with great self-command; but she was pale, and there was a curious giddiness stealing over her. She seemed to feel the solid ground slip away from under her feet.

'My heart,' he said, looking at her with a grateful look, 'will always be warm when I think of the Isle, and all that has been done for me here.'

'Now, Lord Erradeen,' said Mrs. Forrester, 'you will just make Oona and me vain with all these bonnie speeches. We are always glad to be friendly and neighbourlike, but what have we been able to do? – just nothing. When you come back again and let your friends see a little more of you, we will all do what we can to make the loch agreeable. But I hope it will be warmer weather, and more pleasure in moving about. You will be back no doubt, if not sooner, in time for the grouse?'[15c]

*The Wizard's Son, Volume II*                    159

He grew pale in spite of himself, and Oona, looking at him, felt the steady earth slip more and more away.

'I don't know,' he said, hurriedly, 'when I may come back – not before I – not sooner than I can – I mean there are a great many things to look after; and my mother –'

His eyes seemed to seek hers again as if asking her sympathy, and appealing to her knowledge. 'Not before I must – not sooner than I can help,' that was what he meant to say. Oona gave him a faint smile of response. It was so wonderful that when she understood him so completely, he should understand her so little, and never suspect that there was anything cruel in those words. But she made the response he required, and strengthened him by that instinctive comprehension of him in which he put so strange a trust. There was an eagerness in all his preparations for going away which he almost forced upon her notice, so strong was his confidence in her sympathy. He lost no time about any of these arrangements, but sent Hamish with his boat to Auchnasheen for Symington, and wrote down his instructions for Shaw, and talked of what he was going to do when he got 'home,' with the most absolute insensibility to any feeling in the matter save his own. And it seemed to Oona that the moments flew, and the quick morning melted away, and before she could collect her thoughts the time came when her mother and she walked down to the beach with him, smiling, to see him off. There had never been a word said between them of that conversation in the garden on the previous night. Only when he was just about to leave, he cast a glance towards the walk where that encounter had taken place, and turned to her with a look such as cannot pass between any but those that have some secret link of mutual knowledge. Her mother was talking cheerfully of the view and the fine morning after the rain, walking before them, when, he gave Oona that look of mutual understanding. 'I owe you everything,' he said, in a low tone of almost passionate fervour. Presently she found herself shaking hands with him as if he had been nothing more than the acquaintance of three days which he was, and wishing him a good journey. And so the Odyssey came to an end, and the history stopped in the course of making. She stood still for a little, watching the boat and the widening lines it drew along the surface of the water. 'Sometimes to watch a boat moving off will give you a giddiness,' Mrs. Forrester said.

# CHAPTER III.[a]

THERE could be no greater contrast than that which existed between Walter Methven, Lord Erradeen, hurrying away with the sense of a man escaped with his life from the shores of Loch Houran, and Oona Forrester left behind upon the isle.

It was not only that he had all at once become the first object in her life, and she counted for little or nothing in his. That was not the question. She had been for sufficient space of time, and with sufficient stress of circumstances to make the impression one which would not die easily, of the first importance in his thoughts: and no doubt that impression would revive when he had leisure from the overwhelming pre-occupation which was in his mind. But it was that he was himself full of an anxiety and excitement strong enough to dwarf every other feeling, which made the blood course through his veins, and inspired every thought; while she was left in a state more like vacancy than anything else, emptied out of everything that had interested her. The vigorous bend of the rowers to the oars as they carried him away was not more unlike the regretful languor of the women as they stood on the beach, Mrs. Forrester waving her handkerchief, but Oona without even impulse enough in her to do that.

As for Walter, he was all energy and impulse. He arranged the portmanteaux which Symington had brought with his own hands, to leave room for the sweep of the oars, and quicken the crossing. His farewells were but half said. It seemed as if he could scarcely breathe till he got away. Every stroke of the oars lightened his heart, and when he was clear of that tragic water altogether, and sprang up upon the rude country waggonette which had been engaged at the inn to carry him to the station, his brow relaxed, and the muscles of his mouth gave way as they had not done since his first day on Loch Houran. He gave a look almost of hatred at the old castle, and then averted his face. When he reached the railway, the means of communication with the world he had known before, he was a different man. The horses had gone too slowly for him, so did the leisurely friendly trains on the Highland railway,[16] with their broad large windows for the sake of the views. Travellers, as a rule, did not wish to go too fast while they skirted those gleaming lochs, and ran along under shadow of the mountains: they liked to have somebody to point out which was Loch Ool and which St. Monan's.[17] It was too slow for Lord Erradeen, but still it was going away. He began to think of all the commonplace accessories of life with a sort of enthusiasm–the great railway stations, the Edinburgh Hotel, with its ordinary guests. He was so sick of everything connected with his Highland property and with its history, that he resolved he would make no pause in Edinburgh, and would not go near Mr. Milnathort. The questions they would no doubt put to him made him impatient even in thought. He would not subject himself to these; he would put away altogether out of his mind, if he could, everything connected with it, and all that he had been seeing and hearing, or, at least, had fancied he heard and saw.

But when Oona turned away from looking after the boat – which she was indeed the first to do, Mrs. Forrester waiting almost as long as it was within sight to wave her handkerchief if the departing guest should look back – she felt herself and her life emptied out all at once. When she began to think of it in the cold light of this sudden conclusion, a sense of humiliation came over her. She blushed with hot shame at this altogether unasked, unreasonable, unnecessary resignation of herself and her interests to a stranger. He was nothing but a stranger, she said to herself; there was no remarkable charm in him one way or another. She had not been at all affected by his first appearance. He was not handsome enough or clever enough, nor had he any special attraction to gain him so high a place. Somehow she had not thought of Walter in her first realisation of the new interest which had pushed away all the other occupations out of her existence: and she had not blushed in the high sense of expanded life and power to help. But now it moved her with a certain shame to think that the sudden departure of a man whom she scarcely knew, and to whom she was nothing, should thus have emptied out her existence and left a bewildering blank in her heart. She went slowly up the walk, and went to her room, and there sat down with a curious self-abandonment. It was all over, all ended and done. When he came into her life it was accidentally, without any purpose in it on either side; and now that he had gone out of it again, there was no anger, no sense of wrong, only a curious consciousness that everything had gone away–that the soil had slipped from her, and nothing was left. No, there was no reason at all to be angry–nobody was to blame. Then she laughed a little at herself at this curious, wanton sort of trouble[a] intended by nobody – which neither he had meant to draw her into, nor she to bring upon herself.

There was one thing however between her and this vacancy. He had left her a commission which any kind-hearted girl would have thought a delightful one – to arrange with the factor how the cotters[b] were to be most effectually helped and provided for. It had been their thought at first – the young man being little better instructed than the girl on such matters – that to make Duncan Fraser and the rest the proprietors of their little holdings would be the most effectual way of helping them, and would do the property of Lord Erradeen very little harm – a thing that Walter, unaccustomed to property, and still holding it lightly, contemplated with all the ease of the landless, never thinking of the thorn in the flesh of a piece of alienated land in the midst of an estate, until it suddenly flashed upon him that his estates being all entailed,[18] this step would be impossible. How was it to be done then? They had decided that Shaw would know best, and that some way of remitting the rents at least during the lifetime of the present Lord Erradeen must be settled upon, and secured to them at once. Oona had this commission left in her hands. She could have thought of none more delightful a few days ago, but now it seemed to make the future vacancy of life all the more evident by the fact that here was one thing, and only one, before her to do. When that was done, what would happen? – a return upon the pleasant occupations, the amusements, the hundred little incidents which had filled the past? After all, the past was only a week back. Can it ever return, and things be again as they were before? – Oona had never reasoned or speculated on these matters till this moment. She had

162        *The Selected Works of Margaret Oliphant, Volume 21*

never known by experiment that the past cannot return, or that which has been be once more; but she became aware of it in a moment now.

Then she got up and stood at her window and looked out on the unchanging landscape, and laughed aloud at herself. How ridiculous it was! By this time it made no difference to Lord Erradeen that she had ever existed. Why should it make any difference to her that he had come and gone? The new generation takes a view of such matters which is different from the old-fashioned sentimental view. After yielding to the new influence rashly, unawares, like a romantic girl of any benighted century, Oona began to examine it like an enlightened young intelligence of her own. Her spirit rose against it, and that vigorous quality which we call a sense of humour. There was something almost ludicrous in the thought that one intelligent creature should be thus subject to another, and that life itself should be altered by an accidental meeting. And if this was absurd to think of in any case, how much more in her own? Nobody had ever had a more pleasant, happy life. In her perfect womanliness and submission to all the laws of nature, she was yet as independent as the most free-born soul could desire. There was no path in all the district, whether it led to the loneliest cottage or the millionnaire's palace, that was not free to Oona Forrester. The loch and the hills were open to her as her mother's garden, to the perfectly dauntless, modest creature, who had never in her life heard a tone or caught a look of disrespect. She went her mother's errands, which were so often errands of charity, far and near, with companions when she cared for them, without companions when she did not. What did it matter? The old cotter[a] people about had a pretty Gaelic name for her; and to all the young ones Miss Oona of the Isle was as who should say Princess Oona, a young lady whom every one was bound to forward upon her way. Her mother was not so clever as Oona, which was, perhaps, a drawback; but she could not have been more kind, more tender, more loving if she had possessed, as our Laureate says, 'the soul of Shakespeare.'[19] All was well about and around this favourite of nature. How was it possible then that she could have come to any permanent harm in two or three days?

Notwithstanding this philosophical view, however, Oona did nothing all that day, and to tell the truth felt little except the sense of vacancy; but next day she announced to her mother that she was going to the Manse to consult with Mr. Cameron about the Truach-Glas cotters,[b] and that probably she would see Mr. Shaw there, and be able to do the business Lord Erradeen had confided to her. Mrs. Forrester fully approved.

'A thing that is to make poor folk more comfortable should never be put off a moment,' that kind woman said, 'for, poor bodies, they have little enough comfort at the best,' and she stood at the porch and waved her hand to her child, as the boat sped out of the shade of the isle into the cold sunshine which had triumphed for an hour or two over the clouds and rain. Oona found Mr. Shaw, as she had anticipated, in the village, and there was a very brisk and not altogether peaceable discussion in the minister's study, over this new idea. The factor, though he was so strongly set against all severe measures, and in reality so much on the side of the cotters,[a] was yet taken aback, as was natural, by the new idea presented to him. He laughed at the notion of making them the owners of their little holdings.

'Why not give Tom Patterson his farm too? He finds it just as hard to pay the rent,' he cried in mingled ridicule and wrath. 'There is no difference in the principle though there may be in the circumstances. And what if Lord Erradeen had a few hundred crofters instead of half-a-dozen? I'm speaking of the principle. Of course he cannot do it. It's all entailed, every inch of the land, and he cannot do it; but supposing he could, and that he were treating them all equally? It's just not to be done. It is just shifting the difficulty. It is putting other people at a disadvantage. A man cannot give away his land and his living. It is just a thing that is not to be done.'

'He knows it is not to be done; he knows it is entailed, therefore –'

'Oh yes, Miss Oona; therefore –' cried the factor. 'Little of it, very little,[b] would have come his way if it had not been entailed. Whether or not it is good for the country, there can be no doubt it's the stronghold of a family. Very likely there would have been no Methvens (and small damage, begging his pardon that is a kind of a new stock), and certainly there would have been no property to keep up a title, but for the entail. It is a strange story, the story of them altogether.' Shaw continued, 'it[c] has been a wonderfully managed property. I must say that for it; no praise to me, so I am free to speak. There was the late lord – the only one I knew. There was very little in him, and yet the way he managed was wonderful; they have just added land to land, and farm to farm. I do not understand it. And now I suppose we've arrived at the prodigal that always appears some time in a family to make the hoards go.'

'No, no,' said the minister, 'you must not call the man a prodigal whose wish is to give to the poor.'

'That is all very well,' said Shaw; 'the poor, where there are half-a-dozen of them, are easily enough managed. Give them their land if you like (if it was not criminal to cut a slice out of an estate), it does not matter much; but if there were a hundred? It is the principle I am thinking of. They cannot buy it themselves, and the State will not buy it for them, seeing they are only decent Scots lads, not blazing Irishmen.[20] I cannot see where the principle will lead to: I am not against the kindness, Miss Oona, far from that: and these half-a-dozen Frasers, what would it matter? but if there were a hundred?[d] The land is just my profession, as the Church is Mr. Cameron's, and I must think of it, all the ways of it; and this is a thing that would not work so far as I can see.'

'But Lord Erradeen acknowledges that,' said Oona. 'What he wants to do is only for his time. To set them free of the rent they cannot pay, and to let them feel that nobody can touch them, so long as he lives –'

164     *The Selected Works of Margaret Oliphant, Volume 21*

'And the Lord grant him wealth of days,' said the minister; 'a long life and a happy one!'

'You will not look at it,' cried the factor, 'from a common-sense point of view. All that is very pretty, and pleasing to the young man's – what shall I call it? – his kindness and his vanity, for both are involved, no doubt. But it will just debauch the minds of the people. They will learn to think they have a right to it; and when the next heir comes into possession, there will be a burning question raised up, and a bitter sense of wrong if he asks for his own again. Oh yes, Miss Oona, so long as the present condition of affairs lasts it will be their own. A man with a rent of two or three pounds is just as liable as if it were two or three hundred. The principle is the same; and as I am saying, if there were a number of them, you just could not do it: for I suppose you are not a communist,[21] Miss Oona, that would do away with property altogether?'

A sudden smile from among the clouds lit up Shaw's ruddy, remonstrative countenance, as he put this question, and Oona smiled too.

'I don't make any theories,' she said; 'I don't understand it. I feel as Lord Erradeen does, that whatever the law may be, I would rather be without a roof to shelter myself than turn one poor creature out of her home. Oh, I don't wonder when I remember the horror in his face! Think! could you sleep, could you rest – you, young and strong, and well off, when you had turned out the poor folk to the hill? – all for a little miserable money?' cried Oona, starting to her feet, 'or for the principle, as you call it? I, for one,' cried the girl, with flashing eyes, 'would never have let him speak to me again.'

'There you have it, Oona; there's a principle, if you like; there is something that will work,' cried the old minister, with a tremulous burst of laughter. 'Just you keep by that, my bonnie dear, and all your kind; and we'll hear of few evictions within the Highland line.'

'That would be all very well,' said the factor, 'if every landlord was a young lad, like Lord Erradeen; but even then it might be a hard case, and Miss Oona would not find it as easy as she thinks; for supposing there were hundreds, as I'm always saying: and supposing there were some among them that could just pay well enough, but took advantage; and supposing a landlord that was poor too, and was losing everything? No, no, Miss Oona, in this world things are not so simple. My counsel is to let them be—just to let them be. I would bid them pay when they can, and that my lord would not be hard upon them. That is what I would do. I would tell them he was willing to wait, and may be to forgive them what was past, or something like that. After what happened the other day, they will be very sure he will not be hard upon them. And that is what I would advise him to do.'

'You are not going to wash your hands of it, after all?' the minister said.

Shaw laughed. 'Not just this time, Mr. Cameron. I always thought he was a fine lad. And now that he has good advisers, and amenable –' he added, with a glance at Oona, which fortunately she did not see.[a] And after this interview she

*The Wizard's Son, Volume II*  165

went home, very silent, depressed as she had no right to be, feeling as if life was over, and all things come to an end.[a]

\*\*\*

# CHAPTER IV.[b]

IT would be difficult to describe the sensations with which Lord Erradeen found himself set at liberty, and on his way back, as he thought at first, to the easy mind, the quiet life, the undisturbed and undisturbing circumstances of his previous existence. He scarcely seemed to breathe till he had crossed the Border, and was outside of Scotland, feeling during that time like a fugitive in full flight, incapable of thinking of anything except that he had eluded his pursuers and had escaped all possible risks and apprehensions. His trial had lasted nights and days, he could not tell how many. Now for the first time he had the calm, the leisure, the sense of safety, which were necessary for a review of all that he had gone through: he had seen the moon light up the pale line of the sea at Berwick, where Tweed falls into the waste of water, and the lights of Newcastle, turning into a shining highway the dark crescent of the Tyne, and then as the train pounded along through the darkness, with the throb and swing of life and speed, through the silence and night, his faculties seemed to come back to him, and his judgment to be restored. Through what a strange episode of existence had he passed since he saw the lights curve round the sides of that river, and the great bridge striding over above the roofs of the sleeping town! And now he had escaped–had he escaped? He had time at least and quiet to think it all out and see where he stood.

He had been for nearly three weeks altogether on Loch Houran, during which time he had gone through the severest mental struggle he had ever known. It seemed years to him now since the moment when he had been suddenly confronted by the strange and mysterious personage who had assumed a tone towards him and claimed a submission which Walter had refused to yield. That this man's appearance had awakened in him a sensation of overwhelming excitement mingled with fear, that he had come in an unaccountable way, that he had been seen apparently by no one in the old castle but himself, that nobody had betrayed any consciousness of knowing who he was or how he was there, and yet that he had come and gone with a perfect acquaintance and familiarity with the place, the family, the estates, the story of the race; these were details which, with a tremulous sensation in his mind, as of a panic nearly over, he gathered together to examine and find out, if possible, what they meant. He had been unable during the time that followed, when he had taken refuge in Auchnasheen, to exercise any discriminating faculty, or use his own judgment upon these facts. At the moment of seeing and hearing occurrences which disturb the mind, reason is hampered in its action. Afterwards you may ask yourself, have

166        *The Selected Works of Margaret Oliphant, Volume 21*

you really heard and seen? but not when a definite appearance is before your eyes, or likely to re-appear at any moment, and a distinct voice in your ears. The actual then over-masters the soul; the meaning of it must be got at later. He had seen this man whose faculties and pretensions were alike so extraordinary, he had listened to the claim he made, he had been bidden to yield up his individual will and to obey under threatening of evil if he refused, and promises of pleasure and comfort if he consented. And Walter had said 'No.' He would have said No had an angel out of heaven appeared before him, making the same demand. He had been subjected to this strange trial at the very height of independence and conscious power, when he had newly begun to feel his own importance, and to enjoy its advantages. It had seemed to him absurd, incredible,[a] that such a claim should be made, even while the personality of the strange claimant had filled him with a sensation of terror, which he summoned all his forces to struggle against, without any success. He had been like two men during that struggle. One a craven, eager to fly, willing to promise anything might he but escape; the other struggling passionately against the stranger and refusing–refusing, night and day. When he went to Auchnasheen the character of the conflict within him had become more remarkable still. The man who claimed his obedience was no longer visible, but he had been rent asunder between the power of his own resisting spirit and some strange influence which never slackened, which seemed to draw him towards one point with a force which his unwillingness to yield made into absolute agony. Still he had resisted, always resisted, though without strength to escape, until the moment had come when by sudden inspiration of natural justice and pity he had broken loose–by that, and by the second soul struggling in him and with him, by Oona's hand holding him and her heart sustaining him. This was the history of these two tremendous weeks, the most eventful in his life. And now he had escaped out of the neighbourhood in which he could feel no safety, out of the influence which had moved him so strangely, and was able to think and ask himself what it was.

The night was dark, and, as has been said, the moon was on the wane. She shed a pale mist of light over the dark country, where now and then there broke out the red glow of pit or furnace fires. The train swung onwards with a rock of movement, a ploughing and plunging, the dim light in the roof swaying, the two respectable fellow-passengers each in his corner amidst his wraps, slumbering uneasily. Walter had no inclination to sleep. He was indeed feverishly awake; all his faculties in wild activity; his mind intensely conscious and living. What did it all mean? The events which had affected him to a passionate height of feeling with which his previous life had been entirely unacquainted – was it possible that there was any other way of accounting for them? To look himself in the face as it were, and confess now at a distance from these influences that the man to whom he had spoken in the language of to-day was one of the fabulous men in whom the ignorant believe, his own early ancestor–the still existing, undying founder of the house, was, he said to himself, impossible. It could not be; anything else – any hypothesis was more credible than this. There was no place for the supernatural in the logic of life as he had learned it. Now that he had recovered control of himself, it was time for him to endeavour to make out a reason for the hallucination in which he had almost lost himself and his sober senses. And accordingly he began to do it; and this is what he said to himself. His imagination had been excited by all that had happened to him; the extraordinary change in his circumstances which seemed almost miraculous, and then the succession of incidents, the strange half-communications that had been made to him, the old, ruinous house in which he had been compelled to shut himself up, the wonderful solitude, full of superstitious suggestions, into which he had been plunged. All these details had prepared his mind for something – he knew not what. He felt a hot flush of shame and mortification come over him as he remembered how easily, notwithstanding all his better knowledge, he, a man of his century, acquainted with all the philosophies of the day, had been overcome by those influences. He had expected something out of nature, something terrible and wonderful. And when such a state of mind is reached, it is certain (he thought) that something will arise to take advantage of it.[a]

Probably all these effects had been calculated upon by the individual, whoever he was, who haunted Kinloch Houran to excite and exploit these terrors. Who was he? Even now, so far out of his reach, so emancipated from his influence that he could question and examine it, Walter felt a certain giddiness come over his spirit at this thought, and was glad that one of his fellow-passengers stirred and woke, and made a shivering remark, How cold it was, before he again composed himself to sleep. It was very cold. There was an icy chill in the air which penetrated through the closed windows. But nothing else could come in – nothing else! and it could be but a sudden reflection from his past excitement that made Walter feel for a moment as if another figure sat opposite to him, gazing at him with calm sarcasm, and eyes that had a smile in them. When the giddiness passed off, and he looked again, there was (of course) no one opposite to him, only the dark blue cushions of the unoccupied place. Who was this man then who held a sort of court in Kinloch Houran, and demanded obedience from its proprietor? He was no creature of the imagination. Excited nerves and shaken health might indeed have prepared the mind of the visitor for the effect intended to be produced upon him; but they could not have created the central figure – the powerful personality from whom such influence flowed. Who was he? The circumstances were all favourable for a successful imposture, or even a mystification. Suppose it to be some member of the family aggrieved by the promotion of a far-off branch, some dependent with so much knowledge of the secrets of the race as to be able to play upon the imagination of a novice, with mysterious threats and promises; perhaps, who could tell, a monomaniac,[22] the leading idea of whose delusion was to take this character upon him? Walter's breast lightened a little as he made out one by one these links of explanation. It was characteristic of his time, and the liberality of mind[23] with which modern thought abjures the idea of absolute imposture, that the sudden suggestion of a monomaniac gave him great relief and comfort. That might explain all – a man of superior powers crazed in this one point,[a] who might have convinced himself that he was the person he claimed to be, and that it was the interest of the family he had at heart. Such a being, acquainted with all the mysterious passages and hiding-places[b] that exist in such old houses, able to appear suddenly from a secret door or sliding panel, to choose moments when nature herself added to the sense of mystery, hours of twilight and darkness when the half-seen is more alarming than anything fully revealed – this would explain so much, that the young man for the moment drew a long breath of relief, and felt half-consciously that he could afford to ignore the rest.

And in the sense of this relief he fell asleep, and dreamed that he stood again at Mrs. Forrester's door in the Isle, and saw the light on the old tower of Kinloch Houran, and felt the attraction, the drawing and dragging as of some force he could not resist; and woke up with the blow he gave himself against the rail that supported the netting on the opposite side of the carriage, against which he struck his head in his rush towards the place to which he had felt himself called. He staggered back into his seat, giddy and faint, yet thankful to feel that it was only a dream; and then had to begin his self-arguments over again, and trace once more every link of the chain.

A monomaniac – yes, that might be the explanation; but whence then that power which drew him, which he had fought against with all the powers of his being at Auchnasheen, which he had never given in to, but which, even in the reflection of it given in his dream, was vivid enough to awaken him to a new branch of the question? Magnetism, mesmerism,[24] he had heard of, and scorned as other names for charlatanism; but when you are searching anxiously for the means of accounting for mysterious phenomena you are glad to seize upon explanations that at another moment would be little satisfactory. Walter said to himself that the madman of Kinloch Houran – the monomaniac, must possess these strange powers. He might know many secrets, though his wits were gone astray. He might be sane enough to have a purpose, and to cultivate every possible means of affecting the mind he wished to work upon. Such curious combinations of madness and wisdom were not beyond human experience. Perhaps at the end of all his arguments, having fully convinced himself, the thread of the reasoning escaped him, for he suddenly shuddered and grew pale, and shrank into his corner, drawing his wraps close round him and raising the collar of his coat to his very eyes, as if to shut out some bewildering, overwhelming sight. But by this time the wintry day was breaking, and the stir of awakened life reached the other travellers, who woke and stretched themselves, shivering in the chill of the dawn, and

*The Wizard's Son, Volume II*     169

began to prepare for their arrival. One of them spoke to Walter, expressing a fear that he was ill, he looked so pale, and offering his services to 'see him home.' The young man indeed felt as if he had come through a long illness when he stepped forth upon the platform at King's Cross,[25] and felt that he had escaped from his fever and his trouble, and had new ways and new thoughts – or rather the repose of old thoughts and old ways – before him for some time to come.

He remained in London all day, and after his bath and his breakfast, felt the rising of a new life, and began to remember all the good things which he had partially forgotten, but which surely were more than enough to counterbalance the evil things, of which, when you set your mind to it, after all, so feasible an explanation could be found. London was at its darkest, and nothing invited him in the foggy and murky streets; nevertheless he lingered with that mixture of old habit and mental indolence which wastes so much time and disperses so many admirable resolutions. He went in the morning to see the house which belonged to him in Park Lane,[26] and which was at present empty. It was one of those which look out from pleasant, large bow-windows upon the brightness of the Park and the cheerful thoroughfare. Even at such a moment it had a kind of brightness – as much light as could be got in London. It gave Walter a real pleasure to think of furnishing it for his mother, of seeing her take her place there and enter upon a larger life, a mode of existence for which he felt – with a glow of pride in her – she was more qualified than for the smaller village routine at Sloebury. His energy even went so far as to direct that the house should be put in order and prepared for occupation. And if he had gone home at once after this feat, not all the threatenings of his mysterious enemy would have prevented a pleasant re-beginning of his old life.[a]

But he did not; he lingered about the streets, about the hotel to which he had gone in the morning, for no particular reason, and it was late when he started for Sloebury – late and dark and cold, and his sleepless night and all the excitements from which he had fled, began to tell upon him. When he reached the familiar station his cheerfulness and good-humour had fled. And all the pleasant anticipations of the home-coming and the comfort with which he had remembered that existence, free of all mystery, in which he had seldom done anything but what seemed good in his own eyes, abandoned him as he stepped into the drizzle of a dark and rainy December night, into the poor and badly-lighted streets that surround a railway everywhere, and turn the worst side of every town[27] to the eyes of strangers. He sent Symington and his baggage off before him, and himself set out to walk, with that incomprehensible pleasure in a little further delay which is so general. Stepping out into the mean streets had all the effect upon Walter's tired frame and capricious and impatient mind, of sudden disenchantment. His imagination perhaps had been affected by the larger atmosphere from which he had come, and he had forgotten the dinginess and poverty, which never before had struck him with the same force. The damp drizzle which was all there was for air, seemed to suffocate him; the pavement was wet and muddy, dirt and wretchedness pervaded everything. Then he began to realise, as he walked, the scene he was going to, which he could call up before him with such perfect distinctness of memory. Home! It used to be the centre, in books, of all pleasant thoughts – the tired wanderer coming to rest and shelter, the prodigal out of hunger and misery to forgiveness and the fatted calf,[28] the 'war-beaten soldier'[29] from his cold sentry's march, the sailor from the wet shrouds and gloomy seas – to good fires and welcomes, kisses and a hot supper. But that primitive symbol of imagination, like so many others, has got perhaps somewhat soiled with ignoble use;[30] and it never was, perhaps, from this point of view that young men of Walter Methven's type regarded the centre of family life, to which they returned when there was nothing better to do, with a sort of penitential sense of the duties that were considered binding there, and the preposterous things that would be expected of them.

Lord Erradeen, who had been longing for that safe and sensible refuge where no exaggeration or superstition prevailed, suddenly felt it rise before him like a picture of still life as he walked towards it. His mother seated knitting at one side of the fire, with a preoccupied look, listening for his step outside, the evening newspaper and a novel from Mudie's[31] on the table. Miss Merivale opposite working crewel work,[32] and putting a question now and then as to when he was expected: the two lamps burning steadily, the tick of the clock in the foreground, so to speak, the soul of the silent scene. The other accessories of the piece were all conventional ones: fire blazing brightly, now and then breaking into the monologue of the clock with a sudden rush and jet of flame, or dropping of ashes; curtains drawn, sofas and chairs within the glow of the warmth, ready for the new-comer's choice. There would be a sudden springing up, a disturbance of the perfect order of all these arrangements, on his entrance. He would be made to sit down in far too warm a corner; his personal appearance would be commented upon; that he was looking well, or ill, or tired, or as fresh as possible. And then the cross-examination would begin. Walter reminded himself that this cross-examination was maddening, and that even as a boy at school he had never been able to bear it. When he had said that he was well, and consented, yes, that he had come home sooner than he expected, but no, that nothing was wrong, what was there more to say? To be sure he had intended to say a great deal more, to pour forth all his troubles into his mother's sympathetic bosom; but that in any case could only have been when the two were alone. And would she understand him if he did so? Cousin Sophy – he could hear her in imagination – would give a sharp shriek of laughter at the idea of anything mysterious, at any suggestion of the supernatural (in which, of course, by this time Walter did not believe himself, but that was another matter). She would shriek even derisively at the idea that mesmerism could have affected any man in his senses. And his mother – what would she do? not shriek with laughter, that was not her way; but smile perhaps with a doubtful look to see whether it was possible that he could be in earnest in this incredible story of his. No, she would not believe him, she would think he was under the influence of some hallucination. She would look at him with a shock of something like contempt, an annoyed dismay that *her* son should be so credulous,[a] or so weak. Walter's imagination leaped back to the other warm and softly-lighted room on the Isle, the innocent mother talking, who would have believed everything, the girl standing by who did understand, and that almost without a word. Ah, if that indeed were home! Thus with a sudden revulsion in his mind, shutting himself up, and double-locking the door of his heart, even before he had come to the door of the house, to which his mother, he knew, would rush to meet him, hearing and distinguishing his step – he went home.

Mrs. Methven, who had been on the watch all day, opened the door to him as he foresaw. She was trembling with anxiety and pleasure, yet self-restrained and anxious not to betray the excitement which probably he would think uncalled for; she took his wraps from him, and helped to take off his great-coat, giving an aid which was quite unnecessary, but which he, on his side commanding himself also, did his best to accept with an appearance of pleasure. 'You have not dined,' she said, 'there is something just ready. We waited half an hour, but I thought you would prefer to come by this train. Come in and get thawed, and let me look at you, while they bring up your dinner.' She took him by the arm as she spoke, and led him into the drawing-room where everything was exactly as he had imagined. And she drew him, as he had imagined, too close to the fire, and drawing the softest chair, said 'Sit down, dear, and get warm.'

'I am not a bit cold. I have walked, you know, from the station. How do you do, Cousin Sophy? Your room is too warm, mother, I always tell you so. However it looks very cheerful after the wet and mud outside,' he said, with an attempt to be gracious.

'The rain makes everything dismal out of doors. Has it been raining all the way? You have had a dreadful journey, my poor boy.'

'Of course it is warmer here than in Scotland,' said Miss Merivale.

And then there was a pause, and his mother looked at him more closely by the light of the lamp. She was just going to say 'You are not looking very well' – when Walter broke in.

'I hear a tray coming, and I am very hungry. I shall go into the dining-room, mother, and join you by-and-by.'[b]

'I will go too and wait upon you, Walter. I mean to wait upon you myself to-night. I hope your lordship has not grown too fine for that,' she said with an attempt at playful ease. It was a relief to leave Miss Merivale, and have her son all to herself. She put his chair to the table for him, and brought the claret which had been warming, and handed him his plate with a smile of content. 'It is pleas-

172     *The Selected Works of Margaret Oliphant, Volume 21*

ant to serve one's boy,' she said, 'and we don't want any third person. I have so much to hear, and to ask –'

An impatient prayer that she would not begin the moment he sat down to worry a fellow with questions was on Walter's lips; but he forbore, doing his very best to command himself. To sit in his old place, to feel his old impulse, to find the claret too warm, and the potatoes cold, was almost too much for him; but still like a hero he forbore. And she took advantage of his magnanimity. She never relaxed her watch upon him. That is the penalty one pays for having one's mother to serve one: a servant is silent at least. She asked him if he would not have a little more, just this little piece which was very nicely done? Some of the vegetables which were better cooked than usual? A little salad? Some stewed fruit with that Devonshire cream[33] which he used to like? A little of his favourite cheese? She was not in general a fussy woman, but she was so anxious, after the *rapprochement*[34] that had taken place on the eve of his going away, to please him, to preserve that tenderer strain of feeling – if it could be done this way! And yet all the time she was restraining herself not to say too much, not to worry him. A woman has to exercise such wiles often enough for her husband's benefit; but it is hard to go through the process again for her son.

He bore it all with a devouring impatience, yet self-restraint too – not entreating her in words to let him alone for heaven's sake! as he would so fain have done. Perhaps there was something to be said on his side also; his mind was laden with care and anxiety, and wanted repose above all; and this wistful over-anxiety and desire to propitiate by details was irritating beyond description. He did not know how to put up with it. Love itself is sometimes very hard to put up with – embarrassing, officious, not capable of perceiving that to let its object alone is the best. Mrs. Methven did not know how to propitiate him – whether to show her interest or to put on a form of indifference. All her urgency about his dinner, was it not to spare him the questions which she knew he did not love? But that succeeded badly, and her curiosity, or rather her anxiety, was great.

'How did you like Kinloch Houran?' she ventured to say at last. What a question! It seemed to Walter that a glance at his face would have shown her how inappropriate it was.

'Like Kinloch Houran!' he said. 'If you want a categorical answer, mother – and I know you are never satisfied with anything else – not at all!'

'I am sorry for that, Walter, since it seems a place you must have a great deal to do with. Auchnasheen, then, was that better? You must teach me to pronounce the name.'

'Auchnasheen, if possible, was worse,' he said. 'I shall never be able to endure either the one or the other, or forget the associations – don't[a] make me think of them, please. When I got home I thought I should be able to escape all that.'

'My dear, I beg your pardon: I did not know. Was the weather then so bad? They say it always rains – and the place very dull, of course, so far in the wilds? But you said in your letter that the lake was lovely, and that there were some pleasant people –'

He put up his hand, begging her to go no further. 'It was lovely enough if you like, but I hate the place; isn't that enough? I shall never go back with my free will.'

Mrs. Methven looked at him in astonishment. 'I thought –' she said, 'you remember how fantastic you thought it, and mediæval – that you had to make a periodical visit to the old home of the race?'

His very lips trembled with irritation. He had written about all that in the first days of his absence, and even after his arrival at Loch Houran, making fun of the old world stipulation. She might have divined, he thought, that it was a very different matter now. 'I am sorry to keep you so long here, out of your own comfortable corner,' he said. 'You never like sitting in the dining-room. It is brutal of me to keep you here.'

'No, Walter, it is my pleasure,' she cried; then, poor soul, with that most uncalled-for, unprofitable desire for information, 'And there are so many things I want to know –'

He commanded himself with a great effort. 'Mother,' he said, 'I have not enjoyed my visit to Scotland. There are a great many things that perhaps I may be able to talk of hereafter if you will give me time, but that I don't want even to think of now. And I'm tired with my journey; and everything is not *couleur de rose*,[35] as you seem to think. Let me alone, if you can, for to-night.'

'Let you alone – if I can!' She was so startled, so bitterly disappointed, that for a moment or two she could not speak. And this aggravated Walter still more.

'Mother,' he cried, getting up from his unsatisfactory meal, 'I hope you are not going to make a scene the first night.'

Thus, without any intention, with indeed the strongest desire to adopt a better way, this was how young Lord Erradeen resumed his intercourse with his mother. And yet Oona's mother, with all her little gentle affectations, with her kind effusiveness which there was no withstanding, had given him the sincerest sense of home and a refuge from trouble. Was it Oona's presence that explained all, or was there something more subtle underneath? There followed on this occasion no scene; but when Mrs. Methven returned to the drawing-room alone, leaving Walter, as she said, in peace to smoke his cigar after his dinner, Miss Merivale's keen eyes perceived at once that the traveller's meal had not been a happy ceremonial.

'I dare say he is tired,' she said.

'Yes, he is tired – almost too tired to eat. Smoke is the grand panacea,' said Mrs. Methven, with a smile.

'The worst of smoke is that it is so unsociable,' said Miss Merivale, cheerfully, picking up her book. 'I think I'll go to bed and leave you free for your talk with Walter when the cigar's done. Oh yes, you will get on better by yourselves. You

174         *The Selected Works of Margaret Oliphant, Volume 21*

will get more out of him if you are alone. But I dare say you won't get very much out of him. It will come by scraps – a little at a time; and he will be quite astonished that you don't know – by instinct, I suppose. Men are all like that.'

It was very kind of Cousin Sophy. Mrs. Methven gave her a kiss of gratitude as she took her candle and went away. But the expedient after all did little good. Walter lingered over his cigar, growing less and less inclined for any confidences, while his mother lingered in the drawing-room, hoping he would come to her; and Cousin Sophy, by far the most comfortable of the three, established herself cosily in her easy-chair by her bed-room fire, with a yellow novel.[36] Miss Merivale had aspirations beyond Mudie. She thought the French writers far more subtle and searching in their analysis of character than her compatriots ever were, and she liked their boldness, and the distinctness with which they cut away all pretences and showed humanity as it was.[37] She had no opinion of humanity – but yet she was in her way very good-natured, and would even go out of her way to show kindness to one of her fellow-creatures, as she had done to-night. Though her own room looked comfortable, and was so indeed up to a certain point, Miss Merivale, if nobody else, was aware that there was a draught which there was no eluding, – a draught which, whatever you might do, caught you infallibly in the back of the neck. She had taken down the curtains and put them up again. She had changed the position of her seat. She had bought a folding screen. She had even changed her chair and procured a high-backed old-fashioned thing, something like that cushioned sentry-box in which porters delight;[38] but in no way could she escape this draught, except in bed, and it was much too early to go to bed. Therefore she had made a distinct sacrifice of personal comfort in coming so soon up-stairs.[a] She sat there and mused, asking herself what boys were born for, or at least by what strange mistake Providence ever committed them to the charge of women; and why it was that they could not be happy or natural with the people they belonged to. 'I feel almost sure now,' she said to herself, 'that I shall have a stiff neck to-morrow, to no purpose, and that those two down-stairs[b] are sitting in separate rooms, and will not say a word to each other.'

It was a curious, very curious reading of an English home, could any spectator have looked through the secure covering of that respectable roof, or through the curtains that veiled the windows, and seen the two rooms in which these two persons sat each alone. How was it? Why was it? The mother had no thought but for her son. The son was not unkind or heartless, but full of good qualities. And yet at a moment when he had much to tell, and she was eager to hear, they sat in two separate rooms, as if they were fellow-lodgers and no more. Cousin Sophy, who was a sensible woman, with much kind feeling towards both, though she was not perhaps the kind of person from whom any high degree of unselfish devotion was to be looked for, sat and shook her head, and 'wondered at it,' as the ladies at Camelot did over Elaine.[39] But it was a greater wonder than Elaine.

Was it, perhaps, the beginning of the fulfilment of that threat that everything would go ill with him, which had been made at Kinloch Houran? But if so it was no new ill, but only the further following out of an evil that had been growing for years.

# CHAPTER V.[a]

SOMETHING of the same perversity which had turned all his good resolutions to nothing on the night of his arrival, affected Walter when he went out next morning into Sloebury. The place had narrowed and grown small in every way. There was no horizon, only lines of brick houses; no space, only the breadth of a street; no air to breathe for a man who had come from the wide solitude of the hills, and the keen freshness of the Highland breezes. Everything here was paltry, and monotonous, and small; the people who met him – and he met everybody, and there was not a man who could claim the slightest acquaintance with him, or a woman who had seen him once in her neighbour's drawing-room who did not now claim acquaintance with Lord Erradeen – seemed to have dwindled along with the scene. They had never been distinguished by intelligence or originality, but he had not been aware how paltry they were before. Had he seen Jeremy's new turn-out?[b] all the men inquired of him. He had already heard of it from Miss Merivale, who had given him a sketch of the history of the town, and what had happened during his absence, at breakfast. It was a high phaeton,[40c] 'which I suppose must be the fashion,' Miss Merivale said. 'You should really see it,' cried all the young men, with details about the harness[d] and the high-stepping mare which were endless. What did Lord Erradeen care for young Jeremy's phaeton or the high-stepping mare? but it was the only topic at Sloebury – that, and a report which Miss Merivale had also furnished him with about Julia Herbert. 'Your old flame: no doubt it was to console herself in your absence,' said Cousin Sophy. This was disagreeable too. Walter did not care to hear that the girl who had distinguished himself and been distinguished by him should make herself remarkable in a flirtation with another man. He did not want her indeed, but he objected to the transfer of her affections. And everything around looked so barren, stale, flat, and unprofitable. Perhaps it was the quickening of life which his recent experiences, painful though they had been, had brought him, which made him feel how dead-alive everything was. At Loch Houran his mind had gone back to the safe and peaceable commonplace of his native town with something like an enthusiasm of preference for its calm common sense, and superiority to the fever and excitements of that life upon the edge of the supernatural. Now it seemed to him that superstition itself, not to speak of the heats and chills of human passion, were higher things than this cynic-steadiness, this limit of matter-of-fact. What would Sloebury think of those things that had been so real to him, that had rent his very being asunder? He could imagine the inextinguishable laughter with which his story would be greeted, and blushed at

176    *The Selected Works of Margaret Oliphant, Volume 21*

the possibility of betraying himself. A seer of ghosts and visions, a victim of mesmerism! He would become in a moment the scorn, as he was at present,ᵃ the envy, of the town. Not a soul of them would understand. His experiences must be buried in his own bosom, and no one here must ever know that he had got beyond that surface of life to which all their knowledge was confined. When he met Underwood indeed this determination wavered a little: but then Underwood looked at him with an eagerness of inspection which was still more offensive. What did the fellow mean? Did he think it likely that he, a stranger, a person whom the better people disapproved, should be chosen as the confidant of Lord Erradeen?

'You have come back very soon,' the captain said; as indeed did everybody whom he met.

'No – not sooner than I intended,' said Walter, coldly. 'It was business merely that took me there at all.'

Underwood examined his face with a curiosity that had knowledge in it. 'I know that country so well,' he said. 'I should like to know what you think of it. Of course you were at Auchnasheen? I have been weeks there, with the late lord – and at the old castle too,' he added, with a keen look.

'You were interested in the architecture, I suppose.'

Underwood said nothing for a moment. Then suddenly – 'I wish you'd come and talk to me about it!' he cried. 'Any time that you will come I'll shut out everybody else. I'll keep myself free –'

'My dear fellow,' Walter said in a supercilious tone, 'why should I make Sloebury pay the penalty, and banish your friends from you for my selfish advantage?' To remember the time when this man had taken notice of him and been his superior, gave him a sense of impatient indignation. 'Besides, I don't know that there is anything to say.'

'Oh, as you please,' said Underwood; but when they passed each other, he turned back and laid a hand on Walter's sleeve. 'I keep early hours now,' he said. 'After ten I am always free.'

Lord Erradeen walked away, half-angry, half-amused, by the man's presumption, who, after all, was a nobody; but yet, he made a secret note in his mind, almost outside of his consciousness. After ten – It might, in the dreadful blank of those hours after ten at Sloebury (or even before ten for that matter), be a resource.

He had not gone very much further when he fell into another lion's mouth. But how wrong, how cruel, to apply such a phrase to the red and smiling mouth, fresh as the cherries in the song,⁴¹ of Miss Julia Herbert, on her way from the rectory where she paid her old aunt a daily visit, to the cottage in which she was her mother's stay and solace! She had been flirting a great deal in Walter's absence, no one could deny. A young Wynn, a relation on the other side of the house, had been staying there, on leave from his regiment, and on such an occasion what else was there to do? But young Wynn was gone, and his circumstances were not such as to have stood in competition for one moment with Lord Erradeen. As soon as she saw him, Julia began to smile and wave her hand. If there was a little sense of guilt in her, so much the more reason for even an excess of friendliness now. And perhaps there was in Walter a certain desire to let the little world about, which had insisted upon her little infidelities, perceive that she was as much under his influence as ever, as soon as he chose to appear. This was not the way in which the world regarded the matter, if Walter had known. Instead of looking at him as the conquering hero, who had but to show himself, the spectators said pityingly that Julia Herbert had got hold of poor Lord Erradeen again.

'Oh, Walter!' she cried; then changed her tone with a very pretty blush, and said, 'I ought to have said Lord Erradeen;[a] but it was the surprise. And so you have come home?'

'I have come *back,*' he said, with a little emphasis.

'I see it all. Forgive me that I should be so silly – *back,* of course; that means a few days, that means you have come for your boxes, or to see your mother, or to know her wishes respecting the new furniture of the banqueting hall. Shall it be mediæval or renaissance? If you ask my advice –'

'I do; of course, I do. It is for that chiefly I am here.'

'That is what I thought. Renaissance, then. There, you have my opinion – with plenty of cupids and good, fat garlands –'

She laughed, and Walter laughed too, though he was not very much amused. But, of course, he could not speak to a lady as he had spoken to Underwood.

'Come now, tell me about it,' the young lady said. 'You cannot refuse such a little bit of novelty to one who never sees anything new except a novel: and there is so little novelty in them! About what? Oh, about Scotland, and the scenery, and the old castle: and who you met, and what you did. Mayn't I show a little curiosity – in one whom,' she added with that exaggeration of sentiment which leaves room for a laugh, 'I have known all my life?'

'That, I hope, is not all the claim I have on your interest,' said Walter in the same tone.

'Oh, no, not half. There have been moments! – And then the romance of you, Lord Erradeen! It is delightful to touch upon the borders of romance. And your rank! I feel a great many inches higher, and ever so much elevated in my own esti-mation, by being privileged to walk by your lordship's side. When are you going to take your seat and help to rule your country? They say the House of Commons is to be preferred for that.[42] But there is nothing so delightful as a peer.'

'How lucky for me that you should think so. I may walk with you, then, to the –'

'Corner,' said Julia, 'not too far; oh, certainly, not too far: or we shall have all the old ladies, male and female, making comments.'

'I don't care for the old ladies – or their comments,' said Walter: the fun was languid, perhaps, but yet it afforded a little occupation when one had nothing else to do.

'You? Oh, of course not, as you will escape presently, and know all my wiles by heart already, it cannot make much difference to you. It is I who have to be considered, if you please, my lord. They will say there is *that* Julia Herbert at her old tricks, trying to take in poor Lord Erradeen – a poor, innocent young man in the snares of that designing baggage! They will probably add that the police should put a stop to it,' Miss Herbert said.

'The deluded old ladies! Without knowing that it is exactly the other way –'

'Now that is the prettiest speech you ever made,' said Julia. 'I never heard you say anything so nice before. You must have been in very good society since you went away. Tell me, who was it?' she asked with her most insinuating look.

They were old practitioners both. They understood each other: they had flirted since they had been in long clothes,[43] and no harm had ever come of it. This is, no doubt, what Miss Herbert would have said had any feminine critic interposed; but there was something more serious, as the feminine critic would have divined, at once, in Julia's eye. She meant more, not less, than she said; and she was anxious to know, having her eyes upon all contingencies like a wise general, what rivals might have come in the way.

'I have met scarcely any one,' said Walter. 'You cannot conceive what a lonely place it is. Oh, of course there are people about. I was promised a great many visitors had I stayed. On the other hand, even in winter, it is wonderfully beautiful. Coming back to this perfectly flat country, one discovers for the first time how beautiful it is.'

'Yes,' said Julia, indifferently; the beauty of the country did not excite her. 'I have seen a photograph of your old castle. You can only get to it by water, Captain Underwood says. Oh, he has been a great authority on the subject since you went away. One of your castles is on Loch Houran; but the others –'

'If you like to call them castles,' said Walter, gently flattered by these queries, 'there are two of them on Loch Houran. One I call a ruin, and the other a shooting-box –'[44]

'Oh, you lucky, lucky person; and a house in town, and another grand place in Scotland! Aren't you frightened to trust yourself among poor people who have nothing!ᵃ Don't you feel alarmed lest we should rush at you and tear you to pieces, and divide your spoils? I am very romantic. I should have the old castle,' she said with a side glance of provocation and invitation.

Her watchful eyes perceived a change in his countenance as she spoke. There were limits, it was evident, to the topics her flying hand might touch. She went on cleverly without a pause –

'You wonder what I should do with it? Restore it, Lord Erradeen. Build the walls up again, and make everything as it used to be. I should enjoy that – and then the furnishing, how delightful! Don't you know that the aim and object of every rational being now is to make a little Victorian house look like a big Queen Anne one?[45] or if not that, an Eastern harem with quantities of draperies, and mats and cushions.[46] How much more delightful to have the real thing to work upon!'

'But my house is not a Queen Anne house, or an Oriental –'

'You don't like to say the word, you good, delicate-minded young man! Of course not; but a castle like the *Mysteries of Udolpho*. At all events you must ask mamma and me to pay you a visit, and I shall take my lute like Emily[47] in that beautiful story, and a small but well-chosen collection of books; and then what-ever happens–suppose even that you shut my lover up in one of your dungeons –'

'Which I should certainly do; nay, hang him on the gallows-hill.'

'No, no,' she said, 'not hang him; let him; let him have the death of a gentle-man. Here we are at the corner. Oh, you are going my way? Well, perhaps that makes a difference. You meant to pay your respects to mamma? I don't think that I can in that case, Lord Erradeen, interfere with the liberty of the subject; for you have certainly a right, if you wish it, to call on mamma.'

'Certainly I have a right. I am prepared to obey you in every other respect; but Mrs. Herbert has always been very kind to me, and it is one of my objects –'

'How much improved you are!' cried Julia. 'How nice you are! How grateful and condescending! Tell me whom you have been consorting with while you have been away. The Scotch have good manners, I have always heard. Who is your nearest neighbour in your old castle, Lord Erradeen?'

Walter cast about in his mind for a moment before he replied. He had no mind to profane the sanctity of the Isle by betraying its gentle inmates to any stranger's curiosity. He said – 'I think my nearest neighbour is a Mr. William-son – not a distinguished name or person – who has a gorgeous great house and everything that money can buy. That means a great deal. It has all been made by sugar, or some equally laudable production.'

'And Mr. Williamson – no, it is not distinguished as names go – has a daugh-ter, Lord Erradeen?'

'I believe so, Miss Herbert.'

'How solemn we are! It used to be Julia – and Walter. But never mind, when one gets into the peerage one changes all that. "One fair daughter, and no more, whom he loved passing well!"'[48]

'There is but one, I think; sons in an indefinite number, however, which less-ens, I suppose, in a commercial point of view, the value of the lady.'

'Lord Erradeen, you fill me with amazement and horror. If that is how you have been taught by your Scotch neighbours –'

'Miss Herbert, I am following the lead you have given me – trying humbly to carry out your wishes.'

And then they looked at each other, and laughed. The wit was not of a high order, but perhaps that is scarcely necessary to make a duel of this kind between a young man and a young woman amusing. It was more than amusing to Julia. She was excited, her bosom panted, her eyes shone – all the more that Walter's calm was unbroken. It was provoking beyond measure to see him so tranquil, so ready to respond and follow her lead, so entirely unlikely to go any further. He was quite willing to amuse himself, she said to herself, but of feeling in the matter he had none, though there had been moments.[a]

And it did not once occur to her that her antagonist was clever enough to have eluded her investigations, or that the smile upon his face was one of secret pleasure in the secret sanctuary whose existence he had revealed to no one – the little isle in the midst of Loch Houran and the ladies there. He went back to them while all this lively babble went on, seeing them stand and wave their hands to him, as he was carried away over the wintry water. He had come away with relief and eagerness to be gone; but how fair it all looked as he turned back out of this scenery so different from his loch, and from the side of a girl who wanted to 'catch' him, Walter knew. Odious words! which it is a shame to think, much less speak, and yet which are spoken constantly, and, alas! in some cases, are true.

Notwithstanding this lively consciousness of the young lady's meaning (which in itself is always flattering and propitiates as much as it alarms), Walter accompanied Julia very willingly to the cottage. He had not thought of going there so soon. It was a kind of evidence of interest and special attraction which he had not meant to give, but that did not occur to him at the moment. The mother and daughter exerted themselves to the utmost to make his visit agreeable. They insisted that he should stay to luncheon, they sang to him and made him sing, and talked and made him talk, and burned delicate incense before him, with jibes and flouts and pretences at mockery. They had the air of laughing at him, yet flattered him all the time. He was such a prize, so well worth taking a little trouble about. The incense tickled his nostrils, though he laughed too, and believed that he saw through them all the time. There was no deception, indeed, on either side; but the man was beguiled and the woman excited. He went away with certain fumes in his brain, and she came down from the little domestic stage upon which she had been performing with a sense of exhaustion, yet success. Miss Williamson, a country beauty, or perhaps not even a beauty, with red hair and a Scotch accent, and nothing but money to recommend her! Money was much to ordinary mortals, but surely not enough to sweep away all other considerations from the mind of a young favourite of fortune. No! Julia believed in a certain generosity of mind though she was not herself sufficiently well off to indulge in it, and she could not think that money, important as it was, would carry the day.

In the mean time,[b] it was apparent to all the world that Lord Erradeen had spent the greater part of his first day at Sloebury, at the Cottage; he had stayed to luncheon, he had promised to come back to practise those duets. A young man who has just come into his kingdom, and is therefore in circumstances to marry, and likely in all human probability to be turning his thoughts that way, cannot do such things as this with impunity. If he had not meant something why should he thus have *affiché'd*[49] his interest in her daughter, Mrs. Herbert asked herself in polyglot jargon. There was no reason why he should have done so, had he not meant it. Thus Walter walked into the snare though it was so evident, though he saw it very well, and though the sportswoman herself trailed it on the ground before him and laughed and avowed her deep design. In such cases fun and frankness are more potent than deceit.

Walter continued in Sloebury for two or three weeks. He found the stagnation of every interest intolerable. He had nothing to do, and though this was a condition which he had endured with much composure for years before, it pressed upon him now with a force beyond bearing. And yet he did not go away. He betook himself to the Cottage to practise those duets almost every day; and presently he fell into the practice of visiting Captain Underwood almost every night; but not to confide in him as that personage had hoped. Underwood soon learned that a reference to Loch Houran made his companion silent at once, and that whatever had happened there the young lord meant to keep it to himself. But though Walter did not open his heart, he took advantage of the means of amusement opened to him. He suffered Captain Underwood to discourse to him about the turf;[50] about horses, of which the young man knew nothing; about the way in which both pleasure and profit might be secured, instead of the ruin to which it is generally supposed that pursuit must lead. Underwood would have been very willing to 'put' his young friend 'up' to many things, and indeed did so in learned disquisitions which perhaps made less impression than he supposed upon a brain which was preoccupied by many thoughts. And they played a great deal, that deadly sort of play between two, which is for sheer excitement's sake, and is one of the most dangerous ways of gambling. Walter did not lose so much as might have been expected, partly because his interest was apt to flag, and partly that his companion had designs more serious than those of the moment, and was in no hurry to pluck his pigeon[51] – if pigeon it was, of which he was not yet sure.

Thus the young man held himself up to the disapproval of the town, which, indeed, was ready to forgive a great deal to a peer, but 'did not like,' as all authorities said, 'the way he was going on.' He was behaving shamefully to Julia Herbert, unless he meant to marry her, which she and her mother evidently believed to the derision of all spectators; and to mix himself up so completely with Underwood, and abandon the society of his own contemporaries, were things which it was very difficult to forgive. He did not hunt as he had intended, which would have been an amusement suited to his position, partly because there was a good deal of frost, and partly because it was not an exercise familiar to Walter, who had never had the means of keeping horses. And the football club belonged to the previous ages, with which he now felt so little connection. Therefore, it happened after a time, notwithstanding the charm of his rank, that Sloebury felt itself in the painful position of disapproving of Lord Erradeen. Strange to say, he was very little different from Walter Methven, who was a young fellow who had wasted his time and chances – a kind of good-for-nothing. It was something of an insult to the community in which he lived, that he should be 'caught' by the most undisguised flirt, and should have fallen under the influence of the person most like a common adventurer of any in Sloebury. He owed it at least to those who had contemplated his elevation with such a rush of friendly feeling that he should be more difficult to inveigle. Had he still been plain Walter Methven, he could not have been more easily led away.

The house in which Walter was the first interest, and which had risen to such high hopes in his elevation, was held in the strangest state of suspense by this relapse into his old ways. The only element of agreeable novelty in it was the presence of Symington, who had taken possession of the house at once, with the most perfect composure and satisfaction to himself. He was the most irreproachable and orderly retainer ever brought into a house by a young man returning home. He gave no trouble, the maids said; he was not proud, but quite willing to take his meals in the kitchen, and did not stand upon his dignity. Presently, however, it appeared that he had got everything in his hands. He took the control of the dinner table, made suggestions to the cook, and even to Mrs. Methven herself when she ordered dinner, and became by imperceptible degrees the chief authority in the house. In this capacity he looked with puzzled and disapproving eyes at his young lord. His first inquiries as to where the horses were kept, and where he was to find his master's hunting things, being answered impatiently, with an intimation that Walter possessed neither the one nor the other, Symington took a high tone.

'You will, no doubt, take steps, my lord, to supply yourself. I hear it's a fine hunting country: and for a young gentleman like you with nothing to do –'

'Don't you think I can manage my own affairs best?' the young man said.

'It's very likely ye think so, my lord,' with great gravity, Symington said. He was laying the table for luncheon, and spoke sometimes with his back to Walter as he went and came.

'I suppose you are of a different opinion?' Walter said, with a laugh.

'Not always – not always, my lord. I've seen things in you that were very creditable – and sense too – and sense too!' said Symington, waving his hand. 'I'm just thinking if I were a young gentleman in your lordship's place, I would get more enjoyment out of my life. But we never know,' he added piously, 'what we might be capable of, if we were exposed to another's temptations and put in another's place.'

'Let me hear,' said Walter, with some amusement, 'what you would do if you were in my place.'

'It's what I have often asked mysel',' said Symington, turning round, and polishing with the napkin in his hand an old-fashioned silver salt cellar. 'Supposing ye were rich and great that are at present nobody in particular, what would ye do?

*The Wizard's Son, Volume II*   183

It's an awful difficult question. It's far more easy to find fault. We can all do that. Your lordship might say to me, 'That silver is no what it ought to be.' And I would probably answer, 'It's been in a woman's hands up till now,' which he[a] had never taken into consideration. And I may misjudge your lordship in the same way.'

'Do you mean to say that I too have been in a woman's hands? But that is uncivil, Symington, to my mother.'

'I would on no hand be unceevil to my lady; and it was not that I was meaning. To my thinking, my lord, you just dinna get enough out of your life. There is a heap of satisfaction to be got out of the life of a lord, when he has plenty of money, and five-and-twenty years of age like you. It is true your lordship is courting, which accounts for many things.'

'What do you mean by courting? Come, we have had enough of this,' Lord Erradeen said.

'I did not expect, my lord, that you would bide it long, though you were very good-natured to begin with. Courting is just a very well kent amusement, and no ill in it. But I will not intrude my remarks on your lordship. There is one thing though, just one thing,' Symington said, re-arranging the table with formal care. 'You'll no be going north again, my lord, as well as I can reckon, for nigh upon another year?'

'What have you to do with my going north?' Walter cried impatiently.

'Your lordship forgets that I will have to go with ye, which gives me a hantle[52] to do with it,' said Symington imperturbably; 'but that will no be at least till it's time for the grouse? It will always be my duty: – and my pleasure, and my pleasure!' he added with a wave of his hand, 'to follow your lordship to the place ye ken of, and do my best for you: but in the mean time I'm thinking this place suits me real well, and I will just bide here.'

'Bide here, you old Solomon!'[53] Walter cried, between laughter and wrath; 'how do you know that you are to bide anywhere, or that I mean you to stay with me at all?'

Symington waved his hand dismissing this question with the contempt it merited. 'I am just a person much attached to the family,' he said, 'and ye would not find it comfortable, my lord, up yonder, without me. But in the mean time ye will get a younger lad with my advice. And I'll just bide where I am with my lady, your mother, who is a lady of great judgment. I am getting an auld man; and your lordship is a young one; and if you are over-quiet at present, which is my opinion, it is no to be expected or desired that the like of that can last. Ye will aye find me here, my lord, when you want me. It will suit me far better at my years than running to and fro upon the earth at the tail of a young lad. But as long as I can draw one foot after another, I will go with your lordship *up yonder,* and never fail ye,' Symington said.

# CHAPTER VI.[a]

THE manner of life of which Symington disapproved went on till Christmas was over, and the new year had begun. It was not a new kind of life, but only the old, heightened in some of its features; less tragical in its folly because the young man was now no longer dependent upon his own exertions, yet more tragical in so far that life had now great opportunities for him, and means of nobler living, had he chosen. He received business letters now and then from Mr. Milnathort and from Shaw at Loch Houran which he read with impatience or not at all. Business disgusted him. He had no desire to take the trouble of making up his mind on this or that question. He let his letters collect in a pile and left them there, while he went and practised his duets, or lighted his cigar with the pink paper of the telegram which called his attention to letters unanswered, and went out to play ecarte[54] with Underwood. He did not care for the ecarte. He did not care for the duets. Poor Julia's devices to secure him became day by day more transparent to him, and Underwood's attempts to gain an influence. He saw through them both, yet went on day by day. The Herberts, mother and daughter, spoke of him with a secure proprietorship, and Julia, though never without that doubt which adventurers know, had almost a certainty of the coronet upon her handkerchief which she worked upon a cigar-case for him by way of making quite sure what a viscount's coronet[55] was. It is a pretty ornament. She was rather ashamed of her old-fashioned name, but that above it made everything right. Underwood for his part shook off the doubt which had been in his mind as to whether Lord Erradeen was a pigeon to be plucked. He thought of a campaign in town carried on triumphantly by means of his noble victim. It was worth waiting for after all.

And thus Christmas passed. Christmas, that season of mirth! There was the usual number of parties, at all of which Lord Erradeen was a favoured guest, and allowed himself to be exhibited as Miss Herbert's thrall. In these assemblies she used to talk to him about Miss Williamson. 'Oh yes, a lady in Scotland, whose wealth is untold; hasn't Lord Erradeen told you? It is to be a match, I understand,' Julia would say with a radiant countenance. 'Sugar – or cotton, I don't remember which. When one has estates in the West Highlands, that is part of the programme. One always marries – sugar. That is a much prettier way of putting it than to say one marries money.' This tantalised Sloebury a little, and painfully mystified Mrs. Methven, who had never heard Miss Williamson's name; but it did not change the evident fact that Lord Erradeen must either be engaged, or on the point of being engaged–or else that he was using Julia Herbert very ill. When the new year began, and it was suddenly announced that he was going away, there was a flutter and thrill of excitement over all the town. The rector, who met Walter on his way to the railway, and who was aware of all the expectations connected with him, stared aghast at the intimation. 'Going away!'

*The Wizard's Son, Volume II*                                    185

he said, then put forth a tremulous smile. 'Ah, I see! going on some visits, to pot a few pheasants before the season is over.'

'I don't think that would tempt me,' Walter said. 'I am going to town, and my mother will follow shortly. It is a removal, I fear–'

'You are going from Sloebury! But then – but then –' The old clergyman gasped for breath.

'My friends think I have wasted a great deal too much time in Sloebury,' Lord Erradeen said, and he waved his hand to the rector, who went home with his lower lip dropped, and his cheeks fallen in, in a consternation beyond words. His excitement was as great, though of a different kind, as on that day when he ran in from church with his surplice still on, and the most extraordinary disregard of decorum to carry the news of Walter's elevation in rank to his wife. 'That fellow is going off without a word,' cried Mr. Wynn. 'He has been amusing himself, that's all; but you never will listen to me. The girl has been going too far, a great deal too far, her mother ought not to have allowed it. And now I shall hear nothing else wherever I go,' the rector said. He was almost ready to cry, being old and a nervous man by nature. 'I thought it was settled this time, and that we should have no further trouble with her,' which was a contradiction of himself after the words he had begun with. Mrs. Wynn soothed him as best she could, though indeed she had been the one who had all along doubted Lord Erradeen's 'intentions,' and bade the rash Julia beware.

'Perhaps,' she said, 'they have come to an understanding, my dear. For it was quite true what he told you: he has wasted too much time in Sloebury. A young man in his position should not hang about in a place like this.'

'A young man in his position – should not raise expectations that are never to come to anything,' the rector said; which was a truth so undeniable that even his peace-making wife could find nothing to reply.

The change of sentiment which led Walter away from Sloebury was accomplished almost in a moment. In a capricious and wayward mind, a touch is sometimes enough to change the entire direction of a life. He had been kept indoors by a cold, and for want of something else to do had read his letters, and even answered one or two of them. There were several from Shaw relating the course of events at Loch Houran; but these might not perhaps have moved him, had he not found inclosed in one of them a note, now somewhat[a] out of date, from Oona. It was very short and very simple. 'I found I was not authorised to do anything with the poor Frasers except to tell them you would not be hard upon them: and I took it upon me to assure old Jenny that whatever happened you would never take the coo, and Granny that she should die in peace in her own house even – which she would like, I think, for the credit of the glen – if she should live to be a hundred. I think you will not disown my agency by doing anything contrary to this. My mother sends her best regards.' There was nothing more: but the words acted upon Walter's dissatisfied mind like the sudden prick of a lance. It seemed to him that he saw her again standing, with a somewhat wistful look in her eyes, watching him as his boat shot along the gleaming water–her mother with her waving handkerchief, her nodding head, her easy smile, standing by. Oona had said nothing, made no movement, had only stood and looked at him. How little she said now! and yet she was the only living creature (he said to himself in the exaggeration of a distracted mind) who had ever given him real help. She had ever given him her hand without hesitation or coquetry or thought of herself, to deliver him from his enemy–a hand that had purity, strength in its touch, that was as soft – as snow, he had said: cool, and pure, and strong. The thought of it gave him a pang which was indescribable. He rose up from where he sat among a litter of paper and books, the accumulations of an idle man, and went hurriedly to the drawing-room, where his mother sat alone by her fire–so much the more alone because he was in the next room, a world apart from her. He came in with a nervous excitement about him.

'Mother,' he said, 'I am going to town to-morrow.'

She put down her book and looked at him. 'Well, Walter?' she said.

'You think that is not of much importance; but it is, as it happens. I am going away from Sloebury. I shall never do any good here. I can't think why I have stayed – why *we* have stayed indeed; for it cannot have much attraction for you.'

She put down the book altogether now. She was afraid to say too much or too little in this sudden, new resolution, and change of front.

'I can understand your feeling, Walter. You have stayed over Christmas out of consideration for –' She would have said 'me' if she could, but that was impossible. 'For the traditions of the season,' she added, with a faint smile.

'That is a very charitable and kind way of putting it, mother. I have stayed because I am a fool – because I can't take the trouble to do anything but what suggests itself at the moment. Perhaps you think I don't know? Oh, I know very well, if that did any good. I am going to get the house ready, and you will join me when it is fit for you to live in.'

'I, Walter?' she said, with a startled tone. Her face flushed and then grew pale. She looked at him with a curious mixture of pleasure and pain. It seemed like opening up a question which had been long settled. Death is better than the reviving flutters of life when these are but to lead to a little more suffering and a dying over again. She added, somewhat tremulously, 'I think perhaps it would be better not to consider the question of removal as affecting me.'

'Mother,' he said, almost wildly, his eyes blazing upon her, 'your reproaches are more than I can bear.'

'I mean no reproach,' she said, quietly. 'It is simple enough. Your life should not be fettered by cares which are unnecessary. I am very well here.'

## The Wizard's Son, Volume II

187

'We can't go all over it again,' he said. 'We discussed that before. But you will say I have been as selfish, as careless as ever I was: and it is true – worse. Ah, I wonder if this was part of the penalty? Worse, in the old way. That would be a sort of a devilish punishment, just like him–if one were so silly as to believe that he had the power.'

'Of whom are you speaking, Walter?' asked his mother, startled. 'Punishment – who can punish you? You have done nothing to put yourself in any one's power.'

He gazed at her for a moment as she looked at him with anxious eyes, investigating his face to discover, if she could, what he meant. Then he burst into an excited laugh.

'I am getting melodramatic,' he said, 'by dint of being wretched, I suppose.'

'Walter, what is this? If there is indeed anything hanging over you, for God's sake tell me.'

She got up hurriedly and went to him in sudden trouble and alarm, but the sensation of the moment did not carry him any further. He put away her hand almost impatiently. 'Oh, there is nothing to tell,' he said, with irritation. 'You take everything *au pied de la lettre*.[56] But I am going to town to-morrow, all the same.'

And this he did, after a night in which he slept little and thought much. It may be thought that Oona Forrester's letter was a small instrument to effect so much, but it is not thus that influences can be reckoned. His mother had done a great deal more for him than Oona, but nothing she could have done or said could have moved him like the recollection of that small, soft hand by which he had held as if it were the anchor of salvation. It kept him from a sort of despair as he remembered it, through this turbulent night, as he lay awake in the darkness, asking himself could this be what his adversary meant? Not misfortune or down-fall, which was what he had thought of, feeling himself able to defy such threats: but this self-abandonment to his natural defects, this more and more unsatisfactoriness of which he was conscious to the bottom of his heart. It did not occur to him that in the dread that came over him, and panic-stricken sense of the irresistible, he was giving the attributes of something far more than man to his maniac, or monomaniac, of Kinloch Houran. It was not the moment now to question what that being was, or how he had it in his power to affect the life and soul of another. The anguish of feeling that he was being affected, that the better part was being paralysed in him and the worse made stronger, was what occupied him now. When he got a little sleep in the midst of his tossings and troublings of mind and body, it was by the soothing recollection of Oona's refreshing, strengthening touch, the hand that had been put into his own and had given him the strength of two souls.

And so it was that next morning, when he ought to have been practising those duets at Julia Herbert's side, he was hurrying up to London as fast as steam and an express train could carry him. It was not perhaps the best place to go to for spiritual reformation, but at least it was a beginning of something new. And in the force of this impulse he went on for some time, proceeding at once to Park Lane, to push forward the preparations of the house, securing for himself a servant in the place of Symington, and establishing himself, for the interval that must elapse before the house was ready for him, in chambers. In this way he found occupation for a week or two. He made an effort to answer his letters. He suffered himself to go through certain forms of business with the London lawyers who were the correspondents of Mr. Milnathort; and so for a short time found himself in the position of having something to do, and, still more strange, of doing it with a lightness of mind and enlivenment of life which was extraordinary, and without a reflection in respect to the duets and the ecarte. They were over, these *délaissements*,[57] and that was all about it.[a]

It was not such plain sailing however after the beginning. Established in chambers which were pleasant enough, with plenty of money, with youth and health, and what was still more, as he thought, with rank and a title which had the effect of making everybody civil and more than civil to him, Lord Erradeen suddenly awoke to the fact that he was less than nobody in the midst of that busy world of London in which there are so many people who love a lord. Yes; but before you can love a lord, invite him, caress him, make his time pass agreeably, you must know him. And Walter knew nobody. The most curious, the most rueful-comic, insignificant-important of all preliminaries! The doors were open, and the entertainment ready, and the guest willing; but there was no master of the ceremonies to bring him within the portals. It had not occurred to him until he was there, nor had he thought, even had his pride permitted him to ask for them, of the need of introductions, and some helping hand to bring him within the reach of society. Society, indeed, had as yet scarcely come back to town,[58] but yet there was a sprinkling at the club windows, men were to be seen in Pall Mall and Piccadilly,[59] and even a few carriages with ladies in them frequented the Park.[60b] But what did that matter to him who knew nobody? He had no club. He was a stranger from the country. No house was open to him; he went about the streets without meeting a face he knew. To be sure, this must not be taken as an absolute fact, for there were people he knew, even relations, one very respectable clan of them, living at Norwood,[61] in the highest credit and comfort, who would have received him with open arms. And he knew Mr. Wynn, the rector's nephew, a moderately successful barrister, who called upon and asked him to dinner with extreme cordiality, as did one or two other people connected with Sloebury. But in respect to the society to which he felt himself to belong, Walter was like the Peri at the gate of Paradise.[62] He knew nobody. Had ever any young peer with means to keep up his rank, been in such a position before? It gave him a certain pleasure to think upon one other, born to far higher fortunes than himself, who had entered London like this in inconceivable solitude. Byron![63] a magnificent example that went far to reconcile him to his fate. Walter thought a great deal of the noble poet in these days, and studied him deeply, and took pleasure in the comparison, and consolation in the feeling that he could enter thoroughly into all those high, scornful-wistful, heroic utterances about mankind. The Byronic mood has gone out of fashion; but if you can imagine a youth richly endowed by fortune, feeling that his new honours should open every door to him, and also a little that he was fit to hold his own place with the best, yet perceiving no door move on its hinges, and forced to acknowledge with a pang of surprise and disappointment, and that sense of neglected merit which is one of the most exquisite pangs of youth, that nobody cared to make his acquaintance, or even to inquire who was Lord Erradeen! It is all very well to smile at these sentiments where there has been no temptation to entertain them. But the young peer, who knew nobody, entered completely into Byron's feelings. He pondered upon the extraordinary spectacle of that other young peer strolling haughtily, with his look like a fallen angel,[64] up between the lordly ranks to take his hereditary seat: all the representatives of the old world staring coldly at him, and not one to be his sponsor and introduce him there. The same thing Walter felt would have to happen in his own case, if he had courage enough to follow the example of Byron;[65] and he felt how hollow were all his honours, how mean the indifferent spectators round him, how little appreciated himself, with all the keenness of youthful passion and would-be cynicism.[66] Unfortunately, he was not a Byron, and had no way of revenging himself upon that world.

This curious and irritating discovery, after all his good resolutions, had, it need scarcely be said, the reverse of an elevating influence upon him. He sought the amusement from which his equals shut him out in other regions. Strolling about town in an aimless way, he picked up certain old acquaintances whose renewed friendship was of little advantage. There will always be black sheep everywhere, and it is no unprecedented case for a boy from a public school, or youth from the university, to come across, six or seven years after he has left these haunts of learning, stray wanderers, who in that little time have fallen to the very depth of social degradation. When such a thing happens to a young man, the result may be a noble pity and profound impression of life's unspeakable dangers, and the misery of vice; or it may be after the first shock a sense that his own peccadilloes are not worth thinking of, seeing how infinitely lower down others have fallen. Walter stood between these two. He was sincerely sorry, and anxious to succour the fallen; but at the same time he could not but feel that in his position, who never could come to that, the precautions which poor men had to take were scarcely necessary. And what could he do? A young man must have something to amuse himself and occupy his time.

It was while he was sliding into the inconceivable muddle of an indolent mind and a vacant life that Underwood came to town. The captain's motives and intentions in respect to him were of a very mixed character, and require further elucidation: but the effect of his appearance in the mean time was a rapid acceleration of the downward progress. Underwood was 'up to' many things which Lord Erradeen was not 'up to' as yet, and the young man did not any longer, except by intervals, despise the society of the elder one, who brought, it could not be denied, a great many fresh excitements and occupations into his life. Under Captain Underwood's instructions he became acquainted with the turf, which, as everybody knows, is enough to give a young man quite enough to do, and a good many things to think of. And now indeed the time had come when the captain began to feel his self-banishment to Sloebury, and his patience, and all his exertions, so far as Walter was concerned, fully repaid. There was no repetition of that Byronic scene in the House of Lords.[67] Instead of proudly taking his seat alone, and showing the assembled world how little he cared for its notice, Walter discovered that he was indifferent to the world altogether, and asked himself, What is the good of it? with the philosophy of a cynic. What was the good of it, indeed? What was it but a solemn farce when you came to look into it? The House of Commons might be something, but the House of Lords was nothing; and why should a man trouble himself to become a member of it? Then as to the clubs. What was the use of struggling to get admission to White's, or Boodle's,[68] or any other of those exalted institutions which Walter only knew by name—when at Underwood's club, where he was received with acclamation, you had the best dinner and the best wine in London, and no petty exclusiveness?[69] Walter was not by any means the only titled person in that society. There were quantities indeed of what the captain called 'bosses'[70] on its books. Why then should Lord Erradeen take the trouble to sue and wait for admittance elsewhere with these doors so open to him? In the midst of this new influx of life, it is scarcely necessary to say that the house in Park Lane came to a standstill. It stood through all the season profitless, of use to nobody; and Walter's life went on, alas, not to be described by negations, a life without beauty or pleasure; though pleasure was all its aim.

At Sloebury the commotion made by his departure had been great. At the Cottage there had been a moment of blank consternation and silence, even from ill words. Then Mrs. Herbert's energies awoke, and her vivacity of speech. Fire blazed from this lady's eyes, and bitterness flowed from her tongue. She fell upon Julia (who, indeed, might have been supposed the greatest sufferer) with violent reproaches, bidding her (as was natural) remember that *she* had always been against it: a reproach in which there was really some truth. Julia, too, had a moment of prostration in which she could hold no head at all against the sudden disappointment and overthrow, and still more overwhelming realisation of what everybody would say. She retired to her room for a day, and drew down the blinds and had a headache in all the forms. During that period, no doubt, the girl went through sundry anguishes, both of shame and failure, such as the innocent who make no scheming are free from; while her mother carried fire and flame to the Rectory, and even betrayed to various friends her burning sense of wrong, and that Julia had been shamefully used. But when Julia emerged out of the shelter of that headache she put down all such demonstrations. She showed to Sloebury, all on the watch to see 'how she took it,' a front as dauntless and eyes as bright as ever. In a campaign the true soldier is prepared for anything that can happen, and knows how to take the evil with the good. Had she weakly allowed herself to love Walter the result might have been less satisfactory; but she had been far too wise to run such a risk. Afterwards, when rumours of the sort of life he was leading reached Sloebury, she confided to her mother, in the depths of their domestic privacy, that it was just as well he was going a little wrong.

'Oh, a little wrong!' cried Mrs. Herbert vindictively. 'If all we hear is true it is much more than a little. He is just going to the bad as fast as his legs can carry him – with *that* Captain Underwood to help him on; and he richly deserves it, considering how he has behaved to you.'

'Oh, wait a little, mamma,' Julia said. 'I know him better than any one. He will come round again, and then he will be ready to hang himself. And the prodigal will come home, and then – Or, perhaps Tom[a] Herbert will ask me up to town for the end of the season, after all the best is over, as he is sometimes kind enough to do. And I shall carry a little roast veal, just a sort of specimen of the fatted calf, with me to town.' Thus the young lady kept up her heart and bided her time.

Mrs. Methven bore the remarks of Sloebury and answered all its questions with a heavier heart. She could not take any consolation in Walter's wrongdoing, neither could she have the relief of allowing that he was to blame. She accounted for the rearrangement of everything, which she had to consent to after taking many measures for removal, by saying that she had changed her mind. 'We found the house could not be ready before the end of the season,' she said heroically, 'and what should I do in London in the height of the summer with nobody there?' She bore a fine front to the world but in reality the poor lady's heart had sunk within her. Oddly enough, Julia, the wronged, who at heart was full of good nature, was almost her only comforter. Julia treated Lord Erradeen's absence as the most natural thing in the world.

'I know what took him away in such a hurry,' she said. 'It was Miss Williamson. Oh, don't you know about Miss Williamson? his next neighbour at that Lock – something or other, a girl made of money – no, sugar. The next thing we shall hear is that you have a daughter-in-law with red hair. What a good thing that red hair is so fashionable![71] She is so rich, he was quite ashamed to mention it; that is why he never told you; but Walter,' she cried, with a laugh, 'had no secrets from me.'

Mrs. Methven, in dire lack of anything to cling to, caught at Miss Williamson as at a rock of salvation. If he had fallen in love, *did* not that account for everything? She could only pray God that it might be true.

192 *The Selected Works of Margaret Oliphant, Volume 21*

Symington had been bringing in the tea while Miss Herbert discoursed. When he came back to remove the tea things after she was gone, he 'took it upon him,' as he said, 'to put in his word.' 'If you will excuse me, my lady,' he said (a title which in a sort of poetical justice and amendment of fate Symington considered due to my lord's mother), 'my lord could not do better than give his attention to Miss Williamson, who is just the greatest fortune in all the country-side. But, even if it's not that, there is nothing to be out of heart about. If he's taking a bite out of the apples of Gomorrah,[72] he'll very soon find the cinders cranshing[73] in his mouth. But whatever he is after, when it comes to be the time to go *up yonder* there will be an end to all that.'

'My good Symington,' said Mrs. Methven, 'do you think it is necessary to excuse my son to me? It would be strange if I did not understand him better than any one.' But notwithstanding this noble stand for Walter, she got a little consolation both from the thought of Miss Williamson, and of that mysterious going *up yonder,* which must be a crisis in his life.

Thus winter ran into summer, and the busy months of the season went over the head of young Lord Erradeen. It was a very different season from that which he had anticipated. It contained no Byronic episode at all. The House of Lords never saw its new member, neither did any of those gay haunts of the fashionable world of which he had once dreamed. He went to no balls, or crowded dazzling receptions, or heavy dinners. He did not even present himself at a *levée.*[74] He had indeed fallen out of his rank altogether, that rank which had startled him so, with a kind of awe in the unexpected possession. His only club was that one of indifferent reputation to which Underwood had introduced him, and his society, the indifferent company which collected there. He began to be tolerably acquainted with race-courses, great and small, and improved his play both at billiards and whist, so that his guide, philosopher, and friend declared himself ready on all occasions to take odds on Erradeen. He spent a great deal of his time in these occupations, and lost a great deal of his money. They were almost the only things that gave him a semblance of an occupation in life. He was due at the club at certain hours to pursue this trade, which, like any other trade, was a support to his mind, and helped to make the time pass. At five-and-twenty one has so much time on hand, that to spend it is a pleasure, like spending money, flinging it to the right hand and the left, getting rid of it: though there is so much to be got out of it that has grown impossible to the old fogeys, no old fogey is ever so glad to throw it away.

And thus the days went on. They were full of noise and commotion, and yet, as a matter of fact, they were dullish as they dropped one after another. And sometimes as he came back to his rooms in the blue of the morning, and found as the early sun got up, that sleep was impossible, or on such a moment as a Sunday morning, when there was little or nothing 'to do,' Walter's thoughts were not of an agreeable kind. Sometimes he would wake from a doze with the beautiful light streaming in at his windows, and the brown London sparrows beginning

*The Wizard's Son, Volume II*     193

to twitter, and would jump up in such a restlessness and fierce impatience with himself and everything about him as he could neither repress nor endure. At such moments his life seemed to him intolerable, an insult to reason, a shame to the nature that was made for better things. What was the good of going on with it day after day? The laughter and the noise, who was it that called them the crackling of thorns[75] – a hasty momentary blaze that neither warmed nor lighted? And sometimes, even in the midst of his gaiety, there would suddenly come into his mind a question – Was this what was to happen to him if he resisted the will of the dweller on Loch Houran? Psha! he would say to himself, what was happening to him? Nothing but his own will and pleasure, the life that most young fellows of his age who were well enough off to indulge in it pos-sessed–the life he would have liked before he became Lord Erradeen: which was true; and yet it did not always suffice him for an answer. At such times curious gleams of instinct, sudden perceptions as by some light fitfully entering, which made an instantaneous revelation too rapid almost for any profit, and then dis-appeared again – would glance across Walter's soul.

On a fine evening in June he was walking with Underwood to the club to dine. The streets were cool with the approach of night, the sky all flushed with rose red and every possible modification of heavenly blue, the[a] trees in the squares fluttering out their leaves in the coolness of the evening, and shaking off the dust of day, a sense of possible dew going to fall even in London streets, a softening of sounds in the air. He was going to nothing better than cards, or perhaps, for a caprice, to the theatre, where he had seen the same insane burlesque[76] a dozen times before, no very lively prospect: and was cogitating in his mind whether he should not run off to the Continent, as several men were talking of doing, and so escape from Underwood and the club, and all the rest of the hackneyed round: which he would have done a dozen times over but for the trouble of it, and his sense of the bore it would be to find something to amuse him under such novel circumstances. As they went along, Underwood talking of those experiences which were very fine to the boys in Sloebury, but quite flat to Walter now–there suddenly appeared to him, standing on the steps of a private hotel, in a light over-coat like a man going to dinner, a middle-aged, rustic-looking individual, with a ruddy, good-humoured countenance, and that air of prosperity and well-being which belongs to the man of money. 'I think I have seen that man somewhere before,' said Walter. Underwood looked up, and the eyes of all three met for a moment in mutual recognition. 'Hallo, Captain Underwood!' the stranger said. Underwood was startled by the salutation; but he stopped, willingly or unwill-ingly, stopping Walter also, whose arm was in his. 'Mr. Williamson! You are an unexpected sight in London,' he said.

'No, no, not at all,' said the good-humoured man, 'I am very often in London. I am just going in to my dinner. I wonder if I might make bold, being a countryman and straight from Loch Houran, to say, though we have never met before, that I am sure this is Lord Erradeen?'

Walter replied with a curious sense of amusement and almost pleasure. Mr. Williamson, the father of the fabulous heiress who had been invented between Julia Herbert and himself!

'I am very glad to make your acquaintance, Lord Erradeen; you know our lands march,[77] as they say in Scotland. Are you engaged out to your dinner, gentlemen, may I ask, or are ye free to take pot luck?[78] My daughter Katie is with me, and we were thinking–or at least she was thinking – for I am little learned in such matters–of looking in at the theatre to see a small piece of Mr. Tennyson's that they call the *Falcon*,[79] and which they tell me, or rather she tells me, is just most beautiful. Come now, be sociable; it was no fault of mine, my lord, that I did not pay my respects to ye when ye were up at Loch Houran. And Katie is very wishful to make your acquaintance. Captain Underwood knows of old that I am fond of a good dinner. You will come? Now that's very friendly. Katie, I've brought you an old acquaintance and a new one,' he said, ushering them into a large room cloudy with the fading light.

The sudden change of destination, the novelty, the amusing associations with this name, suddenly restored Walter to a freshness of interest of which the *blasé*[80] youth on his way to the noisy monotony of the club half an hour before could not have thought himself capable. A young lady rose up from a sofa at the end of the room and came forward, bending her soft brows a little to see who it was.

'Is it any one I know? for I cannot see them,' in simplest tones, with the accent of Loch Houran, Miss Williamson said.

***

# CHAPTER VII.[a]

THE room was large with that air of bare and respectable shabbiness which is the right thing in a long-established private hotel – with large pieces of mahogany furniture, and an old-fashioned carpet worn, not bare exactly, but dim, the pattern half-obliterated[b] here and there, which is far more correct and *comme il faut*[81] than the glaring newness and luxury of modern caravanseries.[82] As Mr. Williamson, like a true Englishman (a Scotsman in this particular merely exaggerates the peculiarity), loved the costly all the better for making no show of being costly, it was naturally at one of these grimly expensive places that he was in the habit of staying in London. A large window, occupying almost one entire side of the room, filled it with dim evening light, and a view of roofs and chimneys, against which Katie's little figure showed as she came forward asking, 'Is it any one I know?' It was not a commanding, or even very graceful figure, though round and plump, with the softened curves of youth. When the new-comers advanced to meet her, and she saw behind her father's middle-aged form, the slimmer outlines of a young man, Katie made another step forward with an increase of interest. She had expected some contemporaries of papa's, such as he was in the habit of bringing home with him to dinner, and not a personage on her own level. Mr. Williamson, in his good-humoured cordiality, stepped forward something like a showman, with a new object which he feels will make a sensation.

'You will never guess who this is,' he said, 'so I will not keep ye in suspense, Katie. This is our new neighbour at Loch Houran, Lord Erradeen. Think of me meeting him just by chance on the pavey,[83] as ye may say, of a London street, and us next door to each other, to use a vulgar expression, at home!'

'Which is the vulgar expression?' said Katie. She was very fond of her father, but yet liked people to see that she knew better. She held out her hand frankly to Walter, and though she was only a round-about,[84] bread-and-butter[85] little girl with nothing but money, she was far more at her ease than he was. 'I am very glad to make your acquaintance, Lord Erradeen,' she said. 'We were just wondering whether we should meet you anywhere. We have only been a week in town.'

'I don't think we should have been likely to meet,' said Walter with that tone of resentment which had become natural to him, 'if I had not been so fortunate as to encounter Mr. Williamson as he says, on the *pavé*.'[86]

Katie was not pleased by this speech. She thought that Walter was rude, and implied that the society which he frequented was too fine for the Williamsons, and she also thought that he meant a laugh at her father's phraseology, neither of which offences were at all in the young man's intention.

'Oh,' Katie cried, resentful too, 'papa and I go to a great many places – unless you mean Marlborough House[87] and that sort of thing. Oh, Captain Under-wood!' she added next moment in a tone of surprise. The appearance of Captain Underwood evidently suggested to her ideas not at all in accordance with that of Marlborough House.

'Yes,' he said, 'Miss Williamson: you scarcely expected to see me. It is not often that a man is equally intimate with two distinct branches of a family, is it? But I always was a fortunate fellow, and here I am back in your circle again.'

Walter's mind was considerably preoccupied by his own circumstances, and by the novelty of this new meeting; but yet he was quick-witted enough to remark with some amusement the recurrence of the old situation with which he was quite acquainted – the instinctive repugnance of the feminine side everywhere to this companion of his, and the tolerance and even friendliness of the men. Katie did all but turn her back upon Underwood before his little speech was ended. She said, 'Will you ring for dinner, papa?' without making the slightest reply to it: and indeed, after another glance from one to the other, retired to the sofa from which she had risen, with a little air of having exhausted this new incident, and indifference to anything that could follow, which piqued Walter. Had she been a noble person either in fact or in appearance, of an imposing figure and proportions even, it might have seemed less insupportable; but that a little dumpy girl should thus lose all interest in him, classifying him in a moment with his companion, was beyond Lord Erradeen's patience. He felt bitterly ashamed of Underwood, and eager even, in his anger at this presumptuous young woman's hasty judgment, to explain how it was that he was in Underwood's company. But as he stood biting his lip in the half-lighted room, he could not but remember how very difficult it would be to explain it. Why was he in Underwood's company? Because he could get admittance to none better. Marlborough House! He felt himself grow red all over, with a burning shame, and anger against fate. And when he found himself seated by Katie's side at the lighted table, and subject to the questions with which it was natural to begin conversation, his embarrassment was still greater. She asked him had he been here and there. That great ball at the French Embassy[88] that everybody was talking about – of course he had been one of the guests?[a] And at the Duke's – Katie did not consider it necessary to particularise what duke,[89] confident that no Christian, connected ever so distantly with Loch Houran, could have any doubt on the subject. Was the decoration of the new dining-room so magnificent as people said? Walter's blank countenance, his brief replies, the suppressed reluctance with which he said anything at all, had the strangest effect upon Katie. After a while she glanced at Captain Underwood, who was talking with much volubility to her father, and with a very small, almost imperceptible shrug of her little shoulders, turned away and addressed herself to her dinner. This from a little girl who was nobody, who was not even very pretty, who betrayed her plebeian origin in every line of her plump form[b] and fresh little commonplace face, was more than Walter could bear.

'You must think me dreadfully ignorant of the events of society,' he said, 'but the fact is I have not been going out at all. It is not very long, you are aware, since I came into the property, and – there have been a great many things to do.'

'I have always heard,' said Katie, daintily consuming a delicate *entrée*,[90] with her eyes upon her plate as if that was her sole interest, 'that the Erradeen estates were all in such order that there was never anything for the heir to do.'

'You speak,' said Walter, 'as if they changed hands every year.'

'Oh, not that exactly; but I remember two; and I might have remembered others, for we have only been at Loch Houran since papa got so rich.'

'What a pleasant way of remembering dates!'

'Do you think so, Lord Erradeen? Now I should think that to have been rich always, and your father before you, and never to have known any difference, would be so much more pleasant.'

'There may perhaps be something to be said on both sides,' said Walter; 'but I am no judge – for the news of my elevation, such as it is, came to me very suddenly, too suddenly to be agreeable, without any warning.'

*The Wizard's Son, Volume II*        197

Katie reconsidered her decision in the matter of Lord Erradeen; perhaps though he knew nobody, he might not be quite unworthy cultivation, and besides, she had finished her *entrée*. She said, 'Didn't you know?' turning to him again her once-averted eyes.

'I had not the faintest idea; it came upon me like a thunderbolt,' he said. 'You perceive that you must treat me with a little indulgence in respect to dukes, &c. – even if I had any taste for society, which I haven't,' he added, with a touch of bitterness in his tone.

'Oh,' said Katie, looking at him much more kindly; then she bent towards him with quite unexpected familiarity, and said, lowering her voice, but in the most distinct whisper, 'And where then did you pick up that odious man?'

Walter could not but laugh as he looked across the table at the unconscious object of this attack.

'I observe that ladies never like him,' he said; 'at home it is the same.'

'Oh, I should think so,' cried Katie, 'everybody thought it was such a pity that Lord Erradeen took him up – and then to see him with you! Oona Forrester would be very sorry,' Katie added after a pause.

'Miss Forrester!' Walter felt himself colour high with pleasure at the sound of this name, then feeling this a sort of self-betrayal, coloured yet more. 'You know her?'

Katie turned round upon him with a mixture of amusement and disdain. 'Know her! is there any one on the loch, or near it, that doesn't know her?' she said.

'I beg your pardon,' cried Walter. 'I forgot for the moment.' Then he too retired within himself for so long a time that it was Katie's turn to be affronted. He devoted himself to his dinner too, but he did not eat. At last 'Why should she be sorry?' he asked curtly as if there had been no pause.

'How can I tell you now while he sits there?' said Katie, lowering her voice; 'some other time perhaps – most likely you will call in the day-time, in the morning, now that we have made your acquaintance.'

'If you will permit me,' Walter said.

'Oh yes, we will permit you. Papa has always wanted to know you, and so have I since – If you are allowed to[a] come: but perhaps you will not be allowed to come, Lord Erradeen.'

'Will not be *allowed*?[b] What does that mean? and since when, may I ask, have you been so kind as to want to know me? I wish I had been aware.'

'Since – well, of course, since you were Lord Erradeen,' said the girl, 'we did not know of you before: and people like us who have nothing but money are always very fond of knowing a lord – everybody says so at least. And it is true, in a way. Papa likes it very much indeed. He likes to say my friend, the Earl of –, or my friend, the Duke of –. He knows a great many lords, though perhaps you would not think it. He is very popular with fine people. They say he is not at all vulgar considering, and never takes anything upon him. Oh, yes, I know it all very well. I am a new person in the other way – I believe it is far more what you call snobbish – but I can't bear the fine people. Of course they are very nice to me; but I always remember that they think I am not vulgar considering, and that I never pretend to be better than I am.'

There was something in this address spoken with a little heat, which touched Walter's sense of humour, a faculty which in his better moods made his own position, with all its incongruities, ruefully amusing to him. 'I wonder,' he said, 'if I pretend to be better than I am? But then I should require in the first place to know what I am more distinctly than I do. Now you, on that important point, have, I presume, no doubt or difficulty?' –

'Not the least,' she said, interrupting him. 'The daughter of a rich Glasgow man who is nobody – that is what I am – everybody knows; but you, my lord, you are a noble person of one of the oldest families, with the best blood in your veins, with –' She had been eyeing him somewhat antagonistically, but here she broke off, and fell a laughing. 'I don't believe you care a bit about it,' she said. 'Are you going with us to the theatre to see the *Falcon,* Lord Erradeen?'

'What is the *Falcon?*' he said.

'You have not seen it nor heard of it? It is Mr. Tennyson's,' said Katie with a little awe. 'How is it possible you have not heard? Don't you know that lovely story? It is a poor gentleman who has nothing but a falcon, and the lady he loves comes to see him. She is a widow (that takes away the interest a little, but it is beautiful all the same) with a sick child. When he sees her coming he has to prepare an entertainment for her, and there is nothing but his falcon, so he sacrifices it, though it breaks his heart. And oh, to see the terrible stage bird that is brought in, as if that could be his grand hawk! You feel so angry, you are forced to laugh till you cry again. That kind of story should never be brought to the literal,[91] do you think it should?'

'And what happens?' said Walter, young enough to be interested, though not sufficiently well-read to know.

'Oh, you might guess. She had come to ask him for his falcon to save her child. What could it be else? It is just the contrariety of things.'

'You cannot know very much, Miss Williamson, of the contrariety of things.'

'Oh, do you think so? Why shouldn't I? I think I am precisely the person to do so. It seems to me in my experience,' she added, fixing a look upon him which seemed to Walter's conscience to mean a great deal more than it was possible Katie could mean, 'that almost everything goes wrong.'

'That is a most melancholy view to take.'

'But so is everything melancholy,' said the girl. Her little simple physiognomy, her rosy cheeks and blue eyes, the somewhat blunted profile (for Katie had no features, as she was aware) and altogether commonplace air of the little person who produced these wonderful sentiments amused Walter beyond measure. He

*The Wizard's Son, Volume II*   199

laughed perhaps more than was strictly decorous, and drew the attention of Mr. Williamson, who, absorbed in his talk with Underwood, had almost forgotten his more important guest.

'What is the joke?' he said. 'I am glad to see you are keeping his lordship amused, Katie, for the captain and me we have got upon other subjects concerning the poor gentleman, your predecessor, Lord Erradeen. Poor fellow! that was a very sad business: not that I would say there was much to be regretted before the present bearer of the title,' the rich man added with a laugh; 'but at your age you could well have waited a little, and the late lord was a very nice fellow till he fell into that melancholy way.'

'I told you everything was melancholy,' said Katie in an undertone.

'And I,' said the young man in the same suppressed voice, 'shall I too fall into a melancholy way?' He laughed as he said so, but it was not a laugh of pleasure. Could he do nothing without having this family mystery – family absurdity– thrust into his face?

'If you want your cigar,[92] papa –' said Katie getting up, 'and you can't live without that, any of you gentlemen – I had better go. Let laws and learning, wit and wisdom die, so long as you have your cigars. But the carriage is ordered at a quarter to ten, and Lord Erradeen is coming, he says. In any case *you* must come, papa,[a] you know. I can't go without you,' she said, with a little imperative air. It was enough to make any one laugh to see the grand air of superiority which this little person took upon her, and her father greeted her exit with a loud laugh of enjoyment and admiration.

'She is mistress and more, as we say in Scotland,' he said, 'and there must be no trifling where my Katie is concerned. We will have to keep to the minute. So you are coming with us, Lord Erradeen? What will you do, Underwood? I'm doubting if what they call the poetical dramaw will be much in your way.'

To which Underwood replied with some embarrassment that it certainly was not at all in his way. He liked Nelly Somebody in a burlesque,[93] and he was always fond of a good ballet, but as for Shakespeare and that sort of thing, he owned it was above him. Good Mr. Williamson disapproved of ballets,[94] utterly, and administered a rebuke on the spot.

'I hope you are not leading Lord Erradeen into the like of that. It is very bad for a young man to lose respect for women, and how you can keep any after those exhibitions is beyond me. Well, I will not say I take a great interest, like Katie, in poetry and all that. I like a good laugh. So long as it is funny I am like a bairn, I delight in a play: but I am not so sure that I can give my mind to it when it's serious. Lord! we've enough of seriousness in real life. And as for your bare-faced love-making before thousands of people, I just can't endure it. You will think me a prejudiced old fogey, Lord Erradeen. It makes me blush,' said the elderly critic, going off into a laugh; but blush he did, through all the honest red upon his natural cheeks, notwithstanding his laugh, and his claret, and his cigar. Was he a world behind his younger companion who glanced at him with a sensation of mingled shame, contempt, and respect, or was he a world above him? Walter was so confused in the new atmosphere he had suddenly begun to breathe, that he could not tell. But it was altogether new at all events, and novelty is something in the monotony of life.

'I'll see you at the club after,' said Underwood, as they loitered waiting for Miss Williamson at the hotel door. But Walter made no reply.

Now Lord Erradeen, though he had been perverse all his life, and had chosen the evil and rejected the good in many incomprehensible ways, was not – or this history would never have been written – without that finer fibre in him which responds to everything that is true and noble. How strange this jumble is in that confusion of good and evil which we call the mind of man! How often may we see the record of a generous action bring tears to the eyes of one whose acts are all selfish, and whose heart is callous to sufferings of which he is the cause: and hear him with noble fervour applaud[a] the self-sacrifice of the man, who in that language by which it is the pleasure of the nineteenth century to make heroism just half-ridiculous, and to save itself from the highflown, 'never funked and never lied; I guess he didn't know how:'[95] and how he will be touched to the heart by the purity of a romantic love, he who for himself feeds on the garbage – and all this without any conscious insincerity, the best part of him more true and real all the time than the worst! Walter, to whom his own domestic surroundings had been so irksome, felt a certain wholesome novelty of pleasure when he set out between the father and daughter to see what Mr. Williamson called the 'poetical dramaw,' a thing hitherto much out of the young man's way. He had been of late in all kinds of unsavoury places, and had done his best to debase his imagination with the burlesques; but yet he had not been able to obliterate his own capacity for better things. And when he stood looking over the head of Katie Williamson, and saw the lady of the poet's tale come into the poor house of her chivalrous lover, the shock with which the better nature in him came uppermost, gave him a pang in the pleasure and the wonder of it. This was not the sort of heroine to whom he had accustomed himself: but the old Italian romancer, the noble English poet,[96] and the fine passion and high perception of the actors, who could understand and interpret both, were not in vain for our prodigal. When that lady paused in the humble doorway clothed in high reverence and poetry, not to speak of the modest splendour of her mature beauty and noble Venetian dress, he felt himself blush, like good Mr. Williamson, to remember all the less lovely images he had seen. He could not applaud; it would have been a profanation. He was still pure enough in the midst of uncleanness, and high enough though familiar with baseness, to be transported for the moment out of himself.

The other two formed a somewhat comical counterbalance to Walter's emotion; not that they were by any means unfeeling spectators. Mr. Williamson's interest in the story was unfeigned. As Mrs. Kendal[97] poured forth that heart-rending plea of a mother for her child, the good man accompanied her words by strange muffled sounds which were quite beyond his control; and which called forth looks of alarm from Katie, who was his natural guardian, and who herself maintained a dignified propriety as having witnessed this moving scene before. But the running commentary *sotto voce*,[98] which he kept up throughout, might have furnished an amusing secondary comedy to any impartial bystander. 'Bless us all!' said Mr. Williamson, 'two useless servants doing nothing, and not a morsel in the house! How do ye make that out!' 'Lordsake! has he killed the hawk? but that's just manslaughter: and a tough morsel I would say for the lady, when all's done.' 'What is it she's wanting – just the falcon he's killed for her. Tchick! Tchick! Now I call that an awful pity, Katie. Poor lady! and poor fellow! and he has to refuse her! Well, he should not have been so hasty. After all she did not eat a morsel of it; and what ailed that silly old woman there to toss up a bit omelette or something, to save the bird–and they're so clever at omelettes abroad,' the good man said, with true regret. 'Oh, papa, how material you are! Don't you know it's always like that in life?' cried Katie. 'I know nothing of the kind,' said her father, indignantly. 'What is the use of being a poet, as you call it, if ye cannot find some other way and not break their hearts? Poor lad! Now that's a thing I can't understand – a woman like that come pleading to you, and you have to refuse her!' Katie looked round upon her father with her little air of oracle. 'Don't you see, papa, that's the story! It's to wring our hearts he wrote it.' Mr. Williamson paid no attention to this. He went on softly with his 'Tchick! tchick!' and when all was over dried his eyes furtively and got up with haste, almost impatience, drawing a long breath. 'It's just all nonsense,' he said. 'I'll not be brought here again to be made unhappy. So she's to get *him* instead of the bird – but, bless me! what good will that do her? *that* will never save her bairn.'

'It will satisfy the public, more or less,' said a voice behind.

Walter had been aware that some one else had come into the box, who stood smiling, listening to the conversation, and now bent forward to applaud as if aware that his applause meant something. Katie turned half round, with a little nod and smile.

'Did you hear papa?' she said. 'Oh, tell Mr. Tennyson! he is quite unhappy about it. Are you unhappy too, Lord Erradeen? for you don't applaud, or say a word.'

'Applaud!' Walter said. 'I feel that it would be taking a liberty. Applaud what? That beautiful lady who is so much above me, or the great poet who is above all? I should like to go away and draw breath, and let myself down –'

'Toots!' said Mr. Williamson, 'it is just all non-sense. He should not have been so hasty. And now I would just like to know,' he added, with an air of defiance, 'what happened to that bairn: to want a falcon and get a stepfather! that was an ill way to cure him. Hoots! it's all nonsense. Put on your cloak, Katie, and let us get away.'

'But I like you, Lord Erradeen, for what you say,' cried Katie. 'It was too beautiful to applaud. Oh, tell Mrs. Kendal! She looked like a picture. I should like to make her a curtsey, not clap my hands as you do.'

'You will bid me tell Boccaccio next?' said the new-comer. 'These are fine sentiments; but the actors would find it somewhat chilly if they had no applause. They would think nobody cared.'

'Lord Innishouran,' said Katie, 'papa has forgotten his manners. He ought to have introduced to you Lord Erradeen.'

Walter was as much startled as if he had been the veriest cockney whose bosom has ever been fluttered by introduction to a lord. He looked at the first man of his rank (barring those damaged ones at Underwood's club) whom he had met, with the strangest sensation. Lord Innishouran was the son of the Duke[99] – the great potentate of those northern regions. He was a man who might make Walter's career very easy to him, or, alas! rather might have made it, had he known him on his first coming to London. The sense of all that might be involved in knowing him, made the young man giddy as he stood opposite to his new acquaintance. Lord Innishouran was not of Walter's age. The duke was the patriarch of the Highlands, and lived like a man who never meant to die. This gentleman, who at forty-five was still only his father's heir, had taken to the arts by way of making an independent position for himself. He was a *dilettante* in the best sense of the word,[100] delighting in everything that was beautiful. Walter's enthusiasm had been the best possible introduction for him; and what a change there seemed in the young man's world and all his prospects as he walked home after taking leave of the Williamsons with Innishouran's, not Underwood's, arm within his own!

'I cannot understand how it is that we have not met before. It would have been my part to seek you out if I had known you were in town,' his new friend said. 'I hope now you will let me introduce you to my wife. The duke has left town–he never stays a moment longer than he can help. And everything is coming to an end. Still I am most happy to have made your acquaintance. You knew the Williamsons, I suppose, before? They are excellent people–not the least vulgarity about them, because there's no pretension. And Katie is a clever girl, not without ambition. She is quite an heiress, I suppose you know –'

'I don't know – any one, or anything,' Walter said.

'Come, that is going too far,' said the other, with a laugh. 'I presume you don't care for society. That is a young man's notion; but society is not so bad a thing. It never answers to withdraw from it altogether. Yes, Katie is an heiress. She is to have all the Loch Houran property, I believe, besides a good deal of money.'

'I thought,' said Walter, 'there were several sons.'

'One – one only; and he has the business, with the addition also of a good deal of money. Money is a wonderful quality – it stands instead of a great many other things to our friends there. I am fond of intellect myself, but it must be allowed

*The Wizard's Son, Volume II* 203

that the most cultivated mind would not do for any man what his money does at once for that good neighbour of ours – who is a most excellent fellow all the same.'

'I have met him for the first time to-day,' said Walter, 'in the most accidental way.'

'Ah! I thought you had known them; but it is true what I say. I look upon money with a certain awe. It is inscrutable. The most perfect of artists–you and I when we most look up to them, do also just a little look down upon them! No, perhaps that is too strong. At all events, they are there on sufferance. They are not of us, and they know it. Whether they care for us too much, or whether they don't care at all, there is still that uneasy consciousness. But with this good-natured millionnaire, nothing of the sort. He has no such feeling.'

'Perhaps because his feelings are not so keen. Miss Williamson has just been telling me what you say – that her family are considered not vulgar because they never pretend to be better than they are.'

'Ah!' cried Lord Innishouran, startled, 'did Katie divine that? She is cleverer than I thought – and a very fine fortune, and an ambitious little person. I hope her money will go to consolidate some property at home, and not fall into a stranger's hands. I am all for the Highlands, you see, Erradeen.'

'And I know so little about them,' said Walter.

But nevertheless he knew very well what was meant, and there was a curious sensation in his mind which he could not describe to himself, as if some perturbation, whether outside or in he could not tell which, was calmed. He had a great deal of talk with his new friend as they threaded the noisy little circles of the streets, among the shouting link-boys[101] and crowds of carriages, then reached the calm and darkness of the thoroughfares beyond. Lord Innishouran talked well, and his talk was of a kind so different from that of Underwood's noisy coterie, that the charm of the unusual, added to so many other novel sensations, made a great impression upon Walter's mind, always sensitive and open to a new influence. He felt a hot flush of shame come over him when walking thus through the purity of the night, and in the society of a man who talked about great names and things, he remembered the noise of the club, the heated air full of smoke and inanities, the jargon of the race-course[a] and the stables. These things filled him with disgust, for the moment at least, just as the duets had given him a sense of disgust and impatience at Sloebury. His new friend only left him at the door of his rooms, which happened to lie in Lord Innishouran's way, and bade him good night, promising to call on him in the morning. Walter had not been in his rooms so early for many a day. He hesitated whether or not to go out again, for he had not any pleasure in his own society; but pride came to the rescue, and he blushed at the thought of darting out like a truant schoolboy, as soon as the better influence was withdrawn. Pride prevented him from thus running away from himself. He took a book out of the shelves, which he had not done for so long. But soon the book dropped aside, and he began to review the strange circumstances of the evening. In a moment, as it seemed, his horizon had changed. Hitherto, except in so far as money was concerned, he had derived no advantage from his new rank. Now everything seemed opening before him. He could not be unmoved in this moment of transition. Perhaps the life which was called fast had never contained any real temptation to Walter. It had come in and invaded the indolence of his mind and filled the vacant house of his soul, swept and garnished but unoccupied, according to the powerful simile of Scripture;[102] but there was no tug at his senses now urging him to go back to it. And then he thought, with a certain elation, of Lord Innishouran, and pleasurably of the Williamsons. Katie, was that her name? He could not but laugh to himself at the sudden realisation of the visionary Miss Williamson after all that had been said. What would Julia Herbert say? But Julia Herbert had become dim to Lord Erradeen as if she had been a dozen years away.

# CHAPTER VIII.[a]

Next morning Lord Innishouran fulfilled his promise of calling, and made his appearance almost before Walter, following the disorderly usages of the society into which he had fallen, was ready to receive him. The middle-aged eldest son was a man of exact virtue, rising early, keeping punctual hours, and in every way conducting himself as became one whose position made him an example to the rest of the world. And he was one who had a deep sense of the duties of his position. It seemed to him that this young man was in a bad way. 'He is at a crisis, evidently at a crisis,' he had said to his wife, 'and a good influence may be everything for him.' 'He should marry Katie Williamson,' said Lady Innishouran. 'The Erradeens may be odd, as you say, but they always manage to do well for themselves.' 'Not always, not always, my dear; the property seems to grow, but the men come to little,' Innishouran said, shaking his head; and he left his house with the full intention of becoming a 'good influence' to Walter. He proposed at once to put him up at the most irreproachable and distinguished of clubs, and asked him to dinner on the spot. 'I am afraid there is nobody of consequence left whom I can ask to meet you,' he said; 'but in any case Lady Innishouran is anxious to make your acquaintance.'

The Innishourans belonged to the ranks of those very great people for whom the season ends much earlier than for others. The duke had gone home early in June, and his son held that in the end of that month there was nobody of consequence left, except, he said to himself, cabinet ministers, who were perhaps something too much for a young Highland lord.

'And you must take your seat,' he said, 'that is a matter of duty. If we had met earlier the duke would of course have been one of your supporters.[103] I am sure my father will regret it very much. But, however, it can't be helped, and I, you know, don't occupy the necessary position; but there will be no difficulty in that respect.'

This was very different from Walter's fine misanthropic Byronic idea of solitary grandeur, and defiance of the staring ranks of superannuated peers. 'I am no politician,' he said awkwardly. 'I had scarcely thought it was worth the while.' 'It is always worth while to assume the privileges of your position,' Lord Innishouran said. Walter was taken possession of altogether by this good influence. And forthwith his path lay in a course of golden days. It was characteristic of Walter that it gave him no trouble to break his old ties, perhaps because of the fact that he had not, so to speak, made them by any exercise of his will, but simply drifted into them by the exertions of those who meant to benefit by his weakness. He did not, perhaps, put this into words, but yet felt it with a sort of interior conviction which was deeper than all those superficial shades of sentiment which bind some men to the companions of the day, even when they care little for them. Perhaps it was selfishness, perhaps strength – it is difficult sometimes to discriminate.

Thus Captain Underwood, after his interrupted, but latterly almost unbroken, sway over the young man's time and habits, found himself suddenly left in the lurch, and quite powerless over his pupil. The captain tried in the first place the easy tone of use and wont.

'Come, Erradeen,' he said, 'we shall be late. You forget the engagement you made with So-and-so, and So-and-so –'

'I think it was you who made the engagement,' Walter said. 'I am not going to keep it anyhow. I am going with Innishouran to –'

'With Lord Innishouran!' the other cried, overawed. 'So then,' he said, with such a sneer as is often effectual with the young and generous, 'now that you have got in with the big-wigs you mean to throw your old friends over.'

'I don't know much about old friends,' Walter said. 'I don't call the fellows at your club old friends.'

And then Captain Underwood made one of those mistakes which persons of inferior breeding are so apt to make. 'You were glad enough to have them when you had nobody else to take any notice of you,' he said. This was after two or three attempts to recover his old standing, and when he began to feel a certain exasperation. Walter, though he was irritable by nature, had so much the best of the argument at this moment that he kept his temper.

'I don't think,' he said, 'that I ever was very glad. I allowed myself to be drawn into it *faute de mieux*.'[104]

'And now I suppose you think you can throw *me* off too, like an old glove, in your infernal Scotch, cold-blooded way!' cried the captain.

'Am I Scotch?' said Lord Erradeen.

It was not much wonder, perhaps, if Underwood lost his temper. But another time he took matters more wisely. He would not give up in a fit of temper the hold he thought he had obtained upon the young man.[a] He was very unwilling,[b] as may be supposed, to resign his *protégé* and victim, and made spasmodic attempts to regain his 'influence.' At all times this 'influence' had been held precariously, and had it been a virtuous one like that of Lord Innishouran, Walter's mentor and guide might have called forth the sympathy of the spectator; for he had many things to bear from the young man's quick temper, and the constantly recurring dissatisfaction with himself and all things around which made him so difficult to deal with. Underwood, however, after his first disappointment, did not despair. The changeable young fellow, upon whom no one could calculate, whose mind was so uncertain, who would shoot off at a tangent in the most unexpected way, might as suddenly, as he had abandoned, turn to him again.

Miss Williamson received her new acquaintance very graciously when he went to see her next day. She met him with all the ease of an old acquaintance.

'Papa has been so busy,' she said, 'putting John into the business, that we have only got here at the very end of the season. Yes, it is a nuisance; but think how many people there are much better than I, that never come at all. Oona Forrester for instance. You think perhaps she is too good even to wish to come? Not at all; there never was a girl so good as that. Besides, I don't think it would be good. A girl ought to see the world as much as a boy. When you don't know the world, it makes you uninteresting – afterwards; you don't know how to talk to people. Not Oona, you know. I don't think there is any want of interest about her; but most people. Well, did you like Lord Innishouran? He is very kind, and fond of exerting a good influence. I felt that he was the very person for you.'

'You think then that I stand in need of a good influence?' Walter said.

'Yes, after Captain Underwood,' said Katie calmly. 'I think it was very lucky that you met papa, and that Lord Innishouran was at the theatre and came into our box. Perhaps you will look back to it and think—if you had not happened to come here, what people call accidentally, as you passed –'

'I might go a step further,' said Walter, 'and say if I had not happened to be with Captain Underwood, who knew your father, I should never have known what good fortune was standing upon these steps, and never have made the acquaintance of Miss Williamson.'

'You are making fun of me,' said Katie. 'I do not mind in the very least. But still it is just as well, perhaps, that you made the acquaintance of Miss Williamson. What were you going to do with yourself? Nothing so good I am sure as seeing the *Falcon,* and making friends with Lord Innishouran, who can be of a great deal of use to you. *We* cannot do much for you, of course. All sorts of people ask us, but still you know we are not of your class. We are only not vulgar, because – I told you last night.'

Walter laughed with guilty amusement, remembering how Lord Innishouran had justified Katie's estimate of the world's opinion.

*The Wizard's Son, Volume II* 207

'I do not understand,' he said, 'how any one can think of you and vulgarity in the same day.'

'Well,' said Katie, calmly, 'that is my own opinion. But still between me and Oona Forrester there is a great difference. I don't deceive myself about that. And why is it? I am–oh, some hundred times more rich. I can do almost whatever I like; that is to say, I can turn papa, as people say, round my little finger (that is rather vulgar, by the way). I come up here, I go abroad, I meet all kinds of interesting people: and yet I am not like Oona when all is said. Now how is that? It does not seem quite fair.'

She looked at him with an honest pair of blue eyes out of a prepossessing, sensible little face, as she asked this question with all the gravity of a philosophical investigator. Notwithstanding a little figure which threatened in after life to be dumpy, and a profile of which the lines were by no means distinctly drawn, Katie Williamson at twenty had enough of the *beauté du diable*[105] to make her rather an attractive little person. But as Walter looked at her, he too seemed to see a vision of the other with whom she compared herself. He always thought of Oona as she had stood watching his boat pushed off; his mind at the time had been too hurried and eager to remark her look; but that deeper faculty which garners up a face, a look, an act, which we do not seem to notice at the moment, and makes them afterwards more real and present to us than things that are under our eyes, had taken a picture of Oona as she stood in that profoundest deep of emotion, the most poignant moment of her life, with something of the wondering pang in her eyes which was in her heart. How many times since then had he seen her, though he had not seen her at the time! Looking at her in his mind's eye, he forgot altogether the question Katie was putting to him, and the necessity of protesting politely that she did herself wrong. Indeed he was not roused to this till Katie herself, after pausing for reply, said with a little sharpness, 'You don't make me any answer, Lord Erradeen: you ought to tell me I have no reason to be so humble-minded, but that I am as good as Oona. That is what any polite person would say.'

Thus challenged, Walter started with a certain sheepishness, and hastened to inform her, stammering, that comparisons were odious, but that there was nobody who might not be flattered, who ought not to be pleased, who, in short, would not be happy to think themselves on the same level –

Katie broke through his embarrassed explanations with a laugh. 'You quite agree with me,' she said, 'and that is what I like you for. I am not a girl who wants compliments. I am an inquirer. And things are so funny in this world: everything about ourselves is so droll–'

'What is that you are saying about being droll, Katie?' said Mr. Williamson, coming in. 'You do say very daft-like things, my dear, if that is what you mean. And how are you this morning, my Lord Erradeen? none the worse of that *Falcon?* Bless me, that falcon – that just set your teeth on edge the very sight of it. I am glad it was not served up to me. But you will stay to your lunch? We are just going to lunch, Katie and I; and we are both very fond of company. Now just stay. I will take it very kind if you have nothing better to do; and afterwards we'll stroll together to the Caledonian Club,[106] which you ought to be a member of, Lord Erradeen, for auld Scotland's sake. I will put you up if that is agreeable to you. Come, Katie, show Lord Erradeen the way. I have been knocking about all the morning, and I am bound to say I'm very ready for my lunch.'

And in this way affairs went on. Unaccustomed as he was to consider what any change of direction might lead to, it suited Walter very well to have a place where he was always welcome within his reach, and to be urged to stay to lunch, to go to the opera and the theatre, to be the audience for Katie's philosophies, which amused him. The atmosphere was new, and if not, perhaps, exciting, was fresh and full of variety. He had never in his life encountered anything like the easy wealthiness and homeliness, the power to do whatever they pleased, yet extreme simplicity in doing it, which characterised both father and daughter. And there was so much movement and energy about them that he was kept amused. Katie's perfectly just impression of the opinion of the world had no embittering effect upon that little philosopher, whose consciousness of well-being, and of the many ways in which she was better off than her neighbours, gave her a composure and good humour which were delightful. By-and-by,[a] though Walter himself was not aware of this, he began to receive invitations to entertainments at which the Williamsons were to be present, with that understanding on the part of society which is so instinctive, and which, though sometimes without foundation, rarely fails to realise its purpose. He was not indeed at all dependent upon them for his society. Lord Innishouran had opened the way, which once open, is so very easy for a young peer, whose antecedents, even if doubtful, have never compelled general disapproval. He who had known nobody, became in a month's time capable of understanding all the allusions, and entering into that curious society-talk which the most brilliant intellects out of it are confused by, and the most shallow within gain a certain appearance of intelligence from. After a little awkwardness at the beginning, easily explained by the benevolent theory that he had only just come to town, and knew nobody, he had speedily picked up the threads of the new existence, and got himself into its routine. To a new mind there is so much that is attractive in it—a specious air of knowing, of living, of greater experience, and more universal interests is diffused over it. And how indeed should it be possible not to know more in the midst of that constant multiplicity of events, and in sight and hearing of those that pull the strings and move the puppets everywhere? There is something in brushing shoulders with a minister of state that widens the apprehension; and even the lightest little *attaché*[107] gives a feeling that it is cosmopolitan to the circle in which he laughs and denies any knowledge of European secrets. Probably the denial is quite true, but nobody believes it, and the young lady with whom he has flirted knows a little more of the world in consequence—

*The Wizard's Son, Volume II* 209

that is, of the world as it is understood in those regions which claim that name for themselves. This tone Walter acquired so easily that it surprised himself. He did it better than many to the manner born, for to be sure there was to him a novelty in it, which made it feel real, and kept him amused and pleased with himself. He took his seat in the House of Lords, not in the Byronic way, and thought a great deal more of the House of Lords ever after. It seemed to him an important factor in European affairs, and the most august assembly in the world. No – that term perhaps is sacred to the House of Commons, or rather was sacred to the House of Commons, at the time when there were no other popular chambers of legislators[108] to contest the dignity. But a hereditary legislator may still be allowed to think with awe of that bulwark of the constitution[109] in which he has a share.

Lord Erradeen became one of the immediate circle of the Innishourans, where all 'the best people' were to be met. He became acquainted with great dignitaries both of Church and State. He talked to ambassadors – flirted – but no, he did not flirt very much. It was understood that he was to be asked with the Williamsons by all the people who knew them; and even among those who were a little above Miss Katie's range, it was known that there was an heiress of fabulous wealth, whose possessions would sensibly enlarge those of Lord Erradeen, and with whom it was an understood thing – so that flirtation with him was gently discouraged by the authorities. And he himself did not perhaps find that amusement necessary; for everything was new to him–his own importance, which had never up to this time been properly acknowledged, and still more the importance of others with whom it was a wonder to the young man to feel himself associating. The Underwood crew had always secretly angered him, as undeniably inferior to the society from which he felt himself to be shut out. He had been disgusted by their flattery, yet offended by their familiarity, even when in appearance *bon camarade*.[110] And the sense of internal satisfaction now in having attained unmistakably to 'the best people' was very delightful to him, and the air of good society a continual pleasure. Probably that satisfaction, too, might fail by and by, and the perennial sameness of humanity make itself apparent. But this did not occur within the first season, which indeed had begun to wane of its early glories as a season, the duke being gone, and other princes, high and mighty, before Walter appeared in it at all. There was, however, a great deal to be done still in the remnant of June and the early part of July: the heat, the culmination of all things, the sense that these joys will presently be over, and another season, which, in its way, is like another lifetime, departed into the past – producing a kind of whirl and intoxicating impulse. People met three or four times a day in the quickening of all the social wheels before they stopped altogether–in the Park[a] in the morning, at luncheon parties, afternoon receptions, dinners – two or three times in the evening – town growing more and more like the 'village,' which it is sometimes jocularly called.

210   *The Selected Works of Margaret Oliphant, Volume 21*

Through all this Walter spent a great deal of his time with Katie Williamson. Society flattered the probable match. He had to give her his arm to dinner, to dance with her, to talk to her, to get her shawl and call her carriage; her father, in his large good-humoured way, accepting with much placidity a sort of superior footman in Lord Erradeen. 'You are younger than I am,' he would say occasionally, with a laugh. He, too, began to take it for granted. It could not be said that it was Lord Erradeen's fault. He indeed gave in to it with a readiness which was unnecessary, by those continual visits at the hotel, luncheons, dinners, attendances at theatre and opera, which certainly originated in his own will and pleasure. But all that was so simple and natural. He had a sincere liking for Katie. She was a refuge to him from the other society which he had thrown over. Why should he refrain from visiting his country neighbours? There seemed nothing in the world against it, but everything in its favour. They asked him, to be sure, or he would not have gone. Mr. Williamson said – 'We'll see you some time to-morrow,' when they parted; and even Katie began to add – 'We are going to the So-and-so's; are you to be there?' Nothing could be more natural, more easy. And yet a girl who had been properly on her guard, and a young man particular not to have it said that he had 'behaved ill' to a lady, would have taken more care. Had Katie had a mother, perhaps it would not have been; but even in that case, why not? Walter was perfectly eligible. Supposing even that there had been a sowing of wild oats, that had not been done with any defiance of the world, and it was now over; and the Erradeens were already a great family, standing in no need of Katie's fortune to bolster them up. The mother, had she been living, would have had little reason to interfere. It was all perfectly natural, suitable in every way, such a marriage indeed as might have justified the proverb, and been 'made in heaven.'

It would be scarcely correct to say, as is sometimes said, that the last to know of this foregone conclusion, were the parties chiefly concerned. It might indeed be true in respect to Walter, but not to the other principal actor, who indeed was perfectly justified in her impression that he was a conscious agent throughout, and intended everything he was supposed to intend. Katie, for her part, was not unaware of the progress of events upon which all the world had made up its mind. She expected nothing less than to be called upon to decide, and that without any great delay – perhaps before she left town, perhaps shortly after her return home – whether or not she would be Lady Erradeen. She did not think of the coronet upon her handkerchief, as Julia Herbert had done, but of many things which were of more importance. She frankly avowed to herself that she liked Lord Erradeen; as to being in love with him, that was perhaps a different matter. She was much experienced in the world (or thought herself so) though she was so young; having had no mother, and feeling herself the natural guide of her other less enlightened parent. And she was very fond of her father. She could 'turn him round her little finger.' Wherever she wished to go he went; whatever she wished to do, he was ready to carry out her wishes. She was not at all sure that with a husband she would have half so much of her own way. And Katie liked her own way. She could not fancy herself blindly, foolishly in love as people were in books; but she liked Lord Erradeen. So far as that went it was all simple enough; but on the other hand, there were mysteries about the family, and Katie scorned and hated mysteries. Suppose he should ask her to believe in the Warlock lord? Katie knew what would follow; she would laugh in his face, however serious he might be. To her it would be impossible to believe in any such supernatural and antiquated nonsense. She felt that she would scorn even the man who was her husband did he give faith to such fables. She would not listen to any evidence on the subject. Sometimes words had dropped from him which sounded like a belief in the possibility of such influences. To think that she, Katie, should have to defer to superstition, to be respectful, perhaps, of absurdity such as this! *That* she would never do. But otherwise she allowed in her sensible, much-reasoning, composed little mind, that there was very little to object to in Lord Erradeen.

Walter himself was not half so ready to realise the position. He liked Katie, and had not been much accustomed to deny himself what he liked even in his days of poverty. He did not see now why he should not take the good with which the gods provided him in the shape of a girl's society, any more than in any other way. He was a little startled when he perceived by some casual look or word that he was understood by the world in general to be Katie's lover. It amused him at first: but he had so just an opinion of Katie that he was very sure she had no disposition to 'catch' him, such as he had not doubted Julia Herbert to have. He might be vain, but not beyond reason. Indeed it was not any stimulus to vanity to be an object of pursuit to Julia Herbert. It was apparent enough what it would be to her to marry Lord Erradeen, whereas it was equally apparent that to marry anybody would be no object, unless she loved him, to Katie. And Katie, Walter was sure, betrayed no tokens of love. But there were many things involved that did not meet the common eye. Since he had floated into this new form of 'influence,' since he had known the girl whom it would be so excellent for the Erradeen property that he should marry, a halcyon period had begun for Walter. The angry sea of his own being, so often before lashed into angry waves and convulsions, had calmed down. Things had gone well with him: he had come into the society of his peers; he had assumed the privileges of the rank which up to this time had been nothing but a burden and contrariety. The change was ineffable, not to be described; nothing disturbed him from outside, but, far more wonderful, nothing irritated him within. He felt tranquil, he felt *good:* he had no inclination to be angry; he was not swayed with movements of irritation and disgust. The superiority of his society was perhaps not sufficient to account for this, for he began to see the little ridicules of society after a month's experience of it. No, it was himself that was changed; his disturbances were calmed; he and his fate were no longer on contrary sides.[a]

It seemed to the young man that the change all about and around him was something miraculous. He seemed to stand on a calm eminence and look back upon the angry waters which he had escaped with a shiver at the dangers past, and a sense of relief which was indescribable. If he could get Katie to marry him that calm perhaps might become permanent. There would be no guilt in doing this, there would be no wrong to any one. And then he thought of Oona on the beach, looking after his boat. What was she thinking then, he wondered? Did she ever think of him now? Did she remember him at all? Had she not rather dismissed that little episode from her mind like a dream? He sighed as he thought of her, and wondered, with wistful half-inquiries; but, after all, there was no ground for inquiries, and no doubt she had forgotten him long ago. Other questions altogether came into his mind with the thought of Katie Williamson. If he married her would not all the elements of evil which he had felt to be so strong, which had risen into such force, and against which he had been unable to contend—would they not all be lulled for ever? It would be no yielding to the power that had somehow, he no longer reasoned how, got him in its clutches: but it would be a compromise. He had not been bidden to seek this wealthy bride, but in his heart he felt that this way peace lay. It would be a compromise. It would be promoting the interests of the family. Her wealth would add greatly to the importance of the house of Erradeen. And if he made up his mind to a step which had so many advantages, would it not in some sort be the signing of a treaty, the establishment of peace? He thought with a shudder, out of this quiet in which his spirit lay, of those conflicts from which he had escaped. He was like a man on firm land contemplating the horrors of the stormy sea from which he had escaped, but amid which he might be plunged again. It was possible that the disposition in which that sea itself should be braved, rather than accept its alternative, might return to him again. But at the present moment, in full enjoyment of so many more pleasures, and with the struggles of the former period in his mind, he shuddered at the prospect. Katie, it seemed to him, would be a compromise with fate.

The other person most deeply concerned – to wit, Mr. Williamson – was in a state of rapture, and chuckled all day long over the prospect. He would have had Lord Erradeen with them wherever they went. Not a doubt on the subject, not a possibility that all was not plain sailing, crossed his mind. There was no courtship indeed between them, such as was usual in his own more animated class and age. It was not the fashion, he said to himself, with a laugh; but what did the young fellow come for so constantly if it were not Katie? 'It's not for my agreeable conversation,' he said to himself, with another guffaw. When a young man was for ever haunting the place where a girl was, there could not be two opinions about his motives. And it would be very suitable. He said this to himself with

*The Wizard's Son, Volume II*                                                           213

an elation which made his countenance glow. To think of losing Katie had been terrible to him, but this would not be losing Katie. Auchnasheen was next door to Birkenbraes, and they should have Birkenbraes if they liked–they should have anything they liked. John was splendidly provided for by the business and all the immense capital invested in it; but Katie was his darling, and from her he could not be separated. A pretty title for her, and a very good fellow for a husband and no separation! He thought, with a sort of delighted horror as of some danger past, that she was just the girl that might have fallen in love with a lad going out to India or to the ends of the earth, and gone with him, whatever any one could say; and to think by the good guiding of Providence she had lighted on one so ideally suitable as Lord Erradeen! The good man went about the world rubbing his hands with satisfaction. It was all he could do, in his great contentment, not to precipitate matters. He had to put force upon himself when he was alone with Walter not to bid him take courage, and settle the matter without delay.

# CHAPTER IX.[a]

THINGS went on in this way till nearly the end of July, when the parks were brown like heather, and a great many people already had gone out of town. Those who remained kept up their gaieties with a sort of desperation of energy, intent upon getting as much as possible out of the limited time. And what with the drawing closer of the bonds of society, and the additional fervour of the pace at which everything went on, Walter spent almost his entire time in Katie's society, meeting her everywhere, and being, by universal consent, constituted her partner and escort wherever they did meet. She had half begun to wonder herself that nothing further came of it, and that he did not speak the words which would settle every question, so far at least as he was concerned. Miss Williamson, for her own part, reserved her personal freedom. She would not say even to herself that she had finally made up her mind. She would see what he had to say for himself, and then – But Katie was very prudent, and would not be premature. Walter, too, rather wondered at himself that he did nothing conclusive. He perceived for the first time in his life that the position was not one which could be glided over, which he could terminate simply by going away. He had come to that, that Katie must cut the knot, not he: or else, which was most likely, bind it closer. She was a girl of whom nobody could think lightly–not a good girl only, but a little personage of distinct importance. No doubt she would make such a wife as a man might be very well satisfied with, and even proud of in his way. She was even pretty – enough: she was clever, and very well able to hold her own. At the head of a table, at the head of a great house, Katie, though with in every way a pronounced, yet not unrefined Scotch accent[111] (as indeed in the wife of a Scotch lord was very appropriate), would be quite equal to the position.

And peace would come with her: no young man could do more for his family than bring such an accession of fortune into it. It would probably save him from further vexation about small matters of the estate, and those persecutions about leases and investments to which he was now subject. This had been the one drawback of his life since he had known Katie. He had been asked to decide on one side and another: he had concluded against Peter Thomson the sheep farmer, in sheer vexation with Shaw's importunity. He had thought more than once that he saw old Milnathort shake his head, and was subject to the factor's outspoken blame. But if he brought Katie into the family, what would it matter about these small things? One or two unsatisfactory tenants would be little in comparison with that large addition of fortune. And he liked Katie. In herself she was very agreeable to him—a companion whom he by no means wished to lose. There was something in her independence, her almost boyishness, her philosophies and questionings, which made her unlike any other girl with whom he had ever been brought into contact. The thing was not that they were in love with each other, but that they could get on quite well together. Notwithstanding, Walter, being quite content with the circumstances as they were, took no new step, but let the course of events run on day by day.

They had gone together to one of the last celebrations of the waning season – the evening reception at the Royal Academy.[112] Everybody who was in town was there; and Walter, who had now an abundance of acquaintances, went from one group to another, paying his respects to the ladies, but always keeping somewhere within reach of the Williamsons, with whom he had come. Katie expected him to be within reach. It had come to be a habit with her to look round for Lord Erradeen, to beg him to get her what she wanted, to take her to this or that. Her father, though always most dutiful[a] in attendance, yet naturally found persons of his own age to talk with; and he was apt to say foolish things about the pictures, and say them at the top of his voice, which made Katie cautious not to direct his attention to them more than was necessary; but Walter, who on the whole considered her something of an authority on art, and was not unwilling to accept her guidance to some extent, was here a very agreeable companion. She had just intimated to him her desire to look at something of which the artist had been speaking to her – for Katie considered it her duty even in presence of society to show a certain regard for the pictures, as the supposed object of the meeting – and taking his arm, was going on to the corner indicated, when somebody all at once made a little movement towards them with a quick exclamation of pleasure, and saying, 'Walter!' suddenly laid a finger upon Lord Erradeen's unoccupied arm.

This sudden incident produced a curious dramatic effect amid the many groups of this elegant company. Some of the bystanders even were attracted, and one enterprising young painter took in his mind's eye an instantaneous sketch of the three figures enacting a scene in the genteel comedy of life. Walter in the midst, startled,

*The Wizard's Son, Volume II* 215

looking a little guilty, yet not losing his composure, replied readily enough, 'Julia!' holding out his hand to the somewhat eager stranger, who leaned forward towards him with sparkling eyes, and the most arch and smiling expression of pleasure and interest. Katie, on the other hand, held back a little, and looked very gravely at the meeting, with a manifest absence in her countenance of that pleasure which the others expressed, whether they felt it or not. She did not withdraw from Walter's arm, or separate herself in any way, but gazed at the new-comer who addressed him so familiarly with a look of grave inspection. Katie meant to look dignified, and as a girl should look who was the lawful possessor of the attention to which an illegitimate claimant had thus appeared; but her figure was not adapted for expressing dignity. She was shorter than Julia, and less imposing, and her *beauté du diable*[113] could not bear comparison with Miss Herbert's really fine features and charming figure. Julia was as much, or indeed more, a country girl than the other; but she was much handsomer, and had all the instincts of society. Her face was radiant with smiles as she gave her hand to Walter, and half-permitted, half-compelled him to hold it a moment longer than was necessary in his.

'I thought we could not be long of meeting,' she said, 'and that you were sure to be here. I am with my cousins the Tom Herberts. I suppose you know them? They have asked me up for the fag-end of the season. I always told you my season was the very end – and the result is, I am quite fresh when you jaded revellers have had too much of it, and are eager to hurry away.'

And indeed she looked fresh, glowing, and eager, and full of life and pleasure; her vivid looks seemed to take the colour out of Katie, who still stood with her hand upon Walter's arm. For his part he did not know what to do.

'You would not think, to look round these rooms, that it was the fag-end of the season,' he said.

'Ah! that's your usual benevolence to make me think less of my disadvantages,' said Julia. 'You know I don't encourage illusions on that subject. You must come and see me. You must be made acquainted with my cousins, if you don't know them.'

'In the mean time, Lord Erradeen, will you take me to my father, please,' said Katie, on his arm.

'Oh,' cried Julia, 'don't let me detain you now. We have just come. You'll find me presently, Walter, when you are at liberty. No, go, go, we shall have plenty of time afterwards for our talks. I insist upon your going now.'

And she dismissed him with a beaming smile, with a little pat on his arm as if it had been she who was his lawful proprietor, not Katie. Miss Williamson said nothing for the moment, but she resisted Walter's attempt to direct her towards the picture she had meant to visit. 'I think I will go to papa,' she said. 'I must not detain you, Lord Erradeen, from your – friend.'

'That doesn't matter,' said Walter; 'I shall see her again. Let us do what we intended to do. What is the etiquette on such an occasion, Miss Williamson?

216 *The Selected Works of Margaret Oliphant, Volume 21*

Would it be correct for me, a mere man, to introduce two ladies to each other? You know I am a novice in society. I look for instruction to you.'

'I can't tell, I am sure,' said Katie. 'I don't think the case has occurred to me before. You seem to know the lady very well, Lord Erradeen?'

'I have known her almost all my life,' Walter replied, not quite at his ease. 'We have played together, I suppose. She comes from Sloebury where my mother is living. They have all sorts of fine connections, but they are poor, as you would divine from what she said.'

'I did not listen to what she said. Conversation not addressed to one's self,' said Katie with some severity 'one has nothing to do with. I could see of course that you were on the most friendly terms.'

'Oh, on quite friendly terms,' said Walter; he could not for his life have prevented a little laugh from escaping him, a laugh of consciousness and amusement and embarrassment. And Katie, who was full of suspicion, pricked up her little ears.

'I should have said on terms that were more than friendly,' she said in a voice that was not without a certain sharp tone.

Walter laughed again with that imbecility to which all men are subject when pressed upon such a question.

'Can anything be better than friendly?' he said. 'Poor Julia! she has a very kind heart. Was not this the picture you wanted to see?'

'Oh,' cried Katie, 'I have forgotten all about the picture! This little incident has put it out of my head. Human interest is superior to art. Perhaps if you had not left Sloebury, if your circumstances had not changed, your friendship might have changed into – something warmer, as people say.'

'Who can tell?' cried Walter in his vanity; 'but in that case we should have been two poverties together, and that you know would never do.'

'I am no judge,' cried Katie; 'but at all events you are not a poverty now, and there is no reason – Oh, there is papa; he is talking to *that* ambassador – but never mind. Patience for another minute, Lord Erradeen, till we can make our way to him, and then you shall go.'

'But I don't want to go,' Walter said.

'Oh, that is impossible; when Miss – Julia – I am sure I beg your pardon, for I don't know her other name – was so kind as to tell you where to find her. You must want to get rid of me. Papa, give me your arm; I want to show you something.'

'Eh! what do you want to show me, Katie? I'm no judge, you know. You will find it very much better, I'm confident, to show it to young Erradeen.'

'Thank you, Lord Erradeen,' said Katie, making him a curtsey. She took her father's almost reluctant arm, and turned him suddenly away at once from his ambassador, and from Walter, who stood astonished to find himself thus thrown off. 'Look here, papa, it is in this direction,' the young lady said.

*The Wizard's Son, Volume II* 217

Mr. Williamson's voice was rather louder than good manners allowed. 'What! is it a tiff?' he said, with a laugh. 'That's according to all the rules, Katie. I'm astonished you have not had one before.'

Walter heard this speech as well as Katie, and it threw the last gleam of reality on the position in which he stood. That he was looked upon by her father as her lover, and no doubt by herself too, or what would the encounter with Julia have mattered to her, was plain enough. He had known it vaguely before, but only from his own side of the question, and had debated it as a matter of expediency to himself. But when he saw it from the other side, recognising with a shock that they too had something to say in the matter, and coming right up against that barrier of a *must*, which was so obnoxious to his character, everything took a very different aspect. And Julia, too, had assumed an air of property – had made a certain claim of right in respect to him. What! was he to be made a slave, and deprived of free action in respect to the most important act of his life, because he had freely accepted invitations that were pressed upon him? The thing was ridiculous, he said to himself, with some heat. It might be well for him to offer himself to Katie, but to have a virtual demand made upon him, and acknowledge a necessity, that was not to be borne. Still less was he likely to acknowledge any right on the part of Julia Herbert. In her case he was altogether without responsibility, he said to himself; and even in the other, was it a natural consequence of Mr. Williamson's perpetual invitations and hospitality that he should put himself at the disposal of Mr. Williamson's daughter? He seemed to hear that worthy's laugh pealing after him as he took his way hastily in the opposite direction to that in which he had met Julia, with a determination to yield to neither. 'A tiff!' and, 'according to all the rules?' A lovers' quarrel, that was what the man meant; and who was he that he should venture to assume that Lord Erradeen was his daughter's lover?

Walter hurried through the rooms in the opposite direction, till he got near the great staircase, with its carpeted avenue, between the hedges of flowers, and the group of smiling, bowing, picturesque Academicians[114] in every variety of beard, still receiving the late, and speeding the parting guests. But fate was too much here for the angry young man. Before he had reached the point of exit, he felt once more that tap on his arm. 'Walter! I believe he is running away,' said a voice, close to him; and there was Julia, radiant, with her natural protectors beside her, making notes of all that passed.

This time he could not escape. He was introduced to Lady Herbert and Sir Thomas before he could move a step from amid that brilliant crowd. Then Julia, like Katie, declared that she had something she wished to show him, and led him – half-reluctant, half, in the revulsion of feeling, pleased, to have some one else to turn to – triumphantly away.

Sir Thomas, who was tired, protested audibly against being detained; but his wife, more wise, caught him by the arm, and imposed patience.

218       *The Selected Works of Margaret Oliphant, Volume 21*

'Can't you see!' she cried in his ear, 'what a chance it is for Julia – Lord Erradeen, a most eligible young man. And think the anxiety she is, and that one never can be sure what she may do.' 'She is a horrid little coquette; and you may be sure the man means nothing serious, unless he is a fool!' growled Sir Thomas. But his wife replied calmly, 'Most men are fools; and she is not a bad-hearted creature, though she must have some one dangling after her. Don't let us interfere with her chance, poor thing. I shall ask him to dinner,' Lady Herbert said. And Sir Thomas, though he was rather a tyrant at home, and hated late hours, was kept kicking his heels in the vestibule, snarling at everybody who attempted to approach, for nearly an hour by the clock. So far, even in the most worldly bosoms, do conscientious benevolence and family affection go.

'Come, quick!' said Julia, 'out of hearing of Maria. She wants to hear everything; and I have so many things to ask you. Is it all settled? That was She,[a] of course. How we used to laugh about Miss Williamson! But I knew all the time it would come true. Of course that was *she*,[b] Julia said, leaning closely upon his arm and looking up into his face.

'I don't know what you mean by *she*.[c] It is Miss Williamson, certainly,' he said.

'I was sure of it! She is not so pretty as I should have expected from your good taste. But why should she be pretty? She has so many other charms. Indeed, now that I think of it, it would have been mean of her to be pretty – and is it all settled?' Julia said.

She looked at him with eyes half laughing, half reproachful,[d] full of provocation. She was as a matter of fact slightly alarmed, but not half so much as she said.

'I am not aware what there is to settle. We are country neighbours, and I meet them frequently – they go everywhere.'

'Ah! so are we country neighbours, *amis d'enfance:*[115] but I don't go everywhere, Lord Erradeen. Yes, I called you Walter; that was for a purpose, to pique her curiosity, to make her ask who was that forward horrid girl. Did she? I hope she was piqued.'

'I heard nothing about any forward, horrid girl. She is not that sort of person. But I prefer to hear about yourself rather than to discuss Miss Williamson. When did you come? and where are you? What a pity,' Walter said hypocritically, 'that you come so late.'

'Ah, isn't it? but what then? We are too poor to think of the season. This is what one's fine friends always do. They ask us for the last week, when everything is stifled in dust–when all you revellers are dead tired and want nothing so much as to go away–then is the moment for poor relations. But mind that you come to Bruton Street,' Julia said. 'It gives me consequence.[116] They are not very much in society, and a title always tells.'

'You do not leave any ground for my vanity. I am not to suppose that I am asked for any other reason.'

Julia pressed his arm a little with her fingers. She sighed and gave him a look full of meaning.

'The Tom Herberts will think a great deal of you,' she said; 'they will instantly ask you to dinner. As for me—what am I that I should express any feeling? We are country neighbours, as you were saying. But enough of me. Let us return to our – lamb,' cried Julia. 'Tell me, have you seen a great deal of her? How little I thought when we used to laugh about Miss Williamson that it would come true.'

'It has come true, as it began, in your imagination,' said Walter, provoked, and thinking the reiteration vulgar. He was aware that a great many people who knew him were remarking the air with which this new young lady hung upon his arm. They were not equal in this respect. She had few acquaintances, and did not care, nay, would have been pleased that she should be remarked; whereas he began to throb with impatience and eager desire to get away from the comment he foresaw, and from the situation altogether. Julia was very pretty, more pretty and sparkling in the pleasure of having met and secured him thus at the very outset of her too-short and too-late campaign in town, than he had ever known her, and there was nothing that was objectionable in her dress. The Tom Herberts were people against whom nothing could be said. And yet Lord Erradeen, himself not much more than a novice, felt that to everybody whom they met, Julia would be truly a country neighbour, a girl whom no one knew, and whose object, to secure a recreant lover, would be jumped at by many fine observant eyes. There was no return of tenderness in his sentiments towards her. Indeed there had been no tenderness in his sentiments at any time he said to himself with some indignation, which made it all the more hard that he should thus be exhibited as her captive before the eyes of assembled London now. But notwithstanding his impatience he could not extricate himself from Julia's toils. When after various little pretences of going to see certain pictures, which she never looked at, she suffered him to take her back to her friends, Lady Herbert showed herself most gracious to the young man. She begged that as Julia and he were, as she heard, very old friends, he would come to Bruton Street whenever it suited him. Would he dine there to-morrow, next day? It would give Sir Thomas and herself the greatest pleasure. Dear Julia, unfortunately, had come to town so late: there was scarcely anything going on to make it worth her while: and it would be so great a pleasure to her to see something of her old friend. Julia gave him little looks of satirical comment aside while her cousin made these little speeches, and whispers still more emphatic as he accompanied her down-stairs[a] in the train of the Herberts, who were too happy to get away after waiting an hour for the young lady. 'Don't you think it is beautiful to see how concerned she is for my pleasure; and so sorry that I have come so late! The truth is that she is delighted to make your acquaintance. But come, do come, all the same,' she said, her cheek almost touching Walter's shoulder as she looked up in his face.[b]

Need it be doubted that, with the usual malign disposition of affairs at such a crisis, the Williamsons' carriage drew up behind that of the Herberts, and that Walter had to encounter the astonished gaze of good Mr. Williamson, and the amused but not very friendly look of Katie, as he appeared in this very intimate conjunction? Julia's face so full of delighted and affectionate dependence raised towards him, and his own head stooped towards her to hear what she was saying. He scarcely could turn aside now to give them one deprecating glance, praying for a suspension of judgment. When he had put Julia into her cousin's carriage, and responded as best he could to the 'Now remember to-morrow!' which she called to him from the window, he was just in time to see Mr. Williamson's honest countenance, with a most puzzled aspect, directed to him from the window of the next carriage as the foot-man[a] closed the door. The good man waved his hand by way of good-night, but his look was perplexed and uncomfortable. Walter stood behind on the steps of Burlington House[117] amid all the shouts of the servants and clang of the hoofs and carriages, himself too much bewildered to know what he was doing. After a while he returned to get his coat, and walked home with the sense of having woke out of a most unpleasant dream, which somehow was true.

As for Katie, she drove home without a remark, while her father talked and wondered, and feared lest they had been 'ill bred' to Lord Erradeen. 'He came with us, and he would naturally calculate on coming home with us,' the good man said. But Katie took no notice. She was 'a wilful monkey' as he had often said, and sometimes it would happen to her like this, to take her own way. When they reached the hotel, Captain Underwood, of all people in the world, was standing in the hall with the sleepy waiter who had waited up for them. 'I thought perhaps Erradeen might be with you,' the captain said apologetically. Katie, who on ordinary occasions could not endure him, made some gracious reply, and asked him to come in with the most unusual condescension though it was so late. 'Lord Erradeen is not with us,' she said. 'He found some friends, people just newly come to town, so far as I could judge, a Miss Julia – I did not catch her name – somebody from Sloebury.'

'Oh!' said Underwood, excited by his good fortune, 'Julia Herbert. Poor Erradeen! just when he wanted to be with you! Well that's hard; but perhaps he deserved it.'

'What did he deserve? I supposed,' said Katie, 'from the way they talked, that they were old friends.'

Underwood did not in his heart wish to injure Walter – rather the other way; he wanted him to marry Katie, whose wealth was dazzling even to think of. But Walter had not behaved well to him, and he could not resist the temptation of revenging himself, especially as he was aware, like all the rest, that a lovers' quarrel is a necessary incident in a courtship. He smiled accordingly and said, 'I know: they are such old friends that the lady perhaps has some reason to think

*The Wizard's Son, Volume II* 221

that Erradeen had used her rather badly. He is that kind of a fellow you know: he must always have some one to amuse himself with. He used to be dangling after her to no end, singing duets, and that sort of thing. Sloebury is the dullest place in creation–there was nothing else to do.'

Katie made very little demonstration. She pressed her lips tightly together for a moment and then she said, 'You see, papa, it was not ill-bred, but the most polite thing you could have done to leave Lord Erradeen. Good-night, Captain Underwood.' And she swept out of the room with her candle, her silken train rustling after her, as though it was too full of indignation with the world. Her father stood somewhat blankly gazing after her. He turned to the other with a plaintive look when she was gone.

'Man,' said Mr. Williamson, 'I would not have said that. Don't you see there is a tiff, a kind of a coolness, and it is just making matters worse? Will you take anything? No? Well, it is late, as you say, and I will bid you good night.'

It was thus that the effect produced by Julia's appearance was made decisive. Walter for his part, walking slowly along in the depth of the night towards his rooms, was in the most curiously complicated state of feeling. He was angry and indignant both at Miss Herbert's encounter, and the assumption on the part of the Williamsons that it was to them that his attention belonged; and he was disturbed and uneasy at the interruption of that very smooth stream which was not indeed true love, but yet was gliding on to a similar consummation. These were his sentiments on the surface; but underneath other feelings found play. The sense that one neutralised the other, and that he was in the position of having suddenly recovered his freedom, filled his mind with secret elation. After he had expended a good deal of irritated feeling upon the girl whom he felt to be pursuing him, and her whom he pursued, there suddenly came before his eyes a vision, soft, and fresh, and cool, which came like the sweet Highland air in his face, as he went along the hot London street – Oona standing on the beach, looking out from her isle upon the departing guest. What right had he to think of Oona? What was there in that dilemma to suggest to him a being so much above it, a creature so frank yet proud, who never could have entered into any such competition? But he was made up of contradictions, and this was how it befell. The streets were still hot and breathless after the beating of the sun all day upon the unshaded pavements and close lines of houses. It was sweet to feel in imagination the ripple of the mountain air, the coolness of the woods and water. But it was only in imagination. Oona with her wistful sweet eyes was as far off from him, as far off as heaven itself. And in the mean time he had a sufficiently difficult imbroglio of affairs on hand.

Next morning Lord Erradeen had made up his mind. He had passed a disturbed and uneasy night. There was no longer any possibility of delay. Oona, after all, was but a vision. Two or three days – what was that to fix the colour of a life? He would always remember, always be grateful to her. She had come to his succour in the most terrible moment. But when he rose from his uneasy sleep, there was in him a hurrying impulsion which he seemed unable to resist. Something that was not his own will urged and hastened him. Since he had known Katie all had gone well. He would put it, he thought, beyond his own power to change, he would go to her that very morning and make his peace and decide his life. That she might refuse him did not occur to Walter. He had a kind of desire to hurry to the hotel before breakfast, which would have been indecorous and ridiculous, to get it over. Indeed, so strong was the impulse in him to do this, that he had actually got his hat and found himself in the street, breakfastless, before it occurred to him how absurd it was. He returned after this and went through the usual morning routine, though always with a certain breathless sense of something that hurried him on. As soon as he thought it becoming, he set out with a half-solemn[a] feeling of self-renunciation, almost of sacrifice. If 'twere done when 'tis done, then 'twere well it were done quickly.[118] This was not a very lover-like frame of mind. He felt that he was giving up everything that was visionary, the poetry of vague ideals, and even more, the inspiration of that face, the touch of that hand which had been as soft as snow. Katie's hand was a very firm and true one. It would give him an honest help in the world; and with her by his side the other kind of aid, he said to himself, would be unnecessary. No conflict with the powers of darkness would be forced upon him. His heated imagination adopted these words in haste, and did not pause to reflect how exaggerated and ridiculous they would sound to any reasonable ear.

He found Mr. Williamson alone in the room where Katie was usually ready to receive him in her fresh morning toilette and smile of welcome. The good man wore a puzzled look, and was looking over his bill with his cheque-book beside him on the table. He looked up when Lord Erradeen came in, with a countenance full of summings up.

'Yes,' he said, 'I am just settling everything, which is never very pleasant. You need to be made of money when you come to London. Katie is away this morning by skreigh of day. Oh, yes, it was a very sudden resolution. She just took it into her little head. And here am I left to pay everything, and follow as soon as I can. It is breaking up our pleasant party. But what am I to do? I tell her she rules me with a rod of iron. I hope we'll see a great deal of you in autumn, when you come to Auchnasheen.'

Walter went back to his rooms with a fire of resentment in his veins, but yet a sense of exhilaration quite boyish and ridiculous. Whatever might happen, he was free. And now what was to be his next step? To play with fire and Julia, or to take himself out of harm's way? He almost ran against Underwood as he debated this question, hurrying towards his own door.

***

# CHAPTER X.[a]

IT was late in October, when summer was gone even from the smooth English lanes about Sloebury, and autumn, with that brave flourish of flags and trumpets by which she conceals decay, was in full sway over the Scotch hills and moors when Lord Erradeen was next heard of by those interested in him. He had gone abroad at the end of the season, without even returning to Sloebury to see his mother, and very little had been known of him during this disappearance. Mrs. Methven, it is to be supposed, knew something of his movements, but the replies she gave to questions addressed to her were short and vague. She generally answered that he was in Switzerland; but that is rather a wide word, as everybody said, and if she was acquainted more particularly with his whereabouts she chose to keep the information to herself. And in Scotland there was nothing at all known about him. All kinds of business waited till he should be there, or should answer to the appeals made him. Letters elicited no reply, and indeed it was by no means certain that he got the letters that were sent to him. Mrs. Methven writing to Mr. Milnathort, avowed, though with reserve, that she was by no means sure of her son's address, as he was travelling about; and at his club they had no information. So that all the details of the management of the estates, about which their proprietor required to be consulted, had accumulated, and lay hopelessly in the Edinburgh office, sometimes arranging themselves by mere progress of time, though this the angry lawyer, provoked beyond measure, would not allow. The Williamsons had returned to Loch Houran, to their magnificent modern castle of Birkenbraes, in August, for the grouse: it being the habit of the hospitable millionnaire to fill his vast house for those rites of autumnal observance; but neither did they know anything of the wandering peer. 'We saw a great deal of young Erradeen in London,' Mr. Williamson said; 'but at the end he just slipped through our fingers like a knotless thread.' 'That seems to be his most prominent characteristic,' said Lord Innishouran, who for a time flattered himself that he had 'acquired an influence' over this unsatisfactory young man; and the other potentates of the county shook their heads, and remarked that the Erradeens were always strange, and that this new man must be just like the rest.[b]

There was another too who began to be of the same opinion. Notwithstanding the indignant manner in which Katie had darted away after discovering the previous relations of Walter with Julia Herbert, and hearing Underwood's malicious statement that 'he must always have some one to amuse himself with,' there was yet in her mind a conviction that something more must be heard of Lord Erradeen. He would write, she thought, when he found that she had not waited for any explanation from him. It was not possible that after the close intercourse that had existed he would disappear and make no sign. And when months passed by and nothing was heard of him, Katie was more surprised than she would con-

224    *The Selected Works of Margaret Oliphant, Volume 21*

fess. He had 'slipped away like a knotless thread.' Nothing could be more true than this description. From the moment when she turned away from him in the great room at Burlington House, she had heard or seen nothing more of Walter. Her heart[a] was quite whole, and there was not any personal wistfulness in her questionings; but she was piqued, and curious, and perhaps more interested in Lord Erradeen than she had ever been before.

In these circumstances it was very natural, almost inevitable, that she should take Oona into her confidence.[b] For Oona was known, on his first appearance, to have 'seen a great deal' of Lord Erradeen. This she herself explained with some eagerness to mean that she had met him three times – one of these times being the memorable moment of the eviction which he had put a stop to, an incident which had naturally made a great commotion in the country-side. But Mrs. Forrester had never felt the slightest reluctance to talk of their intercourse with the young lord. She had declared that she took a great interest in him, and that she was his first friend on Loch Houran: and anticipated with cheerful confidence the certainty of his coming back, 'more like one of my own boys than anything else,' she said. The fact that the Forresters were the first to know, and indeed the only people who had known him, did indeed at the time of his first appearance identify them with Lord Erradeen in a marked way. The minister and the factor, though not matchmakers, had allowed, as has been said, to steal into their minds, that possibility which is more or less in the air when youth and maiden meet. And there were others who had said – some,[c] that Oona Forrester would make a capital wife for Lord Erradeen, a young man who was a stranger in the country; some, that it would be a good thing for Oona to secure, before any one else knew him, the best match on the loch; and some even, that though Mrs. Forrester looked such a simple person, she had her wits all about her, and never neglected the interests of her family. In the course of time, as Lord Erradeen disappeared and was not heard of any more this gossip drooped and died away. But it left a general impression on the mind of the district that there was a tie of friendship between Lord Erradeen and the ladies of the Isle. They had something to do with him – not love, since he had never come again; but some link of personal knowledge, interest, which nobody else had: any information about him would naturally be carried there first; and Katie, having elucidations to ask as well as confidences to make, lost no time in carrying her budget[119] to the Isle.

The true position of affairs there was unsuspected by any one. The blank which Oona anticipated had closed down upon her with a force even stronger than that which she had feared. The void, altogether unknown to any one but herself, had made her sick with shame and distress. It was inconceivable to her that the breaking off of an intercourse so slight (as she said to herself), the absence of an individual of whom she knew so little, not enough even for the most idiotical love at first sight, should have thus emptied out the interests of life, and made such a vacancy about her. It was a thing not to be submitted to,

*The Wizard's Son, Volume II* 225

not to be acknowledged even, which she would have died sooner than let any one know, which she despised herself for being capable of. But notwithstanding all this self-indignation, repression, and shame, it was there. Life seemed emptied out of all its interest to the struggling, indignant, unhappy girl. Why should such a thing be? A chance encounter, no fault of hers, or his, or any one's. A few meetings, to her consciousness quite accidental, which she had neither wished for nor done anything to bring about. And then some strange difficulty, danger, she could not tell what, in which he had appealed to her for her help. She would have refused that help to no one. It was as natural for her to give aid and service as to breathe. But why, why should a thing so simple have brought upon her all this that followed? She was not aware even that she loved the man; no! she said to herself with a countenance ablaze with shame, how could she love him? she knew nothing of him; and yet when he had gone away the light had been drawn out of her horizon, the heart out of her life. It was intolerable, it was cruel; and yet so it was. Nobody knew with what a miserable monotony the old routine of existence went on for some time after. She was so indignant, so angry, so full of resistance, that it disturbed her temper a little: and perhaps the irritation did her good. She went on (of course, having no choice in the matter) with all her old occupations just as usual, feeling herself in a sort of iron framework within which she moved without any volition of her own. The winter months passed like one long blank unfeatured day. But when the spring came, Oona's elastic nature had at last got the upper hand. There began again to be a little sweetness to her in her existence. All this long struggle, and the slowly acquired victory, had been absolutely unsuspected by those about her. Mysie, perhaps, spectator as servants are of the life from which they are a little more apart than the members of a family, divined a disturbance in the being of her young mistress who was at the same time her child; but even she had no light as to what it was; and thus unobserved, unknown, though with many a desperate episode and conflict more than bloody, the little war began to be over. It left the girl with a throbbing experience of pain such as it is extraordinary to think could be acquired in the midst of so much peace, and at the same time with a sort of sickening apprehension now and then of the possibility of a renewal of the conflict. But no, she said to herself, that was not possible. Another time she would at least be forewarned. She would put on her armour and look to all her defences. Such a cheap and easy conquest should never be made of her again.

She had thus regained the command of herself without in the least forgetting what had been, when Katie came with her story to claim her advice and sympathy. Katie came from her father's castle with what was in reality a more splendid equipage than that which conveyed her with swift prancing horses along the side of the loch. She came attended by a crew of gentlemen, the best in these parts. Young Tom Campbell, of the Ellermore family, was her bow oar. He was furthest off, as being hopelessly ineligible, and not having, even in his own opinion, the least right to come to speech of[120] the heiress, for whom he had a hot boyish passion. Scott of Inverhouran, a Campbell too by the mother's side, and not far off the head of his clan, was stroke; and between these two sat the son of a Glasgow trader, who could have bought them both up, and an English baronet who had come to Birkenbraes nominally for the grouse, really for Katie. Tom of Ellermore was the only one of the crew who might not, as people say, have married anybody, from the Duke's daughter downwards. Katie was accompanied by a mild, grey-haired lady who had once been her governess, and a pretty little girl of fifteen, not indisposed to accept a passing tribute from the least engaged of the gentlemen. Katie deposited her companions and her crew with Mrs. Forrester, and calling Oona aside, rushed up-stairs to that young lady's bed-chamber, where it was evident nobody could pursue them.

'Oh, Oona, never mind *them*,' she cried. 'Your mother will give them their tea and scones; but I want you – I want your advice – or at least I want you to tell me what you think. They will do very well with Mrs. Forrester.' Then she drew her friend into the little elbow-chair in the window, Oona's favourite seat, and threw herself down on the footstool at her feet. 'I want you to tell me –' she said, with a certain solemnity, 'what you think of Lord Erradeen.'

'Of Lord Erradeen?' said Oona, faintly. She was taken so completely by surprise that the shock almost betrayed her. Katie fixed upon her a pair of open, penetrating brown eyes. They were both fair, but Oona was of a golden tint, and Katie of a less distinguished light brownness. Katie, with her little profile somewhat blurred and indistinct in the outlines, had an air of common sense and reason, while Oona's was the higher type of poetry and romance.

'Yes; you know him better than any one about here. But first, I will tell you the circumstances. We saw a great deal of him in London. He went everywhere with us, and met us everywhere –'

'Then, Katie,' cried Oona, with a little burst of natural impatience; 'you must know him a great deal better than I.'

Said Katie calmly – 'I am a quite different person from you, and I saw him only in society. Just hear me out, and you will know what I mean. People thought he was coming after me. I thought so myself more or less: but he never said a word. And the last night we met another girl, who took hold of him as some girls do – you know? Oh, not taking his arm with her hand, as you or I should do, or looking at him with her eyes; but just with a fling, with the whole of her, as those girls do. I was disgusted, and I sent him away. I don't think yet that he wished it, or cared. But of course he was obliged to go. And then Captain–I mean one that knew him – told me – oh, yes, that he was like that; he must always have some one to amuse himself with. I would not see him after: I just came away. Now

*The Wizard's Son, Volume II* 227

what does it mean? Is he a thing of that sort, that is not worth thinking about; or is he – ? – oh, no, I am not asking for your advice: I ask you what you think.'

Oona was not able to quench the agitation that rose up in her heart. It was like a sea suddenly roused by an unforeseen storm.

'I wish,' she said, 'you would not ask me such questions. I think nothing at all. I – never saw him – in that light.'

'What do you think?' said Katie, without changing her tone. She did not look in her friend's face to make any discovery, but trifled with the bangles upon her arm, and left Oona free. As a matter of fact, she was quite unsuspicious of her companion's agitation; for the question, though very important, was not agitating to herself. She was desirous of having an unbiassed opinion, but even if that were unfavourable, it would not, she was aware, be at all likely to break her heart.

Oona on her side was used to having her advice asked. In the interval she schooled herself to a consideration of the question.

'I will tell you, Katie, how I have seen him,' she said, 'here with my mother, and among the poor cotters in the Truach Glas. How could I tell from that how he would behave to a girl? He was very pretty, with my mother. I liked him for it. He listened to her and did what she told him, and never put on an air, or looked wearied, as gentlemen will sometimes do. Then he was very kind to the cotters, as I have told you. To see them turned out made him wild with indignation. You may judge by that the kind of man he was. It was not like doing them a favour; it was mending a miserable wrong.'

'I have heard all this before,' said Katie, with a slight impatience, 'but what has that to do with it? You are telling me facts, when I want your opinion. The one has nothing to do with the other. I can put this and that together myself. But what I want is an opinion. What do you *think?* Don't put me off any longer, but tell me that,' Katie cried.

'What do you want my opinion about?' asked the other, with also, in her turn, some impatience in her voice.

Then Katie ceased playing with her bangles, and looked up. She had never before met with such an unsatisfactory response from Oona. She said with a directness which denoted a natural and hereditary turn for the practical – 'Whether he will come; and if he comes, what it will be for?'

'He will certainly come,' said Oona, 'because he must. You that have lived on the loch so long – you know what the lords of Erradeen have to do.'

'And do you mean to say,' cried Katie, with indignation, 'that an old silly story will bring him–and not me? If that is your opinion, Oona! Do you know that he is a man like ourselves? Lord Innishouran thinks very well of him. He thinks there is something in him. For my part, I have never seen that he was clever; but I should think he had some sense. And how could a man who has any sense allow himself to be led into that?' She jumped up from her seat at Oona's feet in her indignation. 'Perhaps you believe in the Warlock lord?' she said, with fine scorn. 'Perhaps *he* believes in him? If Lord Erradeen should speak of that to me, I would laugh in his face. With some people it might be excusable, but with a man who is of his century!—The last one was a fool – everybody says so: and had his head full of rubbish, when he was not going wrong. By the by!' Katie cried – then stopped, as if struck by a new thought which had not occurred to her before.

'What is it?' said Oona, who had been listening with mingled resignation and impatience.

'When we took Lord Erradeen up he was with that Captain Underwood, who used to be with the old lord. I told him you would be sorry to see it. Now that I remember, he never asked me the reason why; but Captain Underwood disappeared. That looks as if he had given great importance to what I said to him. Perhaps after all, Oona, it is you of whom he was thinking. That, however, would not justify him in coming after me. I am very fond of you, but I should not care to be talked about all over London because a gentleman was in love with *you*!'

Oona had coloured high, and then grown pale. 'You will see, if you think of it, that you must not use such words about me,' she said, with an effort to be perfectly calm. 'There is no gentleman in – as you say – with me. I have never put it in any one's power to speak so.' As she spoke it was not only once but a dozen times that her countenance changed. With a complexion as clear as the early roses, and blood that ebbs and flows in her veins at every touch of feeling, how can a girl preserve such secrets from the keen perceptions of another? Katie kept an eye upon her, watching from under her downcast eyelids. She had the keenest powers of vision, and even could understand, when thus excited, characters of a higher tone than her own. She did not all at once say anything, but paused to take in this new idea and reconcile it with the other ideas that had been in her mind before.[a]

'This is very funny,' said Katie, after an interval. 'I never thought anything dramatical was going to happen to me: but I suppose, as they say in books, that your life is always a great deal more near that sort of thing than you suppose.'

'What sort of thing?' said Oona, who felt that she had betrayed herself, yet was more determined than ever not to betray herself or to yield a single step to the curiosity of the world as embodied in this inquiring spirit. She added, with a little flush of courage, 'When you, a great heiress, come in the way of a young lord, there is a sort of royal character about it. You will—marry for the sake of the world as well as for your own sake; and all the preliminaries, the doubts, and the difficulties, and the obstacles that come in the way, of course they are all like a romance. This interruption will be the most delightful episode. The course of true love never did run –'

'Oh stop!' cried Katie, 'that's all so commonplace. It is far more exciting and original, Oona, that we should be rivals, you and I.'

'You are making a great mistake,' said Oona, rising with the most stately gravity. 'I am no one's rival. I would not be even if–. But in this case it is absurd. I scarcely know Lord Erradeen, as I have told you. Let us dismiss him from the

*The Wizard's Son, Volume II*   229

conversation,' she added, with a movement of her hands as if putting something away. It had been impossible, however, even to say so much without the sudden flush which said more to the eyes of Katie, not herself addicted to blushing, than any words could do to her ears.

'It is very interesting,' she said. 'We may dismiss him from the conversation, but we can't dismiss him from life, you know. And if he is sure to come to Kinloch Houran, as you say, not for me, nor for you, but for that old nonsense, why then he will be – And we shall be forced to consider the question. For my part, I find it far more interesting than I ever thought it would be. You are proud, and take it in King Cambyses' vein.[121] But I'm not proud,' said Katie, 'I am a student of human nature. It will take a great deal of thinking over, and it's very interesting. I am fond of you, Oona, and you are prettier and better than I am; but I don't quite think at this moment that I will give in even to you, till –'

'If you insist on making a joke, I cannot help it,' said Oona, still stately, 'but I warn you, Katie, that you will offend me.'

'Oh, offend you! Why should I offend you?' cried Katie, putting her arm within that of the princess. 'It is no joke, it is a problem. When I came to ask for your opinion I never thought it would be half so interesting. If he has good taste, of course I know whom he will choose.'

'Katie!' cried Oona, with a violent blush, 'if you think that I would submit to be a candidate – a competitor – for any man to choose –'

'How can you help it?' said Katie, calmly. 'It appears it's nature. We have a great deal to put up with, being women, but we can't help ourselves. Of course the process will go on in his own mind. He will not be so brutal as to let us see that he is weighing and considering. And we can have our revenge after, if we like: we can always refuse. Come, Oona, I am quite satisfied. You and me, that are very fond of each other, we are rivals. We will not say a word about it, but we'll just go on and see what will happen. And I promise you I shall be as fond of you as ever, whatever happens. Men would say that was impossible–just as they say, the idiots, that women are never true friends. *That* is mere folly; but this is a problem, and it will be very interesting to work it out. I wonder if those boys have eaten all the scones,' Katie said, with the greatest simplicity, as she led Oona down-stairs.[a] She was so perfectly at her ease, taking the command of her more agitated companion, and so much pleased with her problem, that Oona's proud excitement of self-defence melted away in the humour of the situation. She threw herself into the gaiety of the merry young party down-stairs,[b] among whom Mrs. Forrester was in her element, dispensing tea and the most liberal supply of scones, which Mysie, with equal satisfaction, kept bringing in in ever fresh supplies, folded in the whitest of napkins. Katie immediately claimed her share of these dainties, intimating at once, with the decision of a connoisseur, the kind she preferred: but when supplied remained a little serious, paying no attention to 'the boys,' as she, somewhat contemptuously, entitled her attendants, and thinking over her problem. But Oona, in her excitement and self-consciousness, ran over with mirth and spirits. She talked and laughed with nervous gaiety, so that Hamish heard the sound of the fun down upon the beach where he watched over the boats, lest a passing shower should come up and wet the cushions of the magnificent vessel from Birkenbraes, which he admired and despised. 'Those Glascow persons,' said Hamish, 'not to be disrespectful, they will just be made of money; but Miss Oona she'll be as well content with no cushions at all. And if they'll be making her laugh that's a good thing,' Hamish said.

# CHAPTER XI.[a]

THE first to see the subject of so many thoughts was not any one of those to whom his return was of so much importance.[b] Neither[c] was it at Kinloch Houran that Walter first appeared. On a cold October evening, in one of the early frosts from which everybody augurs a severe winter, and in the early twilight which makes people exclaim how short the days are getting, he knocked suddenly at the door of Mr. Milnathort's house in Edinburgh. Being dark everywhere else, it was darker still in the severe and classic coldness of Moray Place.[122] The great houses gathered round, drawing, one might have thought, a closer and closer circle; the shrubs in the enclosure shivered before the breeze. Up the hill from the Firth[123] came the north-east wind, cutting like a scythe. It was a night when even a lighted window gives a certain comfort to the wayfarer; but the Edinburgh magnates had scarcely yet returned from the country, and most of the houses were dark, swathed in brown paper and cobwebs. But winter or summer made but little difference to the house of Mr. Milnathort, and there a certain light of human welcome was almost always to be found. Lord Erradeen came quickly along the Edinburgh streets, which are grim in the teeth of a north-easter. His frame was unstrung and his spirit unsatisfied as of old. He had been 'abroad'—that is to say, he had been hurrying from one place to another in search of the unattainable one which should not be dull. Most places were dull; there was nothing to do in them. He took in at a draught the capabilities of folly that were there, then passed on in the vain quest. Had he been wholly ignoble he would have been more easily satisfied. But he was not satisfied. In the worst he seemed to want something worse, as in the best he wanted something better. He was all astray upon the world, desiring he did not know what, only aware that nothing was sufficient for his desires. Underwood, who was his companion, had catered vulgarly for the unhappy young man, who used with scorn the means of distraction provided him, and was not distracted, and upon whom disgust so soon followed novelty that his companion was at his wits' end. And now he had come back, obeying an impulse which he neither understood nor wished to obey. A necessity seemed laid upon him; all in a moment it had risen up in his mind, a sense that he must get back.

It was so involuntary, so spontaneous, that it did not even occur to him at first to resist it, or to think of it as anything but a natural impulse.a

He had not been able to rest after this strange inclination came upon him, and it seemed to him in the heat of it that he had always had the same desire, that all the time this was what he had wanted, to get back. He hurried along over land and water, sometimes in the stream of summer tourists coming home, sometimes crossing the other tide of the sick and feeble going away – and when he touched English soil again, that he should have hurried to Edinburgh of all places in the world, was beyond Walter's power of explanation even to himself. He had felt a barrier between himself and the home of his youth. His mother was separated altogether from his new existence. She could not comprehend it, he thought, and his heart turned from the explanations that would be necessary. He could not go to her; and to whom could he go? The suggestion that came into his mind was as fantastical as the whole strange story of his recent life. He was nothing indeed but a bundle of caprices, moved and played upon as if by the winds. And it had seemed a sort of relief to his uncertain mind and consuming thoughts when it occurred to him to come to Moray Place to see the invalid who had known so much about him, while he knew nothing of her. It relieved him, as any resolution relieves an uncertain mind. It was something between him and that future which always failed to his expectations. When he had made up his mind he reflected no more, but went on, and even had an uneasy nap in the railway-carriage[b] as he came north; nor ever asked himself why he was coming till he went up the steps at Mr. Milnathort's door, and then it was too late for any such question. He mounted the long stone staircase with all the throbbings of fatigue in his brain, the sweep and movement of a long journey. Only once before had he been in this house, yet it seemed familiar to him as if it had been his home, and the unchanged aspect of everything affected him as it affects men who have been away for half a life-time–so many things happening to him, and nothing here. This gave him a certain giddiness as he followed the same servant up the same stairs. He was not the same. He had been unconscious of all the peculiarities of his fate when he crossed that threshold before. He had known the good, but not the evil; and now the very carpets, the sound of the door rumbling into the echoes of the tall, silent house, were the same–but he so far from being the same! Then in a moment out of the dim night, the half-lighted stair, he came upon the soft blaze of light in which Miss Milnathort delighted. She lay on her sofa as if she had never stirred, her old-young face in all its soft brightness, her small delicate hands in continual motion. She gave a little cry at the sight of Walter, and held out those hands to him.

'You have come!' she cried. 'I was looking for you;' raising herself on her couch as much as was possible to her, as if she would have thrown herself into his arms. When she felt the pressure of his hands, tears sprang to her eyes. 'I knew,' she cried, 'that you would come. I have been looking for you, and praying for you, Lord Erradeen.'

'Perhaps,' said Walter, moved too, he could scarcely tell why, 'that is how I have come.'

'Oh, but I am glad, glad to see you,' the poor lady said. 'You never came back last year; but I will not reproach you – I am too glad to have you here. And where have you been, and what have you been doing? To see you is like a child coming home.'

'I have been in many different places, and uneasy in all,' said Walter; 'and as for what I have been doing, it has not been much good: wandering about the face of the earth, seeking I don't know what;[124] not knowing, I think, even what I want.'

She held out her hand to him again: her eyes were full of pity and tenderness.

'Oh how I wanted you to come back that I might have spoken freely to you. I will tell you what you want, Lord Erradeen.'

'Stop a little,' he said, 'I don't wish to plunge into that. Let us wait a little. I think I am pleased to come back, though I hate it. I am pleased always more or less to do what I did not do yesterday.'

'That is because your mind is out of order, which is very natural,' she said. 'How should it be in order with so much to think of? You will have been travelling night and day?'

'Rather quickly; but that matters nothing; it is easy enough travelling. I am not so effeminate as to mind being tired; though as a matter of fact I am not tired,' he said. 'So far as that goes, I could go on night and day.'

She looked at him with that mingling of pleasure and pain with which a mother listens to the confidences of her child.

'Have you been home to see your mother?' she asked.

Walter shook his head.

'I have had no thought but how to get to Scotland the quickest way. I have felt as if something were dragging me. What is it? All this year I have been struggling with something. I have sometimes thought if I had come back here you could have helped me.'

'I would – I would! if I could,' she cried.

'It is not a thing that can be endured,' said Walter; 'it must come to an end. I don't know how or by what means; but one thing is certain, I will not go on bearing it. I will rather make an end of myself.'

She put a hand quickly upon his arm.

'Oh do not say that; there is much, much that must be done before you can despair: and *that* is the thought of despair. Some have done it, but you must not. No – not you – not you.'

'What must I do then?'

She caressed his arm with her thin, little, half-transparent hand, and looked at him wistfully with her small face, half child, half old woman, suffused and tremulous.

*The Wizard's Son, Volume II* 233

'Oh!' she said, 'my bonnie lad! you must be good – you must be good first of all.'
Walter laughed; he drew himself back a little out of her reach.

'I am not good,' he said. 'I have never been good. Often enough I have been disgusted with myself, and miserable by moments. But if that is the first thing, I do not know how to attain to it, for I am not good.'

She looked at him without any change in her face while he made this confession. It did not seem to make much impression upon her.

'I can tell you,' she said, 'how to overcome the devil and all his ways; but it costs trouble, Lord Erradeen. Without that you will always be as you are, full of troubles and struggles: but you should thank your God that you cannot be content with ill-doing like those that are the children of perdition. To be content with it – that is the worst of all.'

'Well, then I am in a hopeful way, it appears,' said Walter with a sort of laugh, 'for I am certainly far enough from being content.' After a minute's pause he added–'I said we should not plunge into this subject at once; tell me about yourself. Are you well? Are you better?'

'I am well enough,' she said, 'but never will I be better. I have known that for many years – almost from the moment when, to get away from *him*, I fell off yon old walls, and became what you see.'

'To get away from – whom?' He glanced round him as she spoke with a look which was half alarmed and half defiant. 'I know,' he said, in a low voice, 'what delusions are about.'

'From Him. What he is, or who he is, I know no more than you. I have thought like you that it was my own delusion. I have wondered from year to year if maybe I had deceived myself. But the upshot of all is what I tell you. I am lying here these thirty years and more, because, being very young, I had no command of myself, but was frightened and flew from Him.'

'It is against all possibility, all good sense, against everything one believes. I will not believe it,' cried Walter; 'you were young as you say, and frightened. And I was – a fool – unprepared, not knowing what to think.'

Miss Milnathort shook her head. She made no further reply; and there was a little interval of silence which Walter made no attempt to break. What could he say? It was impossible: and yet he had no real scepticism to oppose to this strange story. In words, in mind, he could not allow that either he or she were more than deceived; but in himself he had no doubt on the subject. His intelligence was easily convinced, indeed, that to attribute the events that happened to him to supernatural influence was in contradiction to everything he had ever been taught, and that it was superstition alone which could invest the mysterious inhabitant of Kinloch Houran with power to act upon his mind across great seas and continents, or to set any occult forces to work for that purpose. Superstition beyond all excuse; and yet he was as thoroughly convinced of it in the depths of his being as he was defiant on the surface. There was perfect silence in the room where these two sat together with a sense of fellowship and sympathy. As for Lord Erradeen, he had no inclination to say anything more. It was impossible, incredible, contrary to everything he believed: and yet it was true: and he did not feel the contradiction to be anything extraordinary, anything to be protested against, in this curious calm of exhaustion in which he was. While he sat thus quite silent Miss Milnathort began to speak.

'Thirty years ago,' she said, 'there was a young Lord Erradeen that was something like yourself. He was a distant cousin once, that never thought to come to the title. He was betrothed when he was poor to a young girl of his own condition in life. When he became Lord Erradeen he was bidden to give her up and he refused. Oh, if he had lived he would have broken the spell! He would not give up his love. I will not say that he was not terribly beaten down and broken with what he heard and saw, and what he had to bear; but he never said a word to me of what was the chief cause. When the summons came he got us all to go to see the old castle, and perhaps, with a little bravado, to prove that he would never, never yield. How it was that I was left alone I can never remember, for my head was battered and stupid, and it was long, long, before I got the command of my senses again. It was most likely when Walter (he was Walter too; it is the great Methven name) was attending to the others, my brother and my mother, who was living then. I was a romantic bit[125] girlie, and fond of beautiful views and all such things. When I was standing upon the old wall, there suddenly came forward to speak to me a grand gentleman. I thought I had never seen such a one before. You have seen him and you know; often and often have I thought I have seen him since. And it may be that I have,' she said, pausing suddenly. It was perhaps the interruption in the soft flowing of her voice that startled Walter. He made a sudden movement in his chair, and looked round him as if he too felt another spectator standing by.

'I am not frightened now,' said the invalid with her calm little voice, 'lying here so long putting things together I am frightened no more. Sometimes I am sorry for him, and think that it is not all ill that is in that burdened spirit. I have taken it upon me even,' she said, folding her little, worn hands, 'to say a word about him now and then when I say my prayers. I never thought at that time that he was anything more than the grandest gentleman I ever saw. He began to speak to me about my engagement, and if I thought of the harm I was doing Walter, and that it was his duty to think of the family above all. It was like death to hear it, but I had a great deal of spirit in those days, and I argued with him. I said it was better for the family that he should marry me, than marry nobody – and that I had no right to take my troth from him. Then he began to argue too. He said that to sacrifice was always best, that I could not love him, if I would not give up everything for him. It might have been Scripture.[126] What could I answer to that? I was just dazed by it, and stood and looked in his face: he looked like a prophet of God, and he said I should give up my love, if I knew what

*The Wizard's Son, Volume II*                                                    235

true love was. I have little doubt I would have done it, after that; but just then my Walter's voice sounded up from where he was calling out to me. 'Where are you, where are you? nothing can be done without you,' he cried. Oh, how well I remember the sound of his voice filling all the air! I turned round and I said, 'No, no, how can I break his heart': – when there came an awful change upon the face you know. His eyes flared like a great light, he made a step forward as if he would have seized me with his hands. And then terror took hold upon me, a kind of horrible panic. They say I must have started back. I mind nothing more for months and months,' the soft little voice said.

The young man listened to this strange tragedy with an absorbed and wondering interest; and the sufferer lay smiling at him in a kind of half childlike, half angelic calm. One would have said she had grown no older since that day; and yet had lived for long ages with her little crushed frame and heart. He was over-awed by the simplicity of the tale. He said after a pause, 'And Walter –? how did it end?'

For a moment she did not say anything, but lay smiling, not looking at him. At last she answered softly with a great gravity coming over her face – 'Lord Erradeen, after some years and many struggles, married the heiress of the Glen Oriel family, and brought a great deal of property to the house. He was to me like an angel from heaven. And his heart was broken. But how could I help him, lying crushed and broken here? What he did was well. It was not the best he could have done; because you see he could not give his heart's love again, and that is essential: but he did no harm. There was just an ending of it for one generation when I fell over yon wall. And his son died young, without ever coming to the age to bear the brunt, and the late lord, poor man, was just confused from the commencement, and never came to any good.'

'What is the best he could have done?'

She turned to him with a little eagerness. 'I have no instruction,' she said, 'I have only the sense that comes with much thinking and putting things together, if it is sense. I have lain here and thought it over for years and years, both in the night when everybody was sleeping, and in the day when they were all thinking of their own concerns. I think one man alone will never overcome that man we know. He is too much for you. If I have gleaned a little in my weakness, think what he must have found out in all these years. But I think if there were two, that were but one – two that had their hearts set upon what was good only, and would not listen to the evil part–I think before them he would lose his strength:[a] he could do no more. But oh, how hard to be like that and to find the other? I am afraid you are far, far from it, Lord Erradeen.'

'Call me Walter – like my predecessor,' he said.

'You are not like him. He was never soiled with the world. His mind was turned to everything that was good. And me, though I was but a small thing, I had it in me to stand by him. Two souls that are one! I am thinking – and I have had a long, long time to think in – that this is what is wanted to free the race from that bondage.'

'Do you mean – that there has never been such a pair to do what you say?'

'Perhaps it is that there never has been a cripple creature like me,' she said with a smile, 'to find it out. And at the best it is just a guess of mine. I have thought of everything else, but I can find nothing that will do. If you will think, however,' said Miss Milnathort, 'you will find it no such a light thing. Two of one mind–and that one mind set intent upon good, not evil. They will have to know. They will have to understand. The woman might miss it for want of knowing. She would have to be instructed in the whole mystery, and set her mind to it as well as the man. Do you think that is too easy? No, oh, no, it is not so very easy, Lord Erradeen.'

'It would be impossible to me,' said Walter with keen emotion, 'my mind is not intent upon good. What I am intent on is–I don't know that there is anything I am intent on: except to pass the time and have my own way.'

Miss Milnathort looked at him with the seriousness which changed the character of her face. 'He that says that,' she said, 'is near mending it, Lord Erradeen.'

'Do you think so?' he cried with a harsh little laugh, 'then I have something to teach you still, ignorant as I am. To know you are wrong, alas! is not the same as being on the way to mend it. I have known that of myself for years, but I have never changed. If I have to decide a hundred times I will do just the same, take what I like best.'

She looked at him wonderingly, folding her hands.

'I think you must be doing yourself injustice,' she said.

'It is you that do human nature more than justice,' said Walter; 'you judge by what you know, by yourself; you prefer what is good; but I – don't do so. It is true: to know what is good does not make one like it, as you think. It is not a mistake of judgment, it is a mistake of the heart.'

'Oh, my dear,' said the poor lady, 'you must be wronging yourself; your heart is tender and good, your eyes filled when I was telling you my story. I have seen that when there was any talk of fine and generous things your eyes have filled and your countenance changed. You have forgotten by times, and turned away from the right way; but you will not tell me that, looking it in the face, you prefer what is wrong. Oh no, Lord Erradeen, no, no.'

'Perhaps,' he said, 'I never look anything in the face; that may be the reason or part of the reason; but the fact is that I do not prefer good because it is good. Oh no, I cannot deceive you. To be fully convinced that one is wrong is very little argument against one's habits, and the life that one likes. It does not seem worth while to test small matters by such a big standard, and, indeed one does not test them at all, but does – what happens to come in one's way at the moment.'

A shade of trouble came over the soft little face. She looked up wondering and disturbed at the young man who sat smiling upon her, with a smile that was half scorn, half sympathy. The scorn, perhaps, was for himself; he made no pretence to himself of meaning better, or wishing to do better than his performance. And Miss Milnathort's distress was great.

'I thought,' she said, faltering, 'that the truth had but to be seen, how good it is, and every heart would own it. Oh, my young lord, you have no call to be like one of the careless that never think at all. You are forced to think: and when you see that your weirdless way leads to nothing but subjection and bondage, and that the good is your salvation, as well for this world as the world to come –'

'Does not every man know that?' cried Walter. 'Is it not instinctive in us to know that if we behave badly, the consequences will be bad one way or another? There is scarcely a fool in the world that does not know that – but what difference does it make? You must find some stronger argument. That is your innocence,' he said, smiling at her.

At that moment the young man, with his experiences which were of a nature so different from hers, felt himself far more mature and learned in human nature than she; and she, who knew at once so much and so little, was abashed by this strange lesson. She looked at him with a deprecating anxious look, not knowing what to say.

'If the victory is to be by means of two whose heart is set on good, it will never be,' said Walter with a sigh, 'in my time. I will struggle and yield, and yield and struggle again, like those that have gone before me, and then, like them, pass away, and leave it to somebody else who will be hunted out from the corners of the earth as I was. And so, for all I can tell, it will go on for ever.'

Here he made a pause, and another tide of feeling stole over him. 'If I were a better man,' he said with a changed look, 'I think I know where – the other – might be found.'

Miss Milnathort's soft, aged, childish countenance cleared, the wistful look vanished from her eyes, her smile came back. She raised herself up among her pillows as if she would have sat upright.

'Oh, my young lord! and does she love you like that?' she cried.

Walter felt the blood rush to his face; he put up his hands as if to stop the injurious thought. 'Love me!' he said.

To do him justice, the idea was altogether new to him. He had thought of Oona often, and wondered what was the meaning of that softness in her eyes as she looked after him; but his thoughts had never ventured so far as this. He grew red, and then he grew pale.

'It is a profanity,' he said. 'How could she think of me at all? I was a stranger, and she was sorry for me. She gave me her hand, and strength came out of it. But if such a woman as that – stood by a true man – Pah! I am not a true man; I am a wretched duffer, and good for nothing. And Oona thinks as much of me, as little of me as–as little as–she thinks of any pitiful, unworthy thing.'

He got up from his chair as he spoke, and began to pace about the room in an agitation which made his blood swell in his veins. He was already in so excitable a state that this new touch seemed to spread a sort of conflagration everywhere; his imagination, his heart, all the wishes and hopes – that 'indistinguishable throng'[127] that lie dormant so often, waiting a chance touch to bring them to life – all blazed into consciousness in a moment. He who had flirted to desperation with Julia Herbert, who had been on the point of asking Katie Williamson to marry him, was it possible all the time that Oona, and she only, had been the one woman in the world for him? He remembered how she had come before his thoughts at those moments when he had almost abandoned himself to the current which was carrying his heedless steps away. When he had thought of her standing upon the bank on her isle, looking after him with indefinable mystery and wistful softness in her eyes, all the other objects of his various pursuits had filled him with disgust. He said to himself, in the excitement of the moment, that it was this which had again and again stopped him and made his pleasures, his follies, revolting to him. This was the origin of his restlessness, his sometimes savage temper, his fierce impatience with himself and everybody around him. In fact, this was far from the reality of the case; but in a flood of new sensation that poured over him, it bore a flattering resemblance to truth, which dignified the caprice of his existence, and made him feel himself better than he had thought. If love had, indeed, done all this for him, struggling against every vulgar influence, must it not, then, be capable of much more – indeed, of all?

Meanwhile Miss Milnathort lay back upon her pillows, excited, yet pleased and soothed, and believing too that here was all she had wished for, the true love and the helping woman who might yet save Erradeen.

'Oona!' she said to herself, 'it's a well-omened name.'

This strange scene of sentiment, rising into passion, was changed by the sudden entry of Mr. Milnathort, whose brow was by no means so cloudless or his heart so soft as his sister's. He came in, severe in the consciousness of business neglected, and all the affairs of life arrested by the boyish folly, idleness, and perhaps vice of this young man, with endless arrears of censure to bestow upon him, and of demands to place before him.

'I am glad to see you, my Lord Erradeen,' he said briefly. 'I have bidden them put forward the dinner, that we may have a long evening; and your things are in your room, and your man waiting. Alison, you forget when you keep Lord Erradeen talking, that he has come off a journey and must be tired.'

Walter had not intended to spend the night in Moray Place, and indeed had given orders to his servant to take rooms in one of the hotels, and convey his luggage thither; but he forgot all this now, and took his way instinctively up another flight of those tall stairs to the room which he had occupied before. It brought him to himself, however, with the most curious shock of surprise and consternation, when he recognised not the servant whom he had brought with him, but old Symington, as precise and serious as ever, and looking as if there had been no break in his punctilious service. He was arranging his master's clothes just as he had done on the winter evening when Lord Erradeen had first been taken possession of by this zealous retainer of the family. Walter was so startled, bewildered, and almost overawed by this sudden apparition, that he said with a gasp –

'You here, Symington!' and made no further objection to his presence.

'It is just me, my lord,' Symington said. 'I was waiting at the station, though your lordship might not observe me. I just went with your lad to the hotel, and put him in good hands.'

'And may I ask why you did that without consulting me; and what you are doing here?' Walter cried, with a gleam of rising spirit.

Symington looked at him with a sort of respectful contempt.

'And does your lordship think,' he said, 'that it would be befitting to take a young lad, ignorant of the family, *up yonder?*' With a slight pause of indignant yet gentle reproach, after these words, he added – 'Will your lordship wear a white tie or a black?' with all the gravity that became the question.

# CHAPTER XII.[a]

THERE is in the winter season, when the stream of tourists is cut off, a sort of family and friendly character about the Highland railways. The travellers in most cases know each other by sight, if no more; and consult over a new-comer[b] with the curiosity of a homely community, amid which a new figure passing in the street excites sentiments of wonder and interest as a novelty. 'Who do you suppose that will be at this time of the year?' they say; and the little country stations are full of greetings, and everybody is welcomed who comes, and attended by kindly farewells who goes away. There was no doubt this time as to who Lord Erradeen was as he approached the termination of his journey; and when he had reached the neighbourhood of the loch, a bustle of guards and porters – that is to say, of the one guard belonging to the train, and the one porter belonging to the station, familiarly known by name to all the passengers – ushered up to the carriage in which he was seated the beaming presence of Mr. Williamson.

'So here ye are,' said the millionnaire. 'Lord Erradeen! I told Tammas he must be making a mistake.'

'Na, na, I was making no mistake,' said Tammas, in a parenthesis.

'And what have ye been making of yourself all this time?' Mr. Williamson went on. 'We have often talked of ye, and wondered if we would see ye again. That was a very sudden parting that we took in London; but Katie is just a wilful monkey, and does what she pleases; but she will be well pleased, and so will I, to

240        *The Selected Works of Margaret Oliphant, Volume 21*

see you at Birkenbraes.' And the good man took his place beside the new-comer,[a] and talked to him with the greatest cordiality during the rest of the journey.

Thus Walter was received on his second arrival with the friendly familiarity natural to the country-side.[b] There seemed to him something significant even in the change of association with which his visit began. He had to promise to present himself at once at Birkenbraes, and the very promise seemed to revive the feelings and purposes which had been growing in his mind during that interval of social success in London which, on the whole, had been the most comfortable period of his life since he came to his fortune. His mind was occupied by this as he was rowed once more round the half-ruined[c] pile of Kinloch Houran to his renewed trial. The afternoon was bright and clear, one of those brilliant October days that add a glory of colour to the departing summer; the water reflected every tint of the ruddy woods, thrown up and intensified everywhere by the dark background of the firs. He thought of the encounter before him with a fierce repugnance and indignation, rebellious but impotent; but there were no longer in it those elements of apprehension and mystery which had occupied all his being when he came here for the first time. It had acquired all the reality of an event not to be escaped from, not to be eluded; in itself something almost worse than death, and involving consequences more terrible than death–from which some way of escape must be found if heaven or earth contained any way of salvation. He had banished it from his mind as long as it was possible, and had wasted in endeavouring to forget it the time which he might have occupied in searching for the means of overcoming his enemy: and now the crisis was again near, and he knew scarcely more than at first what he was to do.

Walter had listened[d] to Miss Milnathort's suggestion with a momentary elevation of mind and hope; but what was he, a 'miserable duffer' as he had truly called himself, to make such an effort? A heart set on good and not evil: he laughed to himself with contemptuous bitterness, when he thought how far this description was from anything he knew of himself. Thus it was from the outset impossible that the redemption of his race could be carried out by him. The only alternative then was to yield. Was it the only alternative? To conduct his own affairs only as the tool and instrument of another, to sacrifice affection, justice, pity, every generous feeling, to the aggrandisement of his family – Walter's heart rose up within him in violent refusal and defiance. And then he thought of Katie Williamson. The storms in his bosom had been quieted from the moment when he had come into contact with her. The evil circumstances around him had changed; even now a lull came over his mind at the thought of her. It was not the highest or the best course of action. At the utmost it would only be to leave once more to those who should come after him the solution of the problem; but what had he to do with those that came after him, he asked himself bitterly? In all probability it would be a stranger, a distant cousin, some one unknown to him as he had been to his predecessor; and in the mean time he would have peace. As he thought of it, it seemed to him that there was something significant even in that meeting with Mr. Williamson. When he came to the loch for the first time, with high hopes and purposes in his mind, meaning to leave all the frivolities of life behind him and address himself nobly to the duties of his new and noble position, it was Oona Forrester whom he had encountered on the threshold of fate. All the circumstances of his intercourse with her flashed through his mind; the strange scene on the isle in which her touch, her presence, her moral support, had saved him from he knew not what, from a final encounter in which, alone, he must have been overthrown. Had he not been a coward then and fled, had he remained and, with that soft strong hand in his, defied all that the powers of darkness could do, how different might have been his position now! But he had not chosen that better part. He had escaped and postponed the struggle. He had allowed all better thoughts and purposes to slip from him into the chaos of a disordered life. And now that he was forced back again to encounter once more this tyranny from which he had fled, it was no longer Oona that met him. Who was he, to expect that Oona would meet him, that the angels would come again to his succour? He could not now make that sudden unhesitating appeal to her which he had made in his first need, and to which she had so bravely replied. Everything was different; he had forfeited the position on which he could confront his tyrant. But a compromise was very possible, and it seemed to him that peace, and a staving off of trouble, were in Katie Williamson's hand.

It is needless to enter into all the sensations and thoughts with which the young man took possession again of the rooms in which he had spent the most extraordinary crisis of his life. It was still daylight when he reached Kinloch Houran, and the first thing he did was to make a stealthy and cautious examination of his sitting-room, looking into every crevice in an accidental sort of way, concealing even from himself the scrutiny in which he was engaged. Could he have found any trace of the sliding panel or secret entrance so dear to romance, it would have consoled him; but one side of the room was the outer wall, another was the modern partition which separated it from his bedroom, and of the others one was filled up with the bookshelves which he had been examining when his visitor entered on the previous occasion, while the fourth was the wall of the corridor which led into the ruinous part of the castle, and had not a possibility of any opening in it.

He made these researches by intervals, pretending other motives to himself, but with the strangest sense that he was making himself ridiculous, and exposing himself to contemptuous laughter, though so far as his senses were cognisant there was nobody there either to see or to laugh. The night, however, passed with perfect tranquillity, and in the morning he set out early on his way to Birkenbraes. If it was there that the question was to be solved, it was better that it should be done without delay.[a]

***

# CHAPTER XIII.[a]

THE party at Birkenbraes was always large. There were, in the first place, many people staying in the house, for Mr. Williamson was hospitable in the largest sense of the word, and opened his liberal doors to everybody that pleased him, and was ready to provide everything that might be wanted for the pleasure of his guests—carriages, horses, boats, even special trains on the railway, not to speak of the steam-yacht that lay opposite the house, and made constant trips up and down the loch. His liberality had sometimes an air of ostentation, or rather of that pleasure which very rich persons often take in the careless exhibition of a lavish expenditure, which dazzles and astonishes those to whom close reckonings are necessary. He had a laugh, which, though perfectly good-natured, seemed to have a certain derision in it of the precautions which others took, as he gave his orders. 'Lord, man, take a special! – what need to hurry? I will send and order it to be in waiting. I have my private carriage, ye see, on the railway – always at the use of my friends.' And then he would laugh, as much as to say, What a simple thing this is – the easiest in the world! If ye were not all a poor, little, cautious set of people, you would do the same. Not afford it? Pooh! a bagatelle like that! All this was in the laugh, which was even more eloquent than *la langue Turque*.[128] There were sure to be some sensitive people who did not like it; but they were very hard to please. And the rich man was in fact so truly kind and willing to make everybody comfortable, that the most sensible even of the sensitive people forgave him. And as the majority in society is not sensitive when its own advantage and pleasure is concerned, his house was always full of visitors, among whom he moved briskly, always pleased, always endeavouring to elicit the expression of a wish which he could satisfy. Katie took less trouble. She was less conscious of being rich. She was willing to share all her own advantages, but it did not appear to her, as to her father, ridiculous that other people should not be rich too. The house was always full of visitors staying there, and there was not a day that there were not neighbours dropping in to lunch or invited to dinner, keeping up a commotion which delighted Mr. Williamson and amused Katie, who was to the manner born, and understood life only in this way. It happened thus that it was into a large party that Walter, coming with a sense that he was under the dominion of fate, and was about to settle the whole tenor of his life, plunged unaware. He heard the sound of many voices before he had got near the great drawing-room, the door of which stood open, giving vent to the murmur of talk from about twenty people within. He had scarcely ever gone up so magnificent a staircase, broad, and light, and bright as became a new palace, with footmen moving noiselessly upon the thick pile of the carpets.

'There is a party, I suppose?' he said, hesitating.

'No more than usual, my lord,' said the elegant functionary in black, who was about to announce him, with a bland and soft smile of superiority and a little pity like his master's for the man who knew no better, 'Two or three gentlemen have dropped in to lunch.'

The drawing-room was a large room, with a huge round bow-window giving upon the loch. It was furnished and decorated in the most approved manner, with quantities of pretty things of every costly description: for Katie, like her father, betrayed the constitution and temperament of wealth, by loving cost almost more than beauty. She was, however, too well instructed to be led into the mistake of making that luxurious modern room into the semblance of anything ancient or faded, while Mr. Williamson was too fond of everything bright and fresh to be persuaded even by fashion into such an anachronism. There was a faint suspicion in the mirrors and gilding and all the conveniences and luxuries, of the style of grandeur peculiar to the saloon of a splendid steamer, to which the steam-yacht,[129] which was the chief object in the immediate prospect as seen from the plate-glass window, gave additional likelihood. Walter for his part was strangely startled, when, out of the seriousness of his own lonely thoughts, and the sense of having arrived at a great crisis, he suddenly stepped into the flutter and talk of this large assembly, which was composed of some half-dozen neighbours on the loch, most of them young men in more or less attendance upon Katie, mingled with strangers of all classes whom Mr. Williamson had picked up here and there. There was a little pause in the hum of voices at his own name, and a slight stir of interest, various of the guests turning round to look as he came in. The master of the house advanced with a large hand held out, and an effusive welcome; but the little lady of Birkenbraes paid Walter the much greater compliment of pursuing her conversation undisturbed, without betraying by a movement that she knew he was there. Katie was not rude. It was not her habit to pay so little attention to a new-comer: she was profoundly conscious of his entrance, and of every step he made among the groups distributed about; but as the matter was a little serious, and his appearance of some importance, she showed a slight stir of mind and thoughts, which could scarcely be called agitation, in this way. It was only when her father called loudly, 'Katie, Katie, do you not see Lord Erradeen?' that she turned, not moving from her place, and suddenly held out her hand with a smile.

'How do you do? I heard you had come,' said Katie; and then returned to her talk. 'As for the influence of scenery upon the mind of the common people, I think it has more influence in the Highlands than anywhere, but very little when all is said. You don't think much of what you see every day, unless, indeed, you think everything of it. You must be totally indifferent, or an enthusiast,' said the philosophical young lady.

Walter meanwhile stood before her, almost awkwardly, feeling the rigidity upon his countenance of a somewhat unmeaning smile.

'And to which class does Miss Williamson belong?' said her companion, who was a virtuous young member of parliament, anxious to study national peculiarities wherever he might happen to be.

'To neither,' said Katie, with a slight coldness, just enough to mark that she did not consider herself as one of the 'common people.' And she turned to Walter with equally marked meaning, 'Have you seen the Forresters since you came, Lord Erradeen?'

'I have seen no one,' said Walter, slightly startled by the question. 'I came[a] only last night, and am here to-day by your father's invitation –'

'I know,' said Katie, with greater cordiality. 'You speak as if I wanted you to account for yourself. Oh, no! only one must begin the conversation somehow–unless I plunged you at once into my discussion with Mr. Braithwaite (Mr. Braithwaite, Lord Erradeen) about the characteristics of the inhabitants of a mountain country. Do you feel up to it?' she added, with a laugh.

'But you avoid the question,' said the member of parliament. 'You say, "neither." Now, if it is interesting to know what effect these natural phenomena have upon the common mind, it is still more interesting when it is a highly cultivated intelligence which is in question.'

'Help me out!' cried Katie, with a glance at Walter. 'I have never been educated – no woman is, you know. How are we to know what the highly cultured feel! Papa is not cultured at all–he does not pretend to it, which is why people approve of him; and as for me!' she spread out her hands like a sort of exclamation. 'And Lord Erradeen cannot give you any information either,' she added, demurely, 'for he has not known the loch very long – and I think he does not like it. No, but you shall see one who can really be of some use this afternoon. Don't you think she is the very person, Lord Erradeen? Oona – for she has lived on the loch, or rather in the loch, all her life.'

'And when shall I see this – nymph is she, or water goddess?'[b] said the genial member. 'That will indeed be to gather knowledge at the fountain-head.'[130c]

'Do you think we may say she is a nymph, Lord Erradeen? Oh yes – what do you call those classical ladies that take care of the water – Naiads?[131] Oona is something of that sort. But better than the classics, for she has water above and water below for a great part of the year. You don't know how many superstitions we have remaining in this wild part of the country. We have ghosts, and wandering Jews,[132] and mysterious lights: Lord Erradeen will tell you –'

Katie paused with the malice bright in her eyes. She did not mean to affront the recovered attendant who might turn out a suitor, and upon whom it was possible she might be induced to smile; so she paused with a little laugh, and allowed Braithwaite to break in.

*The Wizard's Son, Volume II*        245

'Do you call this a wild part of the country, Miss Williamson? Then what must the cultivated portions look like? I see nothing but beautiful villas and palaces, and all the luxuries of art.'

'The comforts of the Saut Market,'[133] said Katie with a shrug of her shoulders. 'It is more easy to carry them about with you than in Bailie Nicol Jarvie's time.[134] But there is luncheon! Papa is always formal about our going in, though I tell him that is out of date nowadays. So you must wait, if you please, Lord Erradeen, and take me.' There was then a pause, until, as they brought up the rear of the procession down-stairs, Katie said, with the slightest pressure on his arm to call his attention, 'That is a Member of Parliament in search of information and statistics. If you hear me talk more nonsense than usual you will know why.'

'Do you expect Miss Forrester this afternoon?' asked Walter quite irrelevant.

Katie's heart gave a little jump. She did not like to be beat. It was the healthful instinct of emulation, not any tremor of the affections. She gave him a keen glance half of anger, half of enjoyment, for she loved a fray.

'Better than that,' she cried gaily, 'we are going down the loch to see her. Don't you remember Mrs. Forrester's scones, Lord Erradeen![a] You are ungrateful, for I know you have eaten them. But you shall come, too.'

If this had been said on the stairs, Walter, probably, would have given a dignified answer to the effect that his engagements would scarcely permit – but they were by this time in the dining-room in the little flutter of taking places which always attends the sitting down of a party, an operation which Katie, with little rapid indications of her pleasure, simplified at once; and Walter found himself seated by her side and engaged in conversation by the enterprising Braithwaite at his other hand before he could utter any remonstrance. Mr. Braithwaite set it down in his journal that Lord Erradeen was a dull young fellow, petted by the women because he was a lord, no other reason being apparent – and wondered a little at the bad taste of Miss Williamson who ought to have known better. As for Katie, she exerted herself to smooth down Walter's slightly ruffled plumes. There was no use, she thought, in handing him over at once to Oona by thus wounding his *amour propre*.[135] She inquired into his travels. She asked where he had disappeared when they all left town.

'I expected we should find you at Auchnasheen for the 12th,'[136] she said. 'You are the only man I know who is philosopher enough not to care for the grouse. One is driven to believe about that time of the year that men can think of nothing else.'

'Perhaps, Katie,' said young Tom of Ellermore, 'if you were to speak to Lord Erradeen, whom we don't know as yet, as we have never had the chance of calling' (here the young men exchanged bows, accompanied by a murmur from Katie, 'Mr. Tom Campbell, Ellermore,' while the colour rose in young Tom's cheek), 'perhaps he would be charitable to us others that are not philosophers.'

'Have ye not enough grouse of your own, Tom Campbell?' cried Mr. Williamson, who, in a pause of the conversation, had heard this address. 'Man! if I were you I would think shame to look a bird in the face.'

'And why?' cried the young fellow; 'that was what they were made for. Do you think otherwise that they would be allowed to breed like *that,* and eat up everything that grows?'

'Heather,' said the head of the house, 'and bracken. Profitable crops, my word!'

Here Walter interrupted the discussion by a polite speech to young Tom, whose eyes blazed with pleasure and excitement at the offer made him.

'But I hope,' he said, 'you will join us yourself. It will be like stealing a pleasure to have such an enjoyment, and the master of it not there.'

'I have other work in hand,' Walter said; at which young Tom stared and coloured still more, and a slight movement showed itself along the table, which Mr. Braithwaite, the knowledge-seeker, being newly arrived, did not understand. Tom cried hastily, 'I beg your pardon,' and many eyes were turned with sudden interest upon Lord Erradeen. But this was what Walter had anticipated as little as the parliamentary inquirer. He grew so red that Tom Campbell's healthy blush was thrown into the shade. 'I ought rather to say,' he added hastily, 'that my time here is too short for amusement.'

There was an uneasy little pause, and then everybody burst into talk. Both the silence and the conversation were significant. Lord Erradeen turned to Katie with an instinctive desire for sympathy, but Katie was occupied, or pretended to be so, with her luncheon. It was not here that sympathy on that point was to be found.

'I wonder,' said Katie, somewhat coldly, 'that you do not remain longer when you are here. Auchnasheen is very nice, and you ought to know your neighbours, don't you think, Lord Erradeen? If it is merely business, or duty, that brings you–'

'I wish I knew which it was,' he said in a low tone.

Katie turned and looked at him with those eyes of common-sense in which there is always a certain cynicism.

'I did not think in this century,' she said, 'that it was possible for any man not to know why he was doing a thing; but you perhaps like to think that an old family has rules of its own, and ought to keep up the past.'

'I should think,' said Mr. Braithwaite, not discouraged by the lower tone of this conversation, 'that the past must have a very strong hold upon any one who can suppose himself a Highland chieftain.'

'A Highland chief!' cried Katie, opening her brown eyes wide: and then she laughed, which was a thing strangely offensive to Walter, though he could scarcely have told why.

'I fear,' he said coldly, 'that though I am to some extent a Highland laird, I have no pretension to be a chief. There is no clan Methven that I ever heard of: though indeed I am myself almost a stranger and of no authority.'

*The Wizard's Son, Volume II*        247

'Mrs. Forrester will tell you, Mr. Braithwaite,' said Katie. 'She is a sort of queen of the loch She is one of the old Macnabs who once were sovereign here. These people,' she said, waving her hand towards the various scions of the great clan Campbell, 'are mushrooms in comparison: which is a comfort to our feelings, seeing that we sink into insignificance as creatures of to-day before them. The very original people for highly consolatory to the upstarts, for we are just much the same as the middling-old people to them. They are worlds above us all.'

Here Tom of Ellermore leant over his immediate neighbours and reminded Katie that the days were short in October, and that it was a stiff row to the isle: and the conversation terminated in the hurried retirement of the ladies, and selection of rugs and wrappers to make them comfortable. Mr. Williamson had, as he said, 'more sense,' than to set out upon any such ridiculous expedition. He stood and watched the preparations, with his thumbs stuck into the armholes of his waistcoat.

'Ye had much better take the yacht,' he said. 'She could get up steam in half an hour, and take you there in ten minutes, and there is plenty of room for ye all, and the cabin in case of rain. But as ye like! A wilful man will have his way. If ye would rather work yourselves than have the work done for ye—and a shower in prospect! But it's your own affair.'

The party, however, preferred the boats, and Katie put her father's remonstrance aside with a wave of her hand.

'It is all these boys are ever good for,' she said, 'and why would you stop them? Besides, it is far nicer than your mechanical steam, and tea on board, and all the rest of it. Lord Erradeen, you are to steer. If you don't know the currents I can tell you. Here is your place beside me: and you can tell me what you have been doing all this time, for there were so many interruptions at lunch I got no good of you,' the young lady said.

Thus Walter was swept along in Katie's train. As he was quite unaware of any understanding between the girls he was of course ignorant that any special significance could attach to his arrival in this manner at the isle. And for his own part he was pleased by the thought of seeing Oona for the first time in an accidental way, without any responsibility, so to speak, of his own. It was a little chilly for a water-party, but on the lochs people are prepared for that and it interferes with no one's pleasure. The afternoon was full of sunshine, and every bit of broken bank, and every island and feathery crest of fir-trees, was reflected and beautified in the still water, that broke with a ripple the fantastic doubling of every substance, but lent a glory to the colour and brilliancy to every outline. The gay party swept along over reflected woods, themselves all brilliant in reflection, and making the loch as gay as a Venetian canal. On the little landing-place at the isle the whole small population was collected to meet them: Mrs. Forrester in her white cap, shivering slightly, and glad to draw round her the fur cloak which Mysie was putting on her shoulders from behind, 'for the sun has not the strength it once had,' she explained, 'now that we are just getting round the corner of the year:' Hamish always in his red shirt, kneeling on the little wooden landing which he had wheeled out to receive the party, in order to catch the prow of the first boat; and Oona, a little apart, standing looking out, with a faint thrill of excitement about her, consequent on having just heard the news of Walter's arrival, but no expectation to make this excitement tangible. They made a pretty show upon the little beach, reflected, too, in the clear depths below – the bit of ribbon on the mother's cap, the knot of pale roses on Oona's breast, culminating in Mysie's stronger tints on one side, and the red of Hamish's garment on the other.

'What a pretty picture it would make,' Katie said. '"Hospitality," you ought to call it, or "Welcome to the isle." But there ought to be a gentleman to make it perfect; either an old gentleman to represent Oona's father, or a young one for her husband. Don't you think so, Lord Erradeen?'

It was perhaps at this moment when he was listening with a somewhat distracted look, smiling against the grain, and standing up in the boat to steer, that Oona saw him first. It cannot be denied that the shock was great. In her surprise she had almost made a false step on the slippery shingle, and Mrs. Forrester grasped her dress with an 'Oona! you'll be in the water if you don't take more care.' Oona recovered herself with a blush, which she would have given anything in the world to banish from her countenance. It was so then! This man, who had, all unawares, produced so much effect upon her life and thoughts, was coming back within her little circle of existence in Katie Williamson's train! She smiled to herself a moment after, holding her head high, and with a sense of ridicule pervading the being which had been momentarily transfixed by that keen arrow of surprise and pain. She said to herself that the humour of it was more than any one could have believed, but that all was well. Oh, more than well! – for was not this the thing of all others that was good for her, that would put the matter on the easiest footing?[a]

All this flew through her mind like lightning while the boat came close, amid the friendly shouts and greetings of the crew, all of them 'neighbours' sons.' Mr. Braithwaite, the English observer, sat by admiring while these brotherly salutations were gone through. Perhaps he did not note in his diary that the young aborigines[137] called each other by their Christian names,[138] but he did make a remark to that effect in his mind. And then there ensued the little tumult of disembarking, in the midst of which Oona, holding out her hand, frankly greeted Lord Erradeen. 'We heard you had come back,' she said, giving him a look of full and confident composure which puzzled Walter. She meant him, and not him only, to perceive the frankness of a reception in which there was not a shade of embarrassment, no recollection of the strange moment they had spent together, or of the encounter that had taken place upon the isle. When one pair of eyes look into another with that momentary demonstration it is a proof of some meaning more than meets the eye. And Walter, whose own eyes were full too of a something, subdued and concealed so far as possible – a deprecating wistful look in which there was pardon sought (though he had consciously done her no wrong; but in doing wrong at all had he not offended Oona as Dante offended Beatrice,[139] although she might never know of what sins he had been guilty?) and homage offered – was still more perplexed by that open gaze in which there was nothing of the softness of the look with which Oona had watched him going away, and which had so often recurred to his mind since. What did it mean? It gave him welcome, but a welcome that felt like the closing of a door. He was far too much occupied with investigating this problem to remark the corresponding look, the slight, almost imperceptible smile, that passed between Oona and Katie as they met. In the midst of all the cheerful din, the merry voices on the air, the boats run up upon the beach, the cheerful movement towards the house, such fine shades of feeling and dramatic purpose can make themselves apparent to those who are in the secret, but to no other. A merrier party never ascended the slope, and that is saying much. Mrs. Forrester led the way in the highest satisfaction.

'Mysie, ye will stand on no ceremony about following,' she said, 'but run on before and see that the tea is masked:[140] but not too much, to get that boiled taste. It is perhaps extravagant, but I like to have just what you may call the first flavour of the tea. And let the scones be just ready to bring ben,[141] for Miss Williamson must not be kept too late on the water at this time of the year. To tell the truth,' she said, turning with her smiles to the member of parliament, a functionary for whom she had a great respect, counting him more important than a young lord, who after all was in the position of a 'neighbour's son'; 'to tell the truth, I have just to be inhospitable at this season and push them away with my own hands: for it is always fresh upon the loch, and a score of young creatures with colds, all because I let them stay half an hour too late, would be a dreadful reflection. This will be your first visit to the loch? Oh, I am sure we are delighted to see you, both Oona and me. We are always pleased to meet with strangers that have an appreciation. Some people would think it was a very lonely life upon the isle; but I assure you if I could give you a list of all the people that come here! It would be rather a good thing to keep a list now that I think of it, you would see some names that would be a pleasure to any one to see. Yes, I think I must just set up a visiting-book, as if we were living in some grand place in London, say Grosvenor Square.[142] What are you saying, Katie, my dear? Oh yes, I have shaken hands with Lord Erradeen. I am very glad to see him back, and I hope he will stay longer and let us see more of him than last year. This is one of our finest views. I always stop here to point it out to strangers,' she added, pausing, for indeed it was her favourite spot to take breath.

And then the group gathered at the turning, and looked out upon Kinloch Houran, lying in shadow, in the dimness of one of those quick-flying clouds which give so much charm to a Highland landscape. The old grey ruin lying upon the dulled surface, steel blue and cold, of the water, which round the island was dancing in sunshine, gave a curious effectiveness to the landscape.

'It is the ghost-castle.' 'It is the haunted house,' said one of the visitors, in a whisper, who would have spoken loud enough but for the presence of Walter, who stood and looked, with great gravity, upon his place of trial. When Katie's voice became audible at his side, advising him in very distinct tones to restore the old place, Walter felt himself shrink and grow red, as if some villany had been suggested to him. He made no reply. He had thought himself of something of the same description in his first acquaintance with Kinloch Houran; but how different his feelings were now!ᵃ

The reader already knows what were Mrs. Forrester's teas. The party filled the pleasant drawing-room in which a fire was burning brightly, notwithstanding the sunshine without, and the scones arrived in bountiful quantity, one supply after another; Mysie's countenance beaming as 'a few more' were demanded; while her mistress did nothing but fill out cups of tea and press her young guests to eat.

'Another cup will not hurt you,' she said. 'That is just nonsense about nerves. If it was green tea,[143] indeed, and you were indulging in it at night to keep you off your sleep – but in a fine afternoon like this, and after your row. Now just try one of these scones; you have not tasted this kind. It is hot from the griddle, and we all think my cook has a gift. Mysie, tell Margaret that we will have a few more. And, Oona, it is the cream scones that Katie likes: but you must tell Lord Erradeen to try this kind, just to please me.'

Thus the kind lady ran on. It gave her the profoundest pleasure to see her house filled, and to serve her young guests with these simple delicacies. 'Dear me, it is just nothing. I wish it was better worth taking,' she answered to Mr. Braithwaite's compliments, who made the usual pretty speeches of the English tourist as to Scotch hospitality. Mrs. Forrester felt as if these compliments were a half-reproach to her for so simple an entertainment. 'You see,' she said, 'it is all we can do; for, besides that there is no gentle-manᵇ in the house, which is against dinner-giving, we are not well situated in the isle for evening visits. The nights are cold at this time of the year, and it is not always easy to strike our bit little landing in the dark; so we have to content ourselves with a poor offering to our friends. And I am sure you are very kind to take it so politely. If my boys were at home, I would have it more in my power to show attention; but if you are going further north, I hope you will make your way to Eaglescairn and see my son, who will be delighted to show you the country about him,' Mrs. Forrester said. The English M.P. could not but think that it was his reputation which had travelled before him, and gained him so delightful a reception.

As for the rest of the party, they were fully entertained by Oona, who was more than usually lively and bright. She said very little to Lord Erradeen, who was by far the most silent of the assembly, but exerted herself for her other guests, with a little flush upon her which was very becoming, and an excitement completely concealed and kept under, which yet acted upon her like a sort of ethereal stimulant quickening all her powers. They were so gay that Mrs. Forrester's anxiety about their return, which indeed she forgot as soon as they were under her roof, was baffled, and it was not till the glow of the sunset was beginning to die out in the west that the visitors began to move. Then there was a hurrying and trooping out, one group following another, to get to the boats. The landscape had changed since they came, and now the upper end of the loch was all cold and chill in the greyness of early twilight, though the sky behind in the southward was still glowing with colour. Benlui[144] lay in a soft mist, having put off his purple and gold, and drawn about him the ethereal violet tones of his evening mantle; but on the slopes beneath, as they fell towards the margin of the water, all colour had died out. Lord Erradeen was one of the last to leave the house, and he was at first but vaguely aware of the little movement and sudden pause of the party upon the first turn of the winding path. He did not even understand for a moment the eager whisper which came almost more distinctly than a shout through the clear still evening air. It was the voice of young Tom of Ellermore.

'Look there! the light – the light! Who says they do not believe in it?' the young fellow said; and then there was a flutter of exclamations and subdued cries of wonder and interest, not without dissentient voices.

'I see some sort of a glimmer,' said one.

'It is as clear as day,' cried another.

'It must be reflection,' a third said.

Walter raised his eyes; he had no sort of doubt to what they referred. His old house lay dark upon the edge of the dark gleaming loch, silent, deserted, not a sign of life about the ruined walls; but upon the tower shone the phantasm of the light, now waning, now rising, as if some unfelt wind blew about the soft light of an unseen lamp. It brought him to himself in a moment, and woke him up from the maze of vague thoughts which had abstracted him even in the midst of the gay movement and bustle. He listened with strange spectatorship, half-stern, half-amused,[a] to all the murmurs of the little crowd.

'If you call that light!' said the voice of Katie; 'it is some phosphorescence that nobody has examined into, I suppose. Who knows what decayed things are there? That sort of glimmer always comes of decay. Oh, yes, I once went to chemistry lectures, and I know. Besides, it stands to reason. What could it be else?'

'You know very well, Katie, what they say—that it is the summons of the warlock lord.'

'I would like to answer the summons,' cried Katie, with a laugh. 'I would send for the health inspector, from Glasgow,[145] and clear it all out, every old crevice, and all the perilous stuff. That would be the thing to do. As for the warlock lord, papa shall invite him to dinner if you will find out where he is to be met with, Tom.'

'Like the commandant in *Don Giovanni*,'[146] somebody said; and there was an echoing laugh, but of a feeble kind.

Walter heard this conversation with a sort of forlorn amusement. He was not excited; his blood was rather congealed than quickened in his veins. But he lingered behind, taking no notice of his late companions as they streamed away to the boats. He seemed in a moment to have been parted miles – nay, worlds away from them. When he thought of the interview that was before him, and of the light-hearted strangers making comments upon the legend of the place with laugh and jest, it seemed to him that he and they could scarcely belong to the same race. He lingered, with no heart for the farewells and explanations that would be necessary if he left them formally: and turning round gazed steadfastly towards Kinloch Houran from behind the shade of the shrubbery. Here Oona found him, as she rushed back to warn him that the boats were pushing off. She began breathlessly –

'Lord Erradeen, you are called –' then stopped, looked at him, and said no more.

He did not answer her for a moment, but stood still, and listened to the sounds below, the impatient call, the plash of the oars in the water, the grating of the keel of the last boat as it was pushed off. Then he looked at Oona, with a smile.

'I am called –?' he said, 'but not that way. Now I must go home.'

Her heart beat so that she could scarcely speak. Was this spell to take possession of her again, against her will, without any wish of his, like some enchantment? She fought against it with all her might.

'If that is so,' she said, 'Hamish will put you across, when you please.'

He took no notice of these indifferent words.

'This time,' he said, 'it is altogether different. I know what is going to happen, and I am not afraid. But it must come to an end.'

What was it to her if it came to an end or not? She tried to check the quick-rising sympathy, to offer no response.

'They will be late on the water, but I hope they will get home before dark,' she replied.

Then he looked at her wistfully, with a look that melted her very heart.

'Don't you know that it will never come to an end unless you stand by me?' he cried.

# CHAPTER XIV.[a]

MRS. FORRESTER was most willing to put Hamish and the boat, or anything else she possessed, at Lord Erradeen's service. 'It is just the most sensible thing you could do,' she said. 'They will be very late, and half of them will have colds. Oona, you will just let Hamish know. But Lord Erradeen, since you are here, will

*The Wizard's Son, Volume II*                              253

you not stay a little longer, and get your dinner before you go? No? Well, I will not say another word if it is not convenient. Just tell Hamish, Oona, my dear.'

Walter followed her so closely when she went upon that mission that she could not escape him. They stood together in the grey of the evening light, upon the beach, while Hamish prepared the boat, Oona's mind in a tumult of apprehension and resistance, with an insidious softness behind, which she felt with despair was betraying her over again into the folly she had surmounted. He had not the same commotion in his mind; his thoughts were altogether bent on what was coming. She was his confidant, his support in it, though he had not said a word to her. He took her into account in the matter as a man takes his wife. She was a part of it all, though it was not of her he was thinking. He spoke after a moment in a tone full of this curious claim, which seemed to him at the moment incontestable.

'It will never come to an end unless you stand by me,' he said. 'Everything can be done if you will stand by me.'

Oona, in her strange agitation, felt as if she had surprised him thinking aloud; as if he did not address her, but merely repeated to himself a fact which was beyond dispute. He said no more, neither did she make any reply. And once more, as if in repetition of the former scene, he turned round as he stepped into the heavy boat, and looked back upon her as Hamish began to ply the oars. She stood and watched him from the beach; there was no wave of the hand, no word of farewell. They were both too much moved for expression of any kind; and everything was different though the same. On the former occasion he had been escaping, and was eager to get free, to get out of reach of an oppression he could not bear; but now was going to his trial, to meet the tyrant, with a certainty that escape was impossible. And for Oona there had been the sensation of a loss unspeakable – a loss which she could neither confess nor explain, which took the heart out of her life; whereas now there was a re-awakening, a mysterious beginning which she could not account for or understand. She stood on the beach till the boat had disappeared, and even till the sound of the oars died out in the distance, in an agitation indescribable. The first despairing sense that the influence against which she had struggled was regaining possession of her, was for the moment lost in an overwhelming tide of sympathy and response to the claim he had made. He had no right to make that claim, and it was intolerable that she should have so little power over herself as to yield to it, and allow herself to become thus the subject of another. Her pride, her reason, had been in arms against any such thraldom; but for this moment Oona was again overcome. She had no power of resistance – her very being seemed to go with him, to add itself to his, as he disappeared across the darkling loch. Stand by him! The words went breathing about her in the air, and in her mind, and everything in her echoed and responded–Stand by him! Yes, to the death. This excitement failed in a sudden chill and shiver, and sense of shame which covered her face with blushes which no one saw, as startled by the gather-

254     *The Selected Works of Margaret Oliphant, Volume 21*

ing dark, and the sound of Mysie's step hastening down to the landing-place with a shawl for her, Oona turned again and ran swiftly up the winding way.

The loch was like lead, with a ripple of mysterious changing lights in the darkness, as the boat shot round under the shadow of Kinloch Houran. All was as still as in a world of dreams, the sound of Hamish's oars in their regular sweep along breaking the intense stillness. Here and there among the trees a light glimmered on the shore–a window of the Manse – the door of the little inn standing open and betraying the ruddy warmth within: but no sound near enough to interrupt the stillness. Walter felt as though he parted with a certain protection when he stepped upon the bit of mossed causeway which served as a landing pier to the old castle, and, bidding Hamish good night, stood alone in that solitude and watched the boatman's red shirt, which had forced its colour even upon the twilight, grow black as it disappeared. The sensation in Walter's mind had little akin with that panic and horror which had once overwhelmed him. No doubt it was excitement that filled up his whole being, and made the pulses throb in his ears, but it was excitement subdued; and all he was conscious of was a sort of saddened expectation – a sense of a great event about to take place which he could not elude or stave off – a struggle in which he might be worsted. 'Let not him that putteth on his armour boast himself like him that putteth it off.'[147] He did not know what might happen to him. But the tremors of his nervous system, or of his agitated soul, or of his physical frame–he could not tell which it was–were stilled. He was intensely serious and sad, but he was not afraid.

Symington, who had been in waiting, listening for his master's return, opened the door and lighted him up the spiral stairs. The room was already lighted and cheerful, the curtains drawn, the fire blazing brightly.

'The days are creeping in,' he said, 'and there's a nip in the air aneath thae hills– so I thought a fire would be acceptable.' In fact the room looked very comfortable and bright, not a place for mysteries. Walter sat down between the cheerful fire and the table with its lights.

There is often at the very crisis of fate a relaxation of the strain upon the mind – a sudden sense as of peril over, and relief. Thus the dying will often have a glimmer in the socket, a sense of betterness and hope before the last moment. In the same way a sensation of relief came on Walter at the height of his expectation. His mind was stilled. A feeling without any justification, yet grateful and consoling, came over him, as if the trial were over, or at least postponed–as if something had intervened for his deliverance. He sat and warmed himself in this genial glow, feeling his pulses calmed and his mind soothed – he could not tell how. How long or how short the interval of consolation was, if a few minutes only, or an hour, or half a lifetime, he could not tell. He was roused from it by the sound of steps in the corridor outside. It was a passage which ended in nothing – in the gloom of the ruinous portion of the house – and consequently it was not usual to hear any sound in it, the servants invariably approaching Lord Erradeen's rooms by the stair. On this occasion, however, Walter, suddenly roused, heard some one coming from a distance, with steps which echoed into the vacancy as of an empty place, but gradually drawing nearer, sounding, in ordinary measure, a man's footstep, firm and strong, but not heavy, upon the corridor outside. Then the door was opened with the usual click of the lock and heavy creak with which it swung upon its hinges. He rose up, scarcely knowing what he did.

'You examined everything last night to find a secret passage,' said the new-comer[a] with a humorous look, 'which indeed might very well have existed in a house of this date. There was actually such a passage once existing, and connected with a secret room which I have found useful in its time. But that was in another part of the house, and the age of concealments and mysteries – of that kind – is past. Won't you sit down?' he added, pleasantly. 'You see I put myself at my ease at once.'

Walter's heart had given such a bound that the sensation made him giddy and faint. He stood gazing at the stranger, only half comprehending what was happening. All that happened was natural and simple in the extreme. The visitor walked round the table to the other side of the fire, and moving the large chair which stood there into a position corresponding to Walter's, seated himself in the most leisurely and easy way. 'Sit down,' he repeated after a moment, more peremptorily, and with almost a tone of impatience. 'We have much to talk over:[b] Let us do it comfortably, at least.'

'I can have nothing to talk over,' said Walter, feeling that he spoke with difficulty, yet getting calm by dint of speaking, 'with an undesired and unknown visitor.'

The other smiled. 'If you will think of it you will find that I am far from unknown,' he said. 'No one can have a larger body of evidence in favour of his reality. What did that poor little woman in Edinburgh say to you?'

'I wonder,' cried Walter, unconscious of the inconsistency, 'that you can permit yourself to mention her name.'

'Poor little thing,' he replied, 'I am sincerely sorry for her. Had I foreseen what was going to happen I should have guarded against it. You may tell her so. Everything that is subject to human conditions is inconsistent and irregular. But on the whole, taking life altogether, there is not so much to be regretted. Probably she is happier *there* than had she embarked, as she was about to do, in a struggle with me. Those who contend with me have not an easy career before them.'

'Yet one day it will have to be done,' Walter said.

'Yes. You consent then that I am not unknown, however undesired,' the stranger said, with a smile. He was so entirely at his ease, at his leisure, as if he had hours before him, that Walter, gazing in an impatience beyond words, felt the hopelessness of any effort to hurry through the interview, and dropped into his seat with a sigh of reluctance and despair.

'Who are you?' he cried; 'and why, in the name of God, do you thus torment and afflict a whole race?'

'The statement is scarcely correct. I was a Highland youth of no pretension once, and you are supposed to be Lord Erradeen, not only a Scotch lord, but an English peer.[148] That is what my tormenting and afflicting have come to, with many solid acres and precious things besides. Very few families of our antiquity have even survived these centuries. Not one has grown and increased to the point at which we stand. I see a great addition within our reach now.'

'And what good has it all done?' Walter said. 'They say that my predecessor was a miserable man, and I know that I–since this elevation, as you think it – have been –'

'Good for nothing. I allow it fully. What were you before? Equally good for nothing; consuming your mother's means, opposing her wishes, faithful to no one. My friend, a man who sets himself against me must be something different from that.'

To this Walter made no reply. He could not be called penitent for the folly of his life; but he was aware of it. And he did not attempt to defend himself. He was entirely silenced for the moment: and the other resumed.

'I have always felt it to be probable that some one capable of resistance might arise in time. In the mean time all that has happened has been gain, and my work has been fully successful. It would rather please me to meet one in the course of the ages who was fit to be my conqueror, being my son. It is a contingency which I have always taken into consideration. But it is not likely to be you,' he said, with a slight laugh. 'I shall know my victor when he comes.'

'Why should it not be I? If it be enough to hate this tyrannical influence, this cruel despotism –'

'As you have hated every influence and every rule all your life,' said the other with a smile. 'That is not the sort of man that does anything. Do you think it is agreeable to me to be the progenitor of a race of nobodies? I compensate myself by making them great against their will – the puppets! I allow you to wear my honours out of consideration to the prejudices of society: but they are all mine.'

'It was not you, however, who got them,' said Walter. 'Can a grandfather inherit what was given to his descendants?'

'Come,' said the stranger, 'you are showing a little spirit – I like that better. Let us talk now of the immediate business in hand. You have something in your power which I did not foresee when I talked to you last. Then there were few opportunities of doing anything–nothing in your range that I had observed, but to clear off incumbrances, which, by the way, you refused to do. Now a trifling exertion on your part –'

'You mean the sacrifice of my life.'

The stranger laughed – this time with a sense of the ludicrous which made his laugh ring through the room with the fullest enjoyment. 'The sacrifice of a life, which has been made happy by – and by – and by –. How many names would you like me to produce? You have perhaps a less opinion of women than I have. Which of them, if they knew all about it, as I do, would pick up that life and unite their own to it? But happily they don't know. She thinks perhaps – that girl on the isle–that I mean her harm. I mean her no harm – why should I harm her? I harm no one who does not step into my way.'

'Man!' cried Walter –'if you are a man – would you hurt her for succouring me? Would you treat her as you treated –'

'That was an accident,' he said quickly. 'I have told you already I would have guarded against it had I divined – But your limited life is the very empire of accident; and those who come across my path must take the consequences. It is their own fault if they put themselves in the way of danger. Let us return to the subject in hand. The woman whom you must marry –'

The words suddenly seemed to close on the air, leaving no sort of echo or thrill in it; and Walter, looking round, saw Symington come in with the scared look he remembered to have seen in the old man's countenance before, though without any sign in him of seeing the stranger. He asked in a hesitating manner, 'Did ye ring, my lord? You'll be wanting your dinner. It is just ready to come up.'

Walter was about to send the old servant hastily away; but a slight sign from his visitor restrained him. He said nothing, but watched, with feelings indescribable, the proceedings of the old man, who began to lay the table, moving to and fro, smoothing the damask cloth, folding the napkin, arranging the silver. Symington did everything as usual: but there was a tremor in him, unlike his ordinary composure. Sometimes he threw an alarmed and tremulous look round the room, as if something terrifying might lurk in any corner; but while doing so brushed past the very person of that strange visitor in the chair without a sign that he knew any one to be there. This mixture of suppressed panic and inconceivable unconsciousness gave Walter a suffocating sensation which he could not master. He cried out suddenly, in a loud and sharp tone which was beyond his own control, 'Symington! Is it possible you don't see –'

Symington let the forks and spoons he was holding drop out of his hands. He cried out, quavering, 'Lord, have a care of us!' Then he stopped trembling to gather up the things he had dropped, which was a great trouble, so nervous and tremulous was he. He collected them all at the very foot of the man who sat smiling in the great chair.

'You gave me a terrible fright, my lord,' the old man said, raising himself with a broken laugh: 'that was what you meant, no doubt. All this water about and damp makes a man nervish. See! what should I see? I am no one of those,' Symington added, with a great attempt at precision and a watery smile, 'that see visions and that dream dreams.'[149]

'Why should you disturb the man's mind for nothing,' said the visitor in that penetrating voice which Walter felt to go through him, penetrating every sense. He had grown reckless in the strange horror of the circumstances.

'Don't you hear that?' he cried sharply, catching Symington by the arm.

The old man gave a cry, his eyes flickered and moved as if they would have leapt from their sockets. He shook so that Walter's grasp alone seemed to keep him from falling. But he remained quite unconscious of any special object of alarm.

'Me! I hear naething,' he cried. 'There is nothing to hear. You have listened to all those old stories till ye are just out of yourself. But no me,' Symington said with a quavering voice, but a forced smile. 'No me! I am not superstitious. You will no succeed, my lord, in making a fool of me. Let me go. The trout is done by this time, and I must bring up my dinner,' he cried with feverish impatience, shaking himself free.

Walter turned round half-dazed to say he knew not what to the occupant of that chair. But when he looked towards it there was no one there: nor in the room, nor anywhere near was the slightest trace of his visitor to be found.

# CHAPTER XV.ᵃ

It may be supposed that the dinner which was served to Lord Erradeen after this episode was done but little justice to. The trout was delicious, the bird cooked to perfection; but the young man, seated in sight of the apparently vacant chair, where so lately his visitor had been seated, could scarcely swallow a morsel. Was he there still, though no one could see him? or had he departed only to return again when Symington and the meal had been cleared away, and the evening was free? There was a sickening sensation at Walter's heart as he asked himself these questions, and indeed, throughout this portion of his life, his experience was that the actual presence of this extraordinary person was very much less exciting and confusing than the effect produced during his apparent absence, when the idea that he might still be there unseen, or might appear at any moment, seemed to disturb the mental balance in a far more painful way. In the present case the effect was overpowering. Walter had been talking to him almost with freedom: it was impossible, indeed, thus to converse – even though the conversation was something of a struggle, with a man possessed of all the ordinary faculties, and in appearance, though more dignified and stately than most, yet in no way unlike other men – without a gradual cessation of those mysterious tremors with which the soul is convulsed in presence of anything that appears supernatural. The personage who inhabited, or (for it was impossible to think of him as inhabiting a ruin) periodically visited Kinloch Houran had nothing in him save his stateliness of aspect which need have separated him from ordinary men. He would have attracted attention anywhere, but except as a person of unusual distinction, would have startled no one; and even when the young man so cruelly subject to his influence talked with him, it was impossible to keep up the superstitious terror which nature feels for the inexplainable. But as soon as he withdrew, all this instinctive feeling returned. Walter's nerves and imagination sprang up into full play again, and got command of his reason. By moments it seemed to him that he caught a glimpse still of an outline in the chair, of eyes looking at him, of the smile and the voice which expressed so full a knowledge of all his own past history and everything that was in him. This consciousness gave to his eyes the same scared yet searching look which he had seen in those of Symington, took his breath from him, made his head whirl, and his heart fail. Symington waiting behind his chair, but eagerly on the watch for any sign, saw that his young lord was ghastly pale, and perceived the half stealthy look which he cast around him, and especially the entire failure of his appetite. This is a thing which no Scotch domestic can bear.

'You are no eating, my lord,' he said in a tone of gentle reproach, as he withdrew the plate with the untasted trout. ('That many a poor gentleman would have been glad of!' he said to himself.)

'No, I am not particularly hungry,' Walter said, with a pretence at carelessness.

'I can recommend the bird,' said Symington, 'if it's no just a cheeper,[150] for the season is advanced, it's been young and strong on the wing; and good game is rich, fortifying both to the body and spirit. Those that have delicate stomachs, it is just salvation to them – and for those that are, as ye may say, in the condition of invalids in the mind –'

Symington had entirely recovered from his own nervousness. He moved about the room with a free step, and felt himself fully restored to the position of counsellor and adviser, with so much additional freedom as his young master was less in a position to restrain him, and permitted him to speak almost without interruption. Indeed Walter as he ineffectually tried to eat was half insensible to the monologue going on over his head.

'Ye must not neglect the body,' Symington said, 'especially in a place like this where even the maist reasonable man may be whiles put to it to keep his right senses. If ye'll observe, my lord, them that see what ye may call visions are mostly half starvit creatures, fasting or ill-nourished. Superstition, in my opinion, has a great deal to do with want of meat. But your lordship is paying no attention. Just two three mouthfuls, my lord! just as a duty to yourself and all your friends, and to please a faithful auld servant,' Symington said, with more and more insinuating tones. There was something almost pathetic in the insistance with which he pressed 'a breast of pairtridge that would tempt a saint' upon his young master. The humour of it struck Walter dully through the confusion of his senses. It was all like a dream to him made up of the laughable and the miserable; until Symington at last consented to see that his importunities were unavailing, and after a tedious interval of clearing away, took himself and all his paraphernalia out of the room, and left Walter alone. It seemed to Lord Erradeen that he had not been alone for a long time, nor had any leisure in which to collect his faculties; and for the first few minutes after the door had closed upon his too officious servant a sense of relief was in his mind. He drew a long breath of ease and consolation, and throwing himself back in his chair gave himself up to momentary peace.

But this mood did not last long. He had not been alone five minutes before there sprang up within him something which could be called nothing less than a personal struggle with – he could not tell what. There is a quickening of excitement in a mental encounter, in the course of a momentous discussion, which almost reaches the height of that passion which is roused by bodily conflict, when the subject is important enough, or the antagonists in deadly earnest. But to describe how this is intensified when the discussion takes place not between two, but in the spiritual consciousness of one, is almost too much for words to accomplish. Lord Erradeen in the complete solitude of this room, closed and curtained and shut out from all access of the world, suddenly felt himself in the height of such a controversy. He saw no one, nor did it occur to him again to look for any one. There was no need. Had his former visitor appeared, as before, seated opposite to him in the chair which stood so suggestively between the fire and the table, his pulses would have calmed, and his mind become composed at once. But there was nobody to address him in human speech, to oppose to him the changes of a human countenance. The question was discussed within himself with such rapidity of argument and reply, such clash of intellectual weapons, as never occurs to the external hearing. There passed thus under review the entire history of the struggle which had been going on from the time of Lord Erradeen's first arrival at the home of his race. It ran after this fashion, though with the quickness of thought far swifter than words.

'You thought you had conquered me. You thought you had escaped me.'

'I did; you had no power in the glen, or on the isle.'

'Fool! I have power everywhere, wherever you have been.'

'To betray me into wickedness?'

'To let you go your own way. Did I tempt you to evil before ever you heard of me?'

'Can I tell? perhaps to prepare me for bondage.'

'At school, at home, abroad, in all relations? Self-lover! My object at least is better than yours.'

'I am no self-lover; rather self-hater, self-despiser.'

'It is the same thing. Self before all. I offer you something better, the good of your race.'

'I have no race. I refuse!'

'You shall not refuse. You are mine, you must obey me.'

'Never! I am no slave. I am my own master.'

'The slave of every petty vice; the master of no impulse. Yield! I can crush you if I please.'

'Never! I am – Oona's then, who will stand by me.'

'Oona's! a girl! who when she knows what you are will turn and loathe you.'

'Fiend! You fled when she gave me her hand.'

'Will she touch your hand when she knows what it has clasped before?'

Then Walter felt his heart go out in a great cry. If any one had seen him thus, he would have borne the aspect of a madman. His forehead was knotted as with great cords, his eyes, drawn and puckered together in their sockets, shone with a gleam of almost delirious hatred and passion. He held back, his figure all drawn into angles, in a horrible tension of resistance as if some one with the force of a giant was seizing him. He thought that he shrieked out with all the force of mortal agony. 'No! If Oona turns from me and all angels – I am God's then at the last!'

Then there seemed to him to come a pause of perfect stillness in the heart of the battle; but not the cessation of conflict. Far worse than the active struggle, it was with a low laugh that his antagonist seemed to reply.

'God's! whom you neither love nor obey, nor have ever sought before.'

The room in which Lord Erradeen sat was quite still all through the evening, more silent than the night air that ruffled the water and sighed in the trees permitted outside. The servants did not hear a sound. Peace itself could not have inhabited a more noiseless and restful place.

# CHAPTER XVI.[a]

IN the early morning there is an hour more like paradise than anything else vouchsafed to our mortal senses as a symbol of the better world to come. The evening is infinitely sweet, but it implies labour and rest and consolation, which are ideas not entirely dissevered from pain; but in the first glory of the morning there is an unearthly sweetness, a lustre as of the pristine world, unsoiled, untried, unalloyed, a heavenly life and calm. The sunshine comes upon us with a surprise, with something of that exultant novelty which it must have had to Adam; the drops of dew shine like little separate worlds; the birds, most innocent of all the inhabitants of earth, have the soft-breathing universe to themselves: all their sweet domestic intercourses, the prattle of the little families, their trills of commentary touching everything that is going on in earth and heaven get accomplished, as the level line of sunshine penetrates from one glade to another, higher and higher, touching as it passes every bough into life. Awakening and vitality are in the very atmosphere which brings a new hope, a new day, a new world of possibility and life. New heavens and a new earth[151] thus present themselves to mortal cognisance, for the most part quite unconscious of them, every day.

262        *The Selected Works of Margaret Oliphant, Volume 21*

If only we brought nothing with us from the old world that ended in the night! But, alas, we bring everything – ourselves, that 'heritage of woe',[152] our thoughts, our desires, baffled or eager, for other objects than those which are in harmony with that new life and blessedness. When the sun rose visibly into the blue, skimming the surface of Loch Houran, and waking all the woods, there stood one spectator upon the old battlements of the ruined castle who was altogether out of harmony with the scene. Walter had not slept all night. He had not even gone through the form of going to bed. He had come out as soon as there was a glimmer of daylight, which, in October, is long of coming, to get what refreshment was possible from the breath of the morning air, and thus had assisted at the re-awakening of earth, and all the development of the new-born day. From where he stood there lay before him a paradise of sky and water, with everything repeated, embellished, made into an ideal of twofold sweetness, brightness, and purity, in the broad mirror of the lake. The autumn woods, the tracts of green field, or late yellow of the unreaped corn, all showed like another fairy-land underneath, a country still purer, more dazzling, and brilliant, more still and fresh, than the morning land above. 'The light that never was on sea or shore'[153] shone in those glorified and softly rippling woods, trending[154] away into the infinite to the point beyond which mortal vision cannot go. What haunts and refuges of happy life might be there! what dreams of poetry beyond the human! That lovely inversion of all things, that more than mortal freshness and sweetness and liquid glow of light, confused the mind with a kind of involuntary bliss, a vision of a place of escape, the never attained country to which the soul, had it wings, might flee away and be at rest.[155]

But that soul had no wings which looked out from Walter's haggard countenance, as he leant on the half-ruined wall. He gazed at the scene before him like one who had no lot or part in it. Its peace and brightness brought but into greater relief the restlessness of his own soul, the gloom and blackness in his heart. He had been struggling all night in a fierce internal controversy which, to his own consciousness, was with another intelligence more powerful than his own, and yet might have been with himself, with the better part that kept up within him a protest for better things, with such representatives of conscience and the higher affections as still existed within him. However it was, he was exhausted with the struggle, his strength was worn out. That lull of pain which does not mean any cure, or even any beginning of healing, but is merely a sign that the power of the sufferer to endure has come to its limit, gave him a kind of rest. But the rest itself was restless and incapable of composure. He moved about like an uneasy spirit along the broken line of the old battlements, pausing here and there to plunge his eyes into the landscape, to take in the morning air with a long inspiration. And so unlike was the mood of his mind to his usual character and habits, that as he moved, Walter gave vent to a low moaning, such as gives a kind of fictitious relief to the old and suffering – an involuntary utterance which it was terrible to hear coming with his breathing from a young man's lips, and in the midst of such a scene. Was he talking to himself? Was he only moaning as a dumb creature moans? By and by he half flung himself, in his weariness, into one of the ruinous embrasures, and remained there, leaning his back against one side of it. And then he said to himself, repeating the words over and over again – 'Neither God's nor Oona's. Neither Oona's nor God's.'

Lord Erradeen had arrived at that lowest depth of self-estimation, which means despair. His own life had been forced upon him, represented before his eyes he could not tell how. He had seen its motives disentangled, its course traced, all its wastes laid bare, with a distinctness against which he could offer no appeal. He could deny nothing; it was true; this was what he had done, with a repetition of folly, of selfishness, of baseness, for which he could offer no sort of excuse, which confounded and abased him. He had known it all, it is true, before; time after time he had pulled himself up and looked at the last scrap of his life, and pronounced it indefensible; then had pushed it from him and gone on again, escaping with all the haste he could from contemplation of the phenomena which were inexplicable, and which he did not desire to attempt to explain even to himself. He had said truly to Miss Milnathort that to know you are wrong is not always equivalent to being on the way to mend it. He had always known he was wrong; he had never been deficient in moral disapproval of others like himself, or even of himself, when in one of the pauses of his career he was brought face to face with that individual. But he had been able to put a sort of accidental gloss upon his own worst actions. He had not intended them; there had been no motive whatever in what he did; he had done so and so by chance – by indolence, because it happened to be put before him to do it; but he had meant nothing by it. Out of this subterfuge he had been driven during the mental conflict of the night. And there was this peculiarity in his state, that he was not thus enlightened and convinced by the exertions of any reformatory influence, by any prophet bidding him repent. Conviction came from entirely the other side, and with a motive altogether different. 'Who are you,' his antagonist said, or seemed to say, 'to take refuge with a pure woman, you who have never been pure? Who are you to lay claim to be God's, after ignoring God's existence altogether; or to be your own master, who have never ruled or guided yourself, but have been the slave of every folly, a feather blown on the wind, a straw carried away by the stream?'

All these accusations had been made as plain to him as the daylight. He had not been allowed to escape; the course of his life had been traced so clearly, that he could not protest, or object, or contradict; he was convinced – the most terrible position in which a man can be. Whether any man, thoroughly persuaded of his own moral wretchedness and debasement ever does escape despair, is a question full of difficulty. The prodigal's sense that in his father's house every servant has enough and to spare while he perishes of hunger is a different matter. 'Father, I have sinned, I am no more worthy to be called thy son; make me as one of thy hired servants.'[156] There are still possibilities to a soul in such a position. But one who is driven from stronghold to stronghold, until at length he is forced to allow that there is no inducement which has not been tried and failed with him, that he has no claim to the succour of God or man, or woman, that he has turned his back upon all, neglected all, wronged every power in heaven and earth that could help, what is he to do? He may be forgiven; but forgiveness, in the entire abasement of that discovery, is not what he wants. He wants a renovation for which there seems no means left; he wants, in the old language – that language which we are said to have outgrown – to be born again: and that is impossible – impossible! What is there in heaven or earth that will prevent him from doing all over again what he has done before, the moment his circumstances permit it? So long as he is what he is – nothing: and how shall he be made other than what he is?

'Ye must be born again.'[157] Ah, what preacher can know that as he does? But how – but how? Neither God's nor Oona's – and who, then, was to help him? He had caught at the woman in his despair; he had not even so much as thought of God till the last moment, and then had flown like a coward to a fetish, meaning nothing but to escape. Why should God bend down from those spotless heavens to acknowledge the wretched runaway's clutch at his divine garments in the extremity of mortal terror? Would Oona have given him that hand of hers, had she known how his was stained? And would God attend to that coward's appeal made only when everything else failed?

The young man sat in the corner of the embrasure pressing himself against the rough stone-work for support. Despair had possession of his soul. What had he to do with the best and highest things, with freedom and love? After all, why should he be his own master, why claim the right to judge for himself? If he had this freedom fully, what would he do with it? Throw it away next day in exchange for some nothing, some pleasure that palled in the tasting. Pleasure! There was no pleasure, but only make-beliefs and deceptions. The old fellow was right, he began to say to himself, with a certain bitter humour. Had he exercised no coercion over the race, had the Methvens been left to their own devices, how much of them would have remained now? Instead of a peerage and great estates they would have died out in a ditch or in a sponging-house generations ago. Their lands would have gone bit by bit: their name would have disappeared – all as he said. And supposing now that Walter was left entirely free to do as he pleased, what reason had he to believe that he would not squander everything he could squander, and bring down the posterity of the race into the dust? That is what he would have done if left to himself. He would have resisted all claims of prudence or duty. He would have followed, he knew it, the caprice of the moment, just as he had done now. If no former Methvens had ruined the family it was in himself to do it. All these thoughts were in favour of the submission which seemed to him now almost the only thing before him. He thought of Miss Milnathort and her anxiety for him, and laughed to himself bitterly at her childish hope. Two that should be one, and that should be set on everything that was good. What a simpleton she was! He set on everything that was good! he was incapable of anything that was good. And Oona – could there be a greater folly than to think that Oona, when she knew, would pick him up out of this ruin, and give him a new starting-ground? He laughed at the thought aloud. Oona! Was not her very name the token of purity, the sign of maidenhood and innocence. And to believe that she would mingle herself in his being which was unclean and false from its very beginning! He laughed at his own folly to think so. In ignorance she had been more kind than ever woman was. She had asked no questions, she had given him her hand, she had stood by him. In ignorance: *but when she knew!* He said to himself that he was not cad enough to let her go on in this ignorance. He would have to tell her what he had been, what he would be again if left to circumstances and his own guidance. He would not deceive her; he was not cad enough for that. And when he had told her, and had given up for ever all hope of really making a stand against the tyrant of his race, or carrying out his theories of happiness, what would remain? What would remain? Subjection – misery –

'No,' said a voice close by him, 'something else – something very good in its way, and with which the greater majority of mankind are quite content, and may be very happy. The second best.'

Walter had started at the sound of this voice. He left his seat with nervous haste; and yet he had no longer any sense of panic. He had a certain doleful curiosity to see the man, whom he had only seen in twilight rooms or by artificial light, in the open air and sunshine. Perhaps this strange personage divined his thoughts, for he came forward with a slight smile. There was nothing in his appearance to alarm the most timid. He was, as Miss Milnathort had called him, a grand gentleman. He had the air of one accustomed to command, with that ease of bearing which only comes to those largely experienced in the world. The path along the ruinous battlements was one that craved wary walking, but he traversed it with the boldest step without a moment's hesitation or doubt. He made a little salutation with his hand as he approached. 'You were laughing,' he said. 'You are taking, I hope, a less highflown view of the circumstances altogether. The absolute does not exist in this world. We must all be content with advantages which are comparative. I always regret,' he continued, 'resorting to heroic measures. To have to do with some one who will hear and see reason, is a great relief. I follow the course of your thoughts with interest. They are all perfectly just; and the conclusion is one which most wise men have arrived at. Men in general are fools. As a rule you are incapable of guiding yourselves; but only the wise among you know it.'

'I have no pretension to be wise.'

'You are modest – all at once. So long as you are reasonable that will do. Adapt your life now to a new plan. The ideal is beyond your reach. By no fault of circumstances, but by your own, you have forfeited a great deal that is very captivating to the mind of youth, but very empty if you had it all to-morrow. You must now rearrange your conceptions and find yourself very well off with the second best.'

There was something in his very tone which sent the blood coursing through Walter's veins, and seemed to swell to bursting the great currents of life. He cried out –

'You have driven me to despair. You have cut off from me every hope. And now you exhort me to find myself very well off, to adapt my life to a new plan. Is that all you know?'

His companion smiled. 'You would like me better to repeat to you again that you have no ground to stand upon, and are as unworthy as one can be at your age. All that is very true. But one aspect of the matter is not all. In the mean time you will have to live and get on somehow. Suicide of course is always open to you, but you are not the sort of man for that; besides, it is begging the question, and solves no problem. No, you must live – on the second level. Your ideal has always been impossible, for you have never had heart or will to keep up to it. Why you should have had this fit of fantastic wilfulness now, and really believed that by means of vague aspirations you were to get the better of me and all your antecedents, I cannot tell. You must now find out practically how you are to live.'

Walter had reached the lowest depths of despair a little while ago. He had consented that it was all true, that there was no further escape for him; but now again a passionate contradiction surged up within him. 'I will not,' he said, vehemently, 'I will not – take your way.'

'I think you will – for why? there is no other half so good. You will be very comfortable, and you will have done a great thing for your house. By-and-by[a] you will settle into a conviction that what you have done is the best thing you could have done. It is one of the privileges of mankind. And I promise you that I will not molest you. Your coming here will be little more than a formula. You will agree with me: why then should there be any controversy between us? Maturity and wealth and well-being will bring you to think with me that a settled advantage like that of one's race is far beyond all evanescent good of the fancy. You will become respectable and happy – yes, quite happy enough – as happy as men have any right to be.'

There was a half-tone[b] of mockery, as if the speaker scorned the picture he drew; and at every word the resistance which had been almost stilled in Walter's mind rose up more warmly. 'Are you happy yourself,' he said, suddenly, 'that you recommend this to me?'

The stranger paused a little. 'The word is a trivial one. I have many gratifications,' he said.

*The Wizard's Son, Volume II* 267

'I don't know what your gratifications can be. Is it worth your while to live through the ages as you say – you, so powerful as you are, with so many great faculties – in a miserable old ruin, to exercise this terrorism upon unoffending men?'

Then Walter's companion laughed aloud. 'To live for ages in a miserable old ruin!' he said. 'That does not seem a very attractive lot indeed. But set your mind at rest, my kind descendant; I live in a miserable ruin no more than you do. My affairs are everywhere. I have the weakness of a man for my own – perhaps in other regions as well – but that is nothing to you.'

'It is everything to me. Give me some explanation of you. If, as you say, you have lived for centuries impossibly, how have you done it? Have you ever come to a blank wall like me – have you ever been abandoned by every hope? or,' cried the young man, 'am I your superior in this horrible experience? No man could stand as I do – given up to despair: and yet go on living like you.'

'It depends upon your point of view. When you have taken my advice (as you will do presently) and have come down from your pinnacle and accepted what is the ordinary lot of mankind, you will find no longer any difficulty in living – as long as is possible; you will not wish to shorten your life by a day.'

'And what is the ordinary lot of mankind?' cried Walter, feeling himself once more beaten down, humiliated, irritated by an ascendancy which he could not resist.

'I have told you – the second best. In your case a wife with a great deal of wealth, and many other qualities, who will jar upon your imagination (an imagination which has hitherto entertained itself so nobly!) and exasperate your temper perhaps, and leave your being what you call incomplete: but who will give you a great acquisition of importance and set you at peace with me. That alone will tell for much in your comfort; and gradually your mind will be brought into conformity. You will consider subjects in general as I do, from a point of view which will not be individual. You will not balance the interests of the few miserable people who choose to think their comfort impaired, but will act largely for the continued benefit of your heirs and your property. You will avail yourself of my perceptions, which are more extended than your own, and gradually become the greatest landowner, the greatest personage of your district; able to acquire the highest honours if you please, to wield the greatest influence. Come, you have found the other position untenable according to your own confession. Accept the practicable. I do not hurry you. Examine for yourself into the issues of your ideal – now that we have become friends and understand each other so thoroughly –'

'I am no friend of yours. I understand no one, not even myself.'

'You are my son,' said the other with a laugh. 'You are of my nature; as you grow older you will resemble me more and more. You will speak to your sons as I speak to you. You will point out these duties to them, as I do to you.'

'In everything you say,' cried Walter, 'I perceive that you acknowledge a better way. Your plans are the second best – you say so. Is it worth living so long only to know that you are embracing mediocrity after all, that you have nothing to rise to? and yet you acknowledge it,' he said.

The stranger looked at him with a curious gaze. He who had never shown the smallest emotion before grew slightly paler at this question: but he laughed before he replied.

'You are acute,' he said. 'You can hit the blot.[158] But the question in hand is not my character, but your practical career.'

The sound of an oar here broke the extreme silence. The morning had fully come, the night coach from 'the south' had arrived at the inn, and Duncan with the postbag was coming along the still water, which cut like a transparent curd before him, and joined again in eddying reflections behind. Duncan bent his back to his oars unconscious of any mystery; his postbag, bringing news of all the world, lay in front of him. He and his boat in every detail of outline and colour swam suspended in the light, in reflection, and swept double over the shining surface. How extraordinary was the contrast between his open-air placidity, his fresh morning countenance, the air of the hills about him, and the haggard countenance of his master, looking upon this country fellow with an envy which was as foolish as it was genuine. Duncan did not know anything about the ideal. And yet in his way he followed his conscience, sometimes with pain and trouble, and at the cost of many a struggle–or else neglected its warnings, and took his own way as his master had done. Walter did not take this into consideration, but looked down upon his boatsman's ruddy, honest countenance and square frame, stretching contentedly to his oars and thinking of nothing, with envy. Would it have been better to be born like that to daily labour and an unawakened intelligence? He turned round to say something, but his visitor had gone. There was not a shadow upon the walls, not the sound of a step. Lord Erradeen had no longer the faintest movement of fear, but in its place a certain impatience and irritability as if this practical joke might be played upon him too often. And presently into the clear air rang the voice of Symington.

'For God's sake, my lord, take care! that is just where the poor lady was killed thirty years ago.'

# CHAPTER XVII.[a]

THE commonplace world has a strange look to a man who has himself come out of any great personal struggle, out of an excitement which no one knows anything about but himself. When he descends, with still the heave of strong emotion in his breast, there is a mixture of contempt and relief in the manner in which he regards the extraordinary stolidity and unimpressionableness of his fellows. He is glad that they are unaware of what has happened to himself, yet cannot help scorning them a little for their want of penetration; and it is a comfort to him to feel himself surrounded with the calm and indifference of strangers, yet he cannot help feeling that had they been of a higher nature, they must have divined the suppressed agitation with which he moves among them, his nerves all trembling with the strain through which they have passed. Thus Walter, when he landed at the village, met the looks of the country folk with a certain expectation of seeing some traces of the wondering curiosity with which they must be asking themselves what ailed Lord Erradeen? and felt himself at once baffled and disappointed and relieved to find them full of their usual friendliness and hospitality, but nothing more.

'We are real glad to see your lordship back,' Mrs. Macfarlane said at the inn, 'and I hope you mean to bide, and no just run away when you are getting acquaint with the country-side.' Big John, who was looking on while his horses were being cared for, gave a tug to his hat in honour of Lord Erradeen, but scarcely withdrew his eyes from the other more interesting spectacle. And finally the minister, who was setting out upon one of his visitations, met his noble parishioner with the most cheerful good morning, without any indication of deeper insight.

'You are welcome home, Lord Erradeen,' he said as the landlady had said, 'and this time I hope we'll see more of you. Are you stepping my way? It is just a most beautiful morning for this time of the year, and I am going to one of my outlying corners; but you young gentlemen, what with your shooting, and stalking, and ploys in general, are not generally much addicted to a simple walk.'

'I am going your way; I am no great sportsman; I want to see Shaw who lives somewhere in this direction, I think.'

'I will show the way with pleasure, Lord Erradeen; but I doubt you will not find him in. He is out upon his rounds before now. He will be tackling you about Peter Thomson, and his farm. And I would be glad to say a word, too, if I might. They had been there all their lives; they never believed it possible that they would be sent away. It is very natural you should want to make the best of your property, but it was a blow; and though he was a little behind in his worldly affairs, he was always good to the poor, and an elder, and well-living person. Such a one is a loss to the country-side; but it is every man's duty, no doubt, to himself and his posterity, to make the best he can of his estate.' This the minister said with an air of polite disapproval, yet acquiescence in a doctrine not to be gainsaid. 'Political economy,'[159] he added, with a laugh, 'did not come into my curriculum, although I was at college in Adam Smith's palmy days.'[160]

'If you think my actions have anything to do with Adam Smith!' cried Walter. It was a peculiarity of this young man, and perhaps of others beside, to resent above all things the imputation of a prudential motive. 'I know nothing about Thomson,' he added. 'I was absent, and I suppose did – whatever I am supposed to have done – on the impulse of the moment, as I am too apt to do.'

'That is a pity,' said the minister, 'especially when the well-being of others is concerned. You will pardon me, my lord, who am an old-fashioned person. The good of

270 *The Selected Works of Margaret Oliphant, Volume 21*

your property (if ye think this is for the good of your property) is always a motive, and some will think a sound one: but to decide what is of great consequence to other folk without thought, because you happen to be tired, or worried, or in an ill way –'

A natural flush of anger came to Walter's face: but notwithstanding all his faults there was something generous in him. He bit his lip to restrain a hasty word which was ready to burst forth, and said, after a moment, 'The reproof is just. I had no right to be so inconsiderate. Still, as you say, the advantage of the property is a motive: there are some,' he added bitterly, with a sense that he was speaking at some third person, 'who think it the best in the world.'

'And so it is in the right view,' said Mr. Cameron; 'that is what I always think when I read what those misguided creatures are wanting in Ireland, to do away with landlords[161] altogether – and some even among ourselves,' he added with that sense of the superiority of 'ourselves' which dwells so calmly in the Scottish bosom. The last was said regretfully, with a shake of the head.

'I dare say,' said Walter, 'they have some reason in what they say.'

'Some, but not the best. They have the kind of reason that lies on the surface – in so much as to have a thing of your own is better than hiring it from another. But in that way Peter Thomson, honest man, would have been doomed without remedy before your time, Lord Erradeen. He has been getting into troubled waters for some years: he would have had to sell the farm and begone if it had been his: but with a good landlord like what I live in hopes to see – a good man in trouble would be helped over the dangerous moment. He would be backed up when he was feeble. Perhaps it was just at all times an ideal: but that was what the old relationship might be.'

'And the ideal is always problematical,' said Walter. He was carrying on the same controversy still, taking the other side. 'Most men I think would prefer to deal with their own even if it meant selling and losing, than to be subject to another man's will – as it appears Thomson has been to mine. That seems ridiculous indeed,' he cried, with a sudden outburst of feeling, 'that a good man, as you say, should depend on the fantastic will of – such a fool as I have been.'

'My Lord Erradeen!' cried the minister in consternation. He thought the young man was going out of his wits, and began to be nervous. There was something, now he looked at him, wild in his air. 'I have no doubt,' he said soothingly, 'that your decision – must have seemed very reasonable. I would not, though my feelings are enlisted and though I regret, go so far as to blame it myself.'

'Why?' said Walter, turning upon him. 'Because? – surely every man ought to have the courage of his opinions.'

'Not for that reason,' said the old minister, with a slight flush. 'I have never been one,' he went on with a smile, 'that have been much moved by the fear of man. No. It is because now they have been forced to make the move it may be better for themselves; they would have struggled on, and perhaps at the end got through, but in Canada they will soon flourish[162] and do well.'

'Not without a struggle there either, I suppose,' said Walter, with a fanciful disposition to resent the idea that Canada was an infallible cure.

'Not without a struggle – there you are right, my lord. There was first the sore, sore tug to pull up the roots of life that were so deeply implanted here; and the long voyage, which was terrible to the father and mother. It is very likely,' he added, 'that the old folk will never get over it. Transplanting does not do at their age. But then the young ones, they are sure to thrive: and the old will die all the sooner, which perhaps is not to be regretted when we get to the evening of life.'

'That is surely an inhuman doctrine,' Walter cried.

'Do ye think so, my young lord? Well! It becomes the young to think so; but for myself I have always seen a foundation of reason in the savage way of making an end of the old and helpless. It is better, far better for the survivors that they should have a horror of it, but for the aged themselves it is not so clear to me. They would be better away. An old man that has outlived all natural love and succour, and that just lives on against his will because he cannot help it, that is a sad sight.'[163]

'But not revolting, as it is to think of the other.'

'The other does not revolt me. If my heritors, yourself the first, were to look in some fine day and bid me out to the banks of the loch and give me a heave into it – in deep clear water mind, none of your muddy, weedy bits – I stipulate for clean water,' the old minister said with a laugh at his own joke.

'If that is all that is to happen to your emigrants,' said Walter, 'they surely would have been as well here.'

'If that had been possible; but you see, Lord Erradeen, though there are few things that ye cannot manage to get your way in, on your level of life, on the lower level when we cannot get what we want, we have to put up with what we can get.'

'Why should you think I can get my way? I have to put up with what I can get, as you say, like everybody else.'

'Well, yes,' said the minister, 'it is a kind of universal rule; and it is just a sign of the disposition that conquers the world, that it will accept what it can get without making a moaning and a fretting over it.'

'The second best,' said Walter with a half-smile[a] of irony: it was strange to come from a teacher so dissimilar to this experienced old man and hear the same doctrine once more repeated. Mr. Cameron nodded his head several times in sign of assent.

'What seems to our blindness often the second best; though you may be sure it is the best for us, and chosen for us by a better judge than we are. This is my way, to the right, up Glen-Dochart, and yonder is Shaw's house, the white one among the trees. I am extremely glad to have had this conversation with you, my lord. And if I can be of use to you at any time in any question that may puzzle ye – oh, I do not stand upon my superior enlightenment, or even on my office, with the like of you that probably belong to another Church;[164b] but I am an old man and have some experience. Good day to you, Lord Erradeen.' The old minister looked back after he had left him, and waved his hand with a benevolent smile.

Lord Erradeen walked on. He waved back a kindly salutation; the meeting, the talk with a man who was his equal, his superior, his inferior, all in one, in wholesome human inconsistency, was a kind of event for him, separating him by a distinct interval, from the agitation of the night and morning, the terrible mental struggle, the philosophy that had fallen on his despair, not as healing dew, but like a baptism of fire, scorching his heart. Strange that the same reasoning should have come before him in this strange way, so accidental and without premeditation! Mr. Cameron took everything from a different point of view. The second best to him meant manly resignation, devout religious faith. To accept it 'because it was chosen for us by a better guide than we,' that was a difference almost incalculable. According to the minister's belief, 'what we wanted' was a thing to be given up nobly when it was proved to be God's will so. But this point of view was so unlike the other that it brought a smile to Walter's lips as he went on. God's will, what had that to do with petty schemes to enrich a family? If it should so happen that he, driven by persecution, by temptations too strong to be resisted, by the feebleness of a spirit not capable of contending with fate, yielded once more to this influence which had operated so strangely upon his race, would that be God's will? – would it be ever possible to look upon it as 'chosen by a better judge'? Walter was not used to the discussion of such problems; and he was weak with mental struggles and want of rest. He lingered for a moment before Shaw's house as he passed it, then rejected, with the sudden capricious impatience of his nature, the intention, only half formed, of seeing Shaw, and walked on with a fantastic sense of relief in having got rid of this disagreeable duty. 'Another time will do just as well,' he said to himself, and hurried on as if his walk had now a more definite, as well as a more agreeable, aim. But, as a matter of fact, he had no aim at all, and did not know where he was going or what he intended. Indeed he intended nothing. Perhaps he would have said 'to think,' had he been closely questioned; but it was a stretch of meaning to apply the term to that confusion of his thoughts in which everything seemed to be turning round and round. It was not like the sharp and keen dialogue of last night, in which, though all went on within his own spirit, there were two minds engaged himself and another. Now he was left to himself; no one contending with him—no one helping, even by contention, to keep him to an actual point, and give energy and definiteness to the mental process going on within him. That process was still going on; but it was as if the wheels of a complicated and delicate machine had lost their guiding principle, and were all circling and whirring in space without an object, with the same show of motion as when fully employed, the same creak, and jar, and grind. Now and then there would come uppermost a phrase made clear out of the confusion – 'the second best': – 'something very good in its way; with which the majority of mankind is quite content and may be very happy;' 'what we call in our blindness the second best': as his two oracles had said to him. Whether it was the practical level which every man

*The Wizard's Son, Volume II*     273

must content himself with after the failure of the ideal, or whether it was the real best, chosen for us by 'a better judge,' this was what both had put before him. The two descriptions, so different, yet both perhaps true, came up before him at intervals with something of strange regularity, as if the words had been printed upon the constantly turning wheels. He walked very quickly along the moorland road, not caring where he went, nor seeing what was round him. The fresh air blew in his face, with the force and keenness which an autumn wind has in a deeply-scooped and somewhat narrow glen among the hills, but seemed only to quicken the pace of the turning wheels, and all that machinery circling giddily, grinding out nothing, making his very soul sick and dizzy as it went on and on.

Suddenly the whirr and movement in his head calmed and stopped. A homely figure, in colour and aspect like an embodiment of those wild, sheep-feeding, rugged, but not majestic slopes that hemmed in the valley on either side, became visible coming down a path that led to the main road on which Walter was. It was that of a man, tall and largely developed, but without any superfluous bulk, roughly clad, roughly shod, lifting his feet high, like one accustomed to bog and heather, with the meditative slow pace of a rustic whose work demanded no hurry, and who had time for thought in all he did. Walter, with the quick senses of his youth, quickened still more by the excitement of the circumstances amid which, once and only once, he had seen Duncan Fraser, recognised him at once, and something like the liveliness of a new impulse moved him. Who could tell but that this man of the hills might be an oracle too, and out of the silence of his lowly life might have brought something to help a soul in peril? Walter waited till the cotter came up to him, who was not on his part so quick to recognise his landlord, of whom he had seen so little, and thought it might be some 'tourist,' or some other Southland person, ignorant of these parts, and wanting information about the way, which was not inducement enough to make Duncan quicken his steps. When they met, he perceived that he had 'seen the face before,' but went no further, and awaited with a certain air of stolid gravity what the stranger might have to say.

'You are – Fraser – of that glen up there? I almost forget how you call it – Truach-Glas.'

'Ay, I am just sae; Duncan Fraser, at your service,' replied the man, not without the slight hauteur of a Highlander interrogated imperatively by a personage in whom he acknowledges no right to do so.

'You don't remember me, apparently,' Walter said.

'No, I cannot just say that I do; and yet I've seen your face before,' said Duncan, with a curious look.

'Never mind that. I want you to tell me if you are contented now, and happy in your glen – now that you are free of all your trouble about rent?'[a]

Duncan's first impulse was to say, What is that to you, I would like to ken? But the words had already set the slower mechanism of his brain to work; and,

274     *The Selected Works of Margaret Oliphant, Volume 21*

after a moment, he took his blue bonnet from his head, and with a bow in which there was a certain rustic dignity, said –

'You'll be the laird, my Lord Erradeen? I have good cause to ken your face that was once to us all just like the face of an angel out o' heaven.'

'You make too much of it,' said Walter, with a smile; for the expression pleased him in spite of himself. 'No one could have done otherwise in my place.'

'The auld wives,' said Duncan, with a little huskiness in his throat, 'do not think sae, sir. They mind you at their Books,[165] morning and night.'

Walter did not know very well what 'minding him at the Books' meant; but he guessed that somehow or other it must refer to prayers; and he said somewhat lightly –

'Do you think that will do me much good?'

Duncan's honest face turned upon him a look of displeasure. The hill-side patriarch put on his bonnet gravely.

'It should, if there's truth in Scripture,' he said, somewhat sternly; 'but nae doubt it is just one of the most awfu' mysteries how a wilful soul will baffle baith God's goodwill and gude folk's prayers.'

This was so curiously unlike anything he had expected, that Lord Erradeen gave his humble monitor one startled glance, and for the moment was silenced. He resumed, however, a minute after, feeling a certain invigoration come to him from his contact with simple nature.

'I acknowledge,' he said, 'though you are a little hard upon me, Fraser, that I have brought this on myself. But I want to know about you, how things are going. Are you satisfied with your position now? And is everything made smooth for you by the remittal of the rent?'

At this Duncan became in his turn confused.

'Nae doubt,' he said, 'it has been a great help, sir – my lord. Ye'll excuse me, but I'm little used to lordships, and I canna get my mouth about it.'

'Never mind my lordship. I want to know the real truth. Your minister has been talking to me about Thomson – the man at the farm.' Walter pointed vaguely to the hill-side, having no idea where Peter Thomson's farm was, about which so much had been said. 'He has been sent away while you have stayed. Let me know which has been the best.'

Duncan looked more embarrassed than ever, and shuffled from one foot to the other, looking down upon the wet and brilliant green of the grass on which he stood.

'We were all muckle obliged to you, my lord; and no one of us has grudged to say sae,' he said.

'But that is not the question,' Walter cried, with a little impatience.

'To flit the old folk would have been impossible,' said Duncan, as if speaking to himself. 'It was just a deliverance, and the Lord's doing, and wonderful in our eyes.[166] But, sir, there is nothing in this world that is pure good. The soil is cauld: there is little will come out of it: and though we're far out o' the way o' the world in our bit glen, I reckon that what ye ca' progress and a' that, has an effeck whether or no. We want mair than our forbears wanted. No, no just education and advancement: my uncle Willie was brought up a minister, and got a' the education my Robbie is ettling at,[167] though my grandfather had, may-be, less to spare than me. But just there is a difference in the ways o't. And maybe if it had come to the worse, and ye had driven us out, instead of being sae generous –'

'It would have been better for you,' said Walter, as his companion paused.

'I'm not saying that. It was just deliverance. I will tell ye mair, my lord. If I had been driven out, me and my auld mother, and my little bairns, I could have found it in my heart to curse ye, sae young, sae rich, sae well off, and sae inhuman. And the auld wife's death would have lain at your door, and the bairns would never have forgotten it, however well they had prospered, no even when they came to be reasonable men, and could see baith sides of the question like me; they would have carried it with them to yon New World, as they call it; it would have grown to be a tradition and a meesery for ever. Now,' said Duncan, with a hoarse half-laugh of emotion, 'the sting is out of it whatever happens.'

'I am glad of that, anyhow,' said Walter.

'And so am I – and so am I! When ye have a sense of being wranged in your heart, it's like a burnin' wound, like thae puir Irish, the Lord help them! And what was our pickle siller[168] to the like of you? But –' Duncan said, and paused, not knowing how to proceed with due respect and gratitude for what his landlord had done.

'But – what you expected has not been realised? the rent, after all, made but a small difference–the relief was not what you hoped?'

'I am just incapable, sir, of making ye a right answer,' said Duncan, with vehemence. 'It's just the effeck of the times, and nae fault o' yours or ours – at least that is all I can make of it. We want mair than our forbears wanted. We are no so easy content. The lads at the college canna live as simple as they once lived. That makes it harder for everybody. The callants![169] I would not bind them to a life like mine; they would have done better for themselves, though it would have killed granny, and been a sore burden upon Jeannie and me.'

'The fact is, Duncan, that to have your own way is not much better than to have some one else's way, and that there is nothing worth making a fight about,' Walter said, with a bitterness which his humble companion did not understand, and still less approved.

'No that, my lord,' said Duncan, 'but just that nothing that is mortal is perfect blessedness, except what is said in the psalm, 'that man – that walketh not astray.'[170] Life is a struggle for the like of us, and maybe for most other folk. We have just to put the evil and the good against one another, and rejoice when the good is a wee predominant over the evil.'

He used longer words perhaps than an Englishman of his rank would have used; and there was a something of Celtic fine manners and natural dignity about him which gave importance to his speech.

'That means – a compromise: no ideal in this world, no absolute good, but only a practicable something that we can get along with.'

Walter said this with a scorn of it, yet growing belief in it, which gave strange vehemence to his tone. He did not expect his rustic companion to understand him, nor did he think of any response.

'It is just this, sir,' said Duncan, 'that here we have nae continuing ceety, but look for one to come.'[171]

END OF VOL. II.

# THE WIZARD'S SON, VOLUME III

## CHAPTER I.[a]

WAS this then the conclusion of all things – that there was nothing so perfect that it was worth a man's while to struggle for it; that any officious interference with the recognised and existing was a mistake; that nothing was either the best or the worst, but all things mere degrees in a round of the comparative, in which a little more or a little less was of no importance, and the most strenuous efforts tended to failure as much as indifference? Walter, returning to the old house which was his field of battle, questioned himself thus, with a sense of despair not lessened by the deeper self-ridicule within him, which asked, was he then so anxious for the best, so ready to sacrifice his comfort for an ideal excellence? That he, of all men, should have this to do, and yet that, being done, it should be altogether ineffectual, was a sort of climax of clumsy mortal failure and hopelessness. The only good thing he had done was the restoration of those half-evicted cotters, and that was but a mingled and uncertain good, it appeared. What was the use of any struggle? If it was his own personal freedom alone that he really wanted, why here it was within his power to purchase it[b] – or at least a moderate amount of it – a comparative freedom, as everything was comparative. His mind by this time had ceased to be able to think, or even to perceive with any distinctness the phrase or *motif* inscribed upon one of those confused and idly-turning wheels of mental machinery which had stood in the place of thought to him. It was the afternoon when he got back, and everything within him had fallen into an afternoon dreariness. He lingered when he landed on the waste bit of grass that lay between the little landing-place and the door of the old castle. He had no heart to go in and sit down unoccupied in that room which had witnessed so many strange meetings. He was no longer indeed afraid of his visitor there, but rather looked forward with a kind of relief to the tangible presence which delivered him from meetings of the mind more subtle and painful. But he had no expectation of any visitor; nor was there anything for him to do except to sit down and perhaps attempt to read, which meant solely a delivering over of himself to his spiritual antagonists – for how was it possible to give his mind to any fable of literature in the midst of a parable so urgent and all-occupying, of his own?

He stood therefore idly upon the neglected turf, watching the ripple of the water as it lapped against the rough stones on the edge. The breadth of the loch was entirely hidden from him by the projection of the old tower, which descended into the water at the right, and almost shut off this highest corner of Loch Houran into a little lakelet of its own. Walter heard the sound of oars and voices from the loch without seeing any one: but that was usual enough, and few people invaded his privacy: so that he was taken by surprise when, suddenly raising his eyes, he was aware of the polished and gilded galley from Birkenbraes, in which already Mr. Williamson, seated in the stern, had perceived and was hailing him. 'Hallo, my Lord Erradeen! Here we've all come to see ye this fine afternoon. I told them we should find ye under your own vine and your own fig-tree.'[1] This speech was accompanied by a general laugh. The arrival of such a party, heralded by such laughter in a desolate house, with few servants and no readiness for any such emergency, to a young man in Walter's confused and distracted condition would not, it may be supposed, have been very welcome in any case, and at present in his exhaustion and dismay he stood and gazed at them with a sort of horror. There was not even a ready servitor like Hamish to assist in the disembarkation. Duncan had rowed cheerfully off upon some other errand after landing his master, and old Symington and old Macalister were singularly ill-adapted for the service. Lord Erradeen did his best, with a somewhat bad grace, to receive the boat at the landing-place. The gravity of his countenance was a little chill upon the merry party, but the Williamsons were not of a kind that is easily discouraged.

'Oh, yes, here we all are,' said the millionnaire. 'I would not let our English visitor, Mr. Braithwaite here, leave without showing him the finest thing on the Loch. So I just told him I knew I might take the liberty. Hoot! we know ye have not your household here, and that it is just an old family ruin, and not bound to produce tea and scones like the Forresters' isle. Bless me! I hope we have a soul above tea and scones,' Mr. Williamson cried with his hearty laugh.

By this time the young, hardy, half-clad rowers had scrambled out, and grouped themselves in various attitudes, such as would suit a new and light-hearted Michael Angelo[2] – one kneeling on the stones holding the bow of the boat, another with one foot on sea and one on shore helping the ladies out. Walter in his dark dress, and still darker preoccupied countenance, among all those bronzed and cheerful youths looked like a being from another sphere: but the contrast was not much to his advantage either in bodily or mental atmosphere. He looked so grave and so unlike the joyous hospitality of a young housekeeper surprised by a sudden arrival, that Katie, always more on her guard than her father, looked at him with a countenance as grave as his own.

'I am not the leader of this expedition, Lord Erradeen,' she said; 'you must not blame me for the invasion. My father took it into his head, and when that happens there is nothing to be done. I don't mean I was not glad to be brought here against my will,' she added, as his face, by a strain of politeness which was far from easy to him, began to brighten a little. Katie was not apt to follow the leading of another face and adopt the woman's *rôle* of submission, but she felt herself so completely in the wrong, an intruder where she was very sure she and her party, exuberant in spirits and gaiety, were not wanted, that she was compelled to watch his expression and make her apologies with a deference quite unusual to her. 'I hope it will not be a very great – interruption to you,' she said after a momentary pause.

'That could never matter,' Walter said, with some stateliness.[a] 'I could have wished to have notice and to have received my friends at Auchnasheen rather than here. But being here – you must excuse the primitive conditions of the place.'

'Hoot! there is nothing to excuse – a fine old castle, older than the flood – just the very thing that is wanted for the picturesque, ye see, Braithwaite; for as ye were remarking, we are in general too modern for a Highland loch. But you'll not call this modern,' said Mr. Williamson. 'Will that old body not open the door to ye when he sees ye have friends? Lord! that just beats all! That is a step beyond Caleb Balderston.'[3]

'Papa!' cried Katie in keen reproof, 'we have been quite importunate enough already. I vote we all go over to Auchnasheen – the view there is much finer, and we could send over for Oona –'

'Is it common in this country,' said the member of Parliament, 'to have two residences so very near? It must be like going next door for change of air when you leave one for the other, Lord Erradeen.'

At this there was that slight stir among the party which takes place when an awkward suggestion is made; the young men and the girls began to talk hurriedly, raising up a sort of atmosphere of voices around the central group. This however was curiously and suddenly penetrated by the reply which – who? – was it Walter? made, almost as it seemed without a pause.

'Not common – but yet not unknown in a country which has known a great deal of fighting in its day. The old castle is our family resource in danger. We do our family business here, our quarrels: and afterwards retire to Auchnasheen, the house of peace (perhaps you don't know that names have meanings hereabouts?)[b] to rest.'

There was a pause as slight, as imperceptible to the ignorant, as evident to the instructed as had been the stir at the first sound of those clear tones. Walter himself to more than one observer had seemed as much startled as any of them. He turned quickly round towards the speaker with a sudden blanching of his face which had been pale enough before; but this was only momentary; afterwards all that was remarkable in him was a strange look of resolution and determined self-control. Perhaps the only one completely unmoved was the Englishman, who at once accepted the challenge, and stepped forward to the individual who it was evident to him was the only duly qualified cicerone[4] in the party, with eager satisfaction.

'That is highly interesting. Of course the place must be full of traditions,' he said.

'With your permission, Walter, I will take the part of cicerone,' said the new voice. To some of the party it seemed only a voice. The ladies and the young men stumbled against each other in their eager curiosity about the stranger. 'I will swear there was nobody near Erradeen when we landed,' said young Tom Campbell in the nearest ear that presented itself; but of course it was the number of people about which caused this, and it could be no shadow with whom the M.P. went forth delighted, asking a hundred questions. 'You are a member of the family?' Mr. Braithwaite said. He was not tall, and his companion was of a splendid presence. The Englishman had to look up as he spoke and to quicken his somewhat short steps as he walked to keep up with the other's large and dignified pace. Katie followed with Walter. There was a look of agitation and alarm in her face; her heart beat she could not tell why. She was breathless as if she had been running a race. She looked up into Lord Erradeen's face tremulously, not like herself. 'Is this gentleman – staying with you?' she said in a scarcely audible voice.

Walter was not agitated for his part, but he had little inclination to speak. He said 'Yes' and no more.

'And we have been – sorry for you because you were alone? Is it a – relation? is it –? You have never,' said Katie, forcing the words out with a difficulty which astonished her, and for which she could not account, 'brought him to Birkenbraes.'

Walter could not but smile. A sort of feeble amusement flew over his mind touching the surface into a kind of ripple. 'Shall I ask him to come?' he said.

Katie was following in the very footsteps of this altogether new and unexpected figure. There was nothing like him, it seemed to her, in all the country-side.[a] His voice dominated every other sound, not loud, but clear. It subdued her little being altogether. She would not lose a word, yet her breath was taken away by an inexplicable terror.

'He is – like somebody,' she said, panting, 'out of a book,' and could say no more.

Old Macalister came towards them from the now open door, at which stood Symington in attendance. The servants had been disturbed by the unusual sounds of the arrival. Malcalister's old face was drawn and haggard.

'Where will ye be taking all thae folk?' he said, no doubt forgetting his manners in his bewilderment. 'Come back, ye'll get into mischief that road,'[b] he cried, putting out his hand to catch the arm of Braithwaite, who, guided by the stranger, was passing the ordinary entrance. He became quite nervous and angry when no heed was paid to him. 'My lord, you're no so well acquaint yourself. Will you let that lad just wander and break his neck?' he cried, with a kind of passion.

'Never mind,' said Walter, with a strange calm which was as unaccountable as all the rest. 'Will you tell your wife to prepare for these ladies – when we come back.'

Here Symington too came forth to explain somewhat loudly, addressing his master and Braithwaite alternately, that the roads were not safe about the old castle, that the walls were crumbling, that a person not acquaint might get a deadly fall, with unspeakable anxiety in his eyes. The party all followed, notwithstanding, led by the stranger, whom even the least of them now thought she could distinguish over Katie's head, but of whom the servants took no notice, addressing the others in front as if he had not been there.

'My lord, ye'll repent if ye'll no listen to us,' Symington said, laying his hand in sudden desperation on Walter's arm.

'You fool!' cried the young man, 'can't you see we have got a safe guide?'

Symington gave a look round him wildly of the utmost terror. His scared eyes seemed to retreat into deep caverns of anguish and fear. He stood back out of the way of the somewhat excited party, who laughed, and yet scarcely could laugh with comfort, at him. The youngsters had begun to chatter: they were not afraid of anything – Still –: though it was certainly amusing to see that old man's face.

Turning round to exchange a look with Macalister, Symington came in contact with Mr. Williamson's solid and cheerful bulk, who brought up the rear. 'I'm saying,' said the millionnaire confidentially, 'who's this fine fellow your master's got with him? A grand figure of a man! It's not often you see it, but I always admire it. A relation, too; what relation? I would say it must be on the mother's side, for I've never seen or heard tell of him. Eh? who's staying with your master, I'm asking ye? Are ye deaf or doited that ye cannot answer a simple question?'

'Na, there is nothing the matter with me; but I think the rest of the world has just taken leave of their senses,' Symington said.

***

# CHAPTER II.ᵃ

JULIA HERBERT had failed altogether in her object during that end of the season which her relations had afforded her. Walter had not even come to call. He had sent a hurried note excusing himself, and explaining that he was 'obliged to leave town,' an excuse by which nobody was deceived. It is not by any easy process that a girl, who begins with all a girl's natural pride and pretensions, is brought down to recognise the fact that a man is avoiding and fleeing from her, and yet to follow and seek him. Hard poverty, and the memories of a life spent in the tiny cottage with her mother, without any enlargement or wider atmosphere, and with but one way of escape in which there was hope or even possibility, had brought Julia to this pass. She had nothing in her life that was worth doing except to scheme how she could dress and present the best appearance, and how she could get hold of and secure that only stepping-stoneᵇ by which she could mount out of it – a man who would marry her and open to her the doors of something better. In every other way it is worth the best exertions of either man or woman to get these doors opened, and to come to the possibility of better things; and a poor girl who has been trained to nothing more exalted, who sees no other way, not-withstandingᶜ that this poor way of hers revolts every finer spirit, is there not something pitiful and tragic in her struggles, her sad and degrading attempt after a new beginning? How much human force is wasted upon it, what heart-sickness, what self-contempt is under-gone,ᵈ what a debasement of all that is best and finest in her?ᵉ She has no pity, no sympathy in her pursuit, but ridicule, contempt, the derision of one half of humanity, the indignation of the other. And yet her object after all may not be entirely despicable. She may feel with despair that there is no other way. She may intend to be all that is good and noble were but this one step made, this barrier crossed, the means of a larger life attained. It would be better for her no doubt to be a governess, or even a seamstress, or to put up with the chill meannesses of a poverty-stricken existence, and starve, modestly keeping up appearances with her last breath.

But all women are not born self-denying. When they are young, the blood runs as warmly in their veins as in that of men; they too want life, movement, sunshine and happiness. The mere daylight, the air, a new frock, however hardly obtained, a dance, a little admiration, suffice for them when they are very young; but when the next chapter comes, and the girl learns to calculate that, saving some great matrimonial chance, there is no prospect for her but the narrowest and most meagre and monotonous existence under heaven, the life of a poor, very poor single woman who cannot dig and to beg is ashamed – is it to be wondered at if she makes a desperate struggle anyhow (and alas! there is but one *how*) to escape. Perhaps she likes too, poor creature, the little excitement of flirtation, the only thing which replaces to her the manifold excitement which men of her kind indulge in – the tumultuous joys of the turf, the charms of play, the delights of the club, the moors, and sport in general, not to speak of all those developments of pleasure,[a] so-called, which are impossible to a woman. She cannot dabble a little in vice as a man can do,[5] and yet return again, and be no worse thought of than before. Both for amusement and profit she has this one way, which, to be sure, answers the purpose of all the others in being destructive of the best part in her, spoiling her character, and injuring her reputation – but for how much less a cause, and with how little recompense in the way of enjoyment! The husband-hunting girl is fair game to whosoever has a stone to throw, and very few are so charitable as to say, Poor soul! Julia Herbert had been as bright a creature at eighteen as one could wish to see. At twenty-four she was bright still, full of animation, full of good humour, clever in her way, very pretty, high-spirited, amusing – and still so young! But how profoundly had it been impressed upon her that she must not lose her time! and how well she knew all the opprobrious epithets that are directed against a young woman as she draws towards thirty – the very flower and prime of her life. Was she to blame if she was influenced by all that was said to this effect, and determined to fight with a sort of mad persistence, for the hope which seemed so well within her reach? Were she but once established as Lady Erradeen, there was not one of her youthful sins that would be remembered against her. A veil of light would fall over her and all her peccadilloes as soon as she had put on her bridal veil. Her friends, instead of feeling her a burden and perplexity, would be proud of Julia; they would put forth their cousinhood eagerly, and claim her – even those who were most anxious now to demonstrate the extreme distance of the connection – as near and dear. And she liked Walter, and thought she would have no difficulty in loving him, had she ever a right to do so. He was not too good for her; she would have something to forgive in him, if he too in her might have something to forgive. She would make him a good wife, a wife of whom he should have no occasion to be ashamed. All these considerations made it excusable – more than excusable, almost laudable – to strain a point for so great an end.

And in her cousin's wife she had, so far as this went, a real friend. Lady Herbert not only felt that to get Julia settled was most desirable, and that, as Lady Erradeen, she would become a most creditable cousin, and one who might return the favours showed to her, but also, which is less general, felt within herself a strong inclination to help and further Julia's object. She thought favourably of Lord Erradeen. She thought he would not be difficult to manage (which was a mistake as the reader knows). She thought he was not so strong as Julia, but once fully within the power of her fascinations, would fall an easy prey. She did not think less of him for running away. It was a sign of weakness, if also of wisdom; and if he could be met in a place from which he could not run away, it seemed to her that the victory would be easy. And Sir Thomas must have a moor somewhere to refresh him after the vast labours of a session in which he had recorded so many silent votes.[6] By dint of having followed him to many a moor, Lady Herbert had a tolerable geographical knowledge of the Highlands, and it was not very difficult for her to find out that Mr. Campbell of Ellermore, with his large family, would be obliged this year to let his shootings. Everything was settled and prepared accordingly to further Julia's views, without any warning on the point having reached Walter. She had arrived indeed at the Lodge, which was some miles down the loch, beyond Birkenbraes, a few days after Walter's arrival, and thus once more, though he was so far from thinking of it, his old sins, or rather his old follies, were about to find him out.

Lady Herbert had already become known to various people on the loch-side.[a] She had been at the Lodge since early in September, and had been called upon by friendly folk on all sides. There had been a thousand chances that Walter might have found her at luncheon with all the others on his first appearance at Birkenbraes, and Julia had already been introduced to that hospitable house. Katie did not recognise Lady Herbert either by name or countenance. But she recognised Julia as soon as she saw her.

'I think you know Lord Erradeen?' was almost her first greeting, for Katie was a young person of very straight-forward methods.

'Oh yes,' Julia had answered with animation, 'I have known him all my life.'

'I suppose you know that he lives here?'

Upon this Julia turned to her chaperon, her relation in whose hands all these external questions were.

'Did you know, dear Lady Herbert, that Lord Erradeen lived here?'

'Oh yes, he has a place close by. Didn't I tell you? A pretty house, with that old castle near it, which I pointed out to you on the lock,'[a] Lady Herbert said.

'How small the world is!' cried Julia; 'wherever you go you are always knocking up against somebody. Fancy Walter Methven living here!'

Katie was not taken in by this little play. She was not even irritated as she had been at Burlington House. If it might so happen that some youthful bond existed between Lord Erradeen and this girl, Katie was not the woman to use any unfair means against it.

'You will be sure to meet him,' she said calmly. 'We hope he is not going to shut himself up as he did last year.'

'Oh tell me!' Julia cried, with overflowing interest, 'is there not some wonderful ghost story? something about his house being haunted; and he has to go and present himself and have an interview with the ghost? Captain Underwood, I remember, told us –'

'Did you know Captain Underwood?' said Katie, in that tone which says so much.

And then she turned to her other guests: for naturally the house was full of people, and as was habitual in Birkenbraes a large party from outside had come to lunch. The Williamsons were discussed with much freedom among the visitors from the Lodge when they went away. Sir Thomas declared that the old man was a monstrous fine old fellow, and his claret worth coming from Devonshire to drink.

'No expense spared in that establishment,' he cried; 'and there's a little girl, I should say, that would be worth a young fellow's while.'

He despised Julia to the bottom of his heart, but he thought of his young friends on the other side without any such elevated sentiment, and decided it might not be a bad thing to have Algy Newton down, to whom it was indispensable that he should marry money. Sir Thomas, however, had not the energy to carry his intention out.

Next day it so happened that Lady Herbert had to return the visit of Mrs. Forrester, who – though she always explained her regret at not being able to entertain her friends – was punctilious in making the proper calls. The English ladies were 'charmed' with the isle. They said there had never been anything so original, so delightful, so unconventional; ignoring altogether, with a politeness which Mrs. Forrester thought was 'pretty,' any idea that necessity might be the motive of the mother and daughter in settling there.

'I am sure it is very kind of you to say so; but it is not just a matter of choice, you know. It is just an old house that came to me from the Macnabs – my mother's side. And it proved very convenient when all the boys were away and nothing left but Oona and me. Women want but little in comparison with gentlemen; and though it is a little out of the way and inconvenient in the winter season, it is wonderful how few days there are that we can't get out. I am very well content

*The Wizard's Son, Volume III* 285

with the Walk when there is a glint of sunshine; but Oona, she just never minds the weather. Oh, you will not be going just yet! Tell Mysie, Oona, to bring ben[7] the tea. If it is a little early what matter? It always helps to keep you warm on the loch, and my old cook is rather noted for her scones. She just begins as soon as she hears there's a boat, and she will be much disappointed if ye don't taste them. Our friends are all very kind; we have somebody or other every day.'

'It is you who are kind, I think,' Lady Herbert said.

'No, no; two ladies – it is nothing we have it in our power to do: but a cup of tea, it is just a charity to accept it; and as you go down to your boat I will let you see the view.'

Julia, for her part, felt, or professed, a great interest in the girl living the life of a recluse on this little island.

'It must be delightful,' she said with enthusiasm; 'but don't you sometimes feel a little dull? It is the sweetest place I ever saw. But shouldn't you like to walk on to the land without always requiring a boat?'

'I don't think I have considered the subject,' Oona said; 'it is our home, and we do not think whether or not we should like it to be different.'

'Oh what a delightful state of mind! I don't think I could be so contented anywhere – so happy in myself. I think,' said Julia with an ingratiating look, 'that you must be very happy in yourself.'

Oona laughed. 'As much and as little as other people,' she said.

'Oh not as little! I should picture to myself a hundred things I wanted as soon as I found myself shut up here. I should want to be in town. I should want to go shopping. I should wish for – everything I had not got. Don't you immediately think of dozens of things you want as soon as you know you can't get them? But you are so good?'

'If that is being good! No, I think I rather refrain from wishing for what I should like when I see I am not likely to get it.'

'I call that goodness itself – but perhaps it is Scotch. I have the greatest respect for the Scotch,' said Julia. 'They are so sensible.' Then she laughed, as at some private joke of her own, and said under her breath, 'Not all, however,' and looked towards Kinloch Houran.

They were seated on the bench, upon the little platform, at the top of the ascent which looked down upon the castle. The sound of Mrs. Forrester's voice was quite audible behind in the house, pouring forth a gentle stream. The sun was setting in a sky full of gorgeous purple and golden clouds; the keen air of the hills blowing about them. But Julia was warmly dressed, and only shivered a little out of a sense of what was becoming: and Oona was wrapped in the famous fur cloak.

'It is so strange to come upon a place one has heard so much of,' Julia resumed. 'No doubt you know Lord Erradeen?'

The name startled Oona in spite of herself. She was not prepared for any allusion to him. She coloured involuntarily, and gave her companion a look of surprise.

'Do you know him?' she asked.

'Oh, so well! I have known him almost all my life. People said indeed –' said Julia, breaking off suddenly with a laugh. 'But that was nonsense. You know how people talk. Oh, yes, we have been like brother and sister – or if not quite that – at least –. Oh yes, I know Walter, and his mother, and everything about him. He has been a little strange since he came here; though indeed I have no reason to say so, for he is always very nice to me. When he came home last year I saw a great deal of him; but I don't think he was very communicative about – what do you call it? – Kinloch –'

'He was not here long,' Oona said.

'No? He did not give himself time to find out how many nice people there are. He did not seem very happy about it when he came back. You see all his habits were formed – it was something so new for him. And though the people are extremely nice, and so hospitable and kind, they were different – from those he had been used to.'

Oona smiled a little. She did not see her new acquaintance from the best side, and there came into her mind a slightly bitter and astonished reflection that Walter, perhaps, preferred people like *this* to other – people. It was an altogether incoherent thought.

'Does he know that you are here?' she said.

'Oh, I don't think he does – but he will soon find me out,' said Julia, with an answering smile. 'He always tells me everything. We are such old friends, and perhaps something – more. To be sure that is not a thing to talk of; but there is something in your face which is so sweet, which invites confidence. With a little encouragement I believe I should tell you everything I ever did.'

She leant over Oona as if she would have kissed her: but compliments so broad and easy disconcerted the Highland girl. She withdrew a little from this close contact.

'The wind is getting cold,' she said. 'Perhaps we ought to go in. My mother always blames me for keeping strangers, who are not used to it, in this chilly air.'

'Ah, you do not encourage me,' Julia said. And then after a pause added, with the look of one preoccupied by her subject – 'Is he there now?'

'I think Lord Erradeen is still at Kinloch Houran, if that is what you mean. That is another house of his among the trees.'

'How curious! two houses so close together. If you see him,' said Julia, rising to join her cousin who had come out to the door of the cottage with Mrs. Forrester, 'if you see him, don't, please don't, tell him you have met me. I prefer that he should find it out. He is quite sure, oh, sooner than I want him, to find me out.'

And then the ladies were attended to the boat in the usual hospitable way.

'You will get back before it is dark,' said Mrs. Forrester. 'I am always glad of that, for the wind is cold from the hills, especially to strangers that are not used to our

Highland climate. I take your visit very kind, Lady Herbert. In these days I can do so little for my friends: unless Sir Thomas would take his lunch with me some day – and that is no compliment to a gentleman that is out on the hills all his time – I have just no opportunity of showing attention. But if you are going further north, my son, the present Mr. Forrester of Eaglescairn, would be delighted to be of any service. He knows how little his mother can do for her friends, perched up here in the middle of the water and without a gentleman in the house. Hamish, have ye got the cushions in, and are ye all ready? You'll be sure to take her ladyship to where the carriage is waiting, and see that she has not a long way to walk.'

Thus talking, the kind lady saw her visitors off, and stood on the beach waving her hand to them. The fur cloak had been transferred to her shoulders. It was the one wrap in which everybody believed. Oona, who moved so much more quickly, and had no need to pause to take breath, did not now require such careful wrapping. She too stood and waved her hand as the boat turned the corner of the isle. But her farewells were not so cordial as her mother's. Julia's talk had been very strange to Oona; it filled her with a vague fear. Something very different from the sensation with which she had heard Katie's confessions on the subject of Lord Erradeen moved her now. An impression of unworthiness had stolen into her mind, she could not tell how. It was the first time she had been sensible of any thought of the kind. Walter had not been revealed to her in any of the circumstances of his past life. She had known him only during his visit at Kinloch Houran, and when he was in profound difficulty and agitation, in which her presence and succour had helped him she could not tell how, and when his appeal to her, his dependence on her, had seized hold of her mind and imagination with a force which it had taken her all this time to throw off, and which, alas! his first appearance and renewed appeal to her to stand by him had brought back again in spite of her resistance and against her will. She had been angry with herself and indignant at this involuntary subjugation – which he had not desired so far as she knew, nor she dreamt of, until she had fallen under it – and had recognised, with a sort of despair and angry sense of impotence, the renewal of the influence, which she seemed incapable of resisting.

But Julia's words roused in her a different sentiment. Julia's laugh, the light insinuations of her tone, her claim of intimacy and previous knowledge, brought a revulsion of feeling so strong and powerful that she felt for the moment as if she had been delivered from her bonds. Delivered – but not with any pleasure in being free: for the deliverance meant the lowering of the image of him in whom she had suddenly found that union of something above her with something below, which is the man's chief charm to the woman, as probably it is the woman's chief charm to the man. He had been below her, he had needed her help, she had brought to him some principle of completeness, some moral support which was indispensable, without which he could not have stood fast. But now another kind of inferiority was suggested to her, which was not that in which a visionary and absolute youthful mind could find any charm, which it was difficult even to tolerate, which was an offence to her and to the pure and overmastering sentiment which had drawn her to him. If he was so near to Miss Herbert, so entirely on her level, making her his confidant, he could be nothing to Oona. She seemed to herself to burst her bonds and stand free – but not happily. Her heart was not the lighter for it. She would have liked to escape, yet to be able to bear him the same stainless regard, the same sympathy as ever; to help him still, to honour him in his resistance to all that was evil.

All this happened on the afternoon of the day which Walter had begun with a despairing conviction that Oona's help must fail him *when she knew*. She had begun to know without any agency of his: and if it moved her so to become aware of a frivolous and foolish connection in which there was levity and vanity, and a fictitious counterfeit of higher sentiments but no harm, what would her feelings be when all the truth was unfolded to her? But neither did she know of the darker depths that lay below, nor was he aware of the revelation which had begun. Oona returned to the house with her mother's soft-voiced monologue in her ears, hearing vaguely a great many particulars of Lady Herbert's family and connections and of her being 'really an acquisition, and Sir Thomas just an honest English sort of man, and Miss Herbert very pretty, and a nice companion for you, Oona,' without reply, or with much consciousness of what it was. 'It is time you were indoors, mamma, for the wind is very cold,' she said.

'Oh yes, Oona, it is very well for you to speak about me: but you must take your own advice and come in too. For you have nothing about your shoulders, and I have got the fur cloak.'

'I am coming, mother,' Oona said, and with these words turned from the door and going to the rocky parapet that bordered the little platform, cast an indignant glance towards the ruined walls so far beneath her on the water's edge, dark and cold, out of the reach of all those autumn glories that were fading in the sky. There was no light or sign of life about Kinloch Houran. She had looked out angrily, as one defrauded of much honest feeling had, she felt, a right to do; but something softened her as she looked and gazed – the darkness of it, the pathos of the ruin, the incompleteness, and voiceless yet appealing need. Was it possible that there was no need at all or vacancy there but what Miss Herbert, with her smiles and dimples, her laughing insinuations, her claim upon him from the past, and the first preference of youth, could supply? Oona felt a great sadness take the place of her indignation as she turned away. If that was so, how poor and small it all was – how different from what she had thought!

# CHAPTER III.[a]

THIS was not the only danger that once more overshadowed the path of Lord Erradeen. Underwood had been left alone in one of those foreign centres of 'pleasure,' so called, whither he had led his so often impatient and unruly pupil. He had been left, without notice, by a sudden impulse, such as he was now sufficiently acquainted with in Walter – who had always the air of obeying angrily and against his will the temptations with which he was surrounded: a sort of moral indignation against himself and all that aided in his degradation curiously mingling with the follies and vices into which he was led. You never knew when you had him, was Captain Underwood's own description. He would dart aside at a tangent, go off at the most unlikely moment, dash down the cup when it was at the sweetest, and abandon with disgust the things that had seemed to please him most. And Underwood knew that the moment was coming when his patron and *protégé* must return home: but notwithstanding he was left, without warning, as by a sudden caprice; the young man, who scorned while he yielded to his influence, having neither respect nor regard enough for his companion to leave a word of explanation. Underwood was astonished and angry as a matter of course, but his anger soon subsided, and the sense of Lord Erradeen's importance to him was too strong to leave room for lasting resentment, or at least for anything in the shape of relinquishment. He was not at all disposed to give the young victim up. Already he had tasted many of what to him were the sweets of life by Walter's means, and there were endless capabilities in Lord Erradeen's fortune and in his unsettled mind, which made a companion like Underwood too wise ever to take offence, necessary to him – which that worthy would not let slip. After the shock of finding himself deserted, he took two or three days to consider the matter, and then he made his plan. It was bold, yet he thought not too bold. He followed in the very track of his young patron, passing through Edinburgh and reaching Auchnasheen on the same momentous day which had witnessed Julia Herbert's visit to the isle. Captain Underwood was very well known at Auchnasheen. He had filled in many ways the position of manager and steward to the last lord. He had not been loved, but yet he had not been actively disliked. If there was some surprise and a little resistance on the part of the household there was at least no open revolt. They received him coldly, and required considerable explanation of the many things which he required to be done. They were all aware, as well as he was, that Lord Erradeen was to be expected from day to day, and they had made such preparations for his arrival as suggested themselves: but these were not many, and did not at all please the zealous captain. His affairs, he felt, were at a critical point. It was very necessary that the young man should feel the pleasure of being expected, the surprise of finding everything arranged according to his tastes.

'You know very well that he will come here exhausted, that he will want to have everything comfortable,' he said to the housekeeper and the servants. 'No one would like after a fatiguing journey to come into a bare sort of a miserable place like this.'

'My lord is no so hard to please,' said the housekeeper, standing her ground. 'Last year he just took no notice. Whatever was done he was not heeding.'

'Because he was unused to everything: now it is different; and I mean to have things comfortable for him.'

'Well, captain! I am sure it's none of my wish to keep the poor young gentleman from his bits of little comforts. Ye'll have *his* authority?'

'Oh, yes, I have his authority. It will be for your advantage to mind what I tell you; even more than with the late lord. I've been abroad with him. He left me but a short time ago; I was to follow him, and look after everything.'

At this the housekeeper looked at the under-factor Mr. Shaw's subordinate, who had come to intimate to her her master's return. 'Will that be all right, Mr. Adamson?' Adamson put his shaggy head on one side like an intelligent dog and looked at the stranger. But they all knew Captain Underwood well enough, and no one was courageous enough to contradict him.

'It will, maybe, be as ye say,' said the under-factor cautiously. 'Anyway it will do us no harm to take his orders,' he added, in an undertone to the woman. 'He was always very far ben with the old lord.'

'The worse for him,' said that important functionary under her breath. But she agreed with Adamson afterwards that as long as it was my lord's comfort he was looking after and not his own, his orders should be obeyed. As with every such person, the household distrusted this confident and unpaid major domo.[8] But Underwood had not been tyrannical in his previous reign, and young Lord Erradeen during his last residence at Auchnasheen had frightened them all. He had been like a man beside himself. If the captain could manage him better, they would be grateful to the captain; and thus Underwood, though by no means confident of a good reception, had no serious hindrances to encounter. He strolled forth when he had arranged everything to 'look about him.' He saw the Birkenbraes boat pass in the evening light, returning from the castle, with a surprise which took away his breath. The boat was near enough to the shore as it passed to be recognised and its occupants; but not even Katie, whose eyesight was so keen, recognised the observer on the beach. He remarked that the party were in earnest conversation, consulting with each other over something, which seemed to secure everybody's attention, so that the ordinary quick notice of a stranger, which is common to country people, was not called forth by his own appearance. It surprised him mightily to see that such visitors had ventured to Kinloch Houran. They never would have done so in the time of the last lord. Had Walter all at once become more friendly, more open-hearted, perhaps feeling in the company of his neighbours a certain safety? Underwood was confounded by this new suggestion. It did not please him. Nothing could be worse for himself than that Lord Erradeen should find amusement in the society of the neighbourhood. There would be no more riot if this was the case, no 'pleasure,' no play; but perhaps a wife – most terrible of all anticipations. Underwood had been deeply alarmed before by Katie Williamson's ascendancy; but when Lord Erradeen returned to his own influence, he had believed that risk to be over. If, however, it recurred again, and, in this moment while undefended by his, Underwood's, protection, if the young fellow had rushed into the snare once more, the captain felt that the incident would acquire new significance.

There[a] were women whom he might have tolerated if better could not be. Julia Herbert was one whom he could perhaps – it was possible – have 'got on with,' though possibly she would have changed after her marriage; but with Katie, Underwood knew that he never would get on. If this were so he would have at once to disappear. All his hopes would be over – his prospect of gain or pleasure by means of Lord Erradeen. And he had 'put up with' so much! nobody knew how much he had put up with. He had humoured the young fellow, and endured his fits of temper, his changes of purpose, his fantastic inconsistencies of every kind. What friendship it was on his part, after Erradeen had deserted him, left him planted there – as if he cared for the d – place where he had gone only to please the young'un! thus to put all his grievances in his pocket and hurry over land and sea to make sure that all was comfortable for the ungrateful young man! That was true friendship, by Jove; what a man would do for a man! not like a woman that always had to be waited upon. Captain Underwood felt that his vested rights were being assailed, and that if it came to this it would be a thing to be resisted with might and main. A wife! what did Erradeen want with a wife? Surely it would be possible to put before him the charms of liberty once more and prevent the sacrifice. He walked along the side of the loch almost keeping up with the boat, hot with righteous indignation, in spite of the cold wind which had driven Mrs. Forrester into the house. Presently he heard the sound of salutations on the water, of oars clanking upon rowlocks from a different quarter, and saw the boat from the isle – Hamish rowing in his red shirt – meet with the large four-oared boat from Birkenbraes and pause while the women's voices exchanged a few sentences, chorused by Mr. Williamson's bass. Then the smaller boat came on towards the shore, towards the point near which a carriage was waiting. Captain Underwood quickened his steps a little, and he it was who presented himself to Julia Herbert's eyes as she approached the bit of rocky beach, and hurrying down, offered his hand to help her.

'What a strange meeting,' cried Julia; 'what a small world, as everybody says! Who could have thought, Captain Underwood, of seeing you here?'

'I might reply, if the surprise were not so delightful, who could have thought, Miss Herbert, of seeing you here? for myself it is a second home to me, and has been for years.'

'My reason for being here is simple. Let me introduce you to my cousin, Lady Herbert. Sir Thomas has got the shootings lower down. I suppose you are with Lord Erradeen.'

Lady Herbert had given the captain a very distant bow. She did not like the looks of him, as indeed it has been stated no ladies did, whether in Sloebury or elsewhere; but at the name of Erradeen she paid a more polite attention, though the thought of her horses waiting so long in the cold was already grievous to her. 'I hope,' she said, 'that Lord Erradoen does not lodge his friends in that old ruin, as he does himself, people say.'

'We are at Auchnasheen, a house you may see among the trees,' said the captain. 'Feudal remains are captivating, but not to live in. Does our friend Walter know, Miss Herbert, what happiness awaits him in your presence here?'

'What a pretty speech,' Julia cried; 'far prettier than anything Walter could muster courage to say. No, Captain Underwood, he does not. It was all settled quite suddenly. I did not even know that he was here.'

'Julia, the horses have been waiting a long time,' said Lady Herbert. 'I have no doubt Lord Erradeen is a very interesting subject – but I don't know what Barber (who was the coachman) will say. I shall be glad to see your friends any day at luncheon. Tell Lord Erradeen, please. We are two women alone, Sir Thomas is on the hills all day; all the more we shall be glad to see him – I mean you both – if you will take pity on our loneliness. Now, Julia, we really must not wait any longer.'

'Tell Walter I shall look for him,' said Julia, kissing her hand as they drove away. Underwood stood and looked after the carriage with varied emotions. As against Katie Williamson, he was overjoyed to have such an auxiliary – a girl who would not stand upon any punctilio[9] – who would pursue her object with any assistance she could pick up, and would not be above an alliance defensive or offensive, a girl who knew the advantage of an influential friend. So far as that went he was glad: but, heavens! what a neighbourhood, bristling with women; a girl at every corner ready to decoy his prey out of his hands. He was rueful, even though he was in a measure satisfied. If he could play his cards sufficiently well to detach Walter from both one and the other, to show the bondage which was veiled under Julia's smiles and complacency, as well as under Katie's uncompromising code, and to carry him off under their very eyes, that would indeed be a triumph; but failing that, it was better for him to make an ally of Julia, and push her cause, than to suffer himself to be ousted by the other, the little parvenue,[10] with her cool impertinence, who had been the first, he thought, to set Walter against him.

He walked back to Auchnasheen, full of these thoughts, and of plans to recover his old ascendancy. He had expedients for doing this which would not bear recording, and a hundred hopes of awakening the passions, the jealousies, the vanity of the young man whom already he had been able to sway beyond his expectations. He believed that he had led Walter by the nose, as he said, and had a mastery over him which would be easily recovered if he but got him for a day or two to himself. It was a matter of fact that he had done him much, if not fatal harm; and if the captain had been clever enough to know that he had no mastery whatever over his victim, and that Walter was the slave of his own shifting and uneasy moods, of his indolences and sudden impulses, and immediate abandonment of himself to the moment, but not of Captain Underwood, that tempter might have done him still more harm. But he did not possess this finer perception, and thus lost a portion of his power.

He went back to Auchnasheen to find a comfortable dinner, a good fire, a cheerful room, full of light and comfort, which reminded him of 'old days,' which he gave a regretful yet comfortable thought to in passing – the time when he had waited, not knowing what moment the old lord, his former patron, should return from Kinloch Houran. And now he was waiting for the other – who was so unlike the old lord – and yet had already been of more use to Underwood, and served him better in his own way, than the old lord had ever done. He was much softened, and even[a] perhaps a little maudlin in his thoughts of Walter as he sat over that comfortable fire. What was he about, poor boy? Not so comfortable as this friend and retainer, who was drinking his wine and thinking of him. But he should find some one to welcome him when he returned. He should find a comfortable meal and good company, which was more than the foolish fellow would expect. It was foolish of him, in his temper, to dart away from those who really cared for him, who really could be of use to him; but by this time the young lord would be too glad, after his loneliness, to come back and find a faithful friend ready to make allowances for him, and so well acquainted with his circumstances here.

So well acquainted with his circumstances! Underwood, in his time, had no doubt wondered over these as much as any one; but that was long ago, and he had in the mean time become quite familiar with them, and did not any longer speculate on the subject. He had no supernatural curiosity for his part. He could understand that one would not like to see a ghost: and he believed in ghosts – in a fine, healthy, vulgar, natural apparition, with dragging chains and hollow groans. But as for anything else, he had never entered into the question, nor had he any thought of doing so now. However, as he sat by the fire with all these comfortable accessories round him, and listened now and then to hear if any one was coming, and sometimes was deceived by the wind in the chimneys, or the sound of the trees in the fresh breeze which had become keener and sharper since he came indoors, it happened, how he could not tell, that questions arose in the captain's mind such as he had never known before.

The house was very still, the servants' apartments were at a considerable distance from the sitting-rooms, and all was very quiet. Two or three times in the course of the evening, old Symington, who had also come to see that everything was in order for his master, walked all the way from these retired regions through a long passage running from one end of the house to the other, to the great door, which he opened cautiously, then shut again, finding nobody in sight, and retired the same way as he came, his shoes creaking all the way. This interruption occurring at intervals had a remarkable effect upon Underwood. He began to wait for its recurrence, to count the steps, to feel a thrill of alarm as they passed the door of the room in which he was sitting. Oh, yes, no doubt it was Symington, who always wore creaking shoes, confound him! But what if it were not Symington? What if it might be some one else, some mysterious being who might suddenly open the door, and freeze into stone the warm, palpitating, somewhat unsteady person of a man who had eaten a very good dinner and drunk a considerable quantity of wine? This thought so penetrated his mind, that gradually all his thoughts were concentrated on the old servant's perambulation, watching for it before it came, thinking of it after it had passed. The steady and solemn march at intervals, which seemed calculated and regular, was enough to have impressed the imagination of any solitary person. And the captain was of a primitive simplicity of mind in some respects. His fears paralysed him; he was afraid to get up, to open the door, to make sure what it was. How could he tell that he might not be seized by the hair of the head by some ghastly apparition, and dragged into a chamber of horrors! He tried to fortify himself with more wine, but that only made his tremor worse. Finally the panic came to a crisis, when Symington, pausing, knocked at the library door. Underwood remembered to have heard that no spirit could enter without invitation, and he shut his mouth firmly that no habitual 'come in' might lay him open to the assault of the enemy. He sat breathless through the ensuing moment of suspense, while Symington waited outside. The captain's hair stood up on his head; his face was covered with a profuse dew; he held by the table in an agony of apprehension when he saw the door begin to turn slowly upon its hinges.

'My lord will not be home the night,' said Symington, slowly.

The sight of the old servant scarcely quieted the perturbation of Underwood. It had been a terrible day for Symington. He was ashy pale or grey, as old men become when the blood is driven from their faces. He had not been able to get rid of the scared and terror-stricken sensation with which he had watched the Birkenbraes party climbing the old stairs, and wandering as he thought at the peril of their lives upon the unsafe battlements. He had been almost violent in his calls to them to come down: but nobody had taken any notice, and they had talked about their guide and about the gentleman who was living with Lord Erradeen, till it seemed to Symington that he must go distracted. 'Where there ever such fools – such idiots! since there is nobody staying with Lord Erradeen but me, his body servant,' the old man had said tremulously to himself. At Symington's voice the captain gave a start and a cry. Even in the relief of discovering who it was, he could not quiet the excitement of his nerves.

'It's you, old Truepenny,'[11] he cried, yet looked at him across the table with a tremor, and a very forced and uncomfortable smile.

'That's not my name,' said Symington, with, on his side, the irritation of a disturbed mind. 'I'm saying that it's getting late, and my lord will no be home to-night.'

'By Jove!' cried Captain Underwood, 'when I heard you passing from one end of the house to the other, I thought it might be – the old fellow over there, coming himself –'

'I cannot tell, sir, what you are meaning by the old fellow over there. There's no old fellow I know of but old Macalister; and it was not for him you took me.'

'If you could have heard how your steps sounded through the house! By Jove! I could fancy I hear them now.'

'Where?' Symington cried, coming in and shutting the door, which he held with his hand behind him, as if to bar all possible comers. And then the two men looked at each other, both breathless and pale.

'Sit down,' said Underwood. 'The house feels chilly and dreary, nobody living in it for so long. Have a glass of wine. One wants company in a damp, dreary old hole like this.'

'You are very kind, captain,' said the old man; 'but Auchnasheen, though only my lord's shooting-box, is a modern mansion, and full of every convenience. It would ill become me to raise an ill name on it.'

'I wonder what Erradeen's about?' said the captain. 'I bet he's worse off than we are. How he must wish he was off with me on the other side of the Channel.'

'Captain! you will, maybe, think little of me, being nothing but a servant; but it is little good you do my young lord on the ither side of the Channel.'

Underwood laughed, but not with his usual vigour.

'What can I do with your young lord,' he said. 'He takes the bit in his teeth, and goes – to the devil his own way.'

'Captain, there are some that think the like of you sore to blame.'

Underwood said nothing for a moment. When he spoke there was a quiver in his voice.

'Let me see the way to my room, Symington. Oh yes, I suppose it is the old room; but I've forgotten. I was there before? well, so I suppose; but I have forgotten. Take the candle as I tell you, and show me the way.'

He had not the least idea what he feared, and he did not remember ever having feared anything before; but to-night he hung close to Symington, following at his very heels. The old man was anxious and alarmed, but not in this ignoble way. He deposited the captain in his room with composure, who would but for very shame have implored him to stay. And then his footsteps sounded through the vacant house, going further and further off till they died away in the distance.

Captain Underwood locked his door, though he felt it was a vain precaution, and hastened to hide his head under the bed-clothes:[a] but he was well aware that this was a vain precaution too.

# CHAPTER IV.[b]

IT was on the evening of the day after Captain Underwood's arrival that Lord Erradeen left Kinloch Houran for Auchnasheen. After labour, rest. He could not but compare as he walked along in the early falling autumnal twilight the difference between himself now, and the same self a year ago, when he had fled from the place of torture to the house of peace, a man nearly frantic with the consciousness of all the new bonds upon him, the uncomprehended powers against which he had to struggle, the sense of panic and impotence, yet of mad excitement and resistance, with which his brain was on flame. The recollection of the ensuing time spent at Auchnasheen, when he saw no one, heard no voice but his own, yet lived through day after day of bewildering mental conflict, without knowing who it was against whom he contended, was burned in upon his recollection. All through that time he had been conscious of such a desire to flee as hurried the pace of his thoughts, and made the intolerable still more intolerable. His heart had sickened of the unbearable fight into which he was compelled like an unwilling soldier with death behind him. To resist had always been Walter's natural impulse; but the impulse of flight had so mingled with it that his soul had been in a fever, counting no passage of days, but feeling the whole period long or short, he did not know which, as one monstrous uninterrupted day or night, in which the processes of thought were never intermitted. His mind was in a very different condition now. He had got over the early panic of nature. The blinding mists of terror had melted away from his eyes, and the novelty and horror of his position, contending with unseen dominations and powers, had almost ceased for the moment to affect his mind, so profoundly exhausted was he by the renewed struggle in which he had been engaged.[c]

The loch was veiled in mist, through which it glimmered faintly with broken reflections, the wooded banks presenting on every side a sort of ghostly outline, with the colour no more than indicated against the dreary confusion of air and vapour. At some points there was the glimpse of a blurred light, looking larger and more distant than it really was, the ruddy spot made by the open door of the little inn, the whiter and smaller twinkle of the manse window, the far-off point, looking no more than a taper light in the distance, that shone from the isle. There was in Walter's mind a darkness and confusion not unlike the landscape. He was worn out: there was in him none of that vivid feeling which had separated between his human soul in its despair and the keen sweetness of the morning. Now all was night within him and around. His arms had fallen from his hands.

He moved along, scarcely aware that he was moving, feeling everything blurred, confused, indistinct in the earth about him and in the secret places of his soul. Desire for flight he had none: he had come to see that it was impossible: and he had not energy enough to wish it. And fear had died out of him. He was not afraid. Had he been joined on the darkling way by the personage of whom he had of late seen so much, it would scarcely have quickened his pulses. All such superficial emotion had died out of him: the real question was so much superior, so infinitely important in comparison with any such transitory tremors as these. But at the present moment he was not thinking at all, scarcely living, any more than the world around him was living, hushed into a cessation of all energy and almost of consciousness, looking forward to night and darkness and repose.

It was somewhat surprising to him to see the lighted windows at Auchnasheen, and the air of inhabitation about the house with which he had no agreeable associations, but only those which are apt to hang about a place in which one has gone through a fever, full of miserable visions, and the burning restlessness of disease. But when he stepped into the hall, the door being opened to him by Symington as soon as his foot was heard on the gravel, and turning round to go into the library found himself suddenly in the presence of Captain Underwood, his astonishment and dismay were beyond expression. The dismay came even before the flush of anger, which was the first emotion that showed itself. Underwood stood holding open the library door, with a smile that was meant to be ingratiating and conciliatory. He held out his hand, as Walter, with a start and exclamation, recognised him.

'Yes,' he said, 'I'm here, you see. Not so easy to get rid of when once I form a friendship. Welcome to your own house, Erradeen.'

Walter did not say anything till he had entered the room and shut the door. He walked to the fire, which was blazing brightly, and placed himself with his back to it, in that attitude in which the master of a house defies all comers.

'I did not expect to find you here,' he said. 'You take me entirely by surprise.'

'I had hoped it would be an agreeable surprise,' said the captain, still with his most amiable smile. 'I thought to have a friend's face waiting for you when you came back from that confounded place would be a relief.'

'What do you call a confounded place?' said Walter, testily. 'You know nothing about it, as far as I am aware. No, Underwood, it is as well to speak plainly. It is not an agreeable surprise. I am sorry you have taken the trouble to come so far for me.'

'It was no trouble. If you are a little out of sorts, never mind. I am not a man to be discouraged for a hasty word. You want a little cheerful society –'

'Is that what you call yourself?' Walter said with a harsh laugh. He was aware that there was a certain brutality in what he said; but the sudden sight of the man who had disgusted him even while he had most influenced him, and of whom he had never thought but with a movement of resentment and secret rage, affected him to a sort of delirium. He could have seized him with the force of passion and flung him into the loch at the door. It would have been no crime, he thought, to destroy such vermin off the face of the earth – to make an end of such a source of evil would be no crime. This was the thought in his mind while he stood upon his own hearth, looking at the man who was his guest and therefore sacred. As for Captain Underwood, he took no offence; it was not in his *rôle* to do so, whatever happened. What he had to do was to regain, if possible, his position with the young man upon whom he had lived and enriched himself for the greater part of the year, to render himself indispensable to him as he had done to his predecessor. For this object he was prepared to bear everything, and laugh at all that was too strong to be ignored. He laughed now, and did his best, not very gracefully, to carry out the joke. He exerted himself to talk and please throughout the dinner, which Walter went through in silence, drinking largely, though scarcely eating at all – for Kinloch Houran was not a place which encouraged an appetite. After dinner, in the midst of one of Underwood's stories, Walter lighted a candle abruptly, and saying he was going to bed, left his companion without apology or reason given. It was impossible to be more rude. The captain felt the check, for he had a considerable development of vanity, and was in the habit of amusing the people to whom he chose to make himself agreeable. But this affront, too, he swallowed. 'He will have come to himself by morning,' he said. In the morning, however, Walter was only more gloomy and unwilling to listen, and determined not to respond. It was only when in the middle of the breakfast he received a note brought by a mounted messenger who waited for an answer, that he spoke. He flung it open across the table to Underwood with a harsh laugh.

'Is this your doing, too?' he cried.

'My doing, Erradeen!'

Underwood knew very well what it was before he looked at it. It was from Lady Herbert, explaining that she had only just heard that Lord Erradeen was so near a neighbour, and begging him, if he was not, like all the other gentlemen, on the hills, that he would come ('and your friend Captain Underwood') to luncheon that day to cheer two forlorn ladies left all by themselves in this wilderness. 'And you will meet an old friend,' it concluded playfully. The composition was Julia's, and had not been produced without careful study.

'My doing!' said Captain Underwood. 'Can you suppose that *I* want you to marry, Erradeen?'

It was a case, he thought, in which truth was best.

Walter started up from his seat.

'Marry!' he cried, with a half-shout[a] of rage and dismay.

'Well, my dear fellow, I don't suppose you are such a fool; but, of course, that is what *she* means. The fair Julia –'[12]

'Oblige me,' cried Lord Erradeen, taking up once more his position on the hearth, 'by speaking civilly when you speak of ladies in my house.'

'Why, bless me, Erradeen, you gave me the note –'

'I was a fool – that is nothing new. I have been a fool since the first day when I met you and took you for something more than mortal. Oh, and before that!' cried Walter bitterly. 'Do not flatter yourself that you did it. It is of older date than you.'

'The fair Julia –' Underwood began; but he stopped when his companion advanced upon him threatening, with so gloomy a look and so tightly strained an arm that the captain judged it wise to change his tone. 'I should have said, since we are on punctilio, that Miss Herbert and you are older acquaintances than you and I, Erradeen.'

'Fortunately you have nothing to do with that,' Walter said, perceiving the absurdity of his rage.

Then he walked to the window and looked out so long and silently that the anxious watcher began to think the incident over. But it was not till Walter, after this period of reflection, had written a note and sent it to the messenger, that he ventured to speak.

'You have accepted, of course. In the circumstances it would be uncivil –'

Walter looked at him for a moment, breaking off his sentence as if he had spoken.

'I have something to tell you,' he said. 'My mother is coming to Auchnasheen.'

'Your mother!' Underwood's voice ran into a quaver of dismay.

'You will see that in the circumstances, as you say, I am forced to be uncivil. When my mother is here she will, of course, be the mistress of the house; and she, as you know –'

'Will not ask me to prolong my visit,' said the captain, with an attempt at rueful humour. 'I think we may say as much as that, Erradeen.'

'I fear it is not likely,' Walter said.

Captain Underwood gave vent to his feelings in a prolonged whistle.

'You will be bored to death. Mark my words, I know you well enough. You will never be able to put up with it. You will be ready to hang yourself in a week. You will come off to me. It is the best thing that could happen so far as I am concerned – wishing to preserve your friendship as I do –'

'Is it friendship, then, that has bound us together?' said Lord Erradeen.

'What else? Disinterested friendship on my part. I take your laugh rather ill, Erradeen. What have I gained by it, I should like to know? I've liked you, and I liked the last man before you. I have put up with a great deal from you – tempers like a silly woman, vagaries of all sorts, discontent and abuse. Why have I put up with all that?'

300     *The Selected Works of Margaret Oliphant, Volume 21*

'Why indeed? I wish you had not,' said the young man scornfully. 'Yes, you have put up with it, and made your pupil think the worse of you with every fresh exercise of patience. I should like to pay you for all that dirty work.'

'Pay me!' the captain said, faltering a little. He was not a very brave man, though he could hold his own; and there was a force of passion and youth in his 'pupil' – with what bitterness that word was said! – that alarmed him a little. Besides, Walter had a household of servants behind him – grooms, keepers, all sorts of people – who held Captain Underwood in no favour. 'Pay me! I don't know how you could pay me,' he said.

'I should like to do it – in one way; and I shall do it – in another,' said Walter still somewhat fiercely. Then once more he laughed. He took out a pocketbook[a] from his coat, and out of that a cheque. 'You have been at some expense on my account,' he said; 'your journey has been long and rapid. I consider myself your debtor for that, and for the – good intention. Will this be enough?'

In the bitter force of his ridicule and dislike, Walter held out the piece of paper as one holds a sweetmeat to a child. The other gave a succession of rapid glances at it to make out what it was. When he succeeded in doing so a flush of excitement and eagerness covered his face. He put out his hand nervously to clutch it with the excited look of the child before whom a prize is held out, and who catches at it before it is snatched away. But he would not acknowledge this feeling.

'My lord,' he said, with an appearance of dignity offended, 'you are generous; but to pay me, as you say, and offer money in place of your friendship –'

'It is an excellent exchange, Underwood. This is worth something, if not very much – the other,' said Walter with a laugh, 'nothing at all.'

Perhaps this was something like what Captain Underwood himself thought, as he found himself, a few hours later, driving along the country roads towards the railway station, retracing the path which he had travelled two days before with many hopes and yet a tremor. His hopes were now over, and the tremor too; but there was something in his breast pocket better, for the moment at least, than any hopes, which kept him warm, even though the wind was cold. He had failed in his attempt to fix himself once more permanently on Lord Erradeen's shoulders – an attempt in which he had not been very sanguine. It was a desperate venture, he knew, and it had failed; but, at the same time, circumstances might arise which would justify another attempt, and that one might not fail: and, in the mean time, his heart rose with a certain elation when he thought of that signature in his breast pocket. *That* was worth an effort, and nothing could diminish its value. Friendship might fail, but a cheque is substantial. He had something of the dizzy feeling of one who has fallen from a great height, and has not yet got the giddiness of the movement out of his head. And yet he was not altogether discouraged. Who could tell what turn the wheel of fortune might take? and, in the mean time, there was that bit of paper. The horse was fresh, and

*The Wizard's Son, Volume III* 301

flew along the road, up and down, at a pace very different from that of Big John's steeds, which had brought Captain Underwood to Auchnasheen. About halfway along he came up to the waggonette from Birkenbraes, in which was Mr. Braithwaite and his luggage, along with two other guests, ladies, bound for the station, and escorted by Mr. Williamson and Katie, as was their way.

'Dear me, is that Underwood?' cried Mr. Williamson with the lively and simple curiosity of rural use and wont. 'So you're there, captain,' he said, as the dog-cart came up behind the heavier carriage.

'No, I'm not here – I'm going,' said Underwood, quickly, 'hurrying to catch the train.'

'Oh, there is plenty of time; we are going too (Bless me,' he said aside, 'how many visitors think you they can have had in yon old place?) I am thinking ye have been with our young neighbour, Lord Erradeen.'

'That is an easy guess. I am leaving him, you mean. Erradeen is a reformed character. He is turning over a new leaf – and full time too,' Captain Underwood cried, raising his voice that he might be heard over the rattle of the two carriages. Notwithstanding the cheque which kept him so warm, he had various grudges against Walter, and did not choose to lose the opportunity for a little mischief.

'It is always a good thing,' said Mr. Williamson, 'to turn over a new leaf. We have all great occasion to do that.'

'Especially when there are so many of them,' the captain cried, as his light cart passed the other. He met the party again at the station, where they had to wait for the train. Katie stood by herself in a thoughtful mood while the departing guests consulted over their several boxes, and Captain Underwood seized the moment: 'I am sorry to lose the fun,' he said, in a confidential tone, 'but I must tell you, Miss Williamson, what is going to happen. Erradeen has been pursued up here into his stronghold by one of the many ladies – I expect to hear she has clutched hold of him before long, and then you'll have a wedding.'

'Is that why you are going away, Captain Underwood?'

'He has gone a little too far, you know, that is the truth,' said the captain. 'I am glad he is not going to take in any nice girl. I couldn't have stood by and seen that. I should have had to warn her people. Even Miss Julia, by Jove! I'm sorry for Miss Julia, if she gets him. But she is an old campaigner;[13] she will know how to take care of herself.'

'Is it because Lord Erradeen is so bad that you are leaving him, or because he is going to be good?' Katie asked. Captain Underwood on ordinary occasions was a little afraid of her; but his virtuous object fortified him now.

'Oh, by Jove! he goes too far,' said Underwood. 'I am not squeamish, heaven knows, but he goes too far. I can speak now that it's all over between him and me. I never could bear to see him with nice girls; but he's got his match in Miss Julia. The fair Julia – that is another pair of shoes.'[14]

302     *The Selected Works of Margaret Oliphant, Volume 21*

'Who was he meaning with his fair Julias?' said Mr. Williamson as they drove away. 'Yon's a scoundrel, if there ever was one, and young Erradeen is well rid of him. But when thieves cast out, honest folk get their ain. Would yon be true?'

Katie was in what her father called 'a brown study,'[15] and did not care to talk. She only shook her head – a gesture which could be interpreted as any one pleased.

'I am not sure,' said Mr. Williamson, in reply. 'He knows more about Lord Erradeen than any person on the loch. But who is the fair Julia, and is he really to be married to her? I would like fine to hear all about it. I will call at Auchnasheen in the afternoon and see what he has to say.'

But Katie remained in her brown study, letting her father talk. She knew very well who the fair Julia was. She remembered distinctly the scene at Burlington House. She saw with the clearest perception what the tactics were of the ladies at the Lodge. Katie had been somewhat excited by the prospect of being Oona's rival, which was like something in a book. It was like the universal story of the young man's choice, not between Venus and Minerva,[16] or between good and evil, but perhaps, Katie thought, between poetry and prose, between the ideal and the practical. She was interested in that conflict and not unwilling in all kindness and honour to play her part in it. Oona would be the ideal bride for him, but she herself, Katie felt, would be better in a great many ways, and she did not feel that she would have any objection to marry Lord Erradeen. But here was another rival with whom she did not choose to enter the lists. It is to be feared that Katie in her heart classified Miss Herbert as Vice, as the sinner against whom every man is to be warned, and turned with some scorn from any comparison with her meretricious attractions. But she was fair and just, and her heart had nothing particular to do with the matter; so that she was able calmly to wait for information, which was not Oona's case.

It had been entirely at random that Lord Erradeen had announced his mother's approaching arrival to Underwood. The idea had come into his mind the moment before he made use of it, and he had felt a certain amusement in the complete success of this hastily-assumed weapon. It had been so effectual that he began to think it might be available in other conflicts as well as this: and in any case he felt himself pledged to make it a matter of fact. He walked to the village when Underwood had gone, to carry at once his intention into effect. Though it was only a cluster of some half-dozen houses, it had a telegraph-office – as is so general in the Highlands[17] – and Walter sent a brief, emphatic message, which he felt would carry wild excitement into Sloebury. 'You will do me a great favour if you will come at once, alone,' was Walter's message. He was himself slightly excited by it. He began to think over all those primitive relationships of his youth as he walked along the quiet road. There was sweetness in them, but how much conflict, trouble, embarrassment! – claims on one side to which the other could not respond – a sort of authority, which was no authority – a duty which did nothing but establish grievances and mutual reproach. His mind was still in the state of exhaustion which Captain Underwood had only temporarily disturbed; and a certain softening was in the weakened faculties, which were worn out with too much conflict. Poor mother, after all! He could remember, looking back, when it was his greatest pleasure to go home to her, to talk to her, pouring every sort of revelation into her never-wearied ears; all his school successes and tribulations, all about the other fellows, the injustices that were done, the triumphs that were gained. Could women interest themselves in all that as she had seemed to interest herself? or had she sometimes found it a bore to have all these schoolboy experiences poured forth upon her? Miss Merivale had very plainly thought it a bore; his voice had given her a headache. But Mrs. Methven[a] never had any headaches, or anything that could cloud her attention. He remembered now that his mother was not a mere nursery woman[18] – that she read a great deal more than he himself did, knew many things he did not know, was not silly, or a fool, or narrow-minded, as so many women are. Was it not a little hard, after all, that she should have nothing of her son but the schoolboy prattle? She had been everything to him when he was a boy, and now she was nothing to him; perhaps all the time she might have been looking forward to the period when he should be a man, and have something more interesting to talk over with her than a cricket-match – for, to be sure, when one came to think of it, she could have no personal interest in a cricket-match. A momentary *serrement*[19] of compunction came to Walter's heart. Poor mother! he said to himself; perhaps it was a little hard upon her. And she must have the feeling, to make it worse, that she had a right to something better. He could not even now get his mind clear about that right.

As he returned from the telegraph-office he too met the waggonette from Birkenbraes, which was stopped at sight of him with much energy on the part of Mr. Williamson.

'We've just met your friend Captain Underwood. If you'll not take it amiss, Lord Erradeen, I will say that I'm very glad you're not keeping a man like that about you. But what is this about – a lady? I hear there's a lady – the fair – What did he call her, Katie? I am not good at remembering names.'

'It is of no consequence,' said Katie, with a little rising colour, 'what such a man said.'

'That's true, that's true,' said her father; 'but still, Erradeen, you must mind we are old friends now, and let us know what's coming. The fair – Toots,[20] I thought of it a minute ago? It's ridiculous to forget names.'

'You may be sure I shall let you know what's coming. My mother is coming,' Walter said.

And this piece of news was so unexpected and startling that the Williamsons drove off with energy to spread it far and near. Mr. Williamson himself was as much excited as if it had been of personal importance to him.

'Now that will settle the young man,' he said; 'that will put many things right. There has not been a lady at Auchnasheen since ever I have been here. A mother is the next best thing to a wife, and very likely the one is in preparation for the other, and ye will all have to put on your prettiest frocks for her approval.' He followed this with one of his big laughs, looking round upon a circle in which there were various young persons who were very marriageable. 'But I put no faith in Underwood's fair – what was it he called her?' Mr. Williamson said.

***

# CHAPTER V.ᵃ

Two days after, Mrs. Methven arrived at Kinloch Houran by the afternoon coach, alone.

She had interpreted very literally the telegram which had brought such a tremor yet such a movement of joy to her heart. Her son wanted her. Perhaps he might be ill, certainly it must be for something serious and painful that she was called; yet he wanted her! She had been very quiet and patient, waiting if perhaps his heart might be touched and he might recall the tie of nature and his own promises, feeling with a sad pride that she wanted nothing of him but his love, and that without that the fine houses and the new wealth were nothing to her. She was pleased even to stand aloof, to be conscious of having in no way profited by Walter's advancement. She had gained nothing by it, she wished to gain nothing by it. If Walter were well, then there was no need for more. She had enough for herself without troubling him. So long as all was well! But this is at the best a forlorn line of argument, and it cannot be doubted that Mrs. Methven's bosom throbbed with a great pang of disappointment when she sat and smiled to conceal it, and answered questions about Walter, yet could not say that she had seen him or any of his 'places in Scotland,' or knew much more than her questioners did. When his message arrived her heart leapt in her breast. There were no explanations, no reason given, but that imperative call, such as mothers love to have addressed to them: 'Come;' all considerations of her own comfort set aside in the necessity for her which had arisen at last. Another might have resented so complete an indifference to what might happen to suit herself. But there are connections and relationships in which this is the highest compliment. He knew that it did not matter to her what her own convenience was, as long as he wanted her. She got up from her chair at once, and proceeded to put her things together to get ready for the journey. With a smiling countenance she prepared herself for the night train. She would not even take a maid. 'He says, alone. He must have some reason for it, I suppose,' she said to Miss Merivale. 'I am the reason,' said Cousin Sophy: 'He doesn't want me. You can tell him, with my love, that to travel all night is not at all in my way, and he need have had no fear on

*The Wizard's Son, Volume III*    305

that subject.'ᵃ But Mrs. Methven would not agree to this, and departed hurriedly without any maid. She was surprised a little, yet would not allow herself to be displeased, that no one came to meet her: but it was somewhat forlorn to be set down on the side of the loch in the wintry afternoon, with the cold, gleaming water before her, and no apparent way of getting to the end of her journey.

'Oh yes, mem, you might drive round the head of the loch: but it's a long way,' the landlady of the little inn said, smoothing down her apron at the door, 'and far simpler just crossing the water, as everybody does in these parts.'

Mrs. Methven was a little nervous about crossing the water. She was tired and disappointed, and a chill had crept to her heart. While she stood hesitating a young lady came up, whose boat waited for her on the beach, a man in a red shirt standing at the bow.

'It is a lady for Auchnasheen, Miss Oona,' said the landlady, 'and no boat. Duncan is away, and for the moment I have not a person to send: and his lordship will maybe be out on the hill, or he will have forgotten, or maybe he wasna sure when to expect you, mem?'

'No, he did not know when to expect me. I hope there is no illness,' said Mrs. Methven, with a thrill of apprehension.

At this the young lady came forward with a shy yet frank grace.

'If you will let me take you across,' she said, 'my boat is ready. I am Oona Forrester. Lord Erradeen is quite well I think, and I heard that he expected – his mother.'

'Yes,' said Mrs. Methven. She gave the young stranger a penetrating look. Her own aspect was perhaps a little severe, for her heart had been starved and repressed, and she wore it very warm and low down in her bosom, never upon her sleeve. There rose over Oona's countenance a soft and delicate flush under the eyes of Walter's mother. She had nothing in the world to blush for, and probably that was why the colour rose. They were of infinite interest to each other, two souls meeting, as it were, in the dark, quite unknown to each other and yet – who could tell? – to be very near perhaps in times to come. The look they interchanged was a mutual question. Then Mrs. Methven felt herself bound to take up her invariable defence of her son.

'He did not, most likely, think that I could arrive so soon. I was wrong not to let him know. If I accept your kindness will it be an inconvenience to you?'

This question was drowned in Oona's immediate response and in the louder protest of Mrs. Macfarlane. 'Bless me, mem, you canna know the loch! for there is nobody but would put themselves about to help a traveller: and above all Miss Oona, that just has no other thought. Colin, put in the lady's box intill the boat, and Hamish, he will give ye a hand.'

Thus it was settled without further delay. It seemed to the elder lady like a dream when she found herself afloat upon this unknown water, the mountains standing round, with their heads all clear and pale in the wonderful atmosphere from which the last rays of the sunset had but lately faded, while down below in this twilight scene the colour had begun to go out of the autumn trees and red walls of the ruined castle, at which she looked with a curiosity full of excitement. 'That is –?' she said pointing with a strange sensation of eagerness.

'That is Kinloch Houran,' said Oona, to whose sympathetic mind, she could not tell how, there came a tender, pitying comprehension of the feelings of the mother, thus thrust alone and without any guide into the other life of her son.

'It is very strange to me – to see the place where Walter – You know perhaps that neither my son nor I were ever here until he –'

'Oh yes,' Oona said hastily, interrupting the embarrassed speech; and she added, 'My mother and I have been here always, and everybody on the loch knows everybody else. We were aware –'

And then she paused too; but her companion took no notice, her mind being fully occupied. 'I feel,' she said, 'like a woman in a dream.'

It was very still on the loch, scarcely a breath stirring (which was very fortunate, for Mrs. Methven, unaccustomed, had a little tremor for the dark water even though so smooth). The autumnal trees alone, not quite put out by the falling darkness, seemed to lend a little light as they hung, reflected, over the loch – a redder cluster here and there looking like a fairy lamp below the water. A thousand suggestions were in the air, and previsions of she knew not what, a hidden life surrounding her on every side. Her brain was giddy, her heart full. By-and-by[a] she turned to her young companion, who was so sympathetically silent, and whose soft voice when she spoke, with the little cadence of an accent unfamiliar yet sweet, had a half-caressing[b] sound which touched the solitary woman. 'You say your mother and you,' she said. 'Are you too an only child?'

'Oh no! there are eight of us: but I am the youngest, the only one left. All the boys are away. We live on the isle. I hope you will come and see us. My mother will be glad –'

'And she is not afraid to trust you – by yourself? It must be a happy thing for a woman to have a daughter,' Mrs. Methven said, with a sigh. 'The boys, as you say, go away.'

'Nobody here is afraid of the loch,' said Oona. 'Accidents happen – oh, very rarely. Mamma is a little nervous about yachting, for the winds come down from the hills in gusts; but Hamish is the steadiest oar, and there is no fear. Do you see now the lights at Auchnasheen? There is some one waiting, at the landing-place. It will be Lord Erradeen, or some one from the house. Hamish, mind the current. You know how it sweeps the boat up the loch?'

'It will just be the wash of that confounded steamboat,' Hamish said.

The voices sounded in the air without conveying any sense to her mind. Was that Walter, the vague line of darker shadow upon the shade? Was it his house she was going to, his life that she was entering once more? All doubts were put to an end speedily by Walter's voice.

The Wizard's Son, Volume III 307

'Is it Hamish?' he cried out.

'Oh, Lord Erradeen, it is me,' cried Oona, in her soft Scotch. 'And I am bringing you your mother.'

The boat grated on the bank as she spoke, and this disguised the tremor in her voice, which Mrs. Methven, quite incapable of distinguishing anything else, was yet fully sensible of. She stepped out tremulously into her son's arms.

'Mother,' he cried, 'what must you think of me for not coming to meet you? I never thought you could be here so soon.'

'I should have come by telegraph if I could,' she said, with an agitated laugh: so tired, so tremulous, so happy, the strangest combination of feelings overwhelming her. But still she was aware of a something, a tremor, a tingle in Oona's voice. The boat receded over the water almost without a pause, Hamish under impulsion of a whispered word, having pushed off again as soon as the traveller and her box were[a] landed. Walter paused to call out his thanks over the water, and then he drew his mother's arm within his, and led her up the bank.

'Where is Jane?' he said. 'Have you no one with you? Have you travelled all night, and alone, mother, for me?'

'For whom should I do it, but for you? And did you think I would lose a minute after your message, Walter? But you are well, there is nothing wrong with your health?'

'Nothing wrong with my health,' he said, with a half-laugh.[b] 'No, that is safe enough. I have not deserved that you should come to me, mother –'

'There is no such word as deserving between mother and son,' she said tremulously, 'so long as you want me, Walter.'

'Take care of those steps,' was all he said. 'We are close now to the house. I hope you will find your rooms comfortable. I fear they have not been occupied for some time. But what shall you do without a maid? Perhaps the housekeeper –'

'You said to come alone, Walter.'

'Oh yes. I was afraid of Cousin Sophy; but you could not think I wanted to impair your comfort, mother? Here we are at the door, and here is Symington, very glad to receive his lady.'

'But you must not let him call me so.'

'Why not? You are our lady to all of us. You are the lady of the house, and I bid you welcome to it, mother,' he said, pausing to kiss her. She had a thousand things to forgive, but in that moment they were as though they had not been.

And there was not much more said until she had settled down into possession of the library, which answered instead of a drawing-room: had dined, and been brought back to the glowing peat fire which gave an aromatic breath of warmth and character to a Highland house. When all the business of the arrival had thus been gone through, there came a moment when it was apparent that subjects of more importance must be entered upon. There was a pause, and an interval of complete silence which seemed much longer than it really was. Walter stood before the fire for some time, while she sat close by, her hands clasped in her lap, ready to attend. Then he began to move about uneasily, feeling the compulsion of the moment, yet unprepared with anything to say. At length it was she who began.

'You sent for me, Walter?' she said.

'Yes, mother.'

Was there nothing more to tell her? He threw into disorder the books[a] on the table, and then he came back again, and once more faced her, standing with his back to the fire.

'My dear,' she said hesitating, 'it is with no reproach I speak, but only – There was some reason for sending for me?'

He gave once more a nervous laugh.

'You have good reason to be angry if you will; but I'll tell you the truth, mother. I made use of you to get rid of Underwood. He followed me here, and I told him you were coming, and that he could not stay against the will of the mistress of the house. Then I was bound to ask you –'

The poor lady drew back a little, and instinctively put her hand to her heart, in which there was a hot thrill of sensation, as if an arrow had gone in. And then, in the pang of it, she laughed too, and cried –

'You were bound, to be sure, to fulfil your threat. And this is why – this is why, Walter –'

She could not say more without being hysterical, and departing from every rule she had made for herself.

Meanwhile, Walter stood before her, feeling in his own heart the twang of that arrow which had gone through hers, and the pity of it and wonder of it, with a poignant realisation of all; and yet found nothing to say.

After a while Mrs. Methven regained her composure, and spoke with a smile that was almost more pathetic than tears.

'After all, it was a very good reason. I am glad you used me to get rid of that man.'

'I always told you, mother,' he said, 'that you had a most absurd prejudice against that man. There is no particular harm in the man. I had got tired of him. He is well enough in his own way, but he was out of place here.'

'Well, Walter, we need not discuss Captain Underwood. But don't you see it is natural that I should exaggerate his importance by way of giving myself the better reason for having come?'

The touch of bitterness and sarcasm that was in her words made Walter start from his place again, and once more turn over the books on the table. She was not a perfect woman to dismiss all feeling from what she said, and her heart was wrung.

After a while he returned to her again.

'Mother, I acknowledge you have a good right to be displeased. But that is not all. I am glad, anyhow – heartily glad to have you here.'

*The Wizard's Son, Volume III*   309

She looked up at him with her eyes full, and quivering lips. Everything went by impulse in the young man's mind, and this look – in which for once in his life he read the truth, the eagerness to forgive, the willingness to forget, the possibility, even in the moment of her deepest pain, of giving her happiness – went to his heart. After all it is a wonderful thing to have a human creature thus altogether dependent upon your words, your smile, ready to encounter all things for you, without hesitation, without a grudge. And why should she? What had he ever done for her? And she was no fool. These thoughts had already passed through his mind with a realisation of the wonder of it all, which seldom strikes the young at sight of the devotion of the old. All these things flashed back upon him at the sight of the dumb anguish yet forgiveness in her eyes.

'Mother,' he cried, 'there's enough of this between you and me. I want you not for Underwood, but for everything. Why should you care for a cad like me? but you do –'

'Care for you? Oh, my boy!'

'I know; there you sit that have travelled night and day because I held up my finger: and would give me your life if you could, and bear everything, and never change and never tire. Why, in the name of God, why?' he cried with an outburst. 'What have I ever done that you should do this for me? You are worth a score of such as I am, and yet you make yourself a slave –'

'Oh, Walter, my dear! how vain are all these words. I am your mother,' she said.

Presently he drew a chair close to her and sat down beside her.

'All these things have been put before me,' he said, 'to drive me to despair. I have tried to say that it was this vile lordship, and the burden of the family, that has made me bad, mother. But you know better than that,' he said, looking up at her with a stormy gleam in his face that could not be called a smile, 'and so do I.'

'Walter, God forbid that I should ever have thought you bad. You have been led astray.'

'To do – what I wanted to do,' he said with another smile, 'that is what is called leading astray between a man and those who stand between him and the devil; but I have talked with one who thinks of no such punctilios. Mother, vice deserves damnation; isn't that your creed?'

'Walter!'

'Oh, I know; but listen to me. If that were so, would a woman like you stand by the wretch still?'

'My dearest boy! you are talking wildly. There are no circumstances, none! in which I should not stand by you.'

'That is what I thought,' he said, 'you and – But they say that you don't know, you women, how bad a man can be: and that if you knew – And then as for God –'

'God knows everything, Walter.'

'Ay: and knows that never in my life did I care for or appeal to Him, till in despair. If you think of it, these are not things a man can do, mother: take refuge with women who would loathe him if they knew; or with God, who does know that only in desperation, only when nothing else is left to him, he calls out that name like a spell. Yes, that is all; like an incantation, to get rid of the fiend.'

The veins were swollen on Walter's forehead; great drops of moisture hung upon it; on the other hand his lips were parched and dry, his eyes gleaming with a hot treacherous lustre. Mrs. Methven, as she looked at him, grew sick with terror. She began to think that his brain was giving way.

'What am I to say to you?' she cried; 'who has been speaking so? It cannot be a friend, Walter. That is not the way to bring back a soul.'

He laughed, and the sound alarmed her still more.

'There was no friendship intended,' he said, 'nor reformation either. It was intended – to make me a slave.'

'To whom, oh! to whom?'

He had relieved his mind by talking thus; but it was by putting his burden upon her. She was agitated beyond measure by these partial confidences. She took his hands in hers, and pleaded with him –

'Oh, Walter, my darling, what has happened to you? Tell me what you mean.'

'I am not mad, mother, if that is what you think.'

'I don't think so, Walter. I don't know what to think. Tell me. Oh, my boy, have pity upon me; tell me.'

'You will do me more good, mother, if you will tell me – how I am to get this burden off, and be a free man.'

'The burden of – what? Sin? Oh, my son!' she cried, rising to her feet, with tears of joy streaming from her eyes. She put her hands upon his head and bade God bless him. God bless him! 'There is no doubt about that; no difficulty about that,' she said; 'for everything else in the world there may be uncertainty, but for this none. God is more ready to forgive than we are to ask.[21] If you wish it sincerely with all your heart, it is done. He is never far from any of us. He is here, Walter – here, ready to pardon!'

He took her hands which she had put upon him, and looked at her, shaking his head.

'Mother, you are going too fast,' he said. 'I want deliverance, it is true; but I don't know if it is *that* I mean.'

'That is at the bottom of all, Walter.'

He put her softly into her chair, and calmed her agitation; then he began to walk up and down the room.

'That is religion,' he said. 'I suppose it is at the bottom of all. What was it you used to teach me, mother, about a new heart? Can a man enter a second time – and be born?[22] That seems all so visionary when one is living one's life. You think

*The Wizard's Son, Volume III*  311

of hundreds of expedients first. To thrust it away from you, and forget all about it; but that does not answer; to defy it and go the other way out of misery and spite. Then to try compromises; marriage, for instance, with a wife perhaps, one thinks –'

'My dear,' said Mrs. Methven, with a sad sinking of disappointment in her heart after her previous exultation, yet determined that her sympathy should not fail, 'if you had a good wife no one would be so happy as I – a good girl who would help you to live a good life.'

Here he came up to her again, and, leaning against the table, burst into a laugh. But there was no mirth in it. A sense of the ludicrous is not always mirthful.

'A girl,' he said, 'mother, who would bring another fortune to the family: who would deluge us with money, and fill out the lines of the estates, and make peace – peace between me and – And not a bad girl either,' he added with a softening tone, 'far too good for me. An honest, upright little soul, only not – the best; only not the one who – would hate me if she knew –'

'Walter,' said Mrs. Methven, trembling, 'I don't understand you. Your words seem very wild to me. I am all confused with them, and my brain seems to be going. What is it you mean? Oh, if you would tell me all you mean and not only a part which I cannot understand!'

There never happens in any house a conversation of a vital kind, which is not interrupted at a critical moment by the entrance of the servants, those legitimate intruders who can never be staved off. It was Symington now who came in with tea, which, with a woman's natural desire to prevent any suspicion of agitation in the family, she accepted. When he had gone the whole atmosphere was changed. Walter had seated himself by the fire with the newspapers which had just come in, and all the emotion and *attendrissement* [23] were over. He said to her, looking up from his reading – 'By-the-bye,[a] mother, Julia Herbert is here with some cousins; they will be sure to call on you. But I don't want to have any more to do with them than we can help. You will manage that?'

'Julia Herbert,' she said. The countenance which had melted into so much softness, froze again and grew severe. 'Here! why should she be here? Indeed, I hope I shall be able to manage that, as you say.'

But oh, what ignoble offices for a woman who would have given her life for him as he knew! To frighten away Underwood, to 'manage' Julia. Patience! so long as it was for her boy.

# CHAPTER VI.[b]

ON the next morning after his mother's arrival, Lord Erradeen set out early for Birkenbraes. Everything pushed him towards a decision; even her prompt arrival, which he had not anticipated, and the clearing away from his path of the simpler and more easy difficulties that beset him, by her means. But what was far more than this was the tug at his heart, the necessity that lay before him to satisfy, one way or the other, the demands of his tyrant. He could not send away that spiritual enemy, who held him in his grip, as he did the vulgar influence of Underwood. *That* had disgusted him almost from the first; he had never tolerated it, even when he yielded to it; and the effort he had made in throwing it over had been exhilarating to him, and gave a certain satisfaction to his mind. But now that was over, and he had returned again to the original question, and found himself once more confronted by that opponent who could not be shaken off – who, one way or other, must be satisfied or vanquished, if life were to be possible. Vanquished? How was he to be vanquished? – by a pure man and a strong – by a pure woman and her love – by the help of God against a spiritual tyranny. He smiled to himself as he hurried along the road, thinking of the hopelessness of all this – himself neither pure nor strong; and Oona, who, if she knew – and God, whom, as his tempter had said, he had never sought nor thought of till now. He hurried along to try if the second best was within his reach; perhaps even that might fail him for anything he knew. The thought of meeting the usual party in the house of the Williamsons was so abhorrent to him, and such a disgust had risen in his mind of all the cheerful circumstances of the big, shining house, that he set out early with the intention of formally seeking an interview with Katie, and thus committing himself from the beginning. The morning was bright and fair, with a little shrill wind about, which brought the yellow leaves fluttering to his feet, and carried them across him as he walked – now detached and solitary, now in little drifts and heaps. He hurried along, absorbed in his own thoughts, shutting his eyes to the vision of the isle, as it lay all golden, russet, and brown upon the surface of the water which gave its colours back; Walter would not look nor see the boat pushing round the corner, with the back of Hamish's red shirt alone showing, as the prow came beyond the shade of the trees. He did not see the boat, and yet he knew it was there, and hurried, hurried on to escape all reminders. The great door at Birkenbraes stood open, as was its wont – the great stone steps lying vacant in the sunshine, and everything still about. It was the only hour at which the place was quiet. The men were out on the hill, the ladies following such rational occupations as they might have to resort to, and the house had an air of relief and repose. Walter felt that he pronounced his own fate when he asked to see Miss Williamson.

'Mr. Williamson is out, my lord,' the solemn functionary said, who was far more important and dignified than the master of the house. 'I asked to see Miss Williamson,' Lord Erradeen repeated, with a little impatience; and he saw the man's eyebrows raised.

So far as the servants were concerned, and through them the whole district, Walter's 'intentions' stood revealed.

Katie Williamson was alone. She was in her favourite room – the room especially given over to her amusements and occupations. It was not a small room, for such a thing scarcely existed in Birkenbraes. It was full of windows, great expanses of plate glass, through which the mountains and the loch appeared uninterrupted, save by a line of framework here and there, with a curious open-air effect. It was in one of the corners of the house, and the windows formed two sides of the brilliant place; on the others were mirrors reflecting the mountains back again. She sat between them, her little fair head the only solid thing which the light encountered. When she rose, with a somewhat astonished air, to receive her visitor, her trim figure, neat and alert, stood out against the background of the trees and rocks on the lower slopes of the hills. A curious transparency, distinctness, and absence of privacy and mystery were in the scene. The two seemed to stand together there in the sight of all the world.

'Lord Erradeen!' Katie said, with surprise, almost consternation. 'But if I had been told, I should have come down-stairs[a] to you. Nobody but my great friends, nobody but women, ever come here.'[b]

'I should have thought that any one might come. There are no concealments here,' he said, expressing the sentiment of the place unconsciously. Then, seeing that Katie's colour rose: 'Your boudoir is not all curtained and shadowy, but open and candid – as you are.'

'That last has saved you,' said Katie, with a laugh. 'I know what you mean – and that is that my room (for it is not a boudoir – I never *boude*)[24] is far too light, too clear for the fashion. But this is my fashion, and people who come to me must put up with it.' She added, after a moment: 'What did you say to Sanderson, Lord Erradeen, to induce him to bring you here?'

'I said I wanted to see Miss Williamson.'

'That was understood,' said Katie, once more with an increase of colour, and looking at him with a suppressed question in her eyes. Her heart gave a distinct knock against her breast, but did not jump up and flutter, as hearts less well regulated will do in such circumstances; for she too perceived what Sanderson had perceived, that the interview was not one to take place amid all the interruptions of the drawing-room. Sanderson was a very clever person, and his young mistress agreed with him; but, nevertheless, made a private memorandum that he should have notice, and that she would speak to papa.

'Yes, I think it must be easily understood. I have come to you with a great deal that is very serious to say.'

'You look very serious,' said Katie; and then she added, hurriedly, 'And I want very much to speak to you, Lord Erradeen. I want you to tell me – who was that gentleman at Kinloch Houran? I have never been able to get him out of my mind. Is he paying you a visit? What is his name? Has he been in this country before? But oh, to be sure, he must have been, for he knew everything about the castle. I want to know, Lord Erradeen –'

'After you have heard what I have got to say –'

'No, not after – before. I tremble when I think of him. It is ridiculous, I know; but I never had any such sensation before. I should think he must be a mesmerist, or something of that sort,' Katie said, with a pale and nervous smile; 'though I don't believe in mesmerism,' she added, quickly.

'You believe in nothing of the kind – is it not so? You put no faith in the stories about my family, in the influence of the past on the present, in the despotism – But why say anything on that subject. You laugh.'

'I believe in superstition,' said Katie somewhat tremulously, 'and that it impresses the imagination, and puts you in a condition to believe – things. And then there is a pride in having anything of the sort connected with one's own family,' she said recovering herself. 'If it was our ghost I should believe in it too.'

'Ghost – is not a word that means much?' Walter said. And then there was a pause. It seemed to him that his lips were sealed, and that he had no longer command of the ordinary words. He had known what he had meant to say when he came, but the power seemed to have gone from him. He stood and looked out upon the wide atmosphere, and the freedom of the hills, with a blank in his mind, and that sense that nothing is any longer of importance or meaning which comes to those who are baffled in their purpose at the outset. It was Katie who with a certain sarcasm in her tone recalled him to himself. 'You came – because you had something serious to say to me, Lord Erradeen.' She was aware of what he intended to say; but his sudden pause at the very beginning had raised the mocking spirit in Katie. She was ready to defy and provoke, and silence with ridicule, the man whom she had no objection to accept as her husband – provided he found his voice.

'It is true – I had something very serious to say. I came to ask you whether you could –' All this time he was not so much as looking at her; his eyes were fixed dreamily and rather sadly upon the landscape, which somehow seemed so much more important than the speck of small humanity which he ought to have been addressing. But at this point Walter recollected himself, and came in as it were from the big, silent, observing world, to Katie, sitting expectant, divided between mockery and excitement, with a flush on her cheeks, but a contraction of her brows, and an angry yet smiling mischief in her eyes.

'To ask you,' he said, 'whether you would – pass your life with me. I am not much worth the taking. There is a poor title, there is a family which we might restore and – emancipate perhaps. You are rich, it would be of no advantage to you. But at all events it would not be like asking you to banish yourself, to leave all you cared for. I have little to say for myself,' he went on after a pause with a little more energy, 'you know me well enough. Whether I should ever be good for anything would – most likely – rest with you. I am at present under great depression – in trouble and fear –'

Here he came to another pause, and looked out upon the silent mountains and great breadths of vacant air in which there was nothing to help: then with a sigh turned again and held out his hand. 'Will you have me – Katie?' he said.

Katie sat gazing at him with a wonder which had by degrees extinguished the sarcasm, the excitement, the expectation, that were in her face. She was almost awestricken by this strangest of all suits that could be addressed to a girl – a demand for herself which made no account of herself, and missed out love and every usual preliminary. It was serious indeed – as serious as death: more like that than the beginning of the most living of all links. She could not answer him with the indignation which in other circumstances she might have felt. It was too solemn for any ebullition of feeling. She felt overawed, little as this mood was congenial to her.

'Lord Erradeen,' she said, 'you seem to be in great trouble.'

He made an affirmative movement of his head, but said no more.

'– Or you would not put such a strange question to me,' she went on. 'Why should I have you? When a man offers himself to a girl he says it is because he loves her. You don't love me –'

She made a momentary breathless pause with a half-hope[a] of being interrupted; but save by a motion of his hand, Walter made no sign. 'You don't love me,' she went on with some vehemence, 'nor do you ask me to love you. Such a proposal might be an insult. But I don't think you mean it as an insult.'

'Not that. You know better. Anything but that!'

'No – I don't think it is that. But what is it then, Lord Erradeen?'

Her tone had a certain peremptory sound which touched the capricious spring by which the young man's movements were regulated. He came to himself. 'Miss Williamson,' he said, 'when you ran away from me in London it was imminent that I should ask you this question. It was expected on all sides. You went away, I have always believed, to avoid it.'

'Why should it have been imminent? I went away,' cried Katie, forgetting the contradiction, 'because some one came in who seemed to have a prior right. She is here now with the same meaning.'

'She has no prior right. She has no right at all, nor does she claim any,' he said hurriedly. 'It is accident. Katie! had you stayed, all would have been determined then, and one leaf of bitter folly left out of my life.'

'Supposing it to be so,' she said calmly, 'I am not responsible for your life, Lord Erradeen. Why should I be asked to step in and save you from – bitter folly or anything else? And this life that you offer me, are you sure it is fit for an honest girl to take? The old idea that a woman should be sacrificed to reform a man has gone out of fashion.[25] Is that the *rôle* you want me to take up?' Katie cried, rising to her feet in her excitement. 'Captain Underwood (whose word I would never take) said you were bad, unworthy a good woman. Is that true?'

'Yes,' he said in a low tone, 'it is true.'

Katie gazed at him for a moment, and then in her excitement sat down and cried, covering her face with her hands. She it was, though she was not emotional, who was overcome with feeling. Walter stood gazing at her with a sort

316     *The Selected Works of Margaret Oliphant, Volume 21*

of stupefaction, seeing the scene pass with a sense that he was a spectator rather than an actor in it, his dark figure swaying slightly against the clearness of the landscape which took so strange a part in all that was happening. It had passed now altogether out of his hands.

As for Katie, it would be impossible to tell what sudden softening, what pity, mingled with keen vexation and annoyance, forced these tears from her eyes. Her heart revolted against him and melted towards him all at once. Her pride would not let her accept such a proposal; and yet she would have liked to accept him, to take him in hand, to be his providence, and the moulder of his fate. A host of hurrying thoughts and sentiments rushed headlong through her mind. She had it in her to do it, better than any silly woman of the world, better than a creature of visionary soul like Oona. She was practical, she was strong, she could do it. But then all her pride rose up in arms. She wept a few hot impatient tears which were irrestrainable: then raised her head again.

'I am very sorry for you,' she said. 'If you were my brother, Lord Erradeen, I would help you with all my might, or if I – cared for you more than you care for me. But I don't,' she added after a pause.

He made an appealing, deprecating movement with his hands, but did not speak.

'I almost wish I did,' said Katie regretfully; 'if I had been fond of you I should have said yes: for you are right in thinking I could do it. I should not have minded what went before. I should have taken you up and helped you on. I know that I could have done it; but then I am not – fond of you,' she said slowly. She did not look at him as she spoke; but had he renewed his claim upon her, even with his eyes, Katie would have seen it, and might have allowed herself to be persuaded still. But Walter said nothing. He stood vaguely in the light, without a movement, accepting whatever she might choose to say. She remained silent for a time, waiting. And then Katie sprang to her feet again, all the more indignant and impatient that she had been so near yielding, had he but known. 'Well!' she said, 'is it I that am to maintain the conversation? Have you anything more to say, Lord Erradeen?'

'I suppose not,' he answered slowly. 'I came to you hoping perhaps for deliverance, at least partial – for deliverance – Now that you will not, there is nothing for it but a struggle to the death.'

She looked at him with a sort of vertigo of amazement. Not a word about her, no regret for losing her, not a touch of sentiment, of gratitude, not even any notice of what she had said! The sensation of awe came back to her as she stood before this insensibility which was half sublime.[a] Was he mad? or a wretch, an egotist, wanting a woman to do something for him, but without a thought for the woman?

'I am glad,' she said, with irrepressible displeasure, 'that it affects you so little. And now I suppose the incident is over and we may return to our occupations. I was busy – with my housekeeping,' she said with a laugh. 'One might sometimes call a struggle with one's bills a struggle to the death.'

*The Wizard's Son, Volume III* 317

He gave her a look which was half-anger, half-remonstrance;[a] and then to Katie's amazement resumed in a moment the tone of easy intercourse which had always existed between them.

'You will find your bills refreshing after this high-flown talk,' he said. 'Forgive me. You know I am not given to romantic sentiment any more than yourself.'

'I don't know,' said Katie, offended, 'that I am less open to the romantic than other people when the right touch is given.'

'But it is not my hand that can give the right touch?' he said. 'I accept my answer as there is nothing else for me to do. But I cannot abandon the country,' he added after a moment, 'and I hope we may still meet as good friends.'

'Nothing has happened,' said Katie with dignity, 'to lessen my friendship for you, Lord Erradeen.' She could not help putting a faint emphasis on the pronouns. The man rejected may dislike to meet the woman who has rejected him, but the woman can have no feeling in the matter. She held out her hand with a certain stateliness of dismissal. 'Papa need not know,' she said, 'and so there will be nothing more about it. Good-bye.'

Walter took her hand in his, with a momentary perception that perhaps there had been more than lay on the surface in this interview, on her side as well as his. He stooped down and kissed it respectfully, and even with something like tenderness. 'You do not refuse it to me, in friendship, even after all you have heard?'

'It shall always be yours in friendship,' Katie said, the colour rising high in her face.

She was glad he went away without looking at her again. She sat down and listened to his footsteps along the long corridor and down the stairs with a curious sensation as if he carried something with him that would not return to her again. And for long after she sat in the broad daylight without moving, leaving the books upon the table – which were not housekeeping[b] books – untouched – going over this strange interview, turning over all the past that had any connection with Lord Erradeen. It seemed all to roll out before her like a story that had been full of interest: and now here was the end of it. Such a fit of wistful sadness had seldom come over the active and practical intelligence of Katie. It gave her for the moment a new opening in nature. But by degrees her proper moods came back. She closed this poetical chapter with a sigh, and her sound mind took up with a more natural regret the opportunity for congenial effort which she had been compelled to give up. She said to herself that she would not have minded that vague badness which he had owned, and Underwood had accused him of. She could have brought him back. She had it in her to take the charge even of a man's life. So she thought in inexperience, yet with the powerful confidence which so often is the best means of fulfilling triumphantly what it aims at. She would not have shrunk from the endeavour. She would have put her vigorous young will into his feeble one, she thought, and made him, with her force poured into him, a man indeed, contemptuous of all miserable temptations, able to sail over and despise them. As she mused her eyes took an eager look, her very fingers twitched with the wish to be doing. Had he come back then it is very possible that Katie would have announced to him her change of mind, her determination 'to pull him through.' For she could have done it! she repeated to herself. Whatever his burdens had been, when she had once set her shoulder to the wheel she would have done it. Gambling, wine, even the spells of such women as Katie blushed to think of – she would have shrunk before none of these. His deliverance would not have been partial, as he had said, but complete. She would have fought the very devils for him and brought him off. What a work it was that she had missed! not a mere commonplace marriage with nothing to do. But with a sigh Katie had to acknowledge that it was over. She could not have accepted him, she said, excusing herself to herself. It would have been impossible. A man who asks you like *that*, not even pretending to care for you – you could not do it! But, alas! what an opportunity lost! Saying this she gave herself a shake, and smoothed her hair for luncheon, and put the thought away from her resolutely. Katie thought of Dante's nameless sinner who made 'the great refusal.'[26] She had lost perhaps the one great opportunity of her life.

# CHAPTER VII.[a]

LORD ERRADEEN retired very quietly, as became a man defeated. Though Katie heard his retiring steps, he hardly did so himself, as he came down the broad softly-carpeted[b] stair-case. There was a sound of voices and of movement in the great dining-room, where a liveried army were preparing the table for one of the great luncheons, under the orders of the too discreet and understanding Sanderson – but nobody about to see the exit of the rejected suitor, who came out into the sunshine with a sort of dim recognition of the scenery of Katie's boudoir; but the hills did not seem so near as they were in that large-windowed and shining place. Failure has always a subduing effect upon the mind even when success was scarcely desired; and Walter came out of the great house with the sense of being cut off from possibilities that seemed very near, almost certain, that morning. This subduing influence was the first that occupied his mind as he came out, feeling as if he were stealing away from the scene of what had been far from a triumph. Perhaps he was a little ashamed of his own certainty; but at all events he was subdued and silent, refraining almost from thought.[c]

He had got securely out of the immediate neighbourhood, and was safe from the risk of meeting any one belonging to it, and being questioned where he had been, before he began to feel the softening of relief, and a grateful sense of freedom. Then his heart recurred with a bound to the former situation. Expedients or compromises of any kind were no more to be thought of; the battle must be fought out on its natural ground. He must yield to the ignominious yoke, or he must conquer. Last year he had fled, and forced himself to forget, and lived in a fever of impulses which he could not understand, and influences which drew him like – he could not tell like what – mesmerism, Katie had said, and perhaps she was right. It might be mesmerism; or it might be only the action of that uncontrolled and capricious mind which made him do that to-day which he loathed to-morrow. But however it was, the question had again become a primary one, without any compromise possible. He must yield, or he must win the battle. He put the losing first, it seemed so much the most likely, with a dreary sense of all the impossibilities that surrounded him. He had no standing ground upon which to meet his spiritual foe. Refusal, what was that? It filled his life with distraction and confusion, but made no foundation for anything better, and afforded no hope of peace. Peace! The very word seemed a mockery to Walter. He must never know what it was. His soul (if he had one)[27] would not be his own; his impulses, hitherto followed so foolishly, would be impotent for everything but to follow the will of another. To abdicate his own judgment altogether, to give up that power of deciding for himself which is the inheritance of the poorest, never to be able to help a poor neighbour, to aid a friend: to be a mere puppet in the hands of another – was it possible that he, a man, was to give himself up, thus bound hand and foot, to a slavery harder than that of any negro ever born? It was this that was impossible he cried within himself.

And then there suddenly came before Walter, like a vision set before him by the angels, a gleam of the one way of escape. When a poor wretch has fallen into a pit, a disused quarry, perhaps, or an old coal-pit, or a still more eerie dungeon, there shines over him, far off, yet so authentic, a pure, clear intensity of light above, a concentrated glory of the day, a sort of opening of heaven in his sight. This is the spot of light, more beautiful than any star, which is all that the walls of his prison permit him to see of the common day, which above-ground[a] is lavished around us in such a prodigal way that we make no account of it. There are times when the common virtues of life, the common calm and peacefulness, take an aspect like this to the fallen soul: – the simple goodness which, perhaps, he has scoffed at and found tame and unprofitable, appearing to the spirit in prison like heaven itself, so serene and so secure. To think he himself has fallen from that, might have possessed and dwelt in it, safe from all censure and dishonour, if he had not been a fool! To think that all the penalties to which he has exposed himself might never have existed at all – if he had not been a fool! To think that now if some miracle would but raise him up to it – And then there are moments in which even the most vicious, the most utterly fallen, can feel as if no great miracle would be required, as if a little help, only a little, would do it – when strength is subdued and low, when the sense of dissatisfaction is strong, and all the impulses of the flesh in abeyance, as happens at times. Walter's mind came suddenly to this conviction as he walked and mused. A good life, a pure heart, these were the things which would overcome – better, far better than any gain, than any sop given to fate; and he felt that all his desires went up towards these, and that there was nothing in him but protested against the degradation of the past. He had, he said to himself, never been satisfied, never been but disgusted with the riot and so-called pleasure. While he indulged in them he had loathed them, sinning contemptuously with a bitter scorn of himself and of the indulgences which he professed to find sweet.[a]

Strange paradox of a soul! which perceived the foulness of the ruin into which it had sunk, and hated it, yet sank deeper and deeper all the while. And now how willing he was to turn his back upon it all, and how easy it seemed to rise with a leap to the higher level and be done with everything that was past! The common goodness of the simple people about seemed suddenly to him like a paradise in which was all that was lovely. To live among your own, to do them good, to be loved and honoured, to have a history pure and of good report,[28] nothing in it to give you a blush; to love a pure and good woman, and have her for your companion all your life – how easy, how simple, how safe it was! And what tyrant out of the unseen could rule a man like this, or disturb his quiet mastery of himself and all that belonged to him? Once upon that standing ground and who could assail you? And it seemed at that moment so easy and so near. Everything round was wholesome, invigorating, clear with the keen purity of nature, fresh winds blowing in his face, air the purest and clearest, inspiring body and soul, not a lurking shade of temptation anywhere, everything tending to goodness, nothing to evil.

'And you think these pettifogging little virtues will deliver *you*,'[b] said some one quietly by his side.

There were two figures walking along in the wintry sunshine instead of one – that was all. The stone-cutter on the road who had seen Lord Erradeen pass and given him a good morning,[c] rubbed his eyes when next he paused to rest and looked along the road. He saw two gentlemen where but one had been, though it was still so early and 'no a drap' had crossed his lips. 'And a pretty man!' he said to himself with mingled amazement and admiration. As for Walter, it was with an instinctive recoil that he heard the voice so near to him, but that not because of any supernatural sensation, though with an annoyance and impatience inexpressible that any one should be able to intrude on his privacy and thus fathom his thoughts.

'This is scarcely an honourable advantage you take of your powers.'

The other took no notice of this reproach. 'A good man,' he said, 'a good husband, a good member of society, surrounded by comfort on all sides and the approbation of the world. I admire the character as much as you do. Shall I tell you what this good man is? He is the best rewarded of all the sons of men. Everything smiles upon him: he has the best of life. Everything he does counts in his favour. And you think that such a man can stand against a purpose like mine? But for that he would want a stronger purpose than mine. Goodness,' he continued reflectively, 'is the best policy in the world. It never fails. Craft may fail, and skill and even wisdom, and the finest calculations; but the good always get their reward. A prize falls occasionally to the other qualities, but theirs is the harvest of life. To be successful you have only to be good. It is far the safest form of self-seeking, and the best.' He had fallen into a reflective tone, and walked along with a slight smile upon his lips, delivering with a sort of abstract authority his monologue, while Walter, with an indescribable rage and mortification and confusion of all his thoughts, accompanied him like a schoolboy overpowered by au authority against which his very soul was rebel. Then the speaker turned upon his companion with a sort of benevolent cordiality. 'Be good!' he said. 'I advise it – it is the easiest course you can pursue: you will free yourself from by far the worst part of the evils common to humanity. Nothing is so bad as the self-contempt under which I have seen you labouring, the shame of vice for which you have no true instinct, only a sham appetite invented by the contradictoriness of your own mind. Be good! it pays better than anything else in life.'

Here Walter interrupted him with an exclamation of anger irrestrainable. 'Stop!' he cried, 'you have tortured me by my sins, and because I had nothing better to fall back upon. Will you make this more odious still?'[a]

'By no means,' said the other, calmly. 'You think I want you to be miserable? You are mistaken – I don't. Seeking the advantage of my race as I do, there is nothing I more desire than that you should have the credit of a spotless life. I love reputation. Be good! it is the most profitable of all courses. I repeat that whatever may fail that never does. Your error is to think that it will free you from me. So far as concerns me it would probably do you more injury than good; for it may well be that I shall have to enforce measures which will revolt you and make you unhappy. But then you will have compensations. The world will believe that only bad advisers or mistaken views could move so good a man to appear on occasions a hard landlord, a tyrannical master. And then your virtue will come in with expedients to modify the secondary effect of my plans and soften suffering. I do not desire suffering. It will be in every way to our advantage that you should smooth down and soften and pour balm into the wounds which in the pursuit of a higher purpose it is necessary to make. Do not interrupt: it is the *rôle* I should have recommended to you, if, instead of flying out like a fool, you had left yourself from the first in my hands.'

'I think you must be the devil,' Walter said.

'No; nor even of his kind: that is another mistake. I have no pleasure in evil any more than in suffering, unless my object makes it necessary. I should like you to do well.[b] It was I, was it not, that set before you the miserableness of the life you have been leading? which you had never faced before. Can you suppose that I should wish greatness to the race and misfortune to its individual members? Certainly not. I wish you to do well. You could have done so, and lived very creditably with the girl whom you have just left, whom you have driven into refusing you. Take my advice – return to her, and all will be well.'

'You have a right to despise me,' said Walter, quivering with passion and self-restraint. 'I did take your advice, and outraged her and myself. But that is over, and I shall take your advice no more.'

'You are a fool for your pains,' he said. 'Go back now and you will find her mind changed. She has thought it over. What! you will not? I said it in your interest, it was your best chance. You could have taken up that good life which I recommend to you with all the more success had there been a boundless purse to begin upon. Poor it is not so easy: but still you can try. Your predecessor was of that kind. There was nothing in him that was bad, poor fellow. He was an agglomeration of small virtues. Underwood was his one vice, a fellow who played cards with him and amused him. No one, you will find, has anything to say against him; he was thought weak, and so he was – against me. But that did not hinder him from being good.'

'In the name of Heaven what do you call yourself, that can speak of good and evil as if they were red and blue!' the young man cried. Passion cannot keep always at a climax. Walter's mind ranged from high indignation, rage, dismay, to a wonder that was almost impersonal, which sometimes reached the intolerable point, and burst out into impatient words. It seemed impossible to endure the calm of him, the reason of him, as he walked along the hilly road like any other man.

'It is not amiss for a comparison,' he answered with a smile. His composure was not to be disturbed. He made no further explanations. While he played upon the young man beside him as on an instrument, he himself remained absolutely calm. 'But these are abstractions,' he resumed, 'very important to you in your individual life, not so important to me who have larger affairs in hand. There is something however which will have to be decided almost immediately about the island property. I told you that small business about the cotters in the glen was a bagatelle. On the whole, though I thought it folly at the time, your action in the matter was serviceable. A burst of generosity has a fine effect. It is an example of what I have been saying. It throws dust in the eyes of the world. Now we can proceed with vigour on a larger scale.'

'If you mean to injure the poor tenants, never! and whatever you mean, no,' cried Walter, 'I will not obey you. Claim your rights, if you have any rights, publicly.'

'I will not take that trouble. I will enforce them through my descendant.'

'No! you can torture me, I am aware, but something I have learned since last year.'

'You have learned,' said his companion calmly, 'that your theatrical benevolence was not an unmixed good, that your *protégés* whom you kept to that barren glen would have been better off had they been dislodged cruelly from their holes. The question in its larger forms is not to be settled from that primitive point of view. I allow,' he said with a smile, 'that on the whole that was well done. It leaves us much more free for operations now. It gives a good impression – a man who in spite of his kind heart feels compelled to carry out –'

'You are a demon,' cried the young man, stung beyond endurance. 'You make even justice a matter of calculation, even the natural horror of one's mind. A kind heart! is that like a spade, an instrument in your hands?'

'The comparison is good again,' said his companion with a laugh; 'your faculty that way is improving. But we must have no trifling about the matter in hand. The factor from the isles is not a fool like this fellow here, whom I tolerate because he has his uses too. The other will come to you presently, he will lay before you –'

'I will not hear him – once for all I refuse –'

'What, to receive your own servant?' said the other. 'Come, this is carrying things too far. You must hear, and see, and consent. There is no alternative, except –'

'Except – if it comes to that, what can you do to me?' asked Walter, ghastly with that rending of the spirit which had once more begun within him, and with the host of fierce suggestions that surged into his mind. He felt as men feel when they are going mad, when the wild intolerance of all conditions which is the root of insanity mounts higher and higher in the brain – when there is nothing that can be endured, nothing supportable, and the impulse to destroy and ravage, to uproot trees and beat down mountains, to lay violent hands upon something, sweeps like a fiery blast across the soul. Even in madness there is always a certain self-restraint. He knew that it would be vain to seize the strong and tranquil man who stood before him, distorting everything in heaven and earth with his calm consistency: therefore in all the maddening rush of impulse *that* did not suggest itself. 'What can you do to me?' How unnecessary was the question! What he could do was sensible in every point, in the torrent of excitement that almost blinded, almost deafened the miserable young man. He saw his enemy's countenance as through a mist, a serene and almost beautiful face – looking at him with a sort of benevolent philosophical pity which quickened the flood of passion. His own voice was stifled in his throat, he could say no more. Nor could he hear for the ringing in his ears, what more his adversary was saying to him – something wildly incoherent he thought, about Prospero, Prospero! 'Do you think I am Prospero to send you aches and stitches?'[29] The words seemed to circle about him in the air, half mockery,[a] half folly. What had that to do with it? He walked along mechanically, rapt in an atmosphere of his own, beating the air like a drowning man.

How long this horror lasted he could never tell. While still those incomprehensible syllables were wavering about him, another voice suddenly made itself heard, a touch came upon his arm. He gave a violent start, recoiling from the touch, not knowing what it was. By degrees, however, as the giddiness went off, he began to see again, to perceive slowly coming into sight those mountains that had formed the background in Katie's room, and to hear the soft wash of the waters upon the beach. He found himself standing close to the loch, far below the road upon which he had been walking. Had he rushed down to throw himself into the water, and thus end the terrible conflict? He could never tell. Or whether it was some angel that had arrested the terrible impulse. When the mist dispersed from his eyes he saw this angel in a red shirt standing close to him, looking at him with eyes that peered out beneath the contraction of a pair of shaggy sandy eyebrows, from an honest freckled face. 'My lord! you'll maybe no have seen Miss Oona?' Hamish said. And Walter heard himself burst into a wild laugh that seemed to fill the whole silent world with echoes. He caught hold of the boatman's arm with a grasp that made even Hamish shrink. 'Who sent you here?' he cried; 'who sent you here? Do you come from God?' He did not know what he said.

'My lord! you mustna take that name in vain. I'm thinking the Almighty has a hand in maist things, and maybe it was just straight from Him I've come, though I had no suspicion o' that,' Hamish said. He thought for the first moment it was a madman with whom he had to do. Walter had appeared with a rush down the steep bank, falling like some one out of the skies, scattering the pebbles on the beach, and Hamish had employed Oona's name in the stress of the moment as something to conjure with. He was deeply alarmed still as he felt the quiver in the young man's frame, which communicated itself to Hamish's sturdy arm. Madness frightens the most stout-hearted. Hamish was brave enough, as brave as a High-lander need be, but he was half alarmed for himself, and much more for Oona, who might appear at any moment. 'I'll just be waiting about and nothing par-ticular to do,' he said in a soothing tone; 'if ye'll get into the boat, my lord, I'll just put your lordship hame. Na, it's nae trouble, nae trouble.' Hamish did not like the situation; but he would rather have rowed twenty maniacs than put Oona within reach of any risk. He took Lord Erradeen by the elbow and directed him towards the boat, repeating the kindly invitation of his country – 'Come away, just come away; I've naething particular to do, and it will just be a pleasure.'

'Hamish,' said Walter, 'you think I am out of my mind: but you are mistaken, my good fellow. *I* think you have saved my life, and I will not forget it. What was that you said about Miss Oona!'[a]

Hamish looked earnestly into the young man's face.

'My lord,' he began with hesitation, 'you see – if a young gentleman is a thocht out of the way, and just maybe excited about something and no altogether his ain man – what's that to the like of me? Never a hair o' hairm would that do to Ham-ish. But when it's a leddy, and young and real tender-hearted! We maun aye think o' them, my lord, and spare them – the weemen. No, it's what we dinna do – they have the warst in a general way to bear. But atween you and me, my lord, that though you're far my shuperior, are just man and man – '

'It is you that are my superior, Hamish,' said Lord Erradeen; 'but look at me now and say if you think I am mad. You have saved me. I am fit to speak to her now. Do you think I would harm her? Not for anything in the world.'

'No if you were – yoursel' – Lord Erradeen.'

'But I am – myself. And the moment has come when I must know. Take my hand, Hamish; look at me. Do you think I am not to be trusted with Oona?'

'My lord, to make Hamish your judge, what's that but daft too? And what right have ye to call my young leddy by her name? You're no a drap's blood to them, nor even a great friend.'

Oona's faithful guardian stood lowering his brows upon the young lord with a mingled sense of the superiority of his office, and of disapproval, almost contemptuous, of the madman who had given it to him. That he should make Hamish the judge was mad indeed. And yet Hamish was the judge, standing on his right to defend his mistress. They stood looking at each other, the boatman holding his shaggy head high, reading the other's face with the keenest scrutiny. But just then there came a soft sound into the air, a call from the bank, clear, with that tone, not loud but penetrating, which mountaineers use everywhere.

'Are you there, Hamish?' Oona cried.

\*\*\*

# CHAPTER VIII.ᵃ

OONA's mind had been much disturbed, yet in no painful way, by the meeting with Mrs. Methven. The service which she had done to Walter's mother, the contact with her, although almost in the dark, the sense of approach to another woman whose mind was full of anxiety and thought for him, agitated her, yet seemed to heal and soften away the pain which other encounters had given her. It gave her pleasure to think of the half-seen face, made softer by the twilight, and of the tremor of expectation and anxiety that had been in it. There was somehow in this a kind of excuse to herself for her involuntary preoccupation with all that concerned him. She had felt that there was an unspoken sympathy between her and the stranger, and that it was something more than chance which brought them together. As the boat pushed off into the loch, and she felt she had left the mother to a certain happiness in her son, her heart beat with a subdued excitement. She felt with them both, divining the soul of the mother who came to him with trembling, not approving perhaps, not fully trusting, but loving; and of the son who was at fault, who had not shown her the tenderness which her love merited in return. The sense of that union so incomplete in fact, and so close in nature, filled Oona with emotion. As the boat glided along the glittering pathway of the lake between the reflected banks, her mind was full of the two who had gone away together arm and arm into the soft darkness. How mysterious was that twilight world, the eye incapable in the dimness of perceiving which was the substance and which the shadow of those floating woods and islands! Sometimes the boat would glide into the tangled reflections of the trees, sometimes strike through what seemed a headland, a wall of rock, a long projecting promontory in this little world of water, where nothing was as it seemed. But it was not half so mysterious as life. It was but lately that this aspect of existence had struck the healthful soul of the Highland girl. Till the last year all had been open and sweet as the day about her ways and thoughts. If she had any secrets at all they had been those which even the angels guard between themselves and God, those sacred enthusiasms for the one Love that is above all: those aspirations towards the infinite which are the higher breath of gentle souls; or perhaps a visionary opening into the romance of life in its present form, which was scarcely less visionary and pure. But nothing else, nothing more worldly, nothing that her namesake, 'heavenly Una with her milkwhite lamb,'[30] need have hesitated to avow.[a]

But since then Oona had gone far[b] and wandered wide in a shadowy world which she shared with no one, and in which there were mystic forces beyond her fathoming, influences which caught the wanderer all unwitting, and drew her hither or thither unawares, against her will. She was no longer the princess and sovereign of life as she had been in the earlier portion of it, but rather its subject or possible victim, moved by powers which she could not understand nor resist, and which overcame her before she was aware of their existence. She thought of all this as her boat made its way, propelled by the long, strong strokes of Hamish, amid the shadows; but not angrily, not miserably as she had sometimes done, with a sadness which (if it was sadness at all) was sweet, and a secret exhilaration for which she could not account. The mother seemed somehow to step into the visionary conflict which was going on, a half-seen, unknown, but powerful champion on the side of – Was it on the side of Oona? She shrank a little from that identification, and said to herself, on the side of good. For that there was a struggle going on between good and evil, which in some mysterious way centred in Lord Erradeen, she was mysteriously aware, she could not tell how.

'Yon young lord will be the better of his mother,' Hamish was saying, his voice coming to her vaguely, running on without any thought of reply, mingled with the larger sound of the oars upon the rowlocks, the long sweep of them through the loch, the gurgle and tinkle of the water as the boat cut through. Hamish was faintly visible and even retained till it grew quite dark some trace of colour in his favourite garment. 'He'll be the better of his mother,' he said; 'there will aye be a want when there's no a leddy in the house. Weeman servants are no to lippen to. A young man when he has not a wife, he will be muckle the better for his mother.'

Oona heard the words vaguely like a chant amid all those sounds of the loch which were the music and accompaniment of her own being. She ran up the slope when they landed, and burst into the little drawing-room which was so bright after the darkness of the evening world, with a pleasure in her little adventure, and in having something to tell which is only known in the deep recesses, the unbroken quiet of rural life. Mrs. Forrester was just beginning, as she herself said, to 'weary' for Oona's return. She had put down her knitting and taken a book. Again she had put aside her book and taken the knitting. Oona was late.

*The Wizard's Son, Volume III*     327

Oona meant the world and life to the solitary lady on the crest of the isle. The house, the little retired nest amid the trees, was full and cheerful when she was there, and though Mysie and the cook, 'ben the house,' gave now and then a sign of life, yet nothing was complete until the sound of the boat drawn up on the shingle, the unshipping oars,[a] the light firm foot on the path, followed by the heavier tread, scattering the gravel, of Hamish, gave token that all the little population were gathered within the circle of their rocks and waters. Then Mrs. Forrester brightened and turned her face towards the door with cheerful expectation: for it became a little too cold now to go down to the beach to meet the boat, even with the fur cloak upon her shoulders, which had been her wont on summer nights, and even on wintry days.

'His mother, poor young man! Dear me, that is very interesting, Oona. I was not sure he had a mother. That's good news: for I always took an interest in Lord Erradeen, like one of our own boys. Indeed, you know, Oona, I always thought him like Rob, though their complexions are different. Dear me! I am very glad you were on the spot, and able to show her a little civility. But he should have been there, oh! he should have been there, to meet her. If any of the boys were to do that to me, I would not know what to think – to leave me to the civility of any person that might be passing. Oh, fie! no, I would not know what to think.'

'I know what you would think,' said Oona, 'that there must have been some mistake, that they did not know the hour of the train, or did not know which train, or that they had been too late of starting, or – something. You would be sure to find a good reason, mamma.'

'Well, that's true, Oona; no doubt it would be something of that kind, for it is impossible that a nice lad (and Lord Erradeen was always that) would show himself neglectful of his mother. Poor lady! and she would be tired after her journey. I am very glad you were there to show her a little attention. She will perhaps think, as so many of those English do, that we're cold and distant in the north. My dear, you can just ring for the tea: and we'll go and call upon her to-morrow, Oona. Well, perhaps not to-morrow; but wait till she is well rested. We'll go on Thursday, and you can just mention it about, wherever you are tomorrow, that everybody may know. It is such a fine thing for a young man to have his mother with him (when he has not a wife), that we must give her a warm welcome, poor lady,' Mrs. Forrester said. She had no reason to call Mrs. Methven poor, but did it as a child does, with a meaning of kindness. She was in fact much pleased and excited by the news. It seemed to throw a gleam of possible comfort over the head of the loch. 'The late lord had no woman about him,' she said to herself after Oona had left the room. She had quite forgotten that she was beginning to 'weary.' 'Did you hear, Mysie,' she went on when 'the tea' appeared with all its wealth of scones, 'that Lord Erradeen was expecting his mother? I am almost as glad to hear it as if one of our own boys had come home.'

'It is a real good thing for the young lord, mem,' said Mysie; 'and no doubt you'll be going to see her, being such near neighbours, and my lord such great friends with the isle.'

'I would not say very great friends, oh no,' said Mrs. Forrester, deprecatory, but with a smile of pleasure on her face. 'There is little to tempt a young gentleman here. But no doubt we will call as soon as she is rested – Miss Oona and me.'

This formed the staple of their conversation all the evening, and made the little room cheerful with a sentiment of expectation.

'And what kind of a person did you find her, Oona? And do you think she will be a pleasant neighbour? And he was at the water-side to meet her, when he saw the boat? And was he kind? and did he show a right feeling?'

These questions Mrs. Forrester asked over and over again. She put herself in the place of the mother who had arrived so unexpectedly without any one to meet her.

'And you will be sure to mention it, whoever you see to-morrow,' she repeated several times, 'that she may see we have all a regard for him. I know by myself that is the first thing you think of,' Mrs. Forrester added with a pleasant smile. 'The boys' were everything they ought to be. There were no eccentricities, nothing out of the way, about them to make public opinion doubtful. Wherever they went, their mother, pleased, but not surprised, heard everything that was pleasant of them. She 'knew by herself' that this was what Walter's mother would want to hear.

And Oona 'mentioned it' to the Ellermore Campbells, with whom she had some engagement next morning, and where she met Miss Herbert from the Lodge. Julia was already popular with her nearest neighbours, and had an attendant at her side in the shape of a friend invited by Sir Thomas as an ardent sportsman, but of whom Julia had taken the command from his first appearance. She was in high spirits, finding everything go well with her, and slightly off her balance with the opening up of new prosperity. She threw herself into the discussion with all the certainty of an old acquaintance.

'I don't understand why you should be so pleased,' said Julia. 'Are you pleased? or is it only a make-believe? Oh, no, dear Oona; I do not suppose you are so naughty as that. You never were naughty in your life – was she? Never tore her pinafore, or dirtied her frock? It is pretty of you, all you girls, to take an interest in Walter's mother; but for my part I like young men best without their mothers,' Miss Herbert said, with a laugh, and a glance towards the attendant squire, who said to himself that here was a girl above all pretences, who knew better than to attempt to throw dust in the eyes of wise men like himself.

Some of the Ellermore girls laughed, for there is nothing that girls and boys are more afraid of than this reputation of never having dirtied their pinafores; while their mother, with the easy conviction of a woman so full of sons and daughters that she is glad, whenever she can, to shirk her responsibilities, said:

*The Wizard's Son, Volume III*

'Well, that is true enough: a young man should not be encumbered with an old woman; and if I were Mrs. Methven –'

'But thank Heaven, you are not at all like Mrs. Methven,' said Julia. 'She is always after that unfortunate boy. It did not matter where he went, he was never free of her. Sitting up for him, fancy! making him give her an account of everything. He had to count up how many times he came to see me.'

'Which perhaps would be difficult,' some one said.

Julia laughed – that laugh of triumph which disturbs feminine nerves.

'He did come pretty often,' she said, 'poor fellow. Oh, most innocently! to get me to play his accompaniments. Don't you know he sings? Oh, yes, very tolerably: if he would but open his mouth, I used to tell him; but some people like to be scolded, I think.'

'By you,' said the attendant in an undertone.

Julia gave him a look which repaid him.

'I always had to take his part. Poor Walter!' she said with a sigh. 'And then when I had him by myself I scolded him. Isn't that the right way? I used to get into great trouble about that boy,' she added. 'When one has known a person all one's life one can't help taking an interest – And he was so mismanaged in his youth.'

'Here is a Daniel come to judgment,'[31] said Jeanie Campbell: 'so much wiser than the rest of us. Lord Erradeen must be years older than you are. Let us call, mother, all the same, and see what sort of a dragon she is.'

'I shall call, of course,' the mother said; 'and I don't want to hear anything about dragons. I am one too, I suppose. Thank you, Oona, for telling me. I should not like to be wanting in politeness. Your mother will be going to-morrow, I shouldn't wonder? Well, we shall go the next day, girls. Erradeen marches with Ellermore, and I know your father wishes to pay every respect.'

'I suppose when you're a lord,' said Tom, who was very far down in the family, and of no account, 'you can go upon a rule of your own; but it would be far greater fun for Erradeen if he would mix himself up more with other people. Did anybody ever find out who that fellow was that was staying with him? Braithwaite thought he must be something very fine indeed – a foreign prince, or that sort. He said such a fellow couldn't be English without being well known. It seems he knew everybody, and everything you could think of. A tremendous swell,[32] according to Braithwaite. Oona, who was he? you ought to know.'

At this all eyes turned to Oona, who grew red in spite of herself.

'I have no way of knowing,' she said. 'I saw such a person once – but I never heard who he was.'

'I am not superstitious,' said Mrs. Campbell, 'but there are people seen about that old castle that – make your blood run cold. No, I never saw anything myself; but your father says – '

'My father never met this fellow,' cried Tom. 'He wasn't a fellow to make any mistake about. Neither old nor young – oh, yes, oldish: between forty and fifty; as straight as a rod, with eyes that go through and through you; and a voice – I think Erradeen himself funks him. Yes, I do. He turned quite white when he heard his voice.'

'There are all kinds of strange stories about that old castle,' said one of the Campbell sisters in an explanatory tone, addressing Julia. 'You must not be astonished if you hear of unearthly lights, and some dreadful ordeal the heir has to go through, and ghosts of every description.'

'I wish, Jeanie,' said Tom, 'when a fellow asks a question, that you would not break in with your nonsense. Who is talking of ghosts? I am asking who a fellow was – a very fine gentleman, I can tell you; something you don't see the like of often –' The young man was much offended by his sister's profanity. He went to the door with Oona, fuming. 'These girls never understand,' he said; 'they make a joke of everything. This was one of the grandest fellows I ever saw – and then they come in with their rubbish about ghosts!'

'Never mind,' Oona said, giving him her hand. The conversation somehow had been more than she herself could bear, and she had come away with a sense of perplexity and indignation. Tom, who was hot and indignant too, was more in sympathy with her than the others who talked about ghosts, which made her angry she could scarcely tell why.

'Let me walk with you,' said Julia Herbert, following. 'I have sent Major Antrobus to look after the carriage. He is a friend of my cousin Sir Thomas, and supposed to be a great sportsman, but not so devoted to slaughter as was hoped. Instead of slaughtering, he is slaughtered, Lady Herbert says. I am sure I don't know by whom. Do let me walk with you a little way. It is so nice to be with you.' Julia looked into Oona's face with something of the ingratiating air which she assumed to her victims of the other sex. 'Dear Miss Forrester –' and then she stopped with a laugh. 'I don't dare to call you by your Christian name.'

'It must be I then that am the dragon, though I did not know it,' Oona said; but she did not ask to be called by her Christian name.

'I see – you are angry with me for what I said of Mrs. Methven. It is quite true, however; that is the kind of woman she is. But I don't excuse Walter, for all that. He was very wicked to her. Ever since he was a boy at school he has been nasty to his mother. Everybody says it is her own fault, but still it was not nice of him, do you think? Oh, *I* think him very nice, in many ways. I have known him so long. He has always been most agreeable to me – sometimes *too* agreeable,' said Julia with a smile, pausing, dwelling upon the recollection. 'But his mother and he never got on. Sometimes those that are the very nicest out of doors are rather disagreeable at home. Haven't you seen that? Oh, I have, a hundred times. Of course the mother is sure to be to blame. She ought to have made a cheerful home for him, you know,

*The Wizard's Son, Volume III*          331

and asked young people, and cheerful people, instead of a set of fogies. But she never would do that. She expected him to put up with her old-fashioned ways.

Oona made no reply. She was disturbed in the ideal that had been rising within her – an ideal not all made up of sunshine and virtue, but where at least the darker shades were of a more elevated description than petty disobediences on one hand and exactions on the other. Life becomes mean and small when dragged down to this prosaic level, which was the natural level in Julia's mind, not pitiful and debasing, as it appeared to Oona. As there was no response to what she had said, Julia resumed, putting her hand with a great show of affection within Oona's arm.

'I want you to let me be your friend,' she said, 'and I don't want you to be deceived. I fear you think too well of people; and when you hear anything against them, then you feel displeased. Oh, yes, I know. You are not pleased with me for telling the truth about the Methvens.'

'I wonder rather,' said Oona, somewhat coldly, 'that being so much a friend of Lord Erradeen you should – betray him; for we should never have known this without you.'

'Oh, betray him; what hard words!' cried Julia, making believe to shrink and hide her face. 'I would not betray him for worlds, poor dear Walter, if I had a secret of his. But this is no secret at all,' she added, with a laugh; 'everybody knows they never got on. And between ourselves, Walter has been a sad bad boy. Oh, yes, there is no doubt about it. I know more of the world than a gentle creature like you, and I know that no man is very good. Oh, don't say a word, for you don't understand. There are none of them very good. What goes on when they are knocking about the world – we don't know what it is: but it is no good. Everybody that knows human nature knows that. But Walter has gone further, you know, than the ordinary. Oh, he has been a bad boy. He took up with Captain Underwood before he knew anything about Kinloch Houran, while he was not much more than a boy: and everybody knows what Captain Underwood is. He has gambled and betted, and done a great many still more dreadful things. And poor Mrs. Methven scolded and cried and nagged: and that has made everything worse.'

Oona's countenance changed very much during this conversation. It flushed and paled, and grew stern with indignation, and quivered with pity. It seemed to her that all that was said must be true: it had not the air of an invention. She asked, with a trembling voice, 'If this is so, how is it that you still care for him? still –' she would have said – pursue him; but Oona's womanly instincts were too strong for this, and she faltered and paused, and said, feebly, 'still – keep him in your thoughts?'

'Oh, we must not be too hard, you know,' said Julia, smiling; 'a man must sow his wild oats. Oh, I should myself had I been a man. I should not have been content with your humdrum life. I should have stormed all over the place and had a taste of everything. Don't you think it is better for them when they have been downright bad? I do; it makes them more humble. They know, if you came to inquire into them, there would not be a word to say for them. I think it is a good thing, for my part; I don't mind. I am not afraid of it. But still it must be confessed that Walter has been, oh! very bad! and unkind to his mother; not what people call a good son. And what is the use of her coming here? She is coming only to spoil sport, to poke her nose into everything. I have no patience with that kind of woman. Now I can see in your face you are quite shocked with me. You think it is I who am bad. But you know I have taken a great fancy to you, and I want you to know.'

'I have no wish to know,' said Oona. She had grown very pale – with the feeling of having been out in a storm and exposed to the beating of remorseless rain, the fierce hail that sometimes sweeps the hills. She heard Julia's laugh ringing through like something fiendish in the midst of her suffering. She was glad to escape, though beaten down and penetrated by the bitter storm. The silence was grateful to her, and to feel herself alone. She scarcely doubted that it was all true. There was something in Miss Herbert's tone which brought conviction with it: the levity and indulgence were abhorrent to Oona, but they sounded true. Julia pressed her hand as she turned back, saying something about Major Antrobus and the carriage, with a laugh at Oona's startled looks, 'Don't look so pale; you are too sensitive. It is nothing more than all of them do. Good-bye, dear,' Julia said. She bent forward with a half-offer[a] of a kiss, from which Oona shrank: and then went away laughing, calling out, 'People will think you have seen one of those ghosts.'

A ghost! Oona went upon her way, silent, aching in heart and spirit. What was a ghost, as they said, in comparison? No ghost but must know secrets that would at the least make levity and irreverence impossible. Nothing but a human voice could mock and jibe at that horror and mystery of evil before which Oona's spirit trembled. She had walked some way alone upon the daylight road, with the wholesome wind blowing in her face, and the calm of nature restoring her to composure, but not relieving the ache in her heart, before she came to the edge of the bank, and called in her clear voice to Hamish in the boat.

# CHAPTER IX.[b]

'LORD ERRADEEN!' His appearance was so unexpected, so curiously appropriate and inappropriate, that Oona felt as if she must be under some hallucination, and was beholding an incarnation of her own thoughts instead of an actual man.

And Walter was himself at so high a strain of excitement that the agitation of her surprise seemed natural to him. It scarcely seemed possible that everybody around, and specially that she, did not know the crisis at which he stood. He took the hand which she instinctively put forward, into both his, and held fast by it as if it had been an anchor of salvation.

'I am a fugitive,' he said. 'Will you receive me, will you take me with you? Have pity upon me, for you are my last hope.'

*The Wizard's Son, Volume III*     333

'Lord Erradeen – has anything – happened? What – have you done?'

She trembled, standing by him, gazing in his face, not withdrawing her hand, yet not giving it, lost in wonder; yet having come to feel that something he had done, some guilt of his, must be the cause.

'I have done – I will tell you everything. I wish to tell you everything: let me come with you, Oona.'

All this time Hamish, standing behind Walter, was making signs to his young mistress, which seemed to no purpose but to increase her perplexity. Hamish shook his shaggy head, and his eyebrows worked up and down. He gesticulated with his arm pointing along the loch. Finally he stepped forward with a sort of desperation.

'I'm saying, Miss Oona, that we're in no hurry. There will always be some-body about that would be glad, real glad, of a visit from you. And as his lordship is a wee disturbed in his mind, and keen to get home, I could just put him up to Auchnasheen – it would take me very little time – and syne come back for you.'

Oona stood startled, undecided between the two – alarmed a little by Wal-ter's looks, and much by the significance of the gestures of Hamish, and his eagerness and anxiety.

'I¹ will no be keeping you waiting long at all – oh, not at all. And my lord will be best at home, being a wee disturbed in his mind – and we're in no hurry – no hurry,' Hamish insisted, doing his best to place himself between the two.

'Hamish thinks I am mad,' said Walter. 'I do not wonder. But I am not mad. I want neither home nor anything else – but you. It is come to that – that nobody can help me but you. First one tries expedients,' he cried, 'anything to tide over; but at last one comes – one comes to the only true –'

'You are speaking very wildly,' said Oona. 'I don't know what you mean, Lord Erradeen; and Hamish is afraid of you. What is it? We are only simple people – we do not understand.'

He dropped her hand which he had held all the time, half, yet only half against her will, for there was something in the way he held it which forbade all idea of lev-ity. She looked at him very wistfully, anxious, not with any offence, endeavouring to put away all prepossession out of her mind – the prejudice in his favour which moved her heart in spite of herself – the prejudice against him, and indignant won-der whether all was true that she had heard, which had arisen from Julia's words. Her eyelids had formed into anxious curves of uncertainty, out of which her soul looked wistfully, unable to refuse help, perplexed, not knowing what to do.

'If you refuse to hear me,' he said, 'I have no other help to turn to. I know I have no right to use such an argument, and yet if you knew – I will urge no more. It is death or life – but it is in your hands.'

Oona's eyes searched into his very soul.

'What can I do?' she said, wondering. 'What power have I? How can I tell if it is – true –' she faltered, and begged his pardon hastily when she had said that word. 'I mean – I do not mean –' she said confusedly. 'But oh, what can I do? it is not possible that I –'

It is cruel to have the burden put upon you of another's fate. Sometimes that is done to a woman lightly in the moment of disappointment by a mortified lover. Was this the sort of threat he meant, or was it perhaps – true? Oona, who had no guile, was shaken to the very soul by that doubt. Better to risk an affront in her own person than perhaps to fail of an occasion in which sincere help was wanted and could be given. She had not taken her eyes from him, but searched his face with a profound uncertainty and eagerness. At last, with the sigh of relief which accompanies a decision, she said to Hamish,

'Push off the boat. Lord Erradeen will help me in,' with something peremptory in her tone against which her faithful servant could make no further protest.

Hamish proceeded accordingly to push off the boat into the water, and presently they were afloat, steering out for the centre of the loch. They were at some distance from the isle on the other side of the low, green island with its little fringe of trees, so different from the rocky and crested isles about, which is known on Loch Houran as the Isle of Rest. The low wall round about the scattered tombs, the scanty ruins of its little chapel, were all that broke the soft greenness of those low slopes. There was nothing like it all around in its solemn vacancy and stillness, and nothing could be more unlike that chill and pathetic calm than the freight of life which approached it in Oona's boat: she herself full of tremulous visionary excitement – the young man in his passion and desperation; even the watchful attendant, who never took his eyes from Lord Erradeen, and rowed on with all his senses on the alert, ready to throw himself upon the supposed maniac at a moment's notice, or without it did the occasion require. There was a pause till they found themselves separated by a widening interval of water from the shore, where at any moment a chance passenger might have disturbed their interview. Here no one could disturb them. Walter placed himself in front of Hamish facing Oona: but perhaps the very attitude, the freedom and isolation in which he found himself with her, closed his lips. For a minute he sat gazing at her, and did not speak.

'You wished – to say something to me, Lord Erradeen?'

It was she again, as Katie had done before, who recalled to him his purpose – with a delicate flush colouring the paleness of her face, half in shame that after all she had to interfere to bring the confession forth.

'So much,' he said, 'so much that I scarcely know where to begin.' And then he added, 'I feel safe with you near me. Do you know what it means to feel safe? But you never were in deadly danger. How could you be?'

'Lord Erradeen, do not mystify me with these strange sayings,' she cried. 'Do they mean anything? What has happened to you? or is it only – is it nothing but –'

'A pretence, do you think, to get myself a hearing – to beguile you into a little interest? That might have been. But it is more serious, far more serious. I told you it was life or death.' He paused for a moment and then resumed. 'Do you remember last year when you saved me?'

'I remember – last year,' she said with an unsteady voice, feeling the flush grow hotter and hotter on her cheek, for she did not desire to be reminded of that self-surrender, that strange merging of her being in another's which was her secret, of which she had been aware, but no one else. 'I never understood it,' she added, with one meaning for herself and one for him. The hidden sense was to her more important than the other. 'It has always been – a mystery –'

'It was the beginning of the struggle,' he said. 'I came here, you know – don't you know? – out of poverty to take possession of my kingdom – that was what I thought. I found myself instead at the beginning of a dreary battle. I was not fit for it, to begin with. Do you remember the old knights had to prepare themselves for their chivalry with fasting, and watching of arms, and all that – folly –' A gleam of self-derision went over his face, and yet it was deadly serious underneath.

'It was no folly,' she said.

'Oh, do you think I don't know that? The devil laughs in me, now and then, but I don't mean it. Oona – let me call you Oona, now, if never again – I had neither watched nor prayed –'

He made a pause, looking at her pitifully; and she, drawn, she knew not how, answered, with tears in her eyes, 'I have heard that you – had strayed –'

'That means accidentally, innocently,' he said. 'It was not so. I had thought only of myself: when I was caught in the grip of a will stronger than mine, unprepared. There was set before me – no, not good and evil as in the books, but subjection to one – who cared neither for good nor evil. I was bidden to give up my own will, I who had cared for nothing else: to give up even such good as was in me. I was not cruel. I cared nothing about worldly advantages; but these were henceforward to be the rule of my life – pleasant, was it not?' he said with a laugh, 'to a man who expected to be the master – of everything round.'

At the sound of his laugh, which was harsh and wild, Hamish, raising himself so as to catch the eye of his mistress, gave her a questioning, anxious look. Oona was very pale, but she made an impatient gesture with her hand to her humble guardian. She was not herself at ease; an agonizing doubt lest Walter's mind should have given way had taken possession of her. She answered him as calmly as she could, but with a tremor in her voice, 'Who could ask that, Lord Erradeen? Oh no, no – you have been deceived.'

'You ask me who! you who gave me your hand – your hand that was like snow – that had never done but kindness all your life – and saved me – so that I defied him. And you ask me who?'

He put out his hand as he spoke and touched hers as it lay in her lap. His face was full of emotion, working and quivering. 'Give it to me, Oona! – will you give it to me? I am not worthy that you should touch me. It has been said to me that you would turn from me – ah, with disgust! – *if you knew*. And I want you to know everything. For you gave it then without pausing to think. Oona! I am going to tell you everything. Give it to me,' he said, holding out his hands one over the other to receive and clasp hers, his eyes moist, his lips appealing with a quivering smile of entreaty. And how may it be told what was in Oona's heart? Her whole being was moved through and through with tenderness, wonder, pity. Her hand seemed to move of itself towards him. The impulse was upon her almost too strong to be resisted, to throw her arms around him, like a mother with a child – to identify herself with him whatever might follow. The womanly instinct that held her back – that kept all these impulses in check and restrained the heart that seemed leaping out of her bosom towards this man whom she loved in spite of herself, and who had need of her, most sacred of all claims – was like a frame of iron round her, against which she struggled, but from which she could not get free. Tears filled her eyes – she clasped her hands together in an involuntary appeal. 'What can I do? What can I do?' she cried.

'You shall hear all,' said he. 'I have tried everything before coming back to that which I always knew was my only hope. I fled away after that night. Do you remember?' (She almost smiled at this, for she remembered far better than he, and the wonder and despair of it, and his boat going away over the silent loch, and his face eager to be gone, and she indignant, astonished, feeling that her life went with him; but of all this he knew nothing.) 'I fled – thinking I could escape and forget. There seemed no better way. There was no one to help me, only to mar and waste – what was all wasted and spoilt already. I want to tell you everything,' he said faltering, drooping his head, withdrawing his eyes from her, 'but I have not the courage – you would not understand me. Nothing that you could imagine could reach to a hundredth part of the evil I have known.' He covered his face with his hands. The bitterness of the confession he dared not make seemed to stifle his voice and every hope.

And Oona's heart quivered and beat against the strong bondage that held it in, and her hands fluttered with longing to clasp him and console him. What woman can bear to hear out such a confession, not to interrupt it with pardon, with absolution, with cries to bring forth the fairest robe? She touched his head with her hands for a moment, a trembling touch upon his hair, and said, 'God forgive you. God will forgive you,' with a voice almost choked with tears.

He raised his head and looked at her with an eager cry. 'I want – not forgiveness. I want life,' he cried, 'life, new life. I want to be born again. Is not that in the Bible? To be born again, to begin again from the beginning, everything new. Help me, Oona! I am not thinking of the past. It is *now* I am thinking of. I am not thinking of forgiveness – punishment if you please, anything! – but a new life. He knew man who said that,' Walter cried, raising his head. 'What use is it to me to forgive me? I want to be born again.'

When he thus delivered himself of his exceeding bitter cry, this woman too, like his mother, answered him with a shining face, with eyes swimming in tears,

*The Wizard's Son, Volume III* 337

and brilliant with celestial certainty. She put out her hands to him without a moment's hesitation, and grasped his and smiled.

'Oh, that is all provided for!' she said. 'Yes, He knew! It is all ready for you – waiting – waiting. Don't you know our Lord stands at the door and knocks, till you are ready to let Him in? And now you are ready. There is nothing more.'

He received the soft hands within his with feelings indescribable, at such a height of emotion that all the lesser shades and degrees were lost. He twined her fingers among his own, clasping them with an entire appropriation.

'Oona,' he said, 'the house is yours, and all in it. Open the door to your Lord, whom I am not worthy to come near – and to everything that is good. It is yours to do it. Open the door!'

They had forgotten Hamish who sat behind, pulling his long, even strokes, with his anxious shaggy countenance fixed like that of a faithful dog upon his mistress, whom he had to guard. He saw the two heads draw very close together, and the murmur of the voices.

'What will she be saying to him? She will be winning him out of yon transport. She will be puttin' peace in his hairt. She has a voice that would wile the bird from the tree,' said Hamish to himself. 'But oh hon! – my bonnie Miss Oona,' Hamish cried aloud.

This disturbed them and made them conscious of the spectator, who was there with them, separate from all the world. Oona, with a woman's readiness to throw her veil over and hide from the eye of day all that is too sacred for the vulgar gaze, raised her face, still quivering with tender and holy passion.

'Why do you say "oh hon?" There is nothing to say "oh hon" for, Hamish. No, no; but the other way.'

Hamish looked across the young lord, whose head was bowed down still over Oona's hands, which he held. The boatman gave him a glance in which there was doubt and trouble, and then raised his shaggy eyebrows, and addressed a look of entreaty and warning to the fair inspired face that hovered over Walter like a protecting angel. 'Ye will not be doing the like of that,' he said, 'without thought?'

And all the time the boat swept on over the reflections in the water, by the low shore of the Isle of Rest where death had easy landing, away among the feathery islets, all tufted brown and crimson to the water's edge, where nothing but the wild life of the woods could find footing: – nothing near them but the one anxious, humble retainer, watching over Oona, for whom no one in heaven or earth, save himself, entertained any fear. He quickened those long strokes in the excitement of his soul, but neither did Walter take any account of where he was going, nor Oona awake out of the excitement of the moment to think of the descent into common life which was so near. Hamish only, having the entire conduct of them, hastened their progress back to ordinary existence – if perhaps there might be some aid of reason and common judgment (as he said to himself) there, to see that the man was in his right senses before Oona should be bound for life.

There was no excitement about the isle. It lay as calm in the sunshine as if nothing but peace had ever passed by that piece of solid earth, with its rocks and trees, that little human world amid the waters; every jagged edge of rock, every red-tinted tree against the background of tall firs, and the firs themselves in their dark motionless green, all shining inverted in the liquid clearness around. The two were still afloat, though their feet were on solid ground; and still apart from all the world, though the winding way led direct to the little centre of common life in which Oona was all in all. But they did not immediately ascend to that gentle height. They paused first on the little platform, from which Kinloch Houran was the chief object. One of those flying shadows that make the poetry of the hills, was over it for a moment, arrested as by some consciousness of nature, while they stood and gazed. There Walter stood and told to Oona the story of Miss Milnathort, and how she had said that two, set upon all good things, would hold the secret in their hands. Two – and here were the two. It seemed to him that every cloud had fled from his soul from the moment when he felt her hands in his, and had bidden her 'open the door.' Oh, fling wide the door to the Christ who waits outside, the Anointed, the Deliverer of men: to peace and truth, that wait upon Him, and mercy and kindness, and love supreme that saves the world! Fling wide the doors![33] Not a bolt or bar but that soft hand shall unloose them, throw them wide, that the Lord may come in. Not a crevice, or corner, or dark hiding-place of evil but shall open to the light. He said so standing there, holding her hand still, not only as a lover caressing, protecting, holds the soft hand he loves, but as a man drowning will hold by the hand held out to save him. It was both to Walter. He told her, and it was true, that from the day when she had put it into his a year ago, he had never lost the consciousness that in this hand was his hope.

Oona was penetrated by all these words to the depths of her heart. What girl could be told that in her hands was the saving of one she loved, without such a movement of the soul to the highest heroism and devotion as raises human nature above itself? Her soul seemed to soar, drawing his with it, into heights above. She felt capable of everything – of the highest effort and the humblest service. That union of the spiritual being above his, and the human longing beneath, came back to her in all the joy of a permitted and befitting mood. She was his to raise him above all those soils of life of which he was sick and weary; and his to sweep away the thorns and briars out of his path; to lead him and to serve him, to mingle her being in his life so that no one henceforward should think of Oona save as his second and helpmeet: yet so to guide his uncertain way as that it should henceforward follow the track of light by which the best of all ages has gone. Even to understand that office of glory and humility demands an enlightenment, such as those who do not love can never attain. To Oona it seemed that life itself became glorious in this service. It raised her above all earthly things. She looked at him with the pity of an angel, with something of the tenderness of a mother, with an identification and willingness to submit which was pure woman. All was justified to her – the love that she had given unsought, the service which she was willing and ready to give.

He stopped before they had reached the height upon which stood home and the sweet and simple existence which embraced these mysteries without comprehending them. A darker shadow, a premonition of evil, came over him.

'And yet,' he said, 'I have not told you all. I have something more still to say.'

# CHAPTER X.ᵃ

WHAT did there remain to say?

He had made his confession, which, after all, was no confession, and she had stopped his mouth with pardon. His cry for new life had overcome every reluctance in her. Her delicate reserve, the instinct that restrained her, had no more power after that. She had stood no longer behind any barrier – at that touch she had thrown her heart wide open and taken him within.

'What more?' she said. 'There can be no more.'

'Much more: and you were to hear all: not only the wretched folly into which I fled, to try if I could forget, but something meaner, nearer – something for which you will despise me. Oh, do not smile; it is past smiling for you and me – for you as well as me now, Oona. God forgive me that have tangled your life in mine!'

'What is it?' she said, giving him an open look of trust and confidence. 'I am not afraid.'

He was. Far worse than the general avowal of sins which she did not understand was the avowal he had to make of something which she could understand. He perceived that it would wound her to the heart – He had no fear now that Oona would throw him off. She had put her hand into his, and was ready to pour the fresh and spotless stream of her life into his. It was no more possible for her to separate herself, to withdraw from him, whatever might happen. He perceived this with a keen pang of remorse, for the first time entering with all his heart into the soul of another, and understanding what it meant. She could not now turn her back upon him, go away from him; and he was about to give her a sharp, profound, intolerable wound.

'Oona,' he said, with great humility, 'it occurred to-day. I cannot tell whether you will be able to see why I did it, or how I did it. This morning –' He paused here, feeling that the words hung in his throat and stifled him. 'This morning – I went – and insulted Katie Williamson, and asked her – to marry me.'

She had been listening with her sweet look of pity and tenderness – sorry, sorry to the depths of her heart, for the evil he had done – sorry beyond tears; but yet ready with her pardon, and not afraid. At the name of Katie Williamson there came up over her clear face the shadow of a cloud – not more than the shadow. When such words as these are said they are not to be understood all at once. But they woke in her a startled curiosity – a strange surprise.

'This morning – it is still morning,' she said, bewildered; 'and Katie –'

'Oona! you do not understand.'

'No. I do not quite – understand. What is it? This morning? And Katie –'

'I asked her this morning to join her land to my land and her money to my money: to be – my wife.'

She drew her hand slowly out of his, looking at him with eyes that grew larger as they gazed. For some time she could not say a word, but only got paler and paler, and looked at him.

'Then what place – have I? – what am – I?' she said, slowly. Afterwards a sudden flush lighted up her face. 'She would not: and then you came – to me?' she said.

A faint smile of pain came to her mouth. Walter had seen that look very recently before – when he told his mother why it was that he had sent for her. Was he capable of giving nothing but pain to those he loved? If he had tried to explain or apologise, it is doubtful whether Oona's faculties, so suddenly and strangely strained, could have borne it. But he said nothing. What was there to say? – the fact which he had thus avowed was beyond explanation. He met her eyes for a moment, then drooped his head. There was nothing – nothing to be said. It was true. He had gone to another woman first, and then, when that failed, as a last resource had come to her. The anguish was so sharp that it brought that smile. It was incredible in the midst of her happiness. Her heart seemed wrung and crushed in some gigantic grasp. She looked at him with wondering, incredulous misery.

'You thought then, I suppose,' she said, 'that one – was as good as another?'

'I did not do that, Oona; it is, perhaps, impossible that you should understand. I told you – I had tried – every expedient: not daring to come to the one and only – the one, the only –'

She waved her hand as if putting this aside, and stood for a moment looking out vaguely upon the loch – upon the sheen of the water, the castle lying darkly in shadow, the banks stretching upward and downward in reflection. They had been glorified a moment since in the new union; now they were blurred over, and conveyed no meaning. Then she said drearily –

'My mother – will wonder why we do not come in –'

'May I speak to her – at once? Let me speak.'

'Oh no!' she cried. 'Say nothing – nothing! I could not bear it.'

And then he seized upon her hand, the hand she had taken from him, and cried out –

'You are not going to forsake me, Oona! You will not cast me away?'

'I cannot,' she said very low, with her eyes upon the landscape, 'I cannot!' Then, turning to him, 'You have my word, and I have but one word: only everything is changed. Let us say no more of it just now. A little time – I must have a little time.'

The Wizard's Son, Volume III 341

And she turned and walked before him to the house. They went in silence, not a word passing between them. Mysie, startled, came out to the door to ascertain who it could be who were preceded by the sound of footsteps only, not of voices. It was 'no canny,' she said. And to think this was Miss Oona, whose cheerful voice always came home before her to warn the house that its pride and joy was approaching! Mysie, confounded, went to open the door of the drawing-room that her mistress might be made to share her uneasiness.

'It will just be Miss Oona, mem, and my lord,' Mysie said, 'but very down, as if something had happened and not saying a word.'

'Bless me!' cried Mrs. Forrester. Her heart naturally leapt to the only source of danger that could affect her deeply. 'It is not a mail day, Mysie,' she said; 'there can be no ill news.'

'The Lord be thanked for that!' Mysie said: and then stood aside to give admittance to those footsteps which came one after the other without any talking or cheerful note of sound. Mrs. Forrester rose to meet them with a certain anxiety, although her mind was at rest on the subject of the mails. It might be something wrong at Eaglescairn: it might be –

'Dear me! what is the matter, Oona? You are white, as if you had seen a ghost,' she said, with a more tangible reason for her alarm.

'I am quite well, mamma. Perhaps I may have seen a ghost – but nothing more,' she said with a half-laugh.[a] 'And here is Lord Erradeen whom we picked up, Hamish and I.'

'And Lord Erradeen, you are just very whitefaced too,' cried Mrs. Forrester. 'Bless me, I hope you have not both taken a chill. That will sometimes happen when the winter is wearing on, and ye are tempted out on a fine morning with not enough of clothes. I have some cherry brandy in my private press, and I will just give you a little to bring back the blood to your cheeks: and come in to the fire. Dear me, Oona, do not shiver like that! and you not one that feels the cold. You have just taken a chill upon the water, though it is such a beautiful morning. And so you have got your mother with you, Lord Erradeen?'

'She came yesterday. She was so fortunate as to meet – Miss Forrester.'

It seemed to him a wrong against which he was ready to cry out to earth and heaven that he should have to call her by that formal name. He paused before he said it, and looked at her with passionate reproach in his eyes. And Oona saw the look, though her eyes were averted, and trembled, with what her mother took for cold.

'You may be sure Oona was very content to be of use: and I hope now you have got her you will keep her, Lord Erradeen. It will be fine for your house and the servants, and all, to have a lady at Auchnasheen. There has not been a lady since the last lord but one, who married the last of the Glen Oriel family, a person that brought a great deal of property with her. I remember her very well. They said she was not his first love, but she was a most creditable person, and well thought upon, and kind to the poor. We were saying to ourselves, Oona

342 *The Selected Works of Margaret Oliphant, Volume 21*

and me, that we would go up the loch to-morrow and call, if you are sure Mrs. Methven is rested from her journey, and will like to see such near neighbours.'

'But, mother –' Oona said.

'But what? There is no but, that I know of. You know that it was all settled between us. We thought to-day she would be tired, and want repose rather than company. But by to-morrow she would be rested, and willing to see what like persons we are in this place. That would be very natural. And I am proud Oona was in the way, to take her across the loch. People that come from flat countries where there is little water, they are sometimes a little timid of the loch, and in the dark too. But she will have got over all that by to-morrow, and to call will be a real pleasure. Did you mention, Oona, at Ellermore and other places that Mrs. Methven had arrived? – for everybody will be keen to see your mother, Lord Erradeen.'

'It is very kind. She will rather see you than any one.'

'Hoots,' said Mrs. Forrester with a smile and a shake of her head, 'that is just flattery; for we have very little in our power except good-will and kindness: but it will give me great pleasure to make your mother's acquaintance, and if she likes mine, that will be a double advantage. But you are not going away, Lord Erradeen? You have this moment come! and Mysie will be reckoning upon you for lunch, and I have no doubt a bird has been put to the fire. Well, I will not say a word, for Mrs. Methven's sake, for no doubt she will be a little strange the first day or two. Oona, will you see that Hamish is ready? And we will have the pleasure of calling to-morrow,' Mrs. Forrester said, following to the door. Her easy smiles, the little movements of her hands, the fluttering of the pretty ribbons in her cap, added to the calm and tranquil stream of her talk so many additional details of the softest quietude of common life. She stood and looked after the young pair as they went down together to the beach, waving her hand to them when they turned towards her, as unconscious of any disturbing influence as were the trees that waved their branches too. Passion had never been in her little composed and cheerful world. By-and-by she felt the chill of the wind, and turned and went back to her fireside. 'No doubt that winter is coming now,' she said to herself, 'and no wonder if Oona, poor thing, was just frozen with the cold on the water. I wish she may not have taken a chill.' This was the greatest danger Mrs. Forrester anticipated, and she did not doubt that a hot drink when Oona went to bed would make all right.

It was very strange to both of the young wayfarers to find themselves alone again in the fresh air and stillness. Since the moment when they had landed in an ecstasy of union, until this moment when they went down again to the same spot, years might have passed for anything they knew. They did not seem to have a word to say to each other. Oona was a step or two in advance leading the way, while behind her came Walter, his head drooping, his courage gone, not even the despair in him which had given him a wild and fiery energy. Despair itself

*The Wizard's Son, Volume III* 343

seemed hopeful in comparison with this. He had risen into another life, come to
fresh hopes, received beyond all expectation the help which he had sought for
elsewhere in vain, but which here alone he could ever find; but now the soul had
gone out of it all, and he stood bewildered, deprived of any power to say or do.
All through his other miseries there had been the thought of this, like a distant
stronghold in which if he ever reached it there would be deliverance. If he ever
reached it! and now he had reached it, but too late. Was it too late? He followed
her helplessly, not able to think of anything he could say to her, though he had
pleaded so eagerly, so earnestly, a little while ago. There comes a time after we
have poured out our whole soul in entreaties, whether to God or man, when
exhaustion overpowers the mind, and utterance is taken from us, and even desire
seems to fail – not that what we long for is less to be desired, but that every effort
is exhausted and a dreary discouragement has paralysed the soul. Walter felt not
less, but more than ever, that in Oona was his every hope. But he was dumb
and could say no more, following her with a weight upon his heart that allowed
him no further possibility, no power to raise either voice or hand. They walked
thus as in a mournful procession following the funeral of their brief joy, half way
down the bank. Then Oona who was foremost paused for a moment, looking
out wistfully upon that familiar prospect, upon which she had looked all her life.
The scene had changed, the sky had clouded over, as if in harmony with their
minds; only over Kinloch Houran a watery ray of sunshine, penetrating through
the quickly gathering clouds, threw a weird light. The ruinous walls stood out
red under this gleam askance of the retreating sun. It was like an indication – a
pointing out, to the executioner of some deadly harm or punishment, of the victim. Oona paused, and he behind her, vaguely turning as she turned, gazing at
this strange significant light, which seemed to point out, 'This is the spot' – was
that what was meant? – 'the place to be destroyed.'

'It was in shadow a moment since,' Oona said, and her voice seemed to thrill the
air that had been brooding over them in a heavy chill, as if under the same influence
that made them voiceless. What did she mean? and why should she care –

'The shadow was better,' he said, but he did not know what he himself meant
more than what she could mean.

'It has come here,' said Oona, 'between you and me. You said you insulted
Katie. I cannot think that it was your meaning to – insult me.'

'Insult – *you*!' his mind was so clear of that, and his own meaning in respect
to the other so evident to him, that the dead quietude of his discouragement
yielded to a momentary impatience. But how was he to make that clear?

'No, I cannot think it. Whatever you meant, whether it was in levity, whether
it was – I do not believe *that*.'

'Oona,' he cried, waking to the desperation of the position, 'will you give me
up, after all we have said?'

344         *The Selected Works of Margaret Oliphant, Volume 21*

She shook her head sadly.

'I will never now deny you what help I can give you, Lord Erradeen.'

He turned from her with a cry of bitterness.

'Help without love is no help. Alms and pity will do nothing for me. It must be two – who are one.'

She answered him with a faint laugh which was more bitter still; but restrained the jest of pain which rose to her lips, something about three who could not be one. It was the impulse of keen anguish, but it would not have become a discussion that was as serious as life and death.

'It is all a confusion,' she said; 'what to say or do I know not. It is such a thing – as could not have been foreseen. Some would think it made me free, but I do not feel that I can ever be free.' She spoke without looking at him, gazing blankly out upon the landscape. 'You said it was no smiling matter to you or me – to you and me. Perhaps,' she interrupted herself as if a new light had come upon her, 'that is the true meaning of what you say – two that are one; but it is not the usual creed. Two for misery –'

'Oh not for misery, Oona! there is no misery for me where you are.'

'Or – any other,' she said with a smile of unimaginable suffering, and ridicule, and indignation.

He answered nothing. What could he say to defend himself? 'If you could see into my heart,' he said after a time, 'you would understand. One who is in despair will clutch at anything. Can you imagine a man trying like a coward to escape the conflict, rather than facing it, and bringing the woman he loved into it?'

'Yes,' she said, 'I can imagine that; but not in the man who is me.' Then she moved away towards the beach, saying, 'Hamish is waiting,' with a sigh of weariness.

'Oona,' said Walter, 'you will give me your hand again before we part?'

'What does it matter if I give it or hold it back? It is yours whether I will or not. You should have told me before. I should have understood. Oh, I am ashamed, ashamed! to think of all I have said to you. How could you betray me first before you told me? In the same morning! It is more than a woman can bear!' she cried.

Perhaps this outburst of passion relieved her, for she turned and held out her hand to him with a smile of pain which was heartrending. 'It did not seem like this when we landed,' she said.

'And it would not seem like this, oh, Oona! if you could see my heart.'

She shook her head, looking at him all the while with that strange smile, and then drew away her hand and repeated, 'Hamish is waiting.' Hamish in the background, standing up against the shining of the water, with his oar in his hand, waited with his anxious eyes upon his young lady, not knowing how it was. He would have pitched Lord Erradeen into the loch, or laid him at his feet with Highland passion, had she given him a sign. He held the boat for him instead to step in, with an anxious countenance. Love or hate, or madness or good meaning, Hamish could not make out what it was.

'To-morrow!' Walter said, 'if I can live till tomorrow in this suspense –'

She waved her hand to him, and Hamish pushed off. And Oona stood as in a dream, seeing over again the scene which had been in her mind for so long – but changed. She had watched him go away before, eager to be gone, carrying her life with him without knowing it, without desiring it: he unaware of what he was doing, she watching surprised, bereaved of herself, innocently and unaware. How poignant had that parting been! But now it was different. He gazed back at her now, as she stood on the beach, leaving his life with her, all that was in him straining towards her, gazing till they were each to the other but a speck in the distance. Two that were one! Oh, not perhaps for mutual joy, not for the happiness that love on the surface seems to mean – rather for the burden, the disappointment, the shame. She waved her hand once more over the cold water, and then turned away. Till to-morrow – 'if I can live till to-morrow' – as he had said.

\*\*\*

# CHAPTER XI.[a]

THE rest of this day passed over Walter like a dream in a fever. Through a kind of hot mist full of strange reflections, all painful, terrible, lurid, with confusion and suffering he saw the people and things about him – his mother questioning him with anxious words, with still more anxious eyes; his servants looking at him wondering, compassionate; and heard now and then a phrase which came to his consciousness and thereafter continued to rise before him from time to time, like a straw cast into a whirlpool and boiling up as the bubbles went and came – something about seeing a doctor, something about sending for Mr. Cameron, with now and then an imploring entreaty, 'Oh, my boy! what ails you? what is wrong?'[b] from Mrs. Methven. These were the words that came back to his ears in a kind of refrain. He answered, too, somehow, he was aware, that there was nothing the matter with him, that he wanted no doctor, no counsellor, in a voice which seemed to come from any point of the compass rather than from his own lips. It was not because of the breach which had so rapidly followed the transport of his complete union with Oona. That, too, had become secondary, a detail scarcely important in the presence of the vague tempest which was raging within him, and which he felt must come to some outburst more terrible than anything he had yet known when he was left to himself. He had come back to Auchnasheen[c] under the guidance of Hamish, distracted, yet scarcely unhappy, feeling that at the end, whatever misunderstanding there might be, he was assured of Oona, her companionship, her help, and, what was greatest of all, her love. She had not hesitated to let him see that he had that; and with that must not all obstacles, however miserable, disappear at the last? But[a] when he landed, the misery that fell upon him was different from the pain of the temporary misunderstanding. He became conscious at once that it was the beginning of the last struggle, a conflict which might end in – he knew not what: death, downfall, flight, even shame, for aught he knew. The impulse was strong upon him to speed away to the hillside and deliver himself over to the chances of this battle, which had a fierce attraction for him on one hand, while on the other it filled him with a mad terror which reason could not subdue.[b]

So strong was this impulse that he hurried past the gate of Auchnasheen and took the path that led up to the moors, with a sense of flying from, yet flying to, his spiritual enemies. He was met there by the gamekeeper, who began to talk to him about the game, and the expediency of inviting 'twa-three' gentlemen to shoot the coverts down by Corrieden,[c] an interruption which seemed to his preoccupied soul too trivial, too miserable, to be borne with. He turned from the astonished speaker in the midst of his explanations, and rushed back with the impatience which was part of his character, exaggerated into a sort of mad intolerance of any interruption. Not there, not there –[d] he began to remember the wild and mad contest which last year had gone on upon those hills, and with an instantaneous change of plan retraced his steps to the house, and burst into his mother's presence, so pale, so wild, with eyes almost mad in their fire, looking out from the curves of his eyelids like those of a maniac. Her terror was great. She came up to him and laid her hands upon him, and cried out, What was it? what was it? After this the active frenzy that had possessed him seemed to sink into a maze of feverish confusion which was less violent, less terrible, more like the operations of nature. He was not aware that he looked at her piteously, and said, 'I want to stay with you, mother' – childlike words, which penetrated with a misery that was almost sweet to Mrs. Methven's very heart. She put her arms round him, drawing down his head upon her bosom, kissing his forehead with trembling lips, holding him fast, as when he was a child and came to her for consolation. He was scarcely aware of all this, and yet it soothed him. The excitement of his brain was calmed. That uneasy haze of fever which confuses everything, the half-delirium of the senses through which the mind looks as through a mist, uneasy, yet with visions that are not all miserable, was a sort of paradise in comparison with the frenzy of a conflict in which every expedient of torture was exercised upon him. He was grateful for the relief. That he did not know what he said or what she said, but heard the answering voices far off, like something musical, was nothing. There was a kind of safety in that society: the enemy could not show himself there. He had to stand off baffled and wait – ah, wait! that was certain. He had not gone away – not Oona, not the mother, could save the victim altogether. They protected him for the moment, they held the foe at arm's length: but that could not be always. Sooner or later the last struggle must come.

The Wizard's Son, Volume III | 347

Walter remained within-doors[a] all day. It was contrary to all his habits, and this of itself added to the alarm of all about him; but it was not inconsistent with the capricious impatient constitution of his mind, always ready to turn upon itself at a moment's notice, and do that which no one expected. During every moment of this long day he had to resist the strong impulse which was upon him – more than an impulse, a tearing and rending of his spirit, sometimes rising into sudden energy almost inconceivable – to go out and meet his enemy. But he held his ground so far with a dumb obstinacy which also was part of his character, and which was strengthened by the sensation of comparative exemption so long as he had the protection of others around him, and specially of his mother's presence. It was with reluctance that he saw her go out of the room even for a moment; and his eager look of inquiry when she left him, his attempts to retain her, his strained gaze towards the door till she returned, gave Mrs. Methven a sort of anguish of pleasure, if those contradictory words can be put together. To feel that she was something, much to him, could not but warm her heart; but with that was the misery of knowing that something must indeed be very far wrong with Walter to make him thus, after so many years of independence, cling to his mother.

'It is like a fever coming on,' she said to Symington, with whom alone she could take any counsel. 'He is ill, very ill, I am sure of it. The doctor must be sent for. Have you ever seen him like this before?'

'My lady,' said old Symington, 'them that have the Methvens to deal with have need of much gumption. Have I seen him like that before? Oh, yes, I have seen him like that before. It is just their hour and the power o' darkness. Let him be for two-three days –'

'But in two or three days the fever may have taken[b] sure hold of him. It may be losing precious time: it may get – fatal force –'

'There is no fears of his life,' said old Symington; 'there is enough fear of other things.'

'Of what? Oh, for God's sake! tell me; don't leave me in ignorance!' the mother cried.

'But that's just what I cannot do,' Symington said. 'By the same taken that I ken nothing mysel.'

While this conversation was going on, Walter, through his fever, saw them conspiring, plotting, talking about him as he would have divined and resented in other moods, but knew vaguely now in his mist of being that they meant him no harm, but good.

And thus the day went on. He prolonged it as long as he could, keeping his mother with him till long after the hour when the household was usually at rest. But, however late, the moment came at last when he could detain her no longer. She, terrified, ignorant, fearing a dangerous illness, was still more reluctant to leave him, if possible, than he was to let her go, and would have sat up all night watching him had she ventured to make such a proposal. But at last Walter summoned up all his courage with a desperate effort, an effort of despair which restored him to himself and made a clear spot amid all the mist and confusion of the day.

'Mother,' he said, as he lighted her candle, 'you have been very good to me to-day! Oh I know you have always been good – and I always ungrateful; but I am not ungrateful now.'

'Oh, Walter! what does that word mean between you and me? If I could but do anything. It breaks my heart to see you like this.'

'Yes, mother,' he said, 'and it may break my heart. I don't know what may come of it – if I can stand, or if I must fall. Go and pray for me, mother.'

'Yes, my dearest – yes, my own boy! as I have done every day, almost every hour, since ever you were born.'

'And so will Oona,' he said. He made no response of affection to this brief record of a life devoted to him, which Mrs. Methven uttered with eyes full of tears and every line of her countenance quivering with emotion. He was abstracted into a world beyond all such expressions and responses, on the verge of an ordeal too terrible for him, more terrible than any he had yet sustained – like a man about to face fearful odds, and counting up what aids he could depend upon. 'And so will Oona,' he repeated to himself, aloud but unawares: and looked up at his mother with a sad glimmer of a smile and kissed her, and said, 'That should help me.' Then, without waiting for her to go first, he walked out of the room, like a blind man, feeling with his hand before him, and not seeing where he went.

For already there had begun within him that clanging of the pulses, that mounting of every faculty of the nerves and blood to his head, the seat of thought, which throbbed as though it would burst, and to his heart, which thundered and laboured and filled his ears with billows of sound. All his fears, half quiescent in the feverish pause of the day, were suddenly roused to action, ranging themselves to meet the last, the decisive, the most terrible assault of all. He went into his room and closed the door upon all mortal succour. The room was large and heavily furnished in the clumsy fashion of the last generation – heavy curtains, huge articles of furniture looming dark in the partial light, a gloomy expanse of space, dim mirrors glimmering here and there, the windows closely shut up and shrouded, every communication of the fresh air without, or such succour of light as might linger in the heavens, excluded. The old castle, with its ruined battlements, seemed a more fit scene for spiritual conflict than the dull comfort of this gloomy chamber, shut in from all human communication. But Walter made no attempt to throw open the closed windows. No help from without could avail him, and he had no thought or time to spare for any exertion. He put his candle on the table and sat down to await what should befall.

The night passed like other nights to most men, even to the greater number of the inhabitants in this house. Mrs. Methven after a while, worn out, and capable of nothing that could help him, dozed and slept, half dressed, murmuring familiar prayers in her sleep, ready to start up at the faintest call. But there came no call. Two or three times in the night there was a faint stir, and once old Symington, who was also on the alert, and whose room was near that of his master, saw Lord Erradeen come out of his chamber with a candle in his hand, the light of which showed his countenance all ghastly and furrowed as with the action of years, and go down-stairs.[a] The old man, watching from the gallery above, saw his master go to the door, which he opened, admitting a blast of night wind which seemed to bring in the darkness as well as cold. Symington waited trembling to hear it clang behind the unfortunate young man. Where was he going to in the middle of the night? But after a few minutes, the door, instead of clanging, closed softly, and Walter came back. It might be that this happened more than once while the slow hours crept on, for the watcher, hearing more than there was to hear, thought that there were steps about the house, and vague sounds of voices. But this was all vanity and superstition. No one came in – with none, save with his own thoughts, did Walter speak. Had his enemy entered bodily, and even with maddening words maintained a personal conflict, the sufferer would have been less harshly treated. Once, as Symington had seen, he was so broken down by the conflict that he was on the eve of a shameful flight which would have been ruin. When he came down-stairs with his candle in the dead of the night and opened the great hall door, he had all but thrown down his arms and consented that nothing remained for him but to escape while he could, as long as he could, to break all ties and abandon all succour, and only flee, flee from the intolerable moment. He had said to himself that he could bear it no longer, that he must escape anyhow, at any cost, leaving love and honour, and duty and every higher thought – for what could help him – nothing – nothing – in earth or heaven.

That which touched him to the quick was not any new menace,[b] it was not the horror of the struggles through which he had already passed, it was the maddening derision with which his impulses were represented to him as the last expedients of the most refined[c] selfishness. When his tormentor in the morning had bidden him, with a smile, 'Be good!' as the height of policy, it had seemed to Walter that the point of the intolerable was reached, and that life itself under such an interpretation became insupportable, a miserable jest, a mockery hateful to God and man; but there was yet a lower depth, a more hateful derision still. Love! what was his love? a way of securing help, a means of obtaining, under pretences of the finest sentiment, some one who would supremely help him, stand by him always, protect him with the presence of a nature purer than his own. Nothing was said to the unhappy young man. It was in the course of his own thoughts that this suggestion arose like a light of hell illuminating all the dark corners of his being. Had he ever said to Oona that he loved her? Did he love her? Was it for any motive but his own safety that he sought her? Katie he had

350 *The Selected Works of Margaret Oliphant, Volume 21*

sought for her wealth, for the increase of importance she could bring, for the relief from torture she could secure to him. And Oona, Oona whom he loved! Was it for love he fled to her? Oh, no, but for safety! All was miserable, all was self, all was for his own interest, to save *him*, to emancipate him, to make life possible for him. He had started to his feet when this intolerable consciousness (for was it not true?) took possession of him. It was true. She was sweet and fair, and good and lovely, a creature like the angels; but he, miserable, had thought only that in her company was safety – that she could deliver him. He sent forth a cry which at the same time sounded like the laughter of despair, and seemed to shake the house; and took up his candle, and opened his door and hurried forth to escape, where he did not know, how he did not know nor care, to escape from the ridicule of this life, the horror of this travestie and parody of everything good and fair. Heaven and earth! to seek goodness because it was the most profitable of all things; to seek love because it was safety; to profane everything dear and sacred to his own advantage! Can a man know this, and recognise it with all the masks and pretences torn off, and yet consent to live, and better himself by that last desecration of all! He went down with hurried steps through the silence of his house, that silence through which was rising the prayers of the mother in whose love too he had taken refuge when in despair, whom he had bidden to go and pray, for his advantage, solely for him, that he might steal from God a help he did not deserve, by means of her cries and tears. 'And so would Oona,'[a] he had said. Oh, mockery of everything sacred! – all for him, for his self-interest, who deserved nothing, who made use of all.

He opened the door, and stood bare-headed, solitary, on the edge of the black and lonely night; behind him life and hope, and torture and misery – before the void, the blank into which the wretched may escape and lose – if not themselves, that inalienable heritage of woe, yet their power to harm those who love them. He loved nobody, it seemed, but for himself – prized nothing but for himself; held love, honour, goodness, purity, only as safeguards for his miserable life. Let it go then, that wretched contemner of all good – disappear into the blackness of darkness, where God nor man should be disturbed by its exactions more!

The night was wild with a raving wind that dashed the tree-tops against the sky, and swept the clouds before it in flying masses; no moon, no light, gloom impenetrable below, a pale glimpse of heaven above, swept by black billows of tumultuous clouds; somewhere in the great gloom, the loch, all invisible, waited for the steps that might stumble upon its margin; the profound world of darkness closed over every secret that might be cast into it. He stood on the threshold in a momentary pause, forlorn, alone, loosing his hold of all that he had clung to, to save him. Why should he be saved who was unworthy? Why trouble earth or heaven? The passion and the struggle died out of Walter's soul: a profound sadness took possession of him; he felt his heart turn trembling within him, now that he had given up the instinct of self-preservation which had driven him to her feet – to Oona whom he loved. God bless her! not for him would be that sweet companionship, and yet of all things the world contained, was not that the best? Two that should be one. All that was external died away from him in his despair. He forgot for the first time since it had been revealed to him, that he had an enemy, a tyrant waiting for his submission. His heart turned to the love which he had thought he dishonoured, without even recollecting that cursed suggestion. It seemed to him now that he was giving it up for Oona's sake, and that only now all the beauty of it, the sweetness of it, was clear to him. Oh, the pity! to see all this so lovely, so fair, and yet have to resign it! What was everything else in comparison with that? But for her sake, for her dear sake!

How dark it was, impenetrable, closing like a door upon the mortal eyes which had in themselves no power to penetrate that gloom! He stepped across the threshold of life, and stood outside, in the dark. He turned his eyes – for once more, for the last time, in the great calm of renunciation, his heart in a hush of supreme anguish, without conflict or struggle – to where she was, separated from him only by silent space and atmosphere, soon to be separated by more perfect barriers; only to turn his head that way, not even to see where she was hidden in the night – so small a satisfaction, so little consolation, yet something before the reign of nothingness began.

All dark; but no,[a] half way between heaven and earth, what was that, shining steady through the gloom? Not a star; it was too warm, too large, too near; the light in Oona's window shining in the middle of the night when all was asleep around. Then she was not asleep, though everything else was, but watching – and if watching, then for him. The little light, which was but a candle in a window, suddenly, brilliantly lighted up the whole heavens and earth to Walter. Watching, and for him; praying for him, not because of any appeal of his, but out of her own heart, and because she so willed it – out of the prodigality, the generous, unmeasured love which it was her choice to give him – not forced but freely, because she so pleased. He stood for a moment with awe in his heart, arrested, not able to make another step, pale with the revolution, the revelation, the change of all things. His own dark thoughts died away; he stood astonished, perceiving for the first time what it was. To have become part of him had brought no joy to Oona, but it was done, and never could be undone; and to be part of her, what was that to Walter? He had said it without knowing what it meant, without any real sense of the great thing he said. Now it fell upon him in a great wonder, full of awe. He was hers, he was *her*, not himself henceforward, but a portion of another, and that other portion of him standing for him at the gates of heaven. His whole being fell into silence, overawed. He stepped back out of the night and closed softly the great door, and returned to his room, in which everything was stilled by a spell before which all evil things fly – the apprehension of that love which is unmerited, unextorted, unalterable. When he reached his room, and had closed the door, Walter, with trembling hands undid the window, and flung it open to the night, which was no more night or darkness, but part of the everlasting day, so tempered that feeble eyes might perceive those lights which hide themselves in the sunshine. What was it he saw? Up in the heavens, where the clouds swept over them, stars shining, undisturbed, though hidden by moments as the masses of earthly vapour rolled across the sky; near him stealing out of his mother's window a slender ray of light that never wavered; further off, held up as in the very hand of love, the little lamp of Oona. The young man was silent in a great awe; his heart stirring softly in him, hushed, like the heart of a child. For him! unworthy! for him who had never sought the love of God, who had disregarded the love of his mother, who had profaned the love of woman: down, down on his knees – down to the dust, hiding his face in gratitude unutterable. He ceased to think of what it was he had been struggling and contending for; he forgot his enemy, his danger, himself altogether, and, overawed, sank at the feet of love, which alone can save.

# CHAPTER XII.ᵃ

Lord Erradeen was found next morning lying on his bed full dressed sleeping like a child. A man in his evening dress in the clear air of morning is at all times a curious spectacle, and suggestive of many uncomfortable thoughts, but there was about Walter as he lay there fast asleep an extreme youthfulness not characteristic of his appearance on ordinary occasions, which made the curious and anxious spectator who bent over him, think instinctively of a child who had cried itself to sleep, and a convalescent recovering from a long illness. Symington did not know which his young master resembled the most. The old man stood and looked at him, with great and almost tender compassion. One of the windows stood wide open admitting the air and sunshine. But it had evidently been open all night, and must have chilled the sleeper through and through. Symington had come at his usual hour to wake Lord Erradeen. But as he looked at him the water came into his eyes. Instead of calling him he covered him carefully with a warm covering, softly closed the window, and left all his usual morning preparations untouched. This done, he went down-stairsᵇ to the breakfast-room where Mrs. Methven, too anxious to rest, was already waiting for her son. Symington closed the door behind him and came up to the table which was spread for breakfast.

'My lady,' he said, 'my lord will no be veesible for some time. I found him sleeping like a bairn, and I had not the heart to disturb him. No doubt he's had a bad night, but if I'm any judge of the human countenance he will wake another man.'

'Oh, my poor boy! You did well to let him rest, Symington. I will go up and sit by him.'

'If ye will take my advice, my lady, ye will just take a little breakfast; a good cup of tea, and one of our fine fresh eggs, or a bit of trout from the loch; or I would find ye a bonnie bit of the breast of a bird.'

'I can eat nothing,' she said, 'when my son is in trouble.'

'Oh, canny, canny, my lady. I am but a servant, but I am one that takes a great interest. He's in no trouble at this present moment; he's just sleeping like a baby, maybe a wee bit worn out, but not a line o' care in his face; just sleepin' – sleepin' like a little bairn. It will do you mair harm than him if I may mak' so bold as to speak. A cup of tea, my lady, just a cup of this fine tea, if nothing else – it will do ye good. And I'll answer for him,' said Symington. 'I'm well acquaint with all the ways of them,' the old servant added, 'if I might venture, madam, to offer a word of advice, it would be this, just to let him bee.'

A year ago Mrs. Methven would have considered this an extraordinary liberty for a servant to take, and perhaps would have resented the advice; but at that time she did not know Symington, nor was she involved in the mysterious circumstances of this strange life. She received it with a meekness which was not characteristic, and took the cup of tea, which he poured out for her, with a lump of sugar too much, by way of consolation, and a liberal supply of cream, almost with humility. 'If he is not better when he comes down-stairs,[a] I think I must send for the doctor, Symington.'

'I would not, my lady, if I were you. I would just watch over him, but let him bee. I would wait for two or three days and just put up with everything. The Methvens are no just a race like other folk. Ye require great judgment to deal with the Methvens. Ye have not been brought up to it, my lady, like me.'

All this Mrs. Methven received very meekly, and only gratified herself with a cup of tea which was palatable to her, after Symington, having done everything he could for her comfort, had withdrawn. She was very much subdued by the new circumstances in which she found herself, and felt very lonely and cast away, as in a strange land where everything was unknown. She sat for a long time by herself, trying to calm her thoughts by what Symington had said. She consented that he knew a great deal more than she did, even of her son in his new position, and had come to put a sort of infinite faith in him as in an oracle. But how hard it was to sit still, or to content herself with looking out upon that unfamiliar prospect, when her heart was longing to be by her son's bedside! Better to let him bee![b] – alas, she knew very well and had known for long that it was better to let him bee. But what was there so hard to do as that was? The shrubberies that surrounded the window allowed a glimpse at one side of the loch, cold, but gleaming in the morning sunshine. It made her shiver, yet it was beautiful: and as with the landscape, so it was with her position here. To be with Walter, ready to be of use to him, whatever happened, that was well; but all was cold, and solitary, and unknown. Poor mother! She had loved, and cherished, and cared for him all the days of his life, and a year since he had scarcely seen Oona; yet it was Oona's love, and not his mother's, which had made him understand what love was. Strange injustice, yet the injustice of nature, against which it is vain to rebel.

While Mrs. Methven, sad and anxious and perplexed, sat in the unfamiliar room, and looked on the strange landscape in which she found no point of sympathy, Oona in the solitude of the isle, was full of similar thoughts.[a] The day which had passed so miserably to Walter had gone over her in that self-repression which is one of the chief endowments[b] of women, in her mother's cheerful society, and amid all the little occupations of her ordinary life. She had not ventured to indulge herself even in thought, unless she had been prepared, as she was not, to open everything to Mrs. Forrester – and thus went through the hours in that active putting aside of herself and her own concerns, which is sometimes called hypocrisy and sometimes selfrenunciation.[c] She smiled, and talked, and even ate against her will, that her mother might not take fright and search into the cause, so that it was not till she had retired into the refuge of her own room that she was at liberty to throw herself down in all the abandonment of solitude and weep out the tears which made her brow heavy, and think out the thoughts with which her mind was charged almost to bursting. Her candle burned almost all the night long, until long after the moment in which the sight of it held Walter back from the wild flight from her and everything to which his maddening thoughts had almost driven him.[d]

The conflict in Oona's mind was longer, if not so violent. With[e] an effort she was able to dismiss herself from the consideration, and with that entire sympathy which may mistake the facts but never the intention, to enter into the mind of her lover. There was much that she could not understand, and did not attempt to fathom, and the process was not one of those that bring happiness, as when a woman, half-adoring, follows in her own exalted imagination the high career of the hero whom she loves. Walter was no hero, and Oona no simple worshipper to be beguiled into that deification. She had to account to herself for the wanderings, the contradictions, the downfalls of a man of whom she could not think, as had been the first impulse of pain, that any woman would satisfy him, that Katie or Oona, it did not matter which[f] – but who it was yet true had offered himself to Katie first, had given himself to vice (as she remembered with a shudder)[g] first of all, and had been roaming wildly through life without purpose or hope. In all the absolutism of youth to know this, and yet to recognise that the soul within may not be corrupt, and that there may be still an agony of longing for the true even in the midst of the false, is difficult indeed. She achieved it, but it was not a happy effort. Bit by bit it became clearer to her. Had she known the character of the interview with Katie, which gave her grievous pain even when she reasoned it out and said to herself that she understood it, the task would have been a little less hard: but it was hard and very bitter, by moments almost more than she could bear. As she sat by the dying fire, with her light shining so steadily, like a little Pharos[34] of love and steadfastness, her mind went through many faintings and moments of darkness. To have to perceive and acknowledge that you have given your heart and joined your life to that of a man who is no hero, one in whom you cannot always trust that his impulses will be right, is a discovery which is often made in after life, but by degrees, and so gently, so imperceptibly, that love suffers but little shock. But to make this discovery at the very outset is far more terrible than any other obstacle that can stand in the way. Oona was compelled to face it from the first moment almost of a union which she felt in herself no possibility of breaking. She had given herself, and she could not withdraw the gift any more than she could separate from him the love which long before she had been betrayed, she knew not how, into bestowing upon him unasked, undesired, to her own pain and shame.

As she sat all through the night and felt the cold steal upon her, into her very heart, and the desolation of the darkness cover her while she pondered, she was aware that this love had never failed, and knew that to[a] abandon him was no more possible to her than if she had been his wife for years. The girl had come suddenly, without warning, without any fault of hers, out of her innocence and lightheartedness, into the midst of the most terrible problem of life. To love yet not approve, to know that the being who is part of you is not like you, has tendencies which are hateful to you, and a hundred imperfections which the subtlest casuistry of love cannot justify – what terrible fate is this, that a woman should fall into it unawares and be unable to free herself? Oona did not think of freeing herself at all. It did not occur to her as a possibility. How she was to bear his burden which was hers, how she was to reconcile herself to his being as it was, or help the good in him to development, and struggle with him against the evil, that was her problem. Love is often tested in song and story by the ordeal of a horrible accusation brought against the innocent, whom those who love him, knowing his nature, stand by through all disgrace, knowing that he cannot be guilty, and maintaining his cause in the face of all seeming proof. How light, how easy, what an elementary lesson of affection! But to have no such confidence, to take up the defence of the sinner who offends no one so much as yourself, to know that the accusations are true – that is the ordeal by fire, which the foolish believe to be abolished in our mild and easy days. Oona saw it before her, realised it, and made up her mind to it solemnly during that night of awe and pain. This was her portion in the world: not simple life and happiness, chequered only with shadows from terrible death[b] and misfortune, such as may befall the righteous,[c] but miseries far other, far different, to which misfortune and death are but easy experiments in the way of suffering. This was to be her lot.

And yet love is so sweet! She slept towards morning, as Walter did, and when she woke, woke to a sense of happiness so exquisite and tender that her soul was astonished and asked why in an outburst of gratitude and praise to God. And it was not till afterwards that the burden and all the darkness came back to her. But that moment perhaps was worth the pain of the other – one of those compensations, invisible to men, with which God still comforts His martyrs.[a] She rose from her bed and came back to life with a face full of new gravity and thoughtfulness, yet lit up with smiles. Even Mrs. Forrester, who had seen nothing and suspected nothing on the previous night except that Oona had perhaps taken a chill, felt, though she scarcely understood, a something in her face which was beyond the ordinary level of life. She remarked to Mysie, after breakfast, that she was much relieved to see that Miss Oona's cold was to have no bad result. 'For I think she is looking just bonnier than usual this morning – if it is not my partiality – like a spring morning,' Mrs. Forrester said.

'Ah mem, and mair than that,' said Mysie. 'God bless her! She is looking as I have seen her look the Sabbath of the Sacrament;[35] for she's no like the like of us, just hardened baith to good and evil, but a' in a tremble for sorrow and joy, when the occasion[36b] comes round.'

'I hope we are not hardened,' said Mrs. Forrester; 'but I know what you mean, Mysie, though you cannot perhaps express it like an educated person; and I was afraid that she was taking one of her bad colds, and that we should be obliged to put off our visit to Mrs. Methven – which would have been a great pity, for I had promised to Lord Erradeen.'

'Do ye not think, mem,' said Mysie, 'that yon young lord he is very much taken up with – the isle and those that are on it?'

'Hoots,' said Mrs. Forrester, with a smile, 'with you and me, Mysie, do you think? But that might well be after all, for I would not wonder but he felt more at home with the like of us, that have had so much to do with boys and young men, and all the ways of them. And you know I have always said he was like Mr. Rob, which has warmed my heart to him from the very first day.'

Perhaps the mother was, no more than Mysie, inclined to think that she and her old maid won the young lord's attention to the isle: but a woman who is a girl's mother, however simple she may be, has certain innocent wiles in this particular. Lord Erradeen would be a great match for any other young lady on the loch, no doubt: but for Oona what prince was good enough? They both thought so, yet not without a little flutter of their hearts at the new idea which began to dawn.

It was once more a perfectly serene and beautiful day, a day that was like Oona's face, adapted to that 'Sabbath of the Sacrament' which is so great a festival in rural Scotland, and brings all the distant dwellers out of the glens and villages. About noon, when the sun was at its height, and the last leaves on the trees seemed to reflect in their red and yellow, and return, a dazzling response to his shining, Hamish, busy about his fishing tackle on the beach, perceived a boat with a solitary rower, slowly rounding the leafy corners, making a circuit of the isle. Hamish was in no doubt as to the rower; he knew everything as well as the two who were most closely concerned. His brow, which for the last twenty-four hours had been full of furrows, gradually began to melt out of those deep-drawn lines, his shaggy eyebrows smoothed out, his mouth began to soften at the corners. There was much that was mysterious in the whole matter, and Hamish had not been able to account to himself for the change in the young pair who had stepped out of his boat on to the isle in an ecstacy[a] of happiness, and had returned sombre, under the shadow of some sudden estrangement which he could not understand. Neither could he understand why it was that the young lord hovered about without attempting to land at the isle. This was so unlike the usual custom of lovers, that not even the easy explanation, half-contemptuous, half-respectful, which the habits of the masters furnish to their servants, of every eccentricity, answered the occasion – and Hamish could not but feel that there was something 'out of the ordinary' in the proceeding. But his perplexity on this subject did not diminish his satisfaction in perceiving that the young lord was perfectly capable of managing his boat, and that no trace of the excitement of the previous day was visible in its regular motion, impelled now and then by a single stroke, floating on the sunny surface of the water within sight of the red roofs and shining windows of the house, and kept in its course out of the way of all rocks and projecting corners by a skill which could not, Hamish felt sure, be possessed by a disordered brain. This solaced him beyond telling, for though he had not said a word to any one, not even to Mysie, it had lain heavily upon his heart that Miss Oona might be about to link her life to that of a daft man. She that was good enough for any king! and what were the Erradeens to make so muckle work about, but just a mad race that nobody could understand? And the[b] late lord had been one that could not hold an oar to save his life, nor yet yon Underwood-man that was his chosen crony. But this lad was different! Oh! there was no doubt that there was a great difference; just one easy touch and he was clear of the stanes yonder, that made so little show under the water – and there was that shallow bit where he would get aground if he didna mind; but again a touch and that difficulty too was cleared. It was so well done that the heart of Hamish melted altogether into softness. And then he began to take pity upon this modest lover. He put his hands to his mouth and gave forth a mild roar which was not more than a whisper in kind intention.

'The leddies are at home, and will ye no land, my lord?' Hamish cried.

Lord Erradeen shook his head, and sent his boat soft gliding into a little bay under the overhanging trees.

'Hamish,' he said, 'you can tell me. Are they coming to-day to Auchnasheen?'

'At half-past two, my lord,' breathed Hamish through his curved hands, 'they'll be taking the water: and it's just Miss Oona herself that has given me my orders: and as I was saying, they could not have a bonnier day.'

It seemed to Hamish that the young lord said 'Thank God!' which was perhaps too much for the occasion, and just a thocht profane in the circumstances;

but a lord that is in love, no doubt there will be much forgiven to him so long as he has a true heart. The sunshine caught Hamish as he stood watching the boat which floated along the shining surface of the water like something beatified, an emblem of divine ease, and pleasure, and calm, and made his face shine too like the loch, and his red shirt glow. His good heart glowed too with humble and generous joy; they were going to be happy then, these Two;[a] no that he was good enough for Miss Oona; but who was good enough for Miss Oona? The faithful fellow drew his rough hand across his eyes. He who had rowed her about the loch since she was a child, and attended every coming and going – he knew it would be 'a sair loss,' a loss never to be made up. But then so long as she was pleased!

At half-past two they started, punctual as Mrs. Forrester always was. Every event of this day was so important that it was remembered after how exact they were to the minute, and in what a glory of sunshine Loch Houran lay as they pushed out, Mysie standing on the beach to watch them, and lending a hand herself to launch the boat. Mrs. Forrester was well wrapped in her fur cloak with a white 'cloud'[37] about her head and shoulders, which she declared was not at all necessary in the sunshine which was like summer.[b]

'It is just a June day come astray,' she said, nodding and smiling to Mysie on the beach, who thought once more of the Sacrament-day with its subdued glory and awe, and all the pacifying influence that dwelt in it. And Oona turned back to make a little friendly sign with hand and head to Mysie, as the first stroke of the oars carried the boat away.

How sweet her face was; how tender her smile and bright! more sorrowful than mirthful, like one who has been thinking of life and death,[c] but full of celestial and tender cheer, and a subdued happiness. Mysie stood long looking after them, and listening to their voices which came soft and musical over the water. She could not have told why the tears came to her eyes. Something was about to happen, which would be joyful yet would be sad. 'None of us will stand in her way,' said Mysie to herself, unconscious of any possibility that she, the faithful servant of the house, might be supposed to have no say in the matter; 'oh, not one of us! but what will the isle be with Miss Oona away!'

# CHAPTER XIII.[d]

Mrs. Methven had time to recover from the agitation and trouble of the morning before her visitors' arrival. Walter's aspect had so much changed when he appeared that her fears were calmed, though not dispelled. He was very pale, and had an air of exhaustion, to which his softened manners and evident endeavour to please her gave an almost pathetic aspect. Her heart was touched, as it is easy to touch the heart of a mother. She had watched him go out in his boat with a faint awakening of that pleasure with which in ordinary circumstances a woman in the retirement of age sees her children go out to their pleasure. It gave her a satisfaction full of relief, and a sense of escape from evils which she had feared, without knowing what she feared, to watch the lessening speck of the boat, and to feel that her son was finding consolation in natural and uncontaminated pleasures, in the pure air and sky and sunshine of the morning. When he came back he was a little less pale, though still strangely subdued and softened. He told her that she was about to receive a visit from his nearest neighbours – 'the young lady,' he added, after a pause, 'who brought you across the loch.'

'Miss Forrester – and her mother, no doubt? I shall be glad to see them, Walter.'

'I hope so, mother – for there is no way in which you can do me so much good.'

'You mean – this is the lady of whom you spoke to me –' Her countenance fell a little, for what he had said to her was not reassuring; he had spoken of one who would bring money with her, but who was not the best.

'No, mother; I have never told you what I did yesterday. I asked that – lady of whom I spoke – to give me her money and her lands to add to mine, and she would not. She was very right. I approved of her with all my heart.'

'Walter! my dear, you have been so – well – and so – like yourself this morning. Do not fall into that wild way of speaking again.'

'No,' he said, 'if all goes well – never again if all goes well;' and with this strange speech he left her not knowing what to think. She endeavoured to recall to her memory the half-seen face which had been by her side crossing the dark water: but all the circumstances had been so strange, and the loch itself had given such a sensation of alarm and trouble to the traveller, that everything was dim like the twilight in her recollection. A soft voice, with the unfamiliar accent of the north, a courteous and pleasant frankness of accost, a strange sense of thus encountering, half-unseen, some one who was no stranger, nor unimportant in her life – these were the impressions she had brought out of the meeting. In all things this poor lady was like a stranger suddenly introduced into a world unknown to her, where great matters, concerning her happiness and very existence, were hanging upon mysterious decisions of others, unknown, and but to be guessed at faintly through a strange language and amidst allusions which conveyed no meaning to her mind. Thus she sat wondering, waiting for the coming of – she could scarcely tell whom – of some one with whom she could do more good for Walter than by anything else,[a] yet who was not the lady to whom he had offered himself only yesterday. Could there be any combination more confusing? And when, amid all this mystery, as she sat with her heart full of tremulous questions and fears, there came suddenly into this darkling, uncomprehended world of hers the soft and smiling certainty of Mrs. Forrester, kind and simple, and full of innocent affectations, with her little airs of an old beauty, and her amiable confidence in everybody's knowledge and interest, Mrs. Methven had nearly laughed aloud with that keen sense of mingled disappointment and relief which throws a certain ridicule upon such a scene. The sweet gravity of Oona behind was but a second impression. The first was of this simple, easy flood of kind and courteous commonplace, which changed at once the atmosphere and meaning of the scene.[b]

'We are all very glad upon the loch to hear that Lord Erradeen has got his mother with him,' said the guileless visitor,[c] 'for everything is the better of a lady in the house. Oh, yes, you will say, that is a woman's opinion, making the most of her own side: but you just know very well it is true. We have not seen half so much of Lord Erradeen as we would have liked – for in my circumstances we have very little in our power. No gentleman in the house; and what can two ladies do to entertain a young man, unless he will be content with his tea in the afternoon? and that is little to ask a gentleman to. However, I must say all the neighbours are very good-natured, and just accept what we have got to give.'

'Your daughter was most kind to me when I arrived,' said Mrs. Methven. 'I should have felt very lonely without her help.'

'That was nothing. It was just a great pleasure to Oona, who is on the loch from morning to night,' said Mrs. Forrester. 'It was a great chance for her to be of use. We have little happening here, and the news was a little bit of excitement for us all. You see, though I have boys of my own, they are all of them away – what would they do here? – one in Canada, and one in Australia, and three, as I need not say, in India – that is where all our boys go[38] – and doing very well, which is just all that heart can desire. It has been a pleasure from the beginning that Lord Erradeen reminds me so much of my Rob, who is now up with his regiment in the north-west provinces, and a very promising young officer, though perhaps it is not me that should say so. The complexion is different, but I have always seen a great likeness. And now, Lord Erradeen, I hope you will bring Mrs. Methven soon, as long as the fine weather lasts, to the isle?'

Mrs. Methven made a little civil speech about taking the first opportunity, but added,' I have seen nothing yet – not even this old castle of which I have heard so much.'

'It is looking beautiful this afternoon, and I have not been there myself, I may say, for years,' said Mrs. Forrester. 'What would you say, as it is so fine, to trust yourself to Hamish, who is just the most careful man with a boat on all the loch, and take a turn as far as Kinloch Houran with Oona and me?'

The suggestion was thrown out very lightly, with that desire to do something for the pleasure of the stranger, which was always so strong in Mrs. Forrester's breast. She would have liked to supplement it with a proposal to 'come home by the isle' and take a cup of tea, but refrained for the moment with great self-denial. It was caught at eagerly by Walter, who had not known how to introduce his mother to the sight of the mystic place which had so much to do with his recent history: and in a very short time they were all afloat – Mrs. Methven, half-pleased, half-disappointed with the sudden changing of all graver thoughts[a] and alarms into the simplicity of a party of pleasure, so natural, so easy. The loch was radiant with that glory of the afternoon which is not like the glory of the morning, a dazzling world of light, the sunbeams falling lower every moment, melting into the water, which showed all its ripples like molten gold. The old tower lay red in the light, the few green leaves that still fluttered on the ends of the branches, standing out against the darker background, and the glory of the western illumination besetting every dark corner of the broken walls as if to take them by joyful assault and triumph over every idea of gloom. Nothing could have been more peaceful than the appearance of this[a] group. The two elder ladies sat in the stern of the boat, carrying on their tranquil conversation – Mrs. Forrester entering well pleased into details about 'the boys,' which Mrs. Methven, surprised, amused, arrested somehow, she could not tell how, in the midst of the darker, more bewildering current, responded to now and then with some half-question, enough to carry on the innocent fulness of the narrative.[b] Oona, who had scarcely spoken at all, and who was glad to be left to her own thoughts, sat by her mother's side, with the eyes of the other mother often upon her, yet taking no part in the talk; while Walter, placed behind Hamish at the other end of the boat, felt this strange pause of all sensation to be something providential, something beyond all his power of arranging, the preface to he knew not what, but surely at least not to any cutting off or separation from Oona. She had not indeed met his anxious and questioning looks: but she had not refused to come, and that of itself was much; nor did there seem to be any anger, though some sadness, in the face which seemed to him, as to Mysie, full of sacred light.[c]

'No, I have not been here for long,' said Mrs. Forrester; 'not since the late lord's time: but I see very[d] little change. If you will come this way, Mrs. Methven, it is here you will get the best view. Yon is the tower upon which the light is seen, the light, ye will have heard, that calls every new lord: oh and that comes many a time when there is no new lord: You need not bid me whisht, Oona! No doubt there will be some explanation of it: but it is a thing that all the world knows.'

Mrs. Methven laughed, more at her ease than she had yet been, and said –

Walter, what a terrible omission: you have never told me of this.'

Walter did not laugh. His face, on the contrary, assumed the look of gloom and displeasure which she knew so well.

'If you will come with me,' he said to Mrs. Forrester, 'I will show you my rooms. Old Macalister is more gracious than usual. You see he has opened the door.'

'Oh I will go with great pleasure, Lord Erradeen: for it is long since I have been inside, and I would like to see your rooms. Oh how do you do, Macalister? I hope your wife and you are quite well, and not suffering with rheumatism. We've come to show Mrs. Methven, that is your master's mother, round the place. Yes, I am sure ye will all be very glad to see her. This is Macalister, a very faithful old servant that has been with the Lords Erradeen as long as I can remember. How long is it – near five and forty years? Dear me, it is just wonderful how time runs on. I was then but lately married, and never thought I would ever live like a pelican in the wilderness in my mother's little bit isle. But your mind just is made to your fortune, and I have had many a happy day there. Dear me, it will be very interesting to see the rooms, we that never thought there were any rooms. Where

362          *The Selected Works of Margaret Oliphant, Volume 21*

is Oona? Oh, never take the trouble, Lord Erradeen, your mother is waiting: and Oona, that knows every step of the castle, she will soon find her way.'

This was how it was that Oona found herself alone. Walter cast behind him an anxious look, but he could not desert the elder ladies, and Oona was glad to be left behind. Her mind had recovered its calm; but she had much to think of, and his presence disturbed her, with that influence of personal contact which interferes with thought. She knew the old castle, if not every step of it, as her mother said, yet enough to make it perfectly safe for her. Old Macalister had gone first to lead the way, to open doors and windows, that the ladies might see everything, and, save for Hamish in his boat on the beach, there was nobody within sight or call. The shadow of the old house shut out the sunshine from the little platform in front of the door; but at the further side, where the trees grew among the broken masses of the ruin, the sun from the west entered freely. She stood for a moment undecided, then turned towards that wild conjunction of the living and the dead, the relics of the past, and the fresh growth of nature, which give so much charm to every ruin.[a] Oona went slowly, full of thought, up to the battlements, and looked out upon the familiar landscape, full of light and freshness, and all the natural sounds of the golden afternoon – the lapping of the water upon the rocks, the rustle of the wind in the trees, the far-off murmurs of life, voices cheerful, yet inarticulate, from the village, distant sounds of horses and wheels on the unseen roads, the bark of a dog, all the easy, honest utterance, unthought of, like simple breathing, of common life. For a moment the voice of her own thoughts was hushed within her, replaced by this soft combination of friendly noises. It pleased her better to stand here with the soft air about her, than amid[b] all the agitation of human influences to accompany the others.[c]

But[d] human influence is more strong than the hold of nature; and by-and-by[e] she turned unconsciously from the landscape to the house, the one dark solid mass of habitable walls, repelling the sunshine, while the tower, with its blunted outline above, and all the fantastic breaches and openings in the ruin, gave full play to every level ray. The loch, all golden with the sunset, the shadows of the trees, the breath and utterance of distant life, gave nothing but refreshment and soothing. But[f] the walls that were the work of men, and that for hundreds of years had gathered sombre memories about them, had an attraction more absorbing. A little beyond where she was standing, was the spot from which Miss Milnathort had fallen. She[g] had heard the story vaguely all her life, and she had heard from Walter the meaning of it, only the other day. Perhaps it was the sound of a little crumbling and precipitation of dust and fragments from the further wall that brought it so suddenly to her memory; but the circumstances in which she herself was, were enough to bring those of the other woman, who had been as herself, before her with all the vividness of reality. As young as herself, and more happy, the promised bride of another Walter, everything before her as before Oona, love and life, the best that Providence[a] can give, more happy than she, nothing to disturb the gladness of her betrothal; and in a moment all over, all ended, and pain and helplessness, and the shadow of death, substituted for her happiness and hope.[b] Oona paused, and thought of that tragedy with a great awe stealing over her, and pity which was so intense in her realisation of a story, in every point save the catastrophe, so like her own, penetrating her very soul. She asked herself which of the two it was who had suffered most – the faithful woman who lived to tell her own story, and to smile with celestial patience through her death in life, or the man who had struggled in vain, who had fallen under the hand of fate, and obeyed the power of outward circumstances, and been vanquished, and departed from the higher meaning of his youth? Oona thought with a swelling and generous throbbing of her heart, of the one –[c] but with a deeper pang of the other; he who had not failed at all so far as any one knew, who had lived and been happy as people say. She leant against the wall, and asked herself if anything should befall her, such as befell Miss Milnathort, whether her Walter would do the same. Would he accept his defeat as the other had done, and throw down his arms and yield? She said no in her heart, but faltered, and remembered Katie. Yet no! That had been before, not after their hearts had met, and he had known what was in hers. No, he might be beaten down to the dust; he might rush out into the world, and plunge into the madness of life, or he might plunge more deeply, more darkly, into the madness of despairing, and die. But he would not yield; he would not throw down his arms and accept the will of the other.[d] Faulty as he was, and stained and prone to evil, this was what he would never do.

And then her thoughts turned to the immediate matter before her – the deliverance of the man whose fate she had pledged herself to share notwithstanding all his imperfections; he who had found means already, since she had bound herself to him, to make her heart bleed; he whom she had loved against her will, against her judgment, before she was aware. He was to be made free from a bondage, a spiritual persecution, a tyrant who threatened him in every action of his life. Oona had known all her life that there was some mysterious oppression under which the house of Erradeen was bound, and there was no scepticism in her mind in respect to a wonder about which every inhabitant of the district had something to say; but from the moment when it became apparent that she too was to belong to this fated house, it had become insupportable and impossible. She felt, but with less agitation and a calmer certainty than that of Walter, that by whatsoever means it must be brought to an end. Had he been able to bear it, she could not have borne it. And he said that she alone could save him – that with her by his side he was safe; strange words, containing a flattery which was not intended, a claim which could not be resisted. He had said it when as yet he scarcely knew her, he had repeated it when he came to her hot from the presence of the other to whom he had appealed in vain. Strange mixture of the sweet and the bitter! She remembered, however, that he had asked her in the simplicity of desperation to give him her hand to help him, a year ago, and this thought banished all the other circumstances from her mind. She had helped him then, knowing nothing – how was she to help him now? Could she but do it by standing forth in his place and meeting his enemy for him! could she but take his burden on her shoulders and carry it for him! He who had suffered so much feared with a deadly terror his oppressor; but Oona did not fear him. On her he had no power. In Walter's mind there was the weakness of previous defeat, the tradition of family subjection; but in her there was no such weakness, either personal or traditionary; and what was the use of her innocence, of her courage, if not to be used in his cause? Could she but stand for him, speak for him, take his place!ª

> 'Up and spokeᵇ she, Alice Brand,
> And made the holy sign;
> And if there's blood on Richard's hand,
> A stainless hand is mine.'³⁹

Oona's heart was full of this high thought. It drove away from her mind all shadows, all recollections of a less exalting kind. She moved on quietly, not caring nor thinking where she went, forming within herself visions of this substitution, which is in so many cases a woman's warmest desire.

But then she paused, and there became visible to her a still higher eminence of generous love – a higher giddy eminence, more precarious, more dangerous, by which deliverance was less secure; not substitution – that was impossible. In her inward thoughts she blushed to feel that she had thought of a way of escape which for Walter would have been ignoble. It was for him to bear his own part, not to stand by while another did it for him. A noble shame took possession of her that she could for a moment have conceived another way. But with this came back all the anxious thoughts, the questions, the uncertainty. How was she to help him? how pour all the force of her life into him? how transfer to him every needed quality, and give him the strength of two in one?

In the full current of her thoughts Oona was suddenly brought to a pause. It was by the instinct of self-preservation which made her start back on the very edge of the ruin. The sickening sensation with which she felt the crumbling masonry move beneath her foot, drove everything out of her mind for the moment.ᶜ With a sudden recoil upon herself, Oona set her back against the edge of the parapet that remained, and endeavoured to command and combat the sudden terror that seized hold upon her. She cast a keen wild lookᵈ round her to find out if there was any way of safety, and called out for help, and upon Walter! Walter! though she felt it was vain. The wind was against her, and caught her voice, carrying it as if in mockery down the loch, from whence it returned only in a vague and distant echo;[a] and she perceived that the hope of any one hearing and reaching her was futile indeed. Above her, on a range of ruin always considered inaccessible, there seemed to Oona a line of masonry solid enough to give her footing. Necessity[b] cannot wait for precedents. She was young and active, and used to exercise, and her nerves were steadied by the strain of actual danger. She made a spring from her insecure standing, feeling the ruin give way under her foot with the impulse, and with the giddiness of a venture which was almost desperate, flung herself upon the higher level. When she had got there, it seemed to her incredible that she could have done it: and what was to be her next step she knew not, for the ledge on which she stood was very narrow, and there was nothing to hold by in case her head or courage should fail. Everything[c] below and around was shapeless ruin, not to be trusted, all honeycombed, with hollow places thinly covered over by remains of fallen roofs and drifted earth and treacherous vegetation. Only in one direction was there any appearance of solidity, and that was above her towards the tower which still stood firmly, the crown of the building, though no one had climbed up to its mysterious heights within the memory of man. Round it was a stone balcony or terrace, which was the spot upon which the mysterious light, so familiar to her, was periodically visible. Oona's heart beat as she saw herself within reach of this spot. She had watched it so often from the safe and peaceful isle, with that thrill of awe, and wonder, and half-terror, which gave an additional pleasure to her own complete and perfect safety. She made a few steps forward, and, putting out her hand with a quiver of all her nerves, took hold upon the cold roughness of the lower ledge. The touch steadied her, yet woke an agitation in her frame, the stir of strong excitement; for death lay below her, and her only refuge was in the very home of mystery, a spot untrodden of men. For the next few minutes she made her way instinctively without thought, holding by every projection which presented itself; but[d] when Oona found herself standing safe within the balustrade, close upon the wall of the tower, and had drawn breath and recovered a little from the exhaustion and strain – when her mind got again the upper hand and disentangled itself from the agitation of the body, the hurry and whirl of all her thoughts were beyond description. She paused as upon the threshold of a new world. What might be about to happen to her? not to perish like the other, which seemed so likely a few minutes ago, yet perhaps as tragic a fate; perhaps the doom of all connected with the Methvens was here awaiting her.[e]

But there[f] is something in every extreme which disposes the capricious human soul to revolt and recoil. Oona still spoke to herself, but spoke aloud, as it was some comfort to do in her utter isolation.[g] She laughed to herself, nature forcing its way through awe and alarm. 'Doom!' she said to herself, 'there is no doom. That would mean that God was no longer over all. What He wills let that

366     *The Selected Works of Margaret Oliphant, Volume 21*

be done.' This calmed her nerves and imagination. She did not stop to say any prayer for her own safety. There arose even in her mind upon the very foundation of her momentary panic, a sudden new force and hope. She who had so desired to stand in Walter's place, to be his substitute, might not this, without any plan or intention of hers, be now placed within her power?[a]

In the mean time everything was solid and safe beneath her feet. The tower stood strong, the pavement of the narrow platform which surrounded it was worn by time and weather, but perfectly secure. Here and there a breach in the balustrade showed like fantastic flamboyant work, but a regiment might have marched round it without disturbing a stone. Oona's excitement was extreme. Her heart beat in her ears like the roaring of a torrent. She went on, raised beyond herself, with a strange conviction that there was some object in her coming, and that this which seemed so accidental was no accident at all, but perhaps – how could she tell? – an ordeal, the first step in that career which she had accepted.[b] She put her hand upon the wall, and guided herself by it, feeling a support in the rough and time-worn surface, the stones which had borne the assault of ages. Daylight was still bright around her, the last rays of the sun dazzling the loch below, which in its turn lent a glory of reflection to the sky above, and sent up a golden sheen through the air from the blaze upon the water. Round the corner of the tower the wind blew freshly in her face from the hills, reviving and encouraging her. Nature was on her side in all its frankness and reality whatever mystery might be elsewhere. When[c] she had turned the corner of the tower, and saw beneath her the roofs of Auchnasheen visible among the trees, Oona suddenly stood still, her heart making, she thought, a pause as well as her feet;[d] then with a bound beginning again in louder and louder pulsation. She had come to a doorway deep set in the wall, like the entrance of a cavern, with one broad, much-worn step, and a heavy old door bound and studded with iron. She stood for a moment uncertain, trembling, with a sense of the unforeseen and extraordinary which flew to her brain – a bewildering pang of sensation. For a moment she hesitated what to do: yet scarcely for a moment, since[e] by this time she began to feel the force of an impulse which did not seem her own, and which she had no strength to resist. The door[f] was slightly ajar, and pushing it open, Oona found[g] herself, with another suffocating pause, then bound, of her heart, upon the threshold of a richly furnished room. She was aware of keeping her hold upon the door with a terrifying anticipation of hearing it close upon her, but otherwise seemed to herself to have passed beyond her own control and consciousness, and to be aware only of the wonderful scene before her. The room was lighted from an opening[h] in the roof, which showed in the upper part the rough stone of the walls in great blocks, rudely hewn, contrasting strangely with the heavy curtains with which they were hung round below. The curtains seemed of velvet, with panels of tapestry in dim designs here and there: the floor was covered with thick and soft carpets. A great telescope occupied a

*The Wizard's Son, Volume III*   367

place in the centre of the room, and various fine instruments, some looking like astronomical models, stood on tables about.[a] The curtained walls were hung with portraits, one of which she recognised as that of the last Lord Erradeen. And in the centre of all supported on a table with a lamp burning in front of it, the light of which (she supposed), blown about by the sudden entrance of the air, so flickered upon the face that the features seemed to change and move, was the portrait of Walter. The cry which she would have uttered at this sight died in Oona's throat. She stood speechless, without power to think, gazing, conscious that this discovery was not for nothing, that here was something she must do, but unable to form a thought. The[b] light fell upon the subdued colours of the hangings and furniture with a mystic paleness, without warmth; but the atmosphere was luxurious and soft, with a faint fragrance in it. Oona held open the door, which seemed in the movement of the air which she had admitted, to struggle with her, but to which she held with a desperate grasp, and gazed spellbound. Was it the flickering of the lamp, or was it possible that the face of the portrait changed, that anguish came into the features, and that the eyes turned and looked at her appealing, full of misery, as Walter's eyes had looked? It seemed to Oona that her senses began to fail her.[c] There[d] was a movement in the tapestry, and from the other side of the room, some one put it aside, and after looking at her for a moment came slowly out.[e] She had seen him only in the night and darkness, but there was not another such that she should mistake who it was.[f] A thrill ran through her of terror, desperation, and daring. Whatever might now be done or said, Oona had come to the crisis of her fate.

He came towards her with the air of courtesy and grace, which seemed his most characteristic aspect. 'Come in,' he said; 'to reach this place requires a stout heart; but you are safe here.'

Oona made him no reply. She felt her voice and almost her breathing arrested in her throat, and felt capable of nothing but to hold fast to the heavy door, which seemed to struggle with her like a living thing.

'You are afraid,' he said; 'but there is no reason to fear. Why should you think I would injure you? You might have fallen, like others, from the ruin; but you are safe here.'

He advanced another step and held out his hand. It seemed to Oona that the door crushed her as she stood against it, but she would not let go her hold; and with all her power she struggled to regain possession of her voice, but could not, paralysed by some force which she did not understand.

He smiled with a slight ridicule in his lofty politeness. 'I tell you not to fear,' he said. 'Yours is not a spirit to fear; you who would have put yourself in his place and defied the demon. You find me no demon, and I offer no hostility, yet you are afraid.'

Oona was astonished by the sound of her own voice, which burst forth suddenly, by no apparent will of her own, and which was strange to her, an unfamiliar tone, 'I am not afraid – I am in – the protection of God –'

He laughed softly. 'You mean to exorcise me,' he said; 'but that is not so easily done; and I warn you that resistance is not the best way. You have trusted yourself to me –'

'No – no –'

'Yes. You fled from the danger to which another in your place succumbed, and you have taken refuge with me. To those who do so I am bound. Come in; there is no danger here.'

It seemed to Oona that there were two beings in her – one which ridiculed her distrust, which would have accepted the hand held out; another – not her, surely, not her frank and unsuspicious self – who held back and clung in terror to the door. She stammered, hearing even in her voice the same conflict, some tones that were her own, some shrill that were not hers – 'I want no protection – but God's.'

'Why then,' he said with a smile, 'did you not remain among the ruins? What brought you here?'

There was an answer – a good answer if she could have found it – but she could not find it, and made no reply.

'You refuse my friendship, then,' he said, 'which is a pity, for it might have saved you much suffering. All the same, I congratulate you upon your prize.'

These last words stopped the current towards him of that natural sentiment of confidence and faith in her fellow-creatures, which was Oona's very atmosphere. Her prize! What did he mean by her prize?

'There could not be anything more satisfactory to your friends,' he said. 'A title – large estates – a position which leaves nothing to be desired. Your mother must be fully satisfied, and your brothers at the ends of the world will all feel the advantage. Other conquests might have been better for the Erradeens, but for you nothing could be more brilliant. It was a chance too, unlikely, almost past hoping for, thus to catch a heart in the rebound.'

She stood aghast, gazing with eyes that were pained by the strain, but which would not detach themselves from his face. Brilliant! advantages! Was she in a dream? or what was the meaning of the words?

'It is against my own policy,' he continued, 'as perhaps you know; still I cannot help admiring your skill, unaided, against every drawback. You have a strong mind, young lady of the isle, and the antecedents which would have daunted most women have been allies and auxiliaries to you.' His laugh was quite soft and pleasant, sounding like gentle amusement, not ridicule. 'I know your family,' he continued, 'of old. They were all men of strong stomachs, able to swallow much so long as their own interest was concerned. With Highland caterans,[40] that is comprehensible; but one so young as you – named like you – after – ' he laughed again that low soft laugh of amusement as if at something which tickled him in spite of himself, 'the emblem of purity and innocence – "heavenly Una with her milk-white lamb."'[41] 'You want,' said Oona, whose voice sounded hoarse in her throat, and sharp to her own ears, 'to make me mad with your taunts; to make me give up –'

'Pardon me, I am only congratulating you,' he said, and smiled, looking at her with a penetrating look of amusement and that veiled ridicule which does not infringe the outward forms of politeness. She gazed back at him with eyes wide open, with such a pang of wondering anguish and shame in her heart as left her speechless; for what he said was true. She had thought of her union with Walter in many ways before, but never in this. Now it all flashed upon her as by a sudden light. What he said was true. She who had never given a thought to worldly advantage, had nevertheless secured it as much as if that had been her only thought. Her senses seemed to fail her in the whirl and heart-sickness of the revelation. It was true. She who had believed herself to be giving all, she was taking to herself rank, wealth, and honour, in marrying Walter. And giving to him what? – a woman's empty hand; no more. Oona was very proud though she did not know it, and the blow fell upon her with crushing effect. Every word had truth in it; her mother would be satisfied; the family would profit by it wherever they were scattered; and she would be the first to reap the advantage.

Oona felt everything swim around her as in the whirl and giddiness of a great fall. Her fall was greater than that of Miss Milnathort, for it was the spirit not the body that was crushed and broken. She could not lift up her head. A horrible doubt even of herself came into her mind in her sudden and deep humiliation. Had this been in her thoughts though she did not know it? No stroke could have been aimed at her so intolerable as this.

He kept his eyes upon her, as if with a secret enjoyment of her overthrow. 'You do not thank me for my congratulations,' he cried.

'Oh!' she cried in the wondering self-abandonment of pain, 'can you be a man, only a man, and strike so deep?' Then the very anguish of her soul gave her a sudden inspiration. She looked round her with her eyes dilating. 'When you can do this,' she said, putting with unconscious eloquence her hand to her heart, 'what do you want with things like those?' The sight of the lamp which burned before Walter's portrait had given her a painful sense of harm and danger when she saw it first. It filled her now with a keen disdain. To be able to pierce the very soul, and yet to use the aid of *that!* She did not know what its meaning was, yet suffering in every nerve, she scorned it, and turned to him with a questioning look which was full of indignation and contempt.

And he who was so strong, so much above her in power and knowledge, shrank – almost imperceptibly, but yet he shrank – startled, from her look and question. '*That?*' he said, 'you who know so little of your own mind, how can you

370 *The Selected Works of Margaret Oliphant, Volume 21*

tell how human nature is affected? – by what poor methods, as well as by great. You understand nothing – not yourself – far less the devices of the wise.'

'Oh, you are wise,' cried Oona, 'and cruel. You can make what is best look the worst. You can confuse our souls so that we cannot tell what is good in us, and what evil. I know, I know, you are a great person. Yet you hide and lurk in this place which no man knows; and work by spells and charms like – like –'

'Like what?' a gleam of anger and shame – or of something that might have betrayed these sentiments on any other face – crossed his usually calm and lofty countenance. Oona, opposite to him, returned his look with a passionate face of indignation and disdain. She had forgotten herself altogether, and everything but the thrill and throbbing of the anguish which seemed to have taken the place of her heart in her. She feared nothing now. The blow which she had received had given her the nobleness of desperation.

'Like a poor – witch,' she said; 'like the wizard they call you; like one who plays upon the ignorant, not like the powerful spirit you are. You that can beat us down to the dust, both him and me. You that can turn sweet into bitter, and good into evil. Oh, how can you for shame take that way too, like a – juggler,' she cried in her passion; 'like a sorcerer; like –'

'You speak like a fool, though you are no fool,' he said, 'not knowing the stuff that we are made of.' He made a step towards her as he spoke, and though his tone was rather sad than fierce, there came upon Oona in a moment such a convulsion of terror as proved what the weakness was of which he spoke. She clung with all her failing force to the door which seemed her only support, and broke out into a shrill cry, 'Walter, Walter, save me!' afraid of she knew not what, panic seizing her, and the light flickering in her fainting eyes.

\*\*\*

# CHAPTER XIV.[a]

WHILE Oona was standing on the verge of these mysteries a trial of a very different kind had fallen to Walter. They had exchanged parts in this beginning of their union. It was his to lead the two elder ladies into those rooms which were to him connected with the most painful moments of his life, but to them conveyed no idea beyond the matter of fact that they were more comfortably furnished and inhabitable than was to be expected in such a ruin. Even to Mrs. Methven, who was interrogating his looks all the time, in an anxious endeavour to know what his feelings were, there seemed nothing extraordinary in the place save this. She seated herself calmly in the chair, which he had seen occupied by so different a tenant, and looking smiling towards him, though always with a question in her eyes, began to express her wonder why, with Auchnasheen so near, it had been thought necessary to retain a dwelling-place among these

The Wizard's Son, Volume III 371

ruins; but since Walter did from time to time inhabit them, his mother found it pleasant that they were so habitable, so almost comfortable, and answered old Macalister's apologies for the want of a fire or any preparations for their coming with smiling assurances that all was very well, that she could not have hoped to find rooms in such careful repair. Mrs. Forrester was a great deal more effusive, and examined[a] everything with a flow of cheerful remark, divided between Lord Erradeen and his old servant, with whom, as with everybody on the loch, she had the acquaintance of a lifetime.

'I must see your wife, Macalister,' she said, 'and make her my compliment on the way she has kept everything. It is really just a triumph, and I would like to know how she has done it. To keep down the damp even in my little house, where there are always fires going, and every room full, is a constant thought – and how she does it here, where it is so seldom occupied –. The rooms are just wonderfully nice rooms, Lord Erradeen, but I would not say they were a cheerful dwelling – above all, for a young man like you.'

'No, they are not a very cheerful dwelling,' said Walter with a smile, which to his mother, watching him so closely, told a tale of pain which she did not understand indeed, yet entered into with instinctive sympathy. The place began to breathe out suffering and mystery to her, she could not tell why. It was cold, both in reality and sentiment, the light coming into it from the cold north-east, from the mountains which stood up dark and chill above the low shining of the setting sun. And the cold affected her from his eyes, and made her shiver.

'I think,' she said, 'we must not stay too long. The sun is getting low, and the cold –'

'But where is Oona?' said Mrs. Forrester. 'I would not like to go away till she has had the pleasure too. Oh, yes, it is a pleasure, Lord Erradeen – for you see we cannot look out at our own door, without the sight of your old castle before our eyes, and it is a satisfaction to know what there is within. She must have stayed out-side among the ruins that she was always partial to. Perhaps Macalister will go and look for her – or, oh! Lord Erradeen, but I could not ask you to take that trouble.'

'My lord,' said old Macalister aside, 'if it had been any other young lady I wad have been after her before now. Miss Oona is just wonderful for sense and judg-ment; but when I think upon yon wall –'

'I will go,' said Walter. Amid all the associations of this place, the thought of Oona had threaded through every movement of his mind. He thought now that she had stayed behind out of sympathy, now that it was indifference, now – he could not tell what to think. But no alarm for her safety had[b] crossed his thoughts. He made a rapid step towards the door, then paused, with a bewilder-ing sense that he was leaving two innocent women without protection in a place full of dangers which they knew nothing of. Was it possible that his enemy could assail him through these unsuspecting simple visitors? He turned back to them with a strange pang of pity and regret, which he himself did not understand. 'Mother,' he said, 'you will forgive me – it is only for a moment?'

'Walter!' she cried, full of surprise; then waved her hand to him with a smile, bidding him, 'Go, go – and bring Miss Forrester.' Her attitude, her smile of perfect security and pleasure, went with him like a little picture, as he went down the spiral stairs. Mrs. Forrester was in the scene too, in all her pretty faded colour and animation, begging him – 'Dear me, not to take the trouble; for no doubt Oona was just at the door, or among the ruins, or saying a word to Hamish about the boat.' A[a] peaceful little picture – no shadow upon it; the light a little cold, but the atmosphere so serene and still. Strange contrast to all that he had seen there – the conflict, the anguish, which seemed to have left their traces upon the very walls.[b]

He hurried down-stairs[c] with this in his mind, and a lingering of all his thoughts upon the wistful smiling of his mother's face – though why at this moment he should dwell upon that was a wonder to himself. Oona was not on the grassy slope before the door, nor talking to Hamish at the landing-place, as her mother suggested. There was no trace of her among the ruins. Then, but not till then, Walter began to feel a tremor of alarm. There came suddenly into his mind the recollection of that catastrophe of which he had been told in Edinburgh by its victim; it sent a shiver through him, but even yet he did not seriously fear; for Oona was no stranger to lose herself upon the dangerous places of the ruin. He went hurriedly up the steps to the battlements, where he himself had passed through so many internal struggles, thinking nothing less than to find her in one of the embrasures, where he had sat and looked out upon the loch. He had been startled as he came out of the shadow of the house, by a faint cry, which seemed to issue from the distance, from the other extremity of the water, and which was indeed the cry for help to which Oona had given utterance when she felt the wall crumbling under her feet, which the wind had carried far down the loch, and which came back in a distant echo. Walter began to remember this cry as he searched in vain for any trace of her. And when he reached the spot where the danger began and saw the traces that some other steps had been there before him, and that a shower of crumbling mortar and fragments of stone had fallen, his heart leaped to his throat with sudden horror. This was calmed by the instant reassurance that had she fallen he must at once have discovered the catastrophe. He looked round him bewildered, unable to conceive what had become of her. Where had she gone? The boat lay at the landing-place, with Hamish in waiting; the whole scene full of rest and calm, and everything silent about and around.[d] 'Oona!' he cried, but the wind caught his voice too, and carried it away to the village on the other bank, to her own isle away upon the glistening water, where Oona was not. Where was she? His throat began to grow parched, his breath to labour with the hurry of his heart. He stood on the verge of the precipice of broken masonry,[e] straining his eyes over the stony pinnacles above, and the sharp irregularities of the ruin. There he saw something suddenly which made his heart stand still: her glove lying where she had dropped it in her hurried progress along the ledge. He did not pause to think how she got there, which would have seemed at another moment impossible, but with a desperate spring and a sensation as of death in his heart, followed, where she had passed, wherever that might be.

Walter neither knew where he was going nor how he made his way along those jagged heights. He did not go cautiously as Oona had done, but flew on, taking no notice of the dangers of the way. The sound of voices, and of his own name, and Oona's cry for help, reached his ear as with a leap he gained the stone balcony of the tower. His feet scarcely touched the stones as he flew to her who called him, nor did he think where he was, or feel any wonder at the call, or at the voices on such a height, or at anything that was happening. His mind had no room for any observation or thought save that Oona called him. He flung himself into the dark doorway as if it had been a place he had known all his life, and caught her as her strength failed her. She who had thought she could put herself in his place, and who had been ready to brave everything for him, turned round with her eyes glazing and her limbs giving way, with strength enough only to throw herself upon his breast. Thus Walter found himself once more face to face with his enemy. The last time they had met, Lord Erradeen had been goaded almost to madness. He stood now supporting Oona on his arm, stern, threatening in his turn.

'If you have killed her,' he cried; 'if you have hurt her as you did before; if you have made her your victim, as you did before!' There was no shrinking in his look now: he spoke out loudly with his head high, his eyes blazing upon the enemy who was no longer his, but *hers*, which had a very different meaning; and though he stood against the door where he had found Oona holding it wide open, this was done unconsciously, with no idea of precaution. The time for that was over now.

And with the sensation of his support, the throb of his heart so near hers, Oona came back to herself. She turned slowly round towards the inhabitant of the tower. 'Walter, tell him – that though he can make us miserable he cannot make us consent. Tell him – that now we are two, not one, and that our life is ours, not his. Oh!' she cried, lifting her eyes, addressing herself directly to him, 'listen to me! – over me you have no power – and Walter is mine, and I am his. Go – leave us in peace.'

'She says true; leave us in peace. In all my life now, I shall do no act that is not half hers, and over her you have no power.'

'You expect me then,' he said, 'to give way to this bargain of self-interest – a partnership of protection to you and gain to her. And you think that before this I am to give way.'

'It is not so,' cried Walter, 'not so. Oona, answer him. I turned to her for help because I loved her, and she to me for – I know not why – because she loved me. Answer him, Oona! if it should be at this moment for death not for life –'

374    *The Selected Works of Margaret Oliphant, Volume 21*

She turned to him with a look and a smile, and put her arm through his, clasping his hand: then turned again to the other who stood looking on. 'If it should be for death,' she said.

There was a moment of intense stillness. He before whom these two stood knew human nature well. He knew every way in which to work upon a solitary being, a soul alone, in his power; but he knew that before two, awake, alive, on the watch one for the other, these methods were without power, and though his experiences were so great the situation was new. They were in the first absolute devotion of their union, invulnerable, no germ of distrust, no crevice of possible separation. He might kill, but he could not move them. This mysterious agent was not above the artifices of defeat. To separate them was the only device that remained to him.

'You are aware,' he said, 'that here if nowhere else you are absolutely in my power. You have come to me. I have not gone to you. If you wish to sacrifice her life you can do so, but what right have you to do it? How dare you take her from those who love her, and make her your victim? She will be your victim, not mine. There is time yet for her to escape. It is for her to go – Die? why should she die? Are you worth such a sacrifice? Let her go –'

'Hold me fast – do not loose me, Walter,' cried Oona wildly in his ear.

And here his last temptation took him, in the guise of love, and rent him in two. To let *her* perish, was that possible? Could he hold her though she was his life, and sacrifice hers? Walter could not pause to think; he tore his hand out of hers, which would not be loosed, and thrust her from him. 'Oona,' he cried, his voice sinking to a whisper, 'go! Oona, go! Not to sacrifice you – no, no, I will not. Anything but that. While there is time, go!'

She stood for a moment between the two, deserted, cast off by him who loved her. It was the supreme crisis of all this story of her heart. For a moment she said nothing, but looked at them, meeting the keen gaze of the tempter, whose eyes seemed to burn her, gazing at Walter who had half-closed his not to see her go. Then with the sudden, swift, passionate action, unpremeditated and impulsive, which is natural to women, she flung herself before him, and seized with her hands the table upon which the light was burning. 'You said,' she cried, breathless, 'that you used small methods as well as great – and this is one, whatever it is.' She thrust it from her violently as she spoke. The lamp fell with a great crash and broke, and the liquid which had supplied it burst out and ran blazing in great globules of flames over the floor. The crash, the blaze, the sudden uproar, was like a wall between the antagonists. The curtains swaying with the wind, the old dry tapestries, caught in the fire like tinder. Oona, as wild with fear as she had been with daring, caught at Walter's hand with the strength of despair, and fled dragging him after her. The door clanged behind them as he let it go, then burst open again with the force of the breeze and let out a great blaze, the red mad gleam of fire in the sunshine and daylight – unnatural, devouring. With a sense that death was in their way before and behind, they went forth clinging to each other, half-stupefied, half-desperate. Then sense and hearing and consciousness itself were lost in a roar as of all the elements let loose – a great dizzy upheaving as of an earthquake. The whole world darkened round them; there was a sudden rush of air and whirl of giddy sensation – and nothing more.[a]

The two mothers meanwhile talked calmly in the room below, where Macalister had lighted the fire, and where, in the cheerful blaze and glow, everything became more easy and tranquil and calm. Perhaps even the absence of the young pair, whose high strain of existence at the moment could not but disturb the elder souls with sympathy, made the quiet waiting, the pleasant talk, more natural. Mrs. Methven had been deeply touched by her son's all unneeded apology for leaving her. She could have laughed over it, and cried, it was so kind, so tender of Walter, yet unlike him, the late awakening of thought and tenderness to which she had never been accustomed, which penetrated her with a sweet and delightful amusement as well as happiness. She had no reason to apprehend any evil, neither was Mrs. Forrester afraid for Oona. 'Oh no, she is well used to going about by herself. There is nobody near but knows my Oona. Her family and all her belongings have been on the loch, I might say, since ever it was a loch; and if any stranger took it upon him to say an uncivil word, there is neither man nor woman for ten miles round but would stand up for her – if such a thing could be,' Mrs. Forrester added with dignity, 'which is just impossible and not to be thought of. And as for ruins, she knows them well.[b] But I would like her to see the books, and what a nice room Lord Erradeen has here, for often we have been sorry for him, and wondered what kind of accommodation there was, and what good it could do to drag the poor young man out of his comfortable house, if it was only once in the year –'

'And why should he come here once in the year?' Mrs. Methven asked with a smile.

'That is just the strange story: but I could not take upon myself to say, for I know nothing except the common talk, which is nonsense, no doubt. You will never have been in the north before?' said Mrs. Forrester, thinking it judicious to change the subject.

'Never before,' Mrs. Methven replied, perceiving equally on her side that the secrets of the family were not to be gleaned from a stranger; and she added, 'My son himself has not yet seen his other houses, though this is the second time he has come here.'

'It is to be hoped,' said the other, 'that now he will think less of that weary London, which I hear is just an endless traffic of parties and pleasure – and settle down to be a Scots lord. We must make excuses for a young man that naturally likes to be among his own kind, and finds more pleasure in an endless on-going than ladies always understand. Though I will not say but I like society very well myself, and would be proud to see my friends about me, if it were not for the quiet way that Oona and I are living, upon a little bit isle, which makes it always needful to consider the weather, and if there is a moon, and all that; and besides that, I have no gentleman in the house.'

'I never had a daughter,' said Mrs. Methven; 'there can be no companion so sweet.'

'You mean Oona? Her and me,' said Mrs. Forrester, with Scotch grammar and a smile, 'we are but one; and you do not expect me to praise myself? When I say we have no gentleman in the house, it is because we cannot be of the use we would wish to our friends. To offer a cup of tea is just all I have in my power, and that is nothing to ask a gentleman to; but for all that it is wonderful how constantly we are seeing our neighbours, especially in the summer time, when the days are long. But bless me, what is that?' Mrs. Forrester cried. The end of her words was lost in a tumult and horror of sound such as Loch Houran had never heard before.[a]

## CHAPTER XV.[b]

THE explosion startled the whole country for miles around.

The old castle was at all times the centre of the landscape, standing sombre in its ruin amid all the smiling existence of to-day. It flashed in a moment into an importance more wonderful, blazing up to the sky in fire and flame and clouds of smoke like a great battle. The whole neighbourhood, as far as sight could carry, saw this new wonder, and sprang into sudden excitement, alarm, and terror. Every soul rushed out of the village on the bank; servants appeared half frantic in front of Auchnasheen, pushing out in skiffs and fishing-cobbles upon the water which seemed to share the sudden passion of alarm, and became but one great reflection, red and terrible, of the flames which seemed to burst in a moment from every point. Some yachtsmen, whose little vessel had been lying at anchor, and who had been watching with great curiosity the moving figures on the height of the gallery round the tower, with much laughing discussion among themselves as to the possibility of having seen the ghost –[c] were suddenly brought to seriousness in a moment as the yacht bounded under their feet with the concussion of the air, and the idle sail flapping from the mast grew blood-red in the sudden glare. It was the work of another moment to leap into their boat and speed as fast as the oars could plough through the water, to the rescue, if rescue were needed. Who could be there? they asked each other. Only old Macalister with his wife, who, safe in the lower story, would have full time to escape. But then, what were those figures[d] on the tower? The young men almost laughed again as they said to each other, 'The warlock lord!' 'Let's hope he's blown himself up and made an end of all that nonsense,' said the sceptic of the party. But just then the stalwart boat-load came across a wild skiff dashing through the water, old Symington like a ghost in the stern, and red-haired Duncan, with bare arms and throat, rowing as for life and death.

'My lord is there!' cried the old man with quivering lips, 'The leddies are there!'

'And Hamish and Miss Oona!' fell stammering from Duncan, half dumb with horror.

The young yachtsmen never said a word, but looked at each other and flew along over the blood-red water. Oona! It was natural they should think of her first in her sweetness and youth.

The two mothers in their tranquil talk sat still for a moment and looked at each other with pale awe on their faces, when that wild tumult enveloped them, paralysing every other sense. They thought they were lost, and instinctively put out[a] their hands to each other. They were alone – even the old servant had left them – and there they sat breathless, expecting death. For a moment the floor and walls so quivered about them that this alone seemed possible; but nothing followed,[b] and their faculties returned. They rose with one impulse and made their way together to the door – then,[c] the awe of death passing, life rising in them, flew down the stair-case[d] with the lightness of youth, and out to the air, which already was full of the red flashes of the rising flames. But once there, a worse thing befell these two poor women. They had been still in the face of death, but now, with life saved, came a sense of something more terrible than death. They cried out in one voice the names of their children. 'My boy!' 'Oona!' Old Macalister, speechless, dragging his old wife after him, came out and joined them, the two old people looking like owls suddenly scared by the outburst of lurid light.

'Oh, what will be happening?' said the old woman, her dazed astonishment contrasting strangely with the excitement and terror of the others.

Mrs. Forrester answered her with wild and feverish volubility.

'Nothing will have happened,' she said. 'Oona, my darling! What would happen? She knows her way: she would not go a step too far. Oh, Oona, where are you? why will you not answer me? They will just be bewildered like ourselves, and she will be in a sore fright; but that will be for me. Oona! Oona! She will be frightened – but only for me. Oona! Oh Hamish, man, can ye not find your young lady? The fire – I am not afraid of the fire. She will just be wild with terror – for me. Oona! Oona! Oona!' cried the poor lady, her voice ending in a shriek.

Mrs. Methven stood by her side, but did not speak. Her pale face was raised to the flaming tower, which threw an illumination of red light over everything. She did not know that it was supposed to be inaccessible. For anything she knew, her boy might be there perishing within her sight; and she could do nothing. The anguish of the helpless and hopeless gave her a sort of terrible calm. She looked at the flames as she might have looked at executioners who were putting her son to death. She had no hope.

Into the midst of this distracted group came a sudden rush of men from the boats, which were arriving every minute, the young yachtsmen at their head.

Mrs. Forrester flung herself upon these young men, catching hold of them as they came up.

'My Oona's among the ruins,' she said breathlessly. 'Oh, no fear but you'll find her. Oh, find her! find her! for I'm going out of my senses, I think. I know that she's safe, oh, quite safe! but I'm silly, silly, and my nerves are all wrong. Oh, Harry, for the love of God, and Patrick, Patrick, my fine lad! And not a brother to look after my bairn!'

'We are all her brothers,' cried the youths, struggling past the poor lady, who clung to them and hindered their progress, her voice coming shrill through the roar of the flames and the bustle and commotion below. Amid this tumult her piercing 'Oona! Oona!' came in from time to time, sharp with the derision of tragedy for anything so ineffectual and vain. Before many minutes had passed the open space in front of the house which stood intact and as yet unthreatened, was crowded with men, none of them, however, knowing what to do, nor, indeed, what had happened The information that Lord Erradeen and Oona were missing was handed about among them, repeated with shakings of the head to every new-comer. Mrs. Methven standing in the midst, whom nobody knew, received all the comments like so many stabs into her heart. 'Was it them that were seen on the walls just before? Then nothing could have saved them.' 'The wall's all breached to the loch: no cannon could have done it cleaner. It's there you'll find them.' 'Find them! Oh, hon,[42] oh, hon! the bodies of them. Let's hope their souls are in a better place.' The unfortunate mother heard what everybody said. She stood among strangers, with nobody who had any compassion upon her, receiving over and over again the assurance of his fate.

The first difficulty here, as in every other case of the kind, was that no one knew what to do; there were hurried consultations, advices called out on every hand, suggestions – many of them impossible – but no authoritative guide to say what was to be done. Mrs. Methven, turning her miserable looks from one to another, saw standing by her side a man of commanding appearance, who seemed to take no share in either advice or action, but stood calmly looking on. He was so different from the rest, that she appealed to him instinctively.

'Oh, sir!' she cried, 'you must know what is best to be done – tell them.'

He started a little when she spoke; his face, when he turned it towards her, was full of strange expression. There was sadness in it, and mortification, and wounded pride. She said after that he was like a man disappointed, defeated, full of dejection and indignation. He gave her a look of keen wonder, and then said with a sort of smile –

'Ah, that is true!' Then in a moment his voice was heard over the crowd. 'The thing to be done,' he said, in a voice which was not loud, but which immediately silenced all the discussions and agitations round, 'is to clear away the ruins. The fire will not burn downward – it has no food that way – it will exhaust itself. The young lady fell with the wall. If she is to be found, she will be found there.'

*The Wizard's Son, Volume III*  379

The men around all crowded about the spot from which the voice came.

'Wha's that that's speaking?'

'I see nobody.'

'What were you saying, sir?'

'Whoever it is, it is the right thing,' cried young Patrick from the yacht. 'Harry, keep you the hose going on the house. I'll take the other work; and thank you for the advice, whoever you are.'

Mrs. Forrester too had heard this voice, and the command and calm in it gave to her troubled soul a new hope. She pushed her way through the crowd to the spot from whence it came.

'Oh,' she cried, 'did you see my Oona fall? Did you see my Oona? No, no, it would not be her that fell. You are just deceived. Where is my Oona? Oh, sir, tell them where she is that they may find her, and we'll pray for you on our bended knees, night and morning, every day!'

She threw herself on her knees, as she spoke, on the grass, putting up her quivering, feverish hands. The other mother, with a horror which she felt even in the midst of her misery, saw the man to whom this heart-rending prayer was addressed, without casting even a glance at the suppliant at his feet, or with any appearance of interest in the proceedings he had advised, turn quietly on his heel and walk away. He walked slowly across the open space and disappeared upon the edge of the water with one glance upward to the blazing tower, taking no more notice of the anxious crowd collected there than if they had not existed. Nor did any one notice the strange spectator going away at the height of the catastrophe, when everybody far and near was roused to help. The men running hurriedly to work did not seem to observe him. The two old servants of the house, Symington and Macalister, stood crowding together out of the reach of the stream of water which was being directed upon the house. But Mrs. Methven took no note of them: only it gave her a strange surprise[a] in the midst of her anguish to see that while her Walter's fate still hung in the balance, there was one who could calmly go away.

By this time the sun had set; the evening, so strangely different from any other that ever had fallen on the loch, was beginning to darken on the hills, bringing out with wilder brilliancy the flaming of the great fire, which turned the tower of Kinloch Houran into a lantern, and blazed upwards in a great pennon of crimson and orange against the blue of the skies. For miles down the loch the whole population was out upon the roads gazing at this wonderful sight; the hillsides were crimsoned by the reflection, as if the heather had bloomed again; the water glowed red under the cool calm of the evening sky. Round about Birkenbraes was a little crowd, the visitors and servants occupying every spot from which this wonder could be seen, and Mr. Williamson himself, with his daughter, standing at the gate to glean what information might be attainable from the passers-by. Katie, full of agitation, unable to bear the common babble inside, had walked on, scarcely knowing what she

380 *The Selected Works of Margaret Oliphant, Volume 21*

did, in her indoor dress, shivering with cold and excitement. They had all said to each other that there could be no danger to life in that uninhabited place.

'Toots, no danger at all!' Mr. Williamson had said, with great satisfaction in the spectacle. 'Old Macalister and his wife are just like rats in their hole, the fire will never come near them; and the ruin will be none the worse – it will just be more a ruin than ever.'

There was something in Katie's mind which revolted against this easy treatment of so extraordinary a catastrophe. It seemed to her connected, she could not tell how, with the scene which had passed in her own room so short a time before. But for shame she would have walked on to Auchnasheen to make sure that Walter was in no danger. But what would he think of her – what would everybody think? Katie went on, however, abstracted from herself, her eyes upon the blaze in the distance, her heart full of disturbed thoughts. All at once she heard the firm quick step of some one advancing to meet her. She looked up eagerly; it might be Walter himself – it might be – When she saw who it was, she came to a sudden pause. Her limbs refused to carry her, her very breath seemed to stop. She looked up at him and trembled. The question that formed on her lips could not get utterance. He was perfectly calm and courteous, with a smile that bewildered her and filled her with terror.

'Is there any one in danger?' he said, answering as if she had spoken. 'I think not. There is no one in danger now. It is a fine spectacle. We are at liberty to enjoy it without any drawback – now.'

'Oh, sir,' said Katie, her very lips quivering, 'you speak strangely. Are you sure that there was no one there?'

'I am sure of nothing,' he said with a strange smile.

And then Mr. Williamson, delighted to see a stranger, drew near.

'You need not be so keen with your explanations, Katie. Of course it is the gentleman we met at Kinloch Houran. Alas! poor Kinloch Houran, we will never meet there again. You will just stay to dinner now that we have got you. Come, Katie, where are your manners? you say nothing. Indeed we will consider it a great honour – just ourselves and a few people that are staying in the house; and as for dress, what does that matter? It is a thing that happens every day. Neighbours in the country will look in without preparation; and for my part, I say always, the more the merrier,' said the open-hearted millionnaire.

The stranger's face lighted up with a gleam of scornful amusement.

'The kindness is great,' he said, 'but I am on my way to the other end of the loch.'

'You are never walking?' cried Mr. Williamson. 'Lord bless us? that was a thing that used to be done in my young days, but nobody thinks of now. Your servant will have gone with your baggage? and you would have a delicacy – I can easily understand – in asking for a carriage in the excitement of the moment; but ye shall not walk past my house where there are conveyances of all kinds that it is just a charity to use. Now, I'll take no denial; there's the boat. In ten minutes they'll get up steam. I had ordered it, ready to send up to Auchnasheen for news. But as a friend would never be leaving if the family was in trouble, it is little use to do that now. I will just make a sign to the boat, and they'll have ye down in no time; it will be the greatest pleasure – if you are sure you will not stay to your dinner in the mean time, which is what I would like best?'

He stood looking down upon them both from his great height; his look had been sad and grave when he had met Katie, a look full of expression which she could not fathom. There came now a gleam of amusement over his countenance. He laughed out.

'That would be admirable,' he said, offering no thanks, 'I will take your boat,' like a prince according, rather than receiving, a favour.

Mr. Williamson looked at his daughter with a confused air of astonishment and perplexity, but he sent a messenger off in a boat to warn the steamer, which lay with its lights glimmering white in the midst of the red reflections on the loch. The father and daughter stood there silenced, and with a strange sensation of alarm, beside this stranger. They exchanged another frightened look.

'You'll be going – a$^a$ long journey?' Mr. Williamson said, faltering, scarcely knowing what he said.

'I am going – for a long time, at least,' the stranger said.$^b$

He seemed to put aside their curiosity as something trifling, unworthy to be answered, and with a wave of his hand to them, took the path towards the beach.

They turned and looked after him, drawing close to each other for mutual comfort. It was twilight, when everything is confusing and uncertain. They lost sight of him, then saw him again, like a tall pillar on the edge of the water. There was a confusion of boats coming and going, in which they could not trace whither he went, or how. Katie$^c$ and her father stood watching, taking no account of the progress of time, or of the cold wind of the night which came in gusts from the hills. They both drew a long sigh of relief when the steamer was put in motion, and went off down the loch with its lights like glow-worms on the yards and the masts. Nor did they say a word to each other as they turned and went home. When inquiries were made afterwards, nothing but the most confused account could be had of the embarkation. The boatman had seen the stranger, but none among them would say that he had conveyed him to the steamer; and on the steamer the men were equally confused, answering at random, with strange glances at each other. Had they carried that passenger down to the foot of the loch? Not even Katie's keen questioning could elicit a clear reply.

But when the boat had steamed away, carrying into the silence the rustle of its machinery and the twinkling of its lights, there was another great explosion from the tower of Kinloch Houran, a loud report which seemed to roar away into the hollow$^d$ of the mountains, and came back in a thousand rolling echoes. A great column of flame shot up into the sky, the stones fell like a cannonade, and then all was darkness and silence. The loch fell into sudden gloom; the men who were labouring at the ruins stopped short, and groped about to find each other through the dust and smoke which hung over them like a cloud. The bravest stood still, as if paralysed, and for a moment, through all this strange scene of desolation and terror, there was but one sound audible, the sound of a voice which cried 'Oona! Oona!' now shrill, now hoarse with exhaustion and misery, 'Oona! Oona!' to earth and heaven.

# CHAPTER XVI.[a]

WHEN the curious and the inefficient dropped away, as they did by degrees as night fell, there were left the three youths from the yacht, Hamish, Duncan, and two or three men from the village, enough to do a greater work than that which lay before them; but the darkness and the consternation, and even their very eagerness and anxiety, confused their proceedings. Such lamps as they could get from Macalister were fastened up among the heaps of ruin, and made a series of wild Rembrandt-like pictures in the gloom,[43] but afforded little guidance to their work. The masses of masonry which they laboured to clear away seemed to increase rather than diminish under their picks and spades – new angles of the wall giving way when they seemed to have come nearly to the foundation. And now and then from above a mass of stones penetrated through and through by the fire, and kept in their place only by mere balance, would topple down without warning, dangerously near their heads, risking the very lives of the workers; upon whom discouragement gained as the night wore on, and no result was obtained. After a while, with a mournful unanimity they stopped work and consulted in whispers what was to be done. Not a sound had replied to their cries. They had stopped a hundred times to listen, one more imaginative than the rest, thinking he heard an answering cry; but no such response had ever come, how was it possible, from under the choking, suffocating mass, which rolled down upon them as they worked, almost stopping their breath? They gave up altogether in the middle of the night in dejection and hopelessness. The moon had risen and shone all round them, appearing through the great chasms in the wall, making a glory upon the loch, but lending no help here, the shadow of the lower part of the house lying black over the new-made ruin. What was the use? They stood disconsolately consulting over[b] the possibilities. If Walter and Oona were under those heaps of ruin, it was impossible that they could be alive, and the men asked each other, shaking their heads, what chance there was of any of those fortunate accidents which sometimes save the victims of such a calamity. The wall had been already worn by time, there were no beams, no archways which could have sheltered them – everything had come down in one mass of ruin. After many and troubled discussions they prepared reluctantly to abandon the

*The Wizard's Son, Volume III* 383

hopeless work. 'Perhaps, in the morning' – it was all that any one could say. The young yachtsmen made a last effort, calling out Walter's name. 'If you can speak, for God's sake speak? any sign and we'll have you out. Erradeen! Erradeen!' they cried. But the silence was as that of the grave. A fall of powdery fragments now and then from the heap, sometimes a great stone solemnly bounding downwards from point to point, the light blown about by the night air lighting up the dark group, and the solitary figure of Hamish, apart from them, who was working with a sort of rage, never pausing, pulling away the stones with his hands. This was all; not a moan, not a cry, not a sound of existence under those shapeless piles of ruin. The only thing that broke the silence, and which came now with a heartrending monotony, almost[a] mechanical, was the cry of 'Oona! Oona!' which Oona's mother,[b] scarcely conscious, sent out into the night.

The men stole softly round the corner of the house which remained untouched, to get to their boats, stealing away like culprits, though there was no want of good-will in them. But they were not prepared for the scene that met them there. The little platform before the door, and the landing-place,[c] were bright almost as day with the shining of the moon, the water one sheet of silver, upon which the boats lay black, the grassy space below all white and clear. In the midst of this space, seated on a stone, was Mrs. Methven. She had scarcely stirred all night. Her companion in sorrow had been taken into the shelter of the house, but she, unknown and half-forgotten,[d] and strong with all the vigour of misery, had remained there, avoiding speech of any one. With all her senses absorbed in listening, not a stroke had escaped her, scarcely a word – for a long time she had stood and walked about, not asking a question, observing, seeing, hearing all that was done. But as the awful hours went on, she had dropped down upon this rough seat, little elevated above the ground, where her figure now struck the troubled gaze of the young men, as if it had been that of a sentinel watching to see that they did not abandon their work. No such thought was in her mind. She was conscious of every movement they had made. For a moment she had thought that their call upon her son meant that they had found some trace of him – but that was a mere instantaneous thrill, which her understanding was too clear to continue to entertain. She had said to herself from the beginning that there was no hope; she had said from the first what the men had said to each other reluctantly after hours of exertion. What was the good? since nothing could be done. Yet all the while as she said this, she was nursing within her bosom, concealing it even from her own consciousness, covering up the smouldering dying fire in her heart, a hope that would not altogether die. She would not even go towards the workers when they called out her son's name to know what it was; but only waited, waited with a desperate, secret, half-heathen thought, that perhaps if she did not cry and importune, but was silent, letting God do what He would, He might yet relent and bring her back her boy. Oh be patient! put on at least the guise of patience! and perhaps He would be touched by the silence of her misery – He who had not heard her prayers.[e]

384     *The Selected Works of Margaret Oliphant, Volume 21*

She sat going over a hundred things in her heart. That Walter should have come back to her, called her to him, opened his heart to her, as a preparation for being thus snatched from her for ever! She said to herself that by-and-by[a] she would thank God for this great mercy, and that she had thus found her son again if only for two days: but in the mean time her heart bled all the more for the thought, and bereavement became more impossible, more intolerable, even from that, which afterwards would make it almost sweet. As she kept that terrible vigil and heard the sound of the implements with which – oh, what was it? – not him, his body, the mangled remains of him, were being sought, she seemed to see him, standing before her, leaning upon her, the strong on the weak, pouring his troubles into her bosom – as he had not done since he was a child; and now he was lying crushed beneath those stones. Oh no, no, Oh no, no – it was not possible. God was not like that, holding the cup of blessing to a woman's lips and then snatching it away. And then with an effort she would say to herself what she had said from the first, what she had never wavered in saying, that there was no hope. How could there be any hope? crushed beneath tons of falling stones – oh, crushed out of recognition, out of humanity! her imagination spared her nothing. When they found him they would tell her it was better, better, she the mother that bore him, that she should not see him again. And all the while the moon shining and God looking on. She was callous to the cry that came continually, mechanically, now stronger, now fainter, from the rooms above. 'Oona, Oona!' Sometimes it made her impatient. Why should the woman cry, as if her voice could reach her child under those masses of ruin? And *she* could not cry who had lost her all![b] her only one! Why[c] should the other have that relief and she none – nor any hope? But all the sounds about her caught her ear with a feverish distinctness. When she heard the steps approaching after the pause of which she had divined the meaning, they seemed to go over her heart, treading it down into the dust. She raised her head and looked at them as they came up, most of the band stealing behind to escape her eye. 'I heard you,' she said, 'call – my son.'

'It was only to try; it was to make an effort; it was a last chance.'

'A last –' though she was so composed there was a catch in her breath as she repeated this word; but she added, with the quiet of despair, 'You are going away?'

The young man who was the spokesman stood before her like a culprit with his cap in his hand.

'My brothers and I,' he said, 'would gladly stay if it was any use; but there is no light to work by, and I fear – I fear – that by this time –'

'There is no more hope?' she said. 'I have no hope. I never had any hope.'

The young man turned away with a despairing gesture, and then returned to her humbly, as if she had been a queen.

'We are all grieved – more grieved than words can say: and gladly would we stay if we could be of any use. But what can we do? for we are all convinced –'

*The Wizard's Son, Volume III*                    385

'No me,' cried Hamish, coming forward in the moonlight. 'No me!' his bleeding hands left marks on his forehead as he wiped the heavy moisture from it; his eyes shone wildly beneath his shaggy brows. 'I was against it,' he cried, 'from the first! I said what would they be doing here? But convinced, that I never will be, no till I find – Mem, if ye tell them they'll bide. Tell them to bide. As sure as God is in heaven that was all her thought – we will find her yet.'

The other men had slunk away, and were softly getting into their boats. The three young yachtsmen alone waited, a group of dark figures about her. She looked up at them standing together in the moonlight, her face hollowed out as if by the work of years.

'He is my only one,' she said, 'my only one. And you – you – you are all the sons of one mother.'

Her voice had a shrill anguish in it, insupportable to hear: and when she paused there came still more shrilly into the air, with a renewed passion, 'Oona! Oona!' the cry that had not ceased for hours. The young man who was called Patrick flung his clenched hand into the air; he gave a cry of pity and pain unendurable.

'Go and lie down for an hour or two,' he said to the others, 'and come back with the dawn. Don't say a word. I'll stay; it's more than a man can bear.'

When the others were gone, this young fellow implored the poor lady to go in, to lie down a little, to try and take some rest. What good could she do? he faltered; and she might want all her strength for to-morrow – using all those familiar pleas with which the miserable are mocked. Something like a smile came over her wan face.

'You are very kind,' she said, 'oh very kind!' but no more. But when he returned and pressed the same arguments upon her she turned away almost with impatience. 'I will watch with my son to-night,' she said, putting him away with her hand. And thus the night passed.

Mrs. Forrester had been taken only half-conscious into Walter's room early in the evening. Her cry had become almost mechanical,[a] not to be stopped; but she, it was hoped, was but half aware of what was passing, the unwonted and incredible anguish having exhausted her simple being, unfamiliar with suffering. Mr. Cameron, the minister from the village, had come over on the first news, and Mysie from the isle to take care of her mistress. Together they kept watch over the poor mother, who lay sometimes with her eyes half closed in a sort of stupor, sometimes springing up wildly, to go to Oona who was ill, and wanting her, she cried, distraught. 'Oona! Oona!' she continued to cry through all.[b] Mysie had removed her bonnet, and her light faded hair was all dishevelled, without the decent covering of the habitual cap, her pretty colour gone. Sorrow seems to lie harder on such a gentle soul. It is cruel. There is nothing in it that is akin to the mild level of a being so easy and common. It was torture that prostrated the soul – not the passion of love and anguish which gave to the other mother the power of absolute self-control, and strength which could endure all things. Mr. Cameron himself, struck to the heart, for Oona was as dear to him as a child of

386         *The Selected Works of Margaret Oliphant, Volume 21*

his own, restrained[a] his longing to be out among the workers in order to soothe and subdue her; and though she scarcely understood what he was saying, his presence did soothe her. It was natural that the minister should be there, holding her up in this fiery passage, though she could not tell why.[b]

And thus the night went on. The moonlight faded outside; the candles paled and took a sickly hue within as the blue dawn came stealing over the world. At that chillest, most awful moment of all the circle of time, Mrs. Forrester had sunk into half-unconsciousness. She was not asleep, but exhaustion had almost done the part of sleep, and she lay on the sofa in a stupor, not moving, and for the first time intermitting her[c] terrible cry. The minister stole down-stairs[d] in that moment of repose. He was himself an old man and shaken beyond measure by the incidents of the night. His heart was bleeding for the child of his spirit, the young creature to whom he had been tutor, counsellor, almost father from her childhood. He went out with his heart full, feeling the vigil insupportable in the miserable room above, yet almost less supportable when he came out to the company of the grey hills growing visible, a stern circle of spectators round about, and realised with a still deeper pang the terrible unmitigated fact of the catastrophe. It was with horror that he saw the other mother sitting patient upon the stone outside. He did not know her, and had forgotten that such a person existed as Lord Erradeen's mother. Had she been there all night? 'God help us,' he said to himself; 'how selfish we are, even to the sharers of our calamity.' She looked up at him as he passed, but said nothing. And what could he say to her? For the first time he behaved himself like a coward, and fled from duty[e] and kindness; for what could he say to comfort her? and why insult her misery with vain attempts? Young Patrick had pressed shelter and rest upon her, being young and knowing no better. But the minister could not tell Walter's mother to lie down and rest,[f] to think of her own life. What was her life to her? He passed her by with the acute and aching sympathy which bears a share of the suffering it cannot relieve. And[g] his own suffering was sore. Oona, Oona, he cried to himself silently in his heart as her mother had done aloud – his child, his nursling, the flower of his flock. Mysie had told him in the intervals, when her mistress was quiet, in whispers and with tears, of all that had happened lately, and of Oona's face that was like the Sabbath of the Sacrament, so grave yet so smiling as she left the isle. This went to the old minister's heart. He passed the ruin where Hamish was still plucking uselessly, half-stupefied, at the stones, and Patrick, with his back against the unbroken wall, had fallen asleep in utter weariness. Mr. Cameron did not linger there, but sought a place out of sight of man, where he could weep: for he was old, and his heart was too full to do without some natural relief.

He went through the[h] ruined doorway to a place where all was still green and intact, as it had been before the explosion; the walls standing, but trees grown in the deep soil which covered the old stone floor. He leaned his white head against the roughness of the wall, and shed the tears that made his old eyes heavy, and relieved his old heart with prayer. He had prayed much all the night through, but with distracted thoughts, and eyes bent upon the broken-hearted creature by whose side he watched. But now he was alone with the great and closest Friend, He to whom all things can be said, and who understands all. 'Give us strength to resign her to Thee,' he said, pressing his old cheek against the damp and cold freshness of the stones, which were wet with other dews than those of nature, with the few concentrated tears of age, that mortal dew of suffering. The prayer and the tears relieved his soul. He lifted his head from the wall, and turned to go back again – if, perhaps, now fresh from his Master's presence he might find a word to say to the other woman who all night long, like Rizpah,[44] had sat silent and watched her son.

But as he turned to go away it seemed to the minister that he heard a faint sound. He supposed nothing but that one of the men who had been working had gone to sleep in a corner, and was waking and stirring to the daylight. He looked round, but saw no one. Perhaps, even,[a] there came across the old man's mind some recollection of the tales of mystery connected with this house; but in the presence of death and sorrow, he put these lesser wonders aside. Nevertheless, there was a sound, faint, but yet of something human.[b] The old stone floor was deep under layers of soil upon which every kind of herbage and even[c] trees grew; but in the corner of the wall against which he had been leaning, the gathered soil had been hollowed away by the droppings from above, and a few inches of the original floor was exposed. The old man's heart began to beat with a bewildering possibility: but[d] he dared not allow himself to think of it: he said to himself, but it must be a bird, a beast, something imprisoned in some crevice. He listened. God! was that a moan? He turned and rushed,[e] with the step of a boy, to where Patrick sat dozing, and Hamish, stupefied, worked on mechanically. He clutched the one out of his sleep, the other from his trance of exhaustion – 'Come here! come here! and listen. What is this?' the old minister said.

\*\*\*

# CHAPTER XVII.[f]

THE two fugitives, holding each other's hands, had fled from the fire without a word to each other. All that needed to be spoken seemed to them both to be over. They hurried on instinctively, but without any hope, expecting every moment when destruction should overtake them. Walter was the last to give up consciousness: but the sickening[g] sense of a great fall, the whirl and resistance of the air rushing madly against him through the void, the sensation mounting up to his brain, the last stronghold of consciousness, and thrill of feeling, as if life were to end there, in a painful rush of blood, were all that were known to him.[h] What happened really was that, holding Oona insensible in his arms, he was carried downwards with the slide and impetus of the part of the ruin on which he was standing, detached by his own weight, rather than thrown violently down by the action of the explosion. The force of the fall, however, was so great, and the mass falling with them so heavy, that some of the stones, already very unsteady, of the pavement below gave way, and carried them underground to one of the subterranean cellars, half filled up with soil, which ran under the whole area of the old castle. How long they lay there unable to move, and for some part of the time at least entirely without consciousness, Walter could never tell. When he recovered his senses he was in absolute darkness and in considerable pain. Oona had fallen across him and the shock had thus been broken. It was a moan from her which woke him to life again. But she made no reply to his first distracted question, and only gave evidence of life by a faint little cry[a] from time to time – too faint to be called a cry – a breath of suffering, no more. The suffocating terrible sensation of the darkness, a roar of something over them like thunder, the oppression of breathing, which was caused by the want of atmosphere, all combined to bewilder his faculties and take away both strength and will to do anything more than lie there quietly and gasp out the last breath.[b] Walter was roused by feeling in Oona an unconscious struggle for breath. She raised first one hand, then another, as if to take away something which was stifling her, and he began to perceive in the vagueness of his awakening consciousness that her life depended upon his exertions. Then, his eyes becoming more accustomed to the darkness, he caught a faint ray of light, so attenuated as to be no more than a thread in the solid gloom. To drag himself towards this, and with himself the still more precious burden, thus in utter helplessness confided to him, was a more terrible work than Walter in all his life had ever attempted before. There was not room to stand upright, and his limbs were so shaken and aching that he could scarcely raise himself upon them; and one of his arms was useless, and, when he tried to raise it, gave him the most exquisite pain. It seemed hours before he could succeed in dragging her[c] to the little opening, a mere crevice between the stones, through which the thread of light had come. When he had cleared the vegetation from it, a piercing cold breath came in and revived him. He raised Oona in his arms to the air, but the weight of her unconsciousness was terrible to him in his weakened condition, and though she began to breathe more easily, she was not sufficiently recovered to give him any help.[d]

Thus she lay, and he crouched beside her, trying to think, for he could not tell how long. He heard sounds above him indeed, but the roar of the falling stones drowned the human noises, and his brain was too much clouded to think of the search which must be going on overhead for his companion and himself. The worst of all was this[e] dazed condition of his brain, so that it was a long time before he could put one thing to another and get any command of his thoughts. In all likelihood consciousness did not fully return until the time when the men above in despair relinquished their work,[f] for some feeble sense of cries and human voices penetrated the darkness, but so muffled and far off that in the

*The Wizard's Son, Volume III*                389

dimness of his faculties he did not in any way connect them with himself, nor think of attempting any reply. Perhaps it was, though he was not aware that he heard it, the echo of his own name that finally brought him to the full possession of himself – and then all his dull faculties centred, not in the idea of any help at hand, but in that of fighting a way somehow to a possible outlet. How was he to do it? The pain of his arm was so great that at times he had nearly fainted with mere bodily suffering, and his mind fluctuated from moment to moment – or was it not rather from hour to hour? – with perplexity and vain endeavour. He was conscious, however, though he had not given any meaning to the sounds he heard, of the strange silence which followed upon the stopping of the work. Something now and then like the movements of a bird (was it Hamish working wildly above, half-mad, half-stupefied,[a] unable to be still?) kept a little courage in him, but the silence and darkness were terrible, binding his very soul.

It was then that he had the consolation of knowing that his companion had come to herself. Suddenly a hand groping found his, and caught it; it was his wounded arm, and the pain went like a knife to his heart, a pang which was terrible, but sweet.

'Where are we?' Oona said, trying to raise herself – oh, anguish! – by that broken arm.

He could not answer her for the moment, he was so overcome by the pain – and he was holding her up with the other arm.

'Do not hold my hand,' he said at last; 'take hold of my coat. Thank God that you can speak!'

'Your arm is hurt, Walter?'

'Broken, I think; but never mind, that is nothing. Nothing matters so long as you have your senses. Oona, if we die together, it will be all right?'

'Yes,' she said, raising her face in the darkness to be nearer his. He kissed her solemnly, and for the moment felt no more pain.

'As well this way as another. Nothing can reach us here – only silence and sleep.'

She began to raise herself slowly, until her head struck against the low roof. She gave a faint cry – then finding herself on her knees, put her arm round him, and they leant against each other. 'God is as near in the dark as in the day,'[45] she said. 'Lord, deliver us – Lord, deliver us!' Then, after a pause, 'What happened? You saved my life.'

'Is it saved?' he asked. 'I don't know what has happened, except that we are together.'

Oona gave a sudden shudder and clung to him. 'I remember now, the flames and the fire: and it was I that broke the lamp. What did it mean, the lamp? I thought[b] it was something devilish – something to harm you.' She shivered more

390 *The Selected Works of Margaret Oliphant, Volume 21*

and more, clinging to him. 'Do you think it is He – that has shut us up in this dungeon, to die?'

Walter made no reply; it was no wonder to him that she should speak wildly. He too was tempted to believe that accident had no part in what had befallen them, that they had now encountered the deadly vengeance of their enemy. He tried to soothe her,[a] holding her close to his breast. 'I think we are in some of the vaults below – perhaps for our salvation.' As her courage failed there was double reason that he should maintain a good heart. 'There must be some outlet. Will you stay here and wait till I try if I can find a way?'

'Oh no, no,' cried Oona, clinging to him, 'let us stay together. I will creep after you. I will not hinder you.' She broke off with a cry, echoing, but far more keenly, the little moan that came from him unawares as he struck his arm against the wall. She felt it far more sharply than he did, and in the darkness he felt her soft hands binding round his neck something warm and soft like their own touch in which she had wound the wounded arm to support it. It was the long white 'cloud' which had been about her throat, and it warmed him body and soul; but he said nothing by way of gratitude. They were beyond all expressions of feeling, partly because they had reached the limit at which reality is too over-powering for sentiment, and partly because there was no longer any separation of mine and thine between them, and they were but one soul.

But to tell the miseries of their search after a way of escape would demand more space than their historian can afford. They groped along the wall, thinking now that they saw a glimmer in one direction, now in another, and constantly brought up with a new shock against the opaque resistance round them, a new corner, or perhaps only that from which they started; under their feet unequal heaps of damp soil upon which they stumbled, and broken stones over which Oona, with childlike sobs of which she was unconscious, caught her dress, falling more than once as they laboured along. In this way they moved round and round their prison, a long pilgrimage. At length, when they were almost in despair, saying nothing to each other, only keeping close that the touch of each to each might be a moral support, they found themselves in what seemed a narrow passage, walls on each side, and something like an arrowslit over their heads, the light from which showed them where they were,[b] and was as an angel of consolation to the two wounded and suffering creatures, stumbling along with new hope. But when they had reached the end of this narrow passage, Walter, going first, fell for a distance of two or three feet into the lower level of another underground chamber like that which he had left, jarring his already strained and racked frame,[c] and only by an immense effort hindered Oona from falling after him. The force of the shock, and instant recovery by which he kept her back and helped her to descend with precaution, brought heavy drops of exhaustion and pain to his forehead. And when they discovered that they were nothing the better for their struggles,

The Wizard's Son, Volume III                    391

and that the place which they had reached at such a cost, though lighter, was without any outlet whatever except that by which they had come, their discouragement was so great that Walter had hard ado not to join in the tears which Oona, altogether prostrated by the disappointment, shed on his shoulder.

'We must not give in,' he tried to say. 'Here there is a little light at least. Oona, my darling, do not break down, or I shall break down too.'

'No, no,' she said submissively through her sobs, leaning all her weight upon him. He led her as well as he was able to a heap of earth in the corner, over which in the roof was a little opening to the light, barred with an iron stanchion, and quite out of reach. Here he placed her tenderly, sitting down by her, glad of the rest,[a] though it was so uninviting. The light came in pale and showed the strait inclosure of their little prison. They were neither of them able to resume their search, but sat close together leaning against each other, throbbing with pain, and sick with weariness and disappointment. It gave Walter a kind of forlorn pride in his misery to feel that while Oona had failed altogether, he was able[b] to sustain and uphold her. They did not speak in their weakness, but after a while dozed and slept, in that supreme necessity of flesh and blood which overcomes even despair, and makes no account of danger. They slept as men will sleep at death's door, in the midst of enemies:[c] and in the depths of their suffering and misery[d] found refreshment. But in that light sleep little moans unawares came with their breathing, for both were bruised and shaken, and Walter's broken arm was on fire with fever and pain. It was those breathings of unconscious suffering that caught the ear of the minister as he made his prayer. His step had not disturbed them, but when he came back accompanied by the others, the light[e] was suddenly darkened and the stillness broken by[f] some one who flung himself upon his knees with a heavy shock of sound and a voice pealing in through the opening –[g] 'Miss Oona,[h] if ye are there, speak! or, oh for the love of the Almighty, whoever is there, speak and tell me where's my leddy?' It was Hamish, half mad with hope and suspense and distracted affection, who thus plunged between them and the light.

They both woke with the sound, but faintly divining what it was, alarmed at first rather than comforted by the darkness[i] into which they were plunged. There was a pause before either felt capable of reply, that additional[j] deprivation being of more immediate terror to them, than there was consolation in the half-heard voice. In this pause, Hamish, maddened by the disappointment of his hopes, scrambled to his feet reckless and miserable, and shook his clenched fist in the face of the minister who was behind him.

'How dare ye,' he cried, 'play upon a man, that is half wild, with your imaginations! there's naebody there!' and with something between a growl and an oath, he flung away, with a heavy step that sounded like thunder to the prisoners. But next moment the rage of poor Hamish all melted away into the exceeding and intense sweetness of that relief which is higher ecstasy than any actual enjoyment given to men, the very sweetness of heaven itself –[a] for as he turned away the sound of a voice, low and weak, but yet a voice, came out of the bowels of the earth; a murmur of two voices that seemed to consult with each other, and then a cry of 'Oona is safe. Oona is here. Come and help us, for the love of God.'

'The Lord bless you!' cried the old minister, falling on his knees. 'Oona, speak to me, if you are there. Oona, speak to me! I want to hear your own voice.'

There was again[b] a pause of terrible suspense. Hamish threw himself down, too, behind the minister, tears running over his rough cheeks,[c] while the young[d] man, who was overawed by the sight,[e] and affected too, in a lesser degree, stood with his face half hidden against the wall.

'I am here,' Oona said feebly,[f] 'all safe – not hurt even. We are both safe; but oh, make haste, make haste, and take us out of this place.'

'God bless you, my bairn. God bless you, my dearest bairn!' cried Mr. Cameron:[g] but his words were drowned in a roar of laughter and weeping from the faithful soul behind him – 'Ay, that will we, Miss Oona – that will we, Miss Oona!' Hamish shouted and laughed and sobbed till the walls rang, then clamorous with his heavy feet rushed out of sight without another word, they knew not where.

'I'll follow him,' said young Patrick; 'he will know some way.'

The minister was left alone at the opening through which hope had come. He was crying like a child, and ready to laugh too like Hamish.

'My bonny dear,' he said; 'my bonny dear –' and could not command his voice.

'Mr. Cameron – my mother. She must be breaking her heart.'

'And mine,' Walter said with a groan. He thought even then of the bitterness of her woe, and of all the miserable recollections that must have risen in her mind: please God not to come again.

'I am an old fool,' said Mr. Cameron, outside: 'I cannot stand out against the joy; but I am going. I'm going, my dear. Say again you are not hurt, Oona. Say it's you, my darling, my best bairn!'

'And[h] me that had not the courage to say a word to yon poor woman,' he said to himself as he hurried away. The[i] light was still grey in the skies, no sign of the sun as yet, but not only the hills distinct around, but[j] the dark woods, and the islands on the water, and even the sleeping roofs so still among their trees on the shores of the loch, had come into sight. The remaining portion of the house which had stood so many assaults, and the shapeless mass of the destroyed tower, stood up darkly against the growing light: and almost like a part of it, like a statue that had come down from its pedestal was the figure of Mrs. Methven, which he saw standing between him and the shore, her face turned towards him. She had heard the hurrying steps and the shout of Hamish, and knew that something had happened. She[k] had risen against her will, against the resolution she had formed, unable to control herself, and stood with one hand under her cloak, holding her heart, to repress, if possible, the terrible throbbing in it. The face she turned towards the minister overawed him in the simplicity of his joy. It was grey, like the morning, or rather ashen white, the colour of death. Even now she would not, perhaps could not, ask anything; but only stood and questioned him with her eyes, grown to twice their usual size, in the great hollows which this night had opened[a] out.

The minister knew that he should[b] speak carefully, and make easy to her the revolution from despair to joy;[c] but he could not. They were both beyond all secondary impulses. He put the fact into the plainest words.

'Thank God! your son is safe,' he cried.

'What did you say?'

'Oh, my poor lady, God be with you. I dared not speak to you before. Your son is safe. Do you know what I mean? He is as safe as you or me.'

She kept looking at him, unable to take it into her mind; that is to say, her mind had flashed upon it, seized it at the first word, yet – with a dumb horror holding hope away from her, lest deeper despair might follow – would not allow her to believe.

'What – did you say? You are trying to make me think –' And then she broke off, and cried out 'Walter!' as if she saw him – as a mother might cry who saw her son suddenly, unlooked for, come into the house when all believed him dead – and fell on her knees, –[d] then from that attitude sank down upon herself, and dropped prostrate on the ground.

Mr. Cameron was alarmed beyond measure. He knew nothing of faints, and he thought the shock had killed her. But what could he do? It was against his nature to leave a stranger helpless. He took off his coat and covered her, and then hurried to the door and called up Macalister's wife, who was dozing in a chair.

'I think I have killed her,' he said, 'with my news.'

'Then ye have found him?' the three old people said together, the woman clasping her hands with a wild 'Oh hon – oh hon!'[e] while Symington came forward, trembling, and pale as death.

'I had hoped,' he said, with quivering lips, 'like the apostles with One that was greater, that it was he that was to have delivered[46] – Oh, but we are vain creatures! and now it's a' to begin again.'

'Is that all ye think of your poor young master? He is living, and will do well. Go and take up the poor lady. She is dead, or fainted, but it is with joy.'

And then he went up-stairs.[f] Many an intimation of sorrow and trouble the minister had carried. But good news had not been a weight upon him hitherto. He went to the other poor mother with trouble in his heart. If the one who had been so brave was killed by it, how encounter her whose soft nature had fallen prostrate at once? He met Mysie at the door, who told him her mistress had slept, but showed signs of waking.

'Oh, sir, if ye could give her something that would make her sleep again! I could find it in my heart to give her, what would save my poor lady from ever waking more,' cried the faithful servant; 'for oh, what will she do – oh, what will we all do without Miss Oona?'

'Mysie,' cried the minister, 'how am I to break it to her? I have just killed the poor lady down-stairs[a] with joy; and what am I to say to your mistress? Miss Oona is safe and well – she's safe and well.'

'Oh, Mr. Cameron,' cried Mysie, with a sob, 'I ken what you are meaning. She's well, the Lord bless her, because she has won to heaven.'

Mrs. Forrester had woke during this brief talk, and raised herself upon the sofa. She broke in upon them in a tone so like her ordinary voice, so cheerful and calm, that they both turned round upon her with a kind of consternation.

'What is that you are saying – safe and well – oh, safe and well. Thank God for it; but I never had a moment's doubt. And where has she been all this weary night; and why did she leave me in this trouble? What are ye crying for, Mysie, like a daft woman? You may be sure, my darling has been doing good, and not harm.'

'That is true, my dear lady – that is true, my dear friend,' cried the minister. 'God bless her! She has done us all good, all the days of her sweet life.'

'And you are crying too,' said Oona's mother, almost with indignation. 'What were you feared for? Do you think I could not trust God, that has always been merciful to me and mine? or was it Oona ye could not trust?' she said with smiling scorn. 'And is she coming soon? For it seems to me we have been here a weary time.'

'As soon – as she can get out of the – place where she is. The openings are blocked up by the ruin.'

'I had no doubt,' said Mrs. Forrester, 'it was something of that kind.'

Then she rose up from the sofa, very weak and tottering, but smiling still, her pale and faded face looking ten years older, her hair all ruffled, falling out of its usual neat arrangement. She put up her hands to her head with a little cry.

'Bless me,' she said, 'she will think I have gone out of my senses, and you too, Mysie, to take my bonnet off and expose me, with no cap. I must put all this right again before my Oona comes.'

Mr. Cameron left her engaged in these operations, with the deepest astonishment. Was it a faith above the reach of souls less simple? or was it the easy rebound of a shallow nature? He watched her for a moment as she put up her thin braids of light hair, and tied her ribbons, talking all the time of Oona.

'She never was a night out of her bed in all her life before; and my only fear is she may have gotten a chill, and no means here of making her comfortable. Mysie, you will go down-stairs,[b] and try at least to get the kettle to boil, and a cup of tea for her. Did the minister say when she would be here?'

'No, mem,' said Mysie's faltering voice; 'naething but that she was safe and well; and the Lord forgive me – I thought – I thought –'

The Wizard's Son, Volume III                                             395

'Never mind what you thought,' said Mrs. Forrester briskly,' but run down-stairs[a] and see if you can make my darling a good cup of tea.'

By the time she had tied her bonnet strings and made herself presentable, the full light of the morning was shining upon the roused world. The air blew chill in her face as she came down the staircase (strangely weak and tottering, which was 'just extraordinary'[b] she said to herself), and emerged upon the little platform outside. Several boats already lay on the beach, and there was the sound of the voices and footsteps of men breaking the stillness. Mrs. Forrester came out with those little graces which were part of herself, giving a smile to old Symington, and nodding kindly to the young men from the yacht who were just coming ashore. 'This is early hours,' she said to them with her smile, and went forward to the little group before the door, surrounding Mrs. Methven, who still lay where Mr. Cameron had left her, incapable[c] of movement. 'Dear me,' said Mrs. Forrester, 'here have I been taking up a comfortable room, and them that have a better right left out of doors. They have given us a terrible night, my child and yours, but let us hope there has been a good reason for it, and that they will be none the worse. They are just coming, the minister tells me. If ye will take the help of my arm, we might step that way and meet them. They will be glad to see we are not just killed with anxiety, which is what my Oona will fear.'

# CHAPTER XVIII.[d]

THE news that Lord Erradeen, and it was supposed several others – some went so far as to say a party of visitors, others his mother, newly arrived as all the world was aware, and to whom he was showing the old castle, with a young lady who was her companion – had perished in the fire, streamed down the loch nobody knew how, and was known and believed to the end of the country[e] before the evening was over. It came to the party at Birkenbraes as they were sitting down to dinner, some time after everybody had come in from gazing at the extraordinary spectacle of the fire,[f] got up, Mr. Williamson assured his guests, entirely for their amusement. The good man, however,[g] had been much sobered out of that jocose mood by his encounter with the strange visitor whom he had first seen at Kinloch Houran,[h] but had begun[i] to draw a little advantage from that too, and[j] was telling the lady next to him with some pride of Lord Erradeen's relation, a very distinguished person indeed. 'I'm thinking in the diplomatic service, or one of the high offices that keep a man abroad all his life. (I would rather for my part live in a cottage at home, but that is neither here nor there.) So as he was leaving and naturally could not trouble the family about carriages just at such a moment, I offered him the boat: and you could[k] see them getting up steam. I find it very useful to have a steam-boat always ready, just waiting at the service of my friends.' The lady had replied as in duty bound, and as was expected of her, that it was a magnificent way of serving your friends, which the million-naire on his side received with a laugh and a wave of his hand, declaring that it was nothing, just nothing, a bagatelle in the way of cost, but a convenience, he would not deny it was a convenience; when that discreet butler who had ush-ered Lord Erradeen into Katie's private sitting-room, leaned over his master's shoulder with a solemn face, and a 'Beg your pardon, sir. They say, sir, that Lord Erradeen has perished in the fire.'

'Lord bless us!' said Mr. Williamson, 'what is that you say?'

'It is only a rumour, sir, but I hear Kinloch Houran is all in a commotion, and it is believed everywhere. The young lord was seen with some ladies going there in a boat this afternoon, and they say that he has perished in the flames.'

Sanderson was fond of fine language, and his countenance was composed to the occasion.

'Lord bless us!' cried Mr. Williamson again. 'Send off a man and horse without a moment's delay to find out the truth. Quick, man, and put down the sherry, I'll help myself! Poor lad, poor lad, young Erradeen! He was about this house like one of our own, and no later than yesterday – Katie, do you hear?' he cried, half rising and leaning over the forest of flowers and ferns that covered the table, 'Katie! do you hear this terrible news? But$^a$ it cannot be true!'

Katie had been told at the same moment, and the shock was so great that everything swam in her eyes, as she looked up blanched and terror-stricken in mechanical obedience to her father's cry. 'That man will have killed him,' she said to herself: and then there came over her mind a horror which was flattering too, which filled her with dismay and pain, yet with a strange sensation of importance. Was it she who was to blame for this catastrophe, was she the cause –

'It seems to be certain,' said some one at the table, 'that Erradeen was there. He was seen on the battlements with a lady, just before the explosion.'

'His mother!' said Katie, scarcely knowing why it was that she put forth this explanation.

'A young lady. There is some extraordinary story among the people that she – had something to do with the fire.'

'That will be nonsense,' said Mr. Williamson. 'What would a lady have to do with the fire? Old stone walls like yon are not like rotten wood. I cannot under-stand for my part –'

'And there could be no young lady,' said Katie. 'Mrs. Methven was alone.'

'Well, well!' said her father. 'I am sorry – sorry for Lord Erradeen; he was just as fine a young fellow – But we will do him no good, poor lad, by letting our dinner get cold. And perhaps the man will bring us better news – there is always exaggeration in the first report. I am afraid you will find that soup not eatable, Lady Mary. Just send it away; there is some fine trout coming.'

He was sincerely sorry;[a] but, after all, to lose the dinner would have spared nothing to poor young Erradeen.

Katie said little during the long meal. Her end of the table, usually so gay, was dull. Now and then she would break in with a little spasmodic excitement, and set her companions talking: then relapse with a strange mingling of grief and horror, and that melancholy elation which fills the brain of one who suddenly feels himself involved in great affairs and lifted to heroic heights. If it was for her – if it was she who was the cause of this calamity – She had dreamed often of finding herself[b] with a high heroic part to fulfil in the world, though it seemed[c] little likely that she would ever realise her dream; but now, Katie said to herself, if this was so,[d] never more should another take the place which she had refused to him. If he had died for her, she would live – for him. She would find out every plan he had ever formed for good and fulfil it. She would be the providence of the poor tenants whom he had meant to befriend. She imagined herself in this poetical position always under a veil of sadness, yet not enough to make her unhappy – known in the county as the benefactor of everybody, described with whispers aside as 'the lady that was to have married poor young Lord Erradeen.' Katie was profoundly sorry for poor Walter – for the first few minutes her grief was keen; but very soon this crowd of imaginations rushed in, transporting her into a new world. If this were so! Already everybody at table had begun to remark her changed looks, and to whisper that they had been sure there was 'something between' Katie and the poor young lord. When the ladies went to the drawing-room they surrounded her with tender cares.

'If you would like to go to your room, my dear, never mind us.'

'Oh, never mind us,' cried the gentle guests, 'we can all understand –'

But Katie was prudent even at this crisis of fate. She reflected that the report might not be true, and that it was premature at least to accept the position. She smiled upon the ladies who surrounded her, and put her handkerchief to her eyes.

'Of course,' she said,' I can't help feeling it – every one will feel it on the loch – and we had seen so much of him! But perhaps, as papa says, when the messenger comes back, we may have better news.'

The messenger did not come back till late, when the party were about to separate. He had found the greatest difficulty in getting information, for all that was known at Auchnasheen was that the young lord and his mother had gone in the boat from the isle with the ladies, to see the old castle. With the ladies! Katie could not restrain a little cry. She knew what was coming. And he had been seen, the man went on, with Miss Oona on the walls – and that was all that was known. This stroke went to Katie's heart. 'Oona!' she cried, with something of sharpness and bitterness in the cry; though[e] in the wail that rose from all around who knew the isle, this tone that broke the harmony of grief was lost. But[f] her little fabric of imaginary heroism fell into the dust: and for the moment the shock of a genuine, if alloyed, sentiment thrown back upon herself, and the secret mortification with which she became conscious of the absurdity of her own self-complacence, kept Katie from feeling the natural pity called forth by such a catastrophe, and the deeper pang which by-and-by awakened her heart[a] to the thought of Oona – Oona no rival, but the friend of her youth, Oona the only companion of her mother, the young and hopeful creature whom everybody loved. To think that she should have indulged a little miserable rivalry – on account of[b] a man for whom she did not care the hundredth part so much as she cared for Oona, before realising this real grief and calamity! Katie's honest little soul was bowed down with shame. She, too, watched that night with many a prayer and tear, gazing from her many-windowed chamber towards the feathery crest of the isle which lay between her and Kinloch Houran. Oh, the desolation that would be there and Oona gone! Oh, the blank upon the loch, and in all the meetings of the cheerful neighbours! Another man on horseback was sent off by break of day for news, and not only from Birkenbraes, but from every house for miles round the messengers hurried. There had been no such excitement in the district for generations.

The news reached the Lodge – Sir Thomas Herbert's shooting-box – early in the morning when the family met at breakfast. The previous night had been occupied with an excitement of their own. Major Antrobus, Sir Thomas's friend, brother in sport and arms, had been from the moment of his arrival a disappointment to Sir Thomas. The first evening Julia had caught him in her toils. She had sung and laughed and talked his heart, so much as remained to him, away. He was the man of all others who, his friends were convinced, was not a marrying man. He had a good estate, a house full of every bachelor comfort, and was useful to those in whom he was interested as only a bachelor can be. Nor was it[c] only to men that he was invaluable as a friend. He had a box at Ascot; he had ways of making the Derby delightful to a party of ladies; he was of infinite use at Goodwood;[47] he knew everybody whom it was well to know. Lady Herbert was almost as inconsolable as her husband at the idea of losing him. And that such a man should be brought by Sir Thomas himself into harm's way, and delivered over to the enemy by the very hands of his friends, was more than flesh and blood could bear. The Herberts saw their mistake before he had been at the Lodge two days. But what could they do? They could not send him away – nor could they send Julia away. Had they done so, that young lady had already made herself friends enough to have secured two or three invitations in a foolishly hospitable country, where everybody's first idea was to ask you to stay with them! Sir Thomas acted with the noble generosity characteristic of middle-aged men of the world in such circumstances. He told his friend, as they smoked their cigars in the evening, a great many stories about Julia, and all she had been 'up to' in her chequered career. He described how Lady Herbert had brought her down here, because of some supposed possibility about Lord Erradeen. 'But young fellows like that are not

The Wizard's Son, Volume III

to be so easily taken in,' Sir Thomas said, and vaunted his own insight in perceiving from the first that there was nothing in it. The major listened, and sucked his cigar, and said nothing; but next day on the way home,[a] when the fire at Kinloch Houran was reddening[b] the skies, took his host aside, and said –

'I say, all that may be true, you know. I don't know anything about that. Girls, you know, poor things! they've devilish hard lines, when they've got no tin. If she's tried it on, you know, once or twice before, that's nothing to me. That's all their mother's fault, don't you know. She's the jolliest girl I ever met, and no end of fun. With her in the house, you know, a fellow would never be dull, and I can tell you it's precious dull at Antrobus on off days, when all you fellows are away. I say! I've asked her – to be mine, you know, and all that; and she's – going to have me, Tom!'

'Going to have you! Oh, I'll be bound she is! and everything you've got belonging to you!' in the keenness of his annoyance, cried Sir Thomas.

The major, who was somewhat red in the face, and whose figure was not elegant (but what trifles were these, Julia truly said, in comparison with a true heart!), hemmed[c] a little, and coughed, and set his chin into his shirt collar. He stood like a man to his choice, and would have no more said.

'Of course she is – if she's going to have me, you know. Fixtures go with the property,' said Major Antrobus, with a hasty[d] laugh. 'And, I say, by-gones are by-gones, you know – but no more of them[e] in the future if we're going to be friends.'

The men had a quarrel, however, before Sir Thomas gave in – which was stopped fortunately before it went too far by his wife, who met them all smiles[f] with both hands extended.

'What are you talking loud about, you two?' she said. 'Major, I'm delighted. Of course I've seen it all along. She'll make you an excellent wife, and I wish you all the happiness in the world.'

'Thank you: he don't think so,' the major said with a growl.

But after this Sir Thomas perceived that to quarrel with a man for marrying your cousin whom he has met in your house is one of the foolishest of proceedings. He relieved his feelings afterwards by falling upon the partner of his life.

'What humbugs[48] you women are! What lies you tell! You said she would make him an excellent wife.'

'And so she will,' said Lady Herbert,' a capital wife! He will be twice as happy, but alas! no good at all henceforward,' she ended[g] with a sigh.

The excitement of this incident was not over, when to the breakfast-table next morning, where Julia appeared triumphant, having overcome all opposition, the news arrived, not softened by any doubt as if the result was still uncertain, but[h] with that pleasure in enhancing the importance of dolorous intelligence which is common to all who have the first telling of a catastrophe. There was a momentary hush of horror when the tale was told, and then Julia, her expression changed in a moment, her eyes swimming in tears, rose up in great excitement from her lover's side.

'Oh, Walter!' she cried, greatly moved. 'Oh that I should be so happy, and he –' And then she paused, and her tears burst forth. 'And his mother – his mother!'

She sat down again and wept, while the rest of the party looked on, her major somewhat gloomy, her cousin (after a momentary tribute of silence to death) with a dawning of triumph in his eye.

'You always thought a great deal of young Erradeen, Ju – at least since he has been Lord Erradeen.'

'I always was fond of him,' she cried. 'Poor Walter! poor Walter! Oh, you can weigh my words if you like at such a time, but I won't weigh them. If Henry likes to be offended I can't help it. He has no reason. Oh, Walter, Walter! I was always fond of him. I have known him since I was *that* high – and his mother, I have always hated her. I have known her since I was *that* high. If you think such things go for nothing it is because you have no hearts. Harry, if you love me as you say, get your dog-cart ready this moment and take me to that poor woman – that poor, poor woman! His mother – and she has only him in all the world. Harry, take me or not but I will go –'

'You said you hated her, Julia,' cried Lady Herbert.

'And so I did: and what does that matter? Shall I keep away from her for that – when I am the only one that has known him all his life – that knew him from a child? Harry –'

'I have ordered the dog-cart, my dear; and you are a good woman, Julia. I thought so, but with all your dear friends and people hang me if I knew.'

Julia gave him her hand: she was crying without any disguise.

'Perhaps I haven't been very good,' she said, 'but I never was hard-hearted, and when I think upon that poor woman among strangers –'

'By Jove, but this is something new,' cried Sir Thomas; 'the girl that liked young men best without their mothers, Antrobus, hey?'

'Oh hush, Tom,' cried his wife; 'and dear Julia, be consistent a little – that you're sorry for your old – friend (don't laugh, Tom; say her old flame if you like, but remember that he's dead, poor fellow), that we can understand. Major Antrobus knows all that story. But this fuss about the mother whom you never could bear. Oh that is a little too much! You can't expect us to take in that!'

Julia turned upon her relations with what at bottom was a generous indignation. 'If you don't know,' she said, 'how it feels to hear of another person's misfortune, when you yourself are happier than you deserve – and if you don't understand that I would go on my knees to poor Mrs. Methven to take one scrap of her burden off her! oh all the more because I never liked her – But what is the use of talking, for if you don't understand, nothing I could say would make you understand. And it does not matter to me now,' cried Julia, less noble feelings breaking in, 'now I have got one who is going to stand by me, who knows what I mean, and will put no bad motive –'

The real agitation and regret in her face gave force to the triumph with which she turned to her major, and taking his arm swept out of the room. He, too, had all the sense of dignity which comes from fine feeling[a] misunderstood, and felt himself elevated in the scale of humanity by his superior powers of understanding. Lady Herbert, who remained behind, was saved by the humour of the situation from exploding, as Sir Thomas did. To think that the delicacy of the major's perceptions should be the special foundation of his bride's satisfaction was, as she declared with tears of angry laughter, 'too good!'

But the second and better news arrived before Julia could set out on her charitable mission. Perhaps it was better that it should end so: for though the first outburst of feeling had been perfectly genuine and sincere, the impulse might have been alloyed by less perfect wishes before she had reached Kinloch Houran. And it is doubtful in any case whether her ministrations, however kind, would have been acceptable to Walter's mother. As it was, when she led her major back, Julia was too clever not to find a medium of reconciliation with her cousins, who by that time had come to perceive how ludicrous any quarrel[b] open to the world would be. And so peace was established, and Julia Herbert's difficulties came in the happiest way to an end.

# CHAPTER XIX.[c]

THE miseries of the night's imprisonment were soon forgotten. Oona, elastic in youthful health, recovered in a few days, she said in a few hours, from its effects,[d] and the keen reality of the after events dimmed in her mind the mystery of that extraordinary moment which appeared now like a dream, too wonderful to be true, too inexplicable and beyond experience to come into natural life at all. They spoke of it to each other with bated breath, but not till some time after their rescue, when the still higher excitement of their near approach to death – a thing which reveals the value and charm of life as nothing else does – had somewhat subsided in their minds. But their recollections were confused, they could not tell how; and as Walter had never been sure after they were over, whether the terrible conflicts which he had gone through were not conflicts between the better and worse parts of his own nature, without any external influence, so they asked each other now whether the mysterious chamber, the burning lamp, the strange accessories of a concealed and mysterious life, were dreams of disordered fancy, or something real and actual. They could not explain these things to each other, neither could they understand what it was that made the throwing down of the light of such vital importance. Was it common fire, acting after the ordinary laws of nature and finding ready fuel in the dry wood and antique furniture? or was it something more mystic, more momentous? They gave little explanation to questioners, not so much because they were unwilling, as because they were unable; and when they discussed it between themselves became more and more confused as the days went on. It became like a phantasmagoria, sometimes suddenly appearing in all the vivid lines of reality, sometimes fading into a pale apparition which memory could scarcely retain.

To the world in general the fact of a great fire, a thing unfortunately not very rare in the records of ancient houses, became after a while a very simple piece of history; and the wonderful escape of Lord Erradeen and Miss Forrester, and their subsequent betrothal and marriage, a pretty piece of natural romance.[a] The tower, now preserving nothing more than a certain squareness in its mass of ruins, showed traces of two rooms that might have been,[b] but everything was destroyed except the stones,[c] and any remains that might have withstood the action of the fire were buried deep under the fallen walls;[d] nor could any trace be found of concealed passages or any way of descent into the house from that unsuspected hiding-place.[e] One thing was certain, however, that the being who had exercised so strange an influence on a year of his life never appeared to Walter more. There were moments in which he felt, with a pang of alarm, that concentration of his thoughts upon himself, that subtle direction and intensification of his mind, as if it had suddenly been driven into a dialogue with some one invisible, which had been the worst of all the sufferings he had to bear; but these, after the first terror, proved to be within the power of his own efforts to resist and shake off, and never came to any agonising crisis like that which he had formerly passed through. His marriage, which took place as soon as circumstances would permit, ended even these last contentions of the spirit. And if in the midst of his happiness he was sometimes tortured by the thought that the change of his life from the evil way to the good one had all the results of the most refined selfishness, as his adversary had suggested, and that[f] he was amply proving the ways of righteousness to be those of pleasantness, and godliness to be great gain, that thought was too ethereal for common use, and did not stand the contact of reality. Mr. Cameron, to whom he submitted it in some moment of confidence, smiled with the patience of old age upon this overstrained self-torment.

'It is true enough,' the minister said,' that the right way is a way of pleasantness, and that all the paths of wisdom are peace.[49] But life has not said out its last word, and ye will have to tread them one time or other with bleeding feet, or all is done – if the Lord has not given you a lot apart from that of other men. And human nature,' the old man said, not without a little recollection of some sermon, at which he smiled as he spoke, 'is so perverse, that when trouble comes, you that are afraid of your happiness will be the first to cry out and upbraid the good Lord that does not make it everlasting. Wait, my young man, wait – till perhaps you have a boy at your side that will vex your heart as children only can vex those that love them – wait till death steps into your house, as step he must –'

'Stop!' cried Walter, with a wild sudden pang of that terror of which the Italian poet speaks, which makes all the earth a desert –

The Wizard's Son, Volume III    403

'Senza quella
Nova, sola, infinita,
Felicitá che il suo pensier figura.'[50a]

He never complained again of being too happy, or forgot that one time or other the path of life must be trod with bleeding feet.

'But I'll not deny,' said the minister, 'that to the like of you, my young lord, with so much in your power, there is no happier way of amusing yourself than just in being of use and service to your poor fellow-creatures that want so much and have so little. Man!' cried Mr. Cameron, 'I would have given my head to be able to do at your age the half or quarter of what you can do with a scratch of your pen! – and you must mind that you are bound to do it,' he added with a smile.

But before[b] this serene course of life began which Walter found too happy, there was an interval of anxiety and pain. Mrs. Methven did not escape, like the rest, from the consequences of the night's vigil. She got up indeed from her faint, and received with speechless thanksgiving her son back from the dead, as she thought, but had herself to be carried[c] to his room in the old castle, and there struggled for weeks in the grips of fever, brought on, it was said, by the night's exposure. But this she would not herself allow. She had felt it,[d] she said, before she left her home, but concealed it, not to be hindered from obeying her son's summons. If this was true, or invented upon the spur of the moment to prove that in no possible way was Walter to blame, it is impossible to say. But the fever ran very high, and so affected her heart, worn and tired by many assaults, that there was a time when everything was hushed and silenced in the old castle in expectation of death. By-and-by,[e] however, that terror gave place to all the innocent joys of convalescence – soft flitting of women up and down, presents of precious flowers and fruits lighting up the gloom, afternoon meetings when everything that could please her was brought to the recovering mother,[f] and all the loch came with inquiries, with good wishes, and kind offerings.[g] Mrs. Forrester, who was an excellent nurse, and never lost heart, but smiled, and was sure, in the deepest depth, that all would 'come right,' as she said, took the control of the sick-room, and recovered there the bloom which she had partially lost when Oona was in danger. And Oona stole into the heart of Walter's mother, who had not for long years possessed him sufficiently to make it bitter to her that he should now put a wife before her. Some women never learn this philosophy;[h] and perhaps Mrs. Methven might have resisted it, had not Oona, her first acquaintance on the loch, her tenderest nurse, won her heart. To have the grim old house in which the secret of the Methvens' fate had been laid up, and in which, even to indifferent lookers-on, there had always been an atmosphere of mystery and terror, thus occupied with the most innocent and cheerful commonplaces, the little cares and simple pleasures of a long but hopeful recovery, was confusing and soothing beyond measure to all around. The old servants, who had borne for many years the presence of a secret which was not theirs, felt in this general commotion a relief which words could not express. 'No,' old Symington said, 'it's not ghosts nor any such rubbitch. I never, for my part, here or elsewhere, saw onything worse than myself; but, Miss Oona, whatever it was that you did on the tap of that tower – and how you got there the Lord above knows, for there never was footing for a bird that ever I saw – it has just been blessed. 'Ding down the nests and the craws will flee away.' What am I meaning? Well, that is just what I canna tell. It's a' confusion. I know nothing. Many a fricht and many an anxious hour have I had here: but I am bound to say I never saw anything worse than mysel'.'

'All yon is just clavers,' said old Macalister, waving his hand. 'If ye come to that there is naething in this life that will bide explaining. But I will not deny that there is a kind of a different feel in the air which is maybe owing to this fine weather, just wonderful for the season; or maybe to the fact of so many leddies about, which is a new thing here – no that I hold so much with women,' he added, lest Oona should be proud, 'they are a great fyke and trouble, and will meddle with everything; but they're fine for a change, and a kind of soothing for a little whilie at a time, after all we've gone through.'

Before the gentle *régime* of the sick-room was quite over, an unusual and unexpected visitor arrived one morning at Loch Houran. It was the day after that on which Mrs. Methven had been transferred to Auchnasheen, and a great festival among her attendants. She had been brought down to the drawing-room very pale and shadowy, but with a relaxation of all the sterner lines which had once been in her face, in invalid dress arranged after Mrs. Forrester's taste rather than her own, and lending a still further softness to her appearance, not to be associated with her usual rigid garb of black and white. And her looks and tones were the most soft of all, as, the centre of everybody's thoughts, she was led to the sofa near the fire and surrounded by that half-worship which is the right of a convalescent where love is. To this pleasant home-scene there entered suddenly, ushered in with great solemnity by Symington, the serious and somewhat stern 'man of business' who had come to Sloebury not much more than a year before with the news of that wonderful inheritance so unexpected and unthought of, which had seemed to Mrs. Methven, as well as to her son, the beginning of a new life. Mr. Milnathort made kind but formal inquiries after Mrs. Methven's health, and offered his congratulations no less formally upon her recovery.

'I need not say to you that all that has happened has been an interest to us that are connected with the family beyond anything that I can express. I have taken the liberty,' he added, turning to Walter, 'to bring one to see you, Lord Erradeen, who has perhaps the best right of any one living to give ye joy. I told her that you would no doubt come to her, for she has not left her chamber, as you know, for many a year; but nothing would serve her but to come herself, frail as she is –'

'Your sister!'[a] Walter cried.

'Just my sister. I have taken the liberty,'[b] Mr. Milnathort repeated, 'to have her

The serious face of the lawyer was more serious than ever: his long upper lip trembled a little. He turned round to the others with anxious self-restraint.

'She is very frail,' he said, 'a delicate bit creature all her life – and since her accident –'

He spoke of this, as his manner was, as if it had happened a week ago.

Walter hurried away to the library, in which he found Miss Milnathort carefully arranged upon a sofa, wrapped up in white furs instead of her usual garments, a close white hood surrounding the delicate brightness of her face. She held out her hands to him at first without a word; and when she could speak, said, with a tremble in her voice:

'I have come to see the end of it. I have come to see – her and you.'

'I should have come to you,' cried Walter,[a] 'I did not forget – but for my mother's illness –'

'Yes?' she said with a grateful look. 'You thought upon me? Oh, but my heart has been with her and you! Oh, the terrible time it was! the first news in the papers, the fear that you were buried there under the ruins, you – and she; and then to wait a night and a day.'[b]

'I should have sent you word at once – I might have known; but I did not think of the papers.'

'No, how should you? you were too busy with your own life. Oh, the thoughts of that night. I just lay and watched for you from the darkening to the dawning. No, scarcely what you could call praying – just waiting upon the Lord. I bade Him mind upon Walter and me – that had lost the battle. And I thought I saw you, you and your Oona. Was not I wise when I said it was a well-omened name?' She paused a little, weeping and smiling. 'I could not tell you all the thoughts that went through my mind. I thought if it was even so, there might have been a worse fate. To break the spell and defeat the enemy even at the cost of your two bonnie lives – I thought it would not be an ill fate, the two of you together. Did I not say it? Two that made up one, the perfect man. That is God's ordinance,[51] my dear? that is His ordinance. Two – not just for pleasure, or for each other, but for Him and everything that is good. You believed me when I said that. Oh, you believed me! and so it was not in vain that I was – killed yon time long ago – ' Her voice was broken with sobs. She leant upon Walter's shoulder who had knelt down beside her, and wept there like a child – taking comfort like a child. 'Generally,' she began after a moment, 'there is little account made, little, little account, of them that have gone before, that have been beaten, Walter. I can call you nothing but Walter to-day. And Oona, though she has won the battle, she is just me, but better. We lost. We had the same heart; but the time had not come for the victory. And now you, my young lord, you, young Erradeen, like him, you have won, Oona and you. We were beaten; but yet I have a share in it. How can you tell, a young man like you, how those that have been defeated, lift their hearts and give God thanks?'ᵃ She made a pause and said, after a moment, 'I must see Oona, too.' But when he was about to rise and leave her in order to bring Oona, she stopped him once more. 'You must tell me first,' she said, speaking very low, 'what is become of *him*?ᵇ Did he let himself be borne away to the clouds in you flames? I know, I know, it's all done; but did you see him? Did he speak a word at the end?'

'Miss Milnathort,' said Walter, holding her hands, 'there is nothing but confusion in my mind. Was it all a dream and a delusion from beginning to end?'

She laughed a strange little laugh of emotion.

'Look at me then,' she said, 'for what have I suffered these thirty years? And you – was it all for nothing that you were so soon beatenᶜ and ready to fall? Have you not seen him? Did he go without a word?'

Walter looked back upon all the anguish through which he had passed, and it seemed to him but a dream. One great event, and then weeks of calm had intervened since the day when driven to the side of the loch in madness and misery, he had found Oona and taken refuge in her boat, and thrown himself on her mercy; and since the night when once more driven distracted by diabolical suggestions, he had stepped out into the darkness, meaning to lose himself somehow in the gloom and be no more heard of – yet was saved again by the little light in her window, the watch-light that love kept burning. These recollections and many more swept through his mind, and the pain and misery more remote upon which this old woman's childlike countenance had shone. He could not take hold of them as they rose before him in the darkness, cast far away into a shadowy background by the brightness and reality of the present. A strange giddiness came over his brain. He could not tell which was real, the anguish that was over, or the peace that had come, or whether life itself – flying in clouds behind him, before him hid under the wide-spreading sunshine – was anything but a dream. He recovered himself with an effort, grasping hold of the latest recollection to satisfy his questioner.

'This I know,' he cried, 'that when we wereᵈ flying from the tower, with flames and destruction behind us, the only words I heard from her were a prayer for pardon – 'forgive him,' that was all I heard.ᵉ And then the rush of the air in our faces, and roar that was like the end of all things. We neither heard nor saw more.'

'Pardon!' said Miss Milnathort, drying her eyes with a trembling hand, 'that is what I have said too, many a weary hour in the watches of the night. What pleasure can a spirit like yon find in the torture of his own flesh and blood? The

*The Wizard's Son, Volume III*

Lord forgive him if there is yet a place of repentance! But well I know what you mean that it is just like a vision when one awaketh. That is what all our troubles will be when the end comes: just a dream! and good brought out of evil and pardon given to many, many a one that men are just willing to give over and curse instead of blessing. Now go and bring your Oona, my bonnie lad! I am thinking she is just me, and you are Walter, and we have all won the day together,' said the invalid clasping her thin hands, and with eyes that shone through their tears, 'all won together! though we were beaten twenty years ago.'

THE END.

# EDITORIAL NOTES

## The Wizard's Son, Volume I

1. THE *Methvens*: a Scottish surname, appropriate for a tale of inheritance, in that it had formerly been attached to 'the lands of Methven', an estate in Perthshire. Dating from at least the thirteenth century, the name survived in a variety of forms such as Methven, Methuen, Meffan, and Meffen.

2. *the peacemakers to whom Scripture allots a special blessing*: see Matthew 5:9, 'Blessed are the peacemakers: for they shall be called the children of God'.

3. *education ... supposed in England to be the best kind*: MOWO had taken the decision to send her sons as dayboys to Eton College, an independent, or Public School, as it is known in England. MOWO frequently raised the topic in her fiction of England and Scotland's different educational systems and their associated class implications. See Jay (1995), pp. 200–1.

4. *years ... of discretion*: a concept arising from Roman Catholic Canon Law, identifying the age at which a child becomes capable of reason, and therefore of taking moral responsibility for his or her actions. The Anglican church makes use of the concept in the Order of Confirmation, described in the Prayer Book, as the 'Laying on of Hands upon those that are Baptized and Come to years of Discretion'.

5. *set the Thames on fire*: achieve something astonishing to distinguish himself. A phrase already well-established by the beginning of the nineteenth-century: see J. Austen, *Persuasion*, ed. J. Todd and A. Blank (1817; Cambridge: Cambridge University Press, 2006), p. 35.

6. *it was Mrs. Methven whom everybody blamed*: MOWO was acutely conscious of the censure she attracted for the way she had raised her two sons. See Jay (1990), pp. 79 and 117; and *Selected Works*, vol. 6, pp. 401, 80.

7. *apothecary ... young doctor*: In the nineteenth-century medical hierarchy, apothecaries, who served an apprenticeship before preparing and dispensing medicines, were often ranked with manual labourers and tradesmen, well below the physician or family doctor. The entry requirement, set by the British medical licensing authorities, that applicants should possess a modern foreign language or Greek, in addition to Latin, was an ill-disguised attempt to restrict the profession to gentlemen.

8. *Though I'm a Tory, I like every man to make his own way*: In the ideological rift between traditional Conservatism, based on loyalty to long-established values and systems, and economic liberalism, Miss Merivale places herself on the liberal conservative wing, though her position is clearly influenced by her resentment at the privileges Walter Methven enjoys, solely on account of his birthright.

9. *sheer democracy*: The notion of universal rights, associated with the French and American

– 409 –

410 *Notes to pages 12–17*

revolutions, is anathema to the conservatively-minded Rector. In practice the Reform acts of 1867–8 had made no great difference to British electoral politics, and universal adult suffrage only came in 1928. 'Tory democracy' was the watchword of the progressive wing of Conservatism espoused by Miss Merivale.

10. *method of examinations*: In 1853 William Ewart Gladstone, as Chancellor of the Exchequer, had commissioned an investigation into the operation and organisation of the Civil Service. The resulting Northcote-Trevelyan report of 1854 recommended entry by competitive examination, and subsequent promotion determined by merit rather than patronage.

11. *Gladstone's name was as a firebrand*: As a young girl, MOWO had shared her mother's political stance, 'Radical and democratic and the highest of aristocrats all in one', but, by the 1880s, she shared the Queen's dislike of Gladstone and his policies. See Jay (1990), pp. 21, 250–1; and *Selected Works*, vol. 6, p. 21. In a letter of 1880 to her Secretary, Sir Henry Ponsonby, Queen Victoria had declared that she would 'sooner abdicate than have anything to do with that half-mad firebrand', quoted in P. Magnus, *Gladstone: A Biography* (1963; London: Penguin, 2001), p. 270.

12. *England had become a mere name, upon which all foreign nations should trample*: Gladstone's 'Midlothian campaign', before the 1880 election which returned him to power, emphasized the twin duties of reining in British imperialism and acting in concert with the rest of Europe.

13. *wild Irishmen*: Agitation for Home Rule for Ireland had gained pace in the early 1880s, as had the fear of Fenian violence. In May 1882, only six months before the first portion of this serialized novel was published, the new Chief Secretary for Ireland had been murdered in Phoenix Park, Dublin.

14. *Americans expectorate*: Frances Trollope's report in *Domestic Manners of the Americans* (1832), of men spitting openly and repeatedly at social events in Cincinnati, encouraged British readers to view it as a national habit.

15. *peace in my days*: see Isaiah 39:8; and 2 Kings 20:19.

16. *public credit*: the national debt.

17. *clever enough for Parliament*: If her frequent habit of despatching the less intelligent husbands of bright heroines to parliament, as in *Miss Marjoribanks* (1866), or *Phoebe, Junior* (1876), is any guide, this is a somewhat double-edged accolade, and thus a joke at the expense of Mrs Methven's over-estimation of her son.

18. *a fellowship at his college*: membership of the governing body of an Oxford college won by competitive examination. Such 'prize' fellowships, awarded mainly to young contenders, did not necessarily carry either teaching or administrative duties and were thus the subject of increasing adverse public comment at this period. 1882 saw the creation of 'ordinary' fellowships, with a fixed tenure of seven years.

19. au courant: staying up-to-date (French).

20. *the difference which a father's larger, more generous sway would have made in him*: MOWO was acutely conscious of the part her own boys' fatherless condition might have played in their behaviour as adults, but here manages to turn her own potential self-pity into Walter's self-indulgence.

21. *militia*: a volunteer, trained and paid force supplementing the regular army. As recently as 1881 the militia infantry had been reassigned as numbered battalions of the regular army, making Underwood's lack of specific credentials that much more suspicious.

22. *Garibaldi*: In 1860, Guiseppe Garibaldi (1807–82), military leader of repeated campaigns to bring about Italian unification, had founded a legion drawn from various nationalities bent on liberating Italy and their respective homelands. His recent death in

Notes to pages 17–40     411

June 1882 had renewed memories of the heroic acclaim England had given him on his visits to the United Kingdom.

23. *the monks and the coffins to come in*: Although MOWO remained largely immune to the charms of music, this seems to be an allusion to Meyerbeer's immensely popular opera, *Robert le diable* (Robert the Devil), with a libretto jointly written by Scribe and Delavigne, which had received its first performance in Paris in 1831. The relevance to *The Wizard's Son* of Robert's relationship to a mysterious stranger who exerts demonic powers will become clear as the novel progresses, as will the power of a good woman's love to help a man defeat temptation. The particular scene in the opera to which MOWO is alluding has the ghosts of nuns rise from their tombs in the cloisters to which Robert has been led by his devilish companion: in a macabre choric dance they celebrate drinking, gambling and lust.

24. *the genius of the place*: in this case, the natural spirit of the rectory. The phrase is derived from the Latin '*genius loci*', describing the local protective spirits of Roman cultic religion.

25. *age of Methusaleh*: Genesis 5:27, 'And all the days of Methuselah were nine hundred sixty and nine years: and he died'.

26. *sensible*: apparent to the senses.

27. *what they call a writer*: a term which MOWO usefully signals to readers is a Scottish term, deriving from the task of a writer, or clerk, preparing writs which required the royal seal or 'signet' of the early Scottish kings, so that those allowed to supervise the Signet's use in Scottish Courts became known as 'writers to the signet'.

28. *in Debrett*: Debrett was the surname of the publisher who, in 1769, launched a book, which was to become a national institution; it offered genealogical information about members of the peerage.

29. *horrified at the thought of whist before dinner*: MOWO had not had the chance of reading her fellow novelist, Anthony Trollope's posthumously published *Autobiography* (1883) by the time she wrote this – he died in December 1882. In it Trollope admitted his custom of retiring to his club and playing 'whist before dinner', berating himself, despite a prodigious output rivalling MOWO's own, for indulging in such a trivial pastime; 'an amusement which has not after all very much to recommend it', A. Trollope, *An Autobiography*, intro. M. Sadleir (London: Oxford University Press, 1968), p. 135.

30. *crotchets*: highly individual opinions.

31. *comforter*: a long woollen scarf worn round the throat as a protection from cold.

32. habitués: regular attenders (French).

33. *canard*: a deliberately false or misleading report (French).

34. *He was a good Churchman, but*: wearing a cassock as daily attire had traditionally been the practice of the Roman Catholic priesthood; in the later decades of the nineteenth century some Ritualist Anglican clergy had started to affect this habit. As a good Anglican, the Reverend Julius Wynn would have followed the rubrics of the Prayer Book, but avoided the excesses of the Ritualist wing of Anglo-Catholicism.

35. *milksop*: a male who is timid, ineffectual or effeminate.

36. *working a coronet in ... new handkerchiefs*: In her fantasy world July would have been busy embroidering a small crown, its size denoting her husband's precise rank in the peerage, into the linen for her trousseau.

37. *hit the blot*: exposed the weak spot in the plan, a phrase deriving from the game of backgammon.

38. *humbug!*: capable of pretence.

39. coup: bold stroke (French).

40. *Something out of the* Arabian Nights: Suitably bowdlerised selections from *One Thousand*

412                                   *Notes to pages 40–57*

*and One Nights* had been standard fare in British nurseries since the late eighteenth-century. This collection of Asian folktales and stories, assembled in Arabic, was known in Britain under the title of its first English translation as *The Arabian Nights' Entertainment* (1706).

41.  *like the mediums*: After her oldest son's death in 1890, MOWO herself became susceptible to the consolations provided by the notion of contact with the spirit world, while also maintaining a healthy scepticism about the possibilities of exploitation lying within organised attempts to establish such communication. See Jay (1995), p. 149.

42.  de haut en bas: condescendingly, as from a superior position (French).

43.  *freckled forehead*: the girl's unshielded exposure to the sun marks her as belonging to the lower servant classes.

44.  *the area*: Designed to admit light into a basement, this space was used to provide convenient access for tradesmen's deliveries to the kitchen and store-rooms located below ground level.

45.  *the god, out of the machinery*: a literal translation of the Latin phrase *deus ex machina*, used to describe the convention in classical Greek drama whereby a crane, or similar device, delivered a god upon the stage, who would then resolve the otherwise insoluble plight in which the human characters found themselves.

46.  *Debrett*: see note 28 above.

47.  *sovereign*: a British gold coin, nominally worth a pound and thus a very generous tip.

48.  *wallowing in the mire, as the Scripture says*: 2 Peter 2:22, 'But it is happened unto them according to the true proverb, The dog is turned to his own vomit again; and the sow that was washed to her wallowing in the mire'.

49.  *portmanteau*: a hinged, stiff leather bag, used as hand-luggage (French).

50.  *reading a French novel*: MOWO here exploits the contrast between Cousin Sophie's 'virginal' status, and the supposedly immoral influence of French novels, much discussed in the British press. An early review in which MOWO had referred to the 'kind of inexorable but passionless dissection' of even 'the vilest of topics' to be found in nineteenth-century French fiction further suggests Cousin Sophie's dispassionate observation of the household which has taken her in. M. O. W. Oliphant, 'Novels', *BM*, 102 (September 1867), pp. 257–80; and *Selected Works*, vol. 1, pp. 367–96.

51.  *Extremes meet, as the proverb says*: from the French, '*les extrèmes se touchent*', an aphorism to be found in the *Pensées* (1669) of Blaire Pascal, the seventeenth-century philosopher, and meaning 'opposites can have much in common'.

52.  bête noir: more properly, *bête noire*, an object of aversion (French).

53.  *Calton Jail*: had replaced the Old Tolbooth prison in 1817. Like many another early nineteenth-century prison its exterior design resembled a medieval castle.

54.  *Arthur's Seat*: the name given to the main peak of a group of crags, or hills, which are only about a mile to the east of Edinburgh Castle.

55.  *Old Town*: A central ravine, running parallel to Princes Street, divides Edinburgh's Old Town, which dates from the medieval period, from the city's neo-classical New Town, developed from the eighteenth-century.

56.  *Castle*: The massive grey presence of Edinburgh Castle, positioned on a rocky outcrop, dominates the city's skyline.

57.  *Prince's Street*: Edinburgh's major east-west thoroughfare. The apostrophe was increasingly dropped during the Victorian period, thus masking the problem of where the punctuation should be placed. Some hold that it should be styled Princes' Street since it was named after Prince George and Prince Frederick, George III's two eldest sons.

58.  *cairngorms*: jewellery adorned with a smoky quartz of various shades of brown, so named

*Notes to pages 57–62* 413

because the quartz crystals are found in the mountain range in the eastern Highlands of Scotland closely associated with the mountain of the same name — Cairn Gorm.

59. *the night train*: The East Coast Mainline from London to Edinburgh had been built by three separate companies in the late 1840s. By 1850 the connections were complete and the route further shortened in 1871; the rolling stock for through journeys such as night travel was jointly owned. MOWO discussed the changes in north-south travel which had occurred in her own lifetime in ''Tis Sixty Years Since', *BM*, 161 (May 1897), pp. 599–664; and *Selected Works*, vol. 13, pp. 445–74.

60. *easterly haar*: the term used for a coastal fog which occurs on the east coast of Scotland.

61. *Moray Place*: In 1822 the Early of Moray had development plans drawn up for his estates, which included Moray Place, resulting in a western extension of Edinburgh's New Town.

62. *fyking*: fidgeting, or making a fuss (Scottish).

63. *manse and his augmentation*: In Scottish law a parish minister could mount an action in the Court of Teinds (teinds being the Scottish equivalent of tithes). In the wake of the Reformation much medieval church property had fallen into lay hands, leaving parish ministers ill-provided.

64. *mid-day gun from the Castle*: A practice begun in 1861, the firing of a gun from the battlements at 1pm from Monday to Saturday was introduced as means of providing an accurate time check on foggy days when the ships in Leith Harbour – two miles away – could not see the time signal erected on Calton Hill.

65. *the crown of St. Giles's*: St. Giles's cathedral bears a framed crown spire.

66. *the poet's warning to yon warrior-maid of his*: This allusion is the first in the chain of references to Edmund Spenser's *Faerie Queen* (1590–6) which will form a leitmotif for the rest of the novel. 'And as she lookt about, she did behold, / How over that same dore was likewise writ, / *Be bold, be bold*, and euery where *Be bold* ... / At last she spyde at that roomes upper end, / Another yron dore, on which was writ, / *Be not too bold*', E. Spenser, 'Faerie Queen', *Spenser: Poetical Works*, ed. J. C. Smith and E. de Selincourt (1596; London: Oxford University Press, 1965), book 3, p. 205, canto 11, stanza 54.

67. *old original club of Edinburgh society*: the Royal Society of Edinburgh, founded in 1783, shared its accommodation on the Mound between 1826 to 1909 with the Society of Antiquaries.

68. *bound about the throat with white ties, like clergymen*: Scottish advocates wear white bow ties rather than the barrister's bands worn by their peers south of the border.

69. *'cod*: still in use in the nineteenth century as a euphemism for God.

70. *arms*: heraldic arms.

71. *as historical as Holyrood*: The palace of Holyrood, at the opposite end of Edinburgh's Royal Mile from the castle, had been constructed in the early sixteenth century to provide the king with a replacement for his guest lodgings, adjacent to the far older Holyrood abbey, founded in 1128.

72. *cicerone*: a guide to antiquities or curiosities of a place.

73. *Baithe Sune and Syne*: both sooner and later (Scottish).

74. *Canongate*: First given to the Augustinian canons at Holyrood Abbey, the area's proximity to the court attracted the Scottish nobility, though King James VI's accession to the English throne in 1603, and the consequent migration south of court life began its slow decline.

75. *silver key*: a payment by way of a piece of silver coin.

76. *clanjamfry*: the odds and ends, or things of little value (Scottish).

77. *warlock-lord*: Frequently used by Sir Walter Scott, the term 'warlock' obtained literary currency, indicating a maleficent sorcerer or wizard, in league with the Devil and so possessing evil powers.

414                                    *Notes to pages 62–71*

78. *pliskies*: mischievous tricks (Scottish).
79. *John Knox*: (1514–72), leader of the Protestant Reformation in Scotland (1514–72). After his return from exile, Knox worked with the Scottish nobility to resist unjust government. The city of Edinburgh gave John Knox a rent-free manse on the north side of the high street to the west of St Giles. This contained 'a warm study of daillis', a study lined with deal panelling, R. Graham, *John Knox: Democrat* (London: Robert Hale, 2001), pp. 196–7.
80. *like Hercules*: The Greek historian, Xenophon, portrayed Socrates recounting an episode in the early life of Hercules in which the mythical hero comes to a fork in the road, where two beautiful goddesses offer opposing counsel as to the path he should take. Having listened to the seductive account of a life of pleasure offered by the first speaker, Hercules opts for the more arduous route promising hardship and suffering en route to attaining true self-discipline. The story serves as a proleptic image of the choice between Katie and Oona that Walter will face.
81. *Cockney*: Strictly-speaking this means 'a Londoner', which Walter, having grown up in Sloebury, could not be called, but here it is indicative of the contempt a Scotsman could muster for someone from the vicinity of the rival capital.
82. *Bailie*: indicating a post-holder with duties equivalent of a magistrate or sheriff.
83. *no credulous Celt, but a sober-minded Englishman*: Proud of her own Scottish lineage, MOWO here satirises the kind of pseudo-ethnography practised by her contemporary, Matthew Arnold (1822–88) in such works as *On the Study of Celtic Literature* (1867) where he characterized the English spirit as 'steadiness with honesty', and the Celtic as 'always ready to react against the despotism of fact', M. Arnold, *The Complete Prose Works of Matthew Arnold*, ed. R. H. Super, 11 vols (Ann Arbor, MI: University of Michigan Press, 1960–77), vol. 3, pp. 341 and 344.
84. diablerie: demonology (French).
85. *mesmerism*: mesmeric experiments were widely current in mid-Victorian England. It was claimed they offered evidence that, through the exercise of hypnotic powers, one person could affect the human body or psyche of another. For a comprehensive account of the cultural significance of mesmerism, see A. Winter, *Mesmerized: Powers of Mind in Victorian Britain* (Chicago, IL and London: University of Chicago Press, 1998).
86. *Moray Place*: see note 61 above.
87. chaise longue: an upholstered chair long enough to accommodate the sitter's legs (French).
88. *auld foozle*: old fogy (Scottish).
89. *old Reformers, 'Ding down the nest, and the crows will flee away'*: The phrase, literally meaning 'knock down the nest and the birds will fly away', enjoyed metaphorical currency during the Scottish Reformation period to imply 'destroy the safe-houses of Roman Catholic priests and they will leave.'
90. mélange: varied mixture (French).
91. *Kinloch Houran*: MOWO set this part of her story in the real Scottish location of Kinloch Hourn, which continues to be a particularly inaccessible settlement in the West Highlands, at the head of Loch Hourn. The path continuing on the south shore of the loch to Barrisdale and beyond may have been used as a coffin-road, a recognised route for transporting the dead from remote homes to cemeteries with burial rights. Such roads attracted tales of ghostly hauntings. The Scottish cemetery-island of Mun in Loch Leven, with its associated legend of phantom lights may also have played a part in MOWO's novel. A further reason for her choice may have been that the clearance of people and sheep from the land in this area remained a contentious issue.
92. *filled out*: more normally 'filled up'. Perhaps the phrase recollects Proverbs 3:10: 'So shall

*Notes to pages 71–81*  415

thy barns be filled with plenty, and thy presses shall burst out with new wine.'

93.  *gas*: The 'illuminating gas', produced from coal, and used for lighting, produces a far brighter light than natural gas or water gas. A harsh bright light was necessary because until the mass-production of a downward-burning gas-mantle at the close of the nineteenth century, the gas flame was obliged to point upwards, away from where the light was most needed.

94.  *Now that bequests of all kinds are being interfered with, and even charities*: MOWO's novel, *Phoebe, Junior* (1876), see *Selected Works*, vol. 19, had included a debate about the questionable benefits of the Victorian thirst for reform of medieval endowments, first given a popular fictional airing in Anthony Trollope's *The Warden* (1855).

95.  *Melville Mortification*: in Scottish Law a mortification referred to the disposal of property or funds for charitable purposes, often applying to the dispersal of medieval endowments during the Scottish Reformation. Melville's Mortification was the title of a real fund held by the University and King's College of Aberdeen.

96.  *collateral*: descended from the same stock, but not in the direct line.

97.  *Marlborough ... obsolete old flag to Windsor*: On the anniversary of the battle of Blenheim (13 August 1704) the Duke of Marlborough is required to send a new flag as acknowledgement to his sovereign of the gift of the Blenheim estate to the original Duke: the flag is then draped over the first Duke's bust in the guardroom at Windsor. Given her long residence in Windsor, the ceremony would have been familiar to MOWO.

98.  *secret cha'mer*: MOWO had published a short story of the supernatural under the title, 'The Secret Chamber' in *BM*, 120 (December 1876), pp. 709–29, in *Selected Works*, vol. 12, pp. 3–25. This contained the germ of the moral challenge Walter Methven will face. See Jay (1995), pp. 159–61, 168–9. For further comment on the relation between the tale and the novel see the Introduction to this volume.

99.  *head garlanded with crape*: As a token of mourning, a black crape 'weeper' was worn bound around the hat and hanging down the back.

100.  *the country of Caleb Balderstone and Ritchie Moniplies*: the names of two faithful family retainers in the novels of Walter Scott, a favourite author of MOWO's as for many another Victorian novelist. Balderstone supplies the comic relief in the tragic *The Bride of Lammermoor* (1819), while Richie (rather than Ritchie as he is spelt here) appears in *The Fortunes of Nigel* (1822), a novel possibly further endeared to MOWO by the surname of its hero, Nigel Olifaunt. When asked if Edinburgh can boast a river to compare with the Thames, that staunchly loyal Scot, Richie replies, 'The Thames! God bless your honour's judgment, we have at Edinburgh the Water of Leith and the Nor' Loch!'

101.  *char-à-banc*: a long, light vehicle with transverse seats looking forward (French).

102.  *tweed, of the ruddy heathery hue which is now so general*: Until the late 1840s Harris tweed had been manufactured for local use, but in the second half of the century it was more widely marketed and found favour with the sporting landed gentry, including Queen Victoria's inner circle. The characteristic colours were implanted by the use of lichen dyes.

103.  *ulster*: a heavy-duty overcoat, with cape and sleeves.

104.  *a ferlie*: a wonder (Scottish).

105.  *corpse-candles*: flickering flames seen in a churchyard or over a grave, and superstitiously believed to appear as an omen of death, or to indicate the route of a coming funeral.

106.  *bagman*: commercial traveller.

107.  *wheen*: few (Scottish).

108.  *cobble*: a small, flat-bottomed, rowing boat typically used for lake or loch fishing.

109.  *Hoo was I to ken*: How was I to know? (Scottish).

110.  *name*: no more (Scottish).

416                    *Notes to pages 81–90*

111. *gangrel*: archaic Scottish word, meaning 'vagrant'.
112. *ain*: own (Scottish).
113. *cattle*: persons (Scottish).
114. fin mot: last word (French).
115. *progged*: poked (Scottish).
116. *There was no electric light in those days*: This does not mean that *The Wizard's Son* was intended as an historical novel. Electric lighting was only slowly making its way into large houses at the end of the nineteenth century. In an article to celebrate Queen Victoria's Diamond Jubilee, MOWO recalled the extraordinary advances in the means of lighting which had occurred in her own lifetime, but also regretted the casting of greater light than had been afforded by the flickering candles of her youth, because 'Ghosts have gone wholly out of fashion with the children, and nobody under fifteen is afraid of them', M. O. W. Oliphant, "Tis Sixty Years Since', *BM*, 161 (May 1897), pp. 599–64; 605; in *Selected Works*, vol. 13, pp. 445–74.
117. *portmanteau*: see note 49 above.
118. *eldritch*: weird, ghostly, unnatural, frightful, hideous.
119. *a mystery of Udolpho*: Much of Ann Radcliffe's four-volume novel, *The Mysteries of Udolpho* (1794), is set in a crumbling Italian castle. The novel was seen as archetypical of the early Gothic novel, even more so after it was satirized in Jane Austen's posthumously published *Northanger Abbey* (1817).
120. *mysteries of Udolpho ... quite explainable*: Walter Scott had long ago remarked upon the rational explanations underlying the apparently supernatural episodes in Radcliffe's Gothic tales: 'All circumstances of her narrative, mysterious and apparently superhuman, were to be accounted for on natural principles at the winding up of the story', W. Scott, *The Lives of the Novelists* (1825; London: Henry Frowde, Oxford University Press, 1906), pp. 326–7.
121. *magic lantern*: an optical device, predecessor of the slide projector, using slides to display a magnified image on a white background in a darkened room. By the 1880s such slide shows were a popular form of entertainment, and the lanterns could be manipulated to produce ghostly or nightmarish effects.
122. *a volume of Dumas*: Alexandre Dumas, père (1802–70) was an immensely popular, much-translated, French dramatist and novelist, whose works of historical adventure included *The Count of Monte Christo* (1844), and *The Three Musketeers* (1844). His prolific output was enabled by a series of collaborators. Serialized in a French newspaper between March and July 1844, *Les Trois Mousquetaires* already enjoyed three, bowdlerized, translations into English by 1846.
123. *breathless ride of d'Artagnan*: The first chapter of Dumas' *The Three Musketeers*, a novel set in the early seventeenth century, recounts the gift to d'Artagnan by his father of an old horse, whose bizarre appearance and gait triggers the Quixotic hero's defensive fight as he is riding to Paris. MOWO's article on Dumas, ostensibly a review of a recent English biography of the author, starts with a sentence celebrating his 'breathless storytelling and equally breathless interest', and includes a lengthy appreciation of The Three Musketeers: M. O. W. Oliphant, 'Alexandre Dumas', *BM*, 114 (July 1873), pp. 111–30; in *Selected Works*, vol. 14, pp. 165–184.
124. *wheen*: see note 106 above.
125. lug: ear (Scottish).
126. *Athos, Porthos and Aramis*: the eponymous three musketeers of the Dumas novel Walter is reading.

*Notes to pages 91–107* 417

127. Pilgrim's Progress ... *Peace*: John Bunyan's Christian allegorical tale, *The Pilgrim's Progress from This World to That Which Is to Come; Delivered under the Similitude of a Dream* (1678) was one of the most-widely read texts of the nineteenth-century. On his way from the City of Destruction to Mount Zion Pilgrim rests at the Palace Beautiful where he is 'laid in a large upper Chamber, whose window opened toward the Sun rising; the name of Chamber was Peace, where he slept till break of day', J. Bunyan, *Pilgrim's Progress*, ed. J. B.Wharey, 2nd edn, revd. R. Sharrock (Oxford: Clarendon Press, 1960), p. 53.

128. *Crusader*: a reference designed to indicate the medieval origin of the castle. A Scottish contingent joined the Richard I (known as Richard the Lionheart) on the third crusade (1189–92), in its attempt to retrieve the Holy Land from Muslim control.

129. *craiks*: (Scottish), croakings.

130. *factor*: agent or steward empowered to administer the estate.

131. *leddy's*: lady's (Scottish).

132. kent: identifiable (Scottish).

133. *Every hardy ... searching air*: W. Scott, *The Lady of the Lake* (1810), in *The Poetical Works of Sir Walter Scott*, ed. J. L. Robertson (London: University Press, 1964), Canto I, Stanza xxvi, p. 214.

134. *'the chase'*: hunting.

135. *before we got Japanese shops at every corner:* In the mid nineteenth-century Japan's lengthy isolationist policy ended and mutual trade with Europe was opened up. In England, the official Japanese section at the 1862 International Exhibition in London was influential in popularizing Japanese art, designs and style.

136. minauderies: coquetteries (French).

137. *crofters*: A term in use in the Highlands and Islands of Scotland to describe those who rented the small landholdings they worked, often in conjunction with some other activity such as fishing.

138. *He pronounced it, alas! Truack*: Rather than the 'k' sound, the Scots pronunciation of 'ch' is more guttural, as in the 'ch' in the name of J. S. Bach.

139. *the sort of thing that happens in Ireland*: The fact that many Irish peasants did not own the land their families had worked, and so were in principle liable to sudden eviction by absentee landlords acting through their bailiffs, had long caused agitation. The Irish National Land League, formed in 1879, was dedicated to transferring the ownership of the land to tenant farmers. Although the majority of its members were opposed to violence, their fierce campaigning and the subsequent imprisonment of its leaders, became known as 'The Land War'. Meanwhile a series of agrarian murders of landlords and their agents in the early 1880s were widely reported in the British and American press.

140. *Ireland is one thing, and Scotland another*: Contrary to this fictional factor's opinion, Scots crofters learned from their Irish neighbours, setting up the Highland Land League which achieved security of tenure and a commission with rent-fixing powers in 1886.

141. *district visitors*: Charitable societies, often organised by religious organisations and on a parochial basis, organised poor areas into districts to be visited on a door to door basis by their representatives, who were usually middle-class and female. For a detailed account see F. K. Prochaska, *Women and Philanthropy in Nineteenth-Century England* (Oxford: Oxford University Press, 1980), pp. 106–37.

142. *grand seigneur*: literally 'great lord', but also suggesting a power of absolute command (French).

143. *dog-cart*: a light horse-drawn vehicle, originally designed to carry retriever dogs over shooting territory.

418                                    *Notes to pages 109–22*

144. Trois Mousquetaires: see notes 121 and 122 above.

145. *this gate*: in this way (Scottish).

146. *no canny ... glowering frae ye*: It's not safe to see you standing there staring fixedly at nothing (Scottish).

147. *India ... Ceylon*: The topic of the way in which the sons of Highland families had long been forced to emigrate in search of employment was one to which MOWO would return in her novel, *Kirsteen: The Story of a Scotch Family Seventy Years Ago* (1890); see *Selected Works*, vol. 22. The nephew MOWO had educated at her own expense had sailed for India in 1875 where he had died in 1879, and her eldest son would depart for Ceylon for a brief spell as the Governor's private secretary in 1884.

148. *mail three times a week ... they thought nothing of it*: The extent to which the British postal service had been revolutionized during her own life-time was one of the subjects to which MOWO would pay considerable attention in "Tis Sixty Years Since', *BM*, 161 (May 1897), pp. 599–604; on pp. 602–4; in *Selected Works*, vol. 13, pp. 445–74.

149. *at the early dinner politely called luncheon*: the emphasis here is on the polite euphemism employed in this female household. By the mid-nineteenth-century fashionable households took afternoon tea between 4.00pm and 5.00pm, in between luncheon, taken between noon and 2.00pm, and dinner, pushed back in the evening to as late as 8.00pm, whereas the lower classes continued to eat their main meal at lunchtime. Though referring to it as 'luncheon', Oona and her mother in fact eat their main meal at lunchtime, then take afternoon tea, followed by a light 'tray' at nine o'clock. S. Mitchell, *Daily Life in Victorian England* (Westport, CT: Greenwood Press, 1996), pp. 126–7.

150. *to make a fellow's commission depend upon his spelling*: There were a high number of Highland Scots recruits to the army. In times past there had been two routes into the army, through purchase, or without purchase through the more rigorous route of Sandhurst. From 1849 all applicants for first commissions in the army were required to pass a qualifying examination. As part of the army reforms undertaken by the Gladstone administration, the sale of army commissions was finally abolished in 1871, and, from 1878, all officer candidates, save those commissioned from the ranks, had to gain entry to the training college at Sandhurst. D. M. Henderson, *Highland Soldier: A Social Study of the Highland Regiments 1820–1920* (Edinburgh: John Donaldson, 1989).

151. *militia*: see note 21 above.

152. *'hap'*: covering (Scottish).

153. *'cloud'*: woman's loose-knitted woollen scarf.

154. *The holy time ... adoration*: lines from Wordsworth's sonnet, 'It Was a Beauteous Evening, Calm and Free', written in 1802 and published in 1807.

155. *the argand lamp*: The Forresters' pride in this oil-lamp, lit by a candle-wick fed by vegetable oil, suggests the remoteness of their island home, by comparison, for instance, with the home of the Edinburgh lawyer, Milnathort, where gas lighting is employed (see note 93 above.)

156. *ulster*: see note 102 above.

157. *gangrel*: see note 110 above.

158. *arguments in favour of a married clergy*: This issue had achieved renewed prominence as a result of the secession of a number of Anglican clergy to Roman Catholicism during the mid-nineteenth-century. Celibate Roman Catholic clergy, especially the Jesuits, were accused of posing a threat to Protestantism's cult of the family, allegedly interfering in domestic matters via the confessional. Within this novel, MOWO defends the notion of the potential efficacy of Protestant celibates by juxtaposing the Anglican Rev. Julius Wynn, all too involved in his relations' lives and affairs, with the bachelor Mr Cameron.

*Notes to pages 122–35*       419

159. *the church of the gentry*: In the process of adopting a Reformed, or Calvinist, theology, the Church of Scotland had rejected government by bishops, preferring presbyterian government by lay elders and ministers. Despite a breakaway movement in 1843, known as the Great Disruption, the Church of Scotland's parochial system meant that it had a nationwide distribution of kirks. Meanwhile an episcopalian church, claiming historical continuity from Christianity's fourth-century roots in Scotland, survived, though its numbers were far smaller and in 1800 it only boasted about seventy clergy. A number of aristocratic supporters, often educated in England, had been encouraged mid-nineteenth-century, both by the Great Disruption, and by Tractarian influences, to build new churches and cathedrals and to reclaim Scotland to the true catholic and apostolic church. For further information see, S. J. Brown, 'Scotland and the Oxford Movement', *The Oxford Movement: Europe and the Wider World 1830–1930* (Cambridge: Cambridge University Press, 2012), pp. 56–77. MOWO maintained a strong interest in Scottish ecclesiastical affairs.

160. *the weird*: fate, or destiny.

161. *Like ... Machomet's coffin*: more usually rendered 'Mahomet'. According to medieval European legends, the founder of Islam's coffin was suspended in mid-air without visible means of support in his tomb in the Hadgira of Medina.

162. *pickle*: few (Scottish).

163. *espièglerie*: mischievousness (French).

164. *cotters*: tenants renting a cottage and land from the landlord.

165. *soon or syne*: see note 73 above.

166. *just like the dove out of the ark*: See Genesis 8. Presumably Mrs Forrester's analogy is based upon the hope offered by the dove's second and third flight from the ark which confirms to Noah that the catastrophic flood has withdrawn sufficiently to support life again. Oona too is on a mission to assure herself that the crofters have sufficient means of support.

167. *disgusted ... political economist*: The Malthusian strain of political economy would appear to be MOWO's target here. Thomas Malthus published two books, *An Essay on the Principle of Population* (1798), and *Principles of Political Economy* (1820). In the former he argued that, since population growth would always exceed a country's ability to feed itself, legislative efforts to alleviate poverty were self-defeating because they allowed those living at subsistence level to multiply. Instead, he believed that natural forces, such as premature death by starvation, disease or war, should be allowed to operate as a check on population growth.

168. *peasant proprietors ... thought to be the strength of France*: while some believed that this class provided a stabilizing factor, providing a link between the interests of the workers and those of the propertied classes, Marxist theorists such as Paul Laforgue, believed that economic competition and distrust of the encroachments of the great landowners, would ultimately lure the beleaguered French peasant proprietors to the side of communism.

169. *Glasgow College*: The Old College site of the University of Glasgow, on the High Street, had closed in 1870 and the campus had moved to new buildings in the poorer west end of the city.

170. *'weirdless'*: ill-fated, improvident (Scottish).

171. *fash'd my thoom*: Scottish expression meaning 'bothered my head'.

172. *plenishing*: furniture (Scottish).

173. *weans*: children (Scottish).

174. *wake*: weak (Scottish).

175. *nae man ava*: no man at all (Scottish).

176. *skreighin'*: schreeching (Scottish).

420                           *Notes to pages 137–56*

177. *and that's Scripter*: Matthew 6:12: 'And forgive us our debts, as we forgive our debtors.'
178. *'drawers-head'*: top surface of the chest of drawers.
179. *feckless*: weak (Scottish).
180. *flitting*: removals (Scottish).
181. *fyle your fingers*: dirty your hands (Scottish).

# The Wizard's Son, Volume II

1.  *the boat is trimmed*: a boat in which the contents have been stowed so as to ensure the craft's secure, efficient balance in the water.
2.  *factotum*: Jack-, or in this case Jill-, of-all-trades.
3.  *maun away*: must be off (Scottish).
4.  *make it our dinner*: see Volume I, note 149 above.
5.  *'Somebody says that in the Bible, I know. Is thy servant a dog that he should do this thing?'*: see 2 Kings 8:13. Walter's rather hazy acquaintance with Biblical narrative is indicated by his naively innocent use of this phrase. In the original tale, Hazael, emissary of the ailing king of Syria, brazenly asks this of the prophet Elisha, who has just foretold the cruelty Hazael will inflict on the Israelites after he has usurped the Syrian throne. Walter too will subsequently be tempted to allow the very cruelty he deplores here.
6.  *It is Ireland one thinks of*: see note 139 above.
7.  *airt*: point of the compass (Scottish).
8.  *the other Una, the spotless lady of romance*: a comparison with the heroine of Edmund Spenser's *Faerie Queene*. See note 66 above.
9.  *Circe's island*: A deliberate slight is intended to Oona, in comparing her island home to that of the sorceress Circe who waylaid the Homeric hero, Odysseus on his voyage home, first using her magic potions to turn his crew into swine.
10. *Armida's garden*: a second slighting reference to Oona's seductive intent. In Tasso's *La Gerusalemme liberate* (1580–1), known in English as *Jerusalem Delivered*, the Saracen witch, Armida, niece of the King of Damascus, lures Rinaldo, a Christian soldier, to her enchanted pleasure garden to prevent his active pursuit of the First Crusade. Just as Armida was modelled on Circe, so her gardens were modelled on classical descriptions of the Elysian fields. Unlike Circe, however, Armida becomes a Christian convert and eventually marries the man she had set out first to kill, then to entrap.
11. *Exceeding peace had made Ben Adhem bold*: a reference to Leigh Hunt's (1784–1859) brief narrative poem, 'Abou Ben Adhem', in which, on a moonlit night, Abou has a vision of an angel recording 'the names of those who love the Lord'. He woke from his dream to see an angel writing in a book 'the names of people who love the Lord.' Discovering his own name is not there, he asks to be considered 'as one that loves his fellow men.' The following night the angel returns to reassure him that his name now heads all the rest. L. Hunt, *The Poetical Works of Leigh Hunt*, ed. H. S. Milford (London: Oxford University Press, 1923), p. 93. The allusion indicates that Mrs Forrester's humanitarianism is greater than her pride in her membership of the Scottish Episcopalian church (see Volume I, note 159 above; see also note 4 above).
12. *the Books*: an accurate translation of the Greek from which we derive the word 'Bible', in that it is a collection of books, varying in content from Judaism to Christianity, and according to the works considered suitable to be included within the canon by different branches of the Christian church.
13. nova, sola, infinita: The happiness of burgeoning love is heralded as 'new, sole and in-

*Notes to pages 156–69* 421

finite' in the nineteenth-century Italian poet, Giacomo Leopardi (1798–1837)'s late poem, 'Amore e Morte'(1832), l. 38. MOWO wrote two essays on this poet: M. O. W. Oliphant, 'Giacomo Leopardi', *BM*, 98 (October 1865), pp. 459–80; and M. O. W. Oliphant, 'Giacomo Leopardi', *CM* (September 1876), pp. 341–57; in *Selected Works*, vol. 14, pp. 287–302. In the Cornhill essay she cites the poem in translation, including the phrase cited here. The poem's theme is the twin birth of love and death.

14. *the Odyssey*: used figuratively here to indicate an intense experience, rather than a lengthy journey.

15. *in time for the grouse*: The grouse-shooting season begins on 12th August and ends on 10th December.

16. *Highland railway*: The Dingwall and Skye railway, launched in the 1870s for east-west transport in Scotland, had been absorbed into the Highlands railway as recently as 1880. Loch Hourn faces the Isle of Skye. The opening up of the Highlands to rail transport in the second half of the nineteenth century began to make them an attractive playground for the rich to enjoy shooting lodges and the like. Walter then takes the train route to London down the East coast.

17. *St. Monan's*: St Monan's is a small fishing port on the east coast of Fife in Scotland, which MOWO would have known well from her holidays in nearby St Andrew's.

18. *entailed*: an entail settles the succession of a landed estate in a prescribed line of descent, thus preventing the current possessor from disposing of it as he will.

19. *As our Laureate says, 'the soul of Shakespeare.'*: a quotation from stanza LXI of Tennyson's lengthy elegy, *In Memoriam* (1850), a particular favourite of MOWO's. In this section of the poem the bereaved poet imagines his dead friend viewing him from his new vantage-point in heaven, and finding him strangely puny. Nevertheless, the poet claims that, judged by earthly standards, his love could not have been greater. In MOWO's somewhat strained application Oona's love for her mother is unaffected by her mother's intellectual inferiority.

20. *blazing Irishmen*: The Irish land agitation (see note 4 above) had seen some properties set ablaze.

21. *a communist*: The Paris Commune and its suppression (1871), had led to increased debate among young idealists from good families as to how far the values and actions of the Paris Commune were compatible with English socialist ideals. The fact that educated men such as H. M. Hyndman (Eton and Cambridge) and William Morris (Marlborough and Oxford) stood in the vanguard of socialist demonstrations in Britain of the 1880s was unsettling, even if the overall numerical threat of such movements was minimal.

22. *a monomaniac*: On 31 October 1882, MOWO wrote to William Blackwood asking him 'what sort of paper you want from me for December. There is a foolish story going about that the Glamis mystery has been cleared up by the death of an old man, either a criminal or a monster, who has been living all the time in the secret chamber. I think it is simply nonsense, but it would not be at all a bad subject for a short story to be called 'The True Story of a Haunted House', Coghill, pp. 309–10, in *Selected Works*, vol. 6, p. 211. The Glamis mystery had formed the basis for her earlier story 'The Secret Chamber' whose relation to *The Wizard's Son* is discussed in the Introduction to this volume.

23. *liberality of mind*: open-mindedness.

24. *Magnetism, mesmerism*: 'Animal magnetism' was an alternative name for mesmerism (see note 4 above).

25. *King's Cross*: The Great Northern Railway terminated at this station.

26. *Park Lane*: Running north-south along the eastern boundary of Hyde Park, this was a fashionable nineteenth-century address.

422                                   *Notes to pages 169–78*

27. *the worst side of every town*: When the railway introduced new routes into long-established towns, it often encountered vested landed interests so that frequently the cheapest course was to opt to build its stations in poorer areas on the perimeters.

28. *prodigal ... forgiveness and the fatted calf*: see Luke 15:11–32.

29. *'warbeaten soldier'*: despite MOWO's quotation marks, no original source has been identified.

30. *home ... soiled with ignoble use*: The 'home, sweet home' motif, fostered by the Victorian cult of domesticity, had triggered a host of sentimental popular art and song.

31. *a novel from Mudie's*: Mudie's Select Library, founded in 1842, was a lending library, which by means of advance bulk orders, had achieved an effective stranglehold over the fiction-publishing industry by the 1880s. In 1881 MOWO had been involved in a risky challenge to Mudie's domination. See Jay (1995), pp. 284–5.

32. *crewel work*: work done with a yarn thicker than embroidery thread, and used to create raised decorative patterns. It had become popular again in the 1860s.

33. *Devonshire cream*: clotted cream, particularly thick dairy cream. For MOWO's use of food imagery see Jay (1995), pp. 303–4.

34. rapprochement: resumption of harmonious relations (French).

35. couleur de rose: as rosy (French).

36. *yellow novel*: This does not denote a racy English 'yellow-back' novel, but the French habit of using a lemon-coloured paper binding for the majority of books, which then permitted owners to have them hard-bound in the style they preferred.

37. *French writers ... humanity as it was*: From Balzac's multi-volumed series of novels and tales, *La Comédie Humaine*, describing French society of the first half-of the nineteenth-century in meticulous detail, to Zola's naturalistic series, *Les Rougon-Macquart*, describing France under the Second Empire (1852–70), French fiction had gained a reputation in Victorian England for tackling subjects considered unsuitable for family consumption, and for an approach which English readers often described as cynical.

38. *cushioned sentry-box ... porters delight*: These enveloping chairs had been developed to protect servants on night duty in cold halls from suffering from draughts.

39. *'wondered at it' as the ladies of Camelot did over Elaine*: Despite the quotation marks, this phrase does not occur in Tennyson's 'Lancelot and Elaine', published in 1859 as part of his epic cycle *Idylls of the King*. It is the knight Gawain who 'wondered at her' (l. 1159) as the corpse of this love-lorn damsel arrives on her barge in Camelot, although in both this poem, and 'The Lady of Shalott' (1832, revised 1842), the courtiers are represented marvelling at the arrival of this mysterious presence.

40. *a high phaeton*: a lightly-sprung, lightweight, open carriage, mounted on four large wheels, designed for speed.

41. *fresh as the cherries in the song*: presumably an allusion to Robert Herrick's song, 'Cherry Ripe', although it is the ripeness rather than freshness of the cherries that the song celebrates. John Everett Millais's 1879 painting, entitled 'Cherry Ripe' had given the phrase and the song fresh currency.

42. *the House of Commons is to be preferred for that*: In nineteenth-century Britain's bicameral political system, the House of Commons was composed of elected members, whereas membership of the House of Lords was either hereditary or by royal appointment. Since the government was and is formed by the party holding the majority of seats in the Commons this is the House where policy is formulated.

43. *since they had been in long clothes*: clothes specifically designed for children were a recent phenomenon, dating from the 1860s. As children grew older, so a girl's skirts grew

*Notes to pages 178–89* 423

longer, and a boy made the transition from knickerbockers to long trousers.

44. *shooting-box*: a small country house used by hunters during the shooting season.

45. *a big Queen Anne one*: The Queen Anne style became architecturally popular in the last quarter of the nineteenth-century: like many revivals it saw no reason to repeat the English Baroque style of the reign of Queen Anne (reigned 1702–14) too slavishly.

46. *Eastern ... mats and cushions*: Early in 1880 the fashionable firm of Liberty & Co. had introduced Anglo-oriental decorative goods into their Regent's Street shop.

47. *take my lute like Emily*: The heroine, Emily St Aubert's sense that her lute has been played and moved from its resting-place by an unknown other is the first mystery encountered in chapter one of Radcliffe's novel, *The Mysteries of Udolpho*. See also notes 118 and 119 above.

48. *one fair daughter, and no more, whom he loved passing well!*: see *Hamlet*, II.ii.427.

49. affiché'd: flaunted (French).

50. *the turf*: horse-racing.

51. *to pluck his pigeon*: fleece his gullible victim.

52. *hantle*: (Scottish), a great deal.

53. *you old Solomon*: perhaps a reference to 1 Kings 3:16–28 where King Solomon demonstrates his judicious wisdom in distinguishing between two plaintiffs: like Solomon, Symington opts for the mother.

54. *ecarte*: Écarté is a two-handed card game (French).

55. *viscount's coronet*: see note 4 above.

56. au pied de la lettre: literally (French).

57. délaissements: acts, or bouts, of neglect (French).

58. *Society ... scarcely ... back to town*: The social season, by long-standing tradition, was the period, coinciding with parliamentary sessions and stretching from early spring to the beginning of July, when aristocrats occupied and entertained from their town-houses.

59. *Pall Mall and Piccadilly*: From Piccadilly Circus it is a short walk to Pall Mall, the street where many of the more famous gentlemen's clubs of the nineteenth century were located.

60. *the Park*: The South Carriage Drive, adjacent to Rotten Row, on the south side of London's Hyde Park, was a fashionable place for those in London society to be seen.

61. *Norwood*: In the late nineteenth century Norwood was a suburban village comprising of middle-class villas surrounded by a hinterland of canal wharfs and factories.

62. *the Peri at the gate of Paradise*: 'The Story of Paradise and the Peri' constituted the fourth part of Thomas Moore's popular oriental romance, 'Lalla Rookh' (1817), and was used as the basis for a cantata by Robert Schumann in 1843. The reference is a favourite of MOWO's, but here the allusion is scarcely apposite in that the peri, a creature from Persian mythology, is required to bring the gift most dear to heaven – a sinner's tear – to gain her readmission to Paradise.

63. *Byron!*: Lord George Gordon Byron (1788–1824), one of the most famous of the late Augustan/early Romantic poets. Like Walter he had come to his peerage by an indirect route, through his great-uncle. In 1882 MOWO had published *The Literary History of England in the End of the Eighteenth and Beginning of the Nineteenth Century*, 3 vols (London: Macmillan & Co., 1882). There she wrote of Byron's coming to London, knowing no-one other than his literary agent and solicitor, and writing 'the kind of letters which any undistinguished young man, with coarsish tastes, and time entirely occupied with the frivolous occurrences of the day, might have written', Oliphant, *The Literary History of England*, vol. 3, pp. 16–17.

64. *his look like a fallen angel*: Byron referred to himself as 'a fallen spirit', G. G. Byron, *Byron's Letters and Journals*, ed. L. A. Marchand, 12 vols (London: John Murray, 1973–82), vol. 2, p. 176).

424                *Notes to pages 189–95*

65. *courage enough to follow the example of Byron*: MOWO described Byron's maiden speech in the House of Lords as being made 'on behalf of the poor rioters in his own county – a very good object', Oliphant, *The Literary History of England*, vol. 3, p. 18.

66. *youthful passion and would-be cynicism*: MOWO described Byron's *Childe Harold* as being 'less of revolt against established laws than of that personal grievance which is felt so bitterly in youth, when things do not go as we wish', Oliphant, *The Literary History of England*, vol. 3, p. 22.

67. *that Byronic scene in the House of Lords*: MOWO described Byron's first appearance and speech in the House of Lords, with its self-advertising sense of being neglected by society, as extraordinary for a man 'educated at Harrow and Cambridge', and thus explicable only by the 'painful' fact 'that the company of his own class was really not agreeable to Byron', Oliphant, *The Literary History of England*, vol. 3, p. 18.

68. *White's, or Boodle's*: the two oldest clubs for gentlemen in London

69. *no petty exclusiveness*: Since membership of the most prestigious London clubs was thought to guarantee a certain social standing, and offer easy access to similarly-placed individuals, gaining membership involved election, either by all members, or a committee.

70. *'bosses'*: First appearing as 'baas' to describe the master or manager in the American colonies, the word did not arrive in Britain until the mid-nineteenth-century, and then only as a slang term.

71. *red hair is so fashionable*: Pre-Raphaelite painting had helped to popularize auburn hair.

72. *the apples of Gomorrah*: a fruit described by the writers of antiquity as attractive to the eye but which dissolves into dust and ashes in the mouth. Also known as Dead Sea fruit, these fruits were associated with Sodom and Gomorrah, the cities of the fertile plain whose wickedness had led God to destroy them. See Genesis 13:10–19:29.

73. *cranshing*: crunching, or being ground to nothing.

74. levée: reception at court.

75. *the crackling of thorns*: see Ecclesiastes 7:5: 'For as the crackling of thorns under a pot, so is the laughter of the fool: this also is vanity.'

76. *burlesque*: Victorian burlesque was a form of parody in which a well-known opera, ballet, or, occasionally, play, was adapted into a comic travesty of the original, often risqué in tone.

77. *our lands march*: our estates have a common boundary (Scottish expression).

78. *pot luck*: a meal, partaken of by an unexpected guest, and therefore composed of whatever items happen to be available.

79. *Tennyson's … the* Falcon: Tennyson's play, though not published until 1884, had first been performed in December 1879. See also notes 276 and 277 below. MOWO complimented Tennyson upon the play personally. Jay (1990) p. 143; in *Selected Works*, vol. 6, p. 99.

80. blasé: world-weary (French).

81. comme il faut: as it should be (French).

82. *caravanseries*: originally large Eastern inns with a central quadrangle, where travellers might rest as they travelled the trade routes.

83. *pavey*: pavement.

84. *round-about*: from every point of view.

85. *bread-and-butter*: meaning ordinary, plain or simple, deriving from the notion of bread and butter being the simplest of regular fares.

86. pavé: pavement (French).

87. *Marlborough House*: From 1863 this had been the London residence of the Prince of Wales and his family, thus Katie is indicating that she and her father have no pretension to move in court circles.

*Notes to pages 196–208* 425

88. *French Embassy*: The French Embassy was fashionably-placed at Albert Gate, one of the entrances to Hyde Park, just off the South Carriage Drive. See also notes 26 and 60 above.

89. *what duke*: The inference to be drawn is that Katie is referring to the Duke of Argyll, the greatest landholder in the area where Walter's Scottish properties were to be found.

90. entrée: a main or meat dish, occurring after the soup and fish courses.

91. *brought to the literal*: given a realistic interpretation on stage.

92. *If you want your cigar*: Custom dictated that women withdrew at the end of dessert allowing their menfolk to indulge in digestifs, cigars and male topics of conversation.

93. *Nelly Somebody in a burlesque*: There were two very well-known actresses of this name who had made a reputation for themselves as burlesque performers: Nellie Farren (1848–1904) and Nelly Power (1854–87).

94. *disapproved of ballets*: Not only did ballerinas flout the Victorian convention for feminine behaviour by making a spectacle of themselves on stage for money, but famous ballerinas such as Marie Taglioni (1804–84) would deliberately shorten her skirts so that her skill at pointe work could be better appreciated by the audience.

95. *'never funked and never lied; I guess he didn't know how'*: in quotation marks to indicate contemporary slang, rather than an attribution to a particular source.

96. *the old Italian romancer, the noble English poet*: Tennyson's play, 'The Falcon', was based upon a tale from the mid-fourteenth-century Decameron, by the Italian poet and storyteller, Boccacio. This tale, 'Federigo degli Alberighi', was cast as the ninth story told on the fifth day of a ten-day cycle of tales.

97. *Mrs. Kendal*: Madge Kendal (1848–1935) and her husband managed the St James's Theatre, London where they produced Tennyson's 'The Falcon' which ran for sixty-seven nights. She and her actor husband customarily played against each other in the leading roles, so helping to maintain a strict code of moral conduct for the actors employed within their theatre, and lending performances there an aura of respectability for middle-class Victorian audiences.

98. sotto voce: in an undertone (Italian).

99. *Lord Innishouran was the son of the Duke*: The current Duke of Argyll's son (b. 1845), had married one of Queen Victoria's daughters, and they had a shared love of the arts.

100. dilettante *in the best sense of the word*: indicating someone who cultivated the fine arts, not as a professional, but for the love of them, rather than its later usage to suggest someone who merely dabbles for self-amusement.

101. *link-boys*: young boys who carried torches to light pedestrians to their carriages.

102. *vacant house ... Scripture*: see Luke 11:24–6: 'When the unclean spirit is gone out of a man, he walketh through dry places, seeking rest; and finding none, he saith, I will return unto my house whence I came out. And when he cometh, he findeth it swept and garnished. Then goeth he, and taketh to him seven other spirits more wicked than himself; and they enter in, and dwell there: and the last state of that man is worse than the first'.

103. *one of your supporters*: a mistake on MOWO's part, since between 1663 and 1999 peers who inherited a title did not have to be ceremonially introduced. Lord Innishouran himself would not become a member of the House of Lords until he succeeded to his father's title.

104. faute de mieux: for want of a better alternative (French).

105. beauté du diable: youthful beauty (French).

106. *Caledonian Club*: Despite this being an invention of MOWO's, such a London club was founded in 1891.

107. *lightest little* attaché: The role might be either that of a junior diplomat, or a member of the administrative staff.

426                                     *Notes to pages 209–44*

108. *other popular chambers of legislature*: From 1848 British colonies had begun to achieve Westminster-style forms of democratic government.

109. *bulwark of the constitution*: Walter Bagehot's classic work, *The English Constitution* (1867) made much play of the contrast between the overweening Emperor Napoleon III and Britain's monarchy, or, in the 1872 edition, the experimental arrangements of France's Third Republic's against Britain's parliamentary system.

110. bon camarade: a good fellow (French).

111. *a pronounced, but not unrefined Scotch accent*: MOWO proudly retained her own Scottish accent. See Jay (1995), p. 17.

112. *evening reception at the Royal Academy*: Founded personally by George III in 1768, the Royal Academy had moved to Burlington House in 1868. The Royal Academy Summer Exhibition has run annually ever since 1769.

113. beauté du diable: see note 105 above.

114. *picturesque Academicians*: the practising artists appointed as Royal Academicians.

115. amis d'enfance: childhood friends (French).

116. *Bruton Street ... gives me consequence*: Given Julia's claim that her relatives are 'not very much in society', it seems surprising that they have taken a house in Bruton Street, a part of fashionable Mayfair.

117. *Burlington House*: see note 112 above.

118. *'If 'twere done when 'tis done, then 'twere well it were done quickly'*: Macbeth I.vii.1–2. In that these are Macbeth's words when pondering on the advantages of proceeding swiftly with the murder of his king, they are certainly not 'lover-like'.

119. *budget*: store of news.

120. *to come to speech of*: to address (Scottish expression).

121. *King Cambyses' vein*: 'for I must speak in passion, and I will do it in King Cambyses' vein', *Henry IV, Part I*, II.iv.430. Katie would appear to have the first part of this quotation in mind, rather than referring to the drunken bombast for which this theatrical character was famed.

122. *Moray Place*: see Volume I, note 61 above.

123. *Firth*: the estuary of the Scottish river Forth, known as the Firth of Forth.

124. *wandering about the face of the earth, seeking I don't know what*: see Job 1:7: 'And the LORD said unto Satan, Whence comest thou? Then Satan answered the LORD, and said, From going to and fro in the earth, and from walking up and down in it'.

125. *bit*: bit of, here used quasi-adjectivally to mean 'small', or 'young'.

126. *I could not love him, if I would not give up everything for him ... Scripture*: see John 15:13: 'Greater love hath no man than this, that a man lay down his life for his friends.'

127. *'indistinguishable throng'*: despite MOWO's quotation marks, no original source has been identified.

128. la langue Turque: In Persian mythology this was held this to be one of three primitive languages: Eve spoke Arabic, but Persian with Adam, while the angel Gabriel spoke Turkish.

129. *steam-yacht*: Steam-powered boats enjoyed a particular vogue in nineteenth-century Scotland, and were often used to serve the Highlands and Islands. By the 1850s there were also elegant, privately-owned steam launches.

130. *to gather knowledge at the fountain head*: MOWO is poking mild fun at the inappropriate register of the parliamentarian's conversation. The phrase recalls both the Latin tag, '*fons et origo*' and Alexander Pope's couplet: 'A little learning is a dang'rous thing;/Drink deep, or taste not the Pierian spring', A. Pope, 'An Essay on Criticism' (1709).

131. *Naiads*: water nymphs.

132. *wandering Jews*: Katie mockingly aligns Walter's 'warlock lord' with this figure of popu-

lar European legend, the wandering Jew, who, having cursed Christ on his way to the Crucifixion, was then condemned to wander the earth until Christ's Second Coming.

133. *Saut Market*: major thoroughfare in the city of Glasgow.

134. *Bailie Nicol Jarvie's time*: a character in Walter Scott's *Rob Roy* (1817). This garrulous Lowland merchant when in the Highlands boasts of his origins in Glasgow's 'saut market'. MOWO may well have had the social panorama of Scott's novel which incorporates both rich and poor, the English and Scots Lowlanders and Highlanders, and a range of classes, when she wrote *The Wizard's Son*.

135. amour propre: self-esteem (French).

136. *the 12th*: see note 15 above.

137. *aborigines*: native Scots.

138. *called each other by their Christian names*: An English-educated man of Braithwaite's class will have learnt to call his schoolfellows by their surnames, whereas Scotland's more democratic educational system and the closeness of those raised in these remote areas will have encouraged more familial relations.

139. *as Dante offended Beatrice*: In Dante's *La Vita Nuova* (1295) the poet tells how, hoping to keep his devotion to Beatrice secret, he had alighted upon a 'screen-lady'. However his apparent devotion to this and a subsequent decoy, provoke outrageous rumours which offend Beatrice when she comes to hear of them. (MOWO's own account of the Vita Nuova, published as M. O. W. Oliphant, 'The Early Years of Dante', *CM*, 32 (October 1875), pp. 471–89, subsequently became Chapter 1 of her historical volume, M. O. W. Oliphant, *The Makers of Florence* (London: Macmillan and Co., 1876). In 1877 she published M. O. W. Oliphant, *Dante* (Edinburgh and London: William Blackwood & Sons, 1877).

140. *masked*: brewed (Scottish).

141. *ben*: adverb, meaning towards the better part of the house, or towards the speaker (Scottish).

142. *Grosvenor Square*: a large garden square in fashionable Mayfair.

143. *green tea*: There are many varieties of green tea, so named because it undergoes less oxidation than other types during processing. Consequently, green tea's reputed beneficial properties also vary greatly from increasing alertness to exercising a calming effect.

144. *Benlui*: a real mountain at the head of Glen Fyne in the southern Highlands.

145. *health inspector, from Glasgow*: and therefore used to the epidemic problems created by dense overcrowding in the city's crumbling tenement buildings.

146. *like the commandant in* Don Giovanni: At the conclusion of Mozart's opera, *Don Giovanni* (1787), the Don, in an act of bravado, invites the speaking statue of a man he has murdered to dinner. When the statue arrives, offering the lecherous Don one last chance to repent, the Don refuses, whereupon hell opens up to drag both the statue and the Don into its maw.

147. *Let not him that putteth on his armour boast himself like him that putteth it off*: a slight misquotation of 1 Kings 20:11.

148. *not only a Scotch lord, but an English peer*: After the Act of Union (1707) between England and Scotland, those who held newly-created peerages became peers of Great Britain, but because there were proportionally many more Scottish peers, they chose a number of representatives to sit in the British House of Lords. The Acts of Union (1800) subsequently changed the terminology to peers of the United Kingdom.

149. *see visions and dream dreams*: see Joel 2:28 and Acts 2:17: 'your sons and your daughters shall prophesy, and your young men shall see visions, and your old men shall dream dreams.'

150. *a cheeper*: a young bird (Scottish).

151. *New heavens and a new earth*: In building her picture of the daily miracle of creation, Oliphant references both Genesis 1 and 2, and the new Jerusalem envisaged in Revelation 21.

428                                   *Notes to pages 262–76*

152. '*heritage of woe*': This allusion to Byron's Gothic narrative poem, 'Lara' (1814), Canto I, Stanza 2, l. 4, implicitly acknowledges MOWO's debt to parts of its plot . The poem begins with the Scottish chieftain, Lara, returning to his ancestral inheritance after a mispent youth abroad. Servants hear 'the sound of words less earthly than his own', when Lara retreats at night to the portrait gallery of his ancestors and on one such occasion they hear a shriek and find Lara unconscious on the floor, his half-drawn sword nearby. The latter part of the poem in which a mysterious visiting Lord, unrecognized by Lara, challenges him to a duel on account of incidents that occurred abroad, and Lara is finally killed by another man who takes up the visitor's cause has little relevance to MOWO's novel.

153. '*The light that never was on sea or shore*': a slight misquotation of Wordsworth's 'The light that never was, on sea or land'. The next couple of sentences owe much to the poem in which this line occurs: 'Elegiac Stanzas. Suggested by a Picture of Peele Castle in a Storm, Painted by Sir George Beaumont' (1807).

154. *trending*: rolling

155. *the soul ... rest*: see Psalm 55:6: 'And I said, Oh that I had wings like a dove! for then would I fly away, and be at rest.'

156. *Father ... hired servants*: see Luke 15:18–19. Also see note 28 above.

157. *Ye must be born again*: see John 3:7.

158. *hit the blot*: see Volume I, note 37 above.

159. *Political economy*: see Volume I, note 167 above.

160. *Adam Smith's palmy days*: Since this novel has a contemporary setting the minister will not literally have sat at the feet of Adam Smith (1723–90). Nevertheless his education will have included this Scottish philosopher's *The Wealth of Nations* (1776) which was to become a foundational text in the study of Political Economy.

161. *Ireland ... landlords*: see Volume I, notes 139 and 140 above.

162. *in Canada they will soon flourish*: During the first half of the nineteenth-century, almost sixty per cent of UK emigrants to the densely-populated Canadian province of Nova Scotia were from Scotland: indeed its name tells of a long history of such migration.

163. *an old man ... is a sad sight*: MOWO repeatedly introduced the topic of euthanasia in her fiction (see *Phoebe, Junior*, in *Selected Works*, vol. 19, p. 234) which had become a matter of public debate in Britain since the 1870s. Allowing the minister, rather than a layman to support the idea here suggests that MOWO could see no strong Christian objection to the practice.

164. *the like of you ... another Church*: Since Walter has been raised south of the border, the minister's assumption is that he will be a member of the Church of England.

165. *mind you at their Books*: Bible-reading (see note 12 above) enjoyed a prominent place at family prayers.

166. *the Lord's doing, and wonderful in our eyes*: see Psalm 118:23: 'This is the Lord's doing; it is marvellous in our eyes'.

167. *ettling at*: eager for (Scottish).

168. *pickle siller*: a grain, and so figuratively, a small amount of silver (Scottish).

169. *callants*: boys (Scottish).

170. *man – that walketh not astray*: quoted from a metrical version of Psalm 1: 'O greatly bless-ed is the man/Who walketh not astray/In counsel of ungodly men,/Nor stands in sinner's way'.

171. *here we have nae continuing ceety, but look for one to come*: see Hebrews 13:14: 'For here have we no continuing city, but we seek one to come'.

*Notes to pages 278–311* 429

# The Wizard's Son, Volume III

1. *under your own vine and your own fig-tree*: see Micah 4:4: 'But they shall sit every man under his vine and under his fig tree; and none shall make them afraid: for the mouth of the Lord of hosts hath spoken it'.
2. *Michael Angelo*: This slightly surprising tableau is a reminder that MOWO had devoted the final chapter of *The Makers of Florence* (1876) to Michelangelo.
3. *Caleb Balderston*: the butler in Walter Scott's *The Bride of Lammermoor* (see Volume I, note 99 above). His second name is Balderstone, but this mistake remains uncorrected in each of the editions consulted for this volume.
4. *cicerone*: see Volume I, note 72 above.
5. *she cannot dabble a little in vice as a man can do*: MOWO here raises both the double standard by which the Victorian social code forgives a young man for sowing his wild oats, whereas any deviation from strictly-defined 'ladylike' behaviour stigmatizes a woman irredeemably, and the habitual categorization of women in extreme binaries, as either angel or whore. For further discussion see the Introduction, pp. xxiii–xxiv.
6. *so many silent votes*: Sir Thomas's parliamentary efforts on behalf of his constituency have never prompted him to making a speech, merely to passing through the lobby when the vote is taken.
7. *bring ben*: see Volume II, note 14 above.
8. *major domo*: a person who undertakes responsibility for household arrangements in the absence of the owner.
9. *punctilio*: over-fastidious scruple.
10. *parvenue*: social climber.
11. *old Truepenny*: See Hamlet, I.v.150. An allusion designed to recall Hamlet's uneasy levity when he is aware of the ghost's lurking presence, but his companions are unaware.
12. *the fair Julia*: Underwood's comically derisory reference to Julia Herbert may be intended to evoke memories of one of the two heroines of Shakespeare's *The Two Gentlemen of Verona* who is prepared to disguise herself as a page, and travel to another, city so intent is she upon retrieving Proteus, her fickle lover.
13. *an old campaigner*: a phrase for scheming manipulative women to which William Makepeace Thackeray had given currency in *The Newcomes* (1855).
14. *another pair of shoes*: another matter.
15. *a brown study*: Katie's mind was elsewhere.
16. *Venus and Minerva*: In the mythical narrative explaining the origins of the Trojan war, Paris, a Trojan mortal, was asked to judge which of the three goddesses, Venus (or Aphrodite), goddess of love, Minerva (or Athena), goddess of wisdom, and Juno (or Hera), queen of the gods, was the fairest.
17. *telegraph office – as is so general in the Highlands*: Britain had been in the forefront of cable-laying to connect its remotest areas and by the 1870s even islands off the west coast of Scotland were connected.
18. *a mere nursery woman*: a woman who had confined herself to looking after infants.
19. serrement: pang (French).
20. *Toots*: an exclamation of mild annoyance.
21. *God is more ready to forgive than we are to ask*: see the Collect for the twelfth Sunday after Trinity in the Book of Common Prayer.
22. *Can a man enter a second time – and be born?*: see John 3:4.
23. attendrissement: tender feeling (French).

430                                   *Notes to pages 313–64*

24. boude: the term 'boudoir' derives from the French verb bouder, meaning to sulk. Walter remarks that this room uncharacteristically receives the full force of the daylight, because at this period a boudoir was used as a term for a lady's evening sitting room, which in grand houses was often separate from her morning room, and her dressing room.

25. *The old idea that a woman should be sacrificed to reform a man has gone out of fashion*: for further discussion of the salvific role of women in MOWO's work see the Introduction, pp. xxi–xxii.

26. *Dante's nameless sinner who made 'the great refusal'*: see D. Alighieri, *The Inferno*, Canto III, pp. 58–61. Dante's 'nameless sinner' is usually identified as Pope Celestine V, whose resignation the poet deemed responsible for permitting further ecclesiastical corruption. MOWO's use of this reference is discussed in the Introduction (pp. xxi–xxii).

27. *His soul (if he had one)*: Charles Darwin's scientific hypotheses appeared to many contemporaries to challenge man's claim to be more than the sum of his physical and rational parts, raising questions as to where to locate humanity's inclinations to the mystical, ethical, moral and aesthetic. Thomas Huxley, Darwin's disciple, summarised the argument thus: 'For of two alternatives one must be true. Either consciousness is the function of something distinct from the brain, which we call the soul, and a sensation is the mode in which this soul is affected by the motion of a part of the brain; or there is no soul, and a sensation is something generated by the mode of a part of the brain', T. Huxley, 'On the Hypothesis that Animals are Automata, and Its History', *Collected Essays*, 8 vols (London: Macmillan, 1893), vol. 1, p. 210.

28. *pure and of good report*: see Philippians 4:8.

29. *Do you think I am Prospero to send you aches and stitches?*: see The Tempest, I.ii.325–6.

30. *'heavenly Una with her milkwhite lamb'*: a quotation from Wordsworth's poem, 'Personal Talk', (1807), l. 42.

31. *'a Daniel come to judgement'*: see *The Merchant of Venice*, IV.i.223: 'A Daniel come to judgment! yea, a Daniel! / O wise young judge, how I do honour thee!'. In this rather curious tribute Jeanie Campbell attempts to flatter both Julia's wisdom and her youth.

32. *swell*: a fashionably-attired person.

33. *Fling wide the doors!*: see Psalm 24:7–9.

34. *Pharos*: lighthouse.

35. *the Sabbath of the Sacrament*: In rural Presbyterian parishes Communion was rarely celebrated more than twice a year, but it was marked by a special period of preparation.

36. *the occasion*: the term by which the periodical Communion service was known in Scottish Presbyterian usage.

37. *cloud* : see Volume I, note 153 above.

38. *Canada ... Australia ... India – that is where all our boys go*: MOWO was perhaps wise to be a little vague here about precisely which 'north-west provinces she had in mind'. A previous reference (p. 144) suggests that MOWO had originally placed Rob Forrester in Australia, where, from 1856, North Western province had designated an electoral region of Victoria. However, the North-Western Provinces had from 1836 designated an administrative region in British India, and the Northwest Territories had entered the Canadian confederation in 1870.

39. *'Up and spoke she, Alice Brand ... mine.'*: An excerpt from a ballad which served as an interlude in Walter Scott's long narrative poem set in Scotland, 'The Lady of the Lake' (1810), Canto IV, Stanza xii, in W. Scott, *The Poetical Works of Sir Walter Scott*, ed. J. L. Robertson (London: Oxford University Press, 1964), p. 243. The reference is apposite in that Alice, because she is free from the crime of killing her brother in battle that has outlawed her

*Notes to pages 364–405*

431

lover, is able to save him from the malevolent preternatural force of the Elfin King.

40. *caterans*: a Gaelic word associated with warrior-bands, had come to refer more insultingly to Highland marauders or cattle-rustlers.

41. '*heavenly Una with her milk-white lamb*': see note 30 above, where, incidentally, 'milk-white' is not hyphenated.

42. *hon*: my dear (Scottish).

43. *Rembrandt-like pictures in the gloom*: The layers of varnish subsequently added to the seventeenth-century Dutch artist, Rembrandt's, paintings made the nineteenth-century art critic John Ruskin declare: 'it is the aim of the best painters to paint the noblest things they can see by sunlight, but of Rembrandt to paint the foulest things he could see by rushlight.' Although the original of Rembrandt's seventeenth-century painting, *The Company of Captain Banning Cocq and Lieutenant Willem van Ruytenburch*, often miscalled 'The Night Watch' on account of the depth of the varnish, always remained in the Netherlands, the National Gallery in London had been in possession of a smaller copy by Gerrit Lundens since 1857.

44. *like Rizpah*: Tennyson had published the bitter maternal lament, 'Rizpah', loosely based on 2 Samuel 21:8–10, in his collection, *Ballads and Other Poems* (1880). The poem tells of a bereaved mother who steals the bones of her highwayman son from the foot of the gibbet, to re-inter them in the churchyard.

45. *God is as near in the dark as in the day*: see Psalm 139:12.

46. '*I had hoped like the apostles … delivered*': see Luke 24:21: 'But we trusted that it had been he which should have redeemed Israel'.

47. *Ascot … the Derby … and Goodwood*: a series of summer meetings at these famous race-courses formed part of the English social season.

48. *humbugs*: hypocrites.

49. *way of pleasantness … peace*: see Proverbs 3:17.

50. '*Senza quella … figura*': an extended form of the quotation from Giacomo Leopardi (see Volume II, note 13 above). It is worth quoting from MOWO's translation in her *Cornhill* essay: 'When in the heart profound, / New love first draws its breath, / Languid and faint, is with it found / A wish for death. / Perhaps because the eyes take fright / Then at this desert, and earth seems / A waste wherein no man can dwell / Without that new sole infinite Joy that has dawned upon his dreams', M. O. W. Oliphant, 'Giacomo Leopardi', *CM* (September 1876), pp. 341–57, in *Selected Works*, vol. 14, pp. 287–302.

51. *God's ordinance*: see Genesis 2:18–24.

# TEXTUAL VARIANTS

The first edition of *The Wizard's Son* has been used as the copy text and has been compared against both the serialised version of the novel, from November 1882 to March 1884, identified as *1882–4*, and the 1894 reprint of the second edition of 1884, identified as *1894*. Volumes II and III of our copy text edition restart the chapter numbering afresh with each new volume, whereas both the 1882–4 and 1894 editions numbers the chapters sequentially throughout. MOWO made extensive cuts in revising the serial text for its appearance in book form, and these long extracts that were omitted from our copy text have been listed here.

| | |
|---|---|
| 7a | parent:] parent; *1894* |
| 8a | kind:] kind; *1894* |
| 8b | money –] holiday, *1882–4, 1894* |
| 8c | for him] now to do *1882–4, 1894* |
| 8d | everybody:] everybody; *1882–4, 1894* |
| 9a | smoothes] smooths *1894.* |
| 12a | others] others, *1882–4, 1894* |
| 12b | Rector,] rector, *1894* |
| 13a | to-morrow?'] tomorrow," *1882–4, 1894* |
| 14a | said,] said *1894* |
| 16a | captain's] Captain's *1882–4, 1894* |
| 16b | captain] Captain *1882–4, 1894* |
| 20a | by and by,] by-and-by, *1894* |
| 22a | gave] give *1882–4, 1894* |
| 23a | advanced] not advanced *1882–4, 1894* |
| 26a | half-a-dozen] half a dozen *1882–4, 1894* |
| 27a | above-board.'] above board." *1882–4, 1894* |
| 28a | more;] more: *1882–4, 1894* |
| 29a | great coat.] greatcoat. *1882–4, 1894* |
| 29b | great coats] greatcoats *1882–4, 1894* |
| 35a | Half-a-dozen] Half a dozen *1882–4, 1894* |
| 39a | extraordinary] extraordinary, *1882–4, 1894* |
| 41a | down-stairs] down stairs *1882–4,* downstairs *1894* |
| 42a | down-stairs] down stairs *1882–4,* downstairs *1894* |
| 42b | shirt sleeves] shirt-sleeves *1882–4, 1894* |
| 47a | it is true –'] is it true—"*1882–4, 1894.* |
| 52a | being,] being *1882–4, 1894* |

– 433 –

434                         *Notes to pages 54–148*

54a         nature] Nature *1882–4, 1894*
54b         man] man, *1882–4, 1894*
57a         half-consciousness] half consciousness *1882–4, 1894*
62a         clanjamfry] clan-jamfry *1882–4, 1894*
64a         strongly!] strongly? *1882–4, 1894*
67a         long] long, *1894*
68a         up-stairs,] up stairs *1882–4*, upstairs *1894*
68b         drawing room.] drawing-room. *1882–4, 1894*
69a         half impatient, half touched,] half-impatient, half-touched *1894*
70a         half–sigh.] half sigh *1882–4, 1894*
71a         up-stairs;] up stairs; *1882–4*, upstairs *1894*.
74a         up-stairs,] up stairs, *1882–4*, upstairs, *1894*
75a         bright] bright, *1882–4, 1894*
79a         ill-will,] ill will, *1882–4, 1894*
88a         half-wish] half wish, *1882–4, 1894*
91a         fire-place,] fireplace, *1894*
91b         book-shelves] bookshelves, *1882–4, 1894*
91c         nineteenth century] nineteenth-century, *1894*
93a         her –] her, – *1882–4, 1894*
94a         half laughing,] half-laughing, *1894*
96a         tack] track, *1894*.
101a        half laughing] half-laughing, *1894*
101b        twenty five,] twenty-five, *1882–4, 1894*
101c        evening.] evening? *1894*
101d        out-door] outdoor *1894*
101e        country] country, *1882–4, 1894*
114a        prison-house?'] prison house?" *1882–4, 1894*
116a        by-and-by,] by and by, *1882–4, 1894*
116b        by-and-by,] by and by, *1882–4, 1894*
117a        longing] longing, *1882–4, 1894*
124a        after-life.] after life. *1882–4, 1894*
128a        daft like] daft-like, *1894*
130a        half-objections,] half objections, *1894*
132a        all.] *1882–4* has no paragraph break after 'all.'
132b        fields.] *1882–4* no paragraph break after 'fields'
133a        game.] *1882–4* no paragraph break after 'game'
133b        soapsuds] soap-suds, *1882–4, 1894*
134a        'weirdless'] "weirdless" *1882–4, 1894*
134b        door.] *1894* no paragraph break after 'door.'
134c        half pleased] half-pleased, *1894*
143a        CHAPTER I.] CHAPTER XVI. *1882–4, 1894*
146a        the] this, *1882–4, 1894*.
147a        mountain-side,] mountain side, *1882–4*, mountain, side *1894*
147b        would – no,] would: no, *1882–4*
148a        of: and] of. And, *1882–4*
148b        might:] might – *1882–4*, might–; *1894*
148c        that we do,'] that do we," *1882–4, 1894*
148d        that we do.] that do we! *1882–4, 1894*

*Notes to pages 149–64* 435

| | |
|---|---|
| 149a | likes – but it] likes – it *1882–4, 1894* |
| 150a | neighbour!] neighbour? *1882–4, 1894.* |
| 152a | aught] anything *1882–4,* aught, *1894* |
| 152b | the one unchangeable form of conjunction for the two mortal companions] the unchangeable one between the two mortal companions, *1882–4* |
| 152c | master – ] master, *1882–4* |
| 154a | threw] through, *1882–4,* through, *1894* |
| 154b | fall] get *1882–4, 1894* |
| 154c | CHAPTER II.] CHAPTER XVII. *1882–4, 1894* |
| 155a | warm window,] warm, window, *1882–4* |
| 156a | By-and-by] By and by *1882–4, 1894* |
| 158a | eyes.] eye. *1894* |
| 158b | cotters] cottars, *1882–4,* cotters, *1894* |
| 158c | grouse?'] grouse." *1882–4* |
| 159a | CHAPTER III.] CHAPTER XVIII. *1882–4, 1894* |
| 161a | trouble] trouble, *1882–4, 1894* |
| 161b | cotters] cottars *1882–4* |
| 162a | cotter] cottar *1882–4* |
| 162b | cotters,] cottars, *1882–4* |
| 163a | cotters,] cottars, *1882–4* |
| 163b | very little,] very little *1882–4* |
| 163c | 'it] "It, *1882–4, 1894* |
| 163d | hundred?] hundred! *1882–4, 1894* |
| 164a | which fortunately she did not see.] which fortunately she did not see. She had made up her mind to go up to the Glen, and convey the good news to the cottars, and, though it was not such entire good news as she wished, and Oona was somewhat disappointed, she paid them the visit notwithstanding, and gave the women to understand that there was nothing to fear from Lord Erradean. It was a long walk, and the afternoon was almost over when Oona came once more in sight of the loch. To get there the sooner, she took a path which cut off a corner, and which communicated, by a little narrow byway leading through the marshy ground at the head of the loch, with the old castle. She was a little startled as she hurried along, to see some one advance, as if to meet her from this way. Her heart jumped with a momentary idea that the slim dark figure against the light in the west, was Lord Erradean himself come back. But another glance satisfied her that this was not so. She was surprised, but not at all alarmed; for there was no one within reach of Loch Houran of whom it was possible to imagine that Oona could be afraid. She was singularly moved, however, she could not tell why, when she perceived, as they approached each other that it was the same person who had come two nights before with the boat from Auchnasheen, and who had sought Walter on the isle. It had been too dark then to distinguish his features clearly, and yet she was very sure that it was he. In spite of herself, her heart beat at this encounter. She did not know what or who he was; but he was Walter's enemy and taskmaster, or so at least it was evident Lord Erradean thought. She felt a nervous feeling steal over her as he came towards her, wondering would he speak to her, and what he would say. She did not, indeed know him, having seen him only under such circumstances, but she could not keep |

436                                    *Notes to page 164*

the consciousness that she did know him, out of her face. It was with a still stronger throb of her heart that she saw he meant to claim the acquaintance.

"Good evening," he said, taking off his hat, "I have not had the advantage of being presented to you, Miss Forrester: but we have met—"

"Yes," she said, with a momentary hesitation and faltering. She had so strong an impulse in her mind to turn and flee, that her amazement with herself was unbounded, and was indeed stronger than the fear.

"I hope," he said, "that nothing I have done or said has made you—afraid to meet me on this lonely road?"

This stirred up all Oona's pride and resolution. "I know no reasons," she said, "why I should be afraid to meet any one, here or elsewhere."

"Ah, that is well," said the stranger; "but," he added, "let me tell you there are many reasons why a young lady so well endowed by nature as yourself might be timid of meeting a person of whom she knows nothing. Lord Erradean, for instance, over whom you were throwing a shield of protection when I saw you last."

Oona felt her thrill of nervous disquietude give way to irritation as he spoke. She restrained with difficulty the impulse to answer hastily, and said after a moment, "I am at home here: there is no one who would venture, or who wishes, to do me harm."

"Harm!" he said; "do you think it no harm to claim your interest, and sympathy, and help, and then without a thought to hurry away?"

"I do not know who you are," said Oona, looking into his face, "that ventures to speak to me so."

"No; you don't know who I am. I am—one of his family," said the stranger. "I have his interest at heart—and yours to a certain extent. I mean to make him rich and great, if he does as I say–but you are inciting him to rebellion. I know women, Miss Forrester. I know what it means when they foster benevolence in a young man, and accept commissions of charity."

Oona coloured high with indignation and anger, but she was too proud to make any reply. The involuntary excitement, too, which had taken possession of her, she could not tell why, took away her breath. She was not afraid of the stranger, but it was irksome beyond description to her to see him stalk along by her side, and she quickened her pace in spite of herself. He laughed softly when he saw this. "You begin to think," he said, "that it is not so certain you will meet with no one who can do you harm."

"Do you mean to harm me?" she said looking more closely in his face.

"You have a fine spirit," he replied. "What a pity then that you are harmed already, and such a vacancy left in your life."

The girl started and her heart began to beat wildly. She began "How do you--" and then stopped short, fluttered and out of breath, not knowing what she said.

"How do I know? You have meddled in a life that does not concern you, and you will have to pay the penalty. After you have executed his commission, how blank everything will be! The past will not come back—it never comes back. You will stay on your isle, and look for him, and he will never come. The ground has gone from under your feet—you are emptied out—" he laughed a little as he spoke, not malignantly, but as a not unfriendly eavesdropper might do who had heard some ridiculous confession. To have her own thoughts thus turned over before her filled her with strange dismay. She had no power to make any reply.

*Notes to pages 164–88*     437

Though there was no definite alarm in her mind, her panic gained upon her. She tried to say something, but the words would not come. The slight trembling which she could not conceal seemed to mollify her strange companion.

"I have no wish to hurt you, " he said in a lofty tone. "What is done is done: but take care how you do more."

"I will take no care," cried Oona, with a flash of sudden power. "I will do what is right, what I think right, and if I suffer it will be at my own pleasure. What I do can be nothing to you." As she spoke the panic which she had been struggling against overcame her powers of resistance wholly. She gathered up her dress in her hand and flew with the speed in which, for a short distance, a girl cannot be surpassed. But as she got out of this stranger's presence, her spirit returned to her with a sense of defiance and opposition which was almost gay. She looked back, and called out to him with a voice that rang like a silver trumpet, "Good-bye—good-night!" waving her hand as she flew along. The dark figure advanced not a step further, but stood still and watched, almost invisible himself against the quickly-darkening background of the brushwood and the distance, the dim hills and gathering night. *1882–4*

| | |
|---|---|
| 165a | And after this interview she went home, very silent, depressed as she had no right to be, feeling as if life was over, and all things come to an end.] *1882–4* omit |
| 165b | CHAPTER IV.] CHAPTER XIX. *1882–4, 1894* |
| 166a | incredible,] incredible *1882–4* |
| 167a | it.] *1882–4* has no paragraph break after 'it.' |
| 168a | this one point,] this point, *1882–4*, this one point *1894* |
| 168b | hiding-places] hiding places, *1882–4* |
| 169a | life.] *1882–4* has no paragraph break after 'life.' |
| 171a | credulous,] incredulous, *1882–4* |
| 171b | by-and-by.'] by and by." *1882–4, 1894* |
| 172a | associations – don't] associations. Don't *1882–4, 1894* |
| 174a | up-stairs.] up stairs. *1882–4* |
| 174b | down-stairs] down stairs *1882–4*, down-stairs, *1894* |
| 175a | CHAPTER V.] CHAPTER XX. *1882–4, 1894* |
| 175b | turn-out?] turn out? *1882–4* |
| 175c | phaeton,] phaeton *1882–4, 1894* |
| 175d | harness] harness, *1882–4* |
| 176a | present,] present *1882–4* |
| 177a | Erradean;] Erradean: *1882–4, 1894* |
| 178a | nothing!] nothing? *1882–4, 1894* |
| 180a | moments.] moments! *1882–4, 1894* |
| 180b | mean time,] meantime, *1882–4*, mean time *1894* |
| 183a | he] ye *1882–4, 1894* |
| 184a | CHAPTER VI.] CHAPTER XXI. *1882–4, 1894* |
| 185a | somewhat] some-how *1882–4* |
| 188a | about it.] about it. Why should there be any consequences to follow? He had meant nothing in either case, nether to marry Miss Herbert nor to make Captain Underwood his chosen companion, and why should they object to his withdrawal? He had not forced the duets upon Julia, or the play upon the captain. He had been invited, urged in both cases. But indeed he was so easy in his mind on those subjects that he did not even take the trouble to argue them out in this way. The argument passed vaguely through the background |

438                              *Notes to pages 188–206*

of his mind, as what might be said if any accusation were made against him: but he did not see that there was any ground for accusation, nor was he conscious of the least tinge of remorse or sense of guilt. *1882–4*

188b    Park.] park. *1882–4*
191a    Tom] my uncle *1882–4*
193a    blue, the] blue; the *1882–4*; blue. The *1894*
194a    CHAPTER VII.] CHAPTER XXII. *1882–4, 1894*
194b    half-obliterated] half obliterated *1882–4, 1894*
196a    about – of course he had been one of the guests?] about — of course he had been there? *1882–4*
196b    form] form, *1882–4, 1894*
197a    allowed to] let, *1882–4*
197b    *allowed?*] *let? 1882–4*
199a    come, papa,] come, *1882–4*
200a    cause: and hear him with noble fervour applaud] cause — with what a noble fervour he will applaud *1882–4*
203a    race-course] racecourse, *1882–4*
204a    CHAPTER VIII.] CHAPTER XXIII. *1882–4, 1894*
206a    man.] man. Was it a want of feeling on the part of Walter thus to separate himself without compunction from the man who had in his ways exerted all his powers to please him? The question is a difficult one. Lord Erradean's eyes (however, he said to himself) had been open all the time: he had always known what Underwood's object was.

And yet as always it was a little difficult to formulate the motives of Underwood. Very few indeed have their motives cut and dried to be classified at the pleasure of the spectator. He was an adventurer by profession, and lived by his wits, preferring that existence of haphazard to other more steady and certain ways of existence. He had been the companion and associate of the late Lord Erradean, who was weak and undefined in all his ways, one of those who are, as people say, easily led away. When that unfortunate person fell into the gloom in which he died, which some people said was disease of the mind and some of the body, Captain Underwood had found his occupation gone; and it had occurred to him that the best thing he could do was to put himself in the path of the new lord, whose claims were very well known in Scotland, and among the hangers-on of the family, though not to himself. He had spent a great deal of time and trouble in securing, as he thought, this new lord. And if he was not altogether in despair now, it was because Walter Methven had already slipped through his hands, and been secured again; a course of incident which might be repeated. And though he had considered Walter as a pigeon to be plucked, as a weakling to be twisted to his own purposes, as a sort of milch cow to supply him with the luxuries and ready money he wanted, it must not be supposed that his intentions to Walter were wholly evil. He had already saved him more than once from plunderers more remorseless than himself, and it had always been a question with him whether he might not employ his knowledge of the family history for Walter's advantage as well as his own. He meant, it is scarcely necessary to say, to secure his own in the first place; but when that was done, he was willing enough to be of use to Walter too. If the young man had ever confided in

*Notes to pages 206–30* 439

him, Underwood would have advised him not to kick against the pricks, to give in to that which was evidently the leading influence in the family, whatever it was, and to shape his life according to that guidance. He would have impressed upon him the uneasy life and untimely end of his predecessor. He had it in him, he felt, to have been the good genius of young Erradean. But that haughty young fellow would not hear a word; and what could he do except treat him as a pigeon to be plucked, though still with a benevolent intention, in accordance with his old allegiance to the family, to save him from other plunderers as far as possible? *1882–4*

206b   He] *1882–4* A new paragraph begins at 'He'
208a   By-and-by,] By and by, *1882–4, 1894*
209a   Park] park *1882–4*
212a   sides.] *1882–4* has no paragraph break after 'sides.'
213a   CHAPTER IX.] CHAPTER XXIV. *1882–4, 1894*
214a   though always most dutiful] always most dutifully *1882–4*, though always most dutifully, *1894*
218a   She] Her, *1882–4*
218b   *She,*] *her,*" *1882–4*
218c   *she.*] *her. 1882–4*
218d   half laughing, half reproachful,] half-laughing, half-reproachful, *1894*
219a   down-stairs] down stairs *1882–4*
219b   up in his face.] up to him. *1882–4*
220a   foot-man] footman *1882–4, 1894*
222a   half-solemn] half solemn *1882–4*
223a   CHAPTER X.] CHAPTER XXV. *1882–4, 1894*
223b   rest.] *1882–4* has no paragraph break after 'rest.'
224a   Walter. Her heart] Walter. Whether it was that he had been drawn back to his allegiance to Miss Herbert – who Katie magnanimously allowed was very pretty – or whether he had been affronted by her own withdrawal, or whether – which was perhaps the most likely of all– he had acted on mere impulse without intention of any kind, she could not tell. Her heart *1882–4*
224b   In these circumstances it was very natural, almost inevitable, that she should take Oona into her confidence.] It was almost a matter of course that she should take Oona into her confidence in this respect. *1882–4*
224c   some,] some *1882–4, 1894*
228a   before.] *1882–4* has no paragraph break after 'before.'
229a   down-stairs] down stairs. *1882–4*
229b   down-stairs,] down stairs, *1882–4*
230a   CHAPTER XI.] CHAPTER XXVI. *1882–4, 1894*
230b   importance.] importance. Save for the fact that old Symington, who in the meantime had taken entire control of her house, and direction of everything in it, had announced to her one day the necessity he was under of leaving her for a short time to attend upon my lord, Mrs Methven was entirely ignorant of her son's whereabouts. And Symington, whom she of course closely interrogated on the subject, did not profess to have had any communication from his master. "But my lord will have nottice," said Symington, "and I make no doubt of finding him there." *1882–4*
230c   Neither] *1882–4* a new paragraph starts at 'Neither'

| | |
|---|---|
| 231a | impulse.] *1882–4* has no paragraph break after 'impulse.' |
| 231b | railway-carriage] railway carriage *1882–4* |
| 235a | strength:] strength; *1882–4* |
| 239a | CHAPTER XII.] CHAPTER XXVII. *1882–4, 1894* |
| 239b | new-comer] new comer *1882–4, 1894* |
| 240a | new-comer,] new comer, *1882–4, 1894* |
| 240b | country-side.] country side. *1882–4* |
| 240c | half-ruined] half ruined *1882–4* |
| 240d | when he came here for the first time ... Walter had listened] when he came here for the first time; and the other circumstances of his life had room to come in with even a certain seductive force in the midst of his excitement. Something swept the current of his thoughts towards Katie, with a secret impulse, as the water of the loch was swept by some force unseen into the current which the boatmen avoided with such care. Walter did not avoid the spiritual stream; he allowed himself to be carried away upon it, with a grateful sense of reconciliation to fate. Katie would smooth away his difficulties, though not in the way Miss Milnathort suggested. She would bring him peace at least for the moment. He had proved himself very little able to contend with the influence which swayed his race; all that he had done hitherto was to run away from it, to make what endeavour he could to forget it, to avoid the tyranny that overshadowed him by abandoning all his duties. But this was not a thing which he could do for ever. And the moment had come when some other course must be decided upon. |
| | This time it was clear he must make up his mind either to conquer the mysterious power which he could no longer ignore– or persuade himself to consider it a delusion– or to yield it altogether. He had listened *1882–4* |
| 241a | early on his way to Birkenraes. If it was there that the question was to be solved, it was better that it should be done without delay.] early on his way to Birkenbraes. The morning was grey and cold, the hills shrouded in mist as he rowed himself across to the other side of the loch. There were horses and carriages awaiting him at Auchnasheen, had he cared to take advantage of them; but the house in which he had suffered so much was odious to him, and he preferred to walk. To an excited and disturbed mind there is nothing so soothing as bodily exercise. Walter went along very quickly as if trying to keep up with the pace of his thoughts; but there was one spot upon which he came to a sudden pause. The road, as became a Highland road, was full of variety, going up and down, now penetrating through clumps of wood, now emerging into full view of the surrounding landscape. He had skirted the "policies" of Auchnasheen, behind which the high road lay, and climbed the rising ground beyond, when suddenly the path came out once more on the side of the loch, and he saw rising out of the gleaming water below, the feathery crest of the Isle with the roofs of the lonely house showing through the branches. Walter stopped with a sudden pang of mingled delight and pain; he stood as if he had been rooted to the ground. There it lay on the surface of the loch, dimly reflected, overhung by low skies, hanging in grey suspense between the dull heaven and dark water. There was no wind to ruffle the trees, or shake off the autumn leaves which made a sort of protest in their brilliant colours against the half tones of the scene. A line of blue smoke rose into the |

*Notes to pages 241–81*    441

still air, the solitary sign of life, unless indeed that gleam of red on the rocks was the shirt of Hamish, fishing as he had been a year ago when first Lord Erradeen set foot upon that hospitable spot. After a while he thought even he could see a figure before the door looking up the loch towards Kinloch Houran. The young man for the moment was transported out of himself. "Oona!" he cried, stretching out his hands to the vacant air which neither heard nor replied. His heart went out of his bosom towards that house in which he had been sheltered in his direst need. Tears gathered into his eyes as he stood and gazed. There was salvation; there was love, and hope, and deliverance—Two, that should be one. He seemed to feel once more in his own the touch of that pure and soft hand "as soft as snow," the touch which gave to him the strength of two souls, and one so spotless, so strong, and simple, and true. He stood holding out his hands in an instinctive appeal to her who neither saw nor knew. For a moment his life once more hung in the balance. Then with a stamp of his foot, and a sense of impatience and humiliation indescribable in words he turned and pursued his way. *1882–4*

242a    CHAPTER XIII.] CHAPTER XXVIII. *1882–4, 1894*
244a    Walter, slightly startled by the question. 'I came] Walter, somewhat astonished, and wondering whether any one could have seen and already betrayed his pause and instinctive exclamation when he came in sight of the isle. "I came *1882–4*
244b    water goddess] water-goddess *1882–4.*
244c    fountain-head.] fountain head. *1882–4, 1894*
245a    Erradeen!] Erradeen? *1882–4*
248a    footing?] *1882–4 has no paragraph break after 'footing?'*
250a    now!] now!' *1882–4*
250b    gentle-man,] gentleman, *1882–4, 1894*
251a    half-stern, half-amused,]half stern half amused, *1882–4*
252a    CHAPTER XIV.] CHAPTER XXIX. *1882–4, 1894*
255a    new-comer] new comer *1882–4*
255b    over:] over. *1882–4, 1894*
258a    CHAPTER XV.] CHAPTER XXX. *1882–4, 1894*
261a    CHAPTER XVI.] CHAPTER XXXI. *1882–4, 1894*
266a    By-and-by] By and by *1882–4, 1894*
266b    half-tone] half tone *1882–4.*
268a    CHAPTER XVII] CHAPTER XXXII. *1882–4, 1894*
271a    half-smile] half smile *1882–4*
271b    Church;] church; *1882–4*
273a    rent?'] rent." *1882-4,* rent?" *1894*
277a    CHAPTER I.] CHAPTER XXXIII. *1882–4, 1894*
277b     purchase it] purchase *1882–4*
279a    with some stateliness.] stately in offence. *1882–4*
279b    hereabouts?)] hereabouts) *1882–4*
280a    country-side.] country side. *1882–4.*
280b    that road,'] that back road," *1882–4*
281a    CHAPTER II] CHAPTER XXXIV. *1882–4, 1894*
281b    stepping-stone] stepping stone *1882–4, 1894*
281c    not-withstanding] notwithstanding *1882–4, 1894*
281d    under-gone,] undergone, *1882–4, 1894*

442                                     *Notes to pages 281–318*

281e        her?] her! *1882–4, 1894*
282a        pleasure,] pleasure *1882–4*
283a        loch-side.]loch side. *1882–4*
284a        lock,'] loch" *1894*
289a        CHAPTER III.] CHAPTER XXXV. *1882–4, 1894*
291a        significance. There] significance. He felt even that something of the kind must
            be the case, or that the Birkenbraes party would never have been so bold as to
            break into the very sanctuary, into the fated precincts of Kinloch Houran. This
            thought brought the moisture suddenly to his forehead. There *1882–4*
293a        He was much softened, and even] He was somewhat *attendri*, even *1882–4*
296a        bed-clothes:] bedclothes: *1882–4*
296b        CHAPTER IV.] CHAPTER XXXVI. *1882–4, 1894*
296c        had almost ceased for the moment to affect his mind, so profoundly exhausted
            was he by the renewed struggle in which he had been engaged.] had been so
            much softened by custom and familiarity that he now scarcely felt its pecu-
            liarity at all, except in a certain sense of contempt, and that subtle conscious-
            ness of superiority which the more enlightened in every sphere can with dif-
            ficulty subdue, towards those who felt, as he had once felt panic-stricken, and
            over whelmed with natural fear. His contempt for the two old servants of the
            house, who recognised with a tremor of all their senses the presence of some
            one whom they could not see, had a certain compassion and kindness mingled
            with it: but it would be difficult to describe the sensation of profound distance
            and difference between himself, informed and enlightened as he now was,
            and those curious and wondering spectators who saw his visitor, and crowded
            round to gaze at him, yet had nothing but a faint thrill of alarm in them to indi-
            cate who and what he was. That strange visitor smiled, with an almost humor-
            ous recognition of this obtuseness, but Walter felt certain anger with the fools
            who had no clearer perception. All this, however, was over now, and he walked
            round the head of the loch towards Auchnasheen with a conscious pause of all
            sensation which was due to the exhaustion of his mind. *1882–4.*
298a        half-shout] half shout *1882–4, 1894*
300a        pocketbook] pocket-book *1882–4, 1894*
303a        Methven] Ruthven *1882–4*
304a        CHAPTER V.] CHAPTER XXXVII. *1882–4, 1894*
305a        subject.' But] subject. "But, *1882–4, 1894*
306a        By-and-by] By and by *1882–4, 1894*
306b        half-caressing] half caressing *1882–4*
307a        were] was *1882–4.*
307b        half-laugh.] half laugh. *1882–4*
308a        He threw into disorder the books] He threw about half the books *1882–4*
311a        By-the-bye,] By the by, *1882–4, 1894*
311b        CHAPTER VI.] CHAPTER XXXVIII. *1882–4, 1894*
313a        down-stairs] down stairs *1882–4*
313b        come here.'] come." *1882–4*
315a        half-hope] half hope *1882–4*
316a        half sublime.] half-sublime. *1894*
317a        half-anger, half-remonstrance;] half anger, half remonstrance; *1882–4*
317b        housekeeping] house-keeping *1882–4, 1894*
318a        CHAPTER VII.] CHAPTER XXXIX. *1882–4, 1894*

| | |
|---|---|
| 318b | softly-carpeted] softly carpeted *1882–4* |
| 318c | thought.] *1882–4* has no paragraph break after 'thought.' |
| 319a | above-ground] above ground *1882–4, 1894* |
| 320a | sweet.] *1882–4* has no paragraph break after 'sweet.' |
| 320b | *you,*'] your soul," *1882–4* |
| 320c | a good morning,] a passing greeting, *1882–4* |
| 321a | this more odious still?'] that odious too?" *1882–4* |
| 321b | well.] work. *1882–4* |
| 323a | mockery,] mocking, *1882–4* |
| 324a | Oona!'] Oona?" *1882–4, 1894* |
| 325a | CHAPTER VIII.] CHAPTER XL. *1882–4, 1894* |
| 326a | avow.] *1882–4* has no paragraph break after 'avow.' |
| 326b | far] far, *1882–4, 1894* |
| 327a | unshipping oars,] unshipping of the oars, *1882–4, 1894* |
| 332a | half-offer] half offer *1882–4, 1894* |
| 332b | CHAPTER IX.] CHAPTER XLI. *1882–4, 1894* |
| 333a | 'I ] "It *1882–4* |
| 339a | CHAPTER X.] CHAPTER XLII. *1882–4, 1894* |
| 341a | half-laugh.] half laugh. *1882–4, 1894* |
| 345a | CHAPTER XI.] CHAPTER XLIII. *1882–4, 1894* |
| 345b | what is wrong?'] what is the matter?" *1882–4* |
| 345c | back to Auchnasheen] to shore *1882–4* |
| 346a | But] *1882–4* A new paragraph starts at 'But' |
| 346b | subdue.] *1882–4* has no paragraph break after 'subdue.' |
| 346c | Corrieden,] Linnheden, *1882–4* |
| 346d | there –] there: *1882–4* |
| 347a | within-doors] within doors *1882–4, 1894* |
| 347b | taken] token *1882–4* |
| 349a | down-stairs.] down stairs. *1882–4* |
| 349b | any new menace,] any menace, *1882–4* |
| 349c | the most refined] a refined *1882–4* |
| 350a | would Oona,'] will Oona," *1882–4* |
| 351a | no,] no – *1882–4* |
| 352a | CHAPTER XII.] CHAPTER XLIV. *1882–4, 1894* |
| 352b | down-stairs] down stairs *1882–4* |
| 353a | down-stairs,] down stairs, *1882–4* |
| 353b | Better to let him bee!] Better to "let him bee!" *1882–4* |
| 354a | rebel. While Mrs. Methven, sad and anxious and perplexed, sat in the unfamiliar room, and looked on the strange landscape in which she found no point of sympathy, Oona in the solitude of the isle, was full of similar thoughts.] rebel. This, however, Mrs. Methven did not know. When Walter left his betrothed, between whom and himself so strange and sudden a breach had come in the solitude of the isle, Oona's heart was rent by many bitter thoughts, which, however, she dared not give herself time either to examine or indulge. *1882–4* |
| 354b | chief endowments] powers *1882–4* |
| 354c | life. She had not ventured to indulge herself even in thought, unless she had been prepared, as she was not to open everything to Mrs. Forrester – and thus went through the hours in that active putting aside of herself and her |

444                                     *Notes to pages 354–61*

own concerns, which is sometimes called hypocrisy and sometimes self-renunciation.] life. Unless she had been prepared, as she was not, to open everything to Mrs. Forrester this was her only alternative. *1882–4*

354d     held Walter back from the wild flight from her and everything to which his maddening thoughts had almost driven him.] had held Walter back, and saved him from the flight which would have ended only in death. *1882–4*

354e     violent. With] violent. There are some people in whose hands it is safe to leave one's case, however appearances may be against one – and Oona was one of these. With *1882–4*

354f     which –] which: *1882–4*

354g     (as she remembered with a shudder)] (which made her shudder) *1882–4*

355a     love had never failed, and knew that to] love was stronger than death, and to *1882–4*

355b     shadows from terrible death] shadows pure, if terrible death *1882–4*

355c     righteous,] righteous – *1882–4*

356a     martyrs.] saints. *1882–4*

356b     occasion] Occasion *1882–4, 1894*

357a     ecstacy] ecstasy *1882–4*

357b     And the] The *1882–4*

358a     these Two;] the Two– *1882–4*

358b     sunshine which was like summer. ] sunshine. *1882–4*

358c     death,] death – *1882–4*

358d     CHAPTER XIII.] CHAPTER XLV. *1882–4, 1894*

359a     with whom she could do more good for Walter than by anything else,] with whom she could help Walter, *1882–4*

359b     commonplace, which changed at once the atmosphere and meaning of the scene.] commonplace. *1882–4*

359c     visitor,] woman, *1882–4*

360a     half-disappointed with the sudden changing of all graver thoughts] half-disappointed to find all graver thoughts *1882–4*

361a     this] the *1882–4*

361b     conversation – Mrs. Forrester entering well pleased into details about "the boys," which Mrs. Methven, surprised, amused, arrested somehow, she could not tell how, in the midst of the darker, more bewildering current, responded to now and then with some half-question, enough to carry on the innocent fulness of the narrative.] conversation. Mrs. Forrester was entirely at her ease thinking of nothing: though to Mrs.Methven after the fears and excitements of the past night this sudden lapse into the natural and ordinary was half-delightful, half-exasperating, wholly unreal, and like a dream. *1882–4*

361c     had not indeed met his anxious and questioning looks: but she had not refused to come, and that of itself was much; nor did there seem to be any anger, though some sadness, in the face which seemed to him, as to Mysie, full of sacred light.] had met his eyes with a soft look of pardon: she had given him her hand without hesitation. The look, which all had observed, had for him the meaning which no one else knew. It meant no ecstasy of happy love, but a deeper, stronger certainty than any such excitement of the moment. "I will never leave thee, nor forsake thee." It was God who said that, and not a woman: but it was reflected in Oona's face. She was not thinking,

*Notes to pages 361–4*    445

as so many happy and proud and gentle souls have thought, of the happiness that love was bringing, the gifts of tenderness and protection and constant support filling up their own being, which henceforward were to be theirs: but of him and of his need, and how she was to fulfil her trust. She looked at him on the other side of those anxious eyes of Hamish, which kept ceaseless watch upon her, without a reproach, or even a consciousness in her look that there was anything to pardon. He was not sufficiently apart from her now to be pardoned. One does not pardon one's self. One goes on to the next trial, trembling yet confident, with a gathering of all one's forces. "This time we shall not fail," her eyes seemed to say. *1882–4*

361d time: but I see very] time, when I had the permission to bring over Willie and Charley, who were just joining their regiments. They are never fond of letting strangers in, the Lords Erradeen. Oh I may say that before you, Lord Erradeen, for you are just new blood, and I am hoping will have new laws. I see very *1882–4*

362a She stood for a moment undecided, then turned towards that wild conjunction of the living and the dead, the relics of the past, and the fresh growth of nature, which give so much charm to every ruin.] *1882–4* omit.

362b amid] with *1882–4*

362c others.] *1882–4* has no paragraph break after 'others.'

362d But] Yet *1882–4*

362e by-and-by] by and by *1882–4, 1894*

362f soothing. But] soothing: but *1882–4*

362g She] Oona *1882–4*

363a Providence] providence *1882–4, 1894*

363b hope.] hope! *1882–4*

363c one –]one, *1882–4*

363d other.] Other. *1882–4*

364a And then her thoughts turned to the immediate matter before her–the deliverance of the man whose fate she had pledged herself to share notwithstanding all his imperfections; he who had found means already, since she had bound herself to him, to make her heart bleed; he whom she had loved against her will, against her judgment, before she was aware. He was to be made free from a bondage, a spiritual persecution, a tyrant who threatened him in every action of his life. Oona had known all her life that there was some mysterious oppression under which the house of Erradeen was bound, and there was no scepticism in her mind in respect to a wonder about which every inhabitant of the district had something to say; but from the moment when it became apparent that she too was to belong to this fated house, it had become insupportable and impossible. She felt, but with less agitation and a calmer certainty than that of Walter, that by whatsoever means it must be brought to an end. Had he been able to bear it, she could not have borne it. And he said that she alone could save him–that with her by his side he was safe; strange words, containing a flattery which was not intended, a claim which could not be resisted. He had said it when as yet he scarcely knew her, he had repeated it when he came to her hot from the presence of the other to whom he had appealed in vain. Strange mixture of the sweet and the bitter! She remembered, however, that he had asked her in the simplicity of desperation to give him her hand to help him, a year ago, and this thought banished all the other cir-

446                                *Notes to page 364*

cumstances from her mind. She had helped him then, knowing nothing–how was she to help him now? Could she but do it by standing forth in his place and meeting his enemy for him! could she but take his burden on her shoulders and carry it for him! He who had suffered so much feared with a deadly terror his oppressor; but Oona did not fear him. On her he had no power. In Walter's mind there was the weakness of previous defeat, the tradition of family subjection; but in her there was no such weakness, either personal or traditionary; and what was the use of her innocence, of her courage, if not to be used in his cause? Could she but stand for him, speak for him, take his place!] It was strange that all this time she had scarcely asked herself who and what this other was who had so long kept mysterious and miserable control over the household of Erradeen. Though the very beginning of her knowledge of Walter had plunged her into the midst of that mystery, she had not dwelt upon it nor even tried to follow it. There was no scepticism about the supernatural in her mind; rather she was so natural that she accepted a being who stood before her according to his semblance, and required no explanations. She had seen and spoken with a man who inspired Walter with a profound and unreasonable terror. Oona, looking at him with eyes of unalarmed and unsuspicious purity and all the kind and fearless freedom which belonged to her house, had neither hated him nor feared. She believed that there was in him something from which the others shrank, some power of giving pain and suggesting evil which justified their fear. But she did not share it. She was not afraid. There was not in her mind any alarm at the thought of encountering in her own person this enemy, of whom she knew scarcely anything more than that he was the enemy of Walter's race, the being of whom there was many a whisper about the loch, and the tradition of whose existence had come down from generation to generation. Could she but meet him, take that upon her own shoulders and spare Walter! She said to herself that, God protecting her, there was no power on earth that could harm, and that she would not be afraid. She would look him in the face, she would hear all that he could say, and refuse, refuse, for herself and all the house that was henceforward to be hers, her consent to his sway. If there was in Walter's mind the weakness of previous defeat, the susceptibility to temptation, which takes strength from the mind and confidence, there was in her no such flaw of nature. *1882–4*

364b   spoke] spake *1882–4*

364c   Oona's heart was full of this high thought. It drove away from her mind all shadows, all recollections of a less exalting kind. She moved on quietly, not caring nor thinking where she went, forming within herself visions of this substitution, which is in so many cases a woman's warmest desire. But then she paused, and there became visible to her a still higher eminence of generous love – a higher giddy eminence, more precarious, more dangerous, by which deliverance was less secure; not substitution – that was impossible. In her inward thoughts she blushed to feel that she had thought of a way of escape which for Walter would have been ignoble. It was for him to bear his own part, not to stand by while another did it for him. A noble shame took possession of her that she could for a moment have conceived another way. But with this came back all the anxious thoughts, the questions, the uncertainty. How was she to help him? how pour all the force of her life into

*Notes to pages 364–6* 447

him? how transfer to him every needed quality, and give him the strength of two in one? In the full current of her thoughts Oona was suddenly brought to a pause. It was by the instinct of self-preservation which made her start back on the very edge of the ruin. The sickening sensation with which she felt the crumbling masonry move beneath her foot, drove everything out of her mind for the moment.] In the crowd of her thoughts – which were all mingled great and small, solemn and trifling, as all human thoughts are in high flood – this ballad floated with the rest through Oona's mind, with an aptness which gave her a momentary amusement, yet helped to increase her visionary exaltation. When this high excitement flagged a little it was with the thought that thus to act for Walter was impossible, was not what was required of her. It was he who must fight though he was weak, not she who felt herself so strong. But then, her hand in his, the whole force of her nature thrown into his, holding him up, breathing courage into his ear, into his soul! Oona's heart rose once more, she felt herself like one inspired. That was the woman's part, a harder part than if all the brunt of the fight had rested upon herself. But where was the wizard, where the black art, where tempter or demon, that could overcome a man thus supported and held up by love behind him, the joint resistance of the two who were one? While all these thoughts were passing through her mind, she had gone on, a few steps at a time, without thinking or perceiving where she went – till in the high flood and fervour of her spirit, suddenly looking up, she found herself on the grey edge of the wall, on the last ledge where any footing was possible, beyond the spot from which her predecessor had fallen. The sickening sensation with which she felt the crumbling masonry move beneath her foot, brought her to herself, and in a moment she realized the danger of her position. Another second and all her hopes and possibilities might have been over for ever. *1882–4*

364d    keen wild look] keen look *1882–4*

365a    echo;] echo: *1882–4*

365b    footing. Necessity] footing, though it had never been attempted before; but necessity *1882–4*

365c    Everything] *1882–4* A new paragraph starts at 'Everything'

365d    itself; but] itself, feeling that there was no other hope or possibility before her. But *1882–4*

365e    all connected with the Methvens was here awaiting her.] all who tried to help the Methvens was awaiting her here. *1882–4*

365f    But there] There *1882–4*

365g    Oona still spoke to herself, but spoke aloud, as it was some comfort to do in her utter isolation.] Oona carried on her self-discussion: but now she spoke aloud, to sustain herself in her utter isolation. *1882–4*

366a    safety. There arose even in her mind upon the very foundation of her momentary panic, a sudden new force and hope. She who had so desired to stand in Walter's place, to be his substitute, might not this, without any plan or intention of hers, be now placed within her power?] safety. A certain scorn of safety, as of fear, and all the vulgar infidelities of superstition rose up in her mind. She raised her head high and went on. So long as God is, where is the fear? And there is no doom but what comes out of His hand. *1882–4*

366b    accepted.] accepted; perhaps, Heaven grant it! A substitution, something to

448                                    *Notes to pages 366–72*

|        | be done for Walter to which her heart and strength rose. *1882–4* |
|--------|---|
| 366c   | When] *1882–4* a new paragraph starts at 'When' |
| 366d   | feet;] feet – *1882–4* |
| 366e   | brain – a bewildering pang of sensation. For a moment she hesitated what to do: yet scarcely for a moment, since] brain with a bewildering pang of sensation – hesitating whether to pass it by, or make sure what was its meaning, yet scarcely hesitating, for *1882–4* |
| 366f   | The door] Going up the step, she found that the door *1882–4* |
| 366g   | open, Oona found] open found, *1882–4* |
| 366h   | lighted from an opening] lighted with a mysterious abstract light from an opening *1882–4*. |
| 367a   | A great telescope occupied a place in the centre of the room, and various fine instruments, some looking like astronomical models, stood on tables about.] Fine instruments, strange and delicate stood on stools and tables, some of them slowly revolving, like astronomical models. *1882–4* |
| 367b   | The] *1882–4* a new paragraph starts at 'The' |
| 367c   | began to fail her.] began to fail. *1882–4* |
| 367d   | There] 1882-4 a new paragraph starts at 'There' |
| 367e   | tapestry, and from the other side of the room, some one put it aside, and after looking at her for a moment came slowly out.] tapestry: and from the other side of the room, some one put it aside and looked at her. *1882–4* |
| 367f   | was.] was. Once more her heart stood still: and then there came upon Oona an impulse altogether beyond her understanding as it was beyond her control. |

      She heard her own voice rise in the silence. She felt words come to her
lips, and was aware that she launched them forth without comprehension,
without a pause. What was she saying? Oaths such as she knew not how
to say. "Accursed wizard!" Was it she who said it, or were the words in the
air. "God confound thee! God destroy thee!" Wrath blazed up in her like a
sudden flame. She struck at the delicate machinery within her reach wildly
with a sort of frenzy, and catching up something, she knew not what, struck
the lamp, not knowing what she did. It fell with a crash, and broke, and the
liquid which had supplied it burst forth, and ran blazing in great globules of
light over the floor. A wild rush was in the air, whether of his steps towards
her, whether of her own hurrying blood she could not tell. "God destroy
thee! God curse thee!" Was it she who spoke – looking at that pale awful
countenance, launching curses which she did not understand? All of Oona
rushed back into the surging brain and beating heart that were possessed by
something not herself. "No," she cried in her own conscious voice, "God pardon you whoever you are," and turned, and heard the great door flung behind
her, and fled and knew no more. *1882–4*

| 370a   | CHAPTER XIV.] CHAPTER XLVI. *1882–4, 1894* |
| 371a   | effusive, and examined] effusive. She was pleased beyond measure to see eve-rything, which was what nobody on the loch had done for many years. Even on the occasion when the Williamsons invaded Lord Erradeen's solitude they had not been admitted to any investigation of this part of the house; and she examined *1882–4* |
| 371b   | no alarm for her safety had] no alarm had *1882–4* |
| 372a   | A] *1882–4* a new paragraph starts at 'A' |

*Notes to pages 372–5* 449

372b    walls.] *1882–4* has no paragraph break after 'walls.'

372c    down-stairs] down stairs *1882–4*

372d    waiting; the whole scene full of rest and calm, and everything silent about and around.] waiting; not a flutter of a veil was to be seen to afford any trace of her; all was silence about and around. *1882–4*

372e    masonry, straining his eyes over the stony pinnacles above, and the sharp irregularities of the ruin.] masonry, looking now to the stony pinnacles above, where nothing but a bird (he thought) could have found the way; now over the ruined battlements to the ledge of rock upon which the waters rose and fell; now down, with an agonised glaze, into the interior, where – thank Heaven for so much certainty – she could not have fallen, but saw nothing, heard nothing, save the rustle of the awful silence which wounded his ear, and the vacancy that made his eyes ache with a feverish strain. *1882–4*

375a    There he saw something suddenly which made his heart stand still: her glove lying where she had dropped it in her hurried progress along the ledge. He did not pause to think how she got there, which would have seemed at another moment impossible, but with a desperate spring and a sensation as of death in his heart, followed, where she had passed, wherever that might be. Walter neither knew where he was going nor how he made his way along those jagged heights. He did not go cautiously as Oona had done, but flew on, taking no notice of the dangers of the way. The sound of voices, and of his own name, and Oona's cry for help, reached his ear as with a leap he gained the stone balcony of the tower. His feet scarcely touched the stones as he flew to her who called him, nor did he think where he was, or feel any wonder at the call, or at the voices on such a height, or at anything that was happening. His mind had no room for any observation or thought save that Oona called him. He flung himself into the dark doorway as if it had been a place he had known all his life, and caught her as her strength failed her. She who had thought she could put herself in his place, and who had been ready to brave everything for him, turned round with her eyes glazing and her limbs giving way, with strength enough only to throw herself upon his breast. Thus Walter found himself once more face to face with his enemy. The last time they had met, Lord Erradeen had been goaded almost to madness. He stood now supporting Oona on his arm, stern, threatening in his turn. 'If you have killed her,' he cried; 'if you have hurt her as you did before; if you have made her your victim, as you did before!' There was no shrinking in his look now: he spoke out loudly with his head high, his eyes blazing upon the enemy who was no longer his, but hers, which had a very different meaning; and though he stood against the door where he had found Oona holding it wide open, this was done unconsciously, with no idea of precaution. The time for that was over now. And with the sensation of his support, the throb of his heart so near hers, Oona came back to herself. She turned slowly round towards the inhabitant of the tower. 'Walter, tell him – that though he can make us miserable he cannot make us consent. Tell him – that now we are two, not one, and that our life is ours, not his. Oh!' she cried, lifting her eyes, addressing herself directly to him, 'listen to me! – over me you have no power – and Walter is mine, and I am his. Go – leave us in peace.' 'She says true; leave us in peace. In all my life now, I shall do no act that is not half hers, and over her you have no power.' 'You expect me then,' he said, 'to give way to this bargain of self-interest – a partnership of protection to you and gain to her. And you think that before this I am to give way.' 'It is not so,' cried Walter, 'not so. Oona, answer him. I turned to her for help because I loved her, and she to me for – I know not why – because she loved me. Answer him, Oona! if it should be at this moment for death not for life –' She turned to him with a look and a smile, and put her arm through his, clasping his hand: then turned again to the other who stood looking on. 'If it should be for death,' she said. There was a moment of intense stillness. He before whom these two stood knew human nature well. He knew every way in which to work upon a solitary being, a soul alone, in his power; but he knew that before two, awake, alive, on the watch one for the other, these methods were without power, and though his experiences were so great the situation was new. They were in the first absolute devotion of their union, invulnerable, no germ of distrust, no crevice of possible separation. He might kill, but he could not move them. This mysterious agent was not above the artifices of defeat. To separate them was the only device that remained to him. 'You are aware,' he said, 'that here if nowhere else you are absolutely in my power. You have come to me. I have not gone to you. If you wish to sacrifice her life you can do so, but what right have you to do it? How dare you take her from those who love her, and make her your victim? She will be your victim, not mine. There is time yet for her to escape. It is for her to go – Die? why should she die? Are you worth such a sacrifice? Let her go –' 'Hold me fast – do not loose me, Walter,' cried Oona wildly in his ear. And here his last temptation took him, in the guise of love, and rent him in two. To let her perish, was that possible? Could he hold her though she was his life, and sacrifice hers? Walter could not pause to think; he tore his hand out of hers, which would not be loosed, and thrust her from him. 'Oona,' he cried, his voice sinking to a whisper, 'go! Oona, go! Not to sacrifice you – no, no, I will not. Anything but that. While there is time, go!' She stood for a moment between the two, deserted, cast off by him who loved her. It was the supreme crisis of all this story of her heart. For a moment she said nothing, but looked at them, meeting the keen gaze of the tempter, whose eyes seemed to burn her, gazing at Walter who had half-closed his not to see her go. Then with the sudden, swift, passionate action, unpremeditated and impulsive, which is natural to women, she flung herself before him, and seized with her hands the table upon which the light was burning. 'You said,' she cried, breathless, 'that you used small methods as well as great – and this is one, whatever it is.' She thrust it from her violently as she spoke. The lamp fell with a great crash and broke, and the liquid which had supplied it burst out and ran blazing in great globules of flames over the floor. The crash, the blaze, the sudden uproar, was like a wall between the antagonists. The curtains swaying with the wind, the old dry tapestries, caught in the fire like tinder. Oona, as wild with fear as she had been with daring, caught at Walter's hand with the strength of despair, and fled dragging him after her. The door clanged behind them as he let it go, then burst open again with the force of the breeze and let out a great blaze, the red mad gleam of fire in the sunshine and daylight – unnatural, devouring. With a sense that death was in their way before and behind, they went forth clinging to each other, half-stupefied, half-desperate. Then sense and hearing and consciousness itself

*Notes to pages 375–7*        451

were lost in a roar as of all the elements let loose – a great dizzy upheaving as of an earthquake. The whole world darkened round them; there was a sudden rush of air and whirl of giddy sensation – and nothing more.] *1882–4* omit

**375b**    And as for ruins, she knows them well.] And as for rough roads or the hillside, I would trust her as soon as the strongest man. *1882–4*

**376a**    before.] before. Walter was half distracted with wonder and alarm. He had looked in every corner where it was possible she could have taken refuge. He sprang now upon the very edge of the battlement, where there was precarious footing though the platform within had crumbled away and stood out there between earth and sky, eagerly scanning the higher points of the ruin. Could she have ventured there, up upon those airy heights, where, so far as he knew, no one had climbed before for ages? Every kind of horrible fear overtook him as he stood and searched everywhere with his eyes. She might have fallen through some of the crevices into the honeycomb of ruins, half filled up, yet affording pits and chasms innumerable. She might, which was more terrible still, have been met by the master of those gloomy ruins and been driven to madness and disaster by the meeting. He stood up, poised between earth and sky, the loch sheer below lapping against the foundations of the castle, the tower rising grey and inaccessible above. Already from the village his figure was seen in mid air, rousing an idle little group round the inn door to amazement and dismay. While he stood thus, it seemed to him that sounds suddenly broke forth from above – a voice bursting out, high, indignant, in words indistinguishable to him: and the voice was not recognisable. It was a human voice, and quivered with passion and vehemence, but that was all. The horrible question crossed his mind, was Oona there at the mercy of his enemy? when suddenly, without an interval, the sound changed into Oona's own voice, and into words of which he could distinguish one only and that was pardon. And before he had time to draw breath there suddenly flashed upon Walter's eyes a vision – was it madness coming upon him? A vision – Oona, her dress and her hair streaming behind her, in the impulse of flight, passing like the wind within the ruinous balustrade, her light figure flashing across the dark openings, her foot scarcely touching the stones over which she flew. With a loud cry he threw out his arms to her, knowing it to be a vision, yet true. Behind her flying figure there flashed out, as if in pursuit, a great sudden blaze, the red mad gleam of fire in the sunshine, fire that flamed up to the sky and rolled along the masonry in a liquid wave of flame. He flung himself towards her he did not know how, and clutched at her wildly as she came flying over the ridges of the ruin. Then sense and hearing and consciousness itself were lost in a roar as of all the elements let loose, a great dizzy upheaving as of an earthquake. The whole world darkened around him; there was a sudden rush of air and whirl of giddy sensation, and nothing more. *1882–4*

**376b**    CHAPTER XV.] CHAPTER XLVII. *1882–4, 1894*

**376c**    ghost –] ghost and its movements, *1882–4*; ghost, *1894*

**376d**    what were those figures] what was that white figure *1882–4*

**377a**    instinctively put out] instinctively looked in each other's faces, and put out, *1882–4.*

**377b**    nothing followed,] no catastrophe followed, *1882–4*

**377c**    door – then,] door, then, *1882–4*

452                                    *Notes to pages 377–87*

377d            stair-case] staircase *1882–4, 1894*
379a            them: only it gave her a strange surprise] them. The only thing that touched
                her with a strange surprise *1882–4*
381a            going – a] going a *1882–4*
381b            'I am going–for a long time, at least,' the stranger said.] "In any case," said the
                stranger, "I am leaving this place." *1882–4*
381c            Katie] *1882–4* a new paragraph starts at 'Katie'
381d            hollow] hollows *1882–4, 1894*
382a            CHAPTER XVI.] CHAPTER XLVIII. *1882–4, 1894*
382b            over] on *1882–4*
383a            almost] because almost *1882–4*
383b            mother,] mother *1882–4*
383c            landing-place,] landing place, *1882–4*
383d            half-forgotten,] half forgotten, *1882–4, 1894*
383e            prayers.] *1882–4* has no paragraph break after 'prayers.'
384a            by-and-by] by and by *1882–4, 1894*
384b            all!] all; *1882–4*
384c            Why] why *1882–4*
385a            almost mechanical,] mechanical *1882–4*
385b            all.] this all. *1882–4*
386a            restrained] gave up *1882–4*
386b            why.] how. *1882–4*
386c            her] that *1882–4*
386d            down-stairs] down stairs *1882–4*
386e            duty] his duty *1882–4*
386f            rest,] rest; *1882–4*
386g            And] For *1882–4*
386h            the] a *1882–4*
387a            even,] even then, *1882–4*
387b            of something human.] a human movement. *1882–4, 1894*
387c            even] several *1882–4*
387d            possibility: but] possibility. But *1882–4*
387e            rushed,] rushed *1882–4, 1894*
387f            CHAPTER XVII.] CHAPTER XLIX. *1882–4, 1894*
387g            THE two fugitives, holding each other's hands, had fled from the fire without
                a word to each other. All that needed to be spoken seemed to them both
                to be over. They hurried on instinctively, but without any hope, expecting
                every moment when destruction should overtake them. Walter was the last
                to give up consciousness: but the sickening] OONA, flying from the catastro-
                phe which she did not understand with neither leisure nor clearness of mind
                to see where her steps were falling, had yet been carried by her excitement,
                she knew not how, over all the dangers of the uncertain path, until she came
                near enough to Walter, who stood out relieved against the blue sky and the
                background of the loch, to throw herself, her strength exhausted, into his
                arms, which were held out to save her. She remembered nothing more – nor
                was he much better aware of what happened. The sickening *1882–4*
387h            consciousness, and thrill of feeling, as if life were to end there, in a painful
                rush of blood, were all that were known to him.] consciousness, in a painful

*Notes to pages 387–93* 453

rush of blood, and thrill of feeling, as if life were to end there, were all that
were known to him. *1882–4*

388a  cry] utterance *1882–4*

388b  breath.] breath.

But it is only when life is vanishing from our grasp that its price and value becomes fully known, even to those who, in other circumstances, might
have been ready enough to throw it away.*1882–4*

388c  her] Oona *1882–4*

388d  help.] *1882–4* has no paragraph break after 'help.'

388e  this] the *1882–4*

388f  work,] work – *1882–4*

389a  half-mad, half-stupefied,]half mad, half stupefied, *1882–4*

389b  now, the flames and the fire: and it was I that broke the lamp. What did it
mean, the lamp? I thought] now. He came out to the door and looked at me.
It was I that broke the lamp. I thought, *1882–4*

390a  reply; it was no wonder to him that she should speak wildly. He too was
tempted to believe that accident had no part in what had befallen them, that
they had now encountered the deadly vengeance of their enemy. He tried to
soothe her,] reply; he did not know what she meant; but it was no wonder to
him that she should speak wildly. There were many things which rose to his
own lips that had no meaning in them. He soothed her, *1882–4*

390b  showed them where they were,] showed what it was, *1882–4*

390c  frame,] frame – *1882–4*

391a  rest,] rest *1882–4, 1894*

391b  able] still able *1882–4*

391c  enemies:] enemies; *1882–4*

391d  suffering and misery] suffering and discouragement *1882–4*

391e  others, the light] others, their half-trance, half-slumber was broken. The light
*1882–4*

391f  darkened and the stillness broken by] darkened by *1882–4*

391g  knees with a heavy shock of sound and a voice pealing in through the opening–] knees, and a voice pealed in, *1882–4*

391h  'Miss Oona,] *1882–4* A new paragraph begins at "Miss Oona"

391i  darkness] renewed darkness *1882–4*

391j  additional] *1882–4* omit

392a  itself –] itself:*1882–4*

392b  again] *1882–4* omit

392c  cheeks,] cheeks: *1882–4*

392d  young] younger *1882–4*

392e  sight,] event, *1882–4*

392f  feebly,] said feebly, *1882–4*

392g  Cameron:] Cameron; *1882–4*

392h  bairn!' 'And] bairn! And *1882–4*

392i  The] *1882–4* a new paragraph begins at 'The'

392j  yet, but not only the hills distinct around, but] yet; but the hills stood distinct around, and *1882–4*

392k  happened. She] happened; and she *1882–4*

393a  opened] laboured *1882–4*

454 *Notes to pages 393–402*

393b     The minister knew that he should] Mr. Cameron felt that he ought to *1882–4*
393c     joy;] joy, *1882–4*
393d     knees, –] knees: *1882–4*
393e     'Oh hon – oh hon!'] "Oh, hon–oh, hon!" *1882–4*
393f     up-stairs] up stairs *1882–4*
394a     down-stairs] down stairs *1882–4*
394b     down-stairs,] down stairs, *1882–4*
395a     down-stairs] down stairs *1882–4*
395b     extraordinary'] extraordinary," *1882–4*
395c     her, incapable] her, restored to consciousness, but incapable *1882–4*
395d     CHAPTER XVIII. CHAPTER L. *1882–4, 1894*
395e     country] county *1882–4, 1894*
395f     fire,] fire – *1882–4*
395g     however,] indeed, *1882–4*
395h     strange visitor whom he had first seen at Kinloch Houran,] stranger, *1882–4*
395i     begun] now begun *1882–4*
395j     and] and when this terrible report reached him *1882–4*
395k     could] might *1882–4*
396a     But] but *1882–4*
397a     sorry;] sorry:*1882–4*
397b     dreamed often of finding herself] often dreamed of finding for herself *1882–4*
397c     though it seemed] but it had seemed *1882–4*
397d     so,] so! *1882–4*
397e     cry; though] sound; but in *1882–4*
397f     But] Thus *1882–4*
398a     catastrophe, and the deeper pang which by-and-by awakened her heart] catastrophe. But by and by her heart awakened with a deeper and truer pang *1882–4*
398b     on account of] of *1882–4*
398c     Nor was it] And it was not *1882–4*
399a     But the next day on the way home,] but at the very hour, *1882–4*
399b     was reddening] was beginning to redden *1882–4*
399c     hemmed] strutted *1882–4*
399d     hasty] husky *1882–4*
399e     them] that *1882–4*
399f     met them all smiles] came in all smiles *1882–4*
399g     ended] ended, *1882–4*
399h     but] but reported *1882–4*
401a     feeling] feelings *1882–4*
401b     quarrel] quarrel, *1882–4*
401c     CHAPTER XIX.] CHAPTER LI. *1882–4, 1894*
401d     effects,] effects:*1882–4*
402a     the mystery of that extraordinary moment which appeared now like a dream, too wonderful to be true, too inexplicable and beyond experience to come into natural life at all. They spoke of it to each other with bated breath, but not till some time after their rescue, when the still higher excitement of their near approach to death – a thing which reveals the value and charm of life as nothing else does – had somewhat subsided in their minds. But their recollections were confused, they could not tell how; and as Walter had never

*Notes to pages 402–4* 455

been sure after they were over, whether the terrible conflicts which he had gone through were not conflicts between the better and worse parts of his own nature, without any external influence, so they asked each other now whether the mysterious chamber, the burning lamp, the strange accessories of a concealed and mysterious life, were dreams of disordered fancy, or something real and actual. They could not explain these things to each other, neither could they understand what it was that made the throwing down of the light of such vital importance. Was it common fire, acting after the ordinary laws of nature and finding ready fuel in the dry wood and antique furniture? or was it something more mystic, more momentous? They gave little explanation to questioners, not so much because they were unwilling, as because they were unable; and when they discussed it between themselves became more and more confused as the days went on. It became like a phantasmagoria, sometimes suddenly appearing in all the vivid lines of reality, sometimes fading into a pale apparition which memory could scarcely retain.

To the world in general the fact of a great fire, a thing unfortunately not very rare in the records of ancient houses, became after a while a very simple piece of history; and the wonderful escape of Lord Erradeen and Miss Forrester, and their subsequent betrothal and marriage, a pretty piece of natural romance.] the more extraordinary, less comprehensible mystery of the strange discovery she had made, and left her instrumentality in the destruction of the tower less and less clear. Sometimes, and this for years after, she would see before her with a shudder the look which the owner of the tower chamber cast upon her as he came out from the inner room, and she fled before him; but as time went on would ask herself was it real or only some dream, some visionary and violent effort of imagination. To no one but Walter did she ever speak of that moment or of the sight she had seen; and between them they had no explanation to give of the mystical furniture of the wizard's room, the lamp which had burned before Walter's portrait, the sad-eyed pictures about the walls, which had all perished without leaving a trace behind. *1882–4*

| | |
|---|---|
| 402b | been,] existed, *1882–4* |
| 402c | stones,] walls, *1882–4* |
| 402d | walls;] ruin; *1882–4* |
| 402e | hiding-place.] *1882–4* has no paragraph break after 'hiding-place.' |
| 402f | and that] that *1882–4* |
| 403a | terror of which the Italian poet speaks, which makes all the earth a desert – 'Senza quella / Nova, sola, infinita, Felicitá che il suo pensier figura.'] terror – as if the very words were an omen of evil. *1882–4* |
| 403b | But before] Before, however, *1882–4* |
| 403c | thought, but had herself to be carried] thought – but after this was not herself able to go further than *1882–4* |
| 403d | felt it,] felt it coming on, *1882–4* |
| 403e | By-and-by,] By and by, *1882–4* |
| 403f | when everything that could please her was brought to the recovering mother,] when everything that could be thought of was brought to please her, *1882–4* |
| 403g | with good wishes, and kind offerings.] and good wishes. *1882–4* |
| 403h | philosophy;] philosophy: *1882–4* |
| 404a | sister!'] sister?" *1882–4* |

456                          *Notes to pages 405–6*

405b          liberty,'] freedom," *1882–4*
405a          Walter,] Walter; *1882–4*
405b          she; and then to wait a night and a day.'] she – and then to wait a night and a
              day –" *1882–4*
406a          thanks?'] thanks!"*1882–4*
406b          *him?*] Him?*1882–4*
406c          beaten] bested*1882–4*
406d          we were] she came*1882–4*
406e          us, the only words I heard from her were a prayer for pardon – 'forgive him,'
              that was all I heard.] her, the word she was saying was 'Pardon! Pardon!' that
              was all I heard.*1882–4*

# SILENT CORRECTIONS

Silent corrections have been made to obvious mistakes in the copy text: in every case but one the correction is legitimated by a prior correct appearance in the serialized version. The exception is the sole occasion when Katie Williamson is referred to as Kate ('Said Kate calmly – I am a quite different person from you,' p. 226) This occurs in all three versions, but since there seems no reason for this name change, in this edition it has been changed back to Katie.

| | |
|---|---|
| p. 76, l. 20 | surpise] surprise |
| p. 112, l. 36 | unobstrusive] unobtrusive |
| p. 122, l. 10 | ministers'] minister's |
| p. 151, ll. 30–1 | Is was the strangest conjunction] It was the strangest conjunction |
| p. 202, l. 11 | damaged ones at Underwoods club] damaged ones at Underwood's club |
| p. 230, l. 16 | Mr Milanthort's house in Edinburgh] Mr. Milnathort's house in Edinburgh |
| p. 237, ll. 14–15 | experinces which were of a nature so different] experiences which were of a nature so different |
| p. 330, l. 40 | cousre] course |